Hudson Strait

Hudson
Bay

D1572009

James
Bay

Churchill R.

Nelson R.

York
Factory

Hayes R.

50° N

Cumberland
House

Norway House

Lake
Winnipeg

Fort William

Lake
Nipissing

Montreal
Lachine

French R.

Ottawa R.

Assiniboine R.

Lake
of the
Woods

Rainy
Lake

Lake
Superior

Sault Ste.
Marie

Georgian
Bay

St. Lawrence R.

Fort Frances
(Fort Lac-la-Pluie)

Lake
Huron

York

Red R.

Grand
Portage

Lake Michigan

Mississippi R.

St. Paul

90° W

Chicago

90° W

60° W

OUTPOST

OUTPOST

JOHN McLOUGHLIN & the FAR NORTHWEST

DOROTHY NAFUS MORRISON

Oregon Historical Society Press

FRONTISPIECE: An early photographic portrait of John McLoughlin. Photography is generally dated as starting not earlier than 1839. Between 1838 and 1840, McLoughlin traveled to London and Montreal. Although the date and photographer are unknown, he appears more youthful than in other portraits. OHS Neg. 245

Oregon Historical Society Press
1200 SW Park
Portland, Oregon 97205
www.ohs.org

First edition

Copyright © 1999 Oregon Historical Society

Library of Congress Cataloging-In-Publication Data

Morrison, Dorothy Nafus
    Outpost: John McLoughlin and the Far Northwest / by Dorothy Nafus Morrison.
        p. cm.
    Includes bibliographical references and index.
    ISBN 0-87595-267-4
    1. McLoughlin, John, 1784-1857. 2. Pioneers—Oregon—Biography. 3. Fur traders—Oregon—Biography. 4. Hudson's Bay Company—Biography. 5. Oregon—History—to 1859. 6. Fur trade—Northwest, Pacific—History—19th century. 7. Northwest, Pacific—Biography. I. Title.
F880.M17M68 1998
979.5'03'092
[B]—DC21   98-3162

CIP

Printed in the United States of America.

Designed and produced by the Oregon Historical Society Press.

The paper used in this publication meets the minimum requirements of American National Standard for Information Sciences—Permanence of Paper for Printed Library Materials, ANSI Z39.48-1984.

To Jim, Anne, David, John
And to all of theirs

The publication of *Outpost: John McLoughlin & the Far Northwest*
has been has been supported by
the M.J. Murdock Publications Fund
of the Oregon Historical Society
and by the generosity of Barbara Davies.

Acknowledgments

The story of John McLoughlin requires a broad canvas. For help in covering it, I have many people to thank—generous people, knowledgeable, stimulating, a pleasure to work with. Without them this would be a poorer book.

Jean Morrison, retired historical officer of Old Fort William, read the Canadian portion of the manuscript twice, and offered suggestions for that nation's history and viewpoint. Thomas Vaughan, the first American reader, gave me much needed encouragement to stick with it and drew on his vast knowledge of facts and sources. Bruce Taylor Hamilton, one of my early contacts, offered valuable advice.

David Hansen, archivist at Fort Vancouver, gave the entire manuscript a careful assessment, made the fort's excellent fur-trade library available, and supplied information. Scott Lansford of the Fort Vancouver library shared its books, and pointed out choice materials that I might otherwise have missed. Doug LaManz helped with photography, as did Steve Brown; and others of the staff were invariably perceptive and accommodating.

Richard Mackie of the Department of Geography, University of British Columbia, and Lloyd Keith, Ph.D. of Shoreline Community College, Seattle, both read the completed manuscript and sent extremely valuable, detailed analyses. John Adams, of Victoria, British Columbia, sent information derived from research for his forthcoming biography of James Douglas. Lawrence L. Dodd, archivist at Whitman College, was enormously kind in volunteering a photocopy of a Narcissa Whitman document, as was Patricia Kennedy of the National Archives of Canada, who sent a photo copy and typescript of McLoughlin's tragic letter of June 4, 1844. And Judith Hudson Beatty of the Hudson's Bay Company Archives in Toronto, not only offered advice, she spent an untold amount of time supplying the new archival numbers for company documents, to supplant those previously used.

Michael Carter and John Bovey of the British Columbia Archives found materials and put me on the track of others, as did George Brandak of the University of British Columbia Library. Margot Kyle and Johanne Pelletier gave assistance with material in the Archives of McGill University. Peter Boyle, Marty Mascarin and Melinda Bell, archivists at old Fort William, steered me to several elusive Canadian addresses, and to a suitable copy of McLoughlin's contract with the Frobisher-McTavish Company. Carole Ritchot of the Archives Nationales de Québec provided a photograph of the contract held there, along with permission to reproduce it.

Many of the book's illustrations came from the extensive photographic archives of the Oregon Historical Society, whose experts served as guides. Others who supplied prints and permissions included Laura Bowler of the Stark Museum of Art, Courtney DeAngelis of the Amon Carter Museum, Jackie Spafford of the Royal Ontario Museum and Sara Montgomery of the National Archives of Canada. Debra Moore of Still Images with the Hudson's Bay Company Archives, gave special help in locating suitable pictures, including the painting used for the book jacket. Oregon has several rich sources of McLoughlin documents. Alden Moberg, Oregoniana Librarian for the Oregon State Library, went out of his way to send material on Burt Brown Barker, and Layne Sawyer provided the microfilm for McLoughlin's signed Intent to Become a Citizen. David Wendell, reference librarian of the Oregon State Archives, sent pictures and documents, and took special pains to find information about McLoughlin's private suits in Clackamas County. Nancy Wilson, curator at the McLoughlin House, shared its unique resources and told me where to see others. O.J. Johnson and the Board of the McLoughlin Memorial Association were generous with permission to use its records, as was John H. Herman, grandson of Burt Brown Barker and literary executor of the Barker estate.

Adair Law, director of the Oregon Historical Society Press—innovative, informed, supremely capable—took great responsibility for pulling it all together and shaping the book, while the book's editor Nancy Trotic, who has incredible attention to detail, watched for lurking pitfalls. Lori Root, book designer, gave the book its professional dress. And Virginia Linnman, sales and marketing manager of the OHS Press, saw that the finished product was properly introduced to its prospective readers.

To librarians—bless them—I am forever indebted. The library of the Oregon Historical Society is a rich treasure trove for all aspects of the area's history, and the members of its staff were without fail kind and helpful, Sieglinde Smith having gone out of her way to suggest special publications. Similarly, the staffs of the OHS Library and Multnomah County Library lugged heavy volumes out of their closed stacks and told me of their favorites, while those at the Beaverton Library repeatedly tapped the bottomless well of Interlibrary Loan.

Of great importance, with special attention, I salute both my writer's groups, who listened week after week for a decade as the manuscript grew. With patience, good humor, and tact (but professional standards) they asked for missing links, or pointed out fuzzy passages and pages that dragged.

And last—from my heart—I mention my wonderful, supportive family, who put up with the process.

Thank you, everyone.

Contents

Prologue

~ The House ~

I t was square and solid, a gracious house with high ceilings and a handsome staircase. It had begun in dignity as Dr. John McLoughlin's home, planned by him and built from timbers sawn in his own mill, with windowsills and trim brought around the Horn. Standing on the lowest level of Oregon City, looking west across the street toward Willamette Falls, it had been one of the finest residences in the Pacific Northwest, an openhearted house where homeless newcomers often found a bed for the night— or rolled up in a quilt on the floor of the upstairs hall, if all the rooms were full.

By 1906, however, it was old and gone to seed, with peeling paint, advertising signs plastered across its front, and a large woolen mill across the street, blocking its river view. The Oregon City Council decided to purchase it, using an annual property tax of one-tenth of one percent until forty-five hundred dollars had been raised. The plan was trounced by popular vote. The Hawley Pulp and Paper Company then bought the house, intending to clear the lot for expansion, and they offered it free to anyone who would move it away. The town? they asked. Could it be used as a public reading room? But the city fathers, having no funds, merely provided space in a park on the second tier of streets, high above the river, saying that someone else would have to do the job. Nobody offered, and when the paper company decided to tear it down, the house became the center of a storm, as its owner had been the center of a greater storm sixty years before.

Again the citizens were divided. One faction said the move should not even be attempted. They recalled that after McLoughlin's death the woolen mill had been built and his home had become the Phoenix Hotel, with a huge addition on the back to lodge the mill's workers. Worse than that, after fire destroyed the mill, the Phoenix had become a tenement and then a "house of negotiable affection." No town should preserve such a building, the group insisted. Tear it down. They published a pamphlet, which righteously stated:

> McLoughlin's former home has been for past decades a haunt of shame and disgrace on South Main Street. It has been used for vile and disreputable purposes so long that no decent, purity loving citizen can associate it with any good purpose. In a state of decay and dissolution it was dumped upon the city to disgrace a park block and destroy the most beautiful park site in our city—a whited sepulcher, a wolf in sheep's clothing.

A second group, with an eye to logistics, thought the argument was a waste of time. The building was too wide for the streets, they said. Too heavy for any machine in the state to budge. It would break apart of its own weight. Even if they contrived the means to move such a mass, it would have to be taken up Singers Hill, where the road passed between a black basalt cliff on one side and a drop-off on the other, with one stretch only half as wide as the house. It would overhang the drop-off and go crashing onto the railway below. The only way to get it past that narrow strip was to take it apart, plank by plank, and reassemble it on the new site, or widen the road by building a trestle. Nobody had the cash to do either one. They'd have to tear it down.

There was a third group, however, who were interested in pioneer days. They acknowledged that the old house had been neglected, that it was "a haunt of wandering tramps and storm-beleaguered animals . . . in a sad state of disrepair, malodorous and weatherbeaten, and as sorry a relic of the past as could well be imagined."

But it was historic, they said. It symbolized the beginning of settlement, of Oregon Territory, of the state. It would remind old and young of the years when its owner ruled the land, giving no quarter, but playing fair. The years when he, a Canadian, saved countless American lives. When war clouds darkened the horizon and he stood firm, a beacon for peace. His home must be preserved.

They refused to give in. They quashed three injunctions. Founded an association. Collected a thousand dollars, took off the roof, took off the chimneys, took off the addition, jacked up the original house, put it on support beams. They made rollers from trees of the surrounding forest, improvised a system of pulleys and cables attached to a winch, and hired men at twenty-five cents per day to carry rollers from the rear, after the house had passed, and lay them

The McLoughlin house mov-
ing to its new site. The horse
walked in a circle, to winch it
along, eight inches per lap.
COURTESY OF MCLOUGHLIN HOUSE
NATIONAL HISTORIC SITE

at the front. For power the workmen hitched up a single horse, which led the
way, turning the winch, turning the pulleys, and worming the massive structure along, eight inches ahead for every slow circuit of the animal. In late
spring 1909, the one-horse-power contraption started out. Watchers gathered
along the route and eyed the narrow slope of Singers Hill, anticipating the
crash. Progress was so slow that the building scarcely seemed to move, but
the movers were ready—men with a plan.

IN 1824, NEARLY A CENTURY BEFORE the attempt to move his house, Dr. John
McLoughlin had come from Canada to the Northwest, as Chief Factor in charge
of the Columbia District of the Hudson's Bay Company. Forty years old and an
experienced fur trader, he had found an almost uncharted land. A few sailing
ships plied the forested coast, collecting furs and seeking the Northwest Passage.
Fur-trading brigades—horses and men and native wives and mixed-blood children—followed the waterways. McLoughlin's company was operating a small
post near the Columbia River's mouth, with a few even smaller ones upstream,
while a handful of American mountain men had abandoned their beaver traps
to eke out a living on scattered farms. But no other white settlements had been
formed, and he was the virtual dictator over the entire area from the Rocky
Mountains to the Pacific, from Alaska to the southern border of Oregon.

The land—rugged mountains, green valleys, and high plateaus—lay quiet,
shrouded in fog, drenched in rain, or warm under the summer sun. Indian
tribes were there, tribes whose names echo in the rivers of today. Tualatin.
Clackamas. Mollala. Umatilla. Walla Walla. Santiam. They fished, farmed, hunt-

ed, and exchanged their products up and down the Columbia in a vast trading network. Although they were wary of whites, they valued ammunition and kettles, blankets and cloth, and therefore they tolerated the company posts.

As a newcomer to this distant land, McLoughlin faced challenges such as he had never known before. In the east he had operated from settled forts over well-known canoe routes, but his new district was virtually unexplored. In the east he was only a few weeks' journey from headquarters, but the Columbia was so remote that if he sent a message to his superiors—by land over the Rockies or by sailing ship to England—he must wait a year or more for a reply.

One of his pressing needs was to build an alliance with his Indian neighbors, who were aloof at first. Calling him the "White-Headed Eagle," for the thatch of white hair that hung thick to his shoulders, they held him in awe for his size—six feet, four inches, which was remarkable for that day—and for his searing temper. Eventually they learned to trust him, because he was kind and fair. "He put men in irons who treated the Indians badly," his daughter later said. "That is the way they kept peace with the Indians."

McLoughlin solved most of his problems with the natives, but those with his own race were more difficult. Instead of a single government, the Northwest had a jerry-built system called joint occupation, which gave the citizens of Britain and the United States equal rights to settle and do business there, guided by neither courts nor laws.

In the resulting vacuum it was impossible for McLoughlin to make long-term plans, and the situation grew worse as more Americans moved in—fur traders, explorers, sea captains, missionaries, government agents. And at last a torrent of immigrants, sweeping across the plains and mountains and ocean for a dozen reasons. To line their own pockets. To save the natives' souls. To expand the United States from sea to sea. Or for land—free land—the irresistible lure.

Surrounded by this horde, McLoughlin was torn between loyalty to his company, friendship for the Indians, and compassion for the trail-worn settlers. He directed an astounding mix of personnel. While the company officers were generally English, Scottish, or Canadian, and fairly well educated, the employees were French Canadian boatmen and laborers, Iroquois from the east, natives of the West Coast, Kanakas (Hawaiians), and American workmen who had strayed from the occasional fur brigade that ventured so far. Sometimes wise, sometimes floundering, but always with profound sympathy, McLoughlin threaded his way among settlers and Indians, fur traders and farmers, Americans and British, Protestants and Catholics. He saved numberless lives, and for the rest of his days he was convinced that he had kept the peace. "I am of opinion if I had acted otherwise than I did," he said, "besides Vancouver being pillaged and the Companys Business Destroyed—England and the United states would be at War."

McLoughlin's career had "spanned a continent and embraced an entire period in the history of the Pacific Northwest." Nevertheless, his last years were lonely and bitter. His relationships with Indians and American settlers moved in opposite directions. With the natives, he began with conflict but achieved peace and friendship. With the immigrants, he began with friendship but ended by being rejected and cruelly hurt. The pattern of his life was that of classical Greek tragedy, in which the hero shows courage and skill but is destroyed by implacable fate, by his virtues, and by his own character flaw.

AS FOR THE HOUSE, on a warm summer day in 1909 it inched its way along, drawn by the patient horse. At the narrow place on Singers Hill, the movers implemented their plan. The house was "sound and well built; the timbering hewed and very heavy." So they modified the arrangement of timbers and jacks, and "loaded the inside of the house next to the cliff with sand, gravel & cement until the weight counterbalanced the overhanging and proceeded with it to the top of the grade." People scarcely breathed as it was rolled cautiously up the slope; but the road held firm and the structure did too, reaching solid ground in safety.

It was night when the house reached its new location, along with the workmen, rolling logs, load of sand, and doubtless tuckered-out horse. Since it was still accompanied by a band of hecklers, the movers decided not to risk a further delay, but worked by torchlight to set the old building on its foun-

The McLoughlin house on its way up the narrow road on the steepest part of Singer's Hill. Since it had been stopped for the night at the base of this grade, this segment was surmounted on the second day of the process. OHS ORHI 35893

The McLoughlin house on the trestle, the most dangerous part of the move. It was here that the workmen weighted the inner side with sand, in order to prevent a collapse.
OHS ORHI 49852

dation without turning it around. It faced west, as it always had, but the new site was on the river side of the street, so its broad front door opened into its own back yard, high above the falls.

During the next few weeks, volunteers pitched in, painting inside and out, replacing the roof, rebuilding the chimneys, cleaning up the lot. On Sunday, September 5, 1909, several hundred citizens attended the dedication—a ceremony that included an introduction by the mayor, speeches by notables, and three numbers by the town band. Carefully kept up and maintained as a museum by the McLoughlin Memorial Association, the house still stands with its back to the street, looking toward the river as it did when it was new.

Honors for its owner were belated, coming after a stormy time, as they had for his home. Handsome and spacious, it was at first admired, then neglected and nearly destroyed, but at last came into its own. Similarly, McLoughlin began with power and prestige, then was attacked and nearly forgotten.

But as the years passed and the settlers reminisced, some of them thought kindly of the white-headed giant who had served them so well. They talked—made speeches—wrote articles. McLoughlin became the subject of more than a dozen books. Streets, schools, and parks were given his name. The U.S. Mint issued a half-dollar with his likeness on one side and Fort Vancouver on the reverse. The state legislature named him the "Father of Oregon." His statue—erect, in a billowing cloak, with cane in one hand and beaver hat in the other—was placed in the United States Capitol, and stands there still.

Dr. John McLoughlin had gained recognition for his role in the growth of his adopted nation. His story, however, began not in the Northwest but in another country, three thousand miles away.

Canada

CHAPTER ONE

Quebec

I cannot accuse no one but myself of my bad fortune
as it was entirely by my own want of conduct
that I came up to this Country.

Dr. John McLoughlin

~ 1 ~

The Litigious Frasers
1746–1778

John McLoughlin's early childhood was spent on the south bank of the St. Lawrence River. His family owned a substantial farm near Rivière-du-Loup, a village of neat cottages clustered along a stream of the same name. It was a scenic area with a waterfall, a steep-sided chasm, forested hills, and small farms that sloped down to the St. Lawrence. Young McLoughlin found much to see, for at that point the river was fifteen miles wide and tidal, an artery of commerce plied by oceangoing ships from Quebec and Montreal.

Although this was a French-speaking region, McLoughlin's ancestry was mixed. His father's people were Scotch-Irish. His mother's mother was French Canadian. And his mother's father was Scottish, the son of Donald Fraser, a Highlander of more courage than luck who had fought for the English when the rebels tried to put Charles Edward Stuart—Bonnie Prince Charlie—on the throne. In 1746, in the battle on Culloden Moor, twelve hundred Scotsmen wielding broadswords had been killed in less than an hour by the English and their Scottish allies, who were backed by cavalry and cannon and lost only seventy-six. It broke the back of the rebellion, but Donald Fraser, McLoughlin's great-grandfather, was among those few who fell.

After this, the English placed Scotland under the iron yoke of empire, executed clan chiefs, banned the kilt and the bagpipe, and gave ownership of clan territories to those who were loyal. One distant relative—wealthy Simon Fraser, who had fought for the Stuarts—was sent to the block. But the Donald Fraser branch of the family was spared, because it had been on England's side, and Donald's son Malcolm, who was a boy of thirteen at the time of Culloden, grew up as a dutiful subject of the Crown.

Malcolm Fraser—he spelled it "ffraser"—was his own man, irascible, domineering, warm-hearted. He spoke Gaelic, English, French, and a bit of Latin,

~3~

and never took "no" gracefully for an answer in any language. When he was quite young, he joined the famous Fraser Highlanders, a regiment raised on Simon Fraser's estate, and as a lieutenant he came to North America to fight the French in the French and Indian War.

Its stakes were the wealth of the New World, and it changed his life. On September 13, 1759, twenty-six-year-old Lieutenant Fraser was with the Highlanders when they climbed the cliffs to the Plains of Abraham above the city of Quebec. There, while bagpipes screamed, the English under General James Wolfe defeated the French under the Marquis de Montcalm and captured

For his military valor in the capture of Quebec, Malcolm Fraser, John McLoughlin's maternal grandfather, was rewarded with a tract of land northeast of the city that equaled roughly 160 square miles. This "View of Quebec" was created more than a century after Fraser's military service. From Robert Brown's *A Graphic and Popular Description of the Countries of the World Illustrated*, part 7. HUDSON BAY COMPANY ARCHIVES, PROVINCIAL ARCHIVES OF MANITOBA, HBCA PP2150 [N14041]

the city of Quebec. The Treaty of Paris then gave Great Britain all the French possessions in Canada except two small islands, marking the end of French rule.

The battle was Malcolm Fraser's great moment. Governments at that time made lavish endowments of land in the New World, and Fraser, who was severely wounded, received the seigneury of Mount Murray, seventy miles northeast of Quebec. The seigneury, a tract of rolling land rich in forests and streams, lay along the north shore of the St. Lawrence River for eighteen miles and stretched nine miles inland. Three decades later his grandson, John McLoughlin, would visit it and know it well.

At first young Malcolm Fraser had so little money that he had to borrow forty-two pounds to buy equipment for operating his estate. Although he had tenants to work his fields, the rents he could ask were incredibly small, perhaps a pair of capons and one dollar in cash per year for a hundred acres. But he prospered. He built a gristmill and a sawmill, as well as an impressive wood-frame house, and he later acquired considerable property in the city of Quebec. Although he probably spent part of his time there, most records place him in Mount Murray.

Shortly after receiving the seigneury, Malcolm either married a young French Canadian named Marie Allaire or entered a longtime alliance with her, the status being uncertain because no record of a marriage has been found. She was French Catholic, while he was a stout Presbyterian, and by bringing her into the family he laid the foundation for countless squabbles over religion. Their first child, Angélique—John McLoughlin's mother—was born about 1760 at Mount Murray, with three boys to follow: Alexander about 1761, Joseph about 1765, and Simon in 1769.

One picture of Angélique survives, drawn in pen and ink in her old age but still showing traces of beauty. She must have grown up in considerable comfort, for her father was the seigneur of Mount Murray, which adjoined the seigneury of Murray Bay, owned by Fraser's close friend John Nairne. The life at Murray Bay has been well documented, some of it by Malcolm Fraser. If, as seems likely, the circumstances of the two families were similar, the Fraser tenants gathered at New Year's for cakes and ale, danced around the maypole on May Day, and asked Fraser to serve as godfather for their children. His family could ride in a carriage, sit in a special pew at church, and receive communion first, and he could require his renters to work a certain number of days per year on the roads or at the manor house.

One old inhabitant, on being asked about the status of a typical seigneur, replied in a voice of awe, "Monsieur, il était le roi, l'empereur du village" (Sire, he was the king, the emperor of the village).

In 1775, when Angélique was about fifteen, Seigneur Malcolm Fraser took up arms once more, to fight on the British side in the American Revolution. He thrived on battles—both international and interfamilial—and he distinguished himself again, this time as captain in a regiment assigned to the defense of Quebec. He was making his rounds in a violent snowstorm shortly before dawn on December 31 when the Americans under Benedict Arnold and General Richard Montgomery attacked. At sight of their signal lights, Fraser immediately ordered the alarm bell and ran down the street shouting "Turn out! Turn out!" thus sending every man to his post in time to repulse the assault. Montgomery was killed and Arnold wounded, the Americans were driven back, and although the war continued farther south, Fraser returned to his estate and the life of a seigneur.

The war had not changed him, for he was still being pursued by conflicts, and meeting them headlong. The first recorded upheaval within the family was due to Angélique. Still in her teens, beautiful, intelligent, and endowed with a full share of her father's combativeness, she was one of the few people rash enough and resolute enough to cross him. To his dismay, she fell in love with a strapping young farmer named John McLoughlin, who lived south of the St. Lawrence River, near the village of Rivière-du-Loup. He was the second of four John McLoughlins. They were:

1. John McLoughlin. Called "Jacques Maclas" in early records, he had been born in Ireland in 1714, and owned land at Rivière-du-Loup by 1780 or before. He married Mary Short, an Irishwoman, by whom he had two daughters and two sons.

2. John McLoughlin. The firstborn child of the above, he was the one who fell in love with Angélique Fraser.

3. Dr. John McLoughlin, the subject of this book. He was the son of John and Angélique.

4. John McLoughlin, son of the doctor.

Their name was pronounced with a "k" sound—"McLocklin." Those who knew Dr. John McLoughlin spelled it by ear, with ingenious variations: McLauchland, McGlaucland, McGloghlin, McLauchlan, MacLochlan. These may indicate the Scottish "ch" rather than the hard "k," but no journals or letters use an "f" in the second syllable.

No one today knows how Angélique Fraser and her John McLoughlin met. It was not remarkable for the owners of a seigneury to have contacts with the substantial farmers of their own neighborhood, and Angélique's father had been in Rivière-du-Loup at least once, in 1775, when he witnessed a lease of land to François Tannau, inhabitant of the area. But the St. Lawrence River is wide, and Rivière-du-Loup is forty miles downstream from Mount Murray.

The McLoughlin family coat of arms. The Latin *Vincet Virtute* translates as "Shall conquer by virtue." From *The McLoughlin Empire and Its Rulers* by Burt Brown Barker. OHS ORHI 99104

In addition, the two families had little in common. John's father used only his mark in signing a deed, while Angélique's father was an educated man who spoke four languages and had kept a war journal of sufficient merit to be published by the Literary and Historical Society of Quebec. The McLoughlins—as far as is known—attended only to their farm and village, while Malcolm Fraser had important connections in the city of Quebec. And in the eighteenth century, when religious hatreds were harsh, the McLoughlins were devout Catholics, while Fraser was a fiercely loyal Scotch Presbyterian.

Angélique's decision therefore resulted in a family upheaval, but as a daughter of rock-ribbed Malcolm Fraser, she stood her ground. She did not care that her young man was from an obscure family, a poor match for the daughter of a seigneur, or that her father detested the Catholic religion, or that the St. Lawrence would separate her from Mount Murray by a long, slow journey with sails or oars. She did not care that her young man's education was skimpy, or that the new life would be hard. John was her choice, she loved him, and she intended to marry him. Let the seigneur roar.

Angélique and her father were too much alike for either to give in easily. In spite of his threats she crossed to the south bank of the river, turned Catholic, and married her young man, probably in 1778. Years later her grand-niece, Sister Marie de St. Thomas d'Aquin, wrote:

> Malcolm Fraser was thunderstruck. He brought up many objections against this unexpected line of conduct, but they were unheeded. His daughter's decision was invincible. Then, in a rage, he disinherited her. She left quietly, insisting that her heart would always be faithful in its love for her father, and they were soon married.

The boyhood family of Dr. John McLoughlin was begun.

~ 2 ~

Across the St. Lawrence
1778–1798

A ngélique left no record of problems or regrets, even though a steep-roofed farm cottage could not have provided the luxuries the daughter of a seigneur was used to. The McLoughlins were a good, stable family, land-owners rather than tenants, who later became prosperous enough to donate land for a church. But as the wife of a farmer, she would probably ride in a farm wagon rather than a carriage, and while she might have some hired servants, she herself would do at least part of the housework. As for her change in religion, she may have welcomed that, because her French Canadian mother, being a Catholic, had doubtless grounded Angélique in that faith.

The first child, Marie Louise, was born in 1780. She was soon followed by another girl, who lived only a short time, and on October 19, 1784, by a boy. Because Rivière-du-Loup had no priest, on December 5, when the baby was six weeks old, the young couple took him to the neighboring village of Kamouraska to have him baptized. It must have been a bitter journey in early winter, with a tiny infant wrapped in shawls and furs, for it was more than thirty cold, windy miles by boat and a still harder trip overland. Although his baptismal name was Jean Baptiste, history knows him as plain John McLoughlin or—more commonly—as Dr. John McLoughlin.

For the early years of Angélique's marriage and the births of the first two children, there are no records of contact between Angélique and her father. But when John was sixteen months old, Seigneur Malcolm, for an unknown reason, bought the young McLoughlins an excellent farm near Rivière-du-Loup, four arpents wide and forty long. An arpent was 191.85 feet, so the farm was not quite a mile and a half long by a sixth of a mile wide, with one narrow end on the St. Lawrence. Early village and parish maps show all the farms of the area as similarly long and narrow, running back from the river like ribbons on the land, in order to give valuable water frontage to as many owners as possible.

According to the records of the Ursuline convent in Quebec, Angélique took baby John and Marie Louise on the long journey across the St. Lawrence River to visit her father soon after the gift of the farm. Grandfather Fraser, seeing the children for the first time, was immediately charmed by the little girl, for she was precocious, with a happy nature that was to grace her entire life.

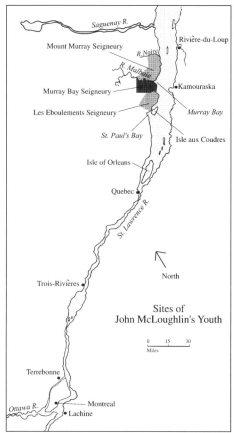

Part of the lower St. Lawrence River, including the places that were significant to McLoughlin and his family when he was a child. His home was near Rivière-du-Loup, he was baptized at Kamouraska, his grandparents lived at the seigneury of Mount Murray, and he moved to Quebec when he was between five and eight years old.

Nothing would please the grandfather but adopting her and bringing her up as his own. Nothing would please Angélique but keeping her. He was adamant. So was she. It was another battle, nearly as acrimonious as the one over her marriage, but this time Angélique lost. As told in convent records, the seigneur declared that Marie Louise should not return to Rivière-du-Loup with her parents and "almost by force, retained her as his adopted child." For nearly a decade she lived at Mount Murray, "attending the Sunday services with her grandfather, and going to a Protestant school instead of the convent." Although John was too young to understand what had happened, he was old enough to miss his sweet-tempered big sister, and to realize that testy Grandfather Fraser often had his fingers in the family pie.

That same year, John's only and much beloved brother David was born, with three more girls to follow. In all, John and Angélique McLoughlin would

Farmland at Rivière-du-Loup where McLoughlin spent his early childhood. This 1952 photograph looks from the St. Lawrence River, southeast toward the hills. The original buildings are no longer in existence. OHS ORHI 78933

have seven children:

Marie Louise	1780
Marie Elizabeth	1782 (died in early childhood)
Jean Baptiste (John)	1784
David	1786
Julienne	1788
Margaret	1789
Honoree	1792

Their farm was on level land, backed by hills and sloping down to the river. Nearby were woods that sheltered deer and wolves and bears, open fields spangled with flowers in spring or dazzling with winter's snow. From the river-bank the children could see white-winged ships sailing up the St. Lawrence to the city of Quebec or down to the wide Atlantic Ocean. Rivière-du-Loup was near, and by the time John was six, the family had a new chapel there in which to attend Mass—St. Patrice, built on the land Grandfather McLoughlin had donated.

In 1791, when Angélique was thirty-one and her youngest brother, Simon, was eighteen, Grandfather Fraser caused another family upheaval, this time by the birth of a daughter. Eventually there were four in his second brood of children—Julienne, Anne, William, and John Malcolm—with birth dates ranging from 1791 to 1800. For a man to have a second family was not unusual, for mortality among women at that time was tragically high. But it was surprising to have a second family while the first wife was still alive, and Marie Allaire lived until at least 1814. "My Grandmother and Mother live together at the Big Farm," Dr. John McLoughlin wrote to his uncle, Dr. Simon Fraser, in that year.

No documents have been found to substantiate Malcolm's divorce and re-marriage, but the children—Angélique's half brothers and sisters—were openly acknowledged, their letters are included in the family correspondence, and the seigneur remembered them in his will. This was a long, peculiar document in which Marie Allaire, mother of the first children, received an income derived from two pieces of her own property on which Malcolm held mortgages. In addition, a certain Mrs. Mary Dugros (sometimes written as Marie Ducros) was given the right to live in the manor house and care for the two youngest sons, plus an annuity of twenty-five pounds, "because she has lived in my house and hath had the management of my household and other affairs at Point Fraser for several years past." She may have been wife or mistress or housekeeper, mother or caretaker of the second brood. But whatever had happened, the situation was certainly one to upset the volatile family, and it must have been known to young John.

It is also said that Fraser fathered several other children by Indian women, but these apparently took their mother's names, and they do not appear in family records.

About the time Grandfather Fraser started his second family, when John was seven, his parents moved to Quebec, where his youngest sister Honoree was born in early 1792. How they financed the move is not clear, but a plaintive letter written by the children's father in 1796 indicates that Fraser was bringing pressure.

Honoured Sir

I received the letter that you honoured me with dated the twentyeth Instant. . . .

. . . I thought that I answered you several times heretofore on that subject. I Refer to Mr. Jones that has them under his Charge I believe and I am sure that he will let you know what Directions I Ever give him whether any or not with Regard to Religion.

I feel it Rather hard that you should Compell a parent to bring his Children up in a Religion that he wass not brought up himself and Consider that it is a weakness to Aquiese. However, If it is your Request I find myself Obliged to Agree With what you Request.

> Honoured Sir
> I am your Dutifull Servant
>
> John McLoughlin

Quebec 27th July 1796
Colonell Fraser

Although the father did not say what pressure the seigneur used to "Compell" the parents to obey, it is reasonable to assume that finances entered the picture.

Whatever had happened, the McLoughlin house was full and lively, with two boys and three girls living at home. John and David were soon old enough to prowl the narrow, crooked streets, where houses stood shoulder to shoulder and carts rattled over the cobbles. The boys could watch ships in the harbor, rising and falling on the twenty-foot tides, and they could climb the wooded bluffs behind the city to the Plains of Abraham, on which Grandfather Malcolm Fraser had fought the French so long ago. The children may have attended school in the city, and at least part of the time they were privately taught by the "Mr. Jones" who had them "under his Charge."

Their older sister, Marie Louise, moved to Quebec in 1795, when she was fifteen and John was eleven, because Grandfather Fraser sent her to the Ursuline convent to be educated and "finished," as was common for girls of good family. In entrusting her to the nuns, the seigneur was gambling that his own Protestant religion would withstand the Catholic faith—a surprising risk for a man of such granite prejudice, and one he would bitterly regret. He doubtless felt he had no choice, for good schools were rare, and a convent education was the best to be had.

Tradition says that during those years John and David made visits to Mount Murray, where they heard bagpipes, watched Scottish games and dances, and listened while Grandfather Fraser spoke Gaelic with the many Highlanders who lived along the St. Lawrence. One of John's granddaughters thought he and David "were brought up by their mother's father"—a circumstance that seems unlikely, although Fraser's influence was undoubtedly strong. Years later, when John was in charge of a frontier fort, one of his men remarked, "The Doctor . . . used to tell anecdotes of old Scotland, probably furnished by his grandfather." And William Tolmie, a fellow fur trader who knew him well, said, "of John McLoughlin's Father I have never heard him speak. Of his maternal grandfather he spoke often."

According to another tradition, while John and David were at Mount Murray they often met Alexander and Simon Fraser, Angélique's younger brothers, who influenced John to enter the fur trade as a physician. However, the careers of both uncles kept them far away. Alexander was a partner in the North West Company and lived on the distant frontier. Simon—Dr. Simon Fraser—had studied medicine at the University of Edinburgh, but he left it at the age of twenty without graduating and became a lieutenant in the Royal Highland Regiment of the British army. Although neither of these uncles was able to pay frequent visits, the boys had doubtless heard of them, and Simon was destined to become John's good angel—a patient, generous refuge in time of trouble.

For some time after their move to Quebec, things were apparently smooth for the McLoughlin family, with the children taught by Mr. Jones and attending a Protestant church, as Grandfather Fraser insisted. The next known squabble was precipitated by an unexpected rebel—sweet-tempered Marie Louise.

When Grandfather Fraser sent her to the Ursulines to be educated, he had not reckoned with the nuns' persuasiveness, or with her early years in Rivière-du-Loup, where her family belonged to the Catholic faith. Neither had he allowed for Marie Louise's share of the family tenacity. Soon after entering the convent school, she accepted the beliefs of the nuns, and she stood by her decision in spite of her grandfather's ferocious opposition. As told in the convent records there was a "storm raised by the disappointed Colonel," but she joined the church with her parents' consent, "while the irascible relative was absent on a journey."

Later, when she was eighteen and took her first formal vows as a nun, Grandfather Fraser was even more furious, but the blustering old man had again met his match. Shout and threaten as he would, he failed to sway her, and she became Sister St. Henry of the Ursulines. For all her long life she remained the happy, gentle individual John had known as a child. A letter from a colleague spoke of her irrepressible laughter; the records of the convent describe her as "radiant with smiles"; and the Abbé Desjardins teased another nun by suggesting that she "try to prevent Sister St. Henry from Laughing." A skilled teacher and greatly beloved, she eventually became Mother Superior of the Ursuline convent in Quebec.

But that was far in the future. At about the time she decided to take the veil, John made an important decision of his own.

~3~

A Very Young Doctor
1798–1803

A t the time of Marie Louise's first vows, John was a teenager, long-legged and gawky, with a mop of shaggy hair and piercing blue eyes. He was bright, energetic, and eager to succeed, and when he was not quite fourteen, he decided to become a physician.

At that time there were two ways to secure medical training and a license: attending a university in Europe or the United States, for there was no medical college in Canada; or apprenticeship to an established doctor, which would mean a vivid but somewhat casual hands-on education close to home. Not wanting to leave the area, or not being able to afford it, he became an apprentice of Dr. James Fisher of Quebec, and in the fall of 1798—just before John's fourteenth birthday—he moved bag and baggage into the Fisher home. It was a good choice, for Dr. Fisher was a prominent physician who helped create laws for the province and has been called the father of medical legislation in Quebec.

As a medical apprentice, John would learn by accompanying his master on his rounds and working under supervision. He would dress in sober, dark clothes, roll pills in the pharmacy, hold the reins as the doctor's team clop-clopped over the cobbled streets. He doubtless learned to draw blood, for physicians believed that bleeding—"the grand preventive as well as the cure"—restored health by drawing off poisons. He would study the use of herbs, such as how to crush sorrel with mortar and pestle and heat it in its own juice until it became a paste for application to a sore. In case of an operation or amputation, he would be taught to give the patient a good swig of alcohol or a dose of laudanum (opium spirits) to deaden the pain. But he would learn nothing about antisepsis, for that lay in the future.

John was an apprentice for four and a half years, the final months being a special pleasure because his brother David was also with Dr. Fisher then, as a beginning student. Now the older boy could help the younger, and perhaps receive a touch of hero worship along with the brotherly squabbling. This year together cemented a tie that lasted all their lives.

By the spring of 1803 McLoughlin was eighteen—a strapping six feet four, with broad shoulders and a booming voice that broke into a stammer when he was excited. After finishing his apprenticeship, which qualified him to set up a practice, he applied for a medical license. But the circumstances were strange. Two years earlier his soldier-uncle, Dr. Simon Fraser, had been wounded in Egypt, after which he had returned to Lower Canada and entered medical practice in Terrebonne, near Montreal. And when John applied for his own medical license, he did it not from Quebec but from Terrebonne, his uncle's hometown. It was an inconvenient choice, because it necessitated a considerable journey and removed him from the city where the provincial offices were located.

Nevertheless, John had made the move by April 1, 1803, when he wrote a respectful petition to the lieutenant governor of the Province of Lower Canada. It said he "humbly showeth" his preparation, "is desirous to practice the same [medicine] in this Province," and "humbly prays" for the privilege of taking an examination for a license. In addition to John's petition, Dr. Fisher submitted an affidavit:

> This will certify that Mr. John McLoughlin, a Canadian, lived with me as an apprentice and student in medicine, surgery and pharmacy for four years and six months, during which he behaved honestly. He possesses talents, and I sincerely believe him a good subject to the British government.

The request was granted. A document dated April 25 says the commissioners "do certify that we have examined John McLoughlin, the Petitioner, and we conceive that he may be licensed to Practice in Surgery and Pharmacy or as an Apothecary." Eight days later, on May 3, an added paragraph ordered the license to be prepared, "by order of His Excellency The Lieut. Governor."

Before that, however, McLoughlin had turned his back on his profession's mainstream, to join the North West Company as an apprentice clerk. This meant leaving Canada and going to the immense forests beyond Lake Superior, bound for five years' service in the fur trade at an apprentice's low salary. The relevant documents, with their significant dates, were:

April 1	Application for medical license, Terrebonne
April 25	Certification by commissioners, Quebec
April 26	Fur-trade contract, Montreal
April 30	Dr. Fisher's affidavit, Quebec
May 3	Commissioners' order to issue license, Quebec

These show that he abandoned his goal of practicing medicine "in this Province" and signed the fur-trade contract just as he finished his training, without waiting to find out whether his license had been granted.

Dr. Henri DeChesne, the son of McLoughlin's sister Honoree, explained the reason in a letter of 1893 to the writer Eva Emery Dye. DeChesne had moved to Oregon, lived for a time in McLoughlin's home, and attended McLoughlin in his last illness, so he knew his uncle well. DeChesne wrote:

> I will tell you what nobody knows on the Pacific Coast, viz: What made the Dr leave Canada and turns his steps towards the N W. . . . The Dr. had just been received M.D. and was taking a walk with a young lady, when in crossing a muddy street (it was in the spring and in Quebec!) over a plank, the lady in front, when in opposite direction came an English officer, who pushed the lady from the plank. Please look into the mud and try to discover the English Officer lying down in it and with it covered from head to feet—In those days there was danger in store for the young gallant and to the N.W. he went to save himself and join his uncles and alas! to forget her.

DeChesne was correct in describing such an episode as dangerous, for it happened only two decades after England lost the American colonies in the Revolutionary War. In any era, attacking an officer would be unwise, and with British-American relations not yet healed, it might have landed the young hothead behind bars.

The details cannot be proven and they may not be entirely accurate, for DeChesne wrote the letter long after the event. But other documents, from three reputable sources, give additional evidence that the newly fledged doctor had fled because of his own mistake.

McLoughlin himself confirmed it. In 1808 he wrote to his Uncle Simon, "I cannot accuse no one but myself of my bad fortune as it was entirely by my own want of conduct that I came up to this Country." In 1814 the event still rankled, and he wrote again, "People talk of the dessert of Siberia, but this is as bad . . . for my part I am sorry I ever came to it however this was perhaps not a matter of Choice but of Necessity on my part."

Further confirmation came from his uncle Alexander Fraser, a partner in the North West Company, who wrote to Simon in 1808, "What and how to dispose of him you are best able to tell." He suggested that John's time in the fur company "should retribute him from the past," but his letter gives no hint of what required retribution, or why the uncle should consider "how to dispose of him."

And gossip about the unfortunate error was circulating years later, when McLoughlin was the powerful head of Fort Vancouver, on the Columbia River. In 1841 the Reverend Herbert Beaver, an Anglican minister who had been stationed at the post, wrote a letter to *Church of England Protestant*

Henri DeChesne's 1893 letter describing why his uncle, John McLoughlin, left Canada. Eva Emery Dye papers, Oregon Historical Society, MSS 1089. OHS ORHI 98569

Magazine saying it was "reported and confirmed" that the doctor "had been compelled to quit Montreal, under Circumstances I will not trust myself to advert to."

Whatever the details, it is known that John McLoughlin was a true descendant of the Highland Frasers—quick-thinking, quick-moving, with a scalding temper. Since DeChesne's letter says "Quebec," without explaining whether he meant the city or the province, the young doctor may have gotten into trouble near home, or he may have gone to Montreal for some other reason and lapsed into his "want of conduct" there. In either case, he took his problem to his loyal uncle, who tried to help.

Simon Fraser's first plan was to send John to the West Indies, which were often a haven for young gentlemen in difficulties, and this idea apparently entranced McLoughlin. "I would much rather have gone to the West Indies as you propos'd," he later wrote.

However, transportation over such a distance may have been difficult, or the uncle may have been unable to secure a quick appointment there. At any rate, he lived in an area where the fur trade was a big business, and a logical second choice.

At that time Montreal—nearly two hundred miles upriver from Quebec—was the last outpost of European settlement, built on a thirty-mile island at the junction of the St. Lawrence and Ottawa Rivers, with Mount Royal—*Mont Real*—nearby. In summer it bustled with sailing ships on the broad St. Lawrence, with wharves piled high and loaded carts rumbling over the cobbles. It was a roistering small city, where as McLoughlin walked the streets he could meet priests in black robes, moccasined Indians, scarlet-clad British army officers, farmers in homespun, and students wearing tunics and bright-colored sashes.

Above all it was a city of furs. Furs were its pride, its passion, its curse, its reason for existence. Mansions of the fur barons dignified Mount Royal. Ships sailed eastward filled with half-cured pelts of beaver and otter, muskrat and mink. In autumn the warehouses along the waterfront were piled to the rafters.

Living so near this fur-trade city, Dr. Simon Fraser went to see Simon McTavish of McTavish, Frobisher—agents for the North West Company, in which John's Uncle Alexander was a partner. It was an easy contact, for the agency headquarters were in Montreal, as was McTavish's home.

Tall, lean, handsome, and so aristocratic he had the sobriquet "Marquis," Simon McTavish admitted his love of "good wine, good oysters, and pretty girls." As a partner and founder of the North West Company—a loosely organized partnership of individuals and small fur-trading groups—he had become the wealthiest, most influential merchant in Montreal, a man with a commanding presence and polished manners, able to deal urbanely with government officials or hobnob with men of the rowdy frontier.

Never one to hold a young fellow's high spirits against him—perhaps even considering them an asset—McTavish conferred with McLoughlin and his uncle, concluded that lanky John was well suited to the fur trade, and offered him a post as apprentice clerk at the low pay of one hundred pounds for five years

The first page of John McLoughlin's four-page 26 April 1803 contract with McTavish Frobisher & Co. At the age of eighteen McLoughlin did "bind and engage himself....in the capacity of a surgeon and apprentice clerk them to serve and go from hence wherever thereunto required and into any part of the Indian or Interior countries as well as those called the Northwest as every other post or posts pace of places where the said company now or at any time hereafter shall carry on trade or be in anywise concerned with the trade carried on by others for the time and term of five years.... He doth faithfully promise...to obey anyone of the said concerns...in all their just and lawful commands, their secrets keep and acquaint them with everything that shall come to his knowledge that may injure, prejudice or in any wise hurt the interests of the said Company...."
ARCHIVES NATIONALES DU QUEBEC. CENTRE DE MONTREAL. DU GREFFE "JOHN GERBRAND BEEK":CN601, S29

of work. John and his uncle both thought he was to receive more if he served as a physician, but if McTavish had this in mind, it was only an unwritten promise.

Although the salary was minimal and the work would be a professional backwater, it was safely out of reach, on the frontier where there were neither courts nor laws. Therefore, on April 26, 1803, McLoughlin signed a contract—four long pages, written in an ornate hand—promising that for the next five years he would obey the company officers and go "whenever whereunto required and into any part of the Indian or Interior Countries." One phrase hinted at John's predicament, for it said he came "with the Consent and Approbation of his uncle, Dr. Simon Fraser." In similar documents the consent of a parent or guardian was mentioned only for younger apprentices, and it was an unusual stipulation for an eighteen-year-old, especially a trained physician. It implied that Dr. Fraser acted as guarantor for his nephew's behavior, although that has not been proven.

Whatever it meant, gangling young McLoughlin accepted the terms and prepared for a long journey to the fur lands. He was fleeing, with no idea when he might return.

~ 4 ~

To the Fur Country

1803

On a soft spring morning in 1803, when the rivers' ice had thawed, McLoughlin left Montreal for Fort Kaministiquia, on the north shore of Lake Superior. Although we have no record of his journey, we know the approximate date, and there was only one way for him to get there—the fur traders' canoe route, which his contemporaries described. A flotilla would set out every two or three days, for a grueling journey of six weeks or more.

McLoughlin must have ridden—probably on a horse, perhaps in a carriage—through the narrow, muddy streets of Montreal, past log cabins, past churches whose spires rose white and slender against the sky, past gray stone cottages with tin roofs and massive iron shutters. Oxcarts plodded back and forth with a shriek of ungreased wooden wheels. Chickens pecked in the ruts, and squealing pigs scrambled out of the way.

At the south edge of town, McLoughlin had to pass through an abandoned gate in the city's crumbling stone wall, then continue for nine miles on a rut-

Lachine, on the same island as Montreal, is nine miles upstream where the St. Lawrence widens to form Lake St. Louis. Canoe brigades left the docks at Lachine every few days during the short season when the streams were free of ice. *The Spring Brigade Leaves Montreal for the West by Franklin Arbuckle.* HUDSON BAY COMPANY ARCHIVES, PROVINCIAL AR-CHIVES OF MANITOBA, HBCA PICTURE COLLECTION, P-412 (N7427).

ted dirt road near a thundering stretch of rapids. Behind him, toward the east, flowed the St. Lawrence River, Montreal's lifeline to Quebec and far beyond. Ahead of him lay Lachine—the point of departure—and an immense forest that could be penetrated only by paddling through lakes and streams.

He doubtless felt misgivings. He knew—everyone knew—that the fur trade was the most glamorous occupation of the day, that fur traders estab-lished canoe routes, named rivers and lakes, made maps, were followed by settlers, and thus helped determine the shape of nations. But however glam-orous, however lucrative it might be, fur trading was a bitter comedown from the medical career he had planned.

And still, as young McLoughlin slogged along, leaving everything and everybody he knew, he was young and strong and it was a blue-sky day of spring, such as the brigades always chose for their departure. When he rounded the last bend he could see the docks of Lachine, the warehouses, and Lake St. Louis, which was a broad section of the St. Lawrence River.

He would find the wharves bustling with workers and with family mem-bers who had come to see their men depart. The *bourgeois*—partners in the North West Company—would be there, some in old-fashioned knee breeches, others in stylish, tight trousers and close-fitted coats cut short in front, with long, tapered backs. They strode along the shore, strode along the piers, mak-ing sure the canoes were properly loaded.

These vessels used on the Great Lakes were enormous—thirty-five to forty feet long and able to carry four tons of crew and freight. They had lightweight frames of cedar, spruce, or ash, over which birch bark was wrapped, sewn with spruce roots and waterproofed with spruce or pine gum. Each canoe, with a Nor'-West pennant fluttering at its prow, was powered by ten to a dozen short, wiry French Canadians called *voyageurs*, who would be checking their craft and stowing its load. This would include six hundred pounds of biscuit, two hundred pounds of pork, three bushels of "pease," the crew's and passengers' personal baggage, and sixty or more packages of trading goods—muskets and blankets, tobacco and beads, lead and powder and knives, all in accurately weighed ninety-pound bundles. The voyageurs would tuck oilcloths over the goods and place within easy reach a sail, axe, towline, cooking kettles, large sponges for bailing, and gum and bark for repairs. Several officers might go as passengers, to attend the company's annual rendezvous at the Lake Superior headquarters. They rode in state, with fashionable beaver hats carefully packed under their seats.

When all was ready, the voyageurs knelt, with the bowsmen and steersmen standing at opposite ends, while young McLoughlin wedged himself in among the bundles and tried to find room for his long legs and oversize feet. Even though an apprentice clerk was a company officer and would not have to paddle, he must learn to sit doubled up and almost motionless for hours on end, being careful not to poke a hole through the fragile bark. It was a genuine hardship, ruefully mentioned in many early accounts.

With everything in place and the canoes low in the water, the people on the pier ceased chattering for the traditional last-minute silence. The voyageurs leaned forward, paddles raised and shining in the sun. The leader gave the shout "*Avant!*" (Forward!) The blades dug deep into the icy water. And the voyageurs began to sing.

Paddle songs—*chansons*—were important because they helped the boatmen through their long days, and a good voice might be worth a bit of extra pay. McLoughlin would hear them often: "*Nous étions trois capitaines de la guerre revenant*" (We were three captains returning from the war); "*En roulant ma boule roulant, En roulant ma boule*" (Roll along, my rolling ball); or, the most beloved of all, "*A la Claire Fontaine.*"

> Unto the crystal fountain
> For pleasure did I stray,
> So fair I found the waters
> My limbs in them I lay.

Sing, nightingale, keep singing,
Thou hast a heart so gay;
Thou hast a heart so merry,
While mine is sorrow's prey.

Long is it I have loved thee,
Thee shall I love alway,
    My dearest;
Long is it I have loved thee,
Thee shall I love alway.

In half an hour the flotilla reached the end of Montreal Island, where they stopped at the rough little chapel of Ste. Anne's, and McLoughlin could join in asking her blessing. Peter Pond, an early trader, said this chapel was "Dedacated to St. Ann who Protects all Voigers. . . .Scarse a Voiger but stops hear and Puts in his mite." Canoemen had been going ashore there for nearly two centuries, to leave a little money in the box and then, strengthened by belief in the blessed saint's protection, push on into the forest from which they might never return.

McLoughlin, growing up along the St. Lawrence, undoubtedly had known voyageurs, and he could speak fluently with them because French was commonly used in Quebec—even by some of his own family. Mainspring of the North West Company's system of transportation, the voyageurs furnished the manpower that moved tons of freight for thousands of miles. Incredibly tough, incredibly daring, they used their own brightly painted paddles, which were often gifts from their voyageur fathers. They wielded them sixteen to eighteen hours per day, forty strokes per minute—or fifty—or sixty—attaining an average speed of four to six miles per hour. They refused to give up. A Nor'Wester named Duncan McGillivray described a race on Lake Winnipeg in which the men of two flotillas spent forty hours paddling, without a break. When one fell out,

the poor fellow almost sinking with the weight of his cloathes cried out to two Canoes that happened to pass within a few yards of him to save his life *pour l'amour de dieu*; but neither the love of God or of the blessed Virgin, whom he powerfully called to his assistance, had the least influence on his hard hearted Countrymen who paddled along with the greatest unconcern, and he must have certainly perished if his own Canoe had not returned [in] time enough to prevent it.

In order to save weight and space, the voyageurs were seldom more than five feet, six inches tall, with broad shoulders and muscular arms. They wore rough breeches fastened at the knee, hooded sky-blue wool jackets, and leather shoes or moccasins without socks. Ribbons or plumes adorned their caps, knives and clay pipes dangled from their belts, and they bound their midsections with wide, colorful, handwoven sashes. They kept their hair long, so that a vigorous shake of the head would drive off the tormenting mosquitoes and black flies. Their appearance reflected their rough lifestyle. An early diary says:

> the face of one man seemed to have been squeezed in a vice, or to have passed through a flattening machine. It was like a cheese-cutter—all edge. Another had one nostril bitten off. He proved the buffoon of the party. He had the extraordinary faculty of untying the strings of his face, as it were, at pleasure, when his features fell into confusion— into a crazed chaos almost frightful. . . . A third man had his features wrenched to the right—exceedingly little, it is true; but the effect was remarkable. He had been slapped on the face by a grizzly bear.

Their pay varied widely by time and place. Wages were generally paid in goods from company supplies, and many workers ended the season in debt. In 1805, guides in the western forests received 800 livres per year—about $350—while bowsmen and steersmen received 500-750 livres, and middlemen 300-500. As an added bonus, those traveling to and from Montreal were given one blanket, one shirt, and one pair of trousers, and winterers—who "wintered" at the outposts—received two of each, plus small articles such as knives, beads, and vermilion. These terms were low, but with twelve livres equal to one pound, even the lowest-paid canoeman received more than McLoughlin's apprentice salary of twenty pounds per year.

The voyageurs were incredibly swift. A passenger once timed them while they unloaded the canoe, took it out of the stream, mended a tear, "reloaded, cooked breakfast, shaved, washed, ate, and reëmbarked—all in *fifty-seven* minutes."

And they loved their life. A former boatman, when he was past seventy, boasted:

> I have now been forty-two years in this country. For twenty-four I was a light canoe-man. . . . Fifty songs a day were nothing to me. I could carry, paddle, walk and sing with any man I ever saw. . . . No

water, no weather, ever stopped the paddle or the song. I had twelve wives in the country; and was once possessed of fifty horses, and six running dogs. . . . I wanted for nothing; and I spent all my earnings in the enjoyment of pleasure. . . . There is no life so happy as a voyageur's life, no place where a man enjoys so much variety and freedom.

The canoe route in 1803, which McLoughlin's flotilla would necessarily follow, went up the Ottawa River, through lakes and streams to Georgian Bay, and then along the north shores of Lakes Huron and Superior. Day after day the routine was the same. When at dawn came the shout *"Leve! Leve!"* (Get up!), McLoughlin must roll out of his blankets at once, for the flotilla was under way in minutes. If the wind and river were favorable, the voyageurs hoisted oilcloth sails, but they generally depended on paddles or poles. After a vigorous workout in the cool morning, perhaps a dozen miles, they pulled up to shore for breakfast. If they had lunch, it was generally a cold one while they were afloat, but sometimes after a hard portage they received an extra meal. About every two hours they paused for a "pipe"—time for the voyageurs to spin a tall tale while they smoked and rested. Whenever they passed a reminder of the crucifixion of Christ, such as the fork of a river or a cross erected over a grave, they removed their hats and crossed themselves while one in each boat repeated a short prayer.

Where possible, the voyageurs rode their canoes through the rapids, hurtling forward in a curtain of spray while the bowsman and steersman expertly used their long paddles to turn sharp angles around the rocks. They reveled in the challenge. One traveler wrote, "During our first day among the rapids old Baptiste, the guide, was constantly in great glee and always laughed when entering a bad rapid." Eventually McLoughlin would be used to such experiences, but on this first trip everything was new.

If the cascades were too dangerous or if the flotilla had to cross overland from one body of water to another, they made a portage. There were thirty-six of them between Lachine and Fort Kaministiquia—welcome chances for McLoughlin to unbend his cramped legs. When approaching a shallow bank, where the bottom might scrape the gummed seal off the canoe's birch-bark skin, the voyageurs often stopped, leaped into waist-deep water, and carried the gentlemen to shore piggyback, safe and dry. Even McLoughlin, who was six feet four, would have to ride on the back of a sinewy canoeman, clinging as best he could to the long, greasy hair.

He and the other officers would then wait while the voyageurs unloaded the cargo—seventy-five or more packages—and carried the empty canoes, or drew them up the rapids by rope. Or the bowsmen and steersmen might take them through the white water, thrusting short, stout paddles against the rocks and singing exuberantly as the spray flew. The rest slung the packages on their backs, two or three ninety-pound packs for each man, supported in slings by straps across the forehead. Bent under their burdens, arms swinging free, "cursing, singing, challenging one another to see who could carry the heaviest load the farthest without stopping," they dogtrotted up the portage trail, with McLoughlin and the other gentlemen following along.

Small as the men were, some of them carried unbelievable loads, earning extra pay. Fur traders' accounts, doubtless embellished, tell about Pierre Bonga, a West Indian who once toted 450 pounds; an Indian called Chief Solomon Voyageur who carried eight packs for half a mile; and a worker named Montferant who carried more than five hundred pounds from four o'clock one morning until ten-thirty at night. Without a stop—or so it was said.

For a long portage, the men took the goods about a third of a mile, called a *pose*, set them down, and returned for more until all were brought that far, after which they began the next *pose*. They reached the end of the trail, reloaded the canoes, and had the flotilla under way again so fast that sedentary Montreal agents often complained of difficulty in keeping up.

At dusk the paddlers brought the boats to shore and cooked a kettle of Indian corn or dried peas—one quart per man—added to strips of fat pork and boiled in gallons of water until thick. "*Mangeurs de lard*" (pork eaters), these men of the lower streams were called, in contrast to those who went beyond the Great Lakes and depended on fish and game and pemmican. McLoughlin, being an officer, would have somewhat better rations, including salted meats, hard bread, fresh eggs for the early stages, and wine or brandy.

At night the voyageurs turned their canoes on their sides to serve as roofs, but McLoughlin would have the comparative luxury of a tent, or at least a canvas shelter. As they pressed on, he would bend his shaggy head under rain and wind and occasional squalls of snow. Severe weather sometimes kept them on shore for hours or days, partly for fear the cargo and men would be lost, but also to protect the fragile birch bark of the canoes. If in spite of all their care they damaged one, the voyageurs stopped and repaired it on the spot, with their ample supply of spruce roots and gum.

They passed through old French country—*Portage de Chaudière* (the Boiler), where churning water sent up clouds of steam; *Portage des Chênes* (the Oaks); and *Lac des Chaudières* (Boiler Lake). At *Portage des Chats* (the Cats), about ten days out, they began to see Indian huts, and McLoughlin undoubtedly noticed the crosses beside almost every rapids—erected in memory of men who had lost their lives there. Captain Rock, towering above the water, had fourteen markers, and one rapids had more than thirty.

After about four weeks the flotilla reached Georgian Bay, the northern arm of Lake Huron. There they tossed overboard a bit of tobacco to appease the wind—*La Vieille*, the Old Woman. "*Souffle, souffle, la vieille*" (Blow, blow, old woman), they would chant. At Sault Ste. Marie, the rough stretch of St. Marys River between Lake Superior and Lake Huron where the water level drops twenty feet in about three-quarters of a mile, McLoughlin could watch with curiosity as oxen pulled them through the primitive stone lock, just large enough for canoes. The first lock anywhere on the Great Lakes, it had been built along the Canadian shore by the Nor'Westers in 1799, to avoid the difficult portage. He would also see the post of the rival XY Company, and he may have met some of its men, insisting on their right to use the canal because it was on public land.

Once in Lake Superior, the flotilla skirted its northern shore, where the winds were unpredictable and violent, sometimes capsizing canoes. Here McLoughlin could realize to the full how far they had come, for the place was awesomely remote from his native soil—lonely—timeless—heavily wooded with dark pine and spruce and tamarack.

Helped by the wind, they scudded past the bleak "fire country," which burned every year, and at last entered Thunder Bay, encircled by forests and backed by a range of mountains. Here they stopped at an island while everyone shaved and changed to his best shirt. Chattering, the voyageurs unfurled their brightest ribbons, while the passengers opened the cassettes under their seats, put on their beaver hats, and smoothed their bedraggled coats as well as they could.

Then, with McLoughlin and the other officers sitting erect and dignified, voyageurs singing, ribbons and pennants flying, the flotilla swept across the bay. A few hundred yards up the Kaministiquia River, past a thick stand of pine and aspen and birch, they caught sight of Fort Kaministiquia, the new depot of the North West Company. The young doctor could see a few roofs projecting above the long palisade, the company flag on a pole, a row of canoes drawn up to the landing stage.

He had reached his first frontier post.

CHAPTER 2

"Lords of the Lakes & Forests"

The Expectations and Prospects in this Country
as my Uncle Alexander can inform you
are very distant and precarious.

DR. JOHN McLOUGHLIN

~ 1 ~

The Fur Companies
1600–1803

The Canada McLoughlin knew was not yet a nation. After Britain defeated France in the French and Indian War, it took over French possessions in North America and formed a single large province called Quebec—the southern part of today's Ontario and Quebec. In 1791, when McLoughlin was seven, the area was split into two provinces. One, called Lower Canada, was approximately the portion of today's Quebec that lies within the St. Lawrence watershed, extending north and a bit west from the lower river. The other, called Upper Canada, was roughly the part of present-day Ontario that lies within the St. Lawrence watershed, stretching north and west along the upper river and the Great Lakes.

Lower Canada was mainly French, while Upper Canada was mainly British. Each had its own capital and its own government, but they shared a governor-general, who reported directly to London. In addition, British territory in North America included today's Maritime Provinces, as well as the vast area that drains into Hudson Bay.

McLoughlin's early homes—Rivière-du-Loup and the city of Quebec—were in Lower Canada, as was Montreal. But when he went to Fort Kaministiquia, he was in Upper Canada, and his later posts were even farther west, outside of both provinces. Upper and Lower Canada were joined in the 1840 Act of Union, but by then McLoughlin was on the Pacific Coast. And he died before 1867, when the Dominion of Canada was created by uniting Ontario, Quebec, New Brunswick, and Nova Scotia.

The land he was to know so well was a fur trader's dream. A glance at a map will show two major bodies of water that penetrate the eastern part of North America: Hudson Strait and Bay in the far north; and the St. Lawrence River and Great Lakes near the center.

A beaver, the rodent that shaped an empire. This illustration comes from Horace T. Martin's *Castorologia, or the History and Traditions of the Canadian Beaver.* OHS ORHI 98819

Around Hudson Bay lies the Canadian Shield, a tremendous horseshoe that covers almost half of present-day Canada, curving from the far north coast of Quebec around the bottom of Hudson Bay and then north again to the Arctic. This is a land of rocks, of swamps, of countless lakes and rivers; of forests in the southern parts and barren steppes in the far north; of frigid winters with driving snow and brief summers when wildflowers grow and loons cry across the lakes. West of the Canadian Shield is the Athabasca drainage, sloping to the Arctic, and beyond that the Rocky Mountains and Pacific Coast.

In most of this north country, fur-bearing animals lived and multiplied, developing glossy, dark coats. Silver fox, otter, muskrat, and beaver offered riches to the fur trapper, while myriad lakes and rivers provided pathways for reaching them. "The waterways . . . were almost miraculous in their range and intricacy," wrote the historian Chester Martin. "A trader could embark at Cumberland House [west of Lake Winnipeg] and, with no portage longer than a single day, could reach the Arctic Ocean, the Pacific, the Atlantic, or the Gulf of Mexico."

When McLoughlin joined the North West Company and moved into this

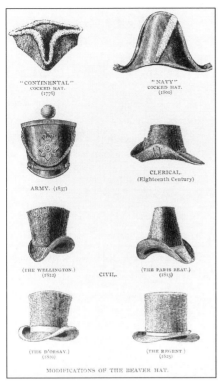

"CONTINENTAL"
COCKED HAT.
(1776)

"NAVY"
COCKED HAT.
(1800)

ARMY. (1837)

CLERICAL.
(Eighteenth Century)

(THE WELLINGTON.)
(1812)

CIVIL.

(THE PARIS BEAU.)
(1815)

(THE D'ORSAY.)
(1820)

(THE REGENT.)
(1825)

MODIFICATIONS OF THE BEAVER HAT.

The most common use of beaver felt was the gentleman's hat—dignified, durable, tall, crowned, and with a wide brim. The felt was firm yet soft and lent itself to other shapes whenever a luxurious and handsome head-covering was desired. From Horace T. Martin's *Castorologia*. OHS ORHI 98821

rich land, he became part of an ancient industry. Its history and practices must be discussed, because they would shape his entire life.

Sagas of the Norsemen, whose dragon ships crossed the Atlantic nearly a thousand years ago, told of exchanging weapons for furs. Later on, the early fishermen sailed into the St. Lawrence to dry their catch, and while there they traded a few items, such as blankets and knives, for beaver robes. Since the Indians had worn these robes fur side in, often as an only garment, they were so ripe that the fishermen called them *castor gras*, "greasy beaver." However, the long guard hairs of the pelts had been worn off, leaving only the underfur, which was so luxuriously warm and soft that on the bone-chilling return journey, the sailors were happy to disregard the stench and use them as sleeping blankets.

Before long, beaver became a prized commodity in European markets, not as skins, but for the underfur alone. The first step in processing it was to remove the long guard hairs, leaving the soft ones underneath, each of which had numerous minute barbs along the shaft. When the underhair was taken off, soaked, and pounded, it meshed into the finest felt in the world—pliant yet firm—for the manufacture of huge, handsome, durable men's hats of many shapes. For more than two hundred years a beaver hat was a status symbol, worn with pride and handed down from father to son. By the early seventeenth century, gentlemen were paying as much as four guineas for them, which was six months' wages for a skilled workman. McLoughlin himself wore one.

For many years the market for beaver was ravenous, and to feed it, trappers followed waterways up and down the coasts of North America. Fur trad-

Beaver underhair has small barbs along each strand, which mesh together to make felt. These hairs are removed and mixed with water, which is poured through mesh and drained to spread it evenly. The hairs are then pounded until the fabric is firm. In this picture, the workman draws back the bowstring and releases it to ensure maximum impact. Other methods of pounding were also used. From *The Growth of Industrial Art* by Benjamin Butterworth. OHS ORHI 98818

ing financed explorers such as Champlain, Joliet, Marquette, and La Salle. In 1792 in the Far West, George Vancouver, captain of the British ship *Discovery*, was looking for the legendary Northwest Passage and seeking furs when he saw "the appearance of an inlet or small river, the land not indicating it to be of any great extent." The sea changed "to river-colored water, the probable consequence of some streams falling into the bay," but he did not think it important, and passed it by. A few weeks later the American Robert Gray, captain of the *Columbia*, was also trading for furs when he sailed into the mouth of a river, named it for his vessel, and established a national claim to the Oregon Country.

One famous member of McLoughlin's company was David Thompson, who made such accurate surveys of the Far West and diagrammed them so meticulously that for more than half a century his findings were the basis for official maps of western Canada. McLoughlin would often see the enormous Thompson map, because it hung for years in the Kaministiquia dining hall.

Another well-known Nor'Wester was Alexander Mackenzie, who in 1793—a decade before Lewis and Clark—fought his way up the Peace River, overland to the Bella Coola, and downstream to North Bentinck Arm, an inlet of the Pacific, in today's British Columbia. There he dipped a stick in vermilion and bear grease and daubed large red letters on a rock:

ALEX MACKENZIE
FROM CANADA
BY LAND

22nd JULY 1793

The partner, Alexander McKay, was with him, along with six voyageurs, two Indians, and a dog. The eight Nor'Westers were the first Europeans to cross the North American continent north of Mexico.

The North West Company traced its roots to independent traders, the "pedlars" who for years had been taking canoes west—ever west—through the rivers and forests, to buy furs from the Indians. During the American Revolutionary War, a group of Montreal "pedlars" had banded together under the leadership of vigorous, intelligent Simon McTavish. Calling themselves the North West Company, they established a base at Grand Portage on Lake Superior, after which large canoes brought in supplies and carried out furs, saving traders the long trek to Montreal.

This first alliance soon collapsed, but in 1783 the traders, again led by Simon McTavish, formed another association under the same name. This time it lasted, although it was a loose series of co-partnerships rather than a tightly controlled organization. Its business affairs—buying supplies and selling furs—were handled by McTavish, Frobisher & Company, the firm with which McLoughlin signed his contract.

The North West Company had two kinds of partners: business agents in Montreal; and wintering partners, who stayed year-round at the outposts. Next in the hierarchy were clerks and apprentice clerks such as McLoughlin—young, inexperienced, lacking a voice in company affairs, but considered officers and slated for advancement. The title referred to rank, not specialty, and clerks might serve in any capacity, even as head of a small post. Below them were workers called *engagés*, some of whom were skilled craftsmen, while

others contributed only their strong arms and backs. They seldom became officers.

The Nor'Westers thrived. They built log trading posts and took canoes up whitewater streams into the fur-rich land drained by the Athabasca River. Two decades before McLoughlin's arrival, they placed a small fleet of sloops and schooners on the Great Lakes, to augment their canoe-based shipping. They were colorful, brash, ruthless—and successful.

Like McTavish, most North West officers were hardy Scots, so McLoughlin, as a Fraser descendant, fitted in very well. Company records

The seal of the Northwest Company. OHS ORHI 37550

over the years listed seven Frasers, four Finlays, five Camerons, six McTavishes, seven McLeods, eight McGillivrays, fourteen Grants, fourteen McKenzies, and so many McDonalds that they were identified by their hometowns. Stewart Wallace, a noted historian of the fur trade, wrote:

> The names of the North West Company partners sound like a roll-call of the clans of Culloden. These men were hardy, courageous, shrewd and proud. They spent a good part of their lives travelling incredible distances in birch-bark canoes, shooting rapids, and navigating inland seas. They were wrecked and drowned. They suffered hunger and starvation. They were robbed and murdered by the Indians, and sometimes by one another. They fell victims of small-pox, syphilis and rum. Yet they conquered half a continent, and they built up a commercial empire, the like of which North America at least has never seen.

Of all the strong Nor'Westers, those with the most power were the Montreal agents, who hired workers, planned routes, decided on new posts, sold furs, and bought trading goods in London. Theirs was a major enterprise. In 1802, the year before McLoughlin joined, its records listed 877 common men, 161 clerks and interpreters, and 20 partners, for a total of 1,058. In addition, there were 80-100 Canadian and Iroquois hunters who had contracts but "ranged free," and 540 canoemen. For another decade the company grew steadily until it had more than two thousand employees and manned a thousand canoes.

The partners reveled on a grand scale, too, as in the Beaver Club of Montreal. Limited to traders who had wintered on the frontier, this club met at the finest hotels, used its own crystal, china, and silver, and opened every meeting with five toasts:

To the Mother of All Saints;
To the King;
To the Fur Trade in All Its Branches;
To Voyageurs, Wives, and Children;
To Absent Members.

After each of these, the partners hurled their glasses into the fireplace, and with the toasts properly honored, serious drinking could begin. One bill from

1808 shows that thirty-one members and guests consumed twenty-nine bottles of Madeira, nineteen bottles of port, fourteen bottles of porter, and twelve quarts of ale, plus a quantity of gin and brandy.

Legend tells about *le grand voyage*, in which the diners would pick up pokers, fire tongs, swords, and canes and drop to the floor, two abreast as if paddling a canoe, while they bawled voyageurs' songs until they toppled over. Although that was doubtless an exaggeration, a guest named Colonel George T. Landmann wrote on one occasion, "By four o'clock in the morning . . . we could all give the war whoop as well as Mackenzie and McGillivray, we could all sing admirably, we could all drink like fishes, and we all thought we could dance on the table without disturbing a single decanter, glass or plate . . . but on making the experiment we discovered that it was a complete delusion." McLoughlin himself would become a member of this famous club, although he seldom had an opportunity to attend a meeting.

In 1803, his first year in the fur trade, McLoughlin's company had two major rivals. One was the venerable Hudson's Bay Company, with its North American headquarters not in Montreal but at York Factory, on the bay itself. It basked in the security of a royal British charter giving it a monopoly over all the lands that drained into Hudson Bay, but even so, it lagged behind the Nor'Westers. In 1800 they exported £144,300 worth of furs to London, while the Hudson's Bay Company sent £38,463.

The other major fur-trading concern was the New North West Company, which had been started by disgruntled Nor'Westers. It was generally called the XY Company, or XYC, because it marked its fur bales with those letters; and like McLoughlin's firm, it had its business headquarters in Montreal. Although it produced smaller returns than the North West Company and employed about a third as many men, it had an approximately equal sum of capital, and it was a growing threat.

During McLoughlin's first years as a fur trader, relations among the three companies were precarious, although their men sometimes built posts near one another, occasionally used a common palisade for protection, celebrated Christmas together, and delivered one another's mail. Lonely, often idle, spending day after day at primitive outposts, they created what diversions they could, in a rowdy life that McLoughlin would never quite embrace.

A wintering partner named Alexander Henry the Younger, writing about a North West dance to which Hudson's Bay men were invited, said that "all were merry . . . but we were very much crowded, 72 men, 37 women and 65 children, and the room being 22/23 feet, made it disagreeably warm."

Robert Kennicott, a student who traveled among the traders in the Great Lakes area, described a function that was jolly but somewhat less than elegant. "The music consisted of a very bad performance of one vile, unvarying tune upon a worse old fiddle, accompanied by a brilliant accompaniment upon a large tin pan."

Sometimes the men showed a wry sense of humor, as when John McKay of the Hudson's Bay Company told its London Committee, "I had the honour of my Neighbors [from a North West fort] company for dinner; your Honours has the honour of bearing the expense."

It was not, however, a life of unbroken revelry, for the traders were after a fortune in furs, and the North Country was essentially ungoverned, with neither courts nor police. The rivalry might lead merely to trickery, as when a Hudson's Bay scout saw Indian tracks in the snow, concluded that the tribe had brought in a fresh supply of skins, and invited the nearby Nor'Westers to a feast. The hosts were lavish with liquor, and while the merriment was at its height, a few of them harnessed dog teams without bells and took the goods.

At other times anger flared, and since law enforcement on the frontier was all but unknown, tragedy resulted. Quarrels with other fur traders led to the killing of Jean Etienne Wadin in 1782, John Ross in 1787, and Joseph King in 1802; but only one of their murderers was brought to trial, and he was acquitted because the judge could not decide on the proper jurisdiction.

Into this situation the tall, rawboned, very young McLoughlin had been plunged, and here he must find his place. No surviving record indicates that he ever had a role in high jinks, and when he became a Nor'Wester in 1803, the violence had not yet reached its peak. But the potential was there, because the rivalry was intense and the stakes were high.

~ 2 ~

Fort Kaministiquia

1803

As the flotilla approached Fort Kaministiquia, McLoughlin could see a long dock lined with canoes, a palisade and arched gate, a few cattle grazing upstream, a few huts of the XY Company across the river, and hulking Mount McKay toward the south. The fort must have appeared lonely, spread across flat, swampy ground and dwarfed by a dark forest. He had learned much since leaving Montreal, for he was toughened to wilderness travel, able to sit for hours in a cramped canoe, sleep on the ground, and bow his head into squalls of rain or snow. Now he must adapt himself to life at a frontier post.

His canoe pulled up to the long landing stage, to be met by workers chattering in excited French and English, for the arrival of each brigade was a chance to hear the latest news, and perhaps receive a message from home. Strong brown arms would steady the canoe, the doctor would grasp the hand of an *engagé*, and he would step out amid barking dogs, dark-eyed children, laborers, and Indians. After the sudden turn his life had taken, after the interminable days afloat, he could at last stand on solid ground, and sleep in a bed, and take his meals at a proper table. But Fort Kaministiquia was a weary distance from Montreal, and everything was strange.

Now that McLoughlin had landed, he had a closer view of the fifteen-foot palisade of new timbers, sharpened at the top, with the bark left on. After walking through its wide gateway, he would find himself on the hard-packed dirt of a large courtyard, with frame buildings around its edge and an imposing hall in the center, "elegantly constructed, though of wood, with a long piazza or portico, raised about five feet from the ground and surmounted by a balcony extending along the whole front." He would notice the smell of skins mingled

Among the voyageurs, the foremen and steersmen were the aristocrats, expert at maneuvering the fragile canoes around the rocks. Equipment and freight were placed with great care to balance the load, because the craft rode low in the water. *Running a Rapid on the Mattawa River*, by Francis A. Hopkins, engraved by C. Butterworth. NATIONAL ARCHIVES OF CANADA C-13585

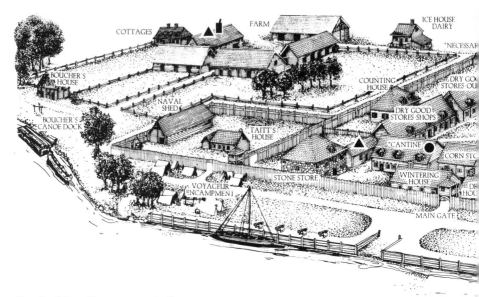

Sketch of Fort Kaministiquia/William.
COURTESY OF OLD FORT WILLIAM, THUNDER BAY, ONTARIO

with the fragrance of new wood, and hear the din of hammers and saws, for the fort had been started only two years before, and it was still unfinished.

The Nor'Westers were building it because they had to abandon their old headquarters at Grand Portage, also on Lake Superior but farther south. After the American Revolutionary War, the Treaty of Paris in 1783 had specified that the boundary between the United States and Canada would run west—partway on the Pigeon River—from Lake Superior to the most northwestern point of the Lake of the Woods, "and from thence on a due west course to the River Mississippi." This was impossible, because none of the Mississippi was that far north—an inconvenient fact that was not then known. In 1794 the Jay Treaty allowed both British and Americans to trade on either side of the border, and it proposed a joint survey, which was not carried out. It seemed certain, however, that Grand Portage would eventually be within the United States, and therefore the North West Company was building a new center at Kaministiquia, the Lake Superior terminus of an old French fur-trading route. It was far enough north to be safe.

McLoughlin's first duty would be to go into the Great Hall and present himself to the senior partners, who had gathered to make plans for the next year. Although his uncle Alexander Fraser was a wintering partner, he did not attend

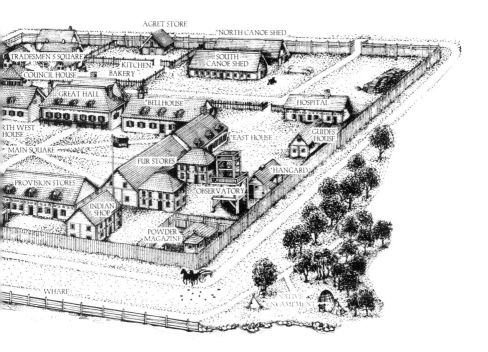

that summer's gathering, and McLoughlin found no familiar faces to welcome him. He would be shown his quarters, the apothecary, the medical office, and the rest of the fort—an astonishing spread of everything needed to make it self-sufficient. When finished, it would include a bakery, blacksmith, tinsmith, jail, cooperage for making kegs, yard for building and repairing canoes, and ship-yard for constructing larger boats and ships. One important building was the shed where furs were beaten to drive out moths, rolled into bundles, and stored.

Since McLoughlin arrived at the time of the summer rendezvous, he found the fort bustling with more than a thousand men. Laborers were housed in camps outside the palisade—one at some distance east for the voyageurs from Montreal, one at a similar distance west for those who had wintered at the small inland posts, and one near the fort for Indians. The voyageurs had been given a regale, a feast, before leaving Montreal, and when they arrived, they celebrated again in their camp. Each man received a quart of rum, half a pound of butter, and a loaf of white bread—a long-anticipated treat, for they had not tasted these deli-cacies for weeks. The Nor'Wester Ross Cox described the scene, with "women, soldiers, voyageurs and Indians dancing, singing, drinking and gambling."

There was also feasting inside the palisade. Washington Irving wrote in *Astoria*—which is fictionalized but based on primary materials—that every summer the canoes "carried up with them cooks and bakers, together with delicacies of every kind, and abundance of choice wines." Traders' journals made similar claims. Agents from Montreal came, bent on adventure along with the business meetings, and winterers left lonely outposts for their one big social time of the year. Night after night in the Great Hall's huge dining room, which seated more than one hundred, they gathered around long tables, where McLoughlin would join them as they gorged on fish, beef, venison, milk and butter, white bread, corn, peas, potatoes, wine, spirits, and desserts. Cox called Kaministiquia "the great emporium for the interior," with a "fashionable season" from May to August when "good living and festivities predominate; and the luxuries of the dinner-table compensate in some degree for the long fasts" of winter quarters.

For a young, somewhat naive doctor, fresh from his city training, it was an astonishing world. The winterers were big, vigorous men who ate a lot, laughed a lot, and sprinkled their conversation with exotic names. The Athabasca. Fort Chipewyan. Great Slave Lake. With bitter resentment and a torrent of frontier oaths, they would recount the latest outrages of the Hudson's Bay and XY Companies. Laughing yet uneasy, they would complain that the United States, the upstart young nation to the south, had forced them to move their headquarters, at immense cost in materials and time. Nobody had expected that puny country to survive, yet there it was, greedy for land—thriving—a potential threat.

While McLoughlin devoured his roast beef and venison, he must have heard tales about narrow escapes from bears and snows and whitewater rapids. With considerable relish, the partners would talk about hunger and fatigue, venomous reptiles, wild beasts, falls from cliffs, and the cold breath of La Vieille, the Old Woman, ever ready to swamp an unwary canoe. When the meal was finished, the tables would be cleared and the men would sing, sometimes until morning. At least once during the rendezvous they had a gala ball, at which they danced with fellow officers or slender young Ojibway girls, gliding and whirling while the timbers rang and the shouts of reveling voyageurs and Indians drifted in through the windows.

Nothing in McLoughlin's life had prepared him for this. He had undoubtedly heard tales about the fur trade and its audacious partners, and he must have known voyageurs when he was a schoolboy, but his life had been sheltered, first by his devout family and then by Dr. Fisher. The son of a simple Scotch-Irish farmer, he now found himself plunged into the privations and excesses of a frontier post.

In addition, he faced unaccustomed responsibilities. As an apprentice clerk, he must learn the fur trade. And as a physician, he must take up the reins of the fort's limited medical facilities, providing the only professional care that hundreds of men would receive for months or years. He would have no one to consult, for the only experienced physician in the area, Dr. Henry Munro, was about to become a full-time trader. Young McLoughlin would be in complete charge. And he was just eighteen years old.

~ 3 ~
An Apprentice Again
1803–1808

Although McLoughlin's new post was so isolated that he could not purchase drugs or instruments, he found a considerable stock in the pharmacy. Among the scores of medicines listed in a later inventory were acacia gum, aloes socotrina, antimon pulvis, crocus indicus, and cantharides, along with camphor, digitalis, opium purificat, "saltpetre," sassafras, and "tapiocha." The instruments included devices for amputating, cupping, and trepanning, as well as lancets, bougies, syringes, one "electrifying machine," and "3 old Silver catheters (very bad)." There was also a collection of medical books, such as *Synopsis Medicina* by Allen, *Ulcers &c* by Bell, *Hydraulicks &c* by Bell, and *Pharmacopia* by Twelfer.

Young, interested in his profession, and eager to succeed, McLoughlin started with a will. He bled his patients, bandaged them, set their bones, dosed them, and supplemented the fort's supplies by preparing medicine from local plants. With a tinge of pride he wrote to his physician-uncle, Simon Fraser,

> among my patients I had one with the King's evil [scrofula] whom I cur'd by applying the common sorrel in form of a poultice to the part affected. The manner of preparing the poultice is as follows: . . . pound it [the sorrel] in a mortar till it is reduced to a kind of pulp, then put it into an unglas'd earthen pot and allow it to macerate in its own juice over a gentle fire until it becomes of a proper consistency and to be applied in as warm as the patient can endure to the naked sore. The patient I had complain'd it hurt him much. . . . I

have adopted Dr. Darwin's theory i.e. that ulcers of this nature are
from deficiency of irritability.

Scrofula is tuberculosis of the lymphatic glands, especially those of the neck,
in which they become large and deteriorate. It was a serious ailment of that
period, and several of McLoughlin's letters discuss his attempts to treat it.

A man of many interests, he once sent his uncle a piece of "petrifid fir,"
and his early letters often asked for books and magazines, both medical and
general. "I must again renew my petion [petition] to you for books, If you had
any historical to spare I would be much oblig'd to You." And a year later, "I
read much on the virtues of Phosphate of Lime in this disease. I would be much
obliged to you if you could send me a little. . . .I would be much oblig'd if you
saw or heard of any new publication worth studying that you would procure
it for me and give to any safe person to give it to me, also if you would let me
know of any new discovery in medicine you hear off."

McLoughlin's relations with his uncle were warm, and he repeatedly
voiced confidence in Fraser's good will. "I would not trouble you if I did not
think but that you would take pleasure in doing me any little kindness as this
in your power." This trust was to last as long as Dr. Fraser lived, and today's
best information on McLoughlin's personal life is the file of family correspondence that the uncle carefully kept.

After several weeks as physician at Fort Kaministiquia, McLoughlin, in
his alternate role as apprentice clerk, was sent to an unidentified outpost for
the winter. There he acted as fur trader, but the next summer he returned to
headquarters as fort physician—a seasonal rotation that became standard.
Although he thought his agreement with McTavish entitled him to extra pay
for his professional services, neither he nor his uncle seemed quite sure of the
terms. McLoughlin later referred to his uncle's request of 1804 "that you
wish'd to know my agreement to which I gave You an Answer but I am sorry
you have not as yet give me Your Opinion on this." The uncertainty would dog
him for years.

For the Nor'Westers, the year 1804 was significant because it saw the
elimination of their most vexing rival, the XY Company. Its head, Alexander
Mackenzie, was a former North West Company partner who had become dissatisfied, because he thought the Montreal agents received too large a share
of the profits and had too much power. In 1799, when his agreement expired,
Mackenzie had stormed out of the summer rendezvous and sailed to England,
where he received a knighthood and published a successful book—by a ghost-

writer—about his discoveries. While he was away, several small companies and disgruntled partners united to form the New North West Company (the XYC), and when he returned he joined it. Sometimes called Sir Alexander Mackenzie and Company, it was a powerful threat to the Nor'Westers.

Mackenzie had a grand vision of forming a comprehensive Fur and Fishery Company, which would ship goods through Hudson Bay instead of by the long canoe route through Montreal, establish posts on the Pacific Coast, and use Americans as middlemen in order to circumvent the British East India Company's monopoly of trade with China. Simon McTavish, however, opposed Mackenzie's plan because he considered it a threat to his own regime, and their two firms became bitter rivals.

The change in 1804 was due to the unexpected death of McTavish—a jolt to the Nor'Westers, for he was only fifty-four and had been in charge ever since the company was formed. However, with the iron-fisted Scot out of the way, the Mackenzie feud was quickly resolved. On November 5 the two companies agreed to merge, signing the contract in Montreal with a scratch of quill pens. The North West Company retained a three-quarters interest in the new concern, while the XY Company—smaller, with fewer members—retained one-quarter. William McGillivray, McTavish's nephew, became the leading Nor'Wester, and three years later, at the insistence of the partners, Fort Kaministiquia was renamed Fort William in his honor.

Although McLoughlin no doubt heard of this change with interest, it made little immediate difference to his work. For the next several years he spent his summers in medical practice at Fort William, where he lived in the doctor's house and gave a few short weeks of professional care to the men who gathered there. No surviving documents picture him as an outstanding physician, but they show that he was a decisive, articulate man with genuine feeling for others and a dignified manner, which made him seem older than his actual age. Daniel Harmon, a partner who knew him well, thought him about thirty, when he was only twenty-three.

Every fall, when most of the men left headquarters, McLoughlin took charge of a frontier post. There he might spend weeks or even months with no English-speaking companion, although he was fluent in French and could easily communicate with the *engagés*. He supervised them in fishing, hunting, building cabins, and cutting wood—jobs necessary for survival in winter. He also traded with the Indians for furs, either at the posts or by going into their camps, and in the spring he supervised the preparation of canoes for the return to headquarters. At the time, this experience seemed remote from his

Engraving of a winter camp. This represents a semi-permanent camp of huts and Indian tepees, such as were occupied at times by Hudson's Bay or North West Company trappers east of the Rockies. Dwellings of the two groups were generally separated rather than mingled as in this picture. "A Winter Camp" from *The Great Fur Land*, by H.M. Robinson. OHS ORHI 98816

chosen profession, but it was actually a stroke of good fortune, for it gave him a chance at administration, where his real talents lay.

Early in his career McLoughlin must have confronted one of the worst problems of the fur trade—alcohol. Ever since the days of the early French traders, liquor had gone hand in hand with other trade goods. It was supremely profitable, being less bulky than kettles and blankets, axes and saws; and once the Indians had a taste, they refused to deal without it. Charles Chaboillez, for example, wrote about one who "came to see if I would give them a large Keg Mixed Rum at Credit or else that they would go at the English & South Traders when they have Skins." As a result, kegs of rum made small mountains on the wharves at Lachine, and its use was growing fast—from 10,098 gallons in 1800 to more than 21,300 in 1803.

The companies seldom traded liquor straight, but stretched it as thin as their customers would accept, which meant that it varied from post to post. Alexander Henry the Younger wrote that in his area, "we do not mix our liquor so strong as we do for tribes who are more accustomed to use it," but he explained that "to make a nine-gallon keg of liquor we generally put in four or five quarts of high wine and then fill up with water."

The mountain portage, on the Kaministiqua River, a few miles upstream from Fort William. McLoughlin crossed this portage every spring and fall from 1803 to 1814 while he was spending his winters as head of an inland post. The artist Paul Kane painted the picture from a sketch he made in 1846 when he crossed the portage with a Hudson's Bay Company brigade, on his way to the Pacific Coast. *The Mountain Portage*, by Paul Kane.
ROYAL ONTARIO MUSEUM, #912.1.18

For the whites it meant profit, but for the natives, who had no traditions of use in moderation, it was a disaster. Traders' journals contain scores of accounts such as that of Daniel Harmon:

To behold a House full of Drunken Indians, as it generally consists of men, women, & children, is truly an unpleasant sight, for they in that condition often quarrel, fight, and pull each other by the hair, and at times you will see ten or twelve or more (of Both sexes) all by the ears at one and the same time, till at last they all fall on the floor, one upon the top of the other, some spilling Rum out of a Kettle or Dish. . .while others are throwing up what they had just drank.

The consequences were not only disgusting, they were dangerous and sometimes fatal. Although the Hudson's Bay historian Douglas McKay made the flinty comment that "drunken Indians were among the casual inconveniences of fur-trading," many individuals were troubled. Alexander Henry the Younger referred to "that baneful source of all evils, spiritous liquor." And William Tomison, an officer in the British army, sent a petition to the commander in chief for Canada, saying, "Good Sir, it grieves us to see a body of Indians destroyed by a set of Men, merely for self Interest."

Officials of both the North West and Hudson's Bay Companies tried to control the sale of "spirits," and their employees faced heavy fines or dismissal if they allowed drinking to interfere with their duties. Liquor, however, was served at the posts, and the companies allowed an extra measure on special occasions or for special effort. James McKenzie wrote that after a New Year's celebration, some of the men "could hardly stand alone . . . such was the effect of the juice of the grape upon their brains." And some traders set a frightful example. In 1802 Harmon wrote, "Of all people in the world, I think the Canadians, when drunk, are the most disagreeable. . . . I had rather have fifty drunken Indians in the fort than five drunken Canadians." He told of one occasion when the Indians were so frightened by the traders' revels that they "hid themselves under beds & elsewhere, and said they thought the White People had become mad."

Whatever McLoughlin thought of this practice, it was scarcely a fit topic for letters to his respectable relatives in Canada, and he kept no journal to tell whether he joined the frolics, or scorned them, or found liquor a deadly personal trap. However, if his opinions at that time were forerunners of his later ones, he was among those who were thoroughly distressed. It may be significant that long afterward, in the Oregon Country, he was known for accepting no alcohol except a rare single glass of wine on special occasions.

Dealing with this and other problems as best he could, McLoughlin spent his second winter, in 1804-5, at an unspecified fort where his Uncle Alexander was also assigned. The next summer, in July 1805, he wrote to his Uncle Simon, "I believe I will not be able to go inland this Year And will winter here" (at Fort Kaministiquia). He did not explain whether he would "not be able" because he was needed at headquarters, or because he was ill. During their winter together, he and his strong-minded relative may have collided, for a year later he wrote that he had "past a much better winter than the preceeding one with my Uncle Alexander."

He was not, however, anticipating a permanent career in the fur trade. In 1806, when the partner William McKay came with the summer brigades, he told McLoughlin that his Uncle Simon was planning to rejoin the army and had already received his commission. This was a surprise, and it gave the young doctor a new idea. "I would if You and the rest of my friends thought proper go and try my fortune in your place as the Expectations and Prospects in this Country . . . are very distant and precarious," he told his uncle. If he could secure release from the rest of his indenture, taking over an established practice would be easier and less costly than starting a new one.

But the rumor proved false. Dr. Fraser remained in Terrebonne, and McLoughlin stayed on the frontier.

To reach Lac la Pluie—Rainy Lake—where he was sent in 1806-7, McLoughlin had to cross the "height of land," beyond which the rivers no longer flowed to the Great Lakes. Fur-company maps show many such heights, but this one—a scrubby area of rocks and trees—was especially significant because its streams were heading north toward Hudson Bay, not toward the St. Lawrence and home.

At this place McLoughlin undoubtedly was put through the usual Nor'-Westers' ritual. As they neared the first northward-flowing stream, the Nor'-Westers would talk darkly about the coming ordeal. "Some men . . ." they would say, and break off, with a great show of sharpening their knives. "Others . . ."

When they reached the stream, they would stop amid a chilling silence, while one veteran cut off a branch of scrub cedar, blindfolded the tyro, ordered him to kneel, and suddenly doused him with ice-cold water. The gasping victim must then repeat, while the knife was held at his throat, *Je suis un homme du Nord*" (Now I am a man of the North) and make two promises: First, never allow a new man to cross the height without subjecting him to the ritual. Second, never kiss a voyageur's wife without her permission.

And the ordeal was over.

After his winter at Rainy Lake, McLoughlin returned to headquarters for the summer of 1807, and then was assigned to Sturgeon Lake—a lonely post north of Lake Superior. With him was Nor'Wester Daniel William Harmon, who had not been well and was sent along in hopes of a medical cure. Harmon kept one of the best surviving accounts of fur traders' lives, and it provides an excellent record of the winter he and McLoughlin spent together.

On August 13, Harmon's journal said, they started out with a flotilla of canoes. These split off one by one for other forts until Harmon, McLoughlin, and four laborers continued in a single craft, arriving by September 1. Sturgeon Lake, about forty miles long and from one to five miles wide, was in low, flat country, swampy in places and broken by many lakes and ponds. It was beautiful but desolate, with no buildings, so "our people are putting up Houses for us to pass the Winter in."

By then McLoughlin had become an active, blustering man with a loud voice and a heavy mane of hair already turning gray. Although he was impulsive and hot-tempered, his friends liked him. On November 9, Harmon wrote:

> We are in a solitary place, where we see no one except the Natives. . . .
> Fortunately for us we have a few good Books, and in perusing them
> we shall pass the greater part of the time—and then again the Doctor
> (who is about my age) is an excellent Companion, good humoured &
> fond of conversation, which with the little I may have to say will serve
> to keep up our spirits, and even make the moments pass away agree-
> ably and I hope I shall have cause to say profitably also. We now have
> about four inches of Snow.

It was not unusual for even a small post to have fairly well stocked shelves of reading material, for most of the company's top officers had once been winterers, and they well knew how much a good book could mean to a lonely man.

On November 15 the lake froze, and by early December McLoughlin and Harmon were catching "great numbers of excellent Trout with Hooks & Lines under the Ice." After cleaning the fish, they made holes in the tails, strung them on small willow branches, and hung them up in the freezing air, which preserved them until warm weather. Throughout the winter, these were the men's chief food.

Even though the two traders were congenial, they had little to do—prepare their meals, take care of the fort, trade with Indians who brought in furs. Harmon once said leisure accounted for "nearly nine-tenths of our time," and as they passed week after week eating a monotonous diet, performing monotonous tasks, McLoughlin became restless. Right after Christmas, accompanied by two Canadians and an Indian, he left "to pay a visit to Mr. Haldane at Red Lake," which meant slogging on snowshoes through high winds and intense cold, two hundred miles each way. They were gone for nearly two months, but on February 19 Harmon wrote, "The Dr. &c. are returned from their long jaunt, whose company I am happy to enjoy after having been for such a length of time alone as it were." Such trips were not unusual. During George Simpson's first winter as Governor of the Northern Department of the Hudson's Bay Company, he made a fifteen-hundred-mile tour of its posts, chiefly on snowshoes.

Winter in the north is long and dark, but at last the northern lights faded, daylight hours increased, the snow melted, and flowers bloomed in the grass. On May 13 McLoughlin packed his few belongings and started out with one workman in a small canoe, to again serve as physician at headquarters.

In that year, 1808, with his apprenticeship at last completed, he was twenty-three years old—a big, bluff man, still with a slight stammer. Sadly distant from his relatives, often homesick and lonely, he must decide whether to remain a Nor'Wester, facing years in the wilderness, or strike out boldly in a medical practice of his own. The course he chose would shape his entire future, and just at that critical time a family problem exploded, one that involved his beloved brother, David.

~4~
Brother David
1808–1811

S ometime during 1807–8, McLoughlin married an Ojibway woman who bore him a son, Joseph. Little is known about her, and the marriage must have been brief. The child lived permanently with McLoughlin, which may indicate that the young wife died, although fathers often took responsibility for their mixed-blood children. Official records have not been found, and a younger boy, David, said only that his father had been married and had one son by his first wife.

It was common for fur traders to take Indian wives, because they thought only girls born in the fur country could survive there, and because native women were valuable helpmates. They gathered berries and other foods, cleaned and packed skins, made leather clothing, and served as interpreters. The North West and Hudson's Bay Companies frowned upon casual romances, but encouraged stable alliances as assets that aided their workmen and promoted friendship with the tribes. Since the frontier boasted neither ministers nor justices of the peace, the couple might merely begin living together, or they might come to the chief officer of the post and tell him their intent. The companies kept careful records of these unions, and at least as early as 1816 the North West Company was issuing marriage certificates, as shown by one for McLoughlin's stepdaughter Nancy McKay. The relationships were often warm, and many of the women performed heroic acts for their husbands' safety.

Some of the marriages were permanent, others were not. A retiring officer might merely provide for his native wife and children and place her with her own people, thinking—or at least piously saying—she would be happier there. This in fact had happened with McLoughlin's wife Marguerite, who had been left by her first husband, Alexander McKay, when he retired from the North West Company. Chief Trader John Work—manager of the Hudson's Bay Company coasting trade—expressed a common view when he wrote to a colleague, "I understand he [John Warren Dease] has taken out his wife and several little ones to Canada, a step which I fear he will repent. Among civilized people neither himself nor her can be happy, to join in anything like civilized society with her is out of the question."

However, the alliances were not always temporary. When North West voyageurs and laborers retired, they often settled near the company fort on the Red River, where they could live with their Indian wives, and many officers were devoted to their native families. Peter Skene Ogden lived a long life with his Julia. James Douglas became governor of British Columbia with his Amelia as the governor's lady. David Thompson moved his wife and children to Lower Canada with him. And David Harmon, who took his large family to New England, wrote in moving words, "How could I spend my days in the civilized world, and leave my beloved children in the wilderness? The thought has in it the bitterness of death. How could I tear them from a mother's love, and leave her to mourn over their absence, to the day of her death? . . . How could I think of her in such circumstances, without anguish?" Back in the provinces, the courts often recognized frontier marriages as legal. As one example, when McLoughlin's uncle Alexander Fraser was a Nor'Wester, he took an Indian wife by whom he had several children, but on retiring he married a white woman. Later, after his death, the children by his two wives engaged in a series of lawsuits, resulting in a court decision that his frontier marriage was valid and that the children by both wives were legal heirs.

In 1808, about the time of McLoughlin's first marriage, his apprenticeship expired, and he hoped that when he became a clerk, the Montreal agents would pay him for serving as physician. "I think they may," he told his uncle, "as I have been doing Dr Munros duty these five years without having any allowance although I recollect your telling me that if required to practice I would have £100 i e Dr Munros Salary."

By then he was disillusioned with life in the fur trade, and regretted that his "want of conduct" had led him into it. He complained that "this sad Experiment has cost me five Years," wrote darkly about going down (leaving the frontier), and said he would prefer living elsewhere on "potatoes and milk" rather than in the fur land. "When a man has been for any time in this Country he is entirely unfit for any other," he said. "The Country is geting ruin'd more and more every year . . . even the length of time to come in could be better employ'd and more agreably spent in any other place than this."

His worries were increased that summer because the brigades brought a letter recounting the financial predicament of his brother David. Although the two had not met for five years, they were close. As children they had explored the streets of Quebec together; they had been fellow apprentices under Dr. Fisher; and in 1827, when their ages were 43 and 41, Dr. John wrote a letter in which he twice called his brother "My Dear Davie." He was therefore concerned when David wanted to continue his education at the University of Edinburgh, which would be expensive. In 1807, before John was aware of the situation, Uncle Simon had offered to pay one-third of his costs, Grandfather Fraser had promised one hundred pounds, and the young man had set out blithely for Scotland—with more self-confidence than cash. But his funds would not cover his Edinburgh expenses, and when John heard of it, he told his Uncle Simon, "There is one thought that unmans my fortitude and that is the fear that my brother David should [not] finish his education through want of means."

In midsummer, while he was worried about his brother and uncertain of his own promotion, he was approached by Roderick McKenzie, a Montreal agent who had come to Fort William for the rendezvous. After asking the doctor what he intended to do, McKenzie offered him sound, if cynical, advice. Threaten to go down, he said, explaining that men often employed this "Stratagem" and predicting that the partners would then do "something handsome."

Thus bolstered and with fire in his heart, McLoughlin had a meeting with William McGillivray, head of the company, who offered him the rank of clerk at the low salary of £150 per year. As calmly as possible, John asked about his prospects for becoming a partner, to which McGillivray replied that they were the same as those of any young man of character. Furthermore, when McLoughlin reminded him of McTavish's agreement, the agent replied that "no promise of the kind could be made *by any body.*" Crushed, McLoughlin reported to his uncle:

> I told him I understood otherwise on my engaging to the Company for that I would not have given five years of my time after studying a profession for the paltry sum of 100 £. With that, he told me to think of his offers and give him an answer that he would not stand on a triffle, but it was impossible for him to give me expectations. I told him that I did not like the proposals and therefore was going down. . . . I am determined to go and settle at Detroit. It is certain that I will not lay up that sum but I will live in a Christian Country and live more happy than I do here. At the same time, I will have this consolation—I am my own master. It is true that I have but little to begin with but little will do.

And then he thought of David and softened. "It was and is still (if I should remain) my intention to help him as much as possible, indeed to be answerable for what necessary amount he should require. . . . My mind is distress'd, so beg you will excuse the incoherency of my stile." John was caught. He wanted to help his brother. He wanted to leave the fur trade. But his accumulated pay was to be four hundred pounds less than he had expected, leaving him only two options: he could give little or no assistance to David, while making a poorly funded and perhaps unsuccessful attempt to set up a private practice; or he could resign himself to another long stint of frontier life at the secure, but mediocre, pay of a company clerk.

He had a right to be dissatisfied, because he, a licensed physician, had received only the rank and salary of a clerk, while records show that others had been much better paid—or even had become partners before their apprenticeship expired. Simon McTavish, who might have straightened it out, was dead, and his successors obviously had no intention of honoring an unverified verbal agreement when the regular apprentice wages fulfilled the letter of the written contract.

The "stratagem," however, worked. Three days later McGillivray sent for him again and increased the offer to two hundred pounds a year, which McLoughlin accepted, asking for half to be paid in advance and forwarded to David. He explained to his uncle, "Nothing but my brother's situation could occasion my drawing money before it was due." He stayed on, dreaming about greener fields, brooding about his old contract, and longing to know what McTavish had actually said.

For three years he sent David money in hundred-pound increments, either "by the first Canoe that goes down" or by directions to draw on his Montreal account. He also repeatedly asked his uncle for the precise terms of the oral agreement, a question that his uncle at first ignored. "I am sorry to find you have never as Yet gave me a positive Answer whether it had been promis'd you for me," McLoughlin wrote in 1809. "If I ask so it is not for to make any Enquiries to others but only as a satisfaction to myself."

The following year he quoted the agreement as he remembered it, and said, "I am sorry you did not commend me in writing the account regarding my engagement as I request'd . . . as it might then have been of great use to me."

McLoughlin's reaction is of interest, because it illustrates his best side and his worst. He had shown sympathy and generosity, with no hint of envy for David's prestigious education. But he could not forget that the company had, in his eyes, broken the contract, and he had badgered his uncle. Years later the same pattern—selfless compassion coupled with endless harping on a grievance—would destroy him.

When at last, in 1810, his Uncle Simon sent the desired reply, it was somewhat confused.

> Mr. McTavish told me the Company would allow you a hundred pounds per annum if requir'd to practice as a surgeon, but he would not advise you to take it for if you went on the common wages the Company would take into consideration the time you serv'd as an apprentice to a surgeon, that is to say, would reckon your services from 1797, that in consequence of this you should be bound for five years only whilst others were for seven years.

Although this clearly reassured McLoughlin that McTavish had offered to pay him one hundred pounds per year if he served as physician, the timing of the apprenticeship was vague. It had indeed lasted only five years, from 1803 to 1808. But if the company had "reckoned" his service from 1797, even a seven-year indenture would have expired in 1804. One point is obvious: the agents did not hesitate to use the professional skills of a young and somewhat naive recruit for a minimum cost.

As for David, his problem eventually involved the whole Fraser family. They were quarrelsome, quick to anger and slow to forgive, but they were also

Dr. Simon Fraser, McLoughlin's Uncle Simon, who arranged the young man's original contact with the North West Company. For more than three decades, Fraser was adviser to his nephew and faithful guide to several of the children. It was through Fraser's descendants that the family letters were preserved, to become the best source of material on McLoughlin's personal life. MCLOUGHLIN HOUSE NATIONAL HISTORIC SITE

warm and loyal, and if any of them needed help, they would rally around. Uncle Alexander offered to secure a loan. Uncle Simon made a contribution. McLoughlin sent funds. Grandfather Malcolm, who had considerable property, was willing but had evidently suffered reverses. He wrote that he could give no further assistance because of "disappointments by those who are greatly indebted to me some of whom . . . I am afraid I must sue. . . . I am obliged to keep out of sight for want of cash as I cannot at this time command ten Dollars." Nevertheless, he urged Simon to send an additional fifty pounds, saying he would guarantee its repayment. And still the money failed to reach David regularly, perhaps because nobody worked out a satisfactory system for transferring it abroad.

Although David managed to enroll in the university and in 1809–10 received a diploma in surgery and a degree in medicine, he was so deeply in debt that he was being held in Edinburgh. Fortunately James Ker, a family friend in Scotland, became aware of the youth's plight. He informed Malcolm Fraser that the uncles had not "sent him a Shilling for a great length of time," and that he himself had advanced David "£120—, to keep him out of Prison." Thanks to this assistance, which Dr. Simon Fraser eventually repaid, David was freed from debt, and in 1811 he received a commission in the British armed services.

That was not, however, the end of the problem, for the confusion brought on a typical Fraser squabble. Simon handled the transactions, and because some of the money didn't go through, Alexander recklessly accused him of mismanagement. Simon was furious, resulting in a feud so acrimonious that the rift never healed. McLoughlin inadvertently got into the fray when he carelessly told his Uncle Simon, "It is very strange that you could not have fallen on some regular plan to remit him money." This spurred the uncle into a royal huff, which the nephew tried to appease: "Your letter surpris'd me not a little I never imagin'd I gave you so much offence by expressing my disappointment at my Brothers not receiveing the remittance I sent him—it is true I May have express'd myself warmly but I believe not impertinently."

A year later, with his uncle still angry, McLoughlin sent an abject apology.

> I am sorry to find that after what I wrote you last year you still recollect what I formerly wrote, their is no situation in life more distressing than when a person wishes to please and finds that he labours in vain. . . . if you will consider, the hurry their is at this place in the Summer of which Mr McKenzie can inform you consequently we have not always time to reflect on what words we may make use of in writeing our friends. . . . I will dismiss this letter with a Sigh being doubtfull how you may Receive it but depend on it I am sorry to have offend'd You.

But the next year the storm was over. "I am happy to find that you and I are again on Good Understanding nothing on my part I think will be wanting to keep it up indeed nothing is worse and more disagreeable than quarrels between Relations."

All his life McLoughlin managed to get along with his prickly family, which was no mean feat. He was the one to whom they all turned for financial help, and he was unfailingly generous. On this occasion, however, the price had been high, because the assistance to his brother had mired him in the fur trade. "Be assured had it not been for the money that I advanced David I would have gone down this year," he wrote to his uncle in 1811. He was having to live with his decision.

~ 5 ~
Physician-Clerk
1808–1814

In 1808, McLoughlin's first year as a clerk, his future was profoundly influenced by the resignation of the prominent Nor'Wester Alexander McKay. As was the occasional practice, McKay provided for his Indian wife and family and left them in the fur country, taking only his eleven-year-old son Tom.

Two years later, still accompanied by Tom, he joined John Jacob Astor's Pacific Fur Company expedition, which sailed around Cape Horn to the mouth of the Columbia River. There the Americans founded Fort Astoria, and there, in 1811, McKay lost his life, leaving fourteen-year-old Tom in the care of the company. For McLoughlin, the event was important because McKay's wife remained in the Fort William-Rainy Lake area.

She was Marguerite, one-half or possibly one-fourth Cree, the daughter of Jean Etienne Wadin, a Nor'Wester who had been shot in a fur-country squabble. Somewhere, sometime during his early years with the company, McLoughlin met Marguerite McKay—gentle, calm, with long black hair that hung loose over her shoulders. According to the custom of the country, she was free as soon as her fur-trader husband left her. She smiled at the tall young doctor; he indulged in a bit of frontier courting; and in the summer or early fall of 1811, when McLoughlin was not quite twenty-seven and Marguerite was thirty-six, they made a "consent of marriage." Although the certificate has not been found, the marriage was probably as formal as was possible on the frontier. The union was happy, and for the rest of his life McLoughlin not only honored her, he insisted that all with whom he associated must treat her with respect.

Marguerite could not read or write, but S. A. Clarke, a historian and early resident of Oregon, said she "was remarkable for the possession of sound judgment and good qualities. That she had much influence with him [McLoughlin] was proof that she was no ordinary woman." She became widely known for her kindness and skill at calming her fiery husband. A grandson later told how McLoughlin would storm in, angrily vowing dreadful retributions against one or another hapless employee, and she would placidly go on with her knitting until, "when the exuberance of wrath had somewhat subsided she made wise suggestions, and in the end was always able to bring him to reason and induce him to do exactly what was right."

For McLoughlin, the year 1811 was significant in another way—he renewed his agreement as clerk in return for a promise that he would "come in for a Share of the advantages of the Country that is in the outfit of 1814." In other words, he would become a partner. He had "offers to go to the Columbia," where the Nor'Westers had established a few small posts, but it is not clear whether they were to take effect in 1811 or 1814.

In marrying Marguerite McKay, he had become a family man, for she had three daughters by Alexander McKay—Nancy, Mary, and a third whose name has not been found. Little is known about them. The David McLoughlin Papers at the Oregon Historical Society Library say:

My mother m. Alexander McKay, by him she had 3 daughters and
one son. One daughter m. Left. McConnick, who died at India. She
came back to England and lived at Woolwich under ½ pay. Another
daughter m. Capt. McCargo, who ran merchant freighter up and down
Lake Superior. The last m. Chief Trader Sinclair, of the H. B. Co.

Based on the time McKay spent in the Red River area, the birth dates of
these girls were between 1795 and 1809, which establishes their ages in 1811
as two to sixteen. Perhaps McLoughlin was unwilling to take such a family—
Marguerite, her three daughters, and his own toddler Joseph—on the long
trip to the West Coast, or perhaps he thought it was too far from his Fraser relatives. Whatever the reason, when he was offered that distant post, he refused.
    In August 1811 he wrote, "In a few days I start for my wintering Grounds
at a place called Vermilion lake, it is a very poor place." His canoes that year
were crowded, and at the lake, while the snow piled high and the wind howled,
the little log cabin must have been full—and more than full—of children's
cries and laughter and paraphernalia. It was McLoughlin's last untroubled year.
    The next summer, while he and his family were again living at Fort
William, the Montreal brigade brought unwelcome but not surprising news.
England and France had been at loggerheads for years. In 1806 the French
had stepped up hostilities by blockading the coast of Britain, at which
England declared all commerce with that country contraband, began to stop
neutral ships to search them for deserters, and instituted a series of blockades
that damaged American trade. During early 1812 tensions were on the rise,
and in June, after the British boarded an American vessel to seize four men,
President James Madison asked Congress to declare war.
    The hostilities spread to the St. Lawrence. Panic-stricken English ladies
fled across the Atlantic, and "traitorous meetings [of French Canadians] were
held even at Murray Bay, under the watchful eye of Malcolm Fraser"—
Grandfather Fraser, a spry seventy-nine. As colonel in the local militia, he was
delighted to pick up arms again, muster a local company, and lead it to
Quebec. He wrote scornfully of "our Southern bad Neighbours who term
themselves *the united States* tho' I believe them to be somewhat disunited in
their declaration of this very unjust war."
    The news reached Fort William in July, while McLoughlin was there for
the rendezvous. Fearing that the Great Lakes would soon be blockaded, the
Nor'Westers immediately decided "to send as many men as could be spared
. . . to *Lac la Pluie* [Rainy Lake] to help getting the packs out in as much haste

as possible." Every available man left at once, to frantically load pelts valued at £200,000 into canoes and take them to Montreal. The "fleet of 44 loaded and 3 light canoes," guarded by 135 Nor'Westers, was to travel in a single large flotilla, which would skirt the shore of Lake Superior and go through the lock at Sault Ste. Marie, into Lake Huron. Since the Americans were patrolling this lake with two armed vessels, the canoes were to hug the wooded shore and scud across the end of Georgian Bay to the mouth of the French River, where they could leave the Great Lakes and finish the trip in safety.

McLoughlin, as physician, would be needed at the summer gathering, and a letter he wrote at Fort William in August indicates that he remained at his post. As the weeks slid by, he and the others who were left behind could only wait in the fort and worry until the news finally came that the canoes, with their men and valuable furs, had reached Montreal.

Although one calamity was averted, the onset of war was nevertheless a grave disappointment to McLoughlin, for he had been looking forward to a partner's share in profits, and the company's trade had collapsed. "I am Greatly afraid this war will injure this country if not ruin it entirely," he wrote to his Uncle Simon on August 12; and in the same letter he expressed another worry. "I receiv'd no letter this Year from David (it is a subject which forces itself on me again) this makes me doubly anxious about him." He obviously did not know that David had received his diploma and was an officer in the British armed forces. The summer brought one bright note, however. In mid-August, Marguerite delivered their first child, a boy whom they named John.

For McLoughlin the following year, 1813, was again a time of trouble, for the war was still raging. The American army invaded Canada, the company's Great Lakes vessel *Nancy* was sunk, and the company buildings and stores at Sault Ste. Marie were burned. Its time-saving canal and lock were also destroyed, which would mean great difficulty in supplying the interior posts.

In addition the brigades brought word of two family tragedies. His Grandfather McLoughlin had died on October 3, 1812, and his father had drowned, probably in the St. Lawrence, on April 28, 1813. These two deaths, so close together, deepened McLoughlin's loneliness and sense of isolation, as shown in a letter to his Uncle Simon. "This year is a Year of Misfortune for me. You have I presume heard of my Fathers Death and the Unfortunate Accident by which he lost his life." In a poignant glimpse of the gulf that had evidently existed in his childhood family, he added, "To me it is very distressing as I never had it in my power to show him any proof of my duty or affection."

He gave the only help he could. Since his Uncle Alexander, who had retired from the fur company, had bought the seigneury of Rivière-du-Loup and was living near the McLoughlin farms, McLoughlin asked him to "give my Mother 50£ and draw on the agents for it." Fifty pounds was a quarter of his annual pay, and it was only a year since his brother's expenses were shrinking his bankroll. But he apparently did not hesitate.

A year later, the express brought a letter from Alexander with extensive news of the family, generating a fresh wave of homesickness. Hungry to see his family, lonely and dejected, McLoughlin wrote to his Uncle Simon,

> Nothing can do me greater pleasure than to hear of the wellfare of my Relations—I hope if alive within a few years to have the pleasure of seeing them at least I hope to go [to] where they are at present. You cannot think how I long to go down, this makes my time pass on very disagreably in the Interior in Winter—it makes my time appear long—I feel loansome, and quite low spirited.

As usual, the Frasers were embroiled in a quarrel, and it was still between the two uncles. McLoughlin continued,

> It certainly grieves me much to find [that] my Brother David has been Instrumental or cause of disagreement between you and my Uncle Alexander I had heard of this before but from no Good authority those who told me said such and Such was the case they thought they had heard, but were not certain.

He asked whether his latest draft had been paid, and said that Simon would shortly be visited by the Nor'Wester Donald McKenzie, who would present him with a "Sea Otter . . . as a mark of the Regard and Respect which is due you."

McLoughlin wrote this letter in 1814, the long-awaited year when he would become a partner, and a few months later the war came to an end. The treaty, however, was not signed until December, which meant that he would not hear of it until the following spring. On the national front little had changed, because all land captured by either party was to be returned. But the Nor'Westers could once more ship their furs in safety and see a restoration of profits, which in the past had provided annual dividends as large as four hundred pounds per share—two thousand dollars in American money. It would mean a vast improvement in McLoughlin's purse.

But as one threat subsided, another arose, one that had been brewing for several years and was potentially serious. It involved the Nor'Westers' giant rival—the "adventurers" of Hudson Bay.

CHAPTER 3

The Great Fur War

I cannot think the Judges will make me pay my Bail
as I certainly have good cause to be absent.

DR. JOHN MCLOUGHLIN

The Honourable Company
1670–1812

E ven before John McLoughlin became a fur trader, he had undoubtedly known about the Hudson's Bay Company, because it
was the oldest branch of "big business" on the North American
continent. He could not, however, have known what a vital role it
would play in his life. It was a bitter rival of his own North West Company.
Both were strong, both wanted the same land, and the young doctor became
a fur trader just in time to be caught in the inevitable clash.

The Hudson's Bay Company traced its beginning to a pair of French
Canadian fur traders—middle-aged, swarthy, bearded Pierre Esprit Radisson;
and Médard Chouart, the Sieur des Groseilliers, a thin, clean-shaven, restless
young man. The early French traders followed streams through unmapped
forests, but these two ventured much farther than any had before. Although
their exact itinerary is not certain, it is generally agreed that in 1654–56 Groseilliers went as far as Lake Michigan, and that in 1659–60 Radisson went
with him to the little-known shores of Lake Superior. They returned to
Quebec with thousands of prime pelts, dark and luxurious. But more than
that, they had an ingenious idea. The finest skins had been secured through
middlemen but had originated near "the Bay of the North Sea." Therefore,
the Frenchmen reasoned, if they could take vessels into Hudson Bay, they
could deal directly with the Indians there and ship the furs straight to
Europe, which would be quicker and cheaper than bartering with third parties and hauling skins over the tortuous canoe route.

Confidently expecting a lavish reward, they offered their idea to the
French colonial governor at Quebec, but he was furious because they had
presumed to trade without a proper license. He may have imprisoned
Groseilliers, and he slapped heavy fines on both of them, at which—understandably annoyed—they left Canada. First they went to Boston, where they

secured financing for a limited venture that failed, and then they sailed to England.

There they indulged in such rosy speculations about a fortune in furs and the legendary Northwest Passage between the Atlantic and Pacific Oceans that a group of intrepid businessmen decided to sponsor a trial expedition of two ships. Using the name "Mr. Gooseberry," because the French word *gro-seillier* means "gooseberry bush," they gave the captains firm instructions:

> You are to saile to such place as Mr. Gooseberry and Mr. Radison shall direct . . . in ord^r to trade with the Indyans there. . . . You are to have in yor thoughts the discovery of the Passage into the South sea and to attempt it as occasion shall offer with the advice and direction of Mr. Gooseberry and Mr. Radison . . . they having told us that it is but 7 daies padling or sailing . . . unto the Stinking Lake and not above 7 daies more to the streight wch. leads into that sea they call the South Sea.

The two ships, *Eaglet* and *Nonsuch*, started bravely, but were caught in a raging Atlantic gale that forced the *Eaglet*, with Radisson aboard, to turn back. The *Nonsuch*, however, managed to reach James Bay, the thumb of Hudson Bay that stretches two hundred miles south, where Groseilliers and the other men spent the winter.

In the spring three hundred Indians came to trade, enabling the *Nonsuch* to bring back a rich cargo of furs. King Charles II then assembled a new group of backers and formed the Hudson's Bay Company, which he legalized by a solemn charter. It was impressive—five large sheets of parchment ornamented by serpentine writing and a hand-colored miniature portrait of the king, aristocratic and elegant with a wide lace jabot and flowing mane of dark curls. On May 2, 1670, the charter received the Great Seal of England, and it named the king's "Deare and entirely beloved Cousin Prince Rupert" as the company's first governor. In this way McLoughlin's future employer—and future nemesis—was launched.

The charter incorporated the new firm as the "Governor and Company of Adventurers of England tradeing into Hudsons Bay," the term "adventurers" meaning those who "ventured" their precious money, but not their precious lives. Although the "Honourable Committee" in London had no concept of the rigors of the fur trade, they were solid, prosperous citizens, and the charter made them the "true and absolute Lordes and Proprietors" of

Rupert's Land, which consisted of

> all those Seas Streightes Bayes Lakes Creekes and Soundes in what-
> soever Latitude they shall bee that lye within the entrance of the
> Streightes commonly called Hudson's Streightes together with all the
> Landes and Territoryes upon the Countryes Coastes and confynes of
> the Seas Bayes Lakes Rivers Creekes and Soundes aforesaid that are
> not actually possessed by or granted to any of our Subjectes or pos-
> sessed by the Subjectes of any other Christian Prince or State.

In simpler terms, the company received a monopoly over all the lands
that drained into Hudson Bay. No one knew its precise extent, but Rupert's
Land stretched northeast nearly to the shores of Labrador, south to the watershed of the St. Lawrence and Great Lakes, and northwest to the Rocky Mountains and Athabasca—the long slope to the Arctic. It encompassed one and a
half million square miles, which is almost half the size of today's United States.
Although the borders were vague, the charter was so durable that a century
and a half later it was still functioning, and McLoughlin became one of the
Hudson's Bay Company's important men.

The company's power was immense. It had been granted exclusive rights
to all mines of gold, silver, and gems, all fisheries, all minerals, all trade. It could
build castles and fortifications, enact laws, establish courts, and make peace
or war "with any Prince or People whatsoever that are not Christians." It
could adopt any business measure it chose, and impose "pains and penalties"
provided they were "reasonable" and not "repugnant" to British law. For all this
the payments were scarcely onerous, being two elk and two black beavers,
given to the king "whensoever and as often as Wee our heires and Successors
shall happen to enter into the Said Countryes."

This token payment—two elk and two black beavers—was actually
made in 1927 when the Prince of Wales came to his Canadian ranch. It was
made again in 1939 to King George and his queen, and in 1959 to Queen
Elizabeth II.

York Factory, on the shore of Hudson Bay, was the field headquarters,
"factory" meaning a business establishment in a foreign country headed by a
"factor," or agent. It stood at the mouth of the Hayes River, in a bleak area of
sodden flats, where the rivers iced thick in winter and bone-chilling winds
whistled in from the sea. Conditions were so difficult that one supervisor wrote
of men working in a swamp to their knees, while mosquitoes stung them "like

The Hudson's Bay Company was using this coat of arms by 1678. A fox is sitting on a beaver hat, at top, and the company motto "Pro Pelle Cutem" is on the ribbon near the bottom. It means "a skin for a pelt," skin being tanned, pelt raw. It was sometimes ironically translated as "skinned for skins." The illustration is from a flag that flew over Fort Vancouver.
OHS ORHI 713

great wasps that wee are nothing in the world but knotts and bumps." McLoughlin would visit York Factory several times, but he would never be stationed there.

During the long dark winters of the early years, the men at the bay waited stolidly for Indians to bring in furs. For the first century the firm was hugely successful, issuing two large stock increases and yearly dividends that ranged from 5 to 12 percent. But eventually the monopoly was challenged, first by the French, who threaded the streams in canoes, and then by nimble companies of Scots, who ranged ever farther afield. By McLoughlin's time, the Hudson's Bay Company profits were in a decline. In 1800 its annual dividend dropped to 4 percent; in 1806 it still paid 4 percent although its trade was not sufficient to maintain that much, requiring it to apply for a loan from the Bank of England. In 1808 the company tried in vain to secure another loan, and in 1809–14 it paid no dividend at all.

The strongest of the other firms—McLoughlin's North West Company—used a radically different system, trading through Montreal and penetrating the forests by canoe routes. Professor K. G. Davies wrote, "On one side were the North Westers, the Cavaliers of the fur trade, flamboyant, extravagant. . . . On the other side stood the Hudson's Bay Company, the Roundheads: sober, persistent, concerned above all with their own rightness and winning the charge at the end of the day."

At first the Bay men derided the Nor'Westers. Andrew Graham of York Factory was sure his English company could keep up the trade "and even overturn all the schemes of the Canadian pilferers without applying to birch-rind canoes and such like wild schemes." But the Nor'Westers' system worked. As the Hudson's Bay Company revenues shrank, it reluctantly began to move south on the Hayes and other rivers and establish its own inland posts, using waterways for transport.

In the resulting competition, McLoughlin's colleagues had several advantages. They staged a summer rendezvous at which the field men shared expertise, but the English posts were strictly on their own. Since canoe birch was plentiful only in the south, the Nor'Westers had the advantage of birchbark canoes for transportation, while the Bay men had to rely on heavy boats built from their northern woods. Even more important, the North West posts were administered by partners who received a share of profits—a powerful spur—but the Bay men had only salaries, and made so little effort that one disgruntled officer described their conduct as "Sleep by the Frozen Sea."

As time went on, it was clear that the Nor'Westers were outdistancing their rivals. By 1795 they controlled 77 percent of Canada's fur trade, while the English company controlled 14 percent and independent traders the rest. In 1800 the value of the North West Company harvest was £144,000, while that of the Hudson's Bay Company was £38,000. In 1806 the old, conservative firm began to pay part of its profits to employees. But five years later it still had only 320 men in the field, while the Nor'Westers had 1,200—a significant difference, even though many of the latter were boatmen, not traders.

These paddlers symbolized the one insuperable handicap of McLoughlin's company—the heavy cost of the arduous canoe route from Quebec. It was expensive in terms of both manpower and the time it tied up company funds. In the fall, after canoes brought estimates of future needs, the Montreal agents would order trade goods from London. These would arrive the following summer—too late to ship to the frontier, because streams would soon freeze. After being stored for the winter in Montreal, the merchandise would be sent to Fort William in the spring and traded the next winter for furs. These would be laboriously sent to London by way of Montreal, for a total time lag of two to three years from purchase of goods to sale of the furs they were traded for. Even though the Nor'Westers tried to compensate by putting three ships on Lake Superior, between Sault Ste. Marie and headquarters, they still had to use canoes from Montreal, and they were infuriated by their rivals' faster route through Hudson Bay.

As the North West Company grew in size and strength, its men began to boldly cross Rupert's Land to establish posts in the far west. They called their rival's charter illegal, saying it had been granted while the land belonged to France, not England, and that Parliament had confirmed it in 1690 for seven years only, without extending it again, which rendered it obsolete. The Hud-

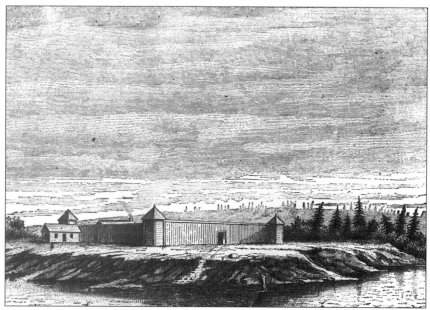

This is the type of secondary post used in the area west of the Great Lakes, where Mc-Loughlin spent his winters from 1803-1814. Some of the posts, such as Fort Frances, were permanent and substantial, while others were often moved or abandoned. FromH.M. Robinson's, *The Great Fur Land.* OHS ORHI 99106

son's Bay Committee itself was not willing to risk a challenge in the courts, and frankly said that if the fur-trade dispute caused serious losses, "it would be very difficult to find redress here even on application to Government."

Simon McTavish had tried to have the charter repealed, or to buy or lease rights to trade through the bay and cross Hudson's Bay lands. In 1803, when McLoughlin was a young recruit, McTavish sent a ship and overland expedition to establish a post on the bay and hold it by force, if necessary. But the English company persuaded the Indians not to trade with the interlopers, causing the venture to pay so little that the Nor'Westers abandoned it. Later, Alexander Mackenzie attempted to buy enough shares to control the British firm, and petitioned for a North West charter on the Pacific Coast. These efforts also failed.

By the time McLoughlin joined the company, the Nor'Westers were freely trading on Hudson's Bay land, while the Bay men were setting up their own posts, sometimes close to the rival establishments. The situation was tense, characterized by an uneasy peace, efforts by each group to outwit the other, and occasional outbursts of violence. But there were also instances of friendly cooperation. McLoughlin's friend Daniel Harmon wrote, "Two of the Hudson's Bay People arrived from Fort des Prairies, who were so obliging as to bring me Letters from several gentlemen in that quarter. The greater part of the North West and Hudson Bay people, live on amicable terms; and when one can with propriety render a service to the other, it is done with cheerfulness."

And then a fiery young Scot cast his eyes on Rupert's Land, changing the fur trade forever.

~ 2 ~

Lord Selkirk's Colony
1803–1815

T he firebrand who so profoundly affected the fur trade was Thomas Douglas, Earl of Selkirk, heir to a Scottish estate. Wealthy, intelligent, fanatical, he wanted to promote British settlement in North America and ease the plight of the crofters—tenant farmers—who were being displaced in the notorious Highland Clearances.

The Clearances had followed the Battle of Culloden of 1746, in which McLoughlin's great-grandfather Donald Fraser had been killed. Afterward, when the Scottish chiefs received ownership of the land, some of them leased or sold it to wealthy speculators, who found more profit in sheep than in farms and ran the crofters out of their homes. Whole villages were seized for pasture, stock was confiscated, and houses were leveled. In exchange the crofters were offered bits of land on the coast—rocky, steep patches of thin soil on the cliff edges, where the Arctic winds blew cold. Or they could become herring fishermen. Or leave the country.

In 1809, the year after McLoughlin became a clerk, the Earl of Selkirk married Jean Wedderburn, a charming, quick-witted young woman whose wealthy family owned a large block of Hudson's Bay stock. Gifted

Thomas Douglas, fifth earl of Selkirk.
NATIONAL LIBRARY OF CANADA NEG. NO. 1346

with a bubbling sense of humor and indomitable loyalty, she was to stand by her husband through difficult times, in Quebec as well as in the British Isles.

Selkirk, being a fervent believer in colonizing, had previously founded two crofters' settlements in eastern Canada, and after his marriage he requested a site for a third colony on Hudson's Bay land along the Red River. The request appalled the Nor'Westers, for they had used that land for decades, it straddled the only route to their fur lands in the west, and it supplied pemmican, without which they could not feed their men in the field.

Pemmican, prepared from buffalo meat, kept indefinitely if protected from wet and mold. It was so nutritious that two pounds of it, with bread and tea, would satisfy eight hungry men. It could be eaten raw, or fried with a little flour, or boiled with potatoes to a thick soup called—in several creative spellings—"rubbaboo." But it was an acquired taste. One trader wrote:

> Take the scrapings from the driest outside corner of a very stale piece of cold roast-beef, add to it lumps of tallowy, rancid fat, then garnish all with long human hairs, on which string pieces, like beads upon a necklace, and short hairs of dogs or oxen, or both, and you have a fair imitation of common pemmican. . . . Carefully made pemmican, flavored with berries and sugar, is nearly good; but of most persons new to the diet it may be said that, in two senses, a little of it goes a long way.

McLoughlin himself ate little or no pemmican, which was seldom used in the Great Lakes area but it was literally a lifesaving staple in the western posts. In 1806, for example, Alexander Henry the Younger said the personnel from Fort Dauphin "are on the eve of starving there are no Buffalo in those parts at present, and they have finished what Pemmican was left last spring."

The land Selkirk wanted was near the buffalo grounds and contained two rival posts: small Fort Douglas, of the Hudson's Bay Company; and the Nor'-Westers' large, solid Fort Gibraltar, protected by oak picketing twelve feet high and equipped with eight stout buildings, one of them an icehouse with a watchtower on top. Several Indian tribes lived in the area, as well as Métis, who were the descendants of Indian mothers and fur-trade fathers. The men hunted buffalo for the North West Company, while the women dried buffalo meat, pounded it, mixed it with berries and melted fat—from marrow or bear grease—and packed it into skin bags.

In 1809 Selkirk decided to place a colony in this essential area and began to buy up stock in the Hudson's Bay Company. Sir Alexander Mackenzie, who

The Northwest Company depended on Indians near Red River for the yearly supply of buffalo. *Indian hunters pursuing the buffalo in the early spring, 1822*, by Peter Rindisbacher. NATIONAL ARCHIVES OF CANADA, C-114467

was then in London, worked with him briefly. But they were at cross-purposes, for Mackenzie hoped to control the Hudson's Bay Company in order to benefit the Nor'Westers, while Selkirk wanted to found a colony for the crofters. After they parted, Mackenzie urged his colleagues to buy shares for themselves, and at the summer rendezvous of 1811 they voted money for the purchase. Being merely a physician-clerk, McLoughlin had no voice in the decision, and his one surviving letter from that year does not mention it, although he must have been aware of the purchase. In any case, the partners' decision was too late. They failed to secure control, Selkirk submitted an offer to finance a colony at Red River, and in March 1811 the Hudson's Bay Company board accepted it, subject to stockholders' approval.

Mackenzie and two other Nor'Westers, William McGillivray's brother Simon and their agent Edward Ellice—all in London—made frantic efforts to block the colony. They bought Hudson's Bay stock, lobbied shareholders, toured coffeehouses, and published pamphlets. "Even if [the settlers] escape the scalping knife . . . their habitations, their crops, their cattle will be destroyed," wrote Simon McGillivray in the *Inverness Journal*, and said they would perish because of dangerous rapids, wild animals, or biting cold. When the shareholders nevertheless approved the plan, the Nor'Westers suggested that the two companies divide the territory, and petitioned the British government for a charter of their own on the Pacific Slope. It was refused. On June 12, 1811, Selkirk received his grant, for which he was to pay a token ten shillings, fur-

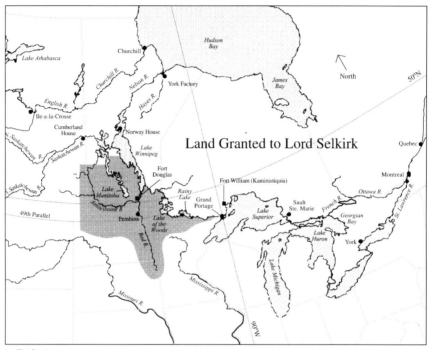

Selkirk Grant

nish the company two hundred servants per year, and provide land for posts and retirees.

It was a fabulous award—a tract of more than 116,000 square miles, which is five times as large as Scotland. Because the border between the United States and Rupert's Land had not yet been agreed upon, the grant included a large chunk of Minnesota, a smaller one of North Dakota, and a corner of South Dakota, as part of the Red River's watershed. Placing an agricultural settlement on Hudson's Bay land was not a new idea. The charter authorized "Plantations Fortes Colonyes or Places of Trade," and the company had for several years been contemplating a Red River settlement for its retired traders and as a source of labor.

The summer of 1812 found McLoughlin in his usual role of physician for the Fort William rendezvous. In the midst of the meetings, the express brought a frantic letter from Simon McGillivray in London, giving the bad news of Selkirk's success. McGillivray grimly predicted, "It will require some time, and I fear cause much expence to us, as well as to himself, before he [Selkirk] is driven to abandon the project . . . yet *he must be driven to abandon*

This sketch, made in 1822, just after the North West and the Hudson's Bay companies merged, shows the location of the settlement on the banks of the Red River, with a canoe and several huts. The dress of the family in the foreground, and the placing of the infant on its mother's back, indicate that they are Métis. *Summer view of Red River in the environs of Fort Douglas* by Peter Rindisbacher. HUDSON BAY COMPANY ARCHIVES, PROVINCIAL ARCHIVES OF MANITOBA, HBCA 1987/363-R-13 1/6 (N70-26A)

it, for his success would strike at the very existence of our Trade." He advised the winterers to send extra men and supplies to the interior posts, and warned them to "prepare your people for a year of Trial . . . the opposition ought to be general and followed up at almost any expence in order to spoil their returns for a year or two."

At the close of the rendezvous, McLoughlin and his family left Fort William for his winter post, somewhere in the area near Rainy Lake. On August 30, 1812, even while they were being paddled through the streams, a haggard, ragtag group of twenty-two Scottish and Irish workmen reached Red River. They had landed at Hudson Bay early the previous winter and in the spring had paddled crude boats up the Hayes River. With them was their governor, Miles Macdonell, a stubborn, high-strung former army captain, honest and able but so abrasive that one subordinate spoke of him as "standing alone like the Poison tree, despised and shunned by every creature."

Within a few weeks a second group arrived, including women and children, but neither the colony nor the Hudson's Bay Company was prepared to receive them. Cold, hungry, housed with the Indians or in cramped little Fort Douglas, some "were grubbing with hoes for wild roots," and mothers sold their shawls to Hudson's Bay employees in order to buy oatmeal for their children. They were so pathetic that the Nor'Westers in well-stocked Fort Gibraltar took pity and sold them pemmican, potatoes, barley, and oats for food, along with seed and livestock in the spring to help them get started.

Governor Macdonell immediately put up Fort Daer, uncomfortably close to Forts Gibraltar and Douglas, for they were all near the juncture of the Red and Assiniboine Rivers. But for the first two years the frontier was calm, with the Métis hunting and processing buffalo and the Nor'Westers freely crossing colony land. McLoughlin, as before, spent his summers at Fort William and winters in the vicinity of Rainy Lake.

The rendezvous of 1814 was special to him as the beginning of his partnership, but it started with an unexpected problem. McLoughlin and four other clerks were slated for promotion, each to receive one share—and only one and one-half shares had been released through retirement or death. He was doubtless much relieved when, as recorded in the minutes, "McTavish McGillivrays and Company (with the assent of Sir A. McK & Co.) gave up 3½ shares for the young men, to be replaced from the first Shares which should fall vacant." In this way all five clerks received their promised appointments, and after eleven years in the fur company, Dr. John McLoughlin, nearly thirty years old, was a partner at last.

This should have been a tremendous satisfaction, but it was marred, because Governor Macdonell had a proclamation tacked onto the gates of North West forts. It crisply said the colonists needed all the available buffalo, and therefore "no person trading in furs or provisions within the territory . . . shall take out any provisions, either flesh, grain or vegetables, procured or raised within the said territory." Although the order applied to both companies, the Nor'Westers were the ones it threatened, for it forbade the export of pemmican, which they depended on to feed their men in the field. Nor did the governor stop with words. Boasting that he had sufficient force to "crush all the Nor'Westers on this river, should they be so hardy as to resist my authority," he confiscated pemmican from the Métis, raided the important post at La Souris, and seized the cargo from two North West canoes.

Many writers have discussed the Red River affair, but even Selkirk supporters criticize this proclamation, calling it bias, or poor judgment, or "an act of madness." Although the governor was legitimately concerned about his colony's needs, he could hardly have found a more effective way to stir up trouble—unnecessary trouble, for the Red River area contained more than enough space and buffalo for them all. The colonists were short of food because they were inexperienced farmers and hunters, not because resources were scarce.

Striving for peace, Governor Macdonell held a series of conferences with Duncan Cameron and other Nor'Westers, at which they worked out a compromise: most of the pemmican would be restored; the North West Company would give assistance in moving oatmeal from York Factory to Red River; and it would receive a limited right to ship furs via Hudson Bay. But the hostilities had been carried too far. McLoughlin's first meeting as a partner was held behind closed doors, where the winterers raged that Macdonell intended to starve them and destroy their company, and that they would resist, at whatever cost. "We will do our best to defend our rights," sputtered Nor'Wester Alexander Macdonell, the governor's cousin. "Nothing but the complete downfall of the Colony will satisfy some, by fair or foul means. So here is at them with all my heart and energy." The partners rejected the compromise and decided to fight back by waging a two-pronged campaign—to frighten the colonists away from Red River, and lure them to free land.

In the War of 1812 the North West Company had raised a unit of militia known as the Corps of Canadian Voyageurs. After the war, William McGillivray obtained the right to grant commissions in the Indian Territories, and in 1814 Duncan Cameron was named captain. He borrowed a scarlet uniform, complete with epaulets and sword, and presented himself to the settlers as "Captain, Voyageur Corps, Commanding Officer, Red River Indian Territory." He spoke to them in Gaelic, entertained them at dinner, and offered them free transportation to Upper Canada, plus free land there, a year's free provisions, and payments of twenty to one hundred pounds.

At the same time, his colleague Alexander Macdonell wrote a rather vague letter to the Métis, saying in part, "I wish that some of your Pilleurs [Pillagers] who are full of mischief and plunder would pay a hostile visit to these sons of gunpowder and riot [the colonists] . . . not that I wish butchery; God forbid." The Métis were not slow to take the hint. They terrorized the settlers by firing shots in the night, trampling crops, and setting fire to buildings.

Such an introduction to partnership was a shattering disappointment to McLoughlin. After plugging away for eleven years at a job he disliked, he had expected to at last reap the profits of partnership—and now the very existence of his company was under threat. His letters of 1814 sound a note of utter despair, as when he again told his uncle he was sorry he ever came to the fur country, and that "though distant from my friends I Still call Canada my home and reckon myself only as a Bird of Passage in this."

The summer, however, brought him one personal pleasure, for his Uncle Alexander's son, Alexander Fraser, stopped at Fort William on his way to the Red River Colony. McLoughlin was overjoyed at the chance to catch up on family news. But he was surprised that his uncle, "with his Knowledge of this part of the world, yet sent his son to it," and although he tried to be tactful, he managed to rile his bristly relative. "I neither advised him [his cousin] to go there or go down and told him he was of sufficient age to decide for himself," he said later. "I wrote my Uncle Alexander Expressing my surprise at his sending his son to this Country—my Uncle I believe has taken offence—I meant none—he has not wrote me since."

In the fall of 1814 young Alexander went to Fort Gibraltar, while McLoughlin took his canoes to Lac la Pluie—Rainy Lake, an important depot for the Athabasca winterers, who "bring to it their peltries and return from it with their outfits of merchandise." McLoughlin was therefore responsible for extensive transportation and storage, the usual Indian trade, and the care of the physical plant—several buildings inside stout log pickets, a small and not very productive garden in sandy soil, and a farm that included a field of wheat, a few oats and potatoes, a herd of horned cattle, and a small water mill.

After the summer's turbulence the peace of the country appealed to him, and he wrote to his Uncle Simon, "It has always been my wish if I had wherewith to buy a farm and settle in the Country certainly a country [life] is the happiest life in the world." It is probable that some time during that year his daughter, Marie Elisabeth—generally called Eliza—was born, although her birth is not on record.

At the next gathering, in 1815, he found tempers even higher than the previous year, for Governor Macdonell had again tacked notices to the forts' gates. This time he ordered the posts to be vacated within six months, under threat of razing them "to the foundations"—and the Nor'Westers swung into action. Duncan Cameron, in his scarlet uniform, obtained warrants from Norman McLeod, who was a justice of the peace. Armed with these, Cameron arrested the governor and John Spencer, the colony's sheriff, "on a criminal charge of burglary and robbery." And he continued his dual campaign with the colonists.

Faced with this carrot-and-stick approach—free land and free transportation versus harassment and terror—most of the settlers fled in North West canoes. The strategy was working, but some of the partners regretted the violence, and the exchange of letters indicated that McLoughlin and Angus Bethune were chief among these. "I could not help thinking that had I been in our good Captain's place I would have left their miserable huts standing," the doctor's friend James Hughes wrote to him. And McLoughlin himself—with less elegance but more heat—said they "had their belly full."

A lighter note was sounded one evening when a gala ball was held in the Great Hall of Fort William, with some unusual guests: several fleeing colonists under Duncan Cameron's wing, as well as his prisoners, Governor Macdonell and Sheriff Spencer. Records show that "Dr. McLachlan," a strapping thirty-one-year-old, was at the gathering, but they do not tell whether Marguerite was with him.

Simon McGillivray, who had come from London, apparently enjoyed the merriment, for he wrote, "All is fun & good humor. Our officers appear in uniform for the first time and dancing kept up till daylight." But to Governor Macdonell, confined in an adjoining bedroom, the affair was somewhat less jolly. "Last night there was a ball to which all the Settlers from Red R. & their women were asked," he wrote. "There was not much drinking but they danced reels incessantly & made a dreadful noise. I could not get a wink of sleep."

McLoughlin was a seasoned Nor'Wester by then, at his second rendezvous as partner, and except for the ball, he found this gathering even stormier than his first. The winterers complained that the year's trading outfits were skimpy. They were incensed because profits had vanished. They objected because the Montreal agents, in figuring the costs of shipping furs to England, charged their accounts in pounds sterling instead of cheaper pounds Halifax, which were generally used in company records. When McGillivray said making the change "would be most injurious to the Concern," they replied that "nevertheless they were determined to try." Some of them threatened to relinquish their shares. McGillivray wrote:

> It is therefore I suppose inferred that the Country is going to the Devil—and people are acting accordingly. It really appears to me that there is some secret but active enemies of the Concern at work in order to sow dissention and if possible destroy the Concern. . . . There seems a general wish to retire from the Country—some from getting old and tired of it—others from a dread of opposition. . . . In short things look discouraging but we must brave out the storm.

It was customary for the winterers at a rendezvous to make assignments at their own "conclave," and early in this session two longtime Nor'Westers, Robert Henry and Simon Fraser, joined the rebellion by refusing the Athabasca post. To replace them, the group unanimously decided on July 17 that McLoughlin, being a new partner, should go there—but by then he was imbued with the general spirit of noncooperation, and boldly refused. This, said McGillivray, was considered extraordinary and in a younger Partner presumptuous conduct.

> The Doctor said he would throw up his share and go to Montreal if required to go to Athabasca. He was told of the consequences, but argued & was stubborn which seemed to excite indignation among the old Partners.
> On the score of *expediency* his nomination to Athabasca or to follow the opposition was rescinded, and as a punishment he was appointed to go to Lac des Isles and then down to Lac La Pluie.

After this the leaders considered the issue closed, because new partners usually did as they were told. But they had not counted on McLoughlin's Irish grit. With reckless abandon, he rejected the assignment to Lac des Iles, declaring that he would leave the fur trade rather than knuckle under. McGillivray plaintively wrote, "Dr. McLaughlin refuses to go to Lac des Isles, and it seems wont go any where unless he may chuse his Department." Tempers were so high that, according to the notes, Mr. McLeod "threatens a prosecution for damages for the injury done the Concern by his [McLoughlin's] unprecedented conduct and dangerous example."

When the session adjourned, the winterers were still seething, and no decision had been made. At the next meeting they stubbornly renewed McLoughlin's assignment to the Athabasca, and this time, after a "conference" with Kenneth McKenzie, he consented. Although no record exists of McKenzie's method of persuasion, he must have applied strong pressure, because subsequent events showed that the doctor was still displeased.

For a short time, however, the meeting was peaceful. McLoughlin had brought some examples of Rainy Lake produce, which indicated his interest in the post's farm, and these intrigued McGillivray. "The Dr. exhibits samples of Lac La Pluie wheat & flour," he wrote, "and I almost regret his removal from thence."

McLoughlin regretted it too. He was still reluctant to go to the Athabasca, and he had one good weapon left—his profession. Three days later McGillivray wrote,

> Dr. McL since his appointment to go inland has entirely neglected the medicines which gives great dissatisfaction. The Winterers com-

plain and as usual, blame the appointment, or in other words the agents. They are told to settle the thing as they please and they send McGillis back to A. River—McLellan on the Expedition and keep the Dr. at Fort William.

Details of the final maneuvering are not known, but it is significant that from this time on, McLoughlin was not assigned to frontier posts. Instead, he spent his winters as ranking officer at Fort William, replacing Kenneth McKenzie, who became a Montreal agent. The doctor had not only secured a desirable appointment, he had firmly established himself as a man to be reckoned with. A young, not very experienced partner, at his second summer meeting he had locked horns with his company, and he had won.

~3~
The Battle of Seven Oaks
1815–1816

Although McLoughlin had proven his clout, he was uneasy, and in the summer of 1815 he wrote a melancholy letter to his Uncle Simon. "Removed so far as I am into the wilderness it is not in my power to communicate any thing very new or agreeable to you." He mentioned his cousin Alexander's visit, his disappointment at not having heard from his brother David, and his longing for news of the relatives. "I assure you that you have no more interesting information to communicate to me than what concerns my family. . .their welfare be assured lies near my heart."

At the close of the rendezvous the partners' canoes glided away from the landing stage, leaving the doctor in charge of Fort William—huge, nearly empty—with winter setting in, when the bay would freeze thick and wind would whip across the ice. Since few men remained at the fort, McLoughlin spent most of his time in management rather than practicing medicine although he and his family lived in the doctor's quarters, in the same building as the "apothecary shop," near the fort's main gate. The size and arrangement of the rooms are not known, but the building was large, and the interior was reasonably well furnished. The inventory of 1816 listed "3 green arm chairs," pine washstand, and birch bedstead—luxurious, compared with the rough log cabins of other years.

About the time the rendezvous ended, a newcomer arrived at the Selkirk colony—a brainy, audacious, long-nosed fur trader who quoted Shakespeare and whose motto was "When you are among wolves, howl!" He was Colin Robertson, a former Nor'Wester who had quarreled with another employee and joined the Hudson's Bay Company instead. Simpson in his Book of Characters called Robertson "a frothy trifling conceited man, who would starve in any other Country and is perfectly useless here."

Acting as agent for Selkirk, who was in Montreal, Robertson had recently set out from there with twenty men in express canoes—the first Hudson's Bay Company use of that route—intending to assist the Red River colony and trade in the Athabasca. At Lake Winnipeg, when he happened to meet a band of settlers fleeing from the Métis, he took charge, escorted them back to Red River, and stayed there, sending the brigade on to the Athabasca without him. He found a major change at the settlement. The imprisoned and unpopular Miles Macdonnell was being replaced by a new governor, Robert Semple, who had just come from York Factory with a fresh group of eighty settlers. Semple was a professorial but somewhat naive writer of travel books—amiable, idealistic, unfamiliar with the fur trade, but supremely self-confident.

Robertson's commission from Selkirk, coupled with his innate shrewdness and drive, gave him considerable power in the colony. In March, when he learned that the Nor'Westers had offered one of his men free passage to Montreal, he used it as a pretext for storming the gates of Fort Gibraltar and seizing its leader, Duncan Cameron of the red uniform and epaulets. Robertson then searched the company papers and found a letter written the summer before by Nor'Wester Alexander Macdonell, the governor's cousin.

"A storm is gathering in the north, ready to burst on the rascals who deserve it," Alexander Macdonell had said. "Little do they know their situation. Last year was but a joke. The new nation [the Métis] under their leaders are coming forward to clear their native soil of intruders and assassins." Worried, apprehensive, he also wrote, "God only knows the result."

Infuriated, Robertson took Cameron back to colony headquarters and began to waylay Nor'Westers' express canoes and break open sealed mail, looking for further evidence of trickery. This generated a wave of hostility by both sides, causing so much turmoil that he wrote in his diary, "The plan I am now executing with the assistance of that establishment [the colony] . . . bids fair for the downfall of the most tyrannical system of commerce that ever existed."

McLoughlin, at Fort William, received news of these events in early spring, and he doubtless felt enormous relief when the weather turned warm and the canoes of wintering partners—in ones and twos and brigades—swept up to the landing stage for the annual gathering. Archibald McLeod, a company agent from Montreal, had arrived but William McGillivray was still on the way when shocking news reached the fort. Robertson had left in March for England, and immediately afterward Governor Semple had ordered the settlers to tear down Fort Gibraltar, float its large timbers and stockade downriver to strengthen the colony's Fort Douglas, and set Gibraltar's remnants afire. This enraged the Métis, for Gibraltar was the center of their economic life, owned by their patrons. As the historian Marjorie Wilkins Campbell wrote:

> The sight of the great fort in flames was too much for the Métis; soon the fire which had been smoldering in every one of them also burst into flame. . . . Like a prairie fire news of the destruction of Fort Gibraltar raced from post to post, and from camp to camp wherever Métis and Indians gathered to hunt buffalo. The ancient war spirit of their Indian mothers, augmented by many a strain of fighting French and Highland Scots paternity, urged them to defend their very existence; and the Nor'Westers were no longer in any mood to enforce restraint.

Since Archibald McLeod was the highest-ranking officer at Fort William, the partners met under his leadership, and decided that with Gibraltar destroyed, pemmican seized, and canoe routes blocked, they must act at once. They organized an expedition to Red River and on June 3 wrote to the leader of the Métis—nineteen-year-old Cuthbert Grant, a resourceful, quick-tempered company clerk, son of a wintering partner and a Cree woman. The letter told him:

> You will, as soon as possible, assemble as many of the Indians as you can, by any means, induce to go to the Red River to meet us there. . . . We shall, and will, be guarded and prudent; we shall commit no extravagances, but we must not suffer ourselves to be imposed upon; nor can we submit quietly to the wrongs heaped upon us by a lawless, unauthorized, and inveterate opponent in trade.

They promised that the Indians would be "well and fully recompensed for their trouble" and said, "There is not the least doubt of the justice of our cause. We start from hence tomorrow in five light canoes; upwards of fifty men in all. . . . we shall be in Red River about the 17th of June." It was signed by the three leading Nor'Westers at the fort—Archibald McLeod, Robert Henry, and McLoughlin.

After sending their message by an express canoe, McLeod, McLoughlin, and a large party of armed men and voyageurs set out for Red River, paddling frantically through waterways and pounding over portages, making the best possible time. Events, however, had moved fast, and they were forty miles short of Red River when they met eight boatloads of fleeing settlers. At first the Nor'Westers, thinking the colony had been merely dispersed, "set up the Indian war-whoop" and banged joyfully on the sides of their canoes. But when McLeod asked whether Robertson and Governor Semple were in the boats, the colonists shouted back the appalling news that a savage fight between Métis and colonists had occurred, in which a number of men, including the governor, had been killed. On hearing the tragic tale, the partners fell silent. They had talked recklessly about violence, but this was more than they wanted.

As the event was later described by participants, when the Métis received the letter from Fort William, sixty or seventy of them, led by Cuthbert Grant, set out on horses, planning to meet the partners somewhere between Fort William and the colony. With them was Thomas McKay—not McLoughlin's stepson, but the "son of Colonel William M'Kay." Colonel McKay, a former Nor'Wester who had become Superintendent of Indian Affairs for the Red River area, was Alexander McKay's brother, and therefore the two Thomas McKays were cousins.

The Métis insisted they had tried to bypass the colony. One of them, François Firmin Boucher, said in a sworn statement:

> The orders were to go past the fort at as great a distance as possible, so as to avoid being seen and having difficulty. Those orders were strictly obeyed. We went as far back as we possibly could; we could not go farther, for there was a swamp, in which it was impossible for the carts to get on, as the horses sunk up to their bellies; but we passed the fort at as great a distance from it as we could.

The most detailed account of subsequent events was written at William McGillivray's request by John Pritchard, a former North West Company employee who was living at Red River. Pritchard said that when a guard in the watchtower of the colony spotted the Métis, Governor Semple ordered two dozen of his people to go with him to meet the horsemen, saying he would merely ask what they wanted. At a clump of trees called Seven Oaks, near

Battle of Seven Oaks, 1816, by Charles W. Jefferys. This painting was used for a Hudson's Bay Company calendar in 1914. The wounded gentleman in the foreground is Robert Semple, governor of the Red River Colony. In the actual confrontation, the two sides were much farther apart. HUDSON'S BAY COMPANY ARCHIVES, PROVINCIAL ARCHIVES OF MANITOBA, HBCA P-378 (N8281)

Main Street of today's Winnipeg, the governor halted his group, and Boucher rode forward. "What do you want?" he called.

"What do *you* want?" the governor brusquely responded.

"We want our fort," said Boucher.

"Go to your fort!"

This scornful reply angered Boucher. "Why did you destroy our fort, you damned rascal?" he shouted back. "If you fire, you're all dead men."

The governor called him a scoundrel, laid his hand on the horse's bridle, and was reckless enough—or naive enough—to grasp the butt end of Boucher's gun. To the overwrought men on both sides, this gesture looked like a threat. Someone fired a shot, and within seconds the uneasy confrontation became a battle.

The settlers were outnumbered, and the Métis quickly slid off their horses to use them as barricades. In a fifteen-minute fusillade, only one Métis was killed, but twenty of the twenty-eight colonists, including Governor Semple, lost their lives. The engagement was called the Battle of Seven Oaks, or sometimes, because it was so lopsided, the Massacre of Seven Oaks.

No one could be sure who shot first. Boucher said "the fire was begun by those of Hudson's Bay." Michael Heden, a settler who escaped by crossing the river in a canoe, said "a shot was instantly fired by one of the party of horsemen."

Pritchard said that "almost immediately a general discharge of fire-arms took place; but whether it began on our side, or that of the enemy, it was impossible to distinguish." However it started, the remaining settlers were so terrified that most of them fled in boats, and these were the ones whom the Nor'Westers met.

Having heard the tale, the partners sent the settlers on, while they continued their own passage to the Hudson's Bay Fort Douglas. Although it is not recorded, it is possible that while McLoughlin was at the fort, he again met his cousin Alexander Fraser, for the young man was still in the area. The partners remained for a few days, gave routine gifts of clothing to their employees among the Métis, and then returned to headquarters to resume the rendezvous. They were shaken. Robert Henry—one of the signers of the letter to Grant—wrote later, "I thank Providence that the Battle was over before we got there, as it was our intention to storm the Fort." And J. D. Cameron wrote that "every neutral person thinks we are in the wrong."

By then McLoughlin was thirty-two years old, gray-haired and generally dignified, but still the hot-blooded dynamo whose unfortunate lapse had catapulted him into the fur trade. The worries of these times doubtless shortened his temper, and a surviving anecdote reveals the tension that all the Nor'-Westers were feeling. It happened soon after the partners returned to Fort William, when a blacksmith in their employ—named Alexander Fraser but not related to McLoughlin's family—agreed to sell several moose skins to a nearby Selkirk scout. William McGillivray, attending the rendezvous at Fort William, decided this was treason, so he called in Fraser, berated him for dealing with the company's enemies, and threatened him with prison if he proceeded with the sale. But Fraser delivered the skins anyway, after which he was sent to face Dr. McLoughlin. The blacksmith later dictated a deposition, and the interview was recorded by J. M. Mondelet, a justice of the peace.

When he came into Dr. Maclaughlin's presence, the Doctor called out to him, "You damned rascal, how durst you sell any thing to our enemies? I would hang you for a copper." The deponent replied, "You can't hang me for that, it is not so easy done."—That the Doctor, who possessed great bodily strength, immediately laid his hands on this deponent's shoulders, and pushed him down upon the floor, and gave him several severe blows. That after this he directed the deponent to be taken to a small square building made of hewn logs, without any light, wherein was a quantity of human excrement. That, after being a short time in this confinement, the stench of the place, and the bruises he had received, made this deponent conceive that if he were kept there much longer his health would be destroyed; and he offered . . . to work for a year without wages for the North-West Company, if they would let him out.

The company, however, hedged until he agreed to serve for three years, after which they would let him go free.

During the next few weeks, Fort William was relatively calm, with most partners on hand for the summer gathering. But the respite would be brief. Selkirk was even then moving west with his canoe brigade, bringing an armed force of one hundred men.

~4~

The Storming of Fort William
1815–1818

In 1816 the Earl of Selkirk and his wife were living in Montreal, where Lady Selkirk was greatly admired for her humor and charm. The earl was less appealing, for he was afflicted with alternating bouts of frenzy and depression, and his tuberculosis was so advanced that he sometimes coughed blood into his lace handkerchiefs. Nevertheless, he had one consuming passion—his settlement. Longing to see it for himself, he asked the governor of the Canadas for protection, and when he received only one officer and half a dozen men, he hired his own army. It consisted of about one hundred Swiss mercenaries from the De Meuron and De Watteville regiments, which had been disbanded after the War of 1812. Most of their personnel remained in the area, and Selkirk agreed to "give the officers and men a portion of land" and pay them eight dollars per month.

In spite of his precarious health, he set out in the spring of 1816, taking his troops, small arms, two brass cannon, and a furnace for making cannonballs. He intended to bypass Fort William by going to the western tip of Lake Superior, then northwest through today's Minnesota to the Red River, and down that stream to the colony. But in midsummer, near Sault Ste. Marie, he met two canoes piloted by Miles Macdonell, who had been released from custody and had returned briefly to Red River. Macdonell "brought the dismal intelligence" of the Battle of Seven Oaks, and Selkirk immediately changed his plan. Hoping to "obtain more complete information" that the Nor'Westers had incited the Métis to act, he had himself appointed justice of the peace and headed for Fort William. "It [the fur trade] is a business which I hate from the bottom of my heart," he wrote to his wife.

On August 12, near the close of the summer gathering, McLoughlin, William McGillivray, and the other partners at Fort William were astonished to see the earl's canoes paddling upstream, heavy with arms and mercenaries. They passed the fort to make camp about a mile up the Kaministiquia River, on the opposite bank.

Shortly afterward, messengers came to Fort William with a demand for the release of several colonists because Selkirk thought they were being held prisoner. The partners immediately complied, but the earl was not satisfied. In his new capacity as justice of the peace, he sent two officers "in a batteau, with nine men, who had arms concealed in the vessel," to deliver a warrant for William McGillivray's arrest.

Even though the Nor'Westers considered this outrageous, they would not defy a legal warrant, so McGillivray crossed the river in a canoe—along with McLoughlin and Kenneth McKenzie with an offer to serve as bail in return for McGillivray's release. Selkirk, however, refused the exchange, placed them all under guard, and sent twenty-five De Meurons to the fort with orders to apprehend every partner on the premises. In spite of the Nor'Westers' attempt to stop them at the gate, the mercenaries' captain, "with much alacrity, aided by several of his men, instantly rushed in, and prevented the gate from being closed." They seized all the partners and paddled them to the camp, where they joined McLoughlin, McGillivray, and McKenzie.

Selkirk had won a round, but at that point his fragile strength gave out. After extracting promises from the Nor'Westers "on their word of honour, that no attempts of resistance should be made, nor any hostile measures countenanced or permitted," he let them climb into canoes again, to return to the fort.

By then McLoughlin, McGillivray, and the other officers were convinced that Selkirk was mad. Seeing no need to honor promises made under duress, they began to destroy every scrap of evidence that might be damaging. As Lieutenant G. A. Fauche of the De Meurons described it:

> We received the intelligence, that a canoe had been sent off during
> the night, loaded with ammunition and arms, and that many papers
> had been burnt in the kitchen of the mess-house, by the partners.
> We found eight barrels of gunpowder lying in a field near the fort,

which had also been taken away, during the night, out of the powder magazine. We also found, in a barn among some hay, about fifty stand of guns, which were apparently fresh loaded and primed.

In the morning, when Selkirk came to the fort, the sight of smoking ashes sent him into a rage. He had his men search every room and shop, and to his satisfaction, they found bales of furs labeled with Hudson's Bay insignia, along with a list of Métis who had been at Seven Oaks. Triumphantly insisting that these were proof of guilt, he declared that the "criminality" was "such as to justify him in sending the partners under an escort to York"—today's Toronto— for trial. He kept only one Nor'Wester at Fort William to represent the company—the recently retired Daniel McKenzie, who said in his deposition that during his entire detention at the fort, "I was in a state of inebriety and actual derangement of mind."

It is of considerable interest that among the papers found on McLoughlin's desk during the raid was the "marriage Contract of Robert McCargo and Nancy McKay," the doctor's stepdaughter. This implies that she had been part of the McLoughlin household, or at least in touch with the family, and it is the only known indication of her given name and approximate age.

In righteous indignation, armed with the confiscated documents, Selkirk had the De Meurons escort the captive partners to the riverbank, and there, although canoes of all sizes were tied up at the dock, he refused every plea for safety. As described in a book of that time:

> One canoe in which three prisoners, Kenneth Mackenzie [McKenzie], Allan Macdonell, and John McLaughlin, were embarked, was considerably under the usual size, and could not carry with safety more than fifteen persons, with their baggage and provisions; yet entirely disregarding the representations and remonstrances made of the danger to be apprehended, his Lordship ordered twenty-one persons to be embarked in it.

McLoughlin had no choice but to jam his long legs into a canoe that they all knew was filled beyond its capacity.

In spite of the crowded canoe, the trip was unremarkable until August 26, when the flotilla encountered a severe storm at the east end of Lake Superior. Some of the surviving accounts say that Lieutenant Fauche, the De Meuron in charge, made the decision to continue in spite of the gale, while Fauche himself stated that "on asking [William McGillivray] whether he thought it dangerous to proceed, he replied that there would not be the least danger, if the guards did their duty."

All agree that one canoe—the one carrying McLoughlin—was dangerously overloaded, and that giant waves washed over its gunwales until it overturned, spilling its passengers into the icy water. Nine of the twenty-one on board were drowned, including McLoughlin's friend Kenneth McKenzie, while the doctor himself "was taken lifeless to the Shore and it was long before he was restored." He said later that he was ill for a month at the home of "a Mr. Grover a Tavern Keeper," who "treated me with the Greatest Kindness."

Although McLoughlin was much weakened by this narrow brush with death, he nevertheless had to report at York, which was then the capital of Upper Canada. It meant another grueling trip, across Lake Huron to the south end of Georgian Bay, overland to Lake Simcoe, south on that lake, and then overland on a road still called Yonge Street. On September 3, when he and the other survivors reached York, they found that the attorney general "had gone on his circuit to Kingston," so they continued east to Montreal. While they were there, the *Montreal Herald* reported that they were "accused of the highest crimes; but after a laborious investigation till Thursday forenoon they were admitted to Bail under moderate recognizances." They were temporarily at liberty, but they would have to face trial, at an undetermined date.

This was McLoughlin's first trip east since he had joined the North West Company, so he took the opportunity to go down the St. Lawrence to visit his mother. She was still living on the "Big Farm," with numerous children, nieces, and nephews nearby, as well as her brother Alexander, who by then was the seigneur of Rivière-du-Loup. McLoughlin owned land in the area, which Alexander offered to buy for fifteen hundred pounds, but the doctor refused because he thought it was worth more. While he was there, he witnessed a family altercation concerning six hundred pounds in the will of his grandfather Malcolm Fraser, who had died the year before. "I Know my Grandmother owed him that sum but she had it in her mind that she had paid him," McLoughlin wrote to his other uncle, Dr. Simon Fraser. "However this and many other subjects I will explain when I have the pleasure of seeing you."

No surviving record tells whether he actually visited his uncle on this trip, but it seems likely, for he spent the rest of the winter in the Montreal area, and Terrebonne was near. On January 21, 1817, at the Mansion House Hotel on St. Paul Street—"the Ritz Carlton of those days"—he was elected to mem-

View of Selkirk Settlement, Manitoba. NATIONAL ARCHIVES OF CANADA, C-8714

bership in the Beaver Club, because he was a partner and had crossed the height of land between Fort William and Lac la Pluie. Whether the meeting indulged in the traditional five toasts or abundance of spirits is not known.

During the winter of 1816–17, while McLoughlin was in the east, Selkirk damaged his reputation by making several mistakes at Fort William. He refused to let North West brigades take pemmican to the winterers in the field, some of whom nearly starved. From "Old Sleepy Head" Daniel McKenzie—the partner who had been kept at the fort—Selkirk bought company food, furs, and trade goods at unfairly low prices, set by himself. And when the Nor'-Westers sent a constable to arrest him for seizing the fort, he refused to submit, saying the warrant was based on "an affidavit full of the grossest perjuries." This would be important in the coming trials, because even in the unsettled fur country, resisting an officer of the law was a serious offense.

The earl himself recognized his blunder and told his wife, "The consequences so naturally and justly arising from my wretchedly ill-advised conduct in September, give room for bitter enough reflections." But she was indomitably loyal. "If we are to be poor for three generations we must absolutely fight this out," she told her brother-in-law, and staunchly explained that Selkirk's letters were "so very sanguine, every difficulty seemed to vanish before him." Her advice to the earl, however, was somewhat different. "For Heaven's sake be less sanguine. You really frighten me."

In June 1817 Selkirk left Fort William to continue his trip to the colony, and for that one summer he had the satisfaction of seeing his dreams unfold. Many settlers had returned, grain waved under the sun, and he walked in peaceful delight from field to field, envisioning roads and bridges, churches and schools. He made his plans with imagination and skill, and before he returned to Montreal, he put a lasting mark on the land.

Since the trial was delayed, McLoughlin had left Montreal in early spring with a company flotilla, and he reached Fort William by midsummer, to serve again as its head. The Hudson's Bay Company had built a small establishment at Pointe de Meuron, a few miles up the Kaministiquia River, and its records say that in November "Dr McClougholin" came upstream "to have a house built" nearby.

In view of the recent conflict, it was inevitable that relations between the new establishment and Fort William would be hostile. The Hudson's Bay post was small, staffed in part by Selkirk's mercenaries, whom a Nor'Wester—doubtless biased—described as "disbanded, intoxicated, and almost uncontrouled soldiers." One of its employees claimed that while he was held prisoner at Fort William, "Dr. McLoughlin struck him and he bore the mark for several days." The man may or may not have been telling the truth, and the doctor's side of the altercation has not survived, but other records show that he would not let even his competitors go hungry. When the smaller fort was in need of food, he gave its men "9 quarts of bleached corn, 1 lb 3/4 of fat, 6 lbs flour, 5 lbs lard, 2 loaves of bread 1½ lb. each, 2 [   ] milk, and 2 bricks of fresh butter." But—still a loyal Nor'Wester—he exacted a promise in return. The men were not to build canoes or put up any buildings until they had repaid a like amount of food; they were not to send for help "to the interior or to the Sault," and they were not to trade with any Indians.

During that winter, as the snow piled into drifts and the wind blew cold, McLoughlin worried about the "disorganisation" due to Selkirk's colony, and about his coming trial. In a letter to Dr. Fraser he expressed hope for acquittal, because as yet the government "has issued no process against any of those concerned in the Battle of the 19th June and this must proceed from a conviction of the truth that the Half Breeds were not the agressors." Afflicted by persistent ill health, which he considered a result of his near drowning, he said he had been "very unwell all this summer indeed at one time I thought I would have gone to the other world."

In the spring of 1818, when the days turned warm again and streams began to thaw, he set out on the long canoe trip east, this time to stand trial at York. Since he would not be called until fall, he paid another visit to Rivière-du-Loup, where he arranged to send his mother some money, and found a family altercation. He calmed his relatives down as best he could, but their quarrels troubled him. When he passed through Montreal on his way back to York, he wrote to his uncle:

Our family at River du Loup do not agree better than they did my
Uncle Joseph is behind Hand three years of his Rent—My Uncle
Alexander has promised to settle this. . . .would you believe that my
disbursements for my family since 1816 to this day amount to about
five hundred pounds Halifax—I would think nothing of it if it made
them comfortable but I am sorry to say I believe they are not some
fatality attends me and my relations. . . . my Grandmother and my
Uncle Alexander are not on better terms than they were. . . . My
Dear Sir you cannot think how painfull these little family feuds are
to me neither are in the write and neither are in wrong or to speak
more correctly they are both in the wrong—but in truth a great deal
must be attributed to go betweens who are repeating one thing to
one and one thing to another.

He was still considering a career outside the fur trade. "Between you
and me I have an offer to enter into Business in the civilized world—if I
do not accept the proposal—it will be from want of capital. This is between
us—no one else must know it." As on his previous trip, he planned to visit
his uncle, and said, "When I come down from York I will be able to go to
see you."

His sister, the happy-hearted Marie Louise, had become the Mother
Superior of the Ursulines in Quebec. He wrote to her, granting authority to
draw on his company account in hope of smoothing the family squabbles, and
he pleaded with her to keep their mother from visiting Dr. Simon Fraser,
because "my Uncle Alexander does not wish it." And then it was time for his
ordeal in court.

The trials, which were held in York, Montreal, and Quebec, were plagued
by missing witnesses, scattered evidence, and uncertain jurisdiction, and were
so confused that Lady Selkirk's lawyer told her, "All becomes a perfect chaos."
There were three main divisions of suits: the British Colonial Office against
Lord Selkirk; Lord Selkirk against the North West Company; and the Nor'-
Westers against colony officials.

To help its readers keep them straight, the *Montreal Courant* published
a "handy list" of more than one hundred cases against the Nor'Westers for
murder, arson, robbery, grand larceny, and malicious shooting, and twenty-nine
cases against Lord Selkirk and the Hudson's Bay Company for riot and larceny, false imprisonment, and assault. The story was a sensation, in which the
men in the street took vehement sides. Some considered Selkirk philan-

thropic and grievously wronged, while the *Montreal Gazette* called him "the unscrupulous land-grabber." Most people acknowledged that Selkirk's grant was probably legal, but "unconscionable and potentially dangerous to the life of the colony."

McLoughlin's case was heard in York on October 30, 1818, he and five other partners being charged as accessories after the fact. It was "not alleged . . . that any of them actually killed Robert Semple," but that they "severally and jointly assisted . . . or received and comforted, the murderers, knowing of their guilt."

McLoughlin was not asked to take the stand. Instead, while others argued it out, he listened quietly—a tall, brawny man with a shock of gray hair, hoping for acquittal but tense with worry. Several witnesses testified that the Métis had been ordered to avoid Fort Douglas, and were actually passing as far from it as possible when they were met by Semple and the colonists. William McGillivray explained the importance of pemmican, and said the previous seizures "had reduced our stocks very low, indeed so low that, unless considerable precaution was used, many of our most distant posts might be exposed to starvation." The Nor'Westers had sent the strong force, he said, to protect these vital provisions, and the gifts to the Métis were not a reward for the massacre, but the same clothing allowance that the company always gave its employees. "All the canoes that go up take more or less of them. . . . It amounts to a heavy sum."

On the second day, the arguments were closed and the jurors left the courtroom, while McLoughlin and the other partners sat in silence. Their suspense was brief. In only forty-five minutes the jury returned with a verdict of not guilty, and for the first time in two years McLoughlin could draw a genuinely free breath.

The trials, however, were not over. Lists of clothing given to the Métis were again cited as evidence of the Nor'Westers' complicity, individuals were arraigned for various crimes, and Selkirk was accused of resisting arrest and seizing the fort.

In the end, although one man was convicted for murder in a frontier brawl, the sentence—hanging—was not carried out. Cuthbert Grant, the leader of the Métis, was charged with the massacre but admitted to bail and allowed to leave; or he may have jumped bail, as some maintain. At any rate he returned to Red River, and the charges were dropped. No marksmen were convicted in the Seven Oaks affair, and no Nor'Wester was fined or imprisoned. But Lord Selkirk was assessed five hundred pounds for resisting arrest and fifteen hundred pounds for the false imprisonment of Daniel McKenzie, whom he had held at Fort William. No one on either side was totally disappointed or totally satisfied. North West supporters said the juries had been "unduly influenced" by Selkirk's passionate addresses and pamphlets, while the Hudson's Bay advocates indignantly insisted that the judges had been bribed. Even today some historians believe Selkirk and the Hudson's Bay Company were trying to destroy the Nor'Westers, while others think the courts were prejudiced.

For the ailing Lord Selkirk it was a disaster, so costly that after his death in 1820, his estate had debts of £160,000. Desperately ill, he returned to England, where his wife, gallant as ever, begged him to "let the wicked flourish; they cannot take from us our own good conscience, and if we do not allow them to bereave us of health and tranquility, we can be happy without the right being proved."

McLoughlin's trial had been too late in the year for him to start for Fort William, so he spent the winter in the York or Montreal area—still not feeling well, and painfully aware that his company's problems were far from solved. The Nor'Westers were facing a fight for survival, in which he, with his growing reputation, was bound to have a significant role.

~5~
The End of an Era
1819–1821

When McLoughlin joined a flotilla for his return to Fort William in the spring of 1819, the trial was behind him. But he had other worries, for he must support his family, and his finances were in deplorable shape.

North West Company accounts were kept in pounds, livres, and sous of North West, or Halifax, currency. One pound Halifax was equal to 12 livres, but one pound sterling was equal to 13 1/3 livres. In other words, one pound of North West currency was worth only nine-tenths of a pound sterling. Sometimes, however, company contracts and business deals used sterling, and to further the confusion, there was occasional use of "Montreal currency," which was different from both. This multiple system explains an apparent discrepancy in McLoughlin's account. The official ledger shows that his annual salary as a clerk was "2400 livres," which, if North West livres were used, would be only 180 pounds sterling. When in 1808 he told his uncle that his salary was "200 pounds," he was obviously thinking in the Halifax system.

The company records were meticulously written with quill pens in a ledger so massive that it has been the butt of many jokes. One, for instance, says that a building inspector recommended always storing it near a wall, because if kept in the center of a room, it might spread the floor joists.

The fading ink in this elephantine book shows that McLoughlin received a total of one hundred pounds during his five-year apprenticeship and two hundred pounds per year as a clerk, with the last of these payments in 1814, when he became a partner. Under normal conditions he would then have had two or three lean years, because a partner's earnings were figured on the annual "outfit." McLoughlin would have been charged the outgo for 1814, and he would not have been credited for profits until the furs for that year were sold. But he would have soon received a hefty annual cut of company profits, because dividends of four hundred pounds per share were quite common. This would have made up for the loss.

However, since the beginning of the fur war, the company had made no profits, and since it had paid out its surplus every summer as dividends, it had no reserves to draw on. As a result, those who became partners in 1814 received nothing. The big book shows McLoughlin's largest savings as 9,147 livres, the amount he had accumulated as a clerk, after which the balance steadily shrank as he withdrew funds for living expenses. His total partnership income was zero.

Generous as McLoughlin was toward his family in the east, he had a healthy respect for money, and he must have thought about the company finances during his long trip from Montreal. But when his canoe drew up to the Fort William pier, it was summer, the time of songbirds and sunshine, and at last he could again be with Marguerite and the children—Joseph, John, Elisabeth, the new toddler Eloisa, and one or possibly two of the McKay daughters, Nancy having been married. He had been away slightly more than a year.

In early summer, singly or in brigades, canoes swept in with a flourish. But things were far from merry, because the winterers were chafing at their nonexistent incomes, and before long the murmur of discontent became a roar. They had been dissatisfied in 1814, during McLoughlin's first rendezvous as a partner, and now, after years of trouble and loss, they were furious—at the Hudson's Bay Company, at the Selkirk colony, and at their own Montreal agents for failing to make peace with the competing firm, or drive out Selkirk, or somehow protect their interests.

It was nearly time to renew their twenty-year partnership agreements, some of which had been signed by the Nor'Westers in 1802 and the rest in

1804, when the North West and XY Companies were merged. William Mc-
Gillivray talked with them one by one or in small groups, trying to secure new
commitments, but they stolidly refused. Samuel Gale, a lawyer in Montreal,
wrote that McGillivray "left Fort William in a melancholy mood," determined
to try again at the next gathering, because without a renewal of the partnerships, the North West Company "would be annihilated."

By this time McLoughlin's integrity and decisiveness were widely known.
He was thirty-four years old, although he appeared older because of his height,
his dignity, and his mane of prematurely gray hair. The acid-tongued Colin
Robertson, who was still employed by the Hudson's Bay Company, spoke of
him as one of the few winterers who possessed "firmness of character," and
explained that "a good dinner, a few fair promises would waltz the remainder
about, to any tune the McGillivray's chose to strike up." The winterers recognized this strength. Knowing that if they bolted from the company it would
not be easy to find other agents to buy supplies and market furs, a number of
them asked McLoughlin to find a solution.

He was never one to dally. To make sure of their options, he wrote first
to George Moffatt, a former North West clerk who had become a prominent
businessman in Montreal and had friends in the Hudson's Bay Company.
Would that company, McLoughlin asked, act as the winterers' agents if they
let their partnerships lapse?

Although Moffatt was not in a position to answer, he handed the query
to Samuel Gale—who had been Selkirk's attorney—and Gale wrote directly
to Lady Selkirk in London, because she had a double connection to the
Hudson's Bay Company: her husband, ill as he was, owned the controlling
interest, and her brother, Andrew Colvile, was a major stockholder and member of its governing committee. Gale's letter said the winterer making the
inquiry—meaning McLoughlin—"possesses influence to withdraw almost
every useful member of the North West Association who are all dissatisfied
& alarmed at being unable to get what is due them from the Montreal
houses."

For the purposes of his company, McLoughlin could hardly have chosen
a worse time. Edward "Bear" Ellice, the North West agent in London, had
already tendered an offer to buy out Lord Selkirk's controlling shares in the
Hudson's Bay Company, and the earl was seriously considering it because of
his strained finances and poor health. If that deal had gone through, the Nor'-
Westers would have secured control of the London company and might have
remained solvent.

Instead, Gale's letter reached Lady Selkirk and Andrew Colvile on a cold, damp, London winter day—Christmas Eve—and, as Selkirk said, McLoughlin's query "seemed to alter the whole face of affairs." Colvile immediately contacted other members of the Honourable Committee, who decided to reject Ellice's offer and deal with the winterers instead, hoping that the Nor'-Westers' firm would collapse.

At this point the two fur companies were like the gingham dog and calico cat who ate each other up, for both had nearly exhausted their resources, and the turmoil on the frontier was increasing. Men at the outposts fought a number of duels. Several starved. Nor'Westers seized five Hudson's Bay posts in the Athabasca. The Bay men, strengthened by Selkirk's De Meuron soldiers and a pair of cannon, captured five North West partners and several laborers at a portage, one of whom—Benjamin Frobisher—died from hardship when he escaped and tried to slog his way to a company fort. It was only a few years since both firms had been thriving, but now the North West Company was floundering and out of funds, the winterers were in rebellion and going broke, Lord Selkirk was dying, and the Hudson's Bay Company's profits had declined so drastically that "Bear" Ellice estimated it was about £100,000 in the red. Frederick Merk, in *Fur Trade and Empire*, summarized the situation:

> Rival posts fought each other at close range; there was undercutting and overbidding; Indians were competitively plied with liquor; there was covert bargaining by each side with faithless employees of the other, and seizure and confiscation of each other's supplies and furs. Such was the musketry of trade. From the arsenal of war were drawn raids, the levelling of each other's trading posts, incitation of Indians and of half-breeds to violence, open fighting and secret stabbing and shooting in the shadows of the forest. . . . By 1820 the struggle had brought the two belligerents to the verge of bankruptcy.

It was inevitable that the Montreal agents would hear about McLoughlin's overture to their rival, and equally inevitable that they would be furious. At the next summer gathering, in 1820, William McGillivray handed McLoughlin the humiliating experience of demotion from his cherished post as head of Fort William. And afterward—with a touch of malicious satisfaction—McGillivray wrote, "The Doctor (who feels very sore at being removed from this place) tried every means to defeat the plan, and he & those whom he got to join him, made themselves ridiculous."

"Ridiculous," however, was scarcely the right word. McGillivray managed to renew the contracts of those who were related to him and a few others, but eighteen winterers—a majority—granted McLoughlin their powers of attorney and asked him to go to Montreal with the fall brigade to see what he could accomplish. Even though the doctor was still feeling ill and exhausted from his two recent trips, representing the winterers seemed so important that after only a few months at home, he grimly set out again. He was accompanied by Angus Bethune, a North West partner who was the son of Marguerite's half sister.

This journey not only would be arduous, it came at a time that necessitated a wrenching decision for McLoughlin and his wife, the same decision that many fur-trade families had to make. Since they lived in isolated areas, they must either allow their children to grow up with no education, or send them to distant schools and not see them for years. By 1820 Marguerite's daughters were in their teens or twenties, with two or perhaps all three of them married. McLoughlin's son Joseph was twelve, and the younger ones were eight-year-old John, six-year-old Elisabeth, and Eloisa, who was three. The details of making the choice can only be surmised, but small John and Elisabeth were curled up in the canoe when it glided away from the dock. They were going to Montreal, where their great-uncle, Dr. Simon Fraser, could keep them under his wing.

Hoping to stave off a total collapse of their company, McLoughlin and Bethune reached Montreal in early autumn, 1820. They first approached the North West Company agents there, but met a stone wall and in October—when all their pleas to the agents had failed—they got in touch with their former contact, Samuel Gale. Since the Earl of Selkirk had recently died, Gale wrote to Lady Selkirk and her brother, telling them with obvious satisfaction that "the Montreal Houses . . . totally rejected the terms proposed and a perfect breach has I believe taken place between McTavish McGillivrays & Company & Messrs. McLoughlin and Bethune."

It was a disappointment, but the winterers were not ready to abandon the field. Gale said they would visit London, "if Mr. McLoughlin who had been ill were sufficiently recovered, & if not Mr. Bethune was to go alone." They were coming, he explained, to make arrangements for the Indian trade after 1823, and he assured Colvile of their complete integrity and good judgment, "notwithstanding their appearance may not announce the capacity." McLoughlin was a dignified man and a courteous one, but his years on the fur-trade frontier had apparently taken their toll.

A similar opinion was expressed a few months later by Colin Robertson, who dined in France with McLoughlin's brother and said that David "bears a strong resemblance to our friend [Dr. John] but it is a polished likeness. What an astonishing difference a little intercourse with the world makes in a man's manners! Dr. McL. [David] is an elegant, gentlemanly young man, stands high at this place, and seems to be a great favorite with the good folks of Boulogne."

Before McLoughlin left Montreal, he placed his son John in the charge of "Mr. Glens," and Elisabeth with "Mrs. Plunkett." He authorized Uncle Simon to draw on his account and said, "I hope when you come to town you will have the Goodness to call at Mrs Plunkett to see how my daughter is and examine her Books, &c—Mrs. Leslie has promised me to take her in Charge for the Winter." With this done, he was ready to start on the weary trek—south from Montreal, down Lake Champlain and the Hudson River to New York City, and then, in November 1820, across the Atlantic on the sailing ship *Albion*.

On board, McLoughlin and Bethune found an unexpected shipmate—Colin Robertson, the Shakespeare-quoting activist who had once seized Fort Gibraltar. After leaving the Selkirk colony, Robertson had gone to Montreal, but returned to Fort Wedderburn on Lake Athabasca, elbow to elbow with the North West Company's Fort Chipewyan. The rivals inevitably clashed, resulting in Robertson's capture by the Nor'Westers, who held him for eight months. Ingenious—sarcastic—he first tried to communicate with his people via notes in a wine keg, and when that failed, he resorted to coded scribbles in a copy of *Henry IV*, which his men managed to decipher. He finally escaped by hurling a plate of dinner biscuits into his jailer's face, fled to New York, and decided to go to England for the negotiations. It was then that he became the rebellious partners' shipmate.

At all costs McLoughlin and Bethune wanted to conceal the purpose of their trip, but the canny Robertson easily guessed it. Acid and clever as always, he delighted in embarrassing them, as he recorded in his journal:

> In the evening the Doctor came into my state room as was his custom, and rattling first off on one point and then on another stumbled rather awkwardly upon an enquiry as to the character of the gentlemen of the committee [of the Hudson's Bay Company], if they were affable and easy in their manners. "You will see them Doctor, by and bye, and you will tell us all about it yourself." "*Me—me*," stammered the poor doctor, with a face as red as a full moon in a frosty morning, "*how, how* am I going to see them?"

Robertson's caustic wit was turned on McLoughlin and Bethune again just before they landed.

> The cloth being withdrawn and the land in sight, the wine went about rather freely, when a subscription was set on foot for the stewards and other servants. Our friend the Doctor had put down his name, and I took up the pen for the same purpose, but perceiving Bethune writing I turned to Abby Carriere—"Come, Abby, put down your name, I don't like to sign between two North Westers."
>
> "Never mind, Mr. R.," replied Monsr. Carriere, "remember our Saviour was crucified between two thieves." The Doctor was in a dreadful passion, but . . . did not like to quarrel with one who stood so high in the Church.

In spite of his teasing, however, Robertson had great respect for McLoughlin. On one occasion the North West agent Ellice made a slurring remark about him, to which Robertson snapped back, "I am afraid, Mr. Ellice, you are not exactly aware of the state of that country. Had the H.B.C. only four such men as McLoughlin, the Athabascas are ours."

While the doctor was in Europe, he seized the chance to pay a brief visit to his brother David, who had left the army to establish a lucrative private practice in France. It must have been a pleasure for the older brother to see for himself that the younger one was doing well, after his early financial woes. They were still close, still ready to lend each other a hand. On February 21, 1821, Dr. John received power of attorney to represent Dr. David in a property settlement in Rivière-du-Loup.

Back in London in early 1821, McLoughlin and his co-conspirator, Bethune, found that William McGillivray was there too, attempting to buy control of the Hudson's Bay Company. This meant that two groups of Nor'-Westers were wooing the Honourable Committee, each weakening the other. Few documents describe the negotiations, which indicates that they were handled privately rather than in formal meetings. Although McLoughlin and Bethune conferred with Andrew Colvile and probably with other members of the committee, they had little power, because the Hudson's Bay Company realized that if it accepted the offer of McLoughlin's group of winterers, the North West Company would be free to hire other men and start over. But if it joined forces with the McGillivrays, the com-

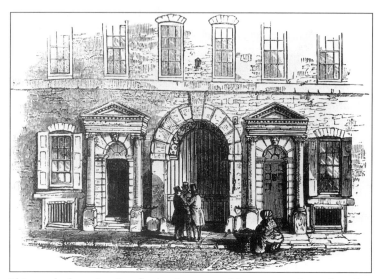

This was the long-time London headquarters of the company. It was here that
the incredible masses of company archives were kept, in journals, letters, and
records of meetings. It was here that McLoughlin twice met his superiors, in
1820-21 and 1838-39. *Hudson's Bay house, Nos. 3 and 4 Fenchurch Street,
London, c. 1840.* HUDSON BAY COMPANY ARCHIVES, PROVINCIAL ARCHIVES OF MANITOBA,
HBCA 1987/363-H-42/12, N79-184

petition would be ended, the combined company would have great strength,
and the dissident winterers would be stranded without a source for supplies or sales.

There is no doubt that McLoughlin and Bethune had inadvertently
worked to their own company's disadvantage and had therefore lost status.
Later on, the McGillivrays bitterly asserted that if the winterers had not
defected, the Nor'Westers might have succeeded in buying control of the
Hudson's Bay Company, or they might have wrung out better terms. While
this was probably true, it was equally true that before going to London, Mc-
Loughlin had tried to reach an agreement with McGillivray and the Montreal
agents. Had the Montrealers been willing then to satisfy some of their complaints, they might have ended the winterers' revolt.

As it was, McLoughlin and Bethune served as catalysts, accentuating the
Nor'Westers' need to make a change and giving the Hudson's Bay Company
an additional bargaining point. They all buckled down, and after several
weeks of hectic activity they worked out the terms. William McGillivray
wished to penalize McLoughlin and Bethune for leading the winterers' revolt,

but he was vetoed, and on March 26, 1821, papers were signed uniting the old enemies under the name of the Hudson's Bay Company.

The fur trade would never be the same again. As Washington Irving wrote in *Astoria*, "The feudal state of Fort William is at an end; its council chamber is silent and deserted; its banquet hall no longer echoes to the burst of loyalty, or the 'auld world' ditty; the lords of the lakes and forests have passed away."

~6~

Coalition
1821–1824

On March 31, 1821, five days after the contract was signed, McLoughlin and Bethune glumly set sail for New York. They had expected to secure better terms for the winterers, but instead their company had been ruthlessly absorbed. Disillusioned, somber, they paced the deck as wind filled the sails overhead.

Four months earlier, on their way to England, they had sparred with Colin Robertson. Now they traveled with Nicholas Garry of the London Committee, who was to meet with the disgruntled Nor'Westers and persuade them to support the coalition. Most Nor'Westers resented Garry—a forty-year-old bachelor, new to the fur trade and a bit priggish—but he and McLoughlin hit it off well, and spent a great deal of time together.

When they landed at New York McLoughlin set out at once for Fort William, but he was cruelly disappointed by the failure of his mission, exhausted from his long trips, and not fully recovered from his near drowning. As a result, by the time he reached Montreal he felt so ill that he decided to return to France, where his brother could care for him. Instead of heading west in a company canoe, he backtracked to New York and sailed from there to France.

That summer, while McLoughlin was with David, Simon McGillivray came to Upper Canada from London to help his brother William and Nicholas Garry launch the new alliance. They conducted one last rendezvous at Fort William, where several Indian chiefs brought twenty of the finest beaver skins and promised that as long as Mount McKay stood, the tribes would remain true to their white friends. In response the Nor'Westers gave each chief a hat, shirt, and red coat trimmed with blue and gold braid. After making a solemn vow that amalgamation would not destroy their relations, Indians and whites smoked the peace pipe together.

On July 10 the winterers gathered in the Great Hall to sit in dour silence as William McGillivray read the new, twelve-thousand-word contract. They learned that in return for the monopoly, the reorganized company was to make the Crown a token payment of five shillings per year—scarcely an onerous amount. They learned that the North West Company would contribute its field system that worked so well—summer gatherings to tap the winterers' expertise, and a share in company profits to motivate the officers—while the Hudson's Bay Company would give its name, charter, gilt-edged monopoly, and access through the bay.

They also learned that under the new "Deed Poll," the officers would be Chief Factors and Chief Traders instead of wintering partners. Fifteen of the twenty-five Chief Factors and seventeen of the twenty-eight Chief Traders were to be former Nor'Westers, the remainder being Hudson's Bay men—a lopsided division that acknowledged the winterers' superior skill and vitality. McLoughlin and Bethune would each receive the top rank of Chief Factor, as would Colin Robertson. Financially, the company profits were to be apportioned in one hundred shares, of which fifty would be divided among the business houses, ten would be funneled into investments, and the remaining forty would be divided into eighty-five parts for the men in the field—one part to each Chief Trader, two to each Chief Factor, and seven split among "eminent retirees." For purposes of administration the land of the company was to be divided into two departments, Northern and Southern.

When McGillivray finished reading and laid the papers down, there was a moment of stunned silence, after which a roar of

disapproval erupted that grew in volume and fury until it filled the hall. Why, the partners asked, did the Hudson's Bay men receive so much power? They had brought only the name, the charter, and the right to use Hudson Bay, while the Nor'Westers had contributed wilderness skill, a fleet of canoes, knowledge of the routes, and posts in the Athabasca—the Mackenzie—the Pacific Slope! Didn't the negotiators realize that the partners would become mere Chief Factors or Chief Traders—little more than servants? Couldn't they see that most of the profits would go not to the winterers but into the greedy maws of the London shareholders and various agents and business groups?

"Amalgamation!" one of the winterers cried out. "This isn't amalgamation but submersion! We are drowned men!"

With the papers signed, however, protests were of no avail, and the officers set to work making the year's assignments. Since Fort William was outside of Rupert's Land, it could no longer serve as headquarters or hold councils, and therefore they decided to gather in the future at York Factory, Fort Garry, or Norway House.

Several years later Simon McGillivray made a speech to the company creditors at Montreal in which he gave an anguished explanation of the reasons he and his brother and Edward Ellice had made the agreement.

> With reduced means, with a losing trade and with credit in jeopardy —with disunion in our councils, and defection among our Partners, if not direct treachery in our camp—with some Partners of our House not only useless, but burthensome to us, and whom we yet feared to cut off, because they had the power to injure us—it was under these almost desperate circumstances, that in the month of December 1820, I opened a negotiation with the Hudson's Bay Company, for a general arrangement upon a new basis. . . . It was effected just in time to save the whole concern from destruction; and our circumstances not being known to our opponents, and they also having their own reasons for wishing to terminate the contest, I obtained liberal, and even advantageous terms for all parties connected with the North-West Company, and yet no one was satisfied.

The biting references to "treachery" and "power to injure us" obviously pointed to McLoughlin and Bethune.

The merger brought a major change, affecting not only the North West Company but the business climate of Montreal, for the now-defunct firm abandoned its agencies, warehouses, and fur-trading activities. William McGillivray estimated that "the yearly disbursements in cash from the office in Montreal to the people employed in various ways, as well as for provisions and stores, was not less than £40,000 pr annum." An advertisement in the *Montreal Herald* for Saturday, September 25, 1824, pictured the reduced condition of the once-proud company offices.

> To Let, for three or Five Years, and Possession immediately given, that Extension Building in St. Gabriel Street; Lately occupied as Offices &c. by the Agents of the North West Company, now fitted for

an Hotel, or Boarding House. The House contains Twenty Bed
Rooms, and Four Parlours and Dining Rooms, all well finished.
    Apply to McGillivray, Thain and Co.

But this came later, and for that summer of 1821, adapting to the new
organization was the job at hand. After the rendezvous, the winterers pushed
off in their canoes, bearing new titles, following new instructions, and heavy
with the knowledge that they would never meet at Fort William again.
    William McGillivray, who was not well, returned to Montreal, but Nicholas
Garry and Simon McGillivray went to Norway House, near Lake Winnipeg,
and then to the whitewashed buildings of York Factory, on the shores of
Hudson Bay. There, when employees of the two companies met for the first
time as colleagues, they bristled with fear and dislike. John Tod, a young
Hudson's Bay clerk, described the opening banquet and the meeting of
Nor'Wester Allan McDonell and Hudson's Bay man Alexander Kennedy, who
had not long before been lunging at each other in a frontier duel.

> One of them still bore the marks of a cut on his face, the other it was
> said on some less conspicuous part of the body. I shall never forget the
> look of scorn and utter defiance with which they regarded each other
> the moment their eyes met. The Highlander's nostrils actually seemed
> to expand, he snorted, squirted, spat, not on the table, but between
> his legs and was as restless as if he had been seated on a hillock of
> ants; the other looked equally defiant, but less uneasy and upon the
> whole, more cool. I thought it fortunate that they were without arms.

But everyone wolfed down a Lucullan feast of venison pie, roast partridge,
and wild duck, plus generous amounts of sherry, and by the time they were
stuffed to the gills, they were able to laugh together.
    McLoughlin did not attend either of these sessions because he was in
France with his brother, but his reputation was solid, and men of both companies respected him. In December George Simpson, recently appointed
Governor of the Northern Department, wrote him a friendly note.

Dear Sir

    I shall be glad to learn that you are long ere now recovered from
your severe illness and hope to have the pleasure of seeing you early
here next Season.

The object of this communication is to intimate the probability of your being appointed to the charge of Lac La Pluie District in order to regulate your Domestic arrangements.

Lac La Pluie being our principal Frontier establishment is supposed to require the presence of a Chief Factor and from your experience in that quarter no one can be so well qualified for it's management.

Until then the legality of the Hudson's Bay charter had not been fully established, but on July 2, 1821, while McLoughlin was still in France, Parliament passed the first of two acts that made it clear. It provided that justices of the peace would handle minor cases in the Indian country and that major offenders would be sent to Upper Canada. Except for the two Canadas, this system would extend to all British territory in North America, including the Athabasca and the Arctic. West of the Rockies, however, it would apply to British subjects only, because the boundary between British and American territory was undecided, and British law did not apply to American citizens.

In December the second act made the "Governor and Company of Adventurers of England tradeing into Hudsons Bay" the authorized license holder in the west for the next twenty-one years, which meant the company had a British monopoly there. This conformed to the empire's colonial system of charters, such as that of the East India Company. The act specified that "the North-west coast of America to the westward of the Stony Mountains should be free and open" to citizens of the United States, and that nothing should be done "to the prejudice or exclusion of any citizens of the United States." But it was nevertheless a potential source of friction with Americans.

Few records have survived of McLoughlin's visit with his brother, but his trip is verified by the Commissioned Officers' Ledger of the Hudson's Bay Company, which says, "Home [London] via Canada 1821   Out via Liverpool and New York March, 1822." In addition, a letter of William McGillivray mentions his presence in France, and on December 31, 1821, McLoughlin wrote from Paris to the home office, asking to draw on his account.

His visit with David was apparently beneficial, for when he left France in February, his health was much improved. He went first to London, where he was given packets of documents related to the amalgamation, to be delivered to Hudson's Bay officials in Canada. In late March he sailed from Liverpool, and he was in Montreal by May.

His severe illness had so shaken him that soon after arriving, he informed his Uncle Simon that he had drawn up his will.

I hope that you will [be] convinced of the great obligation I consider myself under to you for the great kindness you have shown My Boy. . . . allow me to request a continuation of your kindness to my connections and children—should anything happen to me I hope I will leave enough to provide and Educate them You are my Executor and I know you will do them what is right should my Mother want any assistance I will thank you to afford it I will honor your draft on the receipt of it—this is a mere matter of precaution—but it is in case of unforeseen events.

While in Montreal he talked with former North West Company agent Henry McKenzie about a school for his son John, now nearly ten years old, and he arranged to have Thomas Thain of the firm of McTavish, McGillivrays, and Co. draw on his company account for the expenses, which he estimated as about fifty pounds per year. Later on John was sent to a school closer to Uncle Simon, although the boy lived with "Mr Walker Schoolmaster at Terrebonne," not with his uncle.

From Montreal McLoughlin hurried to the Fort William area, to be at last reunited with his family after an absence of two years. The youngest children were five-year-old Eloisa and the toddler David, who had been born soon after McLoughlin left for his long trip to Montreal and Europe. Joseph was probably there also, along with Mary McKay and perhaps the third McKay daughter.

McLoughlin was not home long, for he had to set off almost at once for his first gathering with his new company. He threaded his way through marshes and forests and shallow rivers, going north, ever north, until he reached York Factory, which had become the company's great depot and storehouse. Here, when the brigades had gathered, hundreds of campfires glittered along the shore, while the voyageurs "gambled sang and fought. (Hudson Bay style—kick bite, scratch.)" And here, on July 8, within view of icebergs and the company ship at anchor, McLoughlin gave Governor George Simpson the packet of documents from London, and attended his first Council of the Northern Department of the reorganized Hudson's Bay Company.

As Simpson had indicated in his letter of 1821, McLoughlin was assigned to the Rainy Lake District, where he had been stationed in 1814–15. But this time it was less isolated. Several American surveyors passed through, "on an Exploring party—it is said they came to ascertain the 49 Parallel of north Latitude." Some fur-trade competitors also appeared—twenty-two men in the employ of the American Fur Company, and a trader named Beaulieu who

was working for an independent dealer in Montreal. To counter them, Mc-
Loughlin had three small posts built, and he garnered most of the choice skins.

In 1823, after another gathering at York Factory, McLoughlin was again
sent to Rainy Lake, where he encountered an American named John Tanner,
gravely wounded in a fight and seeking his two half-Indian daughters. After
caring for him until he was able to travel, McLoughlin promised that "all his
efforts would be used" to find the missing girls and that he would "rescue and
protect them until the ensuing spring," when Tanner intended to return.
Trivial as the incident was, it illustrates the doctor's kindness, which tran-
scended race and nationality and business connections.

In the winter of 1823–24 McLoughlin again increased returns for the
Rainy Lake District—a highly commendable accomplishment in the eyes of
profit-conscious Governor Simpson. While there, he wrote reports that have
been called "the best early accounts" of the area, which he described as swampy,
with "innumerable" lakes and rivers—so many that "at least a fifth if not a fourth
of the country is under water." He reported fires that burned repeatedly on
the higher ground, where the soil was generally dry and covered with leaf
mold. He found fine agricultural land on the banks of the Rainy Lake River, and
saw stands of elm and oak, birch and aspen, cedar and pine, along with fruit
trees bearing prunes, cherries, and wild pears. He listed animals and birds,
including caribou, wolverine, beaver, lynx, ravens, "bustards," and loons.

In addition, he paid particular attention to the Indians—their foods and
religion, their courtship and marriage and burial ceremonies. In part he mir-
rored the bias of his time, deploring their "want of cleanliness" and ignorance
of science, but he also found much to admire. Citing their generous care for
widows and orphans, he observed that those in need were "fed as their own
families," and he described married couples as helping one another with daily
tasks. One eloquent passage said:

> But whatever affection or regard they have for their wives, it cannot
> be compared with the tenderness they have for their children, whom
> they in no practice ever correct. . . . And they will much sooner pardon
> or overlook an affront put on them than violence, however so neces-
> sary, toward their children. And for the same cause, nothing pleases
> the parents more than a little attention or favour shown their children.

With the approach of warm weather he went once more to bleak York
Factory, where fur-laden canoes swept in for the rendezvous. On this trip

McLoughlin was accompanied by Marguerite, David, and Eloisa, but they had left Joseph "at St. Mary's. . .in charge of chief factor Bathein" (Bethune).

On July 10, 1824, the Council of the Northern Department convened, and McLoughlin probably received his new assignment on that day. It must have been a stunning surprise, for it meant a gigantic increase in responsibility and difficulty, as well as in physical discomfort. He was to take charge of the Columbia District, the most distant of all the Hudson's Bay lands—farther than the Athabasca—farther than the Rockies—across the "Stony Mountains" and down the Columbia River to the Pacific Coast. Although it was a huge, potentially valuable area, its profits had been meager, and rumor said that the troublesome Americans were threatening to seize control of the river's mouth.

Long before, in 1812, McLoughlin had refused a North West offer to go there, but this time he apparently consented at once. Perhaps in his new company he thought it would be rash to object—or perhaps he saw the post as a promotion, or relished the challenge. Time was short for making such a formidable move, but on July 27, after two frantic weeks of preparation, he and his family started up the Hayes River with two canoes. He was moving into his place in history.

THE PACIFIC NORTHWEST

CHAPTER 4

To the Columbia

As you ascend this River the Climate becomes Colder
till you reach the tops of the Rocky Mountains
whose summit is covered with perpetual Ice and Snow—
the soil is in general very poor and Rocky
the wood however in these places where there is any soil
is much larger than any I have seen on the other side.

DR. JOHN MCLOUGHLIN

~ 1 ~

John Jacob Astor's Company
1810–1824

Taking over the Columbia District was a major change for McLoughlin, one that would carry him across half a continent to the far western fringe of North America. The company posts there could be reached in only two ways, both of them arduous and slow. By sea, ships from London brought bulky goods around Cape Horn at the southern end of South America; moved north toward the Sandwich (Hawaiian) Islands, where they generally stopped for water and supplies; and then continued to Fort George at the mouth of the Columbia River. Overland, a yearly brigade from York Factory carried mail, official documents, and personnel westward by canoe through the Athabasca, crossed the Rocky Mountains by snowshoe or horse, and took boats down the Columbia River—a punishing three-month journey of more than two thousand miles. This was the route McLoughlin would follow.

Distance, however, would be only one part of his problem. His district was huge, encompassing the entire Columbia River basin, and its profits had been so poor that the London Committee were "not sanguine in our expectations" and had considered abandoning it. Its ownership was uncertain, for Britain and the United States were vying for control of the North American continent west of the Rockies and had not agreed on a boundary. Even his headquarters—Fort George—legally belonged to America, which could demand its return at any time. McLoughlin had undertaken a titanic job, and its historical background must be clarified.

The first recorded European sightings of the fog-shrouded Northwest Coast had been made by Spaniards who sailed north from California in the mid-sixteenth century. For the next two hundred years it was seldom seen by Europeans, but in the late 1700s ships of Spain, Russia, Great Britain, and the United States were skirting its wooded shores, in pursuit of the legendary Northwest Passage and a fortune in furs.

Sailors had heard about a great river of the West, flowing to the coast. In 1775 the Spaniard Bruno de Hezeta had reported an apparent opening with a strong current. He did not enter it, but his observation was recorded on early maps. The first mariner known to have ventured inside was the American Robert Gray, captain of the *Columbia*, who on May 11, 1792, "bore away and run in east-north-east between the breakers, having from five to seven fathoms of water. When we were over the bar, we found this to be a large river of fresh water, up which we steered." Gray had entered the mouth of a mighty waterway, which he named the Columbia. He stayed there until May 20, trading for a few furs, then filled his water casks, "stood clear of the bars and bore off to the Northward."

Gray made no attempt to keep his discovery secret. Later that summer, when Captain George Vancouver of Great Britain saw a copy of Gray's chart, he recognized the river as one he had seen earlier that season, but had not entered because it appeared "in no respect remarkable or likely to be an opening of any extent." Shortly after seeing Gray's chart, however, he passed the opening again, and this time he sent Lieutenant William R. Broughton over the bar with the small brig *Chatham*, in which Broughton traveled upriver for a hundred miles.

McLoughlin, in Canada, was a child of eight at that time, and during the next three decades, while he was a rising young fur trader, ships of several nations sailed along the Pacific Coast, trading only from their vessels and seldom touching land. The most numerous were Americans, generally from New England, who loaded their vessels with pelts and sailed to Asia. There they exchanged the furs for silks, teas, and spices, which they sold in Boston for huge profits. As examples, one investment of $40,000 netted $150,000 for its owner, while another of $50,000 brought $284,000.

Four nations were sparring for possession of the Pacific Coast. Russia held the far north, and Spain held Mexico in the south, as far as the upper border of California. Between these two regions, the United States and Great Britain were the contenders. Each of them had a strong claim based on discovery, because Captain Gray, the American, had entered the Columbia River first, but Lieutenant Broughton had gone farther upstream. In addition, both countries cited additional ties: for the Americans, the Louisiana Purchase of 1803 and the Lewis and Clark expedition in 1804–6; for the British, Alexander Mackenzie's penetration to the Pacific in 1793 and that of Simon Fraser in 1808.

There was, however, no question about the title to McLoughlin's headquarters, Fort George. Legally American, it had been founded by the wealthy fur magnate John Jacob Astor, who owned the Pacific Fur Company. Having added

ENTRANCE OF THE COLUMBIA RIVER.
Ship Tonquin, crossing the bar, 25th March, 1811.

Gabriel Franchère, a clerk on the ill-fated *Tonquin*, wrote *Relation d'un Voyage à la Côte du Nord-ouest de L'Amérique Septentrionale*. It was first published in French and republished in English in 1854 as *Journal of a Voyage on the North West Coast of America during the years 1810-1814*. This illustration appeared in the original edition of the book. OHS ORHI 21682

several Montreal fur traders as partners, Astor sent out two parties in 1810, one to cross the Rockies and go down the Columbia, and one to sail around Cape Horn in the *Tonquin* under Captain Jonathan Thorn. Among the Canadian fur traders on the *Tonquin* was Alexander McKay, the first husband of McLoughlin's wife Marguerite, and with McKay was their son, thirteen-year-old Thomas.

Astor's venture was ill-starred. Captain Thorn was cruel and reckless, a man of incredible ignorance and no trading skills. The *Tonquin* reached the mouth of the Columbia in March 1811 at the height of a raging storm. There, overruling his officers' protests, Thorn insisted on crossing the bar at once, with the loss of eight lives.

Two eyewitnesses give different accounts of the building of Fort Astoria. Alexander Ross, a clerk with the party, said they were soaked by rain and plagued by illness, lived on a diet of "boiled fish and wild roots," and used axes because they had no saws, on trees so large that four men sometimes labored for two days in felling one. But Gabriel Franchère, also a clerk, described few problems, said there was ample food, and called the weather "superb."

On June 1, when the *Tonquin* left on a trading voyage, Alexander McKay was on board, but his son Thomas—McLoughlin's stepson—fortunately stayed behind. The ship failed to return, with no explanation until late summer, when a native came to the fort and introduced himself as the ship's interpreter. At a harbor on Vancouver Island, he said, Thorn had disregarded advice, allowed natives to crowd on board, offered low prices, and refused to give the customary presents. Worse, when an Indian offended him, he had a chief "stripped and tied up," which was a mortal insult.

The next day, when the Indians began to swarm back, smiling and bearing bundles of furs, McKay and the crew wanted to set sail at once, but the captain laughed and let the natives come aboard "without reserve." Too late, he discovered his folly. At a signal the Indians drew knives and war clubs from their furs and slaughtered all the Astorians except the interpreter, who leaped into the water. One crewman, however, had apparently survived. Just after the interpreter swam away, he saw the ship explode into splinters, and he concluded that the survivor had managed to reach the ship's powder barrel and set it off, because he was sure to be killed in any case. With his father slain, young Thomas McKay remained at Fort Astoria, where he worked as a laborer and later as a clerk.

The traders' fortunes picked up in early 1812, when the company ship *Beaver* arrived with trading goods and the overland party straggled in, making it possible to build several small inland posts on the Columbia. By then the North West Company also had posts in the area, and McLoughlin himself had been offered a position in one, but had refused. The situation inevitably led to competition and occasional ironic jokes, as when Ross Cox wrote in his journal, "Mr. Pillet [an Astorian] fought a duel with Mr. Montour of the NorthWest, with pocket pistols, at six paces, both hits: one in the collar of the coat and the other in the leg of the trowsers. Two of their men acted as seconds, and the tailor speedily healed their wounds."

The Astor party was weakened by the loss of the *Tonquin* in 1811, with its load of trade goods; and the following year, because war with England had begun, Astor did not send a supply ship. In addition, the *Beaver*, which had gone to China with goods to trade, failed to return, and the men at Fort Astoria received "no tidings" of her or from their other ship, the *Lark*, which was lost at sea. As a result, by 1813 they were so short of merchandise that they decided to abandon the post. In early fall, when a party of Nor'Westers came from their upstream posts with an offer to buy out the Astorians—furs, equipment, and inland establishments—Duncan McDougal, ranking officer at the fort, agreed to the sale in order to salvage something of Astor's investment.

ASTORIA, AS IT WAS IN 1813.

Early pictures of Fort Astoria are widely divergent, some showing it near the waterfront, others more distant, some on a knoll, others on the flats with mountain in the background. This illustration also appeared originally in the book by Franchère. OHS ORHI 21681

The rest of the tale smacks of comic opera. A few weeks later the British sloop of war *Raccoon*, under Captain Black, sailed across the bar, with orders to take the post for the British Crown. The crew, who had anticipated a rich war prize, were sadly disillusioned. "What!" exclaimed the captain. "Is this the fort which was represented to me as so formidable! Good God! I could batter it down in two hours with a four-pounder!"

Even though the establishment had already been sold to Canadians, Black decided that since he had been sent to capture it, he would do exactly that. Marching all available men into the courtyard, he broke "a bottle of Madeira wine . . . on the flagstaff," proclaimed a new name—Fort George—fired three rounds of artillery and musketry, and drank the health of the king. His gallant feat, however, served only to muddy the waters, because after the war, the Treaty of Ghent in 1815 stipulated that everything "taken by either party . . . shall be restored without delay." The status of Fort George was then in doubt, because it had been sold to the Canadians, but had also been "captured" by the English Captain Black. A sale would stand. A seizure would not.

Next, in 1817 Captain James Biddle of the ship *Ontario*, accompanied by John Prevost, was ordered to go to the Columbia and assert the claim of the

The trees of the Northwest were awe-inspiring to early exploring expeditions. This illustration appeared originally in Charles Wilkes *Narrative of the United States' Exploring Expedition, during the years 1838, 1839, 1840, 1841, 1842.* OHS ORHI 55090

United States to its valley. When they reached Valparaiso, however, they had misunderstandings, so Biddle and the *Ontario* went on without Prevost. At the entrance to the Columbia he anchored his ship and crossed the bar with three well-armed boats, manned with fifty officers and seamen. "We nailed up a piece of lead to a tree" on one side of the river and "nailed up a board" on the other side, wrote a member of the crew. The boats and Biddle then returned to the *Ontario* and left the area.

Prevost, however, did not forget his assignment. Left in South America, he managed to sail as a passenger in the British ship *Blossom* and go boldly to the fort, where he arranged a ceremony of restitution, with suitable formality and a drop of rum. The British flag was lowered, "that of the United States hoisted in its stead," and Captain Hickey fired a resounding ship's salute, after which Prevost and the *Blossom* sailed on. The post was left in possession of the Nor'Westers, who undoubtedly switched flags again.

They were still there in 1821, when the Hudson's Bay and North West Companies merged and the new firm acquired all the posts of both companies, including Fort George of the doubtful title. At that time Spain was still claiming the southern part of the Pacific Coast, while Russia had recently issued a ukase closing the entire region north of the fifty-first parallel to any ships but its own. The limits were vague and often ignored.

By 1824, however, when McLoughlin came west, the situation had greatly changed. Spain had ceded to the United States its claims north of California in exchange for retaining its other territories in the New World. And Russia made two agreements. In the one of 1824, with the United States, the tsar's government agreed to withdraw to 54°40' in return for a free hand in the north. In the one of 1825, with Britain, Russia accepted a boundary at the 141st meridian, running north from the Pacific Ocean to the Arctic, except that she retained a coastal strip to 54°—the southern end of today's Alaskan panhandle. This meant that when McLoughlin arrived, Spain and Russia were out of the picture in the central section, leaving just two contenders—Britain and America, who still adhered to the system of joint occupation.

This was the muddled situation in the Pacific Northwest when McLoughlin took over the reins of the Columbia District. His mission was clear. He was to thread his way through the tricky problem of ownership. Turn an unprofitable business into a solvent one. And establish a firm British toehold in the remote Northwest.

~ 2 ~

Over the Stony Mountains
1824

McLoughlin had little time to prepare for his trip to the Columbia, because he did not receive his assignment until July 10 and he had to get over the "Stony Mountains" before winter. The only children to go with him and his wife were the two youngest, Eloisa and David, all the others being out of the home. Marguerite's daughters by Alexander McKay were young adults, Nancy having married Robert McCargo by 1816 and Mary having married Chief Trader William Sinclair in 1823. The third married a "Lieutenant McConnick," but the date and even her given name are not known. Sixteen-year-old Joseph had been left at Sault Ste. Marie. And Elisabeth and John were in school.

Ten-year-old Elisabeth, generally called Eliza, had left Montreal and was studying in the Ursuline convent in Quebec, under the care of the doctor's sister Marie Louise—Sister St. Henry. Eliza was a musical child, and "advanced," which her aunt thought fortunate because "for a life of work, she is not strong."

Although McLoughlin was an affectionate father, he showed the typical attitude of the time in writing, "My object is not to give her a splendid Education
but a good one—at least a good Education for a Girl."

His son John, age twelve, was still studying at Terrebonne, under the
supervision of Uncle Simon. Since John seemed to be doing well, McLoughlin
was interested, hopeful, intent on helping the boy as best he could from such
a distance, but somewhat doubtful of his own role. "I do not know what is best
to be done with him," he wrote to his uncle. "If you think he ought to be
removed to a better school than terre Bonne I would thank you to do it in fact
I will be obliged to you to use your Will and pleasure on this point." Travel to
the Pacific Coast was daunting at best, and it must have been cruelly hard for
the McLoughlins to go so far from these children.

For part of his trip to the Columbia, McLoughlin was to travel with the most
powerful field officer of the Hudson's Bay Company, George Simpson, who at
that time was governor of its Northern Department. In the Hudson's Bay Company, the title "Governor" had two meanings: governor of a department, as
when it referred to Simpson, and governor of the company, who managed the
business from London assisted by the "Honourable Committee." In addition,
it was sometimes popularly, but incorrectly, used for McLoughlin himself.

One part of the Northern Department was McLoughlin's charge—the
Columbia District, which consisted of the entire valley of the Columbia River
and its tributaries. Just north of it was a valuable area called New Caledonia,
lying between the Rocky Mountains and the Pacific. In 1825 New Caledonia
would be attached to the Columbia District, after which McLoughlin would
administer British affairs in all the land west of the Rocky Mountains from the
Russian holdings in Alaska to California, which was then ruled by Spain. The
term "Columbia Department" was not correct, but it was sometimes loosely
used by fur traders, including Governor Simpson and McLoughlin.

George Simpson, who would be a major factor in McLoughlin's life, had
been born about 1787 to an unknown mother and the ne'er-do-well son of a
Calvinist minister. The boy was brought up by his father's family in Scotland,
and was apprenticed to an uncle's sugar brokerage for the West Indies trade.
Andrew Colvile of the Hudson's Bay Company—Selkirk's brother-in-law—
was a partner in this business. He noticed young Simpson, was pleased with his
work, and arranged for him to enter the fur company.

In the spring of 1820 Simpson was sent to the Athabasca. At that time
William Williams, Governor in Chief of Rupert's Land, came under indictment because of the Selkirk disputes, and in the fall Simpson was appointed

governor locum tenens. In this position he learned an enormous amount about the business, and he drastically cut costs, chalking up an excellent record. When the Hudson's Bay and North West Companies merged, he was chosen to head the Northern Department because of his ability and—a paramount concern—because he had not been in the business long enough to make enemies on either side of the fur war. He was intelligent, innovative, hard-working—and also opinionated, stubborn, and flamboyant. Historian E. E. Rich wrote that he was "shrewd, purposeful, and little troubled by scruples. . . . He had an amazing capacity for absorbing detail, for shrewd analysis of complex data, for unscrupulous exploitation of other people's ideas and experience, and he had a marked capacity for exhausting work."

George Simpson was not tall—about five feet seven—but he stood erect, broad-shouldered and imposing, with fiery blue eyes. As governor, he was ruthless but effective, with an overwhelming worship of "oeconomy" that scarcely endeared him to his men. In the first four years of his administration, he reduced the number of company employees from 1,983 to 827 and transferred the displaced workers to the Red River Colony. He closed inefficient posts, reduced wages, opened new routes, and wherever possible substituted heavy York boats for canoes, with a consequent saving in costly manpower.

He was a tireless canoe traveler, rousting his voyageurs out before dawn and keeping them at the paddles for sixteen or more hours—while, it was said, he took comfortable catnaps and occasionally trailed a hand in the lake to make sure the water rose high enough on his wrist to indicate a satisfactory speed. A legend says he once drove his voyageurs so relentlessly that one of them grabbed his collar, lifted him into the water, and held him there until he promised a slower pace. The McLoughlins would have an energetic but hardly comfortable traveling companion.

Since he was expecting a letter of instruction from the London Committee, Simpson decided to wait at York Factory for the company ship. Midsummer, however, was none too soon to start for the Columbia, and McLoughlin's large party would necessarily move more slowly than Simpson's single vessel, so the doctor went ahead. On July 27, 1824, he left with "two Light Canoes [carrying no freight] and Fourteen Men."

Company records of the journey do not mention the family, but later on both Eloisa and David said they crossed the mountains with their father. In Eloisa's words, "We went from the Lake of the Woods to York Factory, and the same spring my father was sent . . . to come on this side of the mountains. Then he came to Fort George—Astoria. The whole family came. . . . We came over the mountains and down the river in boats." Eloisa was seven and David was three, scarcely ages to enjoy sitting still day after day in a canoe or to give the parents much peace.

McLoughlin planned to take his group up the Hayes River to Norway House, just north of Lake Winnipeg, and then proceed via the Saskatchewan River, Frog Portage, the English River, Portage La Biche, and the Athabasca River to Athabasca Pass, where he would cross the Rockies to the upper Columbia River. Simpson, who wanted to try out a slightly different and seldom used route, would start up the Nelson River instead of the Hayes, go through Split Lake to the regular crossing at Frog Portage, and from then on follow the regular trail. It would be a somewhat shorter but more difficult journey than McLoughlin's.

Simpson's journal provides a vivid record of the trip.

August 20: "This channel was overgrown with high Grass & Willows, the Banks Swampy & the Muschetoes innumerable added to which a drizzly Rain rendered the task of Cutting our way most laborious and harassing . . . in the Morning we had a strong hoar Frost and the Fog so thick that we could not see the length of the Canoe ahead."

In early September: "In Lake Primeau we lost nearly a day by a strong head Wind and in making a Traverse [crossing the lake] had much difficulty in keeping the Canoe afloat altho' Two Men were constantly bailing."

At Isle à la Crosse on September 5, finding a letter left there by McLoughlin: "The Dr is still Eight Days a head of me and does not expect I can overtake him before he reaches Nez Perces on the Columbia but in this he is mistaken. . . . the people [voyageurs] almost constantly in the Water dragging the Canoe; the Weather cold raw and disagreeable thick fogs and raining at intervals Daily."

Two weeks later: "It was unsafe to get within reach of the falling Timber, the crashing of which together with the dismal houling of the storm and the fear of having our Canoe blown away interfered seriously with our repose."

September 22: "Mr. McMillan and I walked the whole way and most abominably dirty Walking it was, the banks of the River having been recently overrun by Fire and while still smoking a light rain had fallen so that we were up to the knee every step in Charcoal and ashes, and by the termination of each Days March as black as Sweeps."

In late September Simpson caught up with McLoughlin, and he left a famous description of the doctor on the trail—when he too must have trudged through charcoal and survived "houling storms."

> On the 26th at 7 O'Clock A.M. came up with the Dr before his people had left their Encampment altho we had by that early hour come from his Breakfasting place of the preceding Day; himself and people were heartily tired of the Voyage and his Surprise and vexation at being overtaken in Riviere la Biche notwithstanding his having a 20 Days start of us from York is not to be described; he was such a figure as I should not like to meet in a dark Night in one of the bye lanes in the neighborhood of London, dressed in Clothes that had once been fashionable, but now covered with a thousand patches of different Colors, his beard would do honor to the chin of a Grizzly Bear, his face and hands evidently Shewing that he had not lost much time at his Toilette, loaded with Arms and his own herculean dimensions forming a tout ensemble that would convey a good idea of the high way men of former Days.

From this point they traveled together. Although Simpson's journal does not specifically mention the McLoughlin children, he made sour references to family travel in general, "which is productive of serious injury and inconvenience on account of the great consumption of Provisions. . . . it is attended with much expense and inconvenience on the Voyage, business itself must give way to domestick considerations . . . in short the evil is more serious than I am well able to describe." When he overtook McLoughlin's group he said with a touch of satisfaction, "Continued our route the following Morning but Slackened our speed in order to give the Dr an opportunity of keeping up with us."

Even with Marguerite's help, McLoughlin must have had his hands more than full, trying to keep his children safe and reasonably comfortable without annoying the impatient governor. Years later Eloisa wrote, "George Simpson came with us that year; he was Governor Simpson then." It is perhaps significant that she ventured no comments on her reaction to him, or his to the family.

On October 2 they were high in the mountains at Fort Assiniboine on the Athabasca River, and there, because Simpson had been "extremely unwell for some time past," McLoughlin advised him to take a well-earned break. The governor consented, but only for "the remainder of the day," after which they

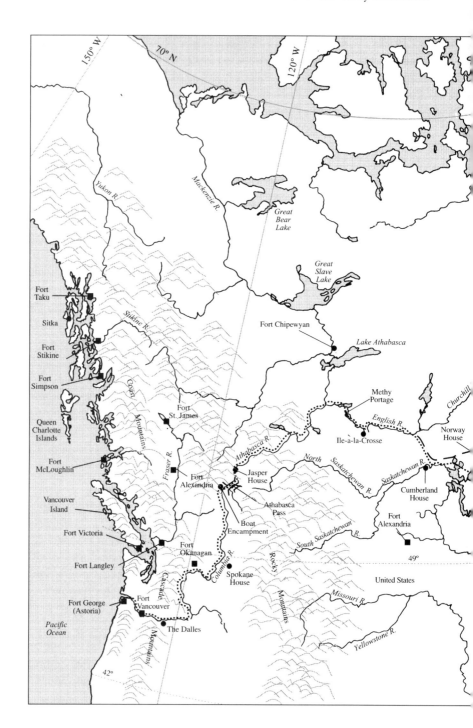

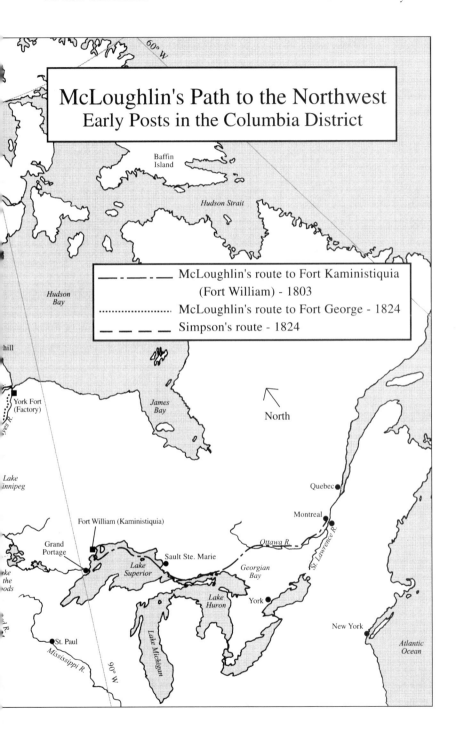

continued up the Athabasca. Here the current was "strong and steady with few rapids except at the Upper parts," and they passed occasional outcroppings of iron and coal.

On October 10 they reached Jasper House high in the Rockies, "beautifully Wild & romantic, on the borders of the Athabasca River which here spreads itself out into a small Lake surrounded by Lofty Mountains." Marguerite's son Thomas McKay, who had become an extremely capable Hudson's Bay clerk, was waiting with horses and men to assist them across the mountains, and it must have been an emotional—but discreetly subdued—meeting between him and his mother.

Marguerite had last seen this son when he left with his father in 1808 as a boy of eleven, and Eloisa and David had never met him before. He had become "a tall very dark man and strange." And he was lame, having permanently injured his hip a decade before, in an accident that has never been explained.

After the brief reunion, McKay and six men went on ahead in order to build a boat, as there were only two on the other side of the pass and the party would need more. On October 12 the rest set out again, with some of the men taking the horses while McLoughlin and Simpson and their people followed in canoes. After about fifty miles, when the river was no longer navigable, they all took to a steep trail with "a cavalcade of Twenty-one Horses."

The pathway over the crest of the Rockies was rugged and frequently covered with fallen timber, for this area had also been overrun by fire. The hunter killed two mountain goats and two mountain sheep, which were "tough and not well flavoured tasting strongly of Musk." As they proceeded, the mountains increased "to a stupendous size," some of them clad in snow. They had to ford the river once on the first day, twice on the second, and about a dozen times on another. On a "hilly cragged & rugged" portion of the path, one of the horses slipped from the riverbank into the swift current, but was saved by the quick action of his driver. The travelers were drenched with sleet and rain, the road grew steadily worse, and "the Mountains rise perpendicular to a prodigious height; the scenery Wild & Majestic beyond description; the track is in many places nearly impassable." It was so difficult a crossing that even the practical-minded Simpson philosophized that nature seemed to have placed the mountains there "for the purpose of interditing all communication between the East and West sides of the Continent."

On October 17 the path was made still worse by an eight-inch fall of snow, and as the party plodded through the drifts, they could see a large number of glaciers. At the top of the pass they came to a small circular lake, from which one stream flowed east through the Missouri drainage system while another

David Thompson was a Nor'-wester who made several significant explorations, kept excellent records, and supplied a great deal of information about previously unknown regions of the west. Athabasca Pass, subject of this picture, was on the usual fur-trade route through Rockies, and McLoughlin traversed it in 1824, 1838 and 1839. *David Thompson in Athabasca Pass*, pen and ink drawing by Charles W. Jefferys. NATIONAL ARCHIVES OF CANADA, C-70258

flowed west via that of the Columbia. Simpson marveled that "this basin should send its Waters to each side of the Continent and give birth to two of the principal Rivers in North America." He and McLoughlin examined the area together, finding it so remarkable that the governor "thought it should be honored by a distinguishing title and it was forthwith named the 'Committee's Punch Bowl.'" The body of water still retains this name, although it is actually a pair of tarns, or mountain pools.

Once past the summit, the party came to a descent so rapid it was called the Grande Côte—the Great Slope. By the next day they were at a lower altitude on the west side of the mountains, where the temperature grew warm and it began to rain—McLoughlin's introduction to that plentiful commodity of the Northwest. On October 19 the party reached Boat Encampment, the station near the junction of the Canoe River and the Columbia where craft were stored for brigades going downriver. They had crossed the formidable Athabasca portage in eight days.

As they expected, Thomas McKay was waiting for them, with boats quite different from the canoes of the east, because birch bark was not available. Some vessels of the West Coast were Indian canoes, made by hollowing out cedar logs, but most of the company boats were built of cedar planks, which were brought by ship to Fort George and then upriver "for making canoes." The ones used on the Columbia generally held up to one and a half tons of freight, and they were so heavy that each one required several men to carry it at a portage. Simpson said they were "called Boats but are more properly speaking Batteaux & wrought by Paddles instead of Oars."

Before setting out, the party paused for a day to finish and gum the craft, "and our provisions running short we were under the necessity of killing three Horses." This indicated an emergency, because fur traders needed their horses for transportation and used them for food only as a last resort. With preparations complete, the travelers left immediately after breakfast on October 21 "in two Boats and a Cedar Canoe." Within a mile they were on the Columbia River, where the current was "bold and strong and the Rapids perfectly safe."

For the next several days, they were dogged by bad weather. Simpson's journal said:

October 22. "The Weather cold raw and disagreeable with occasional Showers of Sleet & Rain."

October 23. "Raining in torrents throughout the Night."

October 25. "Heavy Rain during the Night."

Even so, two of McLoughlin's men put on a lively boxing match, about which Simpson remarked, "I do not know any thing more likely to put a man's bellows in order than a voyage from York Factory to the Columbia."

When they reached the Spokane River, they met a Hudson's Bay employee who was to become important to McLoughlin. He was Peter Skene Ogden, a former Nor'Wester who had become head of Spokane House and was leading a supply brigade from Fort George to the interior posts. Taking advantage of the chance to visit an auxiliary fort, Simpson, McLoughlin, and a few men accompanied Ogden by horse to his post, sixty miles away, leaving Marguerite and the rest of the party at the boats. After inspecting Spokane House and its returns, the governor concluded that the expedition to the Snake Country, then being led by Alexander Ross, should not be "left to a self sufficient empty headed man like Ross," but placed "in the hands of a Commissioned Gentleman and knowing no one in the country better qualified to do it justice than Mr Ogden, I proposed that he should undertake it." He therefore appointed Ogden to lead the Snake brigade, and placed the fort under Finan McDonald.

Simpson and McLoughlin then returned to their boats. As they continued down the Columbia, past Fort Nez Perces near the Walla Walla River, past the mouth of the John Day River, and over a portage at The Dalles, they saw increasing numbers of Indian villages, the occupants being busy with the fall harvest of salmon. They were apparently peaceful and prosperous, "perfectly independent of us for any necessary; arms they merely require for show or defence as they rarely hunt."

On November 6, on the lower Columbia, where there were "Hundreds of Indian Lodges," the Hudson's Bay party accidentally rammed a native canoe that shot across their bow before they could stop. The Indians, however, "thought nothing of it as they rose from under the water round the canoe like so many Seals . . . they appear quite at home in the Water and altho their Canoe was rendered useless by the Blow they took it all in good part and laughed heartily at their misfortune."

A few days later Simpson noted "great numbers of Seals playing about, I fired at them, but they are so quick that on seeing the Flash they are under Water before the Ball can reach them." At nightfall the travelers camped "nearly opposite Mount Hood," in a timbered area where they encountered one of the common discomforts of the trail. The wet, lush woods, in a region blessed with mild winters, were alive with fleas, and at one of the portages the Hudson's Bay party passed through a heavy infestation. As Simpson expressed it, "No sooner had we landed this Evening than all hands were actively employed in dislodging those filthy and loathsome visitants a duty requiring a considerable stock of patience, good Eyesight and active Fingers."

At the Cascades—a long stretch of impassable rapids and rocks—they made another portage. Many Indians were there, and Simpson remarked that Chief Factor Donald McKenzie had once "placed a great part of his property under the charge and in possession of some of the Chiefs," who had cared for it well, with no losses. Early travelers often mentioned the honesty of these tribes.

By November 7, the party was so close to Fort George that "after Supper all hands were busily occupied in shaving scrubbing and changing," in preparation for the voyageurs' time-honored custom of ending every journey in style. They embarked again "about 10 P.M., kept our people at their Paddles until Day break the 8th when we put ashore to Breakfast; wrought hard all day against a strong head Wind and got to Tongue Point about 5 P.M. where we found Chief Factor Kennedy & Mr McDonald amusing themselves Boat Sailing; they embarked with us and we landed at Fort George about Sun Set."

After more than three months on the trail, McLoughlin had reached his Pacific post.

~ 3 ~
Winter at Fort George
1824–1825

By 1824, Fort George was no longer the primitive outpost of the Astorians, but a self-contained village around a central courtyard. It contained several dwelling houses, a seventy-foot mess room, a separate building for the kitchen, a grain store, a bakery, a blacksmith, an Indian store, a shed for packing furs, warehouses for equipment and provisions, a poultry yard in one corner, and a powder magazine with heavy walls, probably of stone. When McLoughlin arrived it was November, the time of year about which Alexander Henry had said, "During the rainy season there is no moving out of doors, except into mud and water. If you step on a stone or billet of wood, ten to one you measure your length on the ground; everything is slippery with green moss."

McLoughlin soon learned that the fort boasted an astonishing inventory, which included such items as coats of mail and ostrich plumes, bought when the North West Company was trying to supply Spanish and Russian ships as well as its own *engagés*. The merchandise horrified Simpson. The fort, he said, had "altogether an air or appearance of Grandeur & consequence which does not become and is not at all suitable to an Indian Trading Post. Everything appears to me on the Columbia on too extended a scale *except the Trade*."

Over-grand it might be, but it was a lonely place—cloaked in rain, almost surrounded by the immense forest of cedar and spruce, and overlooking the Columbia, which here was a wide bay near the river's mouth. Eloisa, who had her eighth birthday on February 3, remembered Fort George as dark and still. Years later she wrote, "There was hardly anything there you know but Indians. The Fort always was shut up and the Indians were not allowed to come in. All the time we were there I did not see one ship until in the Spring that we moved."

Right from the start, McLoughlin had strong reservations about this area, so gloomy and damp and far from all he knew. In early spring he wrote to his uncle,

> I cannot say that I admire much this Country. the Climate is very mild but moist and cloudy to a degree indeed since my Arrival on the 8th Novr we have not seen one clear sun Shineing day and not ten days without rain. . . . the soil is in general very poor and Rocky the wood

The Chinooks were the dominant tribe near Fort George, well known to McLoughlin. Their long houses, constructed of cedar, held several families, each of which had its own section and its own fire. Charles Wilkes *Narrative of the United States' Exploring Expedition*. OHS ORHI 4465A

however in these places where there is any soil is much larger than any I have seen on the other side I saw an Epeneth Blanc [white spruce] of about six fathoms in circumference.

He soon met the Chinook chief Concomely—sturdy and well-built, a powerful man because he dominated the confederacy of the Columbia River tribes. Two of Concomely's daughters had married fur traders, and he was a strong supporter of the Hudson's Bay Company.

Concomely's people were famous for a trading network that extended far up the Columbia and for Chinook Jargon, a simplified tongue based on Chinookan and other Indian languages, French, and English. No records indicate that McLoughlin himself learned to speak it, but many traders did, for it was widely used by both Indians and whites.

The Chinooks were skilled traders and boatmen who secured much of their food from the sea and made extensive use of the immense cedar trees of the forest. They fringed bark for clothing, hollowed out logs for canoes, and split planks for building their long lodges, each of which generally housed several families. Like many coastal tribes, they held and traded for slaves, generally members of other bands whom they had captured or defeated in battle.

This drawing by J.G. Sean shows Indians fishing for salmon using long nets handled by several individuals. Salmon were also caught by upriver tribes, working at waterfalls, with dipnets on poles. OHS ORHI 53858

The British found the Chinooks' appearance remarkable, for they had high, slanting foreheads, achieved by binding infants for several hours of every day into cradleboards equipped with padded head-presses. McLoughlin did not mention the custom, but Simpson, father of many mixed-blood children, had ever an eye to feminine lures, and wrote that "as none but the wretched Slaves have round heads I begin to fall into the Chinook way of thinking that they do not look so well (particularly the Ladies) with round as with Flat Heads." The process was apparently harmless to the brain, for the tribespeople were highly intelligent, and shrewd traders—a people to be respected in business and valued as friends. Many writers remarked on this, such as Paul Kane, who said the Chinooks "are generally considered fully as intelligent as the surrounding tribes who allow their heads to preserve their natural shape."

However, no matter how friendly the Indians might be, McLoughlin knew he probably could not remain in Fort George for long, because it legally belonged to the United States. In addition—and of great importance—the entire area was under the system of joint occupation, which was to shadow McLoughlin's professional life for two decades.

The system had been adopted in 1818, when Britain and the United States were unable to agree on the boundary west of the Rocky Mountains and decided that for the next ten years the land would be open to citizens of both countries. East of the mountains the line was at the forty-ninth parallel, and the Americans wanted the boundary to adhere to that same parallel to the sea. But the British accepted it only to its intersection with the Columbia, and from that point they insisted on following the river to the Pacific. One complication was the British need to use the Columbia in reaching the interior. Another was the scarcity of good ports on the West Coast and the consequent determination of both countries to keep access to the Strait of Georgia and Puget Sound. The land in question was the westdrn third of today's state of Washington, between the forty-ninth parallel and the great curve of the Columbia as it runs south and then west.

The uneasy compromise—joint occupation—reflected the ambivalence of both nations about the value of the West Coast. Neither the Hudson's Bay nor the North West Company had realized much profit from it, and most Americans thought it impossibly remote. Thomas Jefferson had been sufficiently interested in it to send out the Lewis and Clark expedition, but nevertheless in 1813 he told John Jacob Astor, "I view it as the germ of a great, free and independent empire on that side of our continent." As late as 1822, the *New York Gazette* judged it "fit only for the seat of a penal colony," and Senator Thomas Hart Benton called the Rocky Mountains "a convenient, natural and everlasting boundary." In the florid language of the day, he said:

> Along the back of this ridge, the Western limit of the republic should be drawn, and the statue of the fabled god, Terminus, should be raised upon its highest peak, never to be thrown down. In planting the seed of a new power on the coast of the Pacific ocean, it should be well understood that when strong enough to take care of itself, the new Government should separate from the mother Empire as the child separates from the parent at the age of manhood.

McLoughlin, who had to administer the area, could be sure of only one thing. Either line, British or American, would give the United States the south bank of the Columbia, where Fort George stood. The London Committee voiced the same opinion when they wrote in July 1824, "As the Americans are to have possession of Fort George whenever they please, you will immediately proceed in erecting a Fort on the North side of the River." They directed him to find a spot convenient to shipping, high enough to be easily seen from the sea, and "in a dry place with good water."

McLoughlin had ample reasons for moving. Fort George was vulnerable to attack by sea. Its damp climate, with sixty inches of annual rain and persistent ocean winds, was injurious to furs, which had to be stored at headquarters while waiting for a ship. And it lacked open land for agriculture. This particularly vexed Simpson, who was incensed because the company's men had been raising little of their own food. He said they had "shewn an extraordinary predilection for European Provisions without once looking at or considering the enormous price it costs. . . . all this time they may be said to have been eating Gold."

For all these reasons, McLoughlin, Simpson, and the outgoing Chief Factor, Alexander Kennedy, agreed that they must find another site. Although Simon Fraser had considered the Fraser River a horrendous passage, Simpson still favored it, because he thought it would give the company access to its posts in New Caledonia. He therefore sent Chief Trader James McMillan out with a party to look it over, while McLoughlin concentrated his efforts on the Columbia.

One morning in November, the three officers—McLoughlin, Simpson, and Kennedy—set out in an open boat, with Thomas McKay as guide. They planned to cross the river and explore the north shore, which was several miles distant because the river there widened into a bay. But as Simpson told it, before they were halfway across, the boat began to leak so badly that "it became necessary to Bail with Buckets Hats &c, . . . our rigging so rotten that the Sails came down by the run." They touched on a sandbank but fortunately drifted off—"otherwise we must have perished among the breakers; we exhausted our strength at the Oars in order to get ashore but to no avail." They were drifting rapidly toward the open ocean and would almost certainly have been swamped at the bar, but the tide turned and brought them to shore, where they "landed and returned on Foot to the Fort."

After this narrow escape, Simpson decided to stay within the comfort of four walls, while McLoughlin and Kennedy continued the search. Rain or shine—generally rain—they tramped up and down the rough north bank for miles, or explored it by boat, but they found "either high perpendicular Rocks or low points which are overflown by the River in the Season of high Water." Eventually, in late November or early December, they decided on a place nearly a hundred miles inland. As McLoughlin wrote to the Committee, "After Mr. Kennedy and I had examined the North Banks of the Columbia from Chinook Point to this Spot we found no elegible Situation to Build on nigher the Entrance of the River on the North side."

The new location was on the north bank of the Columbia, across and slightly upstream from the mouth of the Willamette River—a major tributary, flowing from the south. The land around the fort sloped upward, from broad tracts of prairie and forest to higher levels densely covered with fir. It was so beautiful that it was known as the Jolie Prairie or Belle Vue Point. Charles Wilkes, an American who visited it later, said that from there, "the noble river can be traced in all its windings, for a long distance through the cultivated prairies, with its groves and clumps of trees; beyond, the eye sweeps over an interminable forest, melting into a blue haze, from which Mount Hood, capped with its eternal snows, rises in great beauty."

Simpson was mildly pleased with the view, but positively entranced by its agricultural potential. "A Farm to any extent may be made there," he wrote. "The pasture is good and innumerable herds of Swine can fatten so as to be fit for the Knife merely on nutricious Roots that are found here in any quantity and the Climate so fine that Indian Corn and other Grain cannot fail of thriving."

Construction began at once, with a work crew on the spot and McLoughlin traveling up and down the river to supervise. The forest rang with the sound of hammers and saws as workmen cut timber and split it for a twelve-foot-high stockade, or hewed it into logs for walls. Laborers at Fort George whipsawed boards for floors. Boats were paddled back and forth, and men lugged supplies up the bank. Years later, Dr. William McKay—Thomas McKay's son—told about the "very large and ungainly craft . . . flat-bottomed, with masts" that was hammered together to carry the fort's livestock—"a few goats, milk-cows and oxen from California, and . . . five work horses that came from Walla Walla, Indian ponies of good size and quality."

At about noon on a rainy Wednesday, March 16, McLoughlin, Simpson, the family, and some of the workers set out in four boats, leaving a crew to watch over Fort George and transport the most essential supplies. The Indians were reluctant to see the whites go, after more than a decade of friendship, and Simpson said Chief Concomely was so distressed that he "actually shed Tears when I shook hands with him at the Water side."

All day, through "incessant rain," the party moved slowly upstream. They made camp that first night at a riverbank site called Oak Point, set out again "at Day break," and camped at dusk at the mouth of the Willamette River, which Simpson—in a phonetic spelling of the original Indian name—called the "Wilhamot."

While they were in camp, they had visits from two important chiefs: Cassicus, who was old Concomely's eldest son, and Casseno. Each of them wanted to send a son east with the governor, to go to the mission school at Red River. But Simpson thought the boys were "too young & delicate to undergo the Labour and hardship of Crossing the Mountain at this early Season," so he declined to take them.

The third day—Friday, March 18—the party was in the boats before sunrise, and it reached the new fort at eleven o'clock in the morning. Dr. John Scouler, physician on the company brig *William and Ann*, saw the fort that summer and said it was "built on the same plan" as Fort George, but smaller. As Simpson described it:

> The Establishment is beautifully situated on the top of a bank about 1 1/4 Miles from the Water side commanding an extensive view of the River the surrounding Country and the fine plain below which is watered by two very pretty small Lakes and studed as if artificially by clumps of Fine Timber. The Fort is well picketted covering a space of about 3/4ths of an acre and the buildings already completed are a Dwelling House, two good Stores an Indian Hall and temporary quarters for the people. It will in Two Years hence be the finest place in North America, indeed I have rarely seen a Gentleman's Seat in England possessing so many natural advantages and where ornament and use are so agreeably combined.

Since the "Dwelling House" was probably for the head of the fort, McLoughlin, Marguerite, and their family could move in at once, but the buildings had been put up so fast that they were by no means "completed." It is known that by the following December McLoughlin's quarters were "in a half-finished state," that they would be moved four years later, and that when they were finally demolished, in 1838, they were still not done. The ones Simpson listed, however, must have been habitable, with at least their external walls and roofs in place. As for the "temporary quarters for the people," these may have been the roughest kind of sheds or huts, or even tents.

The afternoon of that first day was spent in a bustle of getting settled, and Simpson sat up all night "making arrangements." In the morning everyone was up early for the ceremony of dedication, which he recorded in his journal:

> Saturday, March 19th. At Sun rise mustered all the people to hoist the Flag Staff of the new Establishment and in presence of the Gentlemen, Servants, Chiefs & Indians I Baptised it by breaking a

Bottle of Rum on the Flag Staff and repeating the following words in a loud voice, "In behalf of the Honble Hudsons Bay Co^y I hereby name this Establishment *Fort Vancouver* God Save King George the 4th" with three cheers. Gave a couple of Drams to the people and Indians on the occasion. The object of naming it after that distinguished navigator is to identify our claim to the Soil and Trade with his discovery of the River and Coast on behalf of G^t Britain. If the Honble Committee however do not approve the Name it can be altered. At 9 o'Clock A.M. took leave of our Friend the D^r.

With this done, Simpson, Chief Factor Kennedy, and their retinue stepped into canoes, and the boatmen pushed off with a song. Paddles flashed as they started upriver toward the white cone of Mt. Hood. The boats and voices faded into the distance, until they were gone. McLoughlin was on his own.

CHAPTER 5

The Early Years

I have shipped three Swan skins and 10 lbs. Isinglass
as Samples to see what they would Sell for
and to know if worth Collecting.

DR. JOHN MCLOUGHLIN

~ 1 ~

Up the River
1825

With Governor Simpson gone, McLoughlin's immediate concern was to complete the move to Fort Vancouver, because until that was done, his meager forces were dangerously split between the two posts. The move was a major undertaking. In its decade and a half under three companies—Pacific Fur, North West, Hudson's Bay—Fort George had accumulated a vast assortment of furnishings, tools, trade goods, food, and livestock, as well as nearly a year's supply of furs.

A small portion of these had been taken upriver when McLoughlin himself made the move, but most of them were left at the old fort. For transportation, he had no wagons, no roads, no ships—only a few boats and Indian canoes, plus an "old scow" and a "new scow," probably the ark Willie McKay spoke of. The largest vessel in service was the *Otter*, a thirty-ton schooner built by the Nor'Westers while they held Fort George. She was a doubtful resource, being unwieldy, somewhat unsafe, and afflicted with an unfortunate tendency to get stuck or becalmed. But with a four-man crew, she could carry as much as several smaller vessels, and McLoughlin had no other choice. For manpower he relied on the company's salaried employees, including Canadians and Owyhees—also called Kanakas—who were natives of the Sandwich (Hawaiian) Islands engaged by the company when its ships stopped there for supplies. To augment this scanty workforce, he hired local Indians and their slaves.

Fortunately the Columbia itself offered few obstacles, for the segment between Forts George and Vancouver was broad and placid, flowing between densely forested banks, with no rapids requiring a portage. It was, however, tidal for more than a hundred miles, which contributed to its shifting and sometimes contrary currents, swollen in April by the torrents of spring. During the first three weeks of the move, there were only six fair or even showery days, the remainder being an unpredictable mix of rain, wind, and occasional hail.

For this job, McLoughlin appointed John Work—short, slight, and fair-haired, a man whom Governor Simpson called steady and painstaking, but "a queer looking fellow, of Clownish Manners and address . . . nevertheless a Shrewd Sensible Man." Work kept a detailed account of the move and weather:

> Friday [April] 8. Stormy from the S.E. with constant heavy rain in the night & almost all day.
> Saturday 9. Squalls of wind from the S.E. with almost constant rain sometimes very heavy.
> Sunday 10. Stormy from the S.E. with incessant heavy rain in the night & with some short intervals, heavy rain all day. In order to take care of the boats which are kept at anchor in the night, I sleep in one of them myself and make a man sleep in each of the others   We were completely drenched in the night, the mats which cover the property in the boats are quite wet, and with them it is impossible to keep the property dry.

Because the river was not well known, and because the *Otter* was such a cranky little vessel, she repeatedly went aground on the shallows or was stalled. "The wind blew so strong ahead that we were stopped near four hours in the evening," wrote Work on March 22. "During this time the men were employed mending the sail." The next day he noted, "At daylight contd our course under sail but the men mistook the channel and ran the boat aground at 7 Oclock and all efforts could not get her off, & we had to wait till two oclock for the tide." On the first of April "it was calm and we made but little way when pulling against the flood tide. We were four hours getting from Tongue Point to the fort" [Fort George].

After two weeks of agonizingly slow progress with the *Otter*, the scows, and a few canoes, McLoughlin sent a firm letter to Fort George, ordering the preparation of seven boats "forewith . . . four to be manned with two men each, white men and owyhees, and the other three with Indn Slaves." The workers then cobbled together what extra boats they could, although some were "old and crazy," and one was "so rotten" that she promptly stove in her bow.

About four o'clock in the afternoon of April 7, a vessel was seen sailing into the river, and at first McLoughlin's men could not identify her because of the "thick and hazy" weather. Fearing she might be unfriendly, Work and his crew immediately started the *Otter* upriver. But they need not have fled, for the newcomer was the company brig *William and Ann*, bringing the year's supplies from London. The Columbia was considered impassable for oceangoing vessels, so the ship's captain, Henry Hanwell, kept her near the river's mouth and anchored at Fort George four days later. Although her safe arrival was good news, this was an inconvenient time to add a fresh cargo to the goods that were being lightered upstream.

At first the piles of merchandise dwindled all too slowly, and after three weeks the effort was completely halted by a tribal war that broke out nearby. McLoughlin merely told the Governor and Committee that it started because Concomely's son had had one of his slaves assassinate another Chinook chief, but Work's journal explained that "an Indian of the fort Tete Plume, was badly wounded by one [of] Cassernes Slaves, who is supported by his master, The poor man is in the fort and is not expected to live." And the following day he wrote, "The wounded Indian died in the afternoon." "Casserne" was Chief Casseno.

The brig's medical officer, Dr. John Scouler—whose journal mentioned his pleasure at meeting "Dr. McLachlan"—discussed the war as it appeared to him. He said it began with the deaths of two sons of Chief "Comcomli" while they were under the care of a neighboring chief, and that the Indians held medicine men responsible in case of death.

> To revenge this imaginary crime, the remaining son of Comcomli had assassinated the medicine chief, & it was now expected that his friends, who are both numerous & powerful, would attempt to revenge his death. To-morrow in all probability a battle will take place, as old Comcomli is going to visit the graves of his sons, who are buried near the village of the murdered chief.

In the resulting conflict, one man was killed, two were severely wounded, and the tribes of the lower Columbia were in turmoil, threatening one another with reprisal. The situation was dangerous because most company workmen were engaged in transporting goods, which left only a small garrison at Fort George; and the Indians were "collecting about the place, either to revenge the assasination or Support the assasin." It alarmed McLoughlin. He decided he must send a reinforcement downriver, and this, he said, "for a time put a Stop to our transporting the property and even in a great measure to our work at this place."

Later, when peace was restored, the process of moving was delayed again, because the *William and Ann* needed extensive repairs and her carpenter was ill. The job, involving both ironworks and timbers, was not only difficult, it had to be done at once, because the Governor and Committee had ordered Hanwell to go on a trading expedition along the coast. McLoughlin therefore strained his scarce resources by sending a crew downriver, including skilled craftsmen and a caulker to seal the vessel's leaky joints. Again the work at Fort Vancouver was stopped. The ship, however, helped construction in one way, for she had brought a supply of bricks and tiles. They were of "trifling" cost and "a very inferior quality," but nevertheless they were apparently used in building the new establishment's chimneys.

On April 24 the fur brigade from the interior arrived, which temporarily increased McLoughlin's manpower and enabled him to resume the process of lightering goods upstream. By April 26 he had all his boats "constantly employed in transporting the Property from Fort George to this place." On June 7 the company abandoned the old fort. And on June 11, the last boats arrived at Fort Vancouver, bringing the rest of the personnel.

In September, when Dr. Scouler again visited Fort George, he found it rapidly degenerating into "a state of ruin and filth." Later on McLoughlin would reoccupy it as a secondary post, valuable because it stood at the mouth of the Columbia, but for the present he needed all his workmen upstream, so he left the old establishment vacant. He was at last installed in the headquarters he himself had chosen and built, and he was ready to take charge.

~ 2 ~

The First Fort Vancouver
1825–1828

Even while he was moving into his new fort, McLoughlin had to assume the role that would eventually become so important, that of benefactor and host. His first guest was the botanist David Douglas—energetic, twenty-six years old, "a fair, florid, partially bald-headed Scotsman of medium stature, gentlemanly address." Sent by the Royal Horticultural Society of London to survey the flora of the Northwest Coast and collect plant specimens, Douglas came on the *William and Ann*. He went ashore at Fort George on April 12, 1825, and McLoughlin left Fort Vancouver by canoe as soon as messengers brought word of the brig's arrival.

Douglas wrote in his journal, "The chief factor, John McLoughlin, Esq., came down the river from the new establishment, who received me with much kindness. . . . In the most frank and handsome manner he assured me that everything in his power would be done to promote the views of the Society." McLoughlin urged him to make Fort Vancouver his headquarters, and on April 19 Douglas wrote that they started upstream together "at 8 o'clock morning in a small boat with one Canadian and six Indians; we made only forty miles, having no wind and a very strong current against us. We slept in the canoe, which we pulled up on the beach. Our supper was a piece of good sturgeon, a basin of tea, and a slice of bread."

Although Fort Vancouver was scarcely ready for guests, Douglas said that when they arrived,

> a tent was kindly offered, having no houses yet built, which I occupied for some weeks; a lodge of deerskin was then made for me which soon became too small by the augmenting of my collection and being ill adapted for drying my plants and seeds. I am now (August 16) in a hut made of bark of *Thuya occidentalis* which most likely will be my winter lodging.

McLoughlin was troubled because it was "out of our power to make him as comfortable as we would wish," but Douglas was overjoyed at the chance to discover and classify the plants of a new area. He stayed for two years, receiving food and shelter, a horse, and a canoe with men to paddle it. As a special favor, McLoughlin allowed him to accompany a brigade to the interior and take "thirty quires of paper weighing 102 lb," for recording field notes and packing specimens—a heavy load to carry by boat and horse, which Douglas recognized as "far more than I could expect." The botanist also went by company canoe to the coast, where he was hampered by the tribal war but nevertheless identified many specimens. He proved himself a resourceful camper by having his Canadian helper drench the ground "to prevent me from being annoyed with fleas," and by making a tasty meal on a "white-headed" eagle.

At Christmas Douglas was back at Fort Vancouver, where

> rain fell in such torrents, without the least intermission, that my little hut of *Thuya* bark . . . was completely inundated; 14 inches of water was in it. As my lodgings were not of the most comfortable sort,

Mr. McLoughlin kindly invited me to a part of his house in a half-finished state. Therefore on Christmas Day all my little things were
removed to my new dwelling.

This was an all-purpose building called the "Big House," which contained
not only the Chief Factor's living quarters and office, but also the large mess
hall where officers and visitors dined. It was unfinished and would remain so
for years.

Even though Douglas was living in the same building as the Chief Factor,
his journal scarcely mentioned Marguerite McLoughlin, and even then not
by name, for the officers' wives were kept in the background. He gave a
glimpse of her when he said that on Christmas Day the family "took an airing
on horseback." Riding was apparently a favorite recreation, for other writers
also mentioned it. The American John Ball, for example, said several years
later that "we saw little of the women, they never appearing except perhaps
on Sunday or on horseback. As riders they excelled."

In the spring of 1827, two years after his arrival, Douglas reluctantly left
with the spring brigade, to go to York Factory and from there to England. On
March 20, his final day at Fort Vancouver, he wrote, "I cannot forbear expressing my sincere thanks for the assistance, hospitality, and strict attention to my
comfort which I uniformly enjoyed during my stay with them—in a particular manner to Mr. McLoughlin (Chief Factor)." As was his occasional practice, the doctor rode with the brigade as far as Fort Colvile, where he and
Douglas took one last ride together "and returned at dusk for dinner."

The next morning they separated, Douglas continuing overland while the
Chief Factor returned to his fort. The botanist's name was later given to an
important tree of the Northwest—the Douglas fir. Various seeds he had collected were soon growing in British gardens, and on May 11, 1826, the Royal
Horticultural Society awarded McLoughlin a silver medal in acknowledgment
of his aid. The visit had been a pleasure for the doctor, who genuinely enjoyed
a guest, especially one who brought fresh ideas and information.

Acting as host, however, was only part of McLoughlin's new job. In 1825,
when he founded Fort Vancouver, he was forty years old and an experienced
administrator, but he had never before been so isolated. As a Nor'Wester and
later as a Hudson's Bay Chief Factor, he had attended a yearly rendezvous of
able men, where he could exchange ideas, receive instructions, and ask his
superior officers for advice. But in his new position he could not attend summer gatherings, and if questions arose, he had to send them by ship to George

Fort Nez Perce, on the Walla Walla River, was one of the older forts. In 1825 George Simpson and McLoughlin decided to move it to the north side of the Columbia, but abandoned the plan because the Indians objected. This drawing was done by Joseph Drayton of the Wilkes Expedition, in 1841. OHS ORHI 964

Simpson, wherever he might be, or to the head of the company, Governor John Henry Pelly, and the Committee in London. He might wait as long as two years for a reply.

McLoughlin also had an enormous territory to supervise—the entire Columbia District, which included four major posts on the Columbia River and its tributaries:

1.   Fort Vancouver, his headquarters.

2.   Fort Nez Perces, often called Walla Walla, on the river of that name at its junction with the Columbia.

3.   Spokane House, on the Spokane River, with its auxiliaries Kootenai House and Flathead Post. In 1825–26 McLoughlin would abandon Spokane House and build Fort Colvile instead, about seventy-five miles to the north, at Kettle Falls on the Columbia.

4.   Thompson's River, or Kamloops, on the Thompson River, at the
     edge of New Caledonia. This post had an important subsidiary—
     Fort Okanagan, which was at the junction of the Okanagan and
     Columbia Rivers, south of Kamloops by "about Eight Days March
     . . . with loaded Horses."

Most of these forts were in the high, dry plateaus east of the Cascades,
where summers were hot and winters bitterly cold. Forts Vancouver and George
were west of the Cascades, in a country of ample rain, cool summers, and mild
winters with little snow. North of McLoughlin's jurisdiction, in the area called
New Caledonia, were Alexandria Fort, Fort George on the Fraser River, Fort St.
James, McLeod's Fort, and a post on Fraser's Lake, all of which would later become part of his district. Although New Caledonia was difficult to reach, it had
great value as a source of furs, and one of the prime functions of the Columbia
District was to serve as a buffer, keeping American trappers out of the north.

McLoughlin was not only to assist and supply this vast network, he was
to bring it under his firm supervision. Before leaving the Columbia, George
Simpson had told him that "serious loss" had occurred because the leader at
each fort wanted a free hand and considered the Chief Factor at Fort George
as merely "a store keeper or agent." Simpson had given the doctor specific
orders to assume full management of the entire Columbia District, and said
that in case of trouble, he was to make a report "for the information & determination of the Honble. Committee." A year later the Committee reinforced
Simpson's orders by stating that the head of such a remote area must be
"invested with discretionary powers" and by assuring McLoughlin that he was
the supreme authority. This might easily have resulted in conflict, but such
was not the case. The doctor was hot-headed and impulsive, but he was also
a decisive administrator with reasonable expectations, and the leaders at
other posts respected him.

However, he had many difficult obligations, one of which was the completion of his fort. Although it was well located for supplying the inland posts,
the entire area was under the vague system of joint occupation, which was
slated to expire in 1828, and a new agreement might assign the land south of
the Columbia to the United States. If this happened, Fort Vancouver on the
north bank would at best be uncomfortably close to Americans, and McLoughlin might have to abandon the site. He therefore put up "only such Buildings
at this place" as were "Immediately Required," but even that was a strain on
his scarce manpower.

Another of his duties was to set the rate of exchange for blankets, guns, ammunition, beaver traps, beads, cloth, clothing, and other items, and to adjust the terms for individual forts as circumstances demanded. Each fort had its own table, called the standard of trade, in which a large, prime beaver skin was rated as a "made beaver," with other skins and various commodities listed in relative terms. The prices and charges sometimes varied considerably from post to post. The following is a small portion of the standard of trade for the Columbia River in 1824–25:

RETURNS	SKINS MADE BEAVER	
	Fort George	Spokan House
1 Large Prime Beaver	1	1
1 Small " "	1/2	1/2
1 pup " "	1/4	1/4
1 large land otter	1	1
1 prime sea otter	12	
1 musk rat	1/10	1/10
1 mink	1/4	1/4
1 prime deer skin	2	2
1 large wooden canoe, native work	15	
1 good working horse	15	15
1 Chinook Hat 1st quality	4	

CHARGES FOR GOODS	SKINS MADE BEAVER	
	Fort George	Spokan House
Axes Com. ea.	2	2
" Square-headed ea.	3	2
Blankets Plain 3 points ea.	6	6
" Green 4 " "	10	2
Balls Musket & Trading p.lb.	1	
Beads Sky Blue Enam^d p.lb	5	
Cloth Com^n Scarlet fathom	8	10
Files flat 6&7 inches pr doz	6	12
Guns Com. N.W. each	20	18
Guns fine half stocked ea.	30	
Gun Powder per lb.	3	4
Knives Folding ea.	1/2	1/2
Kettles brass & copper pr lb.	2	2 1/2

Rifles English twist		
Barrels ea.	40	30
Tobacco Twist p. lb.	1 1/2	2
Thimbles brass p. doz	1/2	1

This multi-faceted job meant that McLoughlin must handle an endless string of practical details. His early letters show that he controlled the location of men, horses, trappers, and boatmen, had sawmills and gristmills built, sold their products as far away as Hawaii and California, and considered expanding to Lima, Valparaiso, Acapulco, and Russian posts in the north. He decided what crops to grow, what to feed the stock, what to plant in the fort's vegetable garden. He saw that furs were kept clean and dry, directed blacksmiths and carpenters, and made sure that all forts were supplied with personnel, food, transportation, trapping equipment, ammunition, and trade goods. "The additional Shot and Tobacco you sent Enabled us to give all the Requisite Supplies to the Interior," he told the Governor and Committee in 1826, with obvious satisfaction.

He had to provide as much food as possible to the inland forts, because the country east of the Cascades was not well suited for raising crops. "I also sent ninety Bushels of corn and pease and four Kegs Tallow as there was no provisions at Walla Walla and none to be had except Horse Flesh," McLoughlin informed the Governor and Committee in October 1825. Fort Vancouver was not settled soon enough to produce grain that year, but he had workers break the sod of about three hundred acres and plant potatoes, peas, beans, and other vegetables, from which they garnered nine hundred barrels of potatoes, nine and a half bushels of peas, and smaller amounts of the rest. That same fall the overland express from York Factory brought a large shipment of seeds, which were of poor quality and had been damaged on the journey but were nevertheless welcome and resulted in a good yield.

"Our farming goes on as well as we could Expect," McLoughlin wrote in 1826 after the first full harvest, and listed crops of 114 bushels of "pease," 27 of barley, 10 of wheat, and 6 of oats. He said the quantity was small, "owing to the seed being Greatly injured in coming here," but that the wheat, oats, and barley "are the finest I ever saw in any Country." In addition, the fort had "a sufficiency of pease to serve as substitute for Indian Corn," and "the cattle thrive very well, I cannot say so of the pigs." The hogs at Vancouver evidently had a hard time, for McLoughlin wrote to the Governor and Committee, "Our Stock of pigs Increase Slowly, many are Poisoned by Eating a Root that

Grows in these plains"; and he told Governor Simpson that "the Wolves have destroyed several of them."

Another project involved ships, because the Governor and Committee had ordered McLoughlin to set up a system of coastal trade, beginning at once with a voyage by the *William and Ann*. This was not only a radical change from his former reliance on canoes alone to bring supplies and carry away furs, it would mean competing with experienced American traders. And while he struggled to meet the myriad demands, he was plagued with the problem of insufficient manpower. During that first summer, he sent a number of work-men north with the *William and Ann* to conduct the coastal trade, and oth-ers went to the interior with fur brigades. So many left that by fall 1825, his entire staff consisted of only Chief Trader Archibald McDonald, two lower-ranking officers, and seven "common men."

Even though McLoughlin tried to meet his challenges, he did not expect to be on the Columbia long. In March 1825, only four months after arriving, he wrote to his uncle Simon Fraser, "I hope . . . you will have the goodness to continue your cares [for the boy John] till I go down which I think will be in three Years after this, when I hope to have the pleasure of returning you my thanks for this and the Many other obligations I and my family are indebted to you." A year later he was still hopeful, although he had postponed the date. "I have in mind to go down in five Years—but that is merely for your infor-mation."

About then something occurred, an episode that has never been explained. In the summer of 1826, after being on the Columbia for less than two years, Marguerite and the children set out on the long trip upriver and over the mountains to York Factory. John Work wrote that on Tuesday, July 5, the brigade for the interior left, "consisting of 9 boats, six men per boat . . . also their women, and 9 children viz—Dr. McLoughlin's family, Mr. F. McDonald's family and 2 children of Tom McKay" (Marguerite's son). In September they were at Fort Colvile, just south of today's Canadian boundary, and they con-tinued east with the express brigade under Chief Trader John Warren Dease all the way to the headwaters of the Columbia, which was the takeoff point for crossing the Rockies.

There, however, the families' plans were abruptly changed, and they turned back at the western end of the Athabasca portage, "on hearing that the Doctor is not to go out in Spring." Although the reason is undocumented, it seems probable that McLoughlin had expected a transfer, but that Dease met the fall express from York Factory, learned that they were bringing orders for

This is a drawing of McLoughlin's first mill, on a small tributary to the Columbia, about five miles east of Fort Vancouver. OHS ORHI 55091

the Chief Factor to stay on the Columbia, and had the families return. Whatever happened, it must have been a grievous disappointment to the doctor, for his letters often expressed a longing to return to Canada, and he would scarcely have started his wife and children on such a journey unless he felt sure he would follow.

Nevertheless, he buckled down to work, and Fort Vancouver grew. In 1828 the American trapper Jedediah Smith, who spent a winter there, wrote that it had "mechanics of various kinds, to wit, blacksmiths, gunsmiths, carpenters, coopers, tinner and baker. A good sawmill on the bank of the river five miles above, a gristmill worked by hand, but intended to work by water." No white women were at the fort, he said, but "a great number of mixed blood Indian extraction . . . who were treated as wives."

The hand-operated gristmill was described years later by Dr. William McKay, who had watched with delight when he was a small child, living at the fort under the care of his grandmother, Marguerite. At first, McKay said, they used a "great stump that had been hollowed, in which wheat was pounded with a spring pole that worked a heavy pestle." But when they raised more grain, they improved the system. The fort's blacksmith was a former North West employee named William Cannon. He had set up his forge under a majestic fir tree, and this man—quite old, in Willie's eyes—rigged wheels and cogs, made burrs of granite from the nearby hills, and put them together as a mill powered by four yoke of oxen. The little boy "looked on with wonder while all this was done, and with more wonder yet when he saw the beautiful white flour come pouring out as it was ground." This grain, produced in McLoughlin's second year at the post, was the beginning of the wheat-growing industry of the Northwest, with Cannon's ingenious contraption as the first mill.

For several years, however, the grinding of flour remained a primitive operation, less glamorous in practice than it was to Willie. As late as 1836, when the vivacious Narcissa Whitman was a guest at the fort, she wrote, "On visiting the mill did not find it in a high state of improvement It goes by horse power, has a wire bolt. This seemed a hard way of getting bread, but better so than no bread, or to grind by hand."

The fruit industry of the Northwest was also started during those early days. Eloisa McLoughlin's brief biography of her father says:

> There was a gentleman who came from England by Express, and his name was Captain Simpson. . . . He was invited to eat with his friends somewhere before he left home, and somebody gave him eating apples. Somebody said you had better take these seeds, you might go somewhere where you wanted to plant them. He wrapped them up in a paper and put them in his vest pocket; and when he came to Vancouver, and talking about apples, he says, "Here I have got apple seeds in my pocket." They took them out and planted them. . . . My father used to watch the garden so that no one should touch the tree. At first there was only one apple on it, and that everyone must taste. . . . It was a great treat, for everybody had just a little slice. There were a good many it had to go round among.

Narcissa Whitman told the same story. "A gentleman . . . at a party in London put the seeds of the grapes & apples, he eat in his vest pocket, and soon after took a voyage to this country and left them here. Now they are greatly multiplied." And the explanation was corroborated by the missionary Hiram Bingham, who had met Lieutenant Æmelius Simpson in Hawaii and wrote that the young man "says he has himself planted the grape and the apple at that place and they appear to be flourishing."

Fed by the rich soil and abundant rainfall of the Columbia, the plantings were a success. Jedediah Smith in 1829 saw "a fine garden, some small apple trees and grape vines" growing there. A few years later Narcissa Whitman wrote, "Here we find fruit of every description. Apples peaches grapes. Pear plum and Fig trees in abundance. Cucumbers melons beans peas beats cabbage, tammatoes, & every kind of vegitable, to numerous to be mentioned."

Right from the start McLoughlin's physical plant thrived, with a farm, orchard, vineyard, and crude gristmill. These were of great importance, because their output—cattle and pigs, vegetables, fruits, and grain—cut the cost of operating his district. But the most important element in realizing a profit was furs, and for those he must look beyond the palisade.

~3~
The Snake Brigade
1825–1829

As Chief Factor in the Great Lakes area, McLoughlin had been guided by his company's long-established policy of trapping in moderation, in order to preserve the fur-bearing resource, but on the West Coast he adopted a different plan. Sooner or later, when the boundary was settled, part of the Columbia District would fall to the United States, and therefore the Governor and Committee had ordered him to have his trappers turn the area into a "fur desert." They said it was "extremely desirable to hunt as bare as possible all the Country South of the Columbia and West of the Mountains." And the Council of the Northern Department told him, "It is in our interest to reap all the advantage we can for ourselves, and leave it in as bad a state as possible for our successors. . . . our wish is that it [the Snake expedition] should scour the country wherever Beaver can be found." The purpose was twofold: to reap profits while they could, and to discourage Americans from crossing the Rockies.

Not everyone was pleased. Peter Skene Ogden, leader of the Snake brigade, complained, "It is scarcely credible what a destruction of beaver by trapping this season. . . . Did we not hold this country by so slight a tenure it would be most to our interest to trap only in the fall, and by this mode it would take many years to ruin it." And again, "well may it be said beaver have many enemies, while they alone wage war with none."

The area to be trapped out was the vast sweep of forests, mountains, and broken plateaus known to traders as the Snake Country. Its chief section was

Peter Skene Ogden, one of McLoughlin's most trusted and able aids. He was leader of the Snake Brigade, and had an influential role in expanding the company's position in the north. In 1846, after McLoughlin resigned, Ogden would be one of the triumvirate who managed Fort William. OHS ORHI 11419

the Snake River and its tributaries, but its brigades also entered the Great Basin—a semidesert with no outlet to the sea, where the rivers dry up, or sink into the thirsty ground or flow into shallow lakes, many of which are alkaline. The basin contains barren stretches, mountains, patches of forest, and grassy meadows, and it is huge, covering western Utah, most of today's Nevada, and bits of Oregon, Idaho, Wyoming, and California. Much of it is south of the forty-second parallel—the northern edge of today's California, which in Mc-Loughlin's time belonged to Mexico. National boundaries west of the Rockies, however, were poorly defined and frequently ignored.

At that time the chief company officer in the Snake Country was Peter Skene Ogden—thirty years old, a short, rotund man with peculiar speech, "neither falsetto, tenor, nor harsh, still it was an individual voice." A fellow trader, Ross Cox, called him "the humorous, honest, eccentric, law-defying Peter Ogden, the terror of the Indians, and the delight of all gay fellows."

Ogden, son of a judge in Quebec, had entered the fur trade as a clerk in the Astor company. He left briefly to study law but changed his mind again, and at the age of seventeen he became a North West Company apprentice. He was in the Selkirk conflict, and showed such violence that after the merger he was one of three Nor'Westers—Ogden, Cuthbert Grant and Samuel Black—whom the combined company refused to accept. However, to Governor Simpson's "great satisfaction," and due largely to his recommendation, the three had been admitted in 1823, when Ogden was given the rank of Chief Trader and sent to Spokane.

McLoughlin and Simpson had met him there in 1824, while they were on their way to the Columbia. At that time Simpson had appointed Ogden

A typical fur traders' brigade. These generally included the trappers' families, and they carried camping equipment, trade goods, food, spare horses for transportation, and an emergency source of food. Charles Russell painting of a trapping party in W.T. Hamilton's *My Sixty Years on the Plains*. OHS ORHI 98829

head of the Snake expedition—a fractious brigade, trapping in a harsh terrain. Simpson said its men were "the very scum of the country and generally outcasts from the Service for misconduct. . .the most unruly and troublesome gang to deal with in this or perhaps any other part of the World"; and he called the expedition a "forlorn hope . . . the most hazardous and disagreeable office in the Indian Country." In spite of its difficulties, however, this was the largest and most profitable group under McLoughlin's wing.

A fur brigade included two types of trappers: company *engagés*, who were paid a salary; and freemen, including former employees, either discharged or retired. Some were accompanied by their Indian wives, who were

This Indian woman is defending her husband and family from a marauder, an act that was described in numerous accounts. The native wives were essential for their strength and courage, their loyalty, and their ability to care for furs and handle the many emergencies of the trail. From Francis Fuller Victor's *The River of the West*. OHS ORHI 98823

experts in cleaning and packing the furs, and would also help with the work of the camp and care for their husbands in case of injury or illness. The company furnished supplies to its salaried employees, but the freemen were on their own, selling furs and buying clothing, traps, and horses at company posts. Although McLoughlin did not realize it until later, the company paid so little for skins and charged so much for equipment that most of them had to take out fresh loans every year to pay for their outfits.

For this scant—or nonexistent—return, they endured unbelievable hardship, living in tents through the winter, traveling from stream to stream, and hunting for most of their food. In order to set, check, and unload their traps, they submerged their hands for hours in frigid water, sometimes after chopping away ice. When they had cleared their traps and carried the catch to camp, they skinned the animals, stretched the pelts to dry, and used the meat for food. If game proved scarce, they went hungry or, with great reluctance, killed their horses for food—a last resort because they needed the animals for transport. In case of sickness or injury, they were their own doctors, and survived astonishing remedies. In one instance a trapper fell deathly ill after dining on beaver that had eaten water hemlock (poison parsnip). He was "suddenly seized with a violent pain in his Loins and from thence his head and

THE TRAPPER'S LAST SHOT.

If, as the picture's original title indicates, this was truly his "last shot," it was important, because he depended on his gun for both defense and food. The picture's chief interest is the gear and clothing, which were typical. From Francis Fuller Victor's *The River of the West*.
OHS ORHI 91566

shortly after entirely lost all motion of his Limbs, he is now nearly recovered by drinking pepper and [gun] powder mixed in water, for nearly four hours he suffered great pain."

Although McLoughlin understood the brigades' difficulties, he could not maintain contact with them while they were in the field. He knew only that in November 1824, Ogden set out from the Flathead Post with 75 men, 80 guns, 364 beaver traps, and 372 horses, along with a number of trappers' children and Indian wives. McLoughlin later learned that when Ogden stopped at the post, he picked up seven Americans led by Jedediah Smith. The brigade's former leader, Alexander Ross, had happened to meet them the year before, and allowed them to accompany him to the fort—a mistake Ogden later called "that damn'd all cursed day," because, he said, those Americans guided troublemakers to the Hudson's Bay camp.

All during the winter and spring of 1824–25, while McLoughlin was erecting Fort Vancouver, Ogden and his expedition were in the field. Being intelligent and reasonably well educated, he kept a journal that vividly describes the danger and discomforts of a working brigade. One of the hardships was hunger.

Tues. Jan. 10th. [1826] 2 horses killed for food. Seeing our horses killed makes me wretched, for I know full well in the Spring we will require them all.

Tuesday, 16th. [February 1826] Our prospects gloomy; we must continue to starve; now all are reduced to skin and bones; more beggarly looking beings I defy the world to produce.

Sat. 12 Nov. [1826] Within the last 10 days we have had only 6 meals.

The life was not only hard, it was dangerous, because of accidents, illness, exposure to cold, fights with Indians, and drownings. Chief Factor William Connolly lost three men in 1828 at Priest's Rapids on the Columbia, and Ogden lost nine at The Dalles two years later. In 1829 he wrote that only one man remained of those who had accompanied him in 1824. "All have been killed with the exception of two who died a natural death and are scattered over Snake Country. . . . It is almost incredible the number that have fallen."

Ogden's brigade had set out in November 1824, and McLoughlin did not hear from it until the following August 9, when a letter dated June 27 came via Spokane House to Fort Vancouver. Many fur-trade documents are notable for their lively writing, and this letter contains picturesque details and passages in direct dialogue, as does a similar one of July 10.

From the Flathead, Ogden said, he led his men across the Continental Divide to the headwaters of the Missouri—in American territory—and then across the Divide again, into land under joint occupancy. Although this was the trappers' usual route, it was cruelly difficult in winter, when mountain trails were choked with snow. At the Bear River, near the Idaho-Utah border, the seven Americans went up the stream while Ogden followed it down to a large lake, about a hundred miles in length. He had reached Great Salt Lake, a previously uncharted body of water in the Great Basin.

On March 23 the two parties met again in Bear Valley, where an American brigade under Johnson Gardner encamped only one hundred yards away, "hoisted the American Flag and lost no time in informing all hands in the Camp that they were in United States Territories." The night passed without incident, but in the morning Gardner came to Ogden's tent. "Do you know in whose Country you are?" he asked, to which Ogden replied that he did not, as the claims of Great Britain and the United States had not been resolved.

They had been, Gardner snapped. He said the area had been ceded to America, and since Ogden had "no licence to trade or trapp," he must return at once to his native soil. Ogden refused, at which Gardner went to the tent of John Gray, an Iroquois trapper in the British brigade.

Ogden followed and found Gray primed to rebel. "All the Iroquois as well as myself have long wished for an opportunity to join the Americans," Gray told him, saying they had not left sooner because of their "bad luck in not meeting with them [Americans], but now we go & all you Can Say Cannot prevent us." Calling the British "the greatest villains in the World," he said, "We have now been five Years in your Service, the longer we remain the more indebted we become . . . we are now in a free Country and have friends to support us, and go we will." Gardner then gave orders to raise camp, and twenty-three of Ogden's men left, taking most of the expedition's furs, traps, and horses.

Ogden concluded his letter with a warning that, since their rivals paid as much for one beaver skin as the Hudson's Bay Company paid for eight, the Committee should not anticipate another Snake expedition, "for not a freeman will return, and should they, it would be to join the Americans, there is Gentlemen a wide difference with their prices and ours." He said the Americans had developed a source of supplies by driving "waggons overland from St. Louis to the first Spanish Settlement call'd Taa's [Taos] where they fit out their Trappers and receive their furs in return and they say they intend to reach the Columbia also with Waggons not impossible so far as I have seen."

When McLoughlin read this report, his first and characteristic reaction was white-hot anger. He immediately ordered the head of the Flathead Post to send reinforcements to the brigade, and he wrote to the officers of other posts relating the "Mortifying intelligence" of the freemen's desertion. The company, he firmly said, had every right to trap in the Snake because the agreement for joint occupation would not expire until 1828. He urged the officers to resist "to the Utmost of our power any attack on our persons and property." He said he would send another brigade to the Snake Country in order "to counter act the evil impression the vaunting assertions of Gardner and the desertion of our Freemen will have on the Indians and remaining freemen." He complained of the salaried employees' "disgracefull, I might say criminal neglect of their Duty" in not supporting Ogden. And he refused to consider the trappers underpaid. "There is not a man of the party then present who does not well know that none of them were ever induced to Buy a single Article and that they are in Debt much against our will."

In October 1825, McLoughlin was still of the same mind. "The freemen it seems complained of their Traps and the prices they pay for their Goods. As to their Traps they are made Stronger Since last year than they used to be."

He suggested that the company let the trappers buy supplies at Fort Nez Perces at the lower prices of Fort Vancouver. And casually, with no attempt at concealment, he mentioned Ogden's collection of furs that had been "killed on the East side of the Mountains on the Head Waters of the Missisourie." This revealed the brigade's passage across American soil.

McLoughlin was not alone in his nonchalant attitude toward national borders. Ever since the early days of fur trading, trappers had freely ignored boundaries, and although by 1825 that practice was disappearing from the Great Lakes region, it was still customary in the West. Furthermore, crossing the Rockies by way of the Missouri headwaters was the easiest way to reach the Snake, because the Continental Divide loops west and then east, and the trappers' route was a shortcut across the bulge of land. Governor Simpson himself, with no hint of disapproval, referred in his journal to "Letters from Mr. Ogden dated Sources of the Missouri." And McLoughlin had frankly recommended that the Snake party should "hunt all the head branches of Missouries" in order to "destroy the Inducements the American trappers from the other side have to push to the Head waters of the Columbia."

But when the Governor and Committee read his letter, their reaction was far from casual. Never having seen the fur lands, they could not visualize the difficulties of crossing the mountains in winter, and they saw only that Ogden had trespassed. They reminded Governor Simpson that "all collisions with the Americans should be avoided, as well as infringements on their Territory," and they bluntly told McLoughlin that "this should on no account whatever have been done, as it was never our wish that trapping parties should hunt beyond the neutral ground." They took it so seriously that they did not ask the American government to make reparation for the stolen goods, because they feared an investigation might bring embarrassing questions from the Foreign Office. They were mistaken, however, in thinking Ogden had trapped animals on American soil. The brigade had crossed the border and traded for skins caught there, but they had merely passed through, without stopping to set traps. All their hunts, as well as the desertions, had occurred west of the Rockies—in the Oregon Country or in today's Utah, which was then part of Mexico.

In the future McLoughlin would heed the Committee's warning, but in the fall of 1825 it had not yet come. Convinced that he must act at once, he took a canoe up the Columbia to Fort Nez Perces, where he waited until the remnants of the expedition came in—dejected, depleted in numbers, but bringing the "very handsome" and surprising returns of 3,188 made beaver. With results like this, it seemed wise to cash in on the rich source while it lasted, so he had the expedition reinforced and outfitted and sent it off within twelve days, on November 21. It was stronger than before, because he replaced the deserting freemen with regular employees, who were paid salaries and would be more dependable.

The brigade was replenished, but McLoughlin was still uneasy, for he remembered Ogden's warning about the "wide difference" in pay and the growing American post at Taos. Returning to Fort Vancouver, he pored over the huge, handwritten account books and discovered that the past year's cost per made beaver had been 10 shillings, 2½ pence, of which goods issued to the freemen accounted for only 2 shillings—less than 20 percent. The Snake brigade showed a net loss, but the trappers' pay—chiefly in goods—was not large enough to be the cause. After mulling it over, he concluded that the deficit was chiefly "incurred by desertion and by expences in sending clerks and servants to watch over" the freemen. From this he reasoned that if the company paid the trappers better, giving them an incentive for a sizeable catch, they would need less supervision, desertions would shrink, and costs would decline.

Moreover, when he examined individual accounts, he discovered that the company had indeed been charging so much and paying so little that even an expert trapper had to go into debt in order to buy his winter supplies. "Several have Killed a hundred and fifty made Beaver and this was not sufficient to pay their Hunting supplies and their Losses in Horses and traps stolen by the Natives," he told the Governor and Committee.

In his isolated post, McLoughlin's ability to make his own decisions was a major strength. He was painfully aware of the time lag if he wrote to London for advice; he thought he must find a solution at once or risk losing the more reliable men, and he therefore acted on his own responsibility, by drastically raising the men's pay per made beaver and lowering their costs. Instead of asking Simpson or the Committee for permission, he merely wrote to tell them what he had done.

> I can only say that urged by the necessity of the Case and in antici-
> pation of your approval I promised the Freemen 10 [shillings] for
> every large Beaver and half that sum for a cub. . . . I consider the
> measure will be advantageous to the Concern, and if we wished to
> retain these Men we had no alternative left.

Although it was a major change, upending the earlier policy, it was wise. In the following year, 1826, the brigade was strengthened by the presence of

Marguerite's son, Thomas McKay, as Ogden's chief aide, and by the new price system, which heartened its men. Conditions were still rough. Ogden's journal for March 14 [13], 1827, said,

> All obliged to sleep out and two-thirds without blankets to cover them. Still not one complain. This life makes a young man sixty in a few years. Wading in cold water all day, they earn 10 shillings P. beaver. A convict at Botany Bay is a Gentleman living at ease compared to them. Still they are happy. A roving life suits them.

In spite of the hardships, however, the men were so pleased with the new rates that none of them deserted. Ogden later told McLoughlin, "It is to be regretted that the present Plan had not been adopted many years since, for from the exorbitant price the Trappers paid for their Goods and horses is solely to be attributed their desertion and former misconduct."

During a heavy snowfall of the next winter, 1827–28, Ogden had a sweet revenge when he met a party of American trappers who had not learned to make snowshoes. Ogden rejected all their offers to buy equipment, and the local Indians, being loyal Hudson's Bay trading partners, refused to sell any or even carry letters to the rival depot at Salt Lake. On January 23 Ogden's journal said, "The American is now very low spirited. He cannot hire a man to go to his cache nor snowshoes, nor does he suspect that I prevented. This day he offered 8 beaver and $50 for a pair and a prime horse to anyone who would carry a letter to the American camp. In this also he failed." Two days later, he wrote with obvious relish, "They are making snowshoes themselves wh. they ought to have done 2 wks. ago."

Knowing that his stranded competitors could not hunt without suitable footwear, and unwilling to let them starve, Ogden supplied them with meat; and a few days later he had the pleasure of seeing them flounder off on their makeshift gear, headed for their countrymen at Salt Lake.

During that winter, trappers spread the news that McLoughlin had improved the pay scale. It made a difference, for in the spring, when Ogden saw some of his deserters, they told him they were "sorry they had left us and declared had they Anticipated any Reduction on the price of Goods they would have remained." They meant what they said, for during the next few years some of them returned to the brigade.

McLoughlin had run a risk in making this major change without authorization, but his strategy was successful, and the Governor and Committee approved.

They wrote that "we can afford to pay as good a price as the Americans, and where there is risk of meeting their parties it is necessary to pay as much or something more to avoid the risk of a result similar to that of Mr. Ogden. By attempting to make such expeditions too profitable the whole may be lost."

This was the first time, but it would not be the last, that the doctor took the reins into his own hands.

~ 4 ~

Ships & Their Captains
1825–1828

From Fort Vancouver, McLoughlin had only two lifelines to the rest of the world: express canoes from York Factory, which came every fall and left in the spring, carrying mail and traveling "light"—with no freight; and sailing ships from England, which brought food, trade goods, and equipment, took back furs, and served as links with the Sandwich Islands. The Governor and Committee wanted him to build up trade with the Indians on the Northwest Coast, but that would require an extensive use of deep-sea vessels, and he had never dealt with them before.

His first ship was the *William and Ann*, the one that arrived during the move from Fort George. She was a cedar brig of 161 tons, built in Bermuda in 1818 and purchased by the Hudson's Bay Company in 1824 for fifteen hundred pounds. On this, her initial company voyage, she not only needed repairs, she had not been properly loaded. In the opening paragraph of the doctor's first official letter from the Columbia, dated October 6, 1825, he wrote,

> I am sorry to say part of her Cargo was wet, fortunately the Dry Goods are not injured nor indeed is any part of the Cargo except the Flour and Meal. The Barrels of Both are very bad. . . . The Gunpowder is damper than any we have hitherto had and there is no appearance of Water having reached the Powder Barrels. The Pork and Beef are not so good as we have hitherto had and the Barrels are very bad, the Bricks are of a very inferior quality.

McLoughlin had the *William and Ann* repaired and sent her north along the coast, in accordance with her orders.

Trading by ships, called "coasting," was a new enterprise for the company; it would require him to provide goods, manpower, and advice, although he was chronically short of supplies and had never handled shipping before. For this first attempt, he assigned thirteen Kanakas to strengthen the brig's crew, and being a canny merchant, he "sent a share of every Trading Article in the Store" to see what sold best and to "find a Market for Several articles which are a dead Stock on our hands." Since Captain Hanwell had never dealt with Indians, McLoughlin also sent Alexander McKenzie, who "speaks the Chinook language and I consider is fully adequate to do all that was to be done." He told McKenzie to seize every opportunity for spreading news of the company's expansion, in hopes it would influence the Americans to withdraw. "They must be aware," he said, "that we can afford to undersell them by carrying on this business in conjunction with an . . . Inland Trade."

Although McLoughlin had hoped for profits, he was disappointed. Captain Hanwell took the *William and Ann* across the bar on June 2, 1825, and dutifully sailed north, but the coast was a maze of islands and straits, towering mountains, glaciers that came down to the sea, and glittering, blue-green chunks of floating ice. Neither the captain nor his men knew the area, and they had to deal with unfamiliar Indians, some of whom were friendly and some not. As a result, Hanwell was terrified. He gave McKenzie few chances to meet the natives, and spent a great deal of time in the few ports that to his frightened eyes seemed safe. He chanced to meet the American brig *Owhyhee*, whose Captain Kelly came on board, checked the *William and Ann*, and offered friendly advice, but Hanwell remained aloof. As McLoughlin reported,

> Captn Kelly was very communicative the short time he was on board the William & Ann told our people their vessel was not well arranged for the purpose of trade and defence, invited them on board his Vessel, and offered to shew them how she was arranged, and to shew them his Furs, but they did not avail themselves of his invitation.

Because of his timidity and ignorance, Hanwell brought back few furs and very little information. In utter disgust, McLoughlin wrote to Simpson that the captain would not "venture to enter Portland Canal" but sailed instead into Observatory Inlet, "where he was detained twenty nine days without ascertaining if any River discharged into it." After securing only thirty-seven beaver and five land otters, he had visited the Strait of Juan de Fuca, where he traded for skins that would have come to the company posts "by the usual route." McLoughlin considered this a waste of time, and Simpson agreed, saying that the captain's prudence "amounted to pusillanimity."

Although Hanwell wanted to unload his furs at Fort George, saying he could not go up the Columbia without orders, he yielded this point to Mc-Loughlin, who simply "direct[ed] him to come &c. which he accordingly did." It was a major event to have an oceangoing ship, white sails spread, come to anchor at Fort Vancouver, for it proved that the lower Columbia was navigable and ended the backbreaking job of moving goods upriver by boats or canoes. Nevertheless, the captain's trip had been a costly failure, and in addition he had sold liquor to the Indians, which prompted McLoughlin to write him an indignant note. "It is unfortunate the Captain Sells liquor to the Indians—It spoils them—we Sell No liquor to them on any account, Selling liquor to Indians is prohibited by a positive order of the Committee." In saying this, he expressed the official policy, not the reality of the trade. Even though the company dealt in alcohol as little as possible, the traders resorted to the sale of liquor when it was the only way to meet competition.

This first attempt at "coasting" had come to nothing, but for all his problems and all his sputtering to the captain, McLoughlin's official report said merely that he was "very much disappointed" because Hanwell had failed "from difficulties that could not be obviated," such as unfavorable winds. The Chief Factor was angry, but he was also fair. "In justice to him," he continued, "I must say that he always appeared to me most anxious to afford every Satisfaction to his Employers and in all probability his Zeal to act up to the Letter and purport of your Honors Instructions have misled him."

Frustrating though Hanwell's venture had been, he brought back one bit of useful information, for Captain Kelly had told him that six American ships were operating in the area. "There must be a good deal of business done on the Coast if there were six vessels this year on it," McLoughlin shrewdly observed. He decided that trading in the north would be worthwhile, but his recent experience convinced him that in order to succeed at "coasting," he must have authority over company vessels.

He also concluded that he must receive his supplies a year in advance, because otherwise a shipwreck might mean the loss of an entire season's returns. In addition, if he received his goods early, he could equip both land and sea expeditions and send them out in time to catch the lucrative spring trade. Year after year he pleaded for an early supply. "The late arrival of the vessel caused the Brigade to be detained longer at this place than suits the state of our Business in the Interior." "Of Several Articles for Sales to Servants we have this year not more than half the Quantity required in consequence of our not Receiving the additional requisition for Outfit 1826." "We can never do any thing in that branch of the business [coasting] till we have the Outfit a year in advance so as to be able to dispatch the Vessel on it in March."

In 1828 his workers lacked even cords for properly tying the furs, and as late as 1830 he noted that "if an opposition [American] had remained we would have been short of Guns and Green Blankets." The Chief Factor's requests would eventually be granted, but change in company policy was ponderously slow.

At this time, both McLoughlin and the London Committee favored a new and ambitious oceangoing venture—entry to the rich Asian market through an exchange of furs for teas, silks, spices, and other goods. They were, however, blocked by the East India Company, which had a charter-backed monopoly and had decreed that the Hudson's Bay Company could sell skins in Asia but could not carry away goods in exchange. It galled McLoughlin that if he accepted such terms, his ships would have to either sail back empty or merely transport merchandise for the other company, while his American competitors "had the benefit of freight for the whole voyage to China and back."

In the past, various attempts had been made to circumvent the East India Company's charter. The Nor'Westers in Fort George had delivered furs to Perkins & Company of Boston, whose captains took them to China, exchanged them for merchandise, and sailed back to New England, where they sold the goods and kept a percentage of the proceeds. After the coalition, the Hudson's Bay Company had tried the same plan, but it sliced into profits. Therefore, in 1824, "after some negociation," the Committee had signed a contract to sell directly to the East India Company, delivering furs and receiving Asian products in London. It was not a success. Within two years the other company declared it was a "losing concern to them even at the low price at which the Skins were charged." They gave it up, necessitating a return to the former restrictions, which, McLoughlin said, "operated against us as a premium in favor of the Americans." The East India Company remained in full control of the Asian trade, and he was stymied on that front.

Even without trading in China, however, he was so short of vessels that— never loath to try something new—he had a shipyard built at the water's edge. The project was a modest success. In 1826 the thirty-ton sloop *Broughton* was finished, and the *Vancouver*, sixty tons, needed only "to be decked and caulked to be Ready to Launch we have Masts and Spars prepared." Small as she was, the *Broughton* was useful on the Columbia River, but the larger *Vancouver* had multiple problems. Governor Simpson later said that because of "the want of Iron Works and of Iron of the proper sizes . . . the want of a Saw Mill, and the want of time to Season the Timber," her wood "became warped and contracted to such a degree, as to leave Seams so wide, that even with Sheathing it is doubtful they would hold the Oakum" in bad weather. In spite of her rocky start, the *Vancouver* was completed and put into service, but she marked the end of McLoughlin's efforts at shipbuilding. From then on he either secured his vessels from England or did without.

In June 1826, when the tardy *Dryad* finally arrived, her cargo was bad, and McLoughlin reported,

> I am sorry to have to Inform You, the Indian corn is so much injured by Insects that only its being Impossible to get other provisions can justify our giving it in its present state as food to our men. The Iron Especially that for Beaver traps say 3/8 Square Scrap is of a Worse quality than any hitherto sent which causes a Great Loss as by the Breaking of traps the Hunters cannot make the Hunts they would. The powder is very coarse. . . . Some of the Dry Goods are much Injured.

In addition, her captain had a personal problem. "Captn Davidsons talent as a Navigator I know nothing about, but his talent as a Grog Drinker I understand is without parallel," wrote George Simpson, and McLoughlin reported that the captain "is as much addicted to Grog as he is Represented in . . . Governor Simpson's Letter." But as he had with Hanwell, the doctor took pains to be fair. He added that Davidson was "most anxious to accomodate and assist; he Brought his vessel to Douglass's Reach [near Fort Vancouver] . . . Lent us his carpenter for fifteen Days and sent his Boatswain to make the Sails of the *Broughton* and his 2nd mate to finish putting Up her Rigging."

Although the *Dryad*'s late arrival prevented a coastal expedition in 1826, that year saw one noteworthy event: Lieutenant Æmelius Simpson of the Royal Navy—the man who brought the apple seeds—came in November with the express brigade from York Factory. Since he was Governor Simpson's cousin, some of the fort personnel thought he had his job through favoritism, but this was not so. He was a capable officer who was to serve the company well during his short life in the West.

Lieutenant Simpson had been sent to take command of the small schooner *Cadboro*, which arrived the following spring with a permanent assignment to the Columbia. She was new, having been built the year before at Rye, England, and purchased by the Hudson's Bay Company for eight hundred pounds. None of McLoughlin's ships was large, but even in his fleet she was a midget, being only seventy tons—about "fifty-six feet long, seventeen feet at her broadest part, depth of hold eight feet." She had two masts but only one deck, and she was so small that Governor Simpson bluntly said, "The 'Cadboro' is quite unfit for the Trade, there are hundreds of War Canoes on the Coast longer & higher out of the Water than she is." Nevertheless, she was a valiant little vessel, and McLoughlin was glad to have her permanently at hand. Moreover, from this time on, his supply ships were loaded with more skill. In 1827 the *Cadboro* delivered her cargo "in Good order," and the following year the merchandise brought by the *Eagle* was "in excellent condition."

Right from the start, one of McLoughlin's main goals was to establish a chain of forts on the north coast and minimize the use of ships. While George Simpson was on the Columbia in 1824, he had become interested in the Fraser River, which had a broad lower section with little hint of the roaring rapids upstream. Simpson had sent an expedition to explore part of it, and after receiving a favorable report, he convinced the Governor and Committee that it was a promising link to New Caledonia. In 1826 they had requested a post on the Fraser, and a year later Simpson confidently said it would "become our principal Depot for the country west of the Mountains." Although McLoughlin had heard frightful accounts of the upper river's perils, he nevertheless yielded to his superiors and prepared to build the fort.

He intended to use the *William and Ann* as transport, but Captain Hanwell was still too timid to risk his vessel. Since McLoughlin had no authority over captains, he resorted to the little *Cadboro* instead, sending her under young Lieutenant Simpson to sail down the Columbia and north along the coast, while Chief Trader James McMillan led a party overland.

McMillan left Fort Vancouver on June 27, 1827, "proceeded by the Cowlitz [River] across Land to Pugets Sound," and boarded the *Cadboro* there. The combined groups then continued north to the lower Fraser, where Simpson and his men helped construct the new post and remained "untill the Stockades of Fort Langley were Erected and two Bastions and a store Built."

With this accomplished, Lieutenant Simpson left McMillan and part of the crew at Fort Langley, while he himself took the *Cadboro* farther up the coast to trade. But he had started so late, with such limited supplies, that he "saw few furs with the natives and for which they asked a very high price, and traded only two Sea Otters at the rate of six Blankets 2½ pts. and a Calico shirt

Fort Langley, built in 1827 near the mouth of the Fraser River, was the first northern post erected by McLoughlin. George Simpson envisioned it as the future headquarters, but the middle Fraser was not navigable, and could not be used as a depot for supplying posts of the interior. Instead, Langley became important as a shipping center for the coast. OHS ORHI 97458

for Each, and twenty Eight Beaver and Land Otters at a calico shirt Each." The "2½ pts." referred to stripes woven into the edge of the blanket, indicating its weight. A 2½-point blanket had three stripes—two long (about six inches) and one short. It weighed 2½ pounds.

The expedition proved disastrous, because on the way back, while five of his crew were on shore getting fresh water, a man was murdered and a boy wounded by the natives. When McLoughlin heard about it, he called it "shocking proof" of the fur trade's hazards, and said that "a Vessel must be strongly manned to insure the safety of the Crew." For this, his first conflict with the natives, he did not feel ready to retaliate. But he did not forget.

He also found that even though the *Cadboro* and *Broughton* were permanently at hand, he had trouble manning them, because many company contracts forbade sailors to serve on alternate vessels, and the men themselves were often reluctant to make a change. Lieutenant Simpson suggested a solution—that the company should adopt new terms of engagement obligating crews "to Exchange into the Vessel Employed upon the coast if Required." The idea pleased McLoughlin. He forwarded it to London and the Committee adopted it, enabling him to move men from vessel to vessel as they were needed.

Even before he received this authority, he began to use his scarce shipping to develop trade in California and the Sandwich Islands. In November 1827, when Lieutenant Simpson brought the *Cadboro* back from founding Fort Langley, McLoughlin sent him to Monterey to purchase "about three hundred Bushels salt, three Hundred Bushels Indian Corn, about thirty Barrels salted provisions, twenty Barrels flour and twenty firkins Butter." Believing that "we must avail ourselves of all the resources of this Country if we have to Compete for the trade of it with the Americans as we may depend they will turn every thing they possibly can to account," he ordered Simpson to inquire about a market for timber and salmon.

On his return, the lieutenant reported that he could sell planks in California for forty to fifty dollars per thousand feet, and salmon for thirty dollars per 250-pound barrel. The company had previously tried to send salted salmon to England, only to have it spoil; but Monterey was closer, and products sent there arrived in marketable condition. As early as 1830, McLoughlin had nearly three hundred barrels of fish exported from Fort Langley to California and the Sandwich Islands, and in 1836 he wrote that "the expense of keeping up the Establishment at Fort Langley is in general paid by the Salmon Trade."

Soon after McLoughlin came, he also began the shipment of "deals"—boards of several sizes, cut at a small sawmill on a tributary to the Columbia a few miles east of Fort Vancouver. He sent them to California and the Sandwich Islands, a prospect that entranced Governor Simpson. When he came on a tour of inspection in 1828, he envisioned a lumber operation that "might prove as profitable as the entire coastal fur trade," and made a rosy prediction of 200,000 board feet per year, at sixty dollars per thousand feet and a total expense of only £150. But he was too sanguine, for these ventures yielded only modest profits.

It is nevertheless worth noting that in McLoughlin's first three years on the Columbia, with limited manpower and one supply ship per year plus the little *Cadboro* and *Broughton*, he was shipping goods to California, buying sugar products in the Sandwich Islands, and developing a market there for lumber, flour, and salmon.

He continued to expand. In 1829 he sent Lieutenant Simpson to investigate the possibility of trade with "the Russian Establishment of New Archangel," in the north. A year later he looked toward the south and dispatched a vessel "to Lima, touching on her way at California and perhaps at Acapulca with Salmon or Boards to ascertain the demand and price of these articles."

In 1834 one of his captains rescued three Japanese sailors who had been stranded on the coast by a typhoon and a "sickness" that carried off the rest of the crew. As McLoughlin told the Governor and Committee, he could have sent them to the Sandwich Islands and left them "to find a passage to their own country the best way they could," but instead he had them taken to England on the *Eagle*. "I believe they are the first Japanese who have been in the power of the British Nation," he told the Committee. He explained that he thought the Foreign Office would be glad for the opportunity "to open a communication with the Japanese Government," and hoped the men "might convey to their countrymen a respectable idea of the grandeur and power of the British nation."

Unfortunately McLoughlin's plan did not work out as he had hoped, for the government of Japan did not allow the three to return, and they lived out their lives as exiles in China. McLoughlin's attempt, however, was an example of his interest in the international scene. Even in his earliest years on the Columbia, he was anticipating the Pacific Rim.

~ 5 ~

Establishing Peace
1828–1829

Legend says that when McLoughlin came to the Columbia, he achieved immediate peace with the Indians. But that does not square with the facts, for he had several violent encounters, and some distant tribes were permanently hostile. He did, however, build friendship with those along the river and near his forts, based on his company's dual system: to respect the natives, treat them fairly, and make no effort to change their beliefs or way of life; but to respond with vigor if they harmed property or personnel. He wrote that every man in the company was ordered to be kind to the Indians, "and fully understood that any act of wanton murder would expose him to the penalties of a capital indictment in the criminal courts of Canada." It was a humane policy, but also a practical one. As he explained:

> We are traders, and apart from more exalted motives, all traders are desirous of gain. Is it not self evident we will manage our business with more economy by being on good terms with Indians than if at variance. We trade furs, none can hunt fur bearing animals or afford

to sell them cheaper, than Indians. It is therefore clearly our interest, as it is unquestionably our duty to be on good terms with them and the Indians of the Columbia are not such poltroons as to suffer themselves to be illtreated, particularly when the disparity of numbers is so great as to show but one white man to 200 Indians.

Many surviving anecdotes tell of McLoughlin's personal kindness toward the natives. His daughter Eloisa said, "The whites themselves sometimes troubled Indians and then they complained to my Father. He put men in irons who treated the Indians badly. That is the way they kept peace with the Indians." The French Canadian Francis Xavier Matthieu wrote that once, when an Indian was charged with a serious offense, McLoughlin ordered, "Tie him to that cannon. Give him fifteen lashes." Later, when a white man committed the same offense, his punishment was the same. And John Ball, who came west in 1832, said, "The Indians we found always peaceable, these traders having had the good sense and tact to keep them so, by always keeping faith and a good understanding with them."

Closely related to the policy of kindness was respect for the Indians' customs, with a realization that they had their own laws and government, which were not to be disturbed. In 1831–32, when a Cayuse killed a Snake Indian in a dispute over a calf, McLoughlin advised the leader of nearby Fort Walla Walla to let the natives handle it in their own way. "God forbid that I should mean to justify murder," he wrote, "but in dealing with the Indians we ought to make allowance for their manner of thinking."

Still another factor in building friendship was the Indians' desire for British goods and expertise. In 1826, when McLoughlin considered moving Fort Nez Perces—Walla Walla—to the opposite side of the Columbia, "all the Chiefs Exclaimed against it and offerred Horses and Beaver Skins" to have it remain. Their opposition was so strong that the doctor decided moving the fort would expose it to danger, and he left it in place.

This arm of the company policy was benevolent, but the other arm—quick retaliation for an attack—was cast in iron, and it could be ruthless. The London Committee and officers in the field were uncomfortably aware that their men were outnumbered, and they firmly believed they must show strength in order to be safe. The Indians understood this attitude and respected it, because it was rooted in their own concept of justice. They themselves retaliated with force—sometimes tribe against tribe—in case of a wrong. Numerous instances could be cited, such as the warfare that broke out during the move to Fort Vancouver.

INDIAN ENCAMPMENT, PUGET SOUND, WASHINGTON TERRITORY.

This scene could be the Clallam village at the base of today's Dungeness Spit. These are their temporary lodges, covered with woven mats and used only in summer. The Clallams chief foods came from the sea, and cedar trees were useful for canoes, utensils, building materials and clothing. OHS ORHI 4464

In 1827, when the man from the *Cadboro* was killed, McLoughlin did not order retaliation. But the following June, he learned that while a Hudson's Bay party was returning from Fort Langley, the Clallams of Hood Canal—a heavily wooded area west of Puget Sound—had killed Alexander McKenzie and four *engagés* and seized a woman who was accompanying her husband. The reason for the assault is not known, but McLoughlin said the tribe attacked "without having had the least difference with our people," that they did so "merely for the sake of the apparel & Arms" and then "sent us word to come & revenge it, that they were ready." Deeply worried, he wrote:

> To pass over such an outrage would lower us in the opinion of the Indians, induce them to act in the same way, and when an opportunity offered kill any of our people, & when it is considered the Natives are at least an hundred Men to one of us it will be conceived

how absolutely necessary it is for our personal security that we should be respected by them, & nothing could make us more contemptible in their eyes than allowing such a cold blooded assassination of our People to pass unpunished.

Aware of the Indians' respect for strength, he declined the help offered by several Columbia River tribes, because he wanted to avoid any hint that company men could not protect themselves.

Shortly afterward, while he was preparing an expedition against the Clallams, the supply ship *Eagle* sailed up the Columbia River. Since she was a "strong burthensome Vessel" of 193 tons, it would have been logical to use her for transport, but her captain, John Costello Grave, had instructions only "to come to the Columbia & Return direct to England." Grave was willing to use the brig if McLoughlin would take the responsibility, but the doctor considered it unwise because it might "vitiate the Insurance." Instead, he had Chief Trader Alexander Roderick McLeod take a party of fifty-nine servants and freemen by land, while the little *Cadboro* under Lieutenant Simpson set out to meet them at Admiralty Inlet, just north of Hood Canal. The Chief Factor gave McLeod oral instructions to rely on his own judgment, to punish the tribe while remaining "cautious and prudent," and to "get the Woman who was with our people." He considered this important, because of "the influence her father had amongst his tribe to do mischief to the whites," and he insisted that "her liberty was at any consideration to be obtained."

McLeod set out on June 17, 1828, and returned on July 15, after which McLoughlin reported that he had "accomplished the object of his voyage & recov[er]ed the woman . . . without one of our party receiving the least wound or injury."

The cost in native lives, however, had been high. After a lengthy parley, during which the Indians tried to lure the Bay men into ambush, McLeod had ordered Lieutenant Simpson to fire "a few Cannon Shot," landed a force under cover of the barrage, and "burnt the Village with all their property & forty six Canoes." The natives then surrendered the woman in exchange for one of their number who had been captured, and the Hudson's Bay party started back to the Columbia, stopping on the way to destroy another village. Approximately twenty Clallams had been killed, in addition to two slain by the Indians themselves.

This was more destruction than McLoughlin had intended, and he lamented that "it is certainly most unfortunate to be obliged to have recourse to hostile measures against our fellow beings." He still, however, believed that the expedition had been necessary.

> It is a duty we owed our murdered Countrymen & I may say we were forced by necessity, as had we passed over the atrocious conduct of their Murderers, others by seeing them unpunished would have imitated their example & whenever an opportunity offered have murdered any of us that fell in their way, and I beg to assure your Honors that before I decided on this measure I gave it every consideration its importance deserved.

He soon learned that some of his men also thought the action unfortunate. William Todd called it "a failure," and a young clerk, Francis Ermatinger, remarked within McLoughlin's hearing, "For my part I do not wish to go on such Expeditions again we have disgraced ourselves."

Before setting out, McLeod had ordered Ermatinger to keep a journal, and it was full of complaints, most of which criticized the expedition's leadership rather than the company's purpose. It said McLeod had not kept his troops informed, that he conferred with French Canadian workmen in their own language, that Indian property was destroyed without an offer to trade for the woman's freedom "at the price of a few Blankets," and that the Indians had not been told that the expedition was a retaliation for the attack on McKenzie. In several significant passages, the document revealed a conflict between sympathy and the need for security, as when Ermatinger regretted the damage to Indian property but confessed, "I wish we had been allowed to do more to the rascals themselves."

The journal, which Ermatinger freely showed to other clerks, became well known throughout the area, setting off a spate of angry correspondence. McLoughlin ordered the clerk to provide copies for Fort Vancouver and Governor Simpson. Ermatinger refused to supply more than one. The Chief Factor threatened to send him to York Factory. When the London Committee heard of the squabble and asked for particulars, McLoughlin defended McLeod by saying, "There seems to me a most anxious Desire through out the Journal to find fault." He said he had never known of a punitive expedition about which someone did not "conceive that either too much or too little had been done, and it is but justice to all in charge of such Expeditions to state they are the most disagreeable Duty to which a person can be appointed to take Charge of and extremely difficult to manage." With this the Committee agreed, although they thought McLeod had gone too far. When punishment was begun, they said, "there must be no chance of defeat," as that would endanger every post"; but it should be done "as mercifully as possible."

THE NEXT TROUBLE WITH NATIVES, which began only three weeks after McLeod's return, involved Americans. About ten o'clock on the night of August 8, 1828, the sleeping Fort Vancouver was aroused by a tremendous clamor at the gate. When attendants opened it, they found a group of Tillamook Indians supporting a man, faint with hunger and so exhausted he could scarcely stand. Late as it was, they summoned McLoughlin, to whom the man identified himself as a trapper named Arthur Black, probably the only survivor of a brigade under Jedediah Smith, who had been trading in today's southern Oregon. Smith and two others had briefly left the brigade to look for a place to cross the Bridge River, and during their absence the other men had allowed "about a hundred" Kelawatsets—a small tribe of that area—to enter camp. Almost at once, the Indians attacked. Black, who was wounded, "rushed to the woods," to wander until friendly Tillamooks found him and brought him to the fort. He thought it unlikely that Smith or any of the other men were still alive.

Appalled by the tragedy and concerned about possible survivors, McLoughlin paid the Tillamooks well and asked them to search for others. Two days later, to everyone's astonishment, Smith himself, with two of his followers, stumbled through the fort gate, having fled and survived on "a few wild berries which he found on the beach." Saying that all the rest—fifteen men—had been killed, Smith insisted that the attack had occurred because his trappers had merely "secured an Indian & tied him" until a missing axe was returned. He admitted to McLoughlin, however, that before reaching the Umpqua River, his party had fought "two skirmishes with the natives," resulting in the death of two Indians. And Smith's own journal records confrontations that caused nine or more other killings as he came north from California.

Jedediah Smith was a partner in the American firm of Smith, Sublette and Jackson. More than six feet tall, he was a strong, active man who had lost part of one eyebrow in an altercation with a grizzly bear. He disapproved of swearing and using liquor to exploit the natives; he was devoted to prayer; he quoted from the Bible, Methodist hymns, and writings of ancient Greece; and he was planning to publish a book of memoirs. The British had heard of him before, because it was Smith and six followers who had spent the winter at the Flathead Post and set out with Peter Skene Ogden on the ill-fated Snake expedition of 1824–25.

Alarmed at the "melancholy intelligence," McLoughlin was in a dilemma. The incident involved Americans, not his own men, and yet he was convinced that all Europeans would be in danger if he ignored it.

> I know many people will argue that we have no right to make war on the Natives, on the other hand if the business is drop[p]ed, will not our personal security be endangered wherever this report reaches. . . is it not our duty as Christians to endeavour as much as possible to prevent the perpetration of such atrocious crimes—& is their any measure so likely to accomplish so effectually this object as to make these Murderers restore at least the illgotten booty now in their possession.

He decided to investigate and if possible recover the property, estimated as 228 horses and mules, 780 beaver, and 50 or 60 land otters, along with a few sea otters and a large stock of beads, goods, and tobacco.

In the past, he had sent a few brigades into southern Oregon, where the tribes had seemed unfriendly and fearful. In 1826–27, while trapping along the Rogue River, Ogden had learned that the Indians depended on beaver for food and were frightened by rumors that the whites had "no intention but to seize them as Slaves." The natives had shot several of the trappers' horses, but did not attack the men. In the same winter, A. R. McLeod, nearer the coast, had found the Indians independent of beaver as food, but reluctant to trade and quick to "grumble at our presumption in trapping without paying the tribute." He had secured a few furs and distributed trinkets to the Umpquas and other coastal tribes. One Indian was killed when he was hauling a canoe up the riverbank and a gun lying in its bow accidentally went off. The Indians then took revenge by killing one of the company's Iroquois trappers, but there was no further loss of life. Neither Ogden nor McLeod succeeded in building a trade relationship, but they avoided outright violence.

It was in the following year, 1828, that Smith's expedition was annihilated. Since McLeod knew the area and since he was already slated to take a brigade south, McLoughlin ordered him to travel by way of the Kelawatsets, investigate the reason for their attack, punish them only if it seemed justified, try to recover the Americans' goods, and then continue into California. He gave Smith permission to go along, telling him, "McLeod knows these Indians

UMPQUA VILLAGE, HALF MILE BELOW FORT UMPQUA.

The Umpquas were a coastal tribe. Ogden and Work tried to establish trading relations with them but had little success. However, the Umpquas helped McLeod recover the goods of Jedediah Smith. This scene, published in *Frank Leslie's Illustrated Newspaper* in April 1858, shows a typical Umpqua village of long houses built close to the ground. It was half a mile to Fort Umpqua, which McLoughlin built in 1836. OHS ORHI 45811

and knows best whether we can effect any good, he will decide what is to be done." And to McLeod he gave written instructions:

> You know those Indians you know our means, and as a failure in undertaking too much, would make this unfortunate affair worse— & as you are on the spot—you therefore will decide on what is best to be done and depend that whatever that decision may be at least as far as I am concerned every allowance will be made for the situation you are placed in.

As might have been expected, some of the trappers were not pleased. "This was not a very popular measure either with the men or gentlemen," wrote William Todd, "as it was thought we would have difficulty enough to hold our own being already at war to the northward but the Dr. would have his way."

Knowing the Umpquas, McLeod went to them first, and they helped him contact the Kelawatsets. He learned that after hearing of Smith's ruthlessness in northern California, these Indians were convinced that the Americans "were Enemies destroying all the Natives that came within their reach." In addition, they were humiliated because one of their men had been tied up

This scene, also from the April 1858 *Frank Leslie's Illustrated Newspaper*, shows the Umpqua Indians of the coast. There is an infant in a traditional cradle board, and in the background several men are using axes for making a dugout canoe. OHS ORHI 45812

when the axe was missing, and they resented the Americans' slaughter of beaver, a major source of food. The violence, they said, had been triggered when an influential warrior, "wishing to ride a horse for amusement about the Camp," had mounted one, at which a trapper insulted him by brusquely, gun in hand, ordering him to get off. In addition, the Indians said that Smith and his men had boasted that they intended to drive the British from the Columbia, "where we were intruders on their territory." The Kelawatset chief, St. Arnose, said he was surprised that the "King George men"—the British—were "aiding and assisting People that evinced evil intentions" toward them.

McLoughlin later wrote that the Americans, disregarding Smith's orders, had admitted the Indians into camp in order "to gratify their passion for women," and George Simpson, who had recently come to the Columbia, made a similar and more detailed statement in his official report. Neither of them cited a source, and they may have been mistaken, for no other known documents express that view. It is, however, clear that after hearing about the Indians' well-founded fear, their depleted food supply, the American threats, and the insults, McLeod concluded that Smith's party had at least in part brought on its own disaster, so he did not punish the tribe.

Instead he traveled with his Umpqua guides from village to village, listening to the Indians, assuring them that the British wanted peace but were determined to recover Smith's property, and offering gifts and items of trade. In this way he managed to secure a limited amount of the stolen goods—"from

7 to 800 Beaver & Otter Skins in a very damaged state, 40 Horses, and a few other articles of little value." Leaving most of his brigade on the Umpqua, he and a small group carried the goods to Fort Vancouver, which they reached on December 14.

By then Governor Simpson had arrived on a tour of inspection. Although he approved of aid to the Americans, he wrote a curious letter to Smith, alternately generous and carping. He said that "the Gentlemen here [have] the most lively feelings of Sympathy" for Smith's misfortune, but that the "Melancholy catastrophe was occasioned by some harsh treatment on the part of your people." He renounced any claim for damages, but noted that the recovery of the property had entailed "an expense of exceeding £1000." He offered to buy Smith's beaver or keep it at Fort Vancouver until the Americans were able to remove it, but called it "of very bad quality the worst indeed I ever saw." And he assured Smith that he and his followers could remain at the "Establishment" and would be given passage "free of expense" to Red River settlement in the summer, when Simpson and his followers returned.

Proud, insulted, Smith offered reimbursement, but the governor refused to accept it. The Americans then took leave of McLoughlin and went cross-country into northern Idaho, where Smith assumed command of his firm's other brigades. While he was at Fort Vancouver, he had promised that his men would not compete with the Hudson's Bay trappers, and he honored that promise, keeping his brigades on the east side of the Rockies. Although he intended to write a book, he was killed in 1831 while on the Santa Fe Trail.

As for McLeod, his decision to personally bring the goods to Fort Vancouver disgusted McLoughlin. He sputtered to Ogden that the trapper had "loitered his time" and that "had he pushed forward . . . he would have been in the Clamette Country if not across the Bonnaventura [near today's Sacramento] mountains." To McLeod himself he wrote, "I neaver meant or expected you were to run along the Coast from place to place for a few articles. My Idea was that you Should go to the main band of the murderers and make them return what they had and which I conceived you Could have done without any great loss of time."

In January 1829, McLeod left Vancouver to rejoin his men, but his expedition was a failure. His party lost its horses in crossing the Bonnaventura [Sacramento] River; he had serious conflicts with the Indians of northern California; and he brought back very few furs. The disaster reinforced McLoughlin's disillusionment with his aide, and both men were doubtless relieved in 1831 when McLeod was transferred to the Mackenzie District. His reputation had been damaged, for he had been slated for promotion to the rank of Chief Factor but did not receive it for nearly a decade.

NOT LONG AFTER SMITH LEFT FORT VANCOUVER, and while Governor Simpson was still there, McLoughlin had his third major confrontation with Indians, this time with those on the nearby coast. On March 10, 1829, when the *William and Ann* tried to cross the bar in a storm, she "split from stern [stem] to stern." Half of the hull was found on the beach with "a few triffles of Cargo," and the crew were missing and presumed drowned.

This was a severe loss of men and equipment, causing such a shortage of supplies that McLoughlin wrote to Donald Manson at Fort George, "I send you Every thing you ask Except the Guns Which we have not and of course this must be Kept a secret even to our own people." He advised Manson to "Evade the Demand by saying you omitted to write for them or that I did not send them or that I object to sell our Guns for four Skins—as may best suit your purposes." He had to lend his own rifle to Ogden's brigade, and he was "reluctant to Supply Traps to the Indians as we are so short of Goods it may be enableing them to hunt when we will not have wherewith to pay for the furs they Kill."

For several weeks rumors drifted up the river saying that the Indians of the coast had plundered the *William and Ann* and murdered the crew, and by March 25, 1829, when Governor Simpson left for Canada, the question was not yet resolved. At first McLoughlin thought the reports so unreliable that he "defferred taking such measures as so atrocious a deed deserved." But in June a well-known and trusted chief—possibly Casseno—came upriver to tell him that a headman of the Clatsops admitted that his people had picked up twenty-one bales of goods from the wreckage, with no one to protest because "all the crew had been drowned." When McLoughlin received this reliable information, he decided he must act.

Since William Connolly, Chief Factor of New Caledonia, had come to Vancouver to help distribute trade goods, McLoughlin sent him posthaste to overtake the *Cadboro*, which had recently set sail for Fort Langley, and the following day he dispatched forty-four men and five officers in four boats. When they overtook the *Cadboro*, Connolly, as ranking officer, led them down the Columbia to the Clatsop village, where he demanded the missing goods. But "his Messenger returned with an old Brush and a Scoop and said the Clatsops told him take this to your Chief and tell him this is all he will get."

In response, the men prepared to land, and when the Clatsops "fired at the Vessels," "some Balls went through the Bull works." The boats then returned fire, killing one Indian. The rest fled, and the party landed to search and burn the village. As they expected, they found evidence that the Indians had the goods, such as "Rum in Canoes and some in two Punchons which the natives had buried in their Lodges."

A few days later, company search parties discovered five crew members' bodies, dead for several months and in various locations on the beach. One was that of Captain Swan, which had obviously not been molested, for "there was no mark of Violence on the body and two Watches were found on him." After considering all the evidence, McLoughlin concluded that the crew had been drowned, not murdered, although he said that "still several of the gentlemen here think they were." One of the doubters was Governor Simpson, who had left by then but later reported that he was unconvinced.

Even though the material recovered was negligible, McLoughlin thought the destruction of a village would ensure the future safety of his men and possessions—a decision that was later justified, because when other company ships were wrecked, such as the *Isabella* in 1830, the cargo was not disturbed.

These three campaigns of 1828–29—at Puget Sound, the Umpqua River, and the coast—were followed by years of peace and friendship with the Columbia tribes. In 1832 Dr. William Tolmie described the Indian camp in the forest near Fort Vancouver, where the natives gathered in large numbers, performed religious devotions, and danced in a circle "two deep and went round and round," chanting as they moved. Later in that decade, when a fever epidemic decimated the tribes, hundreds of Indians came to Vancouver for medical care, "giving as a reason that if they died they Knew we would Bury them."

The more remote areas, however, remained hostile. Samuel Black, head of Fort Kamloops in today's British Columbia, was killed by a young man who blamed him for giving "bad medicine" that caused a chief's death. In the Blackfoot country of today's Idaho and Montana, Ogden lost two men in 1828, Work lost two in 1831 and five in 1837, and Indian lives were taken in retaliation several other times. In 1832 the Tillamooks on the coast murdered two Hudson's Bay trappers, for which McLoughlin sent out a punitive expedition under Michel Laframboise. The southern brigade through the Rogue River country and northern California had repeated confrontations with natives, some of them fatal. In 1836 McLoughlin had Fort Umpqua built at the mouth of that river, where some of the tribes were friendly, but the area was never secure. In 1837 the chief of the powerful Shastas of mountainous northern California sent an armed escort to make sure the Hudson's Bay trappers were safe. This precaution, said McLoughlin's top aide, James Douglas, "prevented the numberless causes of mutual exasperation," which had previously caused "the worst evils."

But all of these were distant tribes except the Tillamooks, and they were on the coast. The Columbia valley was peaceful, and there would be no major uprisings until after McLoughlin's retirement. Immensely proud of his friendship with the natives, he later said that formerly "it was not considered safe to travel up or down this river with less than 60 men, armed with muskets and fixed bayonets. Now even strangers can come down the River from the Snake Country by twos and threes." Peace along the river would ultimately smooth the way for early immigrants.

Creating this friendly relationship was only one of McLoughlin's major achievements. He is sometimes pictured as a kindly, benevolent gentleman with an unfortunate temper, but he was far more than that. He was an astute businessman with a global outlook, a man who had a vast knowledge of the diverse ramifications of the fur trade and the ability to weave many threads simultaneously. To these qualities he added a good, solid sense for the practical, the decisiveness of a true leader, and compassion for all humanity. During his first four years at Fort Vancouver, he began the major industries of the area, reorganized his company's largest trapping brigade, started a chain of posts in the north, instituted the use of company ships as coasters, won respect from the neighboring Indians, and established his authority over the district's posts—a tremendous list of accomplishments, with limited resources and in so short a time.

The officials in London were aware of this and roundly approved. "Indeed your whole management is marked by a degree of energy, zeal and activity highly creditable to yourself, important to the interests of the service and meeting our warmest commendation," said the Governor and Committee in 1829. In the same year Governor Simpson wrote, "Your whole administration . . . is conspicuous for a talent in planning and for an activity & perseverance in execution which reflect the highest credit on your judgement and habits of business."

McLoughlin would still have to face severe problems—drawbacks in the site of Fort Vancouver, operating a business within the labyrinth of joint occupation, meeting a flood of American settlers—but he was riding high.

CHAPTER 6

The Second Fort Vancouver

In a word, Vancouver is the grand emporium of the company's trade west of the Rocky Mountains.

JOHN DUNN

~ 1 ~

The Grand Emporium
1828–1829

Not long after moving into Fort Vancouver, McLoughlin realized that the site was seriously flawed, because it was more than a mile from the river, and every item of cargo, every pack of furs, every catch of fish, had to be carted in over "a high and rugged road." Moreover, there were no springs on the bluff, and all attempts to dig a usable well had failed. Years later, Dr. William McKay remembered that an old French Canadian employee named La Pierre drove a squealing oxcart down to the river and back twice a day, through summer's dust and winter's mud. "The wheels of his wagon were sawed off a fir log," said McKay. "On these were two puncheons, or casks, which were filled and well lashed on, and the whip was then applied to Lion and Brandy, the two great oxen, as they travelled to the fort."

McLoughlin had selected the location because it was easy to defend and safe from spring floods, but when he found that the water did not rise as high as expected, and that neighboring tribes were friendly, he began to consider a move to lower ground. He could not select a location, however, because the agreement of joint occupation would expire in 1828, and the boundary dispute had not been settled. Neither Britain nor America greatly valued the Columbia, but they both still wanted Puget Sound as a gateway to China, and their mutual dislike exacerbated the dispute. It had been only half a century since the Revolutionary War, and sixteen years since the War of 1812. Britons regarded America as "a rebellious and ungrateful child that had twice . . . made war on its parent," while Americans, in letters to editors and speeches in Congress, began to talk of military stations at the mouth of the Columbia or the entrance to Puget Sound.

McLoughlin himself was doubtful of Fort Vancouver's future. As early as 1825, he warned the Governor and Committee that if Britain lost the land south of the Columbia, the company could not "establish a Post on the north Bank that will pay the Expenses of keeping it up," and that "it is impossible to select the most Eligible situation for a Depot" because of the unsettled boundary. Two years later he repeated the warning, and told Governor Simpson that if they lost the south side of the river, they would be deprived of "the whole of the Snake trade, nine tenths of the Walla Walla, Willameth and a fourth of that of Spokane . . . though it is mortifying to be obliged to abandon a business after such pains have been taken and such expences incurred to organize and establish it, yet it is preferable to do so than to carry on a loosing concern."

His problem was solved when he heard—probably in the spring of 1828— that on August 6, 1827, Britain and America had again failed to decide on the border and had renewed the convention of joint occupation "indefinitely." It meant that for at least a few years, he could operate both north and south of the Columbia, and that he could choose a location for the new fort.

At that time he, Governor Simpson, and the London Committee each advocated a different site. McLoughlin favored the Columbia because of its access to upriver posts. The Committee wished to settle farther north. And Simpson preferred the mouth of the Fraser River, because he thought it supremely safe from the Americans, and an excellent link to company posts in New Caledonia. He had been impressed by the Fraser ever since his tour of inspection in 1824, when James McMillan reported that it was "a fine large bold stream and not barred by dangerous rapids or falls." McLoughlin, however, knew that McMillan had investigated only the lower Fraser. He warned the Governor and Committee that according to firsthand accounts, the Fraser was "difficult and dangerous," and that a great part of it was unnavigable "in the Summer Months."

Simpson himself blew hot and cold. In 1826 he informed the British Foreign Office that because of the river's rapids and falls, "it is not my opinion that it affords a communication by which the interior Country can be supplied from the Coast." But a year later he recommended using it, "if the navigation . . . be practicable of which from the various reports that have reached us there can be no doubt." Finally, in 1828, when he paid a second visit to the Columbia, he decided to descend the Fraser and see it for himself.

On July 12, Simpson and his party set out from York Factory in two canoes— with a bugler in one and a bagpiper in the other, to make a grand entrance at forts along the way. His trek across the Athabasca and the Rockies was routine. But when he ventured into the middle Fraser, his frail craft was tossed beyond control by the churning rapids of a gorge, which was bounded by sheer rock cliffs and echoed with thunderous falls. He said his canoe "shot like the flight of an Arrow, into deep whirlpools which seemed to sport in twirling us about and passing us from one to another, until their strength became exhausted . . . leaving our water logged craft in a sinking state. In this manner, the greater part of two Days was occupied."

Simpson and his party had such a narrow escape that when he finally reached safety, he made an about-face, gamely telling the Governor and Committee, "I should consider the passage down, to be certain Death, in nine attempts out of Ten. I shall therefore no longer talk of it as a navigable stream, altho' for years past I had flattered myself with the idea, that the loss of the Columbia would in reality be of very little consequence to the Honble. Coys. interests on this side [of] the Continent."

He and McLoughlin then decided on a new location for Fort Vancouver, about four hundred yards from the Columbia and a mile west of the first fort—close enough to use the same fields and orchards. Not many details of the move have survived, but some of the structures, including McLoughlin's house, were torn down and rebuilt on the new site. Jedediah Smith, who spent the winter of 1828–29 there, said work began in the spring on a large courtyard, "three hundred feet square, about three quarters of a mile lower down and within two hundred yards of the river."

That fall could not have been comfortable. By September 6, all the "Gentlemen"—Chief Factors, Chief Traders, and clerks—were housed in lodges or tents, while the main residence was taken down and its timbers moved. By October 9, the workmen "began to put up the Posts of the Big House," and by November 2 it was deemed "ready to enter." It was not, however, completed, nor was the rest of the fort.

Nevertheless, rough as it was, this was the beginning of the great Fort Vancouver, hub of the old Northwest. By the time it was built, New Caledonia had been attached to the Columbia District, which made McLoughlin the virtual ruler of the entire sweep of land between the Rockies and the Pacific, from Alaska to the northern border of California. From his headquarters he dispatched orders, mail, and supplies to the other posts—sent land brigades north, south, and into the interior—sent ships to California, Hawaii, South America, and Alaska. At Fort Vancouver he would make his home for nearly two decades, and give lifesaving assistance to American immigrants.

Many of the new fort's visitors were eloquent about the beautiful setting. William Fraser Tolmie, a pleasant, rather stout young Scottish physician who came in 1832, told about his walk on the surrounding plateau, "admiring the

Fort Vancouver, as sketched by Henry J. Warre in 1845. OHS ORHI 803

rich groves of lupin seen amidst the trees mixing with handsome columbines, sunflowers & a great variety of other herbaceous plants in flower." Saying that his heart "bounded with delight & enthusiasm," he described "the colossal Mount Hood" and the Columbia flowing "placidly & majestically along." He also, unfortunately, was interested in "a bushy animal with a large cocked tail, striped white & brown," at which he "let fly & soon settled his hash. Immediately thereafter a most diabolical smell declared him to be a pole cat."

The new fort was enclosed by a stockade of twenty-foot poles, with a massive gate toward the river and another in back. These were probably seven to fourteen feet wide, six or seven inches thick, and heavily studded with large nails, with a small door cut into the center of each for a single person to enter.

Only the most essential buildings were put up at first, with others added as manpower allowed. In 1834 the visiting physician and naturalist John Kirk Townsend said there were ten or twelve major structures—a number that did not include the smaller sheds and "necessaries." The larger ones were dwellings, storehouses, the bakery, and shops for blacksmiths, carpenters, joiners, and a tinner, with a brick or stone powder magazine placed in a corner. Most of them were erected on the customary Hudson's Bay plan of placing sills close to the ground, attaching grooved uprights to the sills, and sliding horizontal timbers into the grooves. The "Big House"—McLoughlin's home—had its main floor elevated several feet, with storage space beneath. There was a piazza across the front from which a double curved stairway led down to the court-yard, and four cannon—later two—stood at the foot of the stairs. The kitchen was a separate building, with a passageway to the house.

Outside the palisade, bit by bit over the years, a village was built, contain-ing laborers' huts, company storehouses, stables, barns, and orchards. A hos-pital, dairy, and "piggery" stood on the extensive plain near the river, and five miles to the east were a gristmill and sawmill. Still farther out, and of great importance, was a thousand-acre farm of pasture and fields, large enough and efficient enough to provide food not only to Fort Vancouver, but to other posts as well. These were growing as much food as possible, to minimize expenses, but only Forts Vancouver and Nisqually and the Cowlitz Farm had land and climate suitable for large-scale agriculture.

McLoughlin was intensely interested in the farm. In early 1836 he read in the *Encyclopoedia of Agriculture* an account of an English reaper which har-vested an imperial acre per hour, "cut down a breadth of five feet at once, was moved by a single horse, and attended by from six to eight persons to tie up the canes." Ever alert to progress, he asked the Governor and Committee to send him two. "Even if they cost £50 each," he said, "it is nothing in compar-ison with the advantage we would derive from having them to cut down our crop." These or something similar were evidently provided. William A. Slacum, a visitor of 1836–37, reported that he had seen such a machine, and Thomas J. Farnham in 1839 described a barn that contained "a mammoth threshing machine."

This is the reaper John McLoughlin saw in the 1836 *Encyclopedia of Agriculture*. He request-ed that the company order two of them. FORT VANCOUVER LIBRARY. PHOTOGRAPHY BY AUTHOR

The center of the whole vast operation was the courtyard, which buzzed with activity. Twenty-five feet high hung a large bell. Eloisa McLoughlin said it was "on three poles . . . covered at the top with a little roof," but a later photograph showed it on a single spar. It ruled the day, clanging at 5:00 A.M. as a signal to be up and begin work, at 8:00 for breakfast, at 9:00 for work again, at 12:00 for dinner, at 1:00 for work, and at 6:00 for supper. During working hours the air was lively with the ring of metal and whine of saws, as smiths made and repaired tools and machinery, carpenters shaped boards, and coopers constructed barrels. Bakers tended roaring fires in the cavernous ovens, turning out bread and sea biscuits for the entire district's ships and brigades. Laborers beat furs weekly to get rid of moths and dust. Clerks kept journals and accounts and copied letters. Indians came for medicines and supplies, and to trade their furs.

Among the year's main events were the departures of trapping brigades and the arrival of overland canoes. "There was great rejoicing when they came," said Eloisa. "We would hear them singing in coming around the point at Vancouver. When they heard someone singing they would call out the 'Express' and there was great excitement." There would be a rush to the river as the brigade swept in, with the company flag at the bow and beribboned voyageurs swinging their paddles in a sparkle of spray. Pulling up with a flourish, they would leap out to shouts and a babel of questions, after which they would have the customary regale of pork, spirits, and flour—treasured ingredients, not tasted for many weeks. They mixed the flour with water and fried it as pancakes.

Through all the activity strode the vigorous, white-haired McLoughlin, carrying his gold-headed cane—not a physical necessity but a symbol of authority, a handy tool. Although the Chief Factor's associates often mentioned his cane, they pictured him as sturdy and energetic, not as limping or frail. His son David said he was "not stuck up," but would visit with laborers as freely as with clerks. "When the voyageurs or Trappers arrived from their trips," recalled David, "he would have the head man of the parties in his office and talk with him for hours at a time . . . he was a fluent talker and had a great memory." And always in the background, seldom mentioned but important, was his wife, caring for her peppery husband. She received many guests—children of Thomas McKay, her granddaughter Catherine Sinclair, the missionaries' wives Narcissa Whitman and Eliza Spalding, and others. A number of fur traders' children were brought up at the fort because their fathers had left or died. When possible, they were housed with their native mothers; otherwise they were placed in the homes of laborers. Francis Ermatinger, whose native wife died, told his brother that "his [McLoughlin's] family has taken care of my little boy," which implies that the doctor's wife had a hand in the orphans' supervision. And Dr. Tolmie wrote in his journal, "Sent calico & tartan to the Drs. rooms who has kindly offered to get them made up by his family." This would mean hand sewing, stitch after patient stitch, by Marguerite McLoughlin and fifteen-year-old Eloisa, who probably made the calico into shirts.

About the time the new fort was founded, McLoughlin took Governor Simpson up the Willamette River to show him its falls, at the site of today's Oregon City. They were a splendid sight, as described by John Kirk Townsend.

> There are here three falls on a line of rocks extending across the river, which forms the bed of the upper channel. The water is precipitated through deep abrazed gorges, and falls perhaps forty feet at an angle of about twenty degrees. It was a beautiful sight when viewed from a distance, but it became grand and almost sublime as we approached it nearer . . . the roar of the cataract was almost deafening and the rays of the bright sun reflected from the white and glittering foam threatened to deprive me of sight.

Simpson was equally impressed, but for a different reason. Envisioning vast profits, he predicted that "Saws enough could be employed, to load the British Navy." He and McLoughlin chose a location suitable for a large mill and establishment where they could trade furs, harvest salmon, and raise cattle. Although the doctor had timber cut there and considered it a better site for a sawmill than the small stream near the fort, he did not develop it then because the mill at Vancouver "sawed sufficient Lumber for our wants," and "the hostile state of the Indian population would not allow of the men being sent away such a Distance from the Fort." His reference to the "hostile state" of the Indians probably reflected his recent trouble with the Clallams and Clatsops of the coast, because the neighboring tribes were peaceful.

On March 25, 1829, soon after visiting the falls, Simpson with his paddlers, bugle, and bagpipes left to continue his trip around the world. He was pleased with the progress on the Columbia, and especially pleased that the farms at Fort Vancouver and other posts were so thriving that "eatables and drinkables" no longer took valuable space in the holds of supply ships. His report to the Governor and Committee praised McLoughlin. "In short, never did a change of system, and a change of management, produce such obvious

George Simpson on a tour of inspection, from the HBC 1926 calendar, by L.L. Fitzgerald (inspired by a painting done by Cyrus C. Cuneo). Simpson was a tireless traveler, and ruthless toward the voyageurs who manned his canoes. He insisted on making a splendid entrance to posts along the way, and often carried a bagpiper and bugler, even on long trips such as his inspection of the Pacific Coast in 1829. HUDSON BAY COMPANY ARCHIVES, PROVINCIAL ARCHIVES OF MANITOBA, HBCA PICTURE COLLECTION, P-390 [N7907]

advantages in any part of the Indian country, as those which the present state of this Establishment in particular, and of the Columbia Department as a whole, at this moment exhibits."

Soon after Simpson's departure, McLoughlin made another significant decision, this time concerning the Willamette Valley—a parklike, rolling land, with the Cascade Range to the east and the Coast Range to the west. It had rich soil, dense forests along the streams, and prairies of luxuriant grass, kept open because the local Indians burned them off in their great fall hunts. Townsend, who saw it in the burning season, wrote:

> The whole country for miles around is most brilliantly illuminated. Here am I sitting cross-legged on the ground, scribbling by the light of the vast conflagration with as much ease as if I had a ton of oil burning by my side. . . . The very heavens themselves appear ignited, and the fragments of ashes and burning grass-blades, ascending and careering about through the glowing firmament, look like brilliant and glorious birds let loose to roam and revel amid this splendid scene.

A typical trading store at a Hudson's Bay Company post in the 1840s. Clerks and Indians are haggling over the price for goods, probably using terms of made beaver. Taken from Ballantyne's "Hudson Bay."

Although a few former mountain men and a few remnants from Fort Astoria or the North West Company posts were living in the valley, it was company policy to discourage them, in the belief that "as the country becomes settled, the Fur trade Must Diminish." As yet, no Hudson's Bay retirees had moved there, because the company's license required it to return employees to Canada or Europe when their terms of enlistment were over, leaving none in the Indian country.

In 1828 a French Canadian freeman named Etienne Lucier—a former Astorian—had asked McLoughlin for seed and implements with which he could establish a farm on the Willamette. The Chief Factor had refused, offering instead a passage to Canada for the man and his family. Lucier accepted, but the express was late, and although he left with it, he turned back because of the cold.

The following year, McLoughlin sent Lucier and other freemen to California with a brigade under A. R. McLeod, "so as to remove them from a place where they were Anxious to begin to farm." But by 1830 the persistent Canadian had come back, and he renewed his request for help. By then an American brig, the *Owhyhee*, had moved into the Columbia, and McLoughlin realized that others would inevitably follow. "I considered it but prudent to accede to his [Lucier's] Demand," he reported to the Governor and Committee, "as I was afraid if I refused him he would join the first opposition which came here." He warned them that refusal to permit a friendly settlement would encourage rivals to establish "a footing in the country."

Lucier was not a company *engagé*, but later, when the company's retiring workmen asked for similar assistance, McLoughlin consented. He was, however, uneasy, and explained to the Governor and Committee that he had "Discouraged our people from settling as long as I could without exciting ill Will towards the Company." Lamenting that "whatever way we View it, it is attended with difficulties," he continued:

> It remains for your Honors to Decide whether you will Allow the Old Servants of the company to settle in it—Who with their children Will Look on the Company as their Benefactors or to prevent them and consequently keep the country to be settled by a people who will most probably feel very differently Inclined towards the Company, and I would therefore recommend to continue the plan I have hitherto followed and as we can get a Market for their Grain we might Make it a Branch of our Business—confer a Benefit on these men and Raise a population which would join us in opposition to that which is likely to come.

Although he was willing to help the retirees, he had no intention of populating the valley with wastrels. He therefore told them he would assist good honest men who had at least fifty pounds in credit at the fort, but they must have families and live on their own farms, not with their native wives' people. Saying that the company was "answerable for them" until they were discharged, which could be done only in Canada, he warned them to be "cautious not to get into any trouble," because "if there was any complaint made against them we would have to take them out of the Country." Since this innovation did not quite fit the rules, he kept retirees' names on the company books as if they were still employed, but he granted no pay and required no work. McLoughlin was a man of rigid personal honesty, but in this instance, as in others, he circumvented the letter of the law in order to accomplish what he considered sensible and right.

His strategy worked, and the number of settlers in the Willamette Valley slowly increased. The area where the retirees lived began near the falls of the

Willamette River, was seven or eight miles wide, and continued south for two or three times that distance. Since its inhabitants were mainly French Canadians, the section was informally called French Prairie, a name that would be prominent in early Northwest politics. From that time on, two national groups were living side by side—American mountain men and French Canadians. The struggle for control had begun.

~ 2 ~

"An Immensity of Trouble"
1829–1830

I n the late 1820s, while McLoughlin was building his new Fort Vancouver, a different kind of competition appeared. Coasters had bypassed the Columbia River until 1827, when Captain John Dominis brought the *Owhyhee* across the bar, spent ten days near the river mouth getting wood, and traded for a few skins. At that time McLoughlin had written with some uneasiness, "Captain Dominie gives twice as much for furs as we do, this of course Excited a great sensation amongst the natives but fortunately he did not remain Long."

That first visit had been brief, but two American brigs came in 1829. One was the *Owhyhee*, again under Captain Dominis, who entered the Columbia on February 14, anchored near Fort George, and waited for his ship's consort, the hermaphrodite brig *Convoy* under Captain D. W. Thompson. It was a long vigil, because the ship did not come until March 10, in the storm that destroyed the *William and Ann*. The log of the *Owhyhee* says the Americans sent the boats of both their vessels to the wreck, salvaged some of the property, and turned it over to the British.

The *Owhyhee* and the *Convoy* were owned by Josiah Marshall of Boston, who had amassed a sizeable fortune in the China trade. In the past, Americans had been seeking the valuable sea otters, but with the population of those animals on the decline, Marshall had told his captains to establish a station on the Columbia for accepting land skins. The visitors did not actually construct a post because, as Dominis wrote, "it would require 40 or 50 men with proper fort built." But they lingered, and McLoughlin knew that under joint occupation they had an incontestable right to be there.

Captain Dominis of the *Owhyhee* was an experienced seaman. He may have had wives in several ports, and he certainly had one in the Sandwich

Islands, for his son married the Hawaiian princess who later became famous
as Queen Liliuokalani. Both Americans had a healthy respect for McLoughlin,
with his well-entrenched company and implacable trading practices. Almost
as soon as he arrived, Captain Thompson of the *Convoy* wrote that "the English
Company here have a great advantage over us, knowing the language well and
the best hunting grounds . . . and they are determined to drive us from the
River." The "Bostons," however, had the pleasurable knowledge that the wreck
of the *William and Ann* had left McLoughlin short of provisions. Captain
Dominis said that "the company have very few goods left," and Captain Thompson indulged in a bit of gloating.

> Our prospects this Season depends much upon the arrival of an Ship
> from England, which is daily expected. Should she not arrive our
> prospects this Season will be tolerable good, as they have but few
> goods here for the present. One of their vessels was totally lost in
> crossing the bar the day I arrived, and vessel, Cargo and all on board
> perished. This unfortunate accident will be favourable for us this
> Season as she had a valuable Cargo on board.

McLoughlin was not at first greatly alarmed. As a result of his entreaties,
the London Committee had sent out two supply ships that year, and although
the *William and Ann* was lost, he expected the *Ganymede* daily with a replen-
ishment. As for the Americans, he later said, "We then considered this opposition as merely coasters who put in to collect a few straggling Skins & certainly had no Idea they intended to set themselves down to contend with us
for the Trade." Nevertheless—to his dismay—Captain Thompson took the
Convoy up the Columbia, passing Fort Vancouver on April 4, 1829, and continuing upriver to the long stretch of rapids called the Cascades. Nine days
later the brig "repassed on her way down & remained between the Cowletz
[River] and falls of the Willamitti from that time until September."

McLoughlin responded at once. As soon as he realized that the Americans
meant to stay, he sent out small trading parties in all directions "to oppose
them," and he sweetened the standard of trade on the lower Columbia. As
early as March 1829, Captain Thompson wrote, "On our arrival here the
English were getting six large Beavers for one Blanket and twenty for a musket, but opposition has reduced it to 1/4 of the former price." Nor was that
the end. Within a few months McLoughlin further "reduced the price of
Guns from Eighteen Beavers to three, of Blankets from five to one Beaver, and

every other article in the same proportion." His position, however, was precarious, because the *Ganymede* did not come until May, and while he was painfully short of trade goods the Americans secured a large number of skins.

Thanks to the incompetence of her captain, the *Ganymede* had a narrow escape in crossing the bar. "I am sorry to say Capt Hayne is so much addicted to Liquor I conceive it would be hazarding the Safety of the Vessel to give him charge of her," McLoughlin told the Committee, saying it was "unpleasant" to make such a report but that "I would not be discharging the duty I owe to Humanity and to the Concern if I withheld this information from you. Mr. Hall his mate is sober and attentive to his duty, and had it not been for his presence of mind the *Ganymede* would have been lost in Chinook Bay." He added that Hayne had sold "Spirits" to the company servants, besides indulging in them himself. "I have several times perceived he had made free with Liquor before Breakfast, often have I seen him intoxicated before dinner, very seldom have I seen him perfectly sober after dinner."

As he had for other troublesome captains, McLoughlin pointed out a positive trait—that Hayne had been "extremely obliging and accommodating"—but the captain was highly unstable. While taking his ship back to England, he became deranged, and "his conduct was so extremely bad, that the Government Authorities displaced him and sent the Vessel home in charge of another Captain."

Nor did McLoughlin's trouble with vessels stop there. In May of the following year, 1830, while the Americans were still on the Columbia, Captain William Ryan of the Hudson's Bay supply ship *Isabella* "mistook Chinook Point for Cape Disappointment and came in through the south Breakers." With her rudder carried away, the *Isabella* was inexorably washed toward shore until Ryan ordered the crew to abandon her, after which they took to boats and rowed upstream to Fort Vancouver.

Two days later, when McLoughlin was informed of the shipwreck, he went down the river with "all the remaining people we could spare." Although they saved most of the cargo, the vessel broke up in the surf. "It is unnecessary to say how much this misfortune has again deranged our Plans," the Chief Factor wrote. "We had to postpone every other object to the saving of the cargo of the *Isabella*, drying and transporting it to this place." He noted that Captain Ryan had abandoned his ship in a panic, when "they had only to slip her cable and she would have drifted into smooth water . . . but in justice to Capt. Ryan I must observe, he abandoned the Vessel in consequence of her stricking so hard he was afraid she would fall to pieces, which she would, if she had not been uncommonly strong." As so often happened, McLoughlin attended to the matter in person—a wise precaution, for the clerk J. F. Harriott said the wreck "caused a great commotion in the lower part of the Columbia, and had not Dr. McLoughlin gone down himself I do not doubt but something very disagreeable would have taken place."

McLoughlin expected two other supply ships in 1830, but they were both late, the brig *Eagle* coming in June and the *Dryad* in August. While he was waiting, the Americans played a watery game of leapfrog. As long as Captain Thompson had the *Convoy* on the Columbia, Dominis took the *Owhyhee* north along the coast. When Thompson left the river to purchase supplies in the Sandwich Islands, Dominis returned and "brought his vessel to Cassino's Camp, where he has remained ever since & sent a party to the Dalles." The village of Chief Casseno was near Fort Vancouver, just across from Belle Vue Point, and with the American ship anchored so close and its land party on the prowl, McLoughlin felt besieged. Compassionate as he was to those in trouble, he was a relentless competitor in business, and he was determined to drive out these interlopers. The only way to do this, he thought, was to extinguish their profits, so he kept at least "20 Men, one Clerk, the Interpreter & a runner constantly on the go," trading in the Indians' villages instead of waiting for them to bring furs to the fort. He said he was willing "to give Indns. even two Blankets for a large Beaver rather than to allow them [the Americans] to procure any quantity as even at this rate the price at which Beaver sell in England will leave us a profit."

But even as he waged a merciless trade war, McLoughlin made friends with his rivals. He sold them lumber, gave them potatoes, and in October, when one of the *Owhyhee*'s mates fell ill, the doctor had him taken to the fort for several months of medical care.

During that winter, Captain Dominis found his profits so poor that he offered to dispose of his trading goods. The hard-pressed McLoughlin, seeing a chance to eliminate or at least reduce the competition, immediately asked Dominis "on what terms he would sell," and they discussed rates. They failed to agree, however, because the captain wanted payment in beaver, bills, or sterling, at a rate McLoughlin found unacceptable, and Dominis said he "could not carry in his vessel" the doctor's counteroffer of payment in lumber. Aware that he had no authority "to buy up an opposition," McLoughlin justified his attempt in a somewhat plaintive letter to Simpson:

> In the Columbia we are peculiarly situated. . . . Our Stores nearly
> empty, dependent for a supply on the arrival of the Vessel to which

if an accident happened, our Trade on this side of the Mountains would be ruined. I would for these reasons have purchased his Goods for the Columbia Trade and paid them in Boards, if he had agreed to my terms as it would have put a stop to the further disorganization of the Indians, would have enabled me to recall our trading parties & employ them to advantage in erecting our intended Saw Mill & at other work about the place.

He had cut prices, but only in the area the Americans had actually invaded. When Samuel Black, Chief Trader at the upstream post of Fort Nez Perces, wanted to make a similar reduction there, McLoughlin refused because "as you well know if your [post] lowered yours the whole trade of Colville Dis^t would be ruined." Black apparently protested, for a few months later McLoughlin assured him that "of course I am perfectly aware how much the reduced price of goods must give you trouble and affect your trade." He pointed out the danger that if the inland posts sold products too cheaply, his storehouses would not have enough goods to meet the increased demand, and said, "The absurdity of doing this at your place with our limited means is exactly similar to a man setting fire to his house when a fire is raging in his vicinity to prevent its being burnt by the fire from his neighbours."

McLoughlin's strategy was successful. In 1830, when the Americans were at last preparing to leave, he congratulated Black, saying that by keeping up prices "in spite of all the means employed by the natives to make you lower them, you prevented the Trade of the Interior being Spoilt." The doctor could take considerable pride in this, for it was a skillful and successful use of the Columbia District as a buffer to keep American trappers from invading the north.

While McLoughlin was in the midst of this trade war, he had several confrontations with company personnel. In 1830 Chief Trader Francis Heron of Fort Colvile demanded more goods and assistants than the doctor could supply, and refused to follow orders. Heron became so strident that Governor Simpson said he was "an idle indolent Lawyer," and that it had been "necessary to go to the Dr.'s assistance & give Heron a Dressing." The feisty clerk had trouble with others as well. Francis Ermatinger called him "the worst man and the greatest drunkard I have ever seen," and complained, "Confound the fellow, I cannot think of him with patience." Eventually the Council of the Northern Department investigated Heron, "his intemperate habits having of late become so notorious as to be the subject of general remark."

In that same year Dr. Hamlyn, a medical officer at Fort Vancouver, wanted to leave and demanded passage to the east, although he had not given the usual notice and his term of enlistment had not expired. When McLoughlin replied that he "could not acceede to his request" because he was needed at the fort, Hamlyn filled the air with complaints. He was so unpleasant and so persistent that McLoughlin finally allowed him to go. "It may be said why give him a passage if you conceive him not entitled to it and that his services are required to this [place]," he wrote to Governor Simpson. "I beg to observe I conceive it of no use to keep a gentleman who says he will not work."

Still another quarrel, more severe and much more disturbing, involved Chief Trader John Warren Dease of Fort Colvile, who fell ill and came to Fort Vancouver in September 1828, to receive medical treatment. For an unknown reason—having apparently improved—Dease started back to his post in the dead of winter, but died at The Dalles because of a sudden hemorrhage, possibly caused by a stomach ulcer. Governor Simpson told J. G. McTavish that a disagreement between Dease and McLoughlin "went as far as it could well do without Powder & Ball," and that the Chief Factor "is quite a changed man since the Death of Dease: you are aware that he had a very Serious quarrel wh. [with] the poor man immediately previous to his death which tis said was the cause of his undertaking the Journey from Vancouver to Colvile at such an unfavorable Season."

These were not McLoughlin's first differences with personnel, and they would not be his last. They point up the difficulty of handling a large number of independent and often aggressive men in an isolated area. In addition, the conflicts shed light on the doctor's own nature—intelligent, kind-hearted, decisive, and fair, but saddled with an explosive temper. Simpson reflected it when he described the doctor in the "Book of Servants' Characters," which he kept in secret, identifying the subjects by a number code. In most of the evaluations Simpson used biting terms, for he was writing for his eyes alone in the unhappy year when his adored infant son died, and he gave his caustic tongue full rein. He called McLoughlin

a very bustling active man who can go through a great deal of business but is wanting in system and regularity and has not the talent of managing the few associates and clerks under his authority: has a good deal of influence with Indians and speaks the Soulteaux [a branch of the Ojibway tongue] tolerably well.—Very zealous in the discharge of his public duties and a man of strict honor and integrity but a great stickler for rights & privileges and sets himself up for a righter of wrongs. Very anxious to obtain a lead among his colleagues with whom he has not much influence owing to his ungovernable violent temper and turbulent disposition, and would be a troublesome man to the Comp'y if he had sufficient influence to form and tact to manage a party. . . . Altogether a disagreeable man to do business with as it is impossible to go with him in all things and a difference of opinion almost amounts to a declaration of hostilities, yet a good hearted man and a pleasant companion.

Critical as this was, Simpson basically admired McLoughlin and his work, and often gave him generous praise. In 1832 he wrote to the Governor and Committee that the

great exertions indefatigable labours and unremitting attention of Chief Factor McLoughlin, who, in the face of every difficulty he has had to contend with, (and they certainly were of no ordinary character), has steadily & uniformly followed up, with a degree of vigour & energy which I have rarely witnessed in this or any other country, every measure and plan which had been determined on at the commencement of his administration in that quarter, and has now brought the business into such a train that . . . will secure to the Honble. Company a branch of trade on the Shores of the Pacific which promises to become one of very great value and importance.

As for the Americans, they remained on the Columbia until July 29, when they weighed anchor and left. They had been in McLoughlin's bailiwick for nearly seventeen months, giving him, as he put it, "an immensity of trouble." They spent the rest of the summer along the coast and then set sail for Boston, taking the respectable haul of 2,900 land skins, mainly otter and beaver, along with fifty-three barrels of salted salmon—the earliest commercial shipment of salmon from the Columbia to the eastern states.

With the *Owhyhee* and *Convoy* gone, McLoughlin's department was at last free from Americans. But he was still wary, and in the fall he said he had "been obliged to Keep our parties running to Indians as much as ever to prevent their having any number of Skins in the event of any coaster coming here."

At the height of the struggle, he had made the gloomy prediction that "as to restoring the trade to the former Tariff we can never Expect it," but once the Americans were out of the picture, his prices made a surprisingly quick recovery. In March 1831, after less than a year, he raised the price of a blanket to two beaver except at Fort George, where he held the figure to half that in order to discourage coasters from making another visit. And by summer the rate was again twenty skins for a gun.

American competition had lasted only from February 1829 to July 1830, but it was significant—the opening salvo of a battle to come. Throughout his early years on the Columbia, McLoughlin had considered the Americans as troublesome but ephemeral competitors, to be undersold, outwitted, and occasionally befriended—as beings from a distant state, who would plague him for a while and then go home. But after this visit he knew they had the ability to move in, that they might return at any time, and that sooner or later they would come to stay.

~ 3 ~
The Intermittent Fever
1830–1832

I n the winter of 1828–29, while George Simpson was visiting Fort Vancouver, he saw McLoughlin's problems with insufficient shipping, overdue trade goods, and recalcitrant captains. Realizing that they interfered with efficiency, when Simpson returned to London he alerted the Governor and Committee, who took steps to improve conditions. They agreed to send trading outfits a year in advance and allocated more vessels to the Columbia, planning to keep two permanently on the coast.

As a result, three vessels arrived in 1830: the *Eagle*, the *Dryad*, and the *Isabella*. Even though the last was wrecked, its cargo was salvaged, and it eased the shortage of ships and goods so effectively that in late summer McLoughlin wrote to Chief Factor John Rowand of the Saskatchewan District, "This is the first year since I am here (which you will hardly believe though nevertheless true) in which I had a suitable Outfit for the Trade and in which I have been able to supply our people adequately."

At the same time, he received word that the Governor and Committee had created a Marine Department, with young Æmelius Simpson as its head. Although McLoughlin disliked coasters and thought the new office unnecessary, he was gratified because the letter assured him that all company ships

James Douglas, McLoughlin's most valued assistant, was a man of intelligence, judgment, and rigid honesty. After McLoughlin was forced to resign, Douglas was one of three chosen to govern Fort Vancouver. He later founded Fort Victoria on Vancouver Island, became Governor of British Columbia, and was knighted by Queen Victoria. BRITISH COLUMBIA ARCHIVES, A-1232

were "subject to your orders from the day of arrival at the Columbia until final departure therefrom." This made him the ultimate authority, with the indisputable right to move captains from ship to ship and send them wherever they were needed.

Another pleasant event of 1830 was the arrival of James Douglas, age twenty-seven, who was assigned to Fort Vancouver as a clerk. McLoughlin and Douglas had both been Nor'-Westers at Fort William in 1819–20, and tradition says that was the beginning of their friendship. Douglas and his wife, Amelia, were given quarters in the "Big House"—elbow to elbow with the McLoughlins—an arrangement that would last for sixteen years. At that time the Douglases had no children, but their family would eventually include five daughters.

Douglas, who was born out of wedlock in 1803, was the son of John Douglas of Scotland, owner of sugar plantations in British Guiana, and Martha Ritchie of Barbados, who was officially described as a "free coloured woman"—a term that indicated she had black blood but was not specific about the amount. When Douglas was a child, his father took him to Scotland, where he attended school, and in 1819 he entered the North West Company, serving that winter as a clerk under McLoughlin. After the amalgamation, Douglas transferred to the Hudson's Bay Company, being carried in its books as a "West Indian" or "Scotch West Indian." It is of interest that, in contrast to the prejudice against children of fur traders and Indian women, Douglas's parentage did not interfere with his advancement. As an officer of superior integrity and ability, he would rise to the company's highest rank of Chief Factor, found Fort Victoria, become governor of British Columbia, and receive knighthood from Queen Victoria.

Other events of 1830 were less pleasant. Captain Minors of the *Dryad* failed to explain the disappearance from his brig's stores of "a stream chain . . . a Bolt of Canvas $ 7, and some Junk . . . besides fifteen buckets of Molasses a cask of Vinagar and several other things." In addition, he refused to take command of a different vessel, even though it would free the *Dryad* for a journey to the north. After Minors had been in revolt for an entire day, McLoughlin went aboard ship, where the crew sided with their captain until the doctor had James Douglas read them their signed agreements. As McLoughlin reported:

> In the course of this discussion Capt Minors repeatedly said in the presence of his Crew that he would not give up the command of his Vessel as long as he could raise an Arm   If I attempted to take his Vessel from him blood would be spilt and from his expression that Mr Duncan Mr Young and the Crew would only obey his orders . . . I am convinced in my own mind that Capt Minors did Tamper with his Crew with a view of getting them to support him in Opposition to us and contrary to what I conceive was his and their duty.

Even after McLoughlin's visit to the ship, Minors remained obdurate. Finally, "seeing all my endeavours to do the business in a genteel manner were in vain and no other alternative remained," the Chief Factor suspended the captain from his post and sent him to England. It was a severe punishment, but when Governor Simpson heard about it, he wrote, "We highly approve of the decisive measures you took with Captn. Minors, who it appears conducted himself with great impropriety." He praised McLoughlin for adhering to the Committee's instructions, and again assured him that "the marine Establishment is as much under your controul and subject to your direction as any other branch of the business." In addition, he informed the Governor and Committee that coastal shipping for the Columbia District was "miserably lame in effective officers," and he asked for captains of a better caliber.

In July 1830, McLoughlin hoped to take a major step. He, George Simpson, and the Governor and Committee had all agreed that the company must strengthen its position in the north, because it was a rich source of skins, and the supply in the Snake Country was on the decline. Ogden said the area he scoured that year was "the poorest in Furs that he had hitherto explored," and McLeod, trapping in the Shasta Valley of northern California, had found "very few Beaver." Deciding to widen his scope, McLoughlin sent Lieutenant Simpson with three vessels to Nass Harbor, at the southern end of today's Alaskan Panhandle. He ordered the lieutenant to explore the area and seek a promising location for a post.

McLoughlin was vitally interested in this new enterprise, which he envisioned as a start on a profitable chain of northern establishments. He had been delayed by frustrating competition from the *Owhyhee* and *Convoy*, and when they left, he expected to forge ahead. But in early summer he was blocked again, this time by an epidemic of "intermittent fever"—malaria—which "began to shake its burning, freezing subjects," and spread with such virulence that it stopped progress on every front. John Kirk Townsend, the physician who visited the Columbia in 1834, described the fever as "a disease of a very fatal character. . . . The symptoms are a general coldness, soreness and stiffness of the limbs and body, with violent tertian ague. Its fatal termination is attributable to its tendency to attack the liver, which is generally affected in a few days after the first symptoms are developed."

It was widespread, afflicting tribes over the entire area, and was so prevalent at Fort Vancouver that at one time, seventy-six victims were in the hospital "exclusive of women and children." Peter Skene Ogden was a patient, as was Dr. John Kennedy, the fort physician, and Kennedy's illness required the harried Chief Factor to personally provide medical care—an exhausting burden when it was added to his other work. McLoughlin wrote to the Governor and Committee:

> I had to attend to the sick who were about fifty in number we had to pack the Furs, to attend to the Indian Trade and to the Indians who frightened by the Mortality amongst them came in numbers to camp alongside of us—giving as a reason that if they died they Knew we would Bury them most reluctantly on our part we were obliged to drive them away and I must add to this the other urgent work of the place so that in fact I was as well as my assistants Messers. J Douglas, Ermatinger, and Bernie Kept constantly employed from day light to eleven at night. I say I was employed but in truth I might say harrassed in mind and body as much as I possibly could be.

Although McLoughlin's writing was generally businesslike and impersonal, his day-to-day correspondence at this time contains many heartfelt references to the fever's toll. "But praise be to God for his great mercies only one of our men Big Pierre [Karaganyate] died," he wrote to Donald Manson, a clerk at Fort George, "though I am sorry to say nine of the women, two children, and several of the Indians about the place, are gone to that bourne whence no traveller returns."

When McLoughlin himself fell ill, he had George T. Allan, a young clerk who was normally in charge of the company farms, act as his deputy, to make rounds and administer medications. Allan was untrained, but he dutifully tramped through the men's houses carrying vials of quinine, handing out medicine and checking on patients. He told about one young *engagé* to whom he gave the medicine, with careful instructions on how much he should take per dose. "But the fellow mistaking swallowed the whole concern at once," said Allan, "eight or ten doses in one. I was awfully alarmed for a time, but I need not have been, for he soon got well, and never had the ague again as long as I was at Fort Vancouver."

The disease was serious for the whites, but it wreaked havoc among the natives, who had no immunity to it and tried to ease their burning fever by plunging into the ice-cold rivers. James Douglas wrote,

> Plomondo [an *engagé*] says that in 1830, the first ague summer, the living sufficed not to bury their dead, but fled in terror to the sea-coast, abandoning the dead and dying to the birds and beasts of prey. Every village presented a scene harrowing to the feelings; the canoes were there drawn up upon the beach, the nets extended on the willow-boughs to dry, the very dogs appeared, as ever, watchful, but there was not heard the cheerful sound of the human voice. The green woods, the music of the birds, the busy humming of the insect tribes, the bright summer sky, spoke of life and happiness, while the abode of man was silent as the grave.

Plomondo—Simon Plomondon—was all too right. In October of that first year, McLoughlin estimated that the fever had carried off three-fourths of the area's natives.

Overburdened as he and his men were, it was impossible for him to carry out his plans to establish a northern post. "Taking the sickly state of our people into consideration, the season of the year when the weather is boisterous and the nights long, and that we are very imperfectly acquainted with the coast I conceived it better to postpone sending to establish that place until spring," he wrote to Archibald McDonald in December 1830.

In winter the fever abated, and in the spring McLoughlin sent Lieutenant Simpson north again, to explore the Nass River and trade for furs. But the Chief

Factor did not have enough able-bodied men to found a fort, and by midsummer he learned that the disease had not run its course. In July 1831 it reappeared, with even greater virulence, and McLoughlin reported,

> Every man in this Establishment except seven has been ill   at One time there were sixty three Patients on the sick list in this Number were Capt Kippling [of the *Vancouver*] his two Mates and seven of the Crew—Indeed all the Crew that Came in her except one have been ill. Some of the Patients have had relapses. some had three attacks and some even four in this latter Number is the Carpenter of the Ganymede and she has been caulked and repaired by the people of the Establishment—Indeed her Cargo has been mostly put on Board by the people of this place as I am of opinion if those of her crew who have been ill were to Work They would relapse . . . and we have to thank God for his Great Mercies that none of our people has as yet died of the fever and all still ill are on the Recovery.

He told Francis Heron at Fort Colvile that "the mortality among the Indians of the Wallahamette has been very great."

With so many ill, the drain on the fort's supply of quinine was immense, and McLoughlin prepared to use a substitute if necessary. In October 1831 he asked Richard Charlton, British consul in the Sandwich Islands, to send a large quantity of the drug, saying that if he could not procure so much, "I request will you have the Goodness to make up the defficiency by sending us thirty pounds of pounded Peruvian Bark for every pound that is deficient."

The bark of the dogwood, a common tree on the coast, was also effective. Townsend, speaking of two critically ill Indian children, said, "Taking one of the parents into the wood with his blanket, I soon chipped off a plentiful supply, returned, boiled it in his own kettle, and completed the preparation in his lodge." He administered "about a scruple of the extract per day," and the children recovered.

With the coming of cold weather, the fever subsided as it had before, only to break out again the following summer. "I am sorry to inform you that the Intermittent Fever is raging with great violence at this place," McLoughlin wrote in September 1832, "but thanks be to god for his mercies none of our people as yet have died." Although this was the last great epidemic year, cases of fever continued to occur from time to time, causing further loss to the natives. Only a fraction of their people remained alive, and the tribes of the Columbia would never again be so strong. Townsend said,

> The Indians of the Columbia were once a numerous and powerful people; the shore of the river, for scores of miles, was lined with their villages; the council fire was frequently lighted, the pipe passed round, and the destinies of the nation deliberated upon . . . the Indian was happy. Now, alas! where is he?—gone;—gathered to his fathers and to his happy hunting grounds; his place knows him no more.

But the number of cases was declining, and this enabled McLoughlin to revive the plan he had abandoned in 1830. He had a good supply of ships, along with authority over their captains, and he decided the time was ripe for a move into the north.

~ 4 ~

Moving North
1829–1834

In moving north, McLoughlin would have to face two strong competitors: American coasters, who worked from sailing ships, with no land bases; and the Russian American Company, which had several Alaskan posts and one—Fort Ross—in California. The Americans' only goal was to secure the greatest possible harvest of furs, but the Russians had permanent establishments, and hoped to turn a profit without destroying the area's resources. Although the three countries had all agreed not to sell arms, liquor, and ammunition to the natives, the Americans habitually disregarded the ban, and the Russians felt they must follow suit. Governor Simpson wrote that "notwithstanding the terms of the convention between Great Britain and Russia . . . Spiritous liquor is disposed of by them [the Russians] in barter for both furs and provisions."

McLoughlin's plan was to found posts in the north, set up a system of trading through ships, and establish a route from the coast into New Caledonia, which would undoubtably become British when the border was decided. Although it was a rich source of furs, it was closed in by mountains, and the Fraser River provided no outlet because its middle section was not navigable. Brigades could reach New Caledonia by only two routes, both of which were difficult and expensive: west from York Factory by canoe and then over the Rocky Mountains by packhorse; or up the Columbia to Okanagan and along an overland trail to the usable portion of the upper Fraser. A third and much easier route would be by ship on one of the rivers that crossed the Alaskan Panhandle, but that was Russian territory and could be entered only with special permission.

McLoughlin knew that the Russians had problems of supply, for they had to depend on the limited resources of Fort Ross, augmented by goods from the Americans' well-stocked vessels. He explained the situation to George Simpson during the governor's 1828–29 visit to the Columbia, and the nimble-witted Simpson immediately scented a potential market. On March 20, 1829, he wrote to the manager of the Russian American Company at Sitka, informing him that the Hudson's Bay Company was planning to extend its northern trade, which he hoped would "enable us to cultivate to Friendship, an acquaintance which we have long been desirous of forming." He recommended adherence to the treaties on arms and liquor, because that would make their dealings with the Indians "less hazardous." He offered to furnish grain, salt pork, and beef, and suggested that his company would sell British manufactures "at a Moderate advance on Prime Cost to cover charges and yield reasonable profit." He himself, Simpson said, was about to leave the area, but Chief Factor McLoughlin would be happy to receive a reply.

Governor Simpson's cousin, Lieutenant Æmelius Simpson, took the letter to Sitka, where he interviewed Captain Pavel E. Chistiakoff of the Russian navy. On his return, the lieutenant reported that Chistiakoff lacked authority to make an agreement, but would forward the letter and had suggested that the Honourable Committee contact the Russian American Company in St. Petersburg. Simpson thought the Russians would purchase merchandise if the British "could supply it in any quantity and at a moderate price, as they find their supplies from California very precarious." He said the Americans traded arms, ammunition, and spirits, and that to oppose them without a sale of these articles would "be a fruitless contest." The Russian government, he said, had already protested American sales, but the United States "either did not appear inclined to restrain those Adventurers, or had not the power to do so." And he found that the Russians depended on their own trapping partners rather than trade with the natives, which left the way open for the British.

The Governor and Committee were already anticipating an expansion to the north, and in December of that same year, even before they received Simpson's report, they wrote to the Russian company offering to furnish supplies "annually at cost price, regardless of profit, with whatever quantity of English products" they needed. Astonishing as the offer was, the Russians declined, but the incident was important to McLoughlin as an encouragement to act.

Early the next year, 1830, he sent Lieutenant Simpson north again, this time to Nass Harbor, telling him to examine its bays and rivers "as high Up as you conveniently can" and to try to find a site for a trading post. The Nass River was close to but not within Russian territory, and Simpson discovered a site on it with "a good Southern Exposure . . . a strong deep soil well calculated to produce vegetables," and pine growing "in great abundance on the banks." He was disappointed to find that only a short distance upstream, the river became "too rapid for boats or Canoes," and, somewhat to his chagrin, he learned that the natives preferred American goods to British. "Arms & ammunition they [the New Englanders] sell without limits & ardent spirits in great abundance," he said. "I regretted being under the necessity of selling a quantity of the latter as I found it impossible to trade without it nor do I see how it can well be avoided till opposition is done off the coast."

The outbreak of fever in the fall of 1830 brought most activity to a halt, although McLoughlin sent the *Dryad* to Monterey with a cargo of salmon and lumber and the *Vancouver* to "Woahoo," in the Sandwich Islands, with deals—planks of various sizes. In winter the disease subsided, and in April he sent Peter Skene Ogden north with two vessels under Lieutenant Simpson, instructing the lieutenant to help build a new fort on the Nass River and then take his ship on a trading expedition along the coast. McLoughlin told him to "strictly observe" the treaty between the British and Russian governments, and specified that "as little Liquor ought to be issued to Indians as well as arms and ammunition as you possibly can."

Carrying a supply of lumber, the convoy sailed a thousand miles to the large estuary of the Nass River—a maze of countless straits and bays, surrounded by fir-clad mountains and fed by meltwater from the ice fields. On a rocky point inside the harbor, forty feet above the high-tide mark and close to timber, Simpson and Ogden had their men build a dwelling house, dining hall, workshop, and store, protected by a stout bastion. After naming the new establishment Fort Simpson, the lieutenant left it in Ogden's care, while he took the *Dryad* still farther north.

But he soon returned, because he had fallen ill with an ailment that Dr. John Kennedy, physician at the new post, diagnosed as liver disease, a poorly understood condition at that time. Although Kennedy wanted to transfer his patient to land, Simpson insisted on staying aboard his schooner, where the doctor visited him daily. In spite of his efforts, however, the condition grew steadily worse. The lieutenant died on September 2, 1831, and the next day his body was brought ashore for burial. When McLoughlin heard about it, he wrote:

> By his death the concern loses the services of a man anxious to promote Its Interests to the utmost of his abilities and I suffer the loss of an acquaintance whose Gentlemanlike conduct and zealous discharge of his duty entitled him to my Respect and Esteem, and though his death at all times would be a loss still in the present situation of our affairs It is particularly so.

Although Simpson was an able officer and his death was a severe blow, McLoughlin also saw it as opportunity. Since coming to the Columbia, he had contended with a series of incompetent captains—timid Hanwell; talented grog drinker Davidson; inept Ryan; Hayne, who was seldom "perfectly sober after dinner"; and Minors, who refused to obey orders "as long as he could raise an Arm." After struggling with these, McLoughlin understandably detested the use of ships.

He also detested the office of marine superintendent, because he thought it weakened his badly needed control over captains, and now, with Lieutenant Simpson dead, the office was vacant. So McLoughlin seized the chance. Instead of appointing a successor, he merely attached the coastal trade to Fort Simpson, under Peter Skene Ogden's management.

He told Ogden to start trading from ships, and in May 1832, Baron Ferdinand von Wrangel, resident governor of the Russian American Company, reported that three Hudson's Bay vessels were trailing the New England coasters and paying two or three times as much per skin. The Americans, Wrangel said, "never hold out very long but hasten to leave the place and proceed to another, where they are immediately followed by Ogden's ships." He added that Ogden had garnered about two thousand skins, but his rivals secured twelve thousand because they were "selling liquor and firearms." While Wrangel's figures were doubtless overstated, they clearly indicated the need to offer arms and liquor, and McLoughlin therefore directed his men to adopt the practice. If the Russians complain about it, he said, "tell them that you are obliged to do so in consequence of its being done by the Americans," and assure them that if the Americans will "discountenance" that trade, the Hudson's Bay Company "will also conform."

Ogden's scant returns and the need for trading in spirits further reinforced McLoughlin's preference for posts rather than ships. He declared that "a Land Establishment can be maintained at much less expense; & the Company is never in want of a Gentleman to take charge of a Land Establishment, but it is extremely difficult to find Naval Officers to manage the coasting Trade." In support of this opinion, he sent headquarters an estimate of comparative expenses, including "the wear & tear of the vessel and Rigging" and the cost of insurance. His results strongly favored stations, and he pointed out another important advantage. "With posts we become better acquainted with the natives, acquire more influence over them, and gain more correct information of the country, which will enable us to extend the trade to the Interior."

In early 1832 the schooner *Vancouver* ran aground in a storm, damaging her so badly that the repairs would take a full year—an accident that left Mc-Loughlin with a shortage of shipping space, plus an idle crew piling up wages. Therefore, since the company had funds in the Sandwich Islands and since the *Eagle* was carrying "a cargo to Woahoo," he sent Chief Factor Duncan Finlayson to scout the market for a ship. "Of course I am aware that we are not authorised to enter into transactions of this nature without your express directions," he wrote to the Governor and Committee, "but when it is considered that vessels such as would suit us are often sold at the Sandwich Islands for 5 or 7 thousand dollars, and that our Naval people who are idle on our hands, will cost us this Year £460 in Wages alone; & that from the want of a vessel our Coasting Trade is not carried on with the energy it ought, your Honours will I trust approve."

He told Finlayson that besides looking for a ship, he should "provide salt at Woahoo and send it by the vessel." If he found a good cook, "we want one." He should ship "a Cask of Molasses" to Fort Langley "to complete the Outfit of that place," and "a Holland or Dutch Bolting Cloth if any fall in your way."

But it was the Chief Factor himself who found the replacement. Captain William McNeill of the American brig *Lama* was not realizing a profit, and when he offered to sell his vessel for sixty-five hundred dollars, McLoughlin was interested. McNeill was about to sail to Woahoo, so the Chief Factor handed him two letters for Finlayson. One, left open, said that if Finlayson had not already bought a vessel, he should consider the *Lama*, but at a maximum price of five thousand dollars, because of her small size. The other, sealed, suggested that Finlayson hire McNeill as captain, because "the man's superior knowledge of the business in comparison to any of our Sea Officers, renders his services more valuable—and knowledge is worth something."

This was risky, because the *Lama* and her skipper were American and might not be welcome in London, but McLoughlin needed a ship, and also a knowledgeable officer. Finlayson, who agreed, not only bought the vessel, he hired the captain and two of the ship's mates. But he was uneasy. "I tremble for the light in which it will be viewed by the Gov. & Council," he told a friend.

He might well tremble, for Governor Simpson approved, but the officers in London were furious. Sputtering that the American vessel "must on no account be sent to this country, as ship and cargo would be liable to seizure," they hauled McLoughlin over the coals for hiring Americans. The sooner he could "get quit of those people the better," they tartly said.

Stung by this unaccustomed censure, McLoughlin wrote a vigorous response, explaining what he had done and defending Finlayson, who had only obeyed orders. "If there is any fault committed I consider that I am the person who must bear the blame and not Mr. Finlayson," he said, and in the end, the Governor and Committee decided to approve the transaction after all. McLoughlin's on-the-spot judgment was vindicated, but he had made the decision in July of 1832 and did not receive the favorable word until October 1834.

The episode of the *Lama* emphasized the growing importance of the company's business in the Sandwich Islands. In 1833 the Governor and Committee responded by establishing an agency there, headed by George Pelly, first cousin of the company's governor, John Henry Pelly. The new agent had formerly been a ship's captain in the East India Company, and was well acquainted with the area.

In the spring of that year, when the fever had temporarily subsided, McLoughlin was able to forge ahead with his chain of northern posts. He added two—Fort McLoughlin on Milbanke Sound, not so far north as the Nass River, and Nisqually, on good pasture land at the southern end of Puget Sound. Nisqually differed from his other posts. Its land was suitable for farming; it was well located for a supply center, because ships could sail to it without making the long voyage up the Columbia; and it was an easy journey from Fort Vancouver via the Cowlitz River. He now had four establishments in the north— Langley, Simpson, McLoughlin, and Nisqually.

In addition he sent a force under Peter Skene Ogden to sail a hundred miles beyond Fort Simpson and investigate the Stikine River. To Ogden's satisfaction, he found that stream navigable, followed it through the Russian-owned coastal strip, and took formal possession of a building site in fur-rich New Caledonia. The location had one potential drawback—it could be reached only by crossing Russian territory.

Ogden did not build the post at that time, but the following spring, in 1834, McLoughlin sent him back to the Stikine, telling him to go at least thirty miles upriver, to a site well within British territory. There he was to establish Fort Stikine, "for which purpose you reduce Fort McLoughlin to twenty men, or even sixteen if you consider it safe and Fort Simpson to twelve."

When Ogden approached the Stikine, however, he found that Baron Wrangel had noticed his exploration of the year before and had hastily planted a new fort, the Redoubt St. Dionysius, at the river's mouth. It was not very impressive. Dr. William Tolmie, who accompanied Ogden, called it "merely a few cedarbark huts, within an enclosure about 6 feet in height, formed of boards fastened to upright poles." But it was protected by the brig *Chichagoff*, which had fourteen guns, and when the *Dryad* appeared, Captain Sarembo of the Redoubt ordered her to stop. He reminded Ogden that the treaties forbade the ships of any country to approach a point occupied by any other, except with permission, and he said the British would have to pass the new Redoubt in order to ascend the Stikine. "He did not deny we had a right to erect an establishment in the interior on English Territory," Ogden later reported, "but [said] we had no right to navigate these Straits, and his orders were to prevent us."

Ogden stayed in the area for eleven days of persistent but futile negotiation, during which the Hudson's Bay officials visited the Redoubt St. Dionysius and the Russians came several times to the *Dryad*. As Tolmie described Sarembo, "He was a thin elderly man of very dark complexion—dressed in a blue surtout, and white vest (unmentionables not observed)—he was accompanied by a short thick set goodnatured vainlooking man, the Indian interpreter." Tolmie's word "unmentionables" was at that time a polite term for trousers.

At first they had trouble communicating, but the Russians solved the problem by bringing over a Spanish speaker with whom, "by guessing and conjecturing," Dr. Tolmie could converse to a limited extent. At the Russians' request, Ogden wrote a protest to Baron Wrangel at Sitka and settled down to wait for a reply.

In the interim he negotiated with the Stikine natives. "This morning the Chiefs again came on board," he reported, "and requested some liquor as a present. Finding them all provided with Russian liquor reduced one third only, I made them a present of a Gallon reduced two thirds." He said they were "determined to prevent us if we attempted to proceed up the River, as by so doing we would injure their trade with the interior."

This was the crux of the dispute. The furs traded in that area originated in New Caledonia, but for years they had been marketed by both Russians and Indians, who were determined to keep that rich source. Governor Simpson acknowledged this fact when he said Fort Stikine was designed "to cut off from the Russians the valuable trade they have hitherto enjoyed . . . from the British Territory in the interior" and would therefore strike "at the very root of their trade."

On June 29, when Baron Wrangel's reply came from Sitka, it did not explicitly forbid the British to pass, but neither did it instruct Captain Sarembo to admit them, and he therefore prepared to enforce the ban. Faced with opposition by both Russians and natives, Ogden decided he had no choice. "However galling it is to be obliged to yield," he said, "I cannot act otherwise without sacrificing lives." He put the *Dryad* under sail and left.

McLoughlin was unaware of these events until December 1834, when the expedition returned to Fort Vancouver. Frustrated and chagrined, with his hopes dashed, the Chief Factor sent the Governor and Committee the pertinent documents—Ogden's report and correspondence with the Russian officers and his own detailed estimate of damage to the company from the "derangement" of its plans. This, he said, was very great, "while the Russians reap all the advantage. . . . And last but not least is the loss of character we suffer in the eyes of the Indians by being prevented by the Russians from erecting the Establishment at Stikine, which we had told them in 1832 and 1833 that we would do so."

The Chief Factor expected the officers in London to be as disappointed as he was, but instead they were delighted with the reports. For several years they had tried to negotiate a better agreement with the Russian American Company, and now they saw McLoughlin's account as a tool for exerting pressure through government channels. Wanting to retain this advantage, they ordered him not to take any further steps toward a Stikine post.

More than that, they noticed his accomplishments of the past decade, when he had established a new headquarters, contended with hostile natives and difficult personnel, handled an epidemic, and forged ahead in the north. As a result, they sent him a special commendation, expressed in that most eloquent voice—money. In 1834, with the encouragement of Governor Simpson, the Council at York Factory passed a resolution praising the

> prosperous and highly promising state of the Columbia Department, arising from the excellent management of Chief Factor McLoughlin . . . it is Resolved 72nd That this Council likewise testify their approbation of that Gentleman's whole administration, by presenting to him

their warmest thanks for his valuable services in the very arduous situation he has filled at Ft. Vancouver during the past 10 years, with so
much credit to himself and advantage to the Concern; and by voting
to him a Gratuity of Five Hundred pounds; with an allowance of one
hundred and fifty pounds p. annum during the years 1830, 1831,
1832 and 1833, in consideration of his professional attendance on the
Sick at that Establishment.

It was a well-earned bonus, for McLoughlin had carried a crushing load
but had received only the standard pay of every Chief Factor—a fixed percentage of profits. The Council, however, could only make a recommendation, subject to "the approbation" of the Governor and Committee, and when
Simpson broached the idea to the London officials, they at first demurred. They
considered it highly unusual—expensive—a disastrous precedent. They debated it and wrote memos about it for nearly two years, but at last they withdrew
their objections and credited McLoughlin's account with eleven hundred
pounds, the full recommended sum, retroactive to the time it was proposed.

Delighted, in November 1836 McLoughlin thanked the London officers.
He had been censored for the Snake brigade's trespass across American soil
and for buying the *Lama*. He had exceeded instructions by changing the rates
of trappers' pay, offering to buy out Captain Dominis, and neglecting to appoint a new marine superintendent. All of these arose from one of his major
strengths—his willingness to shoulder responsibility in unforeseen circumstances. But they were nevertheless a risk, and the bonus, being tangible evidence of the Committee's approval, was extremely welcome. In a passage that
offers a glimpse into the stress of the past few years, he said:

Before bringing this letter to a close, permit me to thank your Honors
for sanctioning the Grant proposed by the Northern Council which
in my estimation is not valued so much in a pecuniary point of view
as in its being a gratifying expression of general approbation, the more
soothing to my feelings from having in the course of my management
had to contend with opinions directly opposed to mine, and to combat
(when in novel circumstances of urgent difficulty which compelled
me to step boldly out of the beaten path of routine) the views and
declared Sentiments of many whose opinions on other subjects I
highly respect. Without some such decided mark of your preference,
I would have been left in doubt with regard to the general estimation

of my services, and it is in this light Gentlemen that I highly prize the Grant, and will be ever proud of the recollection that I owe it to the approbation of your Honors and of my colleagues in the fur Trade. . . .

I have the Honor to be

Honble. Sirs

Your Most Obedt. Servant

JOHN McLOUGHLIN

C.F.

~ 5 ~

My Son John

1825–1834

EVEN WITH HIS BONUS, McLoughlin was not a rich man. Having been paid no dividends as a North West partner, he had begun to draw advances on his Hudson's Bay account as soon as the two companies merged, and he did not receive any income until 1825.

In Hudson's Bay Company accounts, the "outfit" for each year was the business that resulted from the merchandise shipped from London that year. Officers were not credited until the goods from the outfit were traded for furs and the furs were sold, which would be several years later. And the profits from an outfit were generally paid over several years, as its furs were marketed. For example, in 1829 McLoughlin was credited with payments for the outfits of 1823, 1824, 1826, and 1827.

His account for 1822–24 shows only debits, for cash advances or for goods. In 1825 the book shows his first returns, £406.17.6 (406 pounds, 17 shillings, and 6 pence), which was his share of profits on the outfit of 1822. However, this was nearly eaten up by a loss of £392.14.3 on the outfit of 1821. From then on, his debt gradually shrank until on June 1, 1829, he had his first favorable balance—£78.19. It had taken him eight years to become solvent, and only after that did he begin to accumulate an estate.

His heaviest outlay was the expense for his two children, John and Elisabeth, whom he had left in school in Canada. Their care was also a personal worry, and young John's stormy life must be considered in some detail because of its ultimate effect on McLoughlin's career.

When he went to London in 1820 to represent the North West winter-ers, he took eight-year-old John and six-year-old Elisabeth to Montreal and left them under the watchful eye of his uncle, Dr. Simon Fraser. McLoughlin saw them briefly in 1822 on his return from Europe, but when he moved to the Columbia in 1824, he did not bring the two children.

However, he was always anxious about them, and his annual letters to his uncle expressed concern, gratitude, frustration because he could not look after them himself, assurances that he would pay for their needs, and hopeful ref-erences to his ever-receding date for "going down." His company account shows many withdrawals for their costs. "Bill to Simon Fraser due March 1826, £100." "Cash paid Bill to Simon Fraser £150." He was so isolated that at one time he was uncertain of Elisabeth's whereabouts, and "presumed" (correctly) that she was with her aunt, Sister St. Henry, at the Ursuline convent in Quebec.

In 1826, Governor Simpson was sufficiently interested in the children to call on John in Montreal, and on Elisabeth when he made a trip to Quebec. He told Dr. Fraser he was "happy to find that the Young Lady had made great prog-ress" under her aunt's care at the convent, and he trusted that "the Boy under your charge likewise promises well, the Dr is much attached to them both."

Elisabeth was doing well, but Sister St. Henry inadvertently set off a Fraser family squabble when she sent their Uncle Simon a bill of fifty-five pounds for the child's board and education. The conservative uncle was "astonished" by the size of the bill, called it "highly exorbitant," referred her to Governor Simp-son, and "refused to sanction the system she follows." Although the sister's reaction is not on record, the problem was evidently resolved, because Elisabeth remained with her at the convent.

John, however, was still in Montreal, and he was in trouble early. Within two years he had been dismissed from his first school for "soiling [his] breech-es"; by 1826 he had been moved to "Mr Essoms school" instead of Mr. Walker's, with no surviving explanation; and "Messrs Glen Walker and Gill" had repeat-edly urged Dr. Fraser to take John out of the school because he "corrupted the morals of the other boys." Apparently unaware of the problem, McLough-lin asked his uncle to help choose the boy's field. "I do not know what to do with my Son—what do you think he is fit for—I will be obliged to you for your Opinion and . . . I must request you to continue your attentions untill I am able to go down and take charge of him myself."

By 1827 John had acquired "a sufficient Knowledge of Arithmetic and Book Keeping to fit him for an other school his present master Mr Neagle cannot teach him any thing else." Dr. Fraser wrote that the boy was less advanced than he had hoped, but assured McLoughlin that "as I before told you I will do for the best that is to say deal with your son as with my own."

The problem of fitting the boy for a profession was intensified by his ancestry, for his mother was one-half or perhaps one-fourth Indian, and in that prejudiced day the company was reluctant to employ youths of mixed blood, even officers' sons. "I thought and do still think the best thing that can be done for the young man is to make him an Indian Trader," wrote Dr. Fraser, "but Governor Simpson tells me the Company have determined to take none of these Young Men into their service (for reasons which he explained to me & which you must know)."

The uncle himself was by no means free from bias. He told McLoughlin, "I do not think he would succeed as a Physician, he would have to go thro a long course of studies   these boys are remarkable for want of steadiness and application, tho by no means deficient in understanding." And referring to Elisabeth he said, "the Girl cannot be a nun on account of her birth & her education is above the sphere that Society seems to have prescribed for her   it is calculated to make her miserable she is by all reports a fine Girl."

Another vexation for Fraser was the bankruptcy in 1825 of the Montreal firm of McGillivrays, Thain & Company, agents in charge of McLoughlin's account. The partner Thomas Thain fell ill and abruptly fled from Canada to Scotland, where he "succombed to an attack of mental illness and was hospitalized." He left the books in chaos, and the firm collapsed. As a consequence, McLoughlin's finances were in such a tangle that he gave power of attorney to George Simpson and George Moffatt, the Montreal merchant whom he had contacted during the Nor'Westers' rebellion. The doctor's financial account for 1828 shows a debit of £575 paid for "George Simpson's Bill to Frost & Co.," which may have been the settlement of a suit by creditors of the bankrupt company. The situation bedeviled Dr. Fraser. He said he expected the firm to pay him "a dividend along with their other Creditors, but God only knows when that will be."

Although this uncle was McLoughlin's good angel, he was nearly seventy and felt overwhelmed by the burden of coping with derelict agents while educating a boy of difficult temperament and limited prospects. In 1827 he wrote to his half brother John Malcolm Fraser—one of Grandfather Malcolm Fraser's second brood. John Malcolm was living at Rivière-du-Loup, and Simon asked him to "take the young man Master McLoughlin under his protection" and superintend his education in Quebec. The plan fell through, and the fifteen-year-old boy was merely enrolled in another school. He may, however, have felt rejected by Dr. Fraser's attempt to shift the responsibility, for during the past seven years, while he was separated from his parents and moved from school to school, his great-uncle had been his one stable caretaker, his father figure. Whatever the reason, in early 1828 young John erupted in an act so violent that he was summarily expelled from school. It was the first, but not the last, of the boy's recorded tantrums.

As Governor Simpson described the incident, John had gone out one rainy evening without permission, and on his return had beaten a younger student "unmercifully"—presumably for threatening to report the absence. When the school's priest, Dr. Newcombe, complained, John "flew into a violent passion, made use of highly improper Language and providing himself with a bludgeon threatened the Drs life." The schoolmaster then sent for Simpson, who had previously shown interest in John, and the governor tried to interview the boys. However, at his first questions, John "burst out into the most violent gust of rage I ever witnessed, became quite frantic with passion, used the most provoking and unrespectful language to the Schoolmaster and clenching his fist threatened revenge! . . . The poor Schoolmaster was quite horrer struck and alarmed, begged me to take him with me and said he would not poor as was keep him another Week for £500."

The consequences were serious, because until then Simpson had considered John's disposition "even and mild." In fact, he said, "I had taken quite a fancy to the Lad and meant . . . to have given him a Seat in our Counting House occasionally preparatory to recommending him as an apprentice Clerk to the Coy. but I have never been so grossly deceived in a Young Man, and regret it exceedingly on account of his Father for whom I have a very great regard."

He did, however, soften to the extent of giving John a place in the Hudson's Bay Company accounting house at Lachine, which was a considerable favor, in view of the company's reluctance to hire the officers' mixed-blood sons. As for Dr. Fraser, he was so angry that he sent the boy his clothes in a trunk and wrote him a chilly letter of advice, which in his rough draft he signed, "I am Dear John your sincere friend Simon Fraser," but struck it out and substituted merely "Your friend."

For McLoughlin, the incident was a crushing blow. He wrote his son at least two letters, the first of which refused the boy's plea to come to the Columbia, while the second was long and kindly, a bit preachy, and full of fatherly advice. He said he was "surpris'd after the refusal I gave your Request to come and join me you should again make it. You ought to know that if I conceived it to your advantage I would have acced'd to your wish." Urging his son to work hard, he said, "if you feel that pride and ambition (which I hope you have) to Rise in the world, you must see that the only way you can succeed is by Applying yourself Most diligently to your Education. . . . At the same time that application to our Studies increases our knowledge it improves our hearts and elevates our Mind to the Great Author of our Being."

Communication was so slow that McLoughlin was unaware that even before he wrote his letter, Chief Factor James Keith, living in Montreal, had sent John to Quebec to live with the family of H. G. Forsyth—whom he also offended—and on October 26, 1829, the boy had sailed for France to join his bachelor uncle, Dr. David. McLoughlin's representatives in Montreal debited his company account for the cost of passage and for John's later expenses.

In Paris, David McLoughlin seemed quite willing to accept his wayward nephew as a protégé, and even though John had wanted to join his father, he was excited by his new life and determined to succeed. He plunged into a rigorous schedule of preparation for the medical profession and wrote to John Fraser, Dr. Simon Fraser's son, "If I fail it will not be by want of hard application I devote the whole day in studying. I am sorry I did not apply as I ought to have done when I was a boy your good father often told me I should repent of it and I never took or paid the slightest attention. . . . I regret every moment I lost I wish I had to begin over again my studies."

His diligence paid off. "I have passed the examination of Bachelier en lettres and passed it with credit," he wrote to Dr. Fraser in 1833. "As soon as I left the room every gentleman said that it was myself that had passed the best of the whole. I answered to every question put to me by the examinators I was so perfect on it that it is impossible to be rejected. . . . I am to enter in one of the hospitals in summer." He described his long hours of studying chemistry, anatomy, physiology, and physics and said he liked anatomy best of all.

But John's life in Paris was not all work. Dr. David McLoughlin was a prominent physician, and with an entrée to royal circles and an income said to be at least ten thousand pounds a year, he had a lifestyle that delighted John. "You cannot imagine how happy I am here—I spent the winter very gay," he wrote to John Fraser. "I have been to balls even [where] the Royal family was and also I had a moments conversation with the Prince."

He witnessed the July Revolution in 1830 that put an end to the reign of Charles X. In the insurrection of June 5–6, 1832, people fell beside him on the street. And on the anniversary of the "three memorable days of July 1830," he attended a grandiose celebration, with the churches draped in black, the musicians of the National Guard playing funeral music all day, the streets "so crowded that it was impossible to pass," and fireworks blazing in the night sky.

This was exciting, but the boy was young and lonely, and his Great-Uncle Simon coldly neglected—or refused—to answer his letters. In 1831 John wrote to him, "The reason why I did not write so frequent this year is that I was waiting for an answer to the two letters that I wrote you last year." The following spring he told John Fraser, "Since my arrival in Paris I wrote several letters to you and to your father to thank him for his kind attention he had for me while I was under his care. I am astonished that he has not written." And in 1833 he asked his neglectful relative, "Ah what can be the cause of your long silence to me? Am I the cause of it? If so tell me on what occasion. . . . Alas can I ever cease regretting the loss of your love and regard no never."

Even though Dr. Fraser refused to write, McLoughlin's brother David was pleased and unfailingly generous. "You cannot think how kind he is to [me]—he does all what he can for me," wrote John to his great-uncle, and David said the youth was giving him "Great satisfaction   he has taken to his studies with an Ardor and with a tenacity which shows he is not acting under the spur of the Moment but from conviction . . . if his Zeal for Study continues and that he throws the Whole of his mental faculties into the scale he must succeed in distinguishing himself."

But even then, in the care of this kindly uncle, something happened, something unexplained but so serious that David sent him back to Canada. When McLoughlin heard about it, he was both hurt and furious. "This is too painful a subject to dwell on and I will only say if he had felt one hundreth of what I feel he would have acted differently," he wrote to his Uncle Simon. Refusing to abandon hope, he said that if John studied "Zealously" and tried to reform, he should have whatever sum he needed, but otherwise "you will please only give him any small sum necessary to take him out of the Country   I have not the means to support him as an Idler and if I had I would not do it. . . . all has been done for him that could be done and I humbly implore the Almighty that of his infinite Mercy he may touch his heart." Loving his son, thinking he might be sent to India, he said he preferred keeping him in Canada "for the sake of seeing him."

The doctor was also puzzled. "He writes me an Apology for his Misconduct but he does not write me what it was he did," he told John Fraser. "There never was so far as I know a Young [Man] from this Country who had so fine a Prospect to begin life with and how he has thrown it away." The son had complained about his allowance, and McLoughlin told Chief Trader John Mc-

Leod that "my Brother found him Extravagant and sent him Back." Serious trouble over money, however, seems unlikely, because McLoughlin had always supplied ample funds for John's expenses, and the total of six hundred pounds for four years in Paris was not excessive, considering David's lifestyle.

The event occurred early in 1834—only a few months after Dr. David was married—and Roderick Finlayson, a family friend who knew the circumstances, said the marriage "was the cause of Johns coming to Canada." McLoughlin himself referred to a note from his brother, which said he had written to complain of John's behavior and before mailing the letter had shown it to the youth in hope of inducing him to mend his ways. Instead it aroused John's explosive temper, and four days later he committed the act that resulted in his dismissal. "My Brother does not write me what it is and he ought to have done so," McLoughlin lamented.

Although much of the puzzle cannot be solved, the significant events are clear. Young John left Paris under a cloud in the summer of 1834, when he was twenty-two years old, after doing well for nearly five years under his Uncle David's guidance. For McLoughlin it was a mixture of good and ill fortune. His stormy petrel was returning to Canada. But the troubled young man had failed again.

CHAPTER 7

The End of Isolation

It was a Rule with us Never to retreat before an opposition.

DR. JOHN MCLOUGHLIN

~ 1 ~

The Boston Ice Man
1832–1836

U ntil the early 1830s, McLoughlin's only American contacts were a few scattered farmers in the Willamette Valley, an occasional trapper, and the coasters in the north. The first evidence of change appeared at noon on October 29, 1832, in the midst of a cold, dark, rainy spell, when a bedraggled group of visitors trudged through the fort gate. They were Nathaniel Jarvis Wyeth and eleven followers, the forlorn remnant of a group of twenty-four who had set out from Boston in high spirits seven months before. McLoughlin had just dictated a long letter to the Governor and Committee, but he was sufficiently concerned about the newcomers to write again, spelling the then-unfamiliar "Wyeth" as "Dwight."

> This morning a party of eleven Americans under the direction of a Mr. Dwight, from Boston, arrived here. . . . He says he came to ascertain if possible to make a business of curing Salmon in this River, & at the same time to supply the American Trappers in the Rocky Mountains. . . . I would not be surprised to find that his views are in connexion with a plan which I see in a Boston paper of March 1831, to colonise the Willamette.

It was a shrewd observation. Wyeth was tired, ragged, and doubtless none too clean. Most of his men had deserted. His ship was missing and might be lost. But he had grand dreams, and he was the first of his countrymen to bring an organized business to the West Coast. It was characteristic that McLoughlin, even though he foresaw troublesome competition, welcomed the American, assisted him, and made him a friend for life.

Nathaniel Wyeth of Cambridge, Massachusetts, born in 1802, was a tall, handsome, young merchant, with a sensitive face framed by a short, neatly

Nathaniel Wyeth was the first American entrepreneur to attempt to establish a foothold in the Northwest. In economic terms he failed, but he left a lasting mark on the area. Although he and McLoughlin were competitors, they formed a friendship that lasted throughout their lives. OHS ORHI 3632

trimmed beard. In the past, he had spent summers working at his father's resort hotel in Massachusetts and winters directing the ice harvest for the firm of Frederic Tudor, the New England "Ice King." Blessed with an excellent mind, Wyeth had invented devices for the better storage of ice, but he disliked that business so heartily that he once wrote, "I will lose my scalp before I will reengage in it."

His interest in the Pacific Coast had first been stirred by Hall Kelley, a Boston schoolmaster who promoted the Far West with fanatic zeal and planned to lead a group to Oregon. In August 1831, Wyeth applied for a "scituation" with the group, but Kelley's preparations were so elaborate that the departure was delayed. By autumn Wyeth had decided that Kelley's plan was unsound, so he dropped out and organized his own expedition.

Throughout that fall and winter he was in a fever of activity, setting up a joint-stock venture called the Pacific Trading Company. He planned to have a ship sail around Cape Horn with merchandise for trappers on the West Coast and return with furs and salmon, while he himself would lead an overland expedition to the Columbia and handle arrangements there.

Wyeth enrolled young recruits who put up forty dollars each for a share in the profits and the dubious privilege of making the cross-continent trip. He chartered a vessel, the *Sultana*, loaded her with trading goods and supplies, and sent her out with instructions to meet him on the Columbia. Juggling a welter of details, he consulted government officials about laws for the Indian trade and about permissions and licenses. He wrote to his congressman, offering to bring back information on Oregon. He asked his brother for a loan, had his house mortgaged for "about $800," learned "how salmon are pickled and how smoked and how taken," conducted evening meetings of his group, designed uniforms, and planned for music on the march.

> The bugle of which I spoke to him should be of the plainest kind and the most simple to use and the least liable to get out of repair or bro-

ken. It will be used chiefly as a signal for parties at a distance, and sometimes in marching a little music will enliven us. We propose that one
should learn it well and then teach all the rest. We shall have as much
as ten and to be used alternately so as not to be tedious to any one.

His most astonishing innovation was a hybrid wagon, "half boat and half
carriage . . . so constructed that the four wheels could be taken off when we
came to a river, and placed in the wagon . . . to be towed across by a rope."
Cambridge students found the device so amusing that they christened it an
"amphibium" or a "Nat-wyethium."

In early spring, 1832, Wyeth and twenty-four recruits traveled by rail and
steamboat from Boston to St. Louis, where they happened to meet William
Sublette of the Rocky Mountain Fur Company. Since Sublette was about to
lead a brigade west, Wyeth arranged for his help, and, led by these experienced American mountain men, the party started across the plains. Each of
the eager Bostonians was wearing "a coarse woolen jacket and pantaloons, a
striped cotton shirt, and cowhide boots" and carrying a small axe, a musket or

THE SUMMER RENDEZVOUS.

The American trappers held a yearly rendezvous, often on the Green River in Wyoming, or
in the Teton area. Attended by both fur traders and Indians, this was a time for trading the
year's furs, replenishing supplies, replacing worn-out horses and equipment. It was also the
one big social event of the year, with racing, gambling, and feasting. Liquor flowed freely,
and more than one trapper found that by the end of the rendezvous he had spent all of his
profits for the year. From Francis Fuller Victor's *The River of the West*. OHS ORHI 98822

"An American Trapper of the Ancien Régime."
This is an exaggerated depiction of the gear and
appearance of an American trapper, as seen by a
British artist. From Robert Brown's *A Graphic and
Popular Description of the Countries of the World
Illustrated*, part 5. HUDSON BAY COMPANY ARCHIVES,
PROVINCIAL ARCHIVES OF MANITOBA, HBCA PP2150 N13869

rifle with its bayonet tucked into his belt,
and "a large clasped knife for eating and
common purposes." But they had no
bugles, and on Sublette's advice, they left
the "Nat-wyethium" behind.

Even with expert guides, the trail was
punishing. They contended with wolves,
snakes, bears. They built a raft, but it cap-
sized on the Platte River. A band of Black-
feet Indians captured five of their horses.
The men were so tormented by gnats that
the earliest surviving entry in Wyeth's jour-
nal begins, in midsentence, "gray and my face like a plumb pudding the skin
is entirely . . . off one of my ears." Two men deserted, then three. And in July,
at the annual fur-trade rendezvous in Pierre's Hole, west of the Teton Range,
several decided to return with William Sublette's party, who were taking the
company's furs back to St. Louis. Wyeth wrote, "All my men but 11 left me to
these I gave such articles as I could spare from the necesities of my own Party
and let them go."

Shaken by the loss, Wyeth and his loyal eleven continued west with a brigade under Sublette's brother, Milton. At the Humboldt River in late August,
their paths diverged, Milton Sublette going south and Wyeth going west to
Fort Nez Perces, where they were received "in the most hospitable and gentlemanly manner by Peanbron [Pierre Pambrun] the agent for this post."
Pambrun gave them passage on a Hudson's Bay Company barge, which took
them down the Columbia to Fort Vancouver—a five-day float.

Although these guests were Americans—and therefore potential rivals—
McLoughlin felt obligated to assist travelers, and he enjoyed visitors who
brought news of the outside world. He therefore invited Wyeth and one of
the men, John Ball, "to his own table and rooms at the fort," while he housed
the rest outside the palisade. Wyeth wrote:

Here I was received with the utmost kindness and Hospitality by Doct. McLauchland the acting Gov. of the place. . . . Our people were supplied with food and shelter from the rain which is constant they raise at this fort 6000 bush. of wheat 3 of Barley 1500 potatoes 3000 peas a large quantity of punkins   they have coming on apple trees, peach Do. and grapes. Sheep, Hogs, Horses, Cows 600 goats, grist 2, saw mill 2. 24 lb guns powder magazine of stone   the fort is of wood and square they are building a Sch. [schooner] of 70 Tons. . . . I find Doct. McLauchland a fine old gentleman truly philanthropic in his Ideas he is doing much good by introducing fruits into this country which will much facilitate the progress of its settlement.

In November Wyeth received word that the missing *Sultana* had been wrecked in the Pacific—news so daunting that the rest of his men asked to be released from their contracts. "I could not refuse   they had already suffered much . . . they were good men and persevered as long as perseverance would do good," Wyeth wrote, and plaintively added, "I am now afloat on the great sea of life without stay or support but in good hands i.e. myself and providence and a few of the H. B. Co. who are perfect gentlemen."

All winter the stranded Americans remained at Fort Vancouver, disappointed, adrift, but "eating and drinking the good things to be had there and enjoying much the manly society of the place." McLoughlin provided a boat to take Wyeth down the Columbia River to investigate salmon fishing, and up the Willamette River to visit the valley. There he saw the company's lumber mill being built at the falls and "3 or 4 Canadians settled as farmers   they have now been there one year have Hogs, Horses, Cows, have built barns, Houses, and raised wheat, barely [barley], potatoes, turnips, cabages, corn, punkins, mellons." These were the retirees such as Etienne Lucier, whom McLoughlin had furnished with seed and tools.

After visiting the Willamette, Wyeth returned to Fort Vancouver, still at loose ends. When "Doct J. McGlaucland" offered to let the Americans work for their passage to Hawaii, some of them left, but Calvin Tibbetts and Solomon H. Smith started farms and became permanent settlers, and John Ball stayed at the fort. A graduate of Dartmouth College, Ball insisted on earning his way, and although McLoughlin was reluctant to put a guest to work, he finally suggested that Ball might teach the children of the fort.

"Of course I gladly accepted the offer, so he sent the boys to my room to be instructed," wrote Ball. "I found the boys docile and attentive and they made good progress. The doctor often came into the school, and was well satisfied and pleased. One day he said, 'Ball, anyway you will have the reputation of teaching the *first* school in Oregon.'" Among the pupils were Willie McKay and McLoughlin's eleven-year-old David.

Early in February, when a brigade set out under Francis Ermatinger, Wyeth and two of his men went with it. He wrote in his journal:

> I parted with feelings of sorrow from the gentlemen of Fort Vancouver their unremitted kindness to me while there much endeared them to me more so than it would seem possible during so short a time   Doct McGlaucland the Gov. of the place is a man distinguished as much for his kindness and humanity as his good sense and information and to whom I am so much indebted as that he will never be forgotten by me.

In spite of his utter failure, Wyeth was determined to try again. On March 12, 1833, during a stopover at Fort Colvile, he wrote a proposition to Governor Simpson, asking for the right to buy supplies at an advance of "50 pr ct on their original cost" and to purchase furs "at the rate of $5 for full Beavers." In return, he offered to trade only south of the Columbia, and not within a hundred miles of a Hudson's Bay post. From Colvile he went to the rendezvous—this time at Green River—and then east with a party of the Rocky Mountain Fur Company, again led by Milton Sublette. By horse, by bullboat, by canoe, and finally by a Missouri River steamboat, he made his way to St. Louis and from there to the East Coast.

Wyeth was a fast worker. He reached Cambridge on November 6, 1833, and on November 20 he informed his brother Leonard, "To day the thing is closed, the vessell to be sent round the Horn at once." In two weeks he had chartered a ship and put together a "concern . . . to invest $20000." A few months earlier, while traveling with Milton Sublette, he had signed a contract to furnish Sublette's company with trade goods, and therefore he was buying for them, too, bustling from shop to shop. He not only recruited his own party, he arranged to assist several others—the Reverend Jason Lee with four missionaries, the ornithologist John Kirk Townsend, and the botanist Thomas Nuttall.

In the spring of 1834, Wyeth and his New England group met their fellow travelers at Independence, Missouri, and started from there in a caravan of seventy men and 250 horses. In Townsend's words, "Every man in the company seemed to feel a portion of the same kind of enthusiasm; uproarious bursts of merriment, and gay and lively songs, were constantly echoing along the line. We were certainly a most merry and happy company."

The merriment did not last long. Milton Sublette had to turn back because of an infected leg, leaving the brigade to push on without him. When they reached the fur-trade rendezvous, Wyeth met Sublette's brother William, but this was a major disappointment because William refused to honor Milton's order for goods. As a result, Wyeth had a large supply of bulky articles and no market. Deciding to dispose of them at a post of his own, he put up rough log buildings in the southeastern section of today's Idaho "and named it Fort Hall in honor of the oldest member of our concern."

Wyeth described its dedication. "We manufactured a magnificent flag from some unbleached sheeting a little red flannel and a few blue patches, saluted it with damaged powder and wet it in vilanous alcohol, and after all it makes, I do assure you, a very respectable appearance amid the dry and desolate regions of central America."

For the rest of the journey, the groups separated. Lee and the missionaries, who had a band of horned cattle to drive, set out on July 30, while the others finished the fort, left a squad of men to maintain it, and took off on August 6. At Fort Nez Perces they met Lee, and from there to Fort Vancouver they traveled down the Columbia by company barge and individual canoes, arriving on different days. First to reach the fort was Wyeth, on September 14. He said McLoughlin "received us in his usual manner he has here power and uses it as a man should to make those about him and those who come in contact with him comfortable and happy."

Lee and his group arrived the following day, and the naturalists on September 16. Townsend wrote:

On the beach in front of the fort, we were met by Mr. Lee, the missionary, and Dr. John McLoughlin, the chief factor, and Governor of the Hudson's Bay posts in this vicinity. The Dr. is a large, dignified and very noble looking man, with a fine expressive countenance, and remarkably bland and pleasing manners. The missionary introduced Mr. N. and myself in due form, and we were greeted and received with a frank and unassuming politeness which was most peculiarly grateful to our feelings. He requested us to consider his house our home, provided a separate room for our use, a servant to wait upon us, and furnished us with every convenience which we could possibly wish

for. I shall never cease to feel grateful to him for his disinterested kindness to the poor houseless and travel-worn strangers.

As always, McLoughlin was delighted to have knowledgeable visitors. He
housed them, fed them, and lent them a boat manned by Kanakas, and they
roamed the area, collecting plants and birds. Nuttall soon left, but McLoughlin
hired Townsend as a replacement for the fort's resident physician, Dr. Meredith
Gairdner, who was going to Hawaii. Townsend stayed for another year, and
after returning to the States, he publicized his travels in a widely read book
that increased American interest in the Columbia.

As for Wyeth, he was eager as ever, and full of ideas. He had already made
one proposal to Governor Simpson, for which no answer had yet come, and
he now made McLoughlin a new offer. As the doctor explained it to Governor
Simpson:

> Mr. Wyeth . . . told me that he did not come to oppose us, if we would
> put no obstacles in the way of his trading Horses in the Interior or
> Salmon there, as his object was to salt Salmon for exportation, and to
> deal with the American Trappers in the Snake Country. Mr. Wyeths
> Vessel the *May Dacre* arrived a few days before Mr. Wyeth and neither
> the Captain nor Mr. Wyeth have in the least interfered as yet with
> the Trade of Furs at this place or along the Columbia.

The idea appealed to McLoughlin as reasonable and sound. In 1829 Governor Simpson had told him that if rivals appeared, the company should "meet
them fairly and openly as competitors in Trade," and "studiously avoid any dis-
creditable proceeding which might tarnish the reputation of the Honble Co^y."
McLoughlin thought Wyeth's plan would not interfere with the company's harvest of furs, and that cooperating with it was surely a way of meeting him "fairly
and openly." In addition, he was convinced that the Bostonian's venture would
soon collapse, and he feared that if he refused supplies, the resourceful New Englander might bring in goods from some other source. So he decided to deal with
Wyeth as a new outlet and accepted the proposal, but retained trapping rights in
the valuable Flathead Country. The agreement restrained him so little that, without breaking his word, he sent Thomas McKay on a trapping expedition to
the Snake Country and had him build Fort Boise between Wyeth's Fort Hall
and the Hudson's Bay Fort Nez Perces. It was cleverly located—not close to the
American post, but where it would intercept Indians bringing furs.

Although McLoughlin fully expected the Governor and Committee to approve of what he had done, he was disappointed. When the *Eagle* arrived in 1835, she brought a sharp rejection, not to the recent proposal, but to the one Wyeth had made to Governor Simpson in 1833. With it were specific orders that if Wyeth came again, the Chief Factor must "put him down" through vigorous opposition. McLoughlin in the field and the Hudson's Bay officers in London had a basic difference. The Governor and Committee wished to relentlessly drive out competition, while the doctor preferred to be friendly in small things, to cooperate when it was in his company's interest, but to undersell his opponents until their venture became so unprofitable that they gave up. His policy was both sound and practical, but he was unable to convince the London Committee that it had merit. The disagreement was destined to grow, and it would never be satisfactorily resolved.

For the time being, however, there was no conflict, because Wyeth's venture was beset by misfortune and soon collapsed. The *May Dacre* had been struck by lightning and arrived too late for the fall salmon run. Wyeth and all of his men except one fell ill with the all-too-prevalent fever. Seventeen of his people died "by drowning and disease and warfare." He hired Sandwich Islanders to accompany his aide, Captain Joseph Thing, to Fort Hall, but they promptly fled. His one tangible achievement was the erection of several log houses on Wappato Island—today's Sauvie Island—where he set up an establishment, named it Fort William, and planned to use it as a farm. "I have no good news to impart," he wrote to his brother Leonard. "After so long an abstinence I feel hungry for a little success."

Wyeth's surviving letters and journals show that he was a thoroughly decent man, fair, intelligent, with a wry sense of humor. "I assure you the Fort [his Fort William] looks quite as warlike as a pile of ice, but not quite so proffitable," he wrote to Frederic Tudor, his former employer. But he was no longer buoyed by hope. "We have failed in every thing. . . . I shall do all I can one year more, which will I think shew whether anything is to be done here or not, and I will not be long in closing the concern when I find that there is nothing to be made."

In spite of his misfortunes, when Wyeth started home in May 1836, he was already planning a third attempt, and before he left, he wrote out a new proposal: if the Hudson's Bay Company would furnish him with supplies, let him hire men and horses, and guarantee him a market for furs, he would abandon Fort Hall, "if required," and confine his activities to the upper Snake River and to the south and east.

THE END OF ISOLATION The Boston Ice Man

Again the idea seemed sensible to McLoughlin, for if he had an American middleman in the Snake Country, he would no longer have to send a company brigade to that difficult area, but could turn a profit there with little trouble and no risk. Before deciding, he checked with the "Gentlemen" at Fort Vancouver—Duncan Finlayson, John McLeod Jr., and James Douglas—who all agreed. He was so sure of company approval that he confidently consented to Wyeth's plan, and even asked the American what supplies he would like to receive in 1837.

But the members of the Committee were again displeased, and Governor Simpson ordered the Chief Factor to oppose Wyeth "vigorously," rejecting any agreement that might allow their rival "to secure a firm footing in the country." The reply infuriated McLoughlin, because he thought he had protected his company's interests with skill and zeal, without resorting to conflict. Never one to hide his feelings, he poured them out in an angry letter, marking parts of it for emphasis.

Is it possible that Gentlemen unacquainted with . . . our situation at the time and absent from the scene of Action can be as Good judges of What is best to be done as a person on the spot? But What did I give up, Nothing . . . *I take credit to Myself for having secured the Fur trade at this place Entirely to Ourselves While I reserved the Right to oppose him in the Salmon trade . . . I Thwarted his plans* as Effectually as if I had spent our Whole Outfit on that sole object and of Which there can be no better proof than that he has Given up the Business. . . . What can Induce Governor Simpson and the Northern Council to suppose Wyeth was not Vigourously opposed? Is it because there was no quarrelling as in former times. . . . Your Honors may depend on it that it is not those who get into quarrels with their neighbours who Manage best for the Interest of the Concern. . . . Wyeth had only to tap a puncheon of Rum and open a Bale of Goods to make us spend hundreds to secure the trade.

He then asked all senior officers in the area to state their views in writing, and was delighted with the replies. Five gave him strong support. One said he had been absent and therefore could not write. And one favored the plan for Wyeth but feared it might encourage others to come. Along with this barrage, McLoughlin sent the Committee a triumphant statement: "Wyeth is obliged to withdraw, the American trappers are Receding from us—our Returns have not decreased and our Books shew our profits have not Diminished."

~240~

As for Wyeth, after his defeat on the Columbia, he returned to his old "buisness" as a partner in the Tudor company, which soon was shipping ice to Calcutta. He had been the trigger for a serious disagreement between McLoughlin and his company, and was the precursor of a problem that was bound to grow—how to deal with incoming Americans. The Chief Factor's opposition, however, had not been the cause of Wyeth's failure. McLoughlin had undercut Fort Hall, but the Bostonian's insurmountable handicap had been lack of sufficient capital to support his plans.

Even though Wyeth was gone, he was not quite finished with the West Coast, because he still had property there, including Fort Hall. In 1837 McLoughlin sent John McLeod to take an outfit to the fur traders' rendezvous, where Wyeth's agent, Captain Joseph Thing, told him Wyeth "had given over the business, and given him power to sell out." The asking price was $1,000 for Fort Hall, $12 each for traps, and $40 each for horses, which McLeod "very properly" rejected as too high. But Captain Thing "brough[t] down his Furs" to Fort Vancouver.

With the agent at hand, McLoughlin made him a counteroffer for his furs and goods, including five hundred dollars for Fort Hall, which Captain Thing accepted. On January 11, 1838, McLoughlin wrote to the Governor and Committee, "I have this day drawn on Mr. Pelly the Company's agent at Oahu for £1541.1.2 Sterling in favor of Nathaniel Wyeth Esq." He had bought the Bostonian's entire holdings—traps, horses, equipment, Fort Hall in the Snake Country, and Fort William on Wappato Island.

Wyeth had failed to gain a foothold on the Columbia, but nevertheless he made a permanent mark on McLoughlin's domain. At least seven of his men became farmers in the Willamette Valley. His ship brought supplies for sale, the first breach of the Hudson's Bay Company monopoly. One of his followers taught the first school. Wyeth guided the first missionaries and founded an important post on the Oregon Trail. And his four continental crossings would encourage future emigration and help mark its path. For McLoughlin, the Boston ice man's enterprise was a milestone. From that time on, his Columbia River empire would always have Americans nearby.

~ 2 ~

The Macedonian Cry
1834–1840

O ne traveler who came with Wyeth was to have great importance for Mc-Loughlin. He was the tall, bearded Reverend Jason Lee—thirty-one years old, slightly stooped, slow-moving, idealistic. With him were three lay workers—Cyrus Shepard, Philip L. Edwards, and Courtney M. Walker—and Lee's nephew, the Reverend Daniel Lee, good-natured and naive, "a thin bony form surmounted by thin bony features." They marked the beginning of the missionary movement into Oregon.

Interest in bringing Christianity to the Indians had been set off in 1831 by the visit to St. Louis of four young Indians, commonly said to be of the Flathead tribe, although they were actually Nez Perces. Some of their nation had previously attended school at Red River and brought back word about the powerful "black book"—the Bible—which they thought was the white men's source of power. Wanting to learn more of the Americans' skills, the elders sent the four to St. Louis with fur trader Lucien Fontanelle, when he went there for supplies. Two of the Indians became ill and died in the city, one died on the way home, and the last was killed on a hunting trip, so none returned to the tribe. But they were nevertheless significant. William Walker of Ohio, who saw them when he visited St. Louis, found them so fascinating that on January 9, 1833, he wrote about them to G. P. Disosway of New York City. Moved by the letter, Disosway had it published in the *Christian Advocate and Journal*, along with florid additions about the "sincere searchers after truth" who traveled "3,000 miles through thick forests and extensive prairies."

The piece was reprinted many times and became famous as "the Macedonian Cry," named for the passage in the Bible in which a Macedonian asked the apostle Paul for help and "immediately we endeavoured to go into Macedonia, assuredly gathering that the Lord had called us for to preach the gospel unto them." Read from pulpits, discussed at meetings, the letter generated a heated controversy. Some saw the Indians' visit as a sincere hunger for the truth, while others thought they were in pursuit of material things. The Reverend Daniel Lee himself called the *Advocate* piece "a high-wrought account" and said, "These incorrect statements receiving the fullest confidence, many believed that the day had come, and that the call was imperative, to send the gospel to Oregon."

The Reverend Jason Lee came to Oregon in 1836 as a dedicated missionary, established the first mission, and was instrumental in bringing several influential residents into the area. OHS ORHI 8342

First to take action was the Mission Board of the Methodist Church, which in 1834 sent the Reverend Jason Lee and his party to establish a mission among the Flatheads. After joining Wyeth in St. Louis, they traveled with his group, and at his Fort Hall, on Sunday, July 27, in a grove of poplar trees, Lee conducted the first Protestant religious service to be held in the interior west of the Rocky Mountains. He had a congregation of about sixty, including John Kirk Townsend, Thomas Nuttall, and a party of French Canadian trappers and Indians led by Thomas McKay. Townsend wrote that the Indians "sat upon the ground like statues . . . kneeling when the preacher kneeled, and rising when he rose, evidently with a view of paying him and us a suitable respect. . . . A meeting for worship in the Rocky mountains is almost as unusual as the appearance of a herd of buffalo in the settlements. . . . Mr. Lee is a great favorite with the men, deservedly so."

As has been shown, the party then split, and arrived at Fort Vancouver on different days. Having been alerted by Wyeth, McLoughlin was waiting on shore when the missionaries came, at about three o'clock on Monday, September 15, 1834. He promptly ushered them through the broad gate and offered them the facilities of the fort. As Lee described it,

We received every attention from these gentlemen. Our baggage was brought and put into a spacious room without consulting us and the room assigned for our use, and we had the pleasure of sleeping again within the walls of a house. . . . The dinner was as good and served in as good style as in any gentleman's house in the east. Fine muskmelons and water melons and apples were set before us which were, indeed, a luxury, after the dry living we have had for some time. . . . Dr. McLoughlin, the governor of the fort, seems pleased that missions have come to the country and freely offers us any assistance that it is in his power to render. It is his decided opinion that we should commence somewhere in this vicinity.

The Mission Board's original plan had been to establish a mission among the Nez Perces and Flatheads, but McLoughlin told Lee "it was too dangerous," and that the Willamette Valley would be not only safer, but more productive. "To do good to the Indians," he said, the missionaries "must establish themselves where they could collect them around them; teach them first to cultivate the ground and live more comfortably than they do by hunting, and as they do this, teach them religion."

While Lee and his party were seeking a location, McLoughlin fed and housed them and furnished guides, horses, and supplies for a trip to the Willamette. On Sunday he invited Lee to preach at the fort to "a mixed congregation—English, French, Scotch, Irish, Indians, Americans, half breeds, Japanese, &c., some of whom did not understand 5 words of English." From this time on, McLoughlin asked visiting ministers of all faiths to preach at the fort, whenever any of them were there.

The next day Lee resumed his search. "Could I but know the identicle place that the Lord designs for us . . . it would be a matter of great rejoicing," he wrote. "Only God direct us to the right spot where we can best glorify thee." Eventually he decided to settle on the Willamette River, ten miles north of today's Salem in a low-lying area that became known as Mission Bottom.

This heroic illustration is from the HBC Calendar for 1941, and shows McLoughlin and Lee on the waterfront at Fort Vancouver. *McLoughlin Welcomes the Americans, Fort Vancouver, 1834*, a 1941 HBC Calendar illustration by Charles F. Comfort. HUDSON BAY COMPANY ARCHIVES, PROVINCIAL ARCHIVES OF MANITOBA, HBCA PICTURE COLLECTION, P-405 [N14042]

OLD MISSION-HOUSE, OREGON.

The house Jason Lee built at Mission Bottom, when he first came to the Northwest. It was said that he whittled the window sills and other features with a pocket knife. OHS ORHI 1507

Wyeth's *May Dacre* had brought the missionaries' equipment, including farm implements, tools, household goods, books, garden seeds, and live chickens. To supplement their goods, McLoughlin furnished seed for field crops and lent them "seven oxen, one bull, eight cows and their calves," which he had his men drive to the Willamette. He also had a collection taken among the gentlemen of the fort, resulting in a donation of $130.00, and he made a further gift of flour. The missionaries then established a base in the valley, where, Daniel Lee said, they found "about a dozen families, mostly French Canadians, who had been hunters in the service of the Hudson's Bay Company, or free trappers, and had very lately left that employment and begun to farm."

The ardent young newcomers cut timber, hewed boards, and built a house, thirty-two by eighteen feet, with a clay and sand chimney and windowsills whittled by Jason Lee with his pocketknife. Several Indians of the area brought children to be cared for and taught. Cyrus Shepard wrote that he made one little girl "a gown (though not a very fashionable one) from some pieces of tow-cloth, which had been used for baling our goods." The missionaries were busy with a host of secular jobs—farming, caring for the children, teaching, and holding services, and when they or the children were ill, they went to Fort Vancouver for medical help from McLoughlin or his assistants. A colony of Americans was taking root.

THE NEXT GROUP TO ANSWER "the Macedonian Cry" was sent by the American Board of Commissioners for Foreign Missions, under the Congregational

Traders buying furs from the Indians (upper), and Jason Lee preaching to them in the lower Willamette Valley. Lee's mission functioned for several years as a mission and school for the Indians. OHS ORHI 1715

and Presbyterian Churches. In 1835 this board sent out a preliminary party of two—plump, elderly, fussy Samuel Parker, and handsome young Dr. Marcus Whitman.

Parker was "a man of good education and refinement, and exceedingly set in his opinions," while Whitman was considered a well-trained doctor, because he had had several years of "riding" with a practicing physician plus two sixteen-week terms in medical school. He was thirty-three years old, broad-shouldered, muscular and tall, "with high cheek bones and prominent eyebrows, beneath which were grave kindly eyes of gray." After attending the fur traders' rendezvous, Whitman returned east to arrange an expedition, while Parker continued west to Fort Vancouver.

McLoughlin gave Parker the hospitality of the fort, but he was somewhat chagrined because the wordy preacher "*took up* his Residence with us" and stayed for the entire winter. George B. Roberts, a clerk at the fort, called him "a very good old fanatic with some few peculiarities, such as licking his plate." The Chief Factor, being more tolerant, said he seemed to be "a man of piety and zeal but is very unpopular with the other Protestant missionaries." Since Parker was alone and destitute, McLoughlin provided food and lodging, but in the spring he was greatly relieved to give his visitor free passage on a company ship to the Sandwich Islands, from which Parker returned home.

In the summer of that year, 1836, the American Board sent Whitman west again, accompanied this time by his bride Narcissa, by the Reverend Henry Harmon Spalding with his wife Eliza, and by William H. Gray, "a good teacher, cabinet maker and house-joiner." They made their own way to the fur traders' rendezvous, which had never before entertained visitors like these. Narcissa

Narcissa Whitman (wife of Dr. Marcus Whitman) was a beautiful and talented woman, who strove to succeed as a missionary. It was a job that did not suit her well. In her so-called journal—actually a long letter to her family, written over many months— she contributed an intelligent and highly individual look at life in early Oregon. This drawing was made after her death by Oliver Dixon. OHS ORHI 1645

Whitman was a tall, graceful young woman with abundant reddish hair and great personal charm, while Eliza Spalding was plainer, thin and dark and not very well, but with intelligence and a kind heart. After several days, during which Indians and trappers alike were fascinated by the two intrepid young women, the missionaries continued west with a Hudson's Bay party under Chief Trader John McLeod. Although they had expected Parker to meet them, he was on his way east.

McLoughlin's network had brought word that they were coming. "As the boats neared the shore," wrote Gray, "two tall, well-formed, neatly-dressed gentlemen waved a welcome, and in a moment all were on shore. . . . One, whose hair was then nearly white, stepped forward and gave his arm to Mrs. Whitman. The other, a tall, black-haired, black-eyed man, with rather slim body, a light sallow complexion and smooth face, gave his arm to Mrs. Spalding." The "gentlemen"—McLoughlin and James Douglas—led the party into the fort, where the doctor showed them around and invited them to dine at his table, along with his wife and daughter and Douglas.

"We are now in Vancouver. The New York of the Pacific," Narcissa wrote in her diary. "What a delightful place this [is] . . . French is the prevailing language here. English is spoken only by a few." She said McLoughlin "put his Daughter in my care wishes me to hear her recitations."

Housing the missionary women was a special pleasure to Marguerite McLoughlin and her daughter. Eloisa said that as a rule, the families of the fort "lived separate and private entirely," and that when her father had visitors, "he entertained them in the general Mess room, and not in the family mess room." But the missionaries brought change. "We mingled more. Of course we took the ladies into our mess room. But Dr. Whitman always took his meals with us. He brought ladies and Dr. Spaulding too. At the mess room there was much hurry on account of business; they would sit down and get up and go. At our mess there was nothing to hurry, and they would sit down and enjoy themselves."

Narcissa reveled in life at the fort. She described the gardens, the fruits and vegetables, the elaborate table appointments. She made friends with McLoughlin's family, and in a revealing glimpse of the doctor's wife, she said, "Mrs. McLoughlin has a fine ear for music and is greatly delighted she is one of the kindest women in the world. Speaks a little French, but mostly Cree, her native tongue." After riding over the countryside with Marguerite and Eloisa, she said McLoughlin's wife, who rode "gentleman fashion," tried to persuade her and Eliza Spalding to do the same "as being a more easy way," but they declined.

As he had with Lee, McLoughlin offered the missionaries all the facilities of the fort, and Narcissa was greatly impressed. "Doct. McLaughlin gave my Husband a pair of Lether pantaloons today. all the gentlemen here were [wear] them for economy. Riding horseback & carrying a gun is very destructive to cloth pantaloons," she wrote, and said he sold them supplies, "as cheap as can be affoarded & cheaper probably than we can get them from the States. . . . My tin ware has all been made within a week past of the first rate block tin. I have six large milk pans, coffee & tea pots, candle sticks & molds. Covered pails & a baker . . . and besides this the blacksmiths have all been employed in making our farming utensils &c. . . . We see now that it was not necessary to bring anything because we find all here." She mentioned "a few deficiencies in the cloth line," such as the use of blankets for bedding but no sheets.

McLoughlin's son David described his father during these years as "buoyant in spirits," agile and quick, with blue eyes that "can either penetrate into the very heart of a person when excited or be as calm as a lamb in his endearments. . . . he was very polite to strangers and especially to Gentlemen and Ladies—his talk was very loud and always to the point." Energetic, enjoying company, enjoying conversation, McLoughlin was thoroughly pleased to entertain these personable young missionaries. But they placed him in an uncomfortable position, because the officers in London did not approve of such bountiful aid to Americans, even those sent by a church. The Chief Factor, however, was moved both by compassion and by what he considered good business practices. Convinced that the missionaries could not be stopped and that his

wisest course was to set up a normal trading relationship with them, he vigorously insisted that his policy was in the company's best interest.

> If you refuse them they will get their supplies from Wahou [Oahu]
> as they are connected with the Missionaries at the Sandwich Islands
> Who have a Vessel of their own, and if they send her here We may
> be sure that some Adventurers will avail themselves of the opportuni-
> ty to come and open shop in opposition to us, Give us an Immensity
> of trouble, and Make us Incur great Expence . . . can we prevent
> Missionaries dispersing themselves Among these Indians? I say we
> cannot even if we were so Inclined. . . . We ought in policy to secure
> their Good Will and that of those who support them in their Laudable
> Endeavours to do Good, to afford them . . . such assistance as we can
> give without Incurring Expence and this is the plan I have followed.

McLoughlin was dismayed to learn that Whitman and Spalding intended to settle in eastern Oregon, for he considered it hard to reach, hard to supply, and dangerous. He had persuaded Lee to abandon a similar plan, and
now he tried with equal zeal to persuade Whitman and Spalding to choose
another site. They were determined, however, so he housed Narcissa and
Eliza at the fort while their husbands went up the Columbia to find appro-
priate sites. Whitman and Spalding disliked each other, apparently because
Spalding had once been Narcissa's suitor and still smarted from her rejection,
and they chose locations more than a hundred miles apart—the Whitmans at
Waiilatpu on the Walla Walla River, among the Cayuse tribe, and the Spaldings
at Lapwai among the Nez Perces, in today's Idaho. But they cooperated at
times. Whitman worked on Spalding's house at Lapwai, while Spalding returned
to Fort Vancouver to bring both women to their new homes. Again McLoughlin
lent them company boats, and Narcissa was especially overjoyed because he
gave her a "fether bed," which kept her warm in spite of the driving rain.

Distant from Vancouver as these new missionaries were, they would have
great impact on McLoughlin's career. Narcissa Whitman and Eliza Spalding
had shown that it was possible for American women to travel by horse to the
Columbia, which emboldened others to come. Their party took the first
wheeled vehicle past the Green River Rendezvous to Fort Boise—an important segment of the covered wagons' route. Later on, in 1843, Whitman was
to assist the first great immigration over the Oregon Trail, and his mission for
a few crucial years would be a settlers' supply post.

IN 1837, THREE YEARS AFTER it was founded, the Methodist mission received an additional thirteen men, women, and children, who came on the chartered brig *Diana*. Led by Dr. Elijah White, the group included Anna Maria Pittman, a tall, dark-haired young woman—gentle and somewhat embarrassed because it was freely reported that she had come as a probable bride for Jason Lee. On May 17, when their ship reached Fort Vancouver, McLoughlin went aboard to welcome the passengers, and Anna Maria wrote to her parents:

> The next morning we were landed, and conducted to the Dr's dwelling, a very handsome one story house, with a piazza clear across . . . we was introduced to Mrs. McLaughlin she is half white; their daughter Maria [Maria Eloisa] 21 years of age is as white as I am, a lovely girl, she speaks french and english . . . we were all seated around a long table 18 of us, the table set with blue. our first course was Soup, the next boiled salmon, then roasted ducks, then such a roast turkey as I never saw or eat   it was a monster, it was like cutting of slices of pork, then wheat pan cakes, after that bread and butter and cheese all of their own make, and excellent, too.

As soon as Lee knew the *Diana* had arrived, he left Mission Bottom to meet his new assistants, and McLoughlin spotted him through field glasses as he came with two canoes, paddling upriver against a strong wind. The company teased Anna Maria until "a light blush rose to her cheek, and a slight trepidation, which added to the charm of her manner."

After a week at Fort Vancouver, the missionaries set out for the Willamette in a boat and three canoes, supplied by McLoughlin. They were an exuberant young group, singing, racing, with first one craft and then another in the lead. They portaged around the falls of the Willamette and then took their canoes to Mission Bottom, where they set to work at once, cooking, tending fields, and caring for Indian children, seven of whom were quite ill and bedded down with blankets on the floor. Anna Maria wrote to her parents that when they reached the mission, "we found things in old bachelor style we females soon mad[e] a different appearance in the house."

Although Lee knew that Anna Maria had been sent as his possible wife, he was reserved at first.

> I was told that she was sent out on purpose for me, and that she had come with the expectation that I would marry her (this however was a gratuitous assertion) and was asked if I intended to do it. . . . Upon

reflection, I was convinced that she was not a lady that I should have fancied for a wife (there is no accounting for people's *fancies*) though I esteemed her as a lady of deep piety and good sense.

Before many weeks, however, he did a complete about-face and decided that "she was eminently qualified to do all the duties and kind offices of an affectionate companion, and was worthy of my highest regards, esteem and love, and that it was the will and design of our Father in heaven that we twain should become one flesh, as a step, conducive to our mutual happiness and his glory. With these views I made proposals of marriage."

On Sunday, July 16, 1837, when Cyrus Shepard and Susan Downing were slated to be married, Lee—ever dramatic—made a brief speech about the "holy institution of marriage," after which he said, "And now, my friends, I intend to give you unequivocal proof that I am willing, in this respect, at least, to practice what I have so often recommended to you. I then steped forward and led Miss P. to the altar. Surprise seemed to be depicted upon almost every countenance."

AT ABOUT THIS TIME, the Columbia received its third group of missionaries, a pair of Catholic priests. Many employees at Fort Vancouver were devout Catholics, and McLoughlin, with ties to that church through his French Canadian mother and his well-loved sister, had regularly read to them in French and made brief talks, using a French Bible and translations of sermons from the English. In 1834 and again in 1835, he helped them write petitions to Catholic authorities in Quebec, reciting their "sad spiritual conditions," begging for priests, offering financial support, and saying that the Hudson's Bay Company would furnish transportation. Abbé Joseph Norbert Provencher, auxiliary to the Bishop of Quebec, replied that he would try to provide the priests, and he asked Governor Simpson for passage in company boats.

The governor was willing—with reservations. Realizing that the south side of the Columbia was almost certain to fall to America, and hoping to strengthen the British hold farther north, the London Committee wanted company retirees to settle on the Cowlitz River in today's state of Washington. Therefore, Simpson said that if the bishop would place the mission on the Cowlitz and "give his assurance that the missionaries would not locate" south of the Columbia River, he would recommend passage for the priests in the company's express canoes. Somewhat cynically, he offered "such facilities . . . as would not involve any great inconvenience or expence to the Company's service."

In October 1837, Abbé Provencher agreed to locate the priests north of the Columbia, and a year after that, on November 24, 1838, two black-robed missionaries arrived at Fort Vancouver with the fall express. They were Father Francis Norbert Blanchet, whom Gray described as a "black-haired, brown-eyed, smooth-faced, medium-sized Frenchman," and Father Modeste Demers, who had a "fair complexion, something of the bull neck, inclining to corpulency" but "fond of good cheer and good living." McLoughlin was in Europe, so James Douglas, who was in charge of the fort, offered them living quarters, and the next day, at an altar improvised in the schoolhouse, they conducted the first Roman Catholic Mass in the Oregon Country. They opened a mission at Fort Vancouver, where Father Blanchet instructed the Canadians while Father Demers taught the Indians; and, as promised, they established a mission on the Cowlitz.

But they soon changed their plans. In 1836, a year before the priests came, the French Canadians in the Willamette Valley had built the log church of St. Paul's on French Prairie, and within two weeks of his arrival, Father Blanchet

Father Francis Norbert Blanchet. OHS ORHI 206

crossed the Columbia, blessed their church, and conducted services. Before long the company decided to encourage British settlements south of the Columbia, prompting Douglas to inform the priests that the objection had been withdrawn "and you are therefore at liberty to take any means you may consider advisable." A month later, when McLoughlin returned from Europe, he visited St. Paul and found them serving Mass.

For the next several years, Fort Vancouver was the priests' headquarters, for McLoughlin gave them housing, attended their services at least part of the time, and allowed them to use the "old store" as their chapel. But they traveled widely, and set up a number of stations both east and west of the Cascades.

In a relatively short time—1834 to 1837—three strong groups of missionaries had been established in the Northwest: Methodists, based mainly on the Willamette and lower Columbia; Congregational-Presbyterians east of the Cascades; and Catholics, centered at Fort Vancouver and the Willamette Valley but with additional missions east of the mountains. McLoughlin aided all of them by furnishing transportation, food, medical care, and supplies. They were growing in number, extending their influence, and preparing the way for settlers, who soon would come.

~ 3 ~

The Reverend Beaver
1836–1838

One minister who came to Fort Vancouver in the 1830s differed from the others, for he was not American, he left no lasting mark on the area, and he did not become McLoughlin's friend. Sent by the company and probably chosen by George Simpson himself, he was a priest of the Church of England, a rather small, gray-eyed man who had the unlikely name of Herbert Beaver. His religious equipment came first, on the 1836 supply ship *Columbia*—"a church bell, a pulpit, Bibles, prayer books, registers, a surplice, an altar cloth, and a silver communion service." Four months later, on September 6, the Reverend Beaver and his wife Jane arrived on the *Nereide*.

If McLoughlin had foreseen the minister's temperament, or realized the significance of the lavish supplies, he might have made an extra effort to please the Beavers. Instead, he apparently assumed that they would accept the rigors of fort life as others had. He provided living quarters, gave them meals at the officers' dining table, and arranged for services to be held in the mess hall. This was the largest room available, the one in which he had for years led such Sunday observances as he, a layman, could provide. The Reverend Jason Lee and other ministers had also preached in it whenever they came.

Although the amenities of the fort had astonished other visitors, it was actually far from luxurious. In one of Beaver's letters, he spoke of carts and pigs making mud holes in the courtyard, said that from his quarters there were "above a dozen p———s [privies] in open view," and complained of the noise of half a dozen men chopping wood nearby, day after day. McLoughlin shared the inconvenience. He said it would "appear perhaps extraordinary but nevertheless a fact that we have not been able to finish the house I dwell in along with the other officers of the Establishment." This was the "Big House," which was not only crowded, it was in bad condition, as were other buildings, for many of them were a decade old and had been hastily constructed of used timbers. Dr. William Tolmie, who had come in 1833 as fort physician, said that in his own quarters, "the deals composing floor are in some places two or three inches distant from each other, thus leaving wide apertures. This is also true of the deals in the walls & the chinks are numerous, by those to north can look into schoolroom. . . . Shall close all apertures with brown paper pasted or leather."

For a priest of the Church of England, equipped with a bell, altar, and silver communion service, such conditions would be a shock. Furthermore, he was aghast because most of the fort's laborers were French Catholic— "Papists," he called them—and because there were relatively few Protestant officers. He detested the place so thoroughly and so quickly that he decided to return to England on the *Columbia*, which was to sail that fall. When a number of residents—having known him for only a few weeks—petitioned him to stay, he changed his mind, but it was with great reluctance, and he badgered McLoughlin with a shower of complaints.

Beaver's first grievance was the house. He objected to its thin partitions and said the other occupants were "noisy." He complained because the attic was a storeroom, and workmen frequently needed access to it "regardless of Mrs. Beaver's convenience." Calling it "a personal insult and domestic annoyance," the minister protested so vigorously to the London office that McLoughlin reported in self-defense:

> I understand the Revd. Mr. Beaver complains that his Accomodations are not so comfortable as he Expected, that the furniture is coarse

and that the Rooms are not carpeted, and I am told he Intends to apply for carpets to your Honors. . . . I intend doing every thing to Make Mr. Beaver as comfortable as the Circumstances of the Country will Admit, and I consider people ought to satisfy themselves with such things as the country affords. . . . Mr. Beavers house is the Best in the Fort. If he is Allowed carpets and imported furniture—has not every Gentleman in the place a Right to the same Indulgence.

Within a few months McLoughlin was able to provide a better house, but the Reverend had to share that one too, and he was still dissatisfied, for it was a typical fort structure, heated by a large mud and stone chimney. It was made of rough boards, the floors were not planed, and the carpets were Indian mats, which Mrs. Beaver considered "too filthy to step upon." Although the building was doubtless crude, it was acceptable by fort standards, and later, after the Beavers had left, the Catholic priests Fathers Blanchet and Demers occupied it without complaint.

The minister also criticized the meals. He offended the cook by returning the salmon because it was baked instead of boiled, and when McLoughlin did not agree with Mrs. Beaver's "knowledge of the mode of cooking as practiced by civilized beings," he demanded that the kitchen staff should be "required to obey" his orders. He did, however, enjoy the fort liquor, which created another problem.

"His Expenditure of Wine and Brandy is much Greater than the Allowance and I wrote him that we had certain Limits beyond which we could not Exceed," McLoughlin reported to the Committee. Then, trying to be fair, he added that he had "no Intention of reflecting on Mr. Beaver's Conduct as what he has done proceeds from I Believe a hospitable Disposition Without perhaps being aware of the Injury it Might do us and the Evils that might result."

Another irritation was the need to hold church services in the mess room. The minister called it "exceedingly inconvenient, not only on account of the interruption arising from the occupancy of part of the Same building by Several families, who do not attend me, but as it would be impossible to administer in it, with decency, the Sacrament of the Lord's Supper." And he was incensed because some residents met at other times to worship.

He performed a full service every Sunday morning at ten o'clock, with a smaller one at three in the afternoon, and McLoughlin held three others, one of which was in French for the Canadian workmen. The doctor explained that

he used only "a French Bible and a Penser Y Bien . . . having no French sermons my discourses were original compositions or translations from the
English," but Beaver refused to be mollified. The post, he declared, was "the
very strong-hold of Papacy defended and sustained by the head of the establishment himself."

Trying to make peace, McLoughlin offered to hear Beaver's suggestions
and possibly make a "change in our mode of assembling on the Sabbath." He
considered having the Reverend conduct the worship for the workmen, although he wryly observed that "few of the Canadians will understand Mr. B.
in French (and besides there are several errors in his translation) which they
may urge as a plea for not attending Mr. B's services." And in a passage that
reflected his considerably strained patience, along with a trace of amusement,
he said,

> In the first place I cannot discover how schism can be promoted by
> the course now pursued in the Canadian service, of reading a portion
> of scripture a plain practical discourse and uniting in prayer to God
> . . . again I cannot perceive the impropriety of successively assem-
> bling our English and Canadian servants for public worship in the
> same appartment or by the sound of the same Bell.

When the minister first came, McLoughlin was happy to place him in
charge of the somewhat rudimentary fort school, which had been conducted
"without reference to sectarian tenets, intended to benefit all denominations
of Christians." But the Reverend Beaver insisted upon teaching the doctrines
of the Church of England, even though most of the pupils were French
Canadian and therefore Roman Catholic, and he disregarded McLoughlin's
warning that this was certain to cause "an almost general desertion of the
scholars."

Declaring that the Governor and Committee had sent him there to organize a Church of England congregation, Beaver said he could not do so "unless
I am permitted to make use of the only known Means of renovating a people,
who are almost entirely sunk in ignorance and barbarism." McLoughlin tried
without success to persuade him to modify his stance, but as W. Kaye Lamb apt-
ly put it, "neither common sense nor compromise had any part in his makeup."

The Reverend Beaver had come in September 1836, the same month as
the Whitmans and Spaldings. It was the first time educated women had visited the fort, and McLoughlin—delighted—asked them to help with the school.

He especially encouraged Narcissa to teach music, because she had a beautiful voice. "I sing about an hour every evening with the children," she wrote, "teaching them new tunes, at the request of Dr. McLoughlin."

This, too, displeased the Reverend Beaver. He asked McLoughlin whether the school "is under my sole superintendence," to which the Chief Factor firmly replied that he himself was in ultimate charge. The minister then wrote directly to Narcissa and Eliza, saying that it was "unusual in England for any person to take part, without his permission . . . in the parochial duties of the minister." He bluntly asked them to "refrain from teaching, in any respect, the children of the School at Vancouver over which he has charge in virtue of his office."

When McLoughlin heard that the cleric had bypassed him, he was furious, and a blizzard of angry letters passed between them. Again asserting his right and duty, as head of the fort, to make decisions, the Chief Factor declared that the women could teach as long as they remained at Vancouver, and when Beaver continued to insist on his prerogatives, McLoughlin dismissed him from the school. The minister then took back the small supply of books he had brought.

After such an experience, it was understandable that Narcissa Whitman shared the prevailing dislike for the cleric. In one of the few negative passages in her early writings, she told her former pastor that she attended Beaver's services every Sunday. "I enjoy the privaledge much," she wrote. "But to contrast it with the preaching at home, I find a great want of plainness & heart. He is a great way behind the times the standard of piety is low with him and other professed Christians here. He seldom draws the line of distinction between the righteous & wicked & when he does it is so faintly, that it is scarcely preceptable."

In the spring the women left, but even their farewell annoyed Beaver. He complained because the children of the fort had sung at the ladies' departure, and said he was "shocked not at being present, but at hearing that the scholars, by command, had been paraded on the River beach, and sung there an hymn." Sacred music, he contended, should be performed "only on solemn occasions," not as "a common entertainment."

The Reverend and his wife lingered for two years—vexing years for them and everyone else. George T. Allan described Mrs. Beaver as a "rather fierce" woman who wore "the britches." Dr. Thomas M. Anderson, who knew her when he was a boy, remembered that she said she "did not come here to soil her fingers on the dirty brutes, as she called the Indians." But the Beavers apparently made some effort to be pleasant. George B. Roberts said they were both "very kind" to him.

Francis Ermatinger, who spent eight days at the fort, called Beaver "a first rate preacher and a fine man." The Reverend was on good terms with William McKay. And when Eloisa McLoughlin was married, Mrs. Beaver made white dresses for the flower girls, because she wanted it to be "a proper wedding ceremony."

As time passed, Beaver intensified his attacks on the doctor. He submitted sealed reports to headquarters, refusing to hand them to McLoughlin, although the Chief Factor was supposed to review all outgoing communications. The London officers were so opposed to secrecy that once, when Beaver sent Governor Simpson a sealed report, Sir George returned it to Vancouver for the Chief Factor to add his remarks.

But to Beaver the most galling of all the problems was the marital status of the company officers. Disregarding the fact that fur-trade marriages had been the only ones possible and that the unions were stable, the Reverend was convinced that the couples were living in sin. In a possible attempt to placate him, James Douglas had the minister remarry him to his longtime wife Amelia in a double ceremony, the other couple being Eloisa McLoughlin and William Glen Rae. Although McLoughlin did not marry Marguerite at this service, he had Douglas, who was a justice of the peace, perform a civil ceremony.

Matters came to a head in March 1838, when McLoughlin, as part of his job, read the chaplain's reports in which Beaver had called Marguerite "a female of notoriously loose character" and "the kept Mistress of the highest personage in your service at this station." The doctor always insisted that everyone treat his wife with respect, and soon afterward, when he happened to meet Beaver in the fort's yard, he demanded an explanation.

"If, Dr. McLoughlin," shot back the clergyman, "you require to know why a cow's tail grows downward, I can simply cite the fact."

Until then McLoughlin had held his temper in check, but at this show of disrespect to his wife, he erupted. As Beaver himself described the scene that followed,

> I was walking across the Fort-yard to speak to my wife, who was standing at the door of our house, when this monster in human shape . . . advanced towards us, apparently in a violent passion, and upon my making way for him to pass, he came behind me, kicked me several times, and struck me repeatedly with his fists on the back of the neck. Unable to cope with him, from the immense disparity of our relative size and strength, I could not prevent him from wrenching out of my hands a stout stick, with which I was walking, and with

which he next inflicted several severe blows on my shoulders. He then seized me from behind, round my waist, and attempted to dash me on the ground, exclaiming, *'you scoundrel, I will have your life.'* In the meantime, the stick had fallen to the ground; my wife, on the impulse of the moment, picked it up; he took it, to use the epithet of an eye-witness, *'very viciously'* out of her hands, and again struck me with it severely; we were then separated by the intervention of other persons.

According to eyewitness George B. Roberts, as soon as the storm had passed, McLoughlin was, as usual, regretful. On the following day, when the fort personnel had gathered for an auction, he stepped up to the chaplain and in a loud voice said, "Mr. Beaver, I make you this public apology for the indignity I offered you yesterday. I assure you it was unpremeditated."

"Dr. McLoughlin, I won't accept your apology," the chaplain replied, turned on his heel, and walked away.

A few days later, the doctor started his furlough, leaving James Douglas in charge. With a change in leadership, the minister restrained his irritability at first, and things were fairly smooth. But Douglas's patience was soon exhausted. Within six months he sent a scathing report to the Governor and Committee and another to Sir George Simpson, both of which were far stronger than anything written by McLoughlin. Douglas said he had been friendly with the minister for a time, until he asked for an explanation of "certain passages" in the chaplain's report, and the Reverend icily refused.

"I declined holding further intercourse with him," Douglas said. "That Gentleman also usurps a sort of prescriptive right, to libel, by his discoloured statements the character of every person with whom he associates. Were these writings offered only for your perusal, the evil might be bourne in silence, as our characters are too well known to be affected by flimsy misrepresentation; but when . . . the direful passages, designed . . . to blast reputations and procure expulsion from the service, are noised about throughout the settlement, they become an unsufferable nuisance and highly prejudicial to the service."

He cited Beaver's excessive use of wine—225½ gallons in two years, although the annual allowance was sixteen. He was outraged by criticism of "Mrs. McL., who is deservedly respected for her numerous charities, and many excellent qualities of heart . . . I know that Mrs. M's feelings had been dreadfully outraged by the volumes of coarse invictive heaped upon her by a

member of his [Beaver's] family in the public square." He particularly resented the minister's refusal to make a distinction between prostitution and fur-
trade marriages. He said the Beavers rejected their first servant as dishonest,
but that when provided with a "decent, married Sandwich Islander and his
wife," they refused them as "not worth the trouble of training." And in a biting understatement, he said he would have been delighted to have the
Reverend share the teaching of the Indian school, or visit the sick, or carry
counsel into men's homes, none of which had been done.

Douglas did not have to endure the annoyance for long. In the fall of
1838, the Reverend Beaver canceled his engagement with the company and
took passage for England, without Douglas's consent and "entirely upon his
own responsibility." When he reached London, the company paid him one
hundred pounds and told him his services were no longer needed, but he
continued his attacks. In a letter to the *Church of England Protestant
Magazine,* he referred with obvious satisfaction to McLoughlin's long-ago
flight into the fur trade, and said that "it has been reported and confirmed,
that our foe, some years previously, had been compelled to quit Montreal
under circumstances I will not trust myself to advert to." Among his claims
was a statement that McLoughlin had "compelled" the French Canadian settlers to build a Catholic chapel and house in the Willamette Valley, an accu-
sation that was not supported by the records of the Catholic church.

But the Reverend no longer bothered McLoughlin. When he returned
from his furlough in 1839, he was doubtless relieved to find that the minister
was gone.

~4~
Bonneville, Kelley, & Young
1834–1836

T he next American on the Columbia was Benjamin Louis Eulalie de Bonneville, an army captain with a reputation more impressive than his achievements. He had a semiofficial status, for he had been granted a two-year leave
of absence from the army in order to lead a fur-hunting expedition to the Far
West, at his own expense. He set out in May 1832 with 110 men and twenty
wagons and took them through South Pass to the Green River, where he put
up a breastwork of logs and called it Fort Bonneville. This was farther than

wagons had ever before rolled, and it opened a section of what would later be the Oregon Trail. He did not, however, secure enough furs to make a profit. He met Nathaniel Wyeth twice, in 1833 and 1834, and the New Englander proposed that they "make a joint buisness of it," but the plan failed to materialize.

In March and again in September 1834, Bonneville and his men tried to purchase supplies at Fort Nez Perces. The clerk in charge, Pierre Pambrun, received them hospitably, fed and lodged them, but refused to sell them goods for trade. Meager as his assistance had been, when the Governor and Committee heard about it, they thought Pambrun had gone too far, and while McLoughlin agreed, he based it on business rather than political reasons. He wrote:

> As to Bonnaville we never made any arrangement with him, but Mr. Pambrun sold him a Roll of Tobacco and some Dry Goods, at Freemens prices, paid in Beaver at the same rate, but this was injudicious . . . as when this occurred, our Stores were low . . . Mr. Pambrun was tempted to sell by seeing the furs before him, but I explained to him the error he had committed, and I am certain he will not do the like again . . . I must in justice to Mr. Pambrun observe, that he is as anxious to promote the Interest of the Concern as a man possibly can be, and has managed the affairs of Walla Walla, one of the most troublesome posts (if not the most troublesome) in the Country, with the utmost skill and judgement.

McLoughlin's explanation illustrated the long-standing Hudson's Bay policy: to assist wayfarers with their genuine needs but refuse to help them set up a rival establishment, which might cut into the company's trade. In the case of Bonneville, the business-minded McLoughlin thought the attempt to buy Hudson's Bay goods might indicate a new market among American trappers, so he sent Thomas McKay "with a small party and an Outfit of Goods to go to the American Rendezvous" and make some sales. It was late, however, when McKay started, and he "did not reach it till the parties had left."

Rebuffed at Fort Nez Perces, Bonneville started on down the Columbia. But the hardships were greater than he expected, so he turned back at the John Day River, retraced his steps, and arrived on the East Coast in late summer 1835. He became famous because Washington Irving met him at the home of John Jacob Astor, received some of his papers, and wrote *The Adven-*

tures of Captain Bonneville, which portrayed him as a romantic hero—although in fact he had shown little heroism. He had, however, brought his wagons over South Pass to the Green River, farther than any had come before, and Irving's book, which was widely read, became another factor in publicizing the West. Two decades later, in 1852—when Fort Vancouver was held by the U.S. Army—Bonneville returned to the Columbia as a lieutenant colonel, and for three years held command of the post.

IN 1834, WHILE BONNEVILLE was still in the West, the *Cadboro* brought McLoughlin a disturbing letter from Joseph Figueroa, the governor of Upper California. It said:

> In the latter part of the month of August last a man by the name of Joachim [Ewing] Young an Anglo American accompanied by a number of other Foreigners left this country with the intention of going to the Columbia. On leaving these adventurers (forgetting the hospitality with which they were treated by the inhabitants of this territory) committed the crime of robbing upwards of two hundred head of horses belonging to various Mexican citizens. This Misdemeanor is looked upon with horror by all civilized persons as it attacks all social rights and I doubt not but that you will in case these marauders should make their appearance in your quarter take such measures as will be efficient to apprehend them and either chastise them or despoil them of their booty.

Horse-stealing was a serious crime on the frontier. When Young and his band of trappers appeared, McLoughlin relayed the information to the Governor and Committee, and said, "I would have nothing to do with them, and told them my reasons. Young maintained he stole no horses, but admitted the others had. I told him that might be the case, but as the charge was made, I could have no dealings with him till he cleared it up." With Young was Hall Kelley, the Boston schoolmaster who had first interested Wyeth in the Columbia. Kelley had for years been gathering information about Oregon— its furs and fisheries, its soil and climate. He had written books, delivered speeches, made maps, and petitioned Congress for help in forming an emigration society, the one Wyeth had considered joining. In 1833 Kelley had set out with a small party for the Columbia, planning a circuitous route via Mexico—

a grandiose plan, but it reaped disaster. His companions deserted him at New Orleans, his goods were seized for duties at Vera Cruz, and finally, in the summer of 1834, he met Ewing Young in the Mexican province of California. Since Young was on his way to the Columbia, they started together, with half a dozen men and more than a hundred of Young's horses. Unfortunately, their numbers were increased against their will when, as Kelley put it, "a band of *marauders*" overtook and joined them.

While the combined bands were in the mountains of southern Oregon, Kelley was seized by fever, becoming "so unwell that he had to be lifted on and off his horse, and Mr. Kelly's men were so unwell or unwilling, that they would no longer take care of him." He was in serious condition when the party met a Hudson's Bay expedition headed by Michel Laframboise, who "out of humanity" gave him the use of his tent, dosed him with venison broth and quinine, and took him north by horse and canoe, reaching Fort Vancouver in the fall of 1834, at about the same as Young. McLoughlin later said that Kelley promised rewards to the men if they would bring his missing trunk, but that when they did so, it contained, instead of the promised money, "a few old clothes, a piece of an old hand saw an old trying Plane and some old torn accounts."

McLoughlin's earlier visitors had been thoroughly respectable, but the status of these was in doubt. They insisted they were not horse thieves, they were obviously in need, and yet the Chief Factor felt he could not disregard Figueroa's warning. Kelley's appearance was also unfortunate, for he was wearing "a white slouched hat, blanket capot, leather pants with a red stripe down the seam, rather outré even for Vancouver." Troubled, McLoughlin decided that for the time being he would not receive Young, who angrily stormed away, but that it would be inhumane to refuse aid to a sick man, and therefore Kelley could remain. The doctor, however, was unwilling to house a suspected thief among the fort's "gentlemen," so he assigned the visitor to the one-room house of a Canadian family, outside the stockade, and had his meals sent to him there.

Kelley was insulted, and described his quarters as "a cabin, opening on the back side, into a shed, which, having been long a place for dressing fish and wild game, was extremely filthy. The black mud about the doors, back and in front, was abundantly mixed with animal putrescence." Convinced that McLoughlin was deliberately trying to destroy him, he said, "The persecuting monster, anticipating my coming to the place of his abode, was ready, with sword in hand, to cut me down; and, I was treated . . . with every demonstration of inhumanity."

When Kelley's condition grew more serious, McLoughlin had him transferred to the fort hospital, a situation that the Bostonian interpreted as "imprisonment," contrived by the doctor in order to "overhaul my baggage, and to examine its contents." Equally disgruntled with Ewing Young, Jason Lee, and Wyeth, who were still in the area, Kelley complained that they paid him little attention, and that even when Wyeth called on him, "his only object seemed to be to afflict, and to fill my soul with sorrow."

In the spring of 1835, when the schoolmaster had recovered, McLoughlin gave him seven pounds sterling and free passage to the Sandwich Islands. Although Kelley reached home safely, he spent the rest of his life churning out diatribes against McLoughlin and the Hudson's Bay Company, trying to promote the settlement of Oregon, and pleading in vain for government rewards because "the colonization of Oregon was both conceived and achieved by me." By the time he died, in 1874, he was eighty years old and nearly blind.

Kelley was fanatic, indomitable, a tragic character. The historian Frances Fuller Victor wrote that he was "neither a great hero nor a great rascal," being remarkable chiefly for "staggering for fifty years under an idea too big for his brain." And S. A. Clarke, in *Pioneer Days of Oregon History*, said, "He alone was stirring the cauldron of Fate." However, unbalanced as Kelley was, his books were widely read in the United States, and he was among the first to urge emigration and plant the seeds of anti-Hudson's Bay bias.

THE AMERICAN WITH KELLEY was Ewing Young, a trader from Tennessee who carried a two-volume set of Shakespeare in his pack, and was called "a very candid and scrupulously honest man, thorough-going, brave and daring." Young drove his herd of horses through the Willamette Valley on the west side of the river and stopped in Chehalem Valley, across from French Prairie. There he took out a large claim—fifty square miles of forest and meadows with billowing grass that was lush and shoulder-high, ideal for pasturing his herd.

Shortly afterward, when he crossed the river to meet the settlers, he discovered that McLoughlin had posted notices on the trees, calling him a horse thief and advising his neighbors not to deal with him. Furious, Young paddled to Fort Vancouver to meet the doctor face-to-face, in a stormy confrontation between two giants, for Young was six feet two and McLoughlin was two inches taller than that. They reached no accord, and Young—seething with anger—returned to his claim.

There he found that life without access to Fort Vancouver was difficult, because it was the area's only source of supplies. Courtney Walker, who had come with Wyeth, said that before long the Yankee had a company employee deliver a request for supplies to Fort Vancouver, along with beaver pelts to pay for them, but that McLoughlin returned the skins and sent the needed goods. As McLoughlin explained it, "while these accusations remained against him, I could not take any Furs or any thing else from him." Young, however, was too proud to accept a gift, and he paddled to the fort to confront the Chief Factor again. In this conference, McLoughlin suggested that Young should not have allowed the interlopers to accompany him, to which Young replied, "It is not so easy in the place they overtook me for a person to chuse his Company."

The doctor had stood his ground, but he was not entirely convinced of the American's guilt, and he told Lee in a private conversation that "Mr. Young had been met by our People in their trapping excursions and that they always found him act as an honest upright man." He himself, McLoughlin said, had kept his distance in order "to avoid being implicated as the receiver of stolen property, at the same time I wished to accomodate Young, as much as I well could."

In a few months Figueroa wrote again, explaining that Young "had no hand in stealing the horses" and that the thieves had merely attached themselves to the party. McLoughlin then tried to make amends, but the Tennessean would not be mollified, and he remained in the valley, prospering but bitter.

In 1837, when Wyeth sold his goods at Fort William, Young took a revenge of sorts by buying the enormous cauldron the Yankee had used for pickling salmon. It would be, Young said, a fine distillery, which he and another American, Lawrence Carmichael, would use for the manufacture of spirits. The plan set off a furor. Most residents—Hudson's Bay retirees, Wyeth's men, a few ex-trappers, and the missionaries, as well as McLoughlin himself—considered alcohol "that bane that changes men into demons." The Chief Factor offered to lend Young money, while the others created the Oregon Temperance Society, subscribed sixty dollars for purchase of the distillery, and sent it to Young, with a communiqué signed by nearly all the settlers, both Americans and Canadians. It said they had heard of Young's plan "with feelings of *deep regret,*" and that "we do most *earnestly* and *feelingly* request you Gentlemen to forever abandon your enterprise." Still in a rage, Young rejected the money, and said the main reason he had started the project was the "tyrannizing oppression" of McLoughlin, who had treated him "with more disdain than any American's feelings can support."

Although Young and Carmichael eventually agreed to abandon their project, the Reverend Daniel Lee said the people had been alarmed, because they "felt that if that *distillery* went on all was lost." They were grateful to the Chief Factor, liked him, admired him. Lee expressed their good will when he wrote, "It is due to say that Dr. M'Laughlin seconded the efforts of the missionaries and the friends of temperance, and that the course he has taken in regard to spirituous liquors has done much to preserve the general order and harmony of the mixed community of which the settlement is composed."

The episode shows McLoughlin's willingness to support the Americans, even though they were a potential threat to his business. Knowing that they were bound to increase in number, that they had a right to be there, and that he could not in any case stop them, he saw cooperation as his company's wisest course. In the case of the distillery, the settlers had made their first attempt to organize, and he had lent them a hand.

~5~

The Willamette Cattle Company
1836–1838

In late December 1836, while the settlers were trying to block Ewing Young's distillery, another American came to the Columbia—an official one this time, although he tried to conceal it. American interest in the Northwest had been growing, fanned by news from missionaries and travelers and by the writings of Hall Kelley, who accused the Hudson's Bay Company of violating the terms of joint occupancy. As a result, President Andrew Jackson arranged to have William A. Slacum of the U.S. Navy go to the West Coast and investigate. Slacum accordingly went to the Sandwich Islands, chartered the brig *Loriot*, loaded it with a token amount of trade goods, and sailed to the Columbia, prepared to pose as a private merchant.

On reaching Fort George, he sent a message upriver by a Hudson's Bay canoe, asking for a pilot and a stove. Although McLoughlin promptly supplied them, he saw through Slacum's pretense, and informed the Governor and Committee:

> He never gave me to understand that he came in the service of the
> United States, but that he had hired the Vessel to bring him here in

the expectation of meeting some gentleman who were to have come across the Country. . . . however it appeared strange to me that any gentleman merely for the sake of pleasure should come in such a poorly equipped Vessel as the *Lariat*, and in her cross the bar of the Columbia River in winter and expressed my surprise to our Officers and told them, I supposed Mr. Slacum was an agent of the American Government.

In spite of his skepticism, McLoughlin sent James Douglas in a boat manned by voyageurs to bring the visitor to the fort, where he housed Slacum and showed him around. The establishment had grown. In Slacum's report, he estimated that the Fort Vancouver palisade was 750 by 450 feet and contained thirty-four buildings, "including officers' dwelling-houses, workshops for carpenters, blacksmiths, wheelwrights, coopers, tinners, &c., all of wood except the magazine for powder which is of brick; outside and very near the fort there are forty-nine cabins for laborers and mechanics, a large and commodious barn, and seven buildings attached thereto; a hospital and a large boat house on the shore, six miles above the fort. On the north bank, the Hudson's Bay Company have erected a sawmill. . . . There is a large threshing machine, distillery (not at present in operation) and a grist mill." He estimated the population around the fort as about 750 to 800.

On January 10, 1837, McLoughlin provided Slacum with a boat and boatmen for a visit to the Willamette Valley. The American called at "almost every house in the community, and took an account of the produce of their farms, and stock, and the number of inhabitants"—doubtless incomplete, but notable as the area's first census. In addition to missionaries, he found thirty male residents in the valley, thirteen being Canadians and the rest Americans or British. He learned that people were wondering what nation would eventually govern the area, and he assured the French Canadians that "although they were located within the territorial limits of the United States, their pre-emption rights would doubtless be secured when our government should take possession of the country."

As Slacum moved from farm to farm, he heard about the distillery and met Young, who told him that "a cloud hung over him so long through Dr. McLoughlin's influence that he was almost maddened by the harsh treatment he had received from that gentleman." In trying to heal the breach, Slacum received authorization from Chief Factor Duncan Finlayson to tell Young that if he would give up his distillery, he could get supplies at Fort Vancouver "on the same terms as other men." But the American proudly refused.

Everywhere Slacum went, settlers lamented their overriding need—cattle, which were useful as draft animals as well as for food. His official report said, "I found that nothing was wanting to insure comfort, wealth, and every happiness to the people of this most beautiful country, but the possession of neat cattle, all of those in the country being owned by the Hudson's Bay Company, who refuse to sell them under any circumstances whatsoever."

The entire Columbia was short of these animals. The missionaries had brought a few, and McLoughlin was able to lend the settlers some from the company herd, but for years, he said, "we had not the number we required for ourselves." The supply was so small that official policy forbade him to kill any for meat or to sell any, even the "increase" of calves, until they had built up their herd. "As to Beef," he wrote in 1837, "from '25 to '36, we never Killed more than a Bull Calf or Two annually for the purpose of getting rennet . . . it must be recollected that in 1825, when I took charge of this place, we only had 3 Bulls, 23 Cows, 5 Heifers, and 9 Steers . . . we require a Hundred Oxen to do the Work of the Farm and Saw Mill, and which is the reason we did not begin to Kill Cattle sooner." He denied beef even to the British navy. As late as 1839, Captain Edward Belcher, head of a surveying squadron, was furious because McLoughlin gave a limited amount to the ship's officers but refused to supply the sailors as well. In a document found after the Chief Factor's death, he further explained,

> If I sold, they would of course be entitled to the increase, and I would not have the means to assist the new settlers, and the settlement would be retarded, as those purchasers who offered me $200 for a cow would put such a price on the increase as would put it out of the power of poor settlers to buy. This would prevent industrious men settling. For these reasons I would not sell, but loaned, as I say, two cows to each settler.

Confronted by this shortage, the farmers had worked out a plan but could not implement it. Large numbers of half-wild longhorns were roaming the hills of California, and even before Slacum came, an attempt to buy some "was in contemplation"—if they could figure out a way to get there. When Slacum heard of it, he offered to take an expedition on the *Loriot*, and most residents, both French and American, attended a meeting at the Methodist mission, followed by one at Champoeg, a popular landing site on the Willamette River. There they organized the Willamette Cattle Company and selected Philip Leget Edwards, a former schoolteacher, as treasurer.

For the difficult job of leading of the drive, they chose Ewing Young, because he had brought a band of horses when he came from California and knew something of the trail. In response to this tempting offer, Young abandoned his plans for a still. Slacum advanced $500, the settlers added enough to total $1,600, and McLoughlin gave $880 from his company, "so that by purchasing a larger number (as the expense of driving five hundred or a thousand was the same) as it would make the cattle cheaper. The settlers who had money bought stock, while those who had none engaged as drivers at $1 per day, to be paid in cattle at their actual cost." McLoughlin's donation was not mentioned in the missionaries' accounts or Slacum's report, but it fills the otherwise puzzling gap in the financial record, which says that having received $1,600, they spent $2,480 for Mexican cattle.

On January 17, 1837, eleven men set out by canoe from Willamette Falls, to board the *Loriot* at Fort George and head south. P. L. Edwards kept notes, which describe their difficulties in buying animals and herding them through the mountains of southern Oregon. "The last month, what has it been! Little sleep, much fatigue, hardly time to eat, mosquitoes, cattle breaking like so many evil spirits, and scattering to the four winds, men ill natured and quarreling; another month like the past, God avert! Who can describe it?"

But they succeeded in purchasing eight hundred longhorn cattle. Although some strayed and some were drowned in fording rivers, they brought back 630 animals in October, to be distributed to the settlers at the net price of $7.67 each, in proportion to each man's contribution. For his pay as leader, Young received a considerable number, which set him on the road to prosperity as a successful farmer and proprietor of a sawmill. McLoughlin also received a large number because of his donation, but with his willing consent, the settlers "kept the tame and broken-in oxen they had belonging to the Hudson's Bay Company, and gave their California wild cattle in the place, so that they found themselves stocked with tame cattle which cost them only $8 per head." Again the settlers had organized, again McLoughlin had helped them, and this time they created the first cooperative business venture in Oregon.

Slacum did not return from California to the Columbia, but took the *Loriot* back to the Sandwich Islands and then went to Washington, where he gave Congress a lengthy report. In it he blandly ignored the treaty of joint occupation, and protested the "unauthorized introduction of large quantities of British goods within the territorial limits of the United States." The settlers, he said, were "subject to the *protection* and authority, otherwise *thraldom*," of "an immense foreign monopoly established in our own waters."

Although his report was favorable to McLoughlin personally, it made several charges against the Hudson's Bay Company. It said the company's policy "is calculated to perpetuate the institution of slavery, which now exists, and is encouraged, among all Indian Tribes West of the Rocky Mountains"; that the company encouraged the natives to believe that Captain Dominis of the *Owhyhee* had "brought the fever to the River"; and that the Americans "hesitate not to charge the subordinate Agents of the Hudsons Bay Company with instigating the Indians to attack all other parties." All of these claims were false, and when McLoughlin heard of them, he was furious.

In a letter to William Miller, the British consul general at Oahu, he answered Slacum point by point. "It is incorrect that we encourage Slavery and on the reverse we avail ourselves of every opportunity to discourage it. Tho' we cannot prevent Indians having Slaves We tell the Masters it is very improper to keep their fellow beings in Slavery: moreover we have redeemed several and sent them back to their own Country." In several instances, he said, when Indians at the fort had slaves, "by our influence they were liberated. . . . If the plan we adopt is followed they will before long emancipate themselves."

He also said the company could not force its own standards on the natives. As an example, McLoughlin explained that when J. Dugald Cameron—his predecessor in charge of Fort George—emancipated all slaves belonging to employees' wives, "the wives made a present of them to their Indian Relations," who enslaved them again, and gave them worse treatment than "their former mistresses at the Fort." For that reason, the Chief Factor said, he employed some of these slaves but paid them "as other Indians," and when they wished to claim their liberty, "I support them. . . . We disapprove of any one having Slaves and consider every one about the Establishment as free." It was a typical McLoughlin solution—to do the right and sensible thing, by whatever means he could.

In further comments on the Slacum report, he said it was true that the Indians attacked American brigades, but "they also attack ours, and if our parties do not suffer as the others, It is because ours are better organized and better arranged." And he explained that he had indeed told Slacum of the Indians' belief that Captain Dominis had brought the fever, but did so merely to point out the need to speak with care. In talking with the natives, he said, "we made it a point to maintain that Domenes did not give them the fever."

In addition to his anti-Hudson's Bay charges, Slacum gave Oregon a rave review, describing the Willamette Valley as "the finest grazing country in the world" and urging the United States to take possession of it at once. He recommended founding a military post at the mouth of the Columbia. He called the West Coast a place where "our whalers from the coast of Japan might resort for supplies, which, in the course of a few years, would be abundant." And he said, "I hope our claim to 54° of north latitude will never be abandoned; at all events, we should never give up Pugitt's sound, nor permit free navigation of the Columbia." But he qualified this by cagily adding, "unless, indeed a fair equivalent was offered, such as the free navigation of the St. Lawrence."

Some accounts have claimed that Slacum took a petition from the settlers to Congress asking for protection, but that is not generally accepted. His report, however, was widely circulated, stirring further interest in the Oregon Country and reinforcing Kelley's anti-British, anti-Hudson's Bay bias. The tide was rising, and it would soon sweep over the nation.

~ 6 ~

Sails & Steam
1834–1838

In April 1834, when the brig *Nereide* arrived from London, she brought a dispatch from the Governor and Committee saying they had appointed her captain, J. M. Langtry, to succeed Lieutenant Æmelius Simpson as superintendent of the Marine Department, subject only to McLoughlin's orders. The Chief Factor was not pleased. After Simpson's death in 1831, he had deliberately left the office vacant, because he considered it "unnecessary with the number of vessels we have" and thought it would give an administrator undesirable "claims." Neither was he pleased with the *Nereide*, for she had required repairs three times while on the way. Therefore, having already made arrangements for the season, he "did not immediately place the naval department under Captain Langtry," and he decided to have the *Nereide* take the year's returns to London.

This caused a problem, because if the *Nereide* left and Captain Langtry stayed as marine superintendent, he would have to transfer to another vessel, and his papers forbade him to do so without permission "from the Lords Commissioners of the Admiralty." The logical solution was to have the captain accompany his ship, and McLoughlin decided to do this—doubtless with considerable satisfaction. Instead of appointing a superintendent, he gave Duncan Finlayson the management of the coastal trade, replacing Peter Skene Ogden, whom he transferred to New Caledonia.

Another unwelcome bit of news came in the fall, when McLoughlin learned that the Governor and Committee had decided to send him a steamboat. He had once favored the idea. In 1826 he had suggested having two of them built at Fort Vancouver and equipped with British engines, to be used in towing vessels on the Columbia and lower Fraser Rivers, and a year later he had told Governor Simpson that "a small steam boat will be found the best adapted to carry on that trade and perhaps that of the whole Coast." By 1833, however, he had done an about-face, concluding that in spite of their convenience, "we ought not to open a new Channel of expense." Thinking the London Committee backed him, he had confidently told Peter Skene Ogden that they rejected the idea of a steamship as too costly, and that he agreed.

When he heard in 1834 of the Committee's plan, he protested again that the advantages "would not pay her increased expense," and a year later, when the officers in London adhered to their decision, he registered an aggrieved protest. "As to the Steam Boat for the coast, you have decided, and it is useless to say more about the business, and I will only repeat . . . That she is not required and that the expense incurred on her . . . is so much money thrown away." He was so sure the experiment would fail that he asked Simpson whether, if the vessel proved unsuitable, he should keep her or sell her or send her home.

Only a few months later, on March 19, 1836, the tubby little *Beaver* arrived, having rounded the Horn under sail with the machinery in her hold. She was the first steamboat—steamship is too grand a term—on the West Coast, a clumsy craft of only 110 tons but "most substantially put together, her oak timbers being unusually heavy. Her small wheels [side paddles] were placed far forward like the fins of a seal; her square poop stood high out of the water, slanting toward the rudder." Built in 1835 and making her maiden voyage, she carried a crew of thirty, was armed with four six-pounders and a supply of small weapons, and had a rope netting around her deck to prevent unauthorized boarding.

Since she was there and had to be used, McLoughlin decided to take himself, Douglas, their families, and all the gentlemen of the fort on a trial excursion. On June 14, as soon as the mechanics had hoisted her engine out of the hold and rigged it up, the sightseers went aboard. Black smoke billowed, paddles churned, and the whistle blew as the *Beaver* puffed a few miles down the Columbia, rounded Wappato Island, and chugged back, carrying her suitably impressed passengers. The next day she proved her mettle by towing the bark *Columbia* to the sawmill, to load timber for the Sandwich Islands.

The steamship *Beaver* in her final site, after she was wrecked in 1888. She was small, diffi-cult to keep in repair, and had an engine with a voracious appetite for wood. Independent of wind, and able to enter rivers and bays that were too cramped for sailing vessels, she had a long and useful life on the Columbia. *The S.S.* Beaver *as She Lay on Entering Burrard Inlet,* painted in 1889 by W. Ferris. HUDSON BAY COMPANY ARCHIVES, PROVINCIAL ARCHIVES OF MANITOBA, HBCA PICTURE COLLECTION, P-212 [N5399]

Toward the end of the month, she crossed the bar and splashed her way north on her first trading voyage. As McLoughlin had expected, she was so small and chunky that she had trouble with the rough Pacific. Chief Factor Duncan Finlayson, in charge of the coastal trade, commented, "Our progress was much impeded by the steamer's being so heavily laden, the paddles some-times plunging into the waves which shook the vessel much, and in a very heavy sea I would consider a vessel under sail as the safest mode of conveyance."

In spite of her small size, the *Beaver* had a voracious appetite. Finlayson wrote that six axemen required two days to cut enough logs for one run of twelve to fourteen hours, and that "when not supplied with wood from the Forts, we have to stop 2 days to provide fuel for the consumption of one. In such cases our progress is slow and may be estimated . . . at 90 miles in 3 days or 30 per day." He added that even in the sheltered waters of canals, it was not safe to run at night, "owing to the quantity of drift timber which the tide carries along, and which if it came in contact with the Paddles, would break them to pieces, and perhaps cause some serious injury to the vessel and the engine."

Nevertheless, the *Beaver* was independent of wind, and her shallow draft enabled her to enter channels forbidden to larger ships. After giving her a summer's trial in the intricate waterways of the north, Finlayson declared that "she will give the most effectual blow to the opposition which they have ever met with on the coast, and will also lessen in a great measure the traffic carried on amongst the natives themselves." Even McLoughlin, however grudgingly, came to rely on the *Beaver*, and she was to have a long and useful life in the Northwest.

FOR SEVERAL YEARS MCLOUGHLIN HAD DREAMED of expanding his operations in the north, and the decline of returns from other fur lands pointed up the need. The London Committee shared his concern, and at about the time they sent the *Beaver*, they increased his fleet to seven ships, for trading on the coast and carrying cargo back and forth to England. Most of them were satisfactory, but one was the *Nereide*, which returned in September 1836. Knowing that McLoughlin disliked her, the Committee tartly informed him that she was "built as strong as materials could make her," that her appearance was "imposing," and that with ten carronades plus small arms she was "well adapted" for both defense and coastal trade. However, to the Chief Factor's satisfaction, she was in the charge of a different captain, David Home, and the Marine Department was not mentioned.

Since she was on hand, costing the salaries of her crew, McLoughlin used her that winter to supply his northern posts, but he complained that "she draws so much water she cannot ascend Frasers River to Fort Langley, and is so sharp, that if she should ground, she would lay almost on her beam ends; and if this was to happen on the North West Coast, it would expose her to be taken by the Natives and her Crew to be butchered." A further complaint was her capacity, for she had a deeper draft than his other vessels but could carry "little more than half the Cargo." The ship's structure was not the only problem. On May 31, 1837, her entire crew came to McLoughlin and complained about Captain Home's severity and excessive demands. After boarding the vessel and taking depositions, the Chief Factor decided the crew's evidence was insufficient, and James Douglas agreed, calling their charges so dubious "that no Court in England would have entertained them for a moment." Nevertheless, even when McLoughlin issued direct orders, the men refused to "mann the windless" or take the vessel to sea, and at last he had them confined in irons.

For nearly three weeks the *Nereide* rocked at anchor, while McLoughlin paid her visit after visit. He ordered the crew "to be fed on Prisoners allowance"—bread and water. He offered to shorten their hours on watch. When that failed to work, he told them they were "reduced to one Glass of Grog. p. day," at which dreadful prospect all except two returned to their posts. But the last holdouts were so recalcitrant that he finally "had a Dozen lashes given to each of them," and they escaped a second flogging only because, when they saw preparations for tying them up again, they consented to work.

In reporting the incident to the Governor and Committee, McLoughlin pointed out the vulnerability of the company and its need to be firm. "It is true, in the civilised world when a man refuses his Duty you may dismiss him, and replace him with another; in this country we cannot do it, but do our work with the people we have, as we cannot replace them, it therefore leaves us no alternative."

Douglas concurred, saying that McLoughlin's course had been moderate and that "we were forced upon the unpleasant alternative of carrying our point by the use of severe measures." Although flogging was an accepted practice at that time, the Governor and Committee apparently sent a directive to abandon it. When the crew of the *Beaver* mutinied in 1838, Douglas reported that the officers at first made several severe examples, but that later "your orders for the prevention of corporal punishments, have been obeyed."

As for the *Nereide*, on September 10, 1837, she was hung up on the Columbia bar for thirty-six hours, with damage so serious that it appeared "from the wrinkled and uneven state of the sheathing copper that the body of the vessel is likewise much strained." She was towed into nearby Bakers Bay for repairs, and on January 11, 1838, she sailed for the Sandwich Islands with a cargo of lumber, salmon, and farm produce. It was not known whether the repairs would hold up "in rough weather with a heavy sea," but in any case the London officers realized that she was, as McLoughlin had said, poorly adapted for the Columbia, and they called her home to be sold.

Other sailing ships remained, backbone of the trade, to compete with coasters from the United States. Finlayson called the Americans a "vexatious annoyance," and said,

> It is not only the number of skins which these vessels collect, that causes serious loss but the extravagant prices paid for them, as they dispose of the remainder of their cargoes under prime cost, rather

than be at the trouble and expence of carrying it to China. . . . The
Natives also, who are very keen traders, will keep their skins for months
in the expectation of the re-appearance of our opponents unless that
we become equally liberal.

The competition in the far north exposed again the basic difference between McLoughlin's approach and that of the Governor and Committee. As
he had successfully done with the *Owhyhee* and *Convoy*, the Chief Factor
preferred to hold prices at a level that would not shatter the company's business, but would deprive his opponents of a profit and induce them to give up.
The men in London, however, wanted him to make such a drastic change that
their rivals would be unable to secure any furs at all. "Your individual opinion
with respect to an energetic opposition to the American traders . . . is not in
accordance with that of Governor Simpson and the Northern Council and
assented to by us," they sternly wrote.

Surprised and disturbed, McLoughlin picked up his pen. "I know of no
difference of opinion in regard to carrying on the opposition with energy,
except that I consider the same object may be accomplished without incur-
ring the expence of purchasing a steam Boat. . . . Our policy ought to be to
collect a sufficiency of Furs to make our opponents lose money; as to attempt
to prevent their getting any Furs would be to spoil the trade still more and
not answer the purpose more effectually."

He realized, however, that it would be difficult to drive out the Americans by a price policy alone, because they enjoyed another lucrative source
of profit—the sale of supplies to the Russians. The Governor and Committee,
who coveted a share of that business, had tried but failed to make an agreement with the tsar's agents, and they had not forgotten Ogden's humiliating
defeat on the Stikine. They had recently decided to use McLoughlin's report
of that incident as a tool for pressuring Russia through government channels,
and therefore, in January 1837, they asked him to come to London, bringing
all pertinent documents.

This would suit him, because a visit to headquarters was long overdue,
and his ties with the company were showing strain. They had disagreed on the
use of steamships, the relative importance of vessels versus forts, the ultimate
authority over ships, the location of headquarters, and most of all on the best
way to counter American competition. McLoughlin had planned several times
to take a furlough, or perhaps move to a different post, but his departure had
always been postponed. "I see that you and several of my friends expected me

down last year," he had written to Edward Ermatinger in 1835. And in March 1837—before he received the Committee's letter directing him to come—he had asked for permission "to pay a visit to the civilized world in 1838, 1839, or 1840, as may be found most convenient." In late spring, when the Committee's request arrived, he was greatly pleased, and accepted at once.

Although McLoughlin initially planned to sail in the bark *Sumatra* in the summer of 1837 and go around Cape Horn, he was not well at departure time. "I would be extremely happy as you desire it, to have gone home in the *Sumatra* if my health would permit it," he wrote, "but it is not in that state to allow me [to] undertake so long a sea voyage, which I much regret."

During those few months of delay, the fort was in turmoil, undergoing a long-needed major renovation. The exact dates and sequence are not known, but for at least a year workmen were occupied in replacing old buildings and enlarging the courtyard to nearly twice its original size. Francis Ermatinger wrote that one project was to erect "a good and commodious house" for the Chief Factor, because "the men who were called to prop up the old House, still unfinished, caused an alarm by telling the family that it would soon be down upon them." The new "Big House" was forty by seventy feet and similar to the first, elevated from the ground, with storage underneath and two curving flights of stairs that led to a broad veranda all across the front.

By March 1838, the doctor and his family had moved in, as had James Douglas with his wife and three-year-old daughter. The Reverend and Mrs. Beaver also had quarters there, which somewhat mollified the minister as being "more commodious" and "more decent arrangements for conducting public worship, at which the unseemly dining room is dispensed with."

McLoughlin did not have to rub elbows with him for long. On the twenty-second of that month, the Chief Factor set out with the overland express, to make his first trip away from the Columbia in more than thirteen years.

~ 7 ~

Daughters & Sons
1832–1838

On the chilly day of March 1838 when McLoughlin stepped into a canoe to begin his furlough, he must have felt pleased, because his son John— who had caused the family so much anguish—had come to the Columbia and was to be part of the expedition. John's story must be brought up to date, because of its eventual repercussions on his father's life.

All of McLoughlin's children were adults by 1838, and most of them were away. Marguerite's three daughters by Alexander McKay were married and living in the east, and although little is known of them today, they had kept in touch with the family.

Eliza (Marie Elisabeth), who had been taken to Montreal in 1820 to attend school under the care of her great-uncle, Dr. Simon Fraser, had gone to the Ursuline convent in Quebec. In 1833, when she was nineteen, young John had written, "I received a letter from my dear sister in which she announces me her marriage with Mr Epps I hope she shall be happy with him. . . . it seems that the gentleman is very respected in Quebec by all his friends." Her husband was William Randolph Eppes, an officer in the British army who was then stationed in Canada.

Eloisa was married in 1838 to a young Scottish clerk named William Glen Rae, who had come to Vancouver the previous year. George Simpson's Character Book called Rae "a very fine high spirited well conducted young man of tolerably good Education. Stout Strong and active, is quite a mechanical genius and can turn his hand to anything." Rae and his young wife were living at Fort Vancouver when the doctor left on his furlough.

Four years earlier the youngest child, David, had been sent to Montreal, to the care of faithful Dr. Simon Fraser. The only surviving record of his time there is a brief reference by David himself. "I have a clear recollection of Terrebonne the beautiful streets and walks about the town and often when in solitude I brood over the past with feelings of the deepest regret that I should have come to this Country without any prospect of seeing Canada again."

In 1834, after a brief stay in Montreal, David had been sent to Paris. According to McLoughlin, this was done "in consequence of the fine Accounts my Brother gave me of Johns progress," and he told his brother to draw on his agent, George Moffatt, "for any sum he required for the support of my Sons under two hundred per Annum." At one time he was not sure where David was—a poignant reminder of the miles and time that separated McLoughlin from his children. "My youngest son is I believe at Addiscombe College preparing to go to the East Indies," he told Chief Trader John McLeod in 1836, and to his cousin he said, "My Brother writes that he proposes to Educate him for the Engineer Department and send him out to India."

The other sons were nearby. Thomas McKay, who had a farm near the south bank of the Columbia, was about to take another farm and put up a gristmill in the Willamette Valley. Well-known and prosperous, he was a forceful man with moody dark eyes. He was also an excellent teller of stories, which he often began with "It rained, it rained, and it blew, it blew," and finished with "And my God how it did snow." He sometimes accompanied Hudson's Bay brigades or led outfits on his own to the American rendezvous.

McLoughlin's oldest son, Joseph, had followed his father to the Columbia. In 1827–28 he had been a company apprentice; in 1828–30 he had served as a trapper in the California brigade under A. R. McLeod; and after that he was at times a storekeeper at the fort. In 1837 the doctor wrote that Joseph had witnessed a document because "there was no other at the time at the Fort (besides Commissioned Officers) who could sign his name," which indicates that he had received at least a little education. By the time of McLoughlin's furlough, Joseph was living in the Willamette Valley, where he had acquired a farm.

And young John had been in serious trouble, but had at last attained his goal of coming to the Columbia.

By 1836 McLoughlin knew his brother had sent young John back to Canada, but the gravity of the situation was not at first apparent. After his dismissal, the youth had spent the summer of 1834 at Terrebonne with Dr. Simon Fraser. In the fall the young man had moved to Montreal, where he enrolled in McGill University. But he had a problem, because in order to graduate he needed a transcript of his studies in Paris, which his Uncle David neglected to send. "If no letter comes in the course of this month I will not be admitted to pass this session," he wrote to Dr. Fraser. "I have written to him [Dr. David McLoughlin] several letters and I do not know what hinders him from doing as I suppose that he does not wish me to take my diploma so soon."

Apparently Fraser offered advice, because John wrote to his cousin, "On the receipt of your father's letter I immediately went to one of the professors and show it to him and he told me that it was impossible that I could pass without showing my certificate so for my Uncle's [David's] negligence I have lost one year more." At the age of not quite twenty-three, John was stranded in Montreal, while his father, who would have helped him, was on the far side of the continent. According to John's letters, he genuinely wanted to settle down and get his diploma, but without the missing papers, he was stalled.

To a young man of John's mercurial disposition, the situation was intolerable. While he waited and worried, he began to run up debts, waste money, and neglect his studies. Dr. Fraser, nearly seventy and not very well, withdrew his support, and in early 1835 he contacted Chief Factor James Keith, in charge of the company facilities at Lachine. He then told John, "You will on receipt of this letter call immediately on Mr. Keith and request of him . . . to procure you a passage to Fort Vancouver Columbia river. You know or ought to know that I have not the means to maintain you in Montreal that your father tho' much richer than myself would not support you at the rate you have lately done."

When John, for an unknown reason, failed to secure passage to the Columbia, Dr. Fraser tried to place him with the family at Rivière-du-Loup. But Sister St. Henry objected.

> I am extremely sorry for the trouble and sadness which my nephew gives you, but for heavens sake, do not send him to Rivière du Loup. My Uncle Alexander is too infirm to take care of the conduct of the young man. My Mother can barely see to distinguish objects, she is unable to walk alone, besides her sensitiveness increases with the years, she would die of sadness, to see that child run wild in the country, for charity's sake, My dear Uncle, place this child at some estate of your vicinity, do not abandon him . . . you have been as a father to him, I beg of you to finish and crown your deed.

Fraser kept the youth for a while, but—to his dismay—the bills were rolling in.

A medical student with whom John boarded said he was "anxious to know If Mr. Fraser [Uncle Simon] will be accountable for Mr. McL. Board which Will Amount on the 11th of this month to 6-0-0 (pounds) being for two Month's Board."

A confectioner said he had allowed John credit for pastries and sweets, "having been deceived by him as a debt of honor and counting on the respectability of his family. It is true that the sum is not of very great importance but for me it is much."

An attorney asked Fraser to pay £9.16.0, which John owed to John L. Neysmith, a merchant, saying Mr. Neysmith had advanced it only after being assured "that you would be responsible for the bills to him." He hoped Fraser would "pay this little debt in the same way as you have already paid the other creditors."

Sometime that summer—1835—the young man was moved to Rivière-du-Loup, and while there he asked his cousin John Fraser to send him "a complete set of Instruments for extracting teeth," that he might practice dentistry. Whether this materialized or not, and whatever happened, he returned to Quebec, and this time lived with his sister Eliza Eppes. When he wrote a note to his cousin asking for money, his Uncle Simon's patience was completely exhausted. On January 12, 1836, he wrote his nephew a long letter that is remarkably savage, even for the cantankerous Frasers. He said,

> I am convinced you are depraved beyond any hopes of reform. . . . You perhaps live on Mr Eppes who if he is not a very saint . . . must curse the hour he became the husband of the sister of such a wretch as you are you appear to me born to disgrace every being who has the misfortune to be connected with you. If you have any the least affection for your father mother or brothers you will retire to some distant far country that you may never more be heard of. . . .
> . . . you must know that you are illiterate to that degree that if by any favor you should pass an examination for a Physician you would infallibly disgrace the Profession. . . . you have nothing left besides being a day labourer in civilized society or an hunter among savages.

Matters went so far that George Moffatt lent the young man some money "as he was actually under Arrest."

For some time, McLoughlin in far-off Fort Vancouver was ignorant of John's follies, and when he heard about them, he was humiliated, angry, and crushed. "It is impossible for me to express how much I am Disappointed and Grieved," he told his uncle, but he was still not ready to abandon hope. "As I am desirous to give him every fair chance. if as I wrote you last year he Conducts himself as a Gentleman and if he Endeavours to the Utmost to make up for his past misconduct by applying as Zealously as he possibly can to his Studies you will please Allow him any sum you think Necessary Under a hundred and fifty pounds Halifax pr Annum. . . . But let me drop this and pray that God may of his Mercy lead him to see the Error of his ways."

Disappointed, angry, yet loving his son, he blew hot and cold. "He has applied to be Allowed to come to this Country. I have suffered enough of Mortification from the Reports I had of him. he shall not come to this Country." He told his uncle to "not give him one farthing more than you consider absolutely Necessary . . . he must have no pocket Money. . . . if I had been in Canada when he made this most impudent demand I should have sent him at once about his Business and cast him off for ever." But a few days later, unwilling after all to abandon his floundering son, he wrote that "if a hundred and fifty pounds is found too little and that his conduct deserves it you will please allow him what is necessary."

The family had not solved the puzzle of what-to-do-about-John when the young man embarked on a project under James Dickson, a Canadian of fanciful imagination who had set up a "filibustering expedition"—in the original meaning of "filibuster," as an unauthorized military expedition into a foreign country to foment or support a revolution. Dickson intended to go to the Hudson's Bay colony at Red River, where he would liberate the Indians and lead them to California to set up an Indian empire, with himself on the throne. John McLoughlin enlisted, with two other Hudson's Bay sons named Charles McBean and Alexander McLeod, and in July 1836 they were with the group of sixty that sailed on a chartered schooner for Sault Ste. Marie. Near there they landed on an island, stole and slaughtered some cattle, and just west of Detroit they were arrested by a sheriff's posse.

After Dickson managed to pay the fine of $150, the rabble started to sail across Lakes Erie and Huron. John was in command of a vessel that was wrecked in a severe storm, but he and his men escaped drowning, for which he was promoted to "Major of the Cavalry"—an office that the historian Burt Brown Barker called "interesting . . . for an officer in command of a shipwrecked schooner in the army of a dreamer without cavalry." Nevertheless, the bemused John wrote to his cousin John Fraser asking him to order a suitable uniform, with a red coat "worked with silver lace on the chest and collar with large silver epauletts and two pair of pantaloons one black and the other . . . with gold lace on the sides."

The "army" was trudging west of the Great Lakes—depleted in number, hungry, and without funds—when Governor George Simpson chanced to learn of it through a newspaper account. Fearing that if they reached the Red River settlement "they would occasion much excitement and give an infinity of trouble," he contacted Chief Factor Alexander Christie at Fort Garry and told him to do whatever was necessary to "set them at variance with each other and break up the party." He said Christie should hire McLoughlin as clerk and surgeon for a salary of one hundred pounds per year for three years, and McLeod as an apprentice clerk, which would detach them so that "you will have less difficulty in managing the others." To John himself Simpson wrote a friendly note, saying that "your Father requested me by letter last Spring to endeavor to procure a situation in the Service for you," and that the retirement of a "Medical Gentleman" had created a vacancy, which John could have.

Simpson was not the only one who urged John to take a post with the company. Sister St. Henry begged him to "desist from his foolish expectations," and his cousin John Fraser told him that the Dickson foray "is considered by all here a most degraded expedition—the risk of your life is nothing, my dear fellow, look to your honor." He advised John to "go and join your Honorable Father who waits anxiously for his lost son, go and return to him, he will receive you with his arms open, he will soothe the pain and suffering you are feeling, he will restore you to yourself and make a new man of you."

Meanwhile, the "army" plodded on. "We hired dogs to take our trunks as far as Red Lake and what the poor animals could not take we carried it on our back," said John. "We lived on what we could kill and that was very little, a rabbit [a] day was our allowance." By the time they reached Red River, in December 1836, he and young McLeod were glad to accept the security of Simpson's offer, after which John was taken by company express to the Columbia. Although he was first assigned to Fort McLoughlin, his father had him stationed at Fort Vancouver instead, where he arrived in August 1837.

Ever since his schoolboy years, John had been pleading for the chance to join his parents on the Columbia, and when at last he attained his goal, he plunged into the work of the fort, serving as a clerk with energy and skill. "I perfectly agree with you that it did me no credit for having left Montreal, the more I think on the subject the more I see my folly," he later wrote to his cousin.

The doctor, and doubtless his wife as well, could not fail to be overjoyed at such an about-face, and by March 1838, when father and son set out on the long trip, they had become close friends. They were going to travel together for several months over the backbone of the continent, through snow and streams and lakes, all the way to Norway House.

OREGON

CHAPTER 8

The Winds of Change

*The interests of the Colony, and Fur Trade will never
harmonize, the former can flourish, only . . . by establishing
a new order of things, while the fur Trade,
must suffer by each innovation.*

JAMES DOUGLAS

~ 1 ~

McLoughlin in England
1838–1839

I n 1838, with McLoughlin leaving the Columbia for more than a year, the Governor and Committee acknowledged the complexity of his job by appointing not one man but three to take his place. Chief Factor Peter Skene Ogden was given charge of New Caledonia; Samuel Black, recently promoted to the rank of Chief Factor, was to supervise the inland posts of the Columbia River; and James Douglas was to manage "Fort Vancouver and the lower establishments of the Columbia; likewise the Coasting Trade, Expeditions, Shipping &c."

These were excellent choices. Ogden had proven his mettle as head of the Snake brigade, led coasting expeditions, and served in northern posts. Black had spent more than a decade as head of Fort Nez Perces and Kamloops. And although Douglas was only thirty-four, he had shown outstanding integrity and skill. In his Character Book, Simpson described him as "a stout powerful active man of good conduct and respectable abilities:—tolerably well educated, expresses himself clearly on paper.—Well qualified for any service requiring bodily exertion, firmness of mind, and the exercise of sound judgment but furiously violent when roused." With leaders like these, McLoughlin's district would be in good hands.

The Governor and Committee had called McLoughlin "home" ostensibly to help press their claim against Russia, but this was not their only purpose. In spite of the recent commendation and bonus, they were not satisfied with his administration. In November 1837 they had told James Douglas that the Chief Factor had employed "less system than desirable," and had started projects "on the spur of the moment." Their letter continued,

in the Fur trade as in all other branches of business, a regular system of action should be laid down as long in advance as possible, and followed up as far as circumstances may admit; and it is desirable on a general principle that the plan of operation should be submitted both to us and the Council, and that it should not be deviated from unless rendered necessary by pressing unforseen circumstances.

Serious as this criticism was, McLoughlin seemed unaware of it. He and John started up the Columbia by canoe, stopping on March 28 at Fort Nez Perces, where Marcus Whitman—who knew he was coming—met him and gave him a letter of introduction to the American Board of Commissioners for Foreign Missions in Boston, whom McLoughlin hoped to visit. Signed by both Whitman and Spalding, it mentioned the "numerous favors" the Chief Factor had shown them, and said, "We cannot speak too highly of his kindness to us since we have been in this country." Whether McLoughlin actually called on the board is not known.

He expected to meet Thomas McKay and his son William, but they and two other sons—John and Alexander—were at the Whitman mission, Waiilatpu. McKay wanted William to be a doctor, and had arranged for McLoughlin to take the boy to Scotland, where relatives had promised to give him financial aid. But the plan was changed. Fifty years later, William—who by then was Dr. William McKay—said Whitman had convinced Thomas McKay that the Oregon Country would eventually belong to the United States and that "I would succeed better here if I was educated in the States and became an American in thought and feeling." As a result, William was to go east with Jason Lee, who had started upriver only a few days after McLoughlin.

After the brief stop at Walla Walla, McLoughlin and John continued with the express canoes. The Governor and Committee had forwarded a request from the "Geographical Society," which the doctor tried to honor. "I do myself the pleasure," McLoughlin wrote, "to forward observations made on the degree of heat at which water boils at several places between this and York by which a nigh approximation is made to the elevation of those places."

Challenging the Rockies was, as always, an ordeal. Afterward young John wrote that he "came out this spring with my Father. It is no joke to cross the Mountains in the Spring Snow eleven [feet] deep. I think if the Snow was as deep in Canada at that season some of the folks would open their eyes."

When they reached Norway House, the express went north to York Factory, but McLoughlin and a few men continued east toward Montreal. On the way he met his old friend John Tod, with whom he had a lively conversation about the brief Canadian rebellions of the previous year. McLoughlin, who was never one to veil his opinions, was so outspoken about the Canadian colonists' futile attempt to win self-government that Tod said:

> The Doctor, who has at length descended from his roost, I met in Lake Winnipeg—we breakfasted together, & talked incessantly all the while on the late events of Canada—he was strenuous in support of that arch rebel Pappeneau [Louis Papineau] & his party. I took the liberty to say in a jocund way that it was fortunate for him, he had not been with me last winter, otherwise I should have most probably been now carying an account of his trial, for the gratification of his friends.

We can only speculate on what the doctor might have done if he—always an activist—had lived in Canada at the time.

On August 1, 1838, McLoughlin informed the Governor and Committee that he had arrived in Montreal "to day at 1 P.M." His report included some bits of West Coast news: the recent drowning of five men near Fort George, the smallpox that raged among the Plains tribes, and the latest returns of the inland posts. "I intend to start for England in the Great Western steam Boat which some say will sail on the 9th Instant [of the current month]—But others again say she will only sail on the 16th." The *Great Western* was a new steamship, the first built especially for the transatlantic trade. She was rated as 1,440 tons, in contrast to company ships, such as the schooner *Cadboro* of 70 tons, the brig *Dryad* of 200 tons, and the brig *Nereide* of 240 tons, which the Chief Factor considered too large.

Since the *Great Western* would sail from New York within two weeks or less, McLoughlin had little time to see his family. He managed a visit to his Uncle Simon at Terrebonne, and when his Uncle Alexander's children, Elisabeth and William, were not "in time to come with me and see our uncle Dr. Fraser," he urged them to come by themselves. Alexander had recently died, still at odds with Simon, but McLoughlin assured Elisabeth that "you may depend he [Simon] will receive your with kindness and do all he can for you as though [although] your father and uncle were on bad terms—you ought not to be a party in such differences." Whether they came then is not known, but Elisabeth eventually married her Uncle Simon's son, John Fraser, and it was through their descendants that the family letters were found.

McLoughlin probably sailed on the *Great Western* as planned. After a brief stop in London, where negotiations were not yet under way, he went to Paris to visit his highly successful brother. As two physicians following their profession under vastly different circumstances, they had much to discuss, and it is probable that the Chief Factor at last learned the details of young John's fall from grace.

While he was in Paris, McLoughlin wrote an unexplained note.

Paris 13th Sept. 1838

Rue de La Paix No. 8

To The Governor Deputy Governor and Committee
H.H. Bay Co. No. 3 Fen Church Street London

Honble. Sirs

I have this day drawn in favour of Mrs. Catherine OGorman for the sum of ten pounds sterling which please pay and charge to

Your Humble Servant

John McLoughlin.

For two decades his company account contains a long series of enigmatic entries showing regular payments of ten pounds per quarter to "C. O'Gorman," for a total of £730. The first was dated April 23, 1838, while he was traveling up the Columbia, and it must have been authorized by letter several months before he left. The last was made in 1857, the year of his death. Surviving documents offer little enlightenment, but in a letter of 1843 written in Gillingham, Kent, to the company secretary William Smith, Mrs. O'Gorman said, "Dr. McLoughlin (whose daughter I am) . . . " In 1857 she wrote again, referring to "the death of my kind stepfather, Dr. John Maclaughlin . . . a good and substantial friend as well as a relative." She also called him "my late father." Since Catherine O'Gorman lived in England, McLoughlin may have seen her while he was there.

The most logical explanation is that Catherine O'Gorman was the third McKay daughter, the one of unknown name who, according to David, married "Left. McConnick" and lived in England on a pension after his death. Her letters sound as if she knew the doctor, and the McKay children had probably lived in his household when they were young. David may have confused "O'Gorman" with "McConnick," or the widow may have remarried. The evidence is skimpy, and O'Gorman's precise identity is lost. The only certainties are that for nearly two decades she received regular payments from the Hudson's Bay account, that McLoughlin and his wife maintained some contact with all three McKay daughters—for David knew their married names—and that the other two were Nancy, who married Robert McCargo in or before 1816, and Mary, who married Hudson's Bay officer William Sinclair in 1823. Perhaps it is significant that O'Gorman's given name was the same as that of Mary Sinclair's daughter, Catherine.

By mid-November McLoughlin had left Paris and was in the venerable Hudson's Bay House in Fenchurch Street, London, meeting with the Governor and Committee, who hoped to wring a trade concession from Russia. Earlier that fall, in a burst of belligerence, the Committee had ordered James Douglas to prepare a strong force of one hundred men in three vessels for a venture to the north. They told him to keep the expedition a profound secret until after it left the Columbia, "as if it obtains publicity, the Russians and the Indians under their influence may concert measures to frustrate our plans. . . . therefore it may be advisable to let it be understood that the object is to establish a Post on Vancouver's Island or some other part of the Coast." Much as they hoped for a peaceful solution, they were preparing to exert physical force if necessary.

In the negotiations, they used Ogden's repulse at Stikine, backed by McLoughlin's on-the-spot testimony, as a lever in extracting a trade agreement from Russia, and the maneuver succeeded. The British Foreign Office accepted the affair as a serious international incident, important enough to warrant decisive pressure. As a result, in February 1839, while McLoughlin was still in London, the Russian American Company promised concessions, the Hudson's Bay Company waived its claim to indemnity, and the two firms signed an agreement to cooperate in the Northwest.

According to this compact, the Russians were to stop trading in a coastal strip ten miles wide and about 350 miles long, extending from Mount Fairweather to the Portland Canal—today's Alaskan Panhandle. They granted the Hudson's Bay Company a ten-year lease of this area, for which the company agreed to pay "as annual rent 2,000 seasoned Land Otter Skins (excluding Cub and damaged skins) taken and hunted on the west side of the Rocky Mountains during the said term of ten years." The British were also to supply wheat, flour, peas, grits, hulled pot barley, salted beef, butter, and pork hams. Hudson's Bay men must have felt special satisfaction in having control of the panhandle, because it contained the lower Stikine River, where Ogden had been stopped.

The agreement was advantageous to both sides. It ensured the Russians a dependable supply of agricultural products, enabling them to abandon their expensive Fort Ross in California. It gave the Hudson's Bay Company its long-desired market for foodstuffs, coupled with access to New Caledonia and a free hand in setting up northern posts, and it bolstered the efforts of both to crowd out American competitors. It was a satisfactory arrangement that would be renewed and kept in force until 1867, when the United States purchased Alaska.

Fulfilling this contract would require McLoughlin to step up his farming operations, and therefore, during the meetings with him, the Governor and Committee created the Puget's Sound Agricultural Company. It was to be a corporation with £200,000 of capital stock in shares of £100 each, most of its farms being between Puget Sound and the headwaters of the Cowlitz portage. While it was nominally separate from the Hudson's Bay Company, its superintendent was always to be chosen from officers of that firm, and its first three agents were John Henry Pelly, governor of the Hudson's Bay Company; Andrew Colvile, the deputy governor; and George Simpson.

The new company was to receive seeds and grains and animals for breeding, and it could engage only in agriculture, its employees being forbidden to trade in furs. The purpose of the enterprise was not entirely economic, because its creators believed that the presence of fences, buildings, and cultivated fields would help substantiate Britain's future claim to the area north of the Columbia. "The Government is favorable to the object for political reasons," the Governor and Committee frankly told George Simpson.

This must have given McLoughlin a wry satisfaction, for it was essentially the plan he had drawn up in 1832, only to have it summarily rejected. At that time he had "unfolded his views" to Dr. Tolmie, who agreed that "when the trade in furs is knocked up which at no very distant day must happen, the Servants of Coy [the company] may turn their attention to the rearing of cattle." McLoughlin had proposed the formation of the "Oragon Beef & Tallow Company" as a private enterprise, and Governor Simpson had recommended "that cattle rearing on a large scale . . . be established by the Honble. Company, as a branch of the Fur trade." The officers in London, however, had refused, saying it "would be detrimental, if not dangerous to the Fur Trade," to allow individuals to set up independent business, and that the company "has a right to the best exertions, and to the undivided time and attention of every Chief Factor and Chief Trader as well as Clerk & Servant."

At that time McLoughlin had protested with considerable vigor, "I see nothing in the Deed Poll that deprives me of the Right of investing my means in any business I think proper, except in trading directly or indirectly with the Indians." He had failed, however, to make a dent in his company's resolve, and was forced to drop his plan. It was ironic that the one finally adopted was similar in everything but its name.

Even though the Governor and Committee had recently become dissatisfied with McLoughlin's management, when they met him in person, with his tall frame and resonant voice, his grasp of the Columbia situation, and his innovative ideas, he made an excellent impression. They broke bread with him at least once. A surviving letter in the doctor's hand says, "Mr. McLoughlin presents his Respects to the Governor and Committee of the Honble. Hudson Bay Company and will with great pleasure do himself the Honor to dine with them on Wednesday 13th March."

On February 27, 1839, before he left London, the officers passed a resolution that cited the extent and importance of the Columbia District, the contract with the Russians, and the new Puget's Sound Agricultural Company. Because these entailed heavy responsibility, the Committee provided that

> the Chief Factor who shall be appointed to the principal superintendence or management of that District shall in addition to the emoluments arising from his Chief Factorship be allowed a Salary of Five Hundred Pounds p. Annum to commence from the 1st June next.
>
> That John McLoughlin Esquire Chief Factor be appointed to the principal superintendence or management of the Columbia District.

The endorsement he received in 1836 had been welcome, but this new one was a greater triumph, and a source of intense satisfaction.

Business, however, was only one of his objectives. He wanted to see his son David, who had been sent to Paris in 1834, at the age of thirteen, because Dr. David had given such favorable accounts of young John that McLoughlin "could not hesitate to send his Brother." David had not remained in France. His papers indicate that after attending a general school for eighteen months under "an Irishman named McMahone," he transferred to an institution near London. There he passed the examination for the military school at Addiscombe and became an ensign, but his father arrived in London "about that time," paid all his expenses, and took him back to Fort Vancouver. This is supported by records of the Commonwealth Relations Office in London, which show that David was nominated as a cadet for the East India Company's Military Seminary at Addiscombe, joined it on April 14, 1837, passed the Public

This miniature, painted in France, is probably a portrait of the younger brother, Dr. David McLoughlin, although some historians believe it is John McLoughlin himself. It is now at the McLoughlin House National Historic Site.
OHS ORHI 243

Examination on December 11, 1838, but "resigned the service, his name was struck out of list no. 1 of 1839." No reason for McLoughlin's decision has been preserved, nor has any record of the boy's desires.

McLoughlin's financial account for 1839 shows £38.5.0 paid on February 16 to the "Agent of Gt. Western Steam Ship Co. for his Passage to New York." David undoubtedly accompanied him, and after crossing the Atlantic, they spent some time in New York City. While there, McLoughlin sent his Uncle Simon a book about the Columbia area written by Samuel Parker, the stuffy minister who had spent the winter of 1835–36 at Fort Vancouver as a none-too-popular guest.

Again McLoughlin passed through Montreal, and he evidently managed a little time with his family, for he wrote to Dr. Fraser, "I much regret that my Business would not allow me in my Visit to the Civilised World to spend a longer time in the Society of my Relations." These included his frail mother at Rivière-du-Loup, his sister Marie Louise at the Ursuline convent in Quebec, three other sisters, several members of Grandfather Malcolm Fraser's second brood, and his cousin John Fraser, near Montreal.

When the Chief Factor started west from Montreal on the long trek to the Columbia, he left David for a brief visit with his Uncle Simon. On June 6–12 at Red River, McLoughlin attended a meeting of the Council of the Northern Department, then continued to Norway House, which he reached ten days later.

There he found John, who had crossed the mountains to meet him, and there David caught up. "I arrived here just in time to bid My Father and Brother John a good day for they were on the point of starting in light Canoes for York Factory," David said. Although McLoughlin faced a long, hard trek to Fort Vancouver, he delayed it by the side trip, setting out on June 24 with John and returning three weeks later.

Marguerite's daughter, Mary Sinclair, was living in the Rainy Lake area, and while McLoughlin was there, her fifteen-year-old daughter Catherine joined him, to go west for a visit. By July 23 he had his group together, and they left with the Saskatchewan brigade—McLoughlin, his sons John and David, and Catherine Sinclair.

As before, McLoughlin met his friend John Tod at Lake Winnipeg, and afterward Tod wrote to Edward Ermatinger that "the big Doctor has again returned to the quarters with new power and fresh honours, their Honours at home [England] having placed in him the most unbounded confidence in all affairs connected with the Columbia." Tod was clearly impressed with Mc-Loughlin's endorsement by the Governor and Committee—and no doubt equally impressed by the extra pay.

From Lake Winnipeg, McLoughlin and his young relatives threaded the waterways and crossed the Rockies while the snow was melting and the streams were full. He reported that "at the foot of the Grand Cote . . . one of our men falling off his horse was nigh drowned, and . . . it was with the utmost difficulty our people in several places could prevent the Boats whirling round in the whirlpools. At the Rapid below the *rapide des Morts* . . . one of my Boats was caried into the Stream in spite of the people and filled."

After crossing the mountains, they came in three vessels down the Columbia, where they encountered an American, Thomas J. Farnham, who had left the States with a group of fourteen. They had intended to found a business at the mouth of the Columbia, but because of quarrels and misfortunes, Farnham finished the trip alone, and came down the river with Daniel Lee. While they were stopped at the Cascades, Farnham later wrote, they met McLoughlin, "a hearty old gentleman of 50 or 55. . . . He was about five feet eleven inches in height and stoutly built, weighing about two hundred pounds, with large green bluish eyes, a ruddy complexion, and hair of snowy whiteness. . . . He was in high spirits. Every crag in sight was familiar to him . . . we spent ten minutes with the doctor, and received a kind invitation to the hospitalities of his posts." Later, while the Farnham party was portaging around the rapids, McLoughlin's three barges, with their sails of trading blankets, "swept gallantly past."

McLoughlin and Catherine Sinclair arrived at Fort Vancouver on October 17, 1839, with David and John either accompanying them or coming soon after. The doctor was loaded with honors and ready to tackle a greatly expanded job, but he had changed. In his three previous decades on the frontier, he had never fully seen himself as a fur trader. Having been plunged into the business as an expedient, he had clung to his dream of leaving it, and his letters had repeatedly spoken of "going down." But after the trip, his compass veered west, as if he had physically made a half-turn toward the Pacific Coast. From then on he wrote only of the Columbia, of his hopes and triumphs and disappointments there.

Perhaps it was because the officials in London had raised his pay and given him such generous approval. Perhaps after his renewed acquaintance with the world beyond the Rockies, he realized that it was not an Eden after all. Perhaps it was the sheer joy of floating down the Columbia, past the familiar crags and forests, with snow-capped Mt. Hood at his left hand and a stiff wind filling the blanket sail, on the way to his family and his fort.

Or perhaps it was the reunion with his colleagues, who welcomed him home. Dr. Tolmie, who was there to greet him, said years later that he "resumed sole charge . . . having returned with flying colors, much to the satisfaction of subalterns of Bachelors' Hall, for we greatly liked him." He was once more among his friends.

~ 2 ~

Reaching Out
1839–1840

When McLoughlin took up the reins in the fall of 1839, he was at his zenith, warmed by his superiors' approval, by a hefty boost in pay, and by the satisfaction of working with his sons, all of whom were doing well.

Joseph was still managing his farm in the Willamette Valley and occasionally accompanying a brigade. James Douglas described him as "a young man of determined character" and spoke of him as a valuable employee.

John, who had returned to the fort and worked under Douglas while his father was away, was apparently happy on the Columbia. He told John Fraser about "travelling on horseback to red River annoyed by swarms of mus-quitos for all that I never yet had such a pleasant journey it is worth any ones trouble who is fond of seeing beautiful sceneries." He referred with considerable pride to his new work. "I do not believe that there is an office in Montreal that has so much to do as ours. We are in it from ½ past 6 in the morning till nine at night. I have learned more in the way of transacting business here than I should have done in Montreal in the same space of time. If you were to see our establishment you would be highly delighted with it." In this and other writings, his English shows a trace of awkwardness, the remnant of his years in foreign schools.

And David became a company apprentice. "I still feel as happy now," he told John Fraser, "when I am mounted on my horse with my Rifle; my pistols on each side of my saddle and well belted and a bear 300 year [yards] off as when I used to set by a parler window and listened to a Military Band playing."

Delighted with the change, McLoughlin told John Fraser with obvious pride, "I brought back David with me who has been ever since his arrival Employed in our office as is also John and I must say that they are as attentive and smart at their work as most young men." He thought their industry was a result of being "Kept Employed As certainly most Young Men are ruined by not being Kept Busy as Idleness is the Root of all evils."

The Big House must have been full and lively, with three young adults—John, David, and Catherine Sinclair—in the McLoughlin quarters, along with Eloisa, her husband, and their infant son, while James and Amelia Douglas, under the same roof, had two small daughters. Traders' journals carry accounts of weddings, of "singing, dancing and all kinds of fun" in Bachelors' Hall, of a card party in McLoughlin's room in the evening with a supper afterward, and of a "ball in the evening upstairs, which was kept up till 2 o'clock in the morning." The term "upstairs" was commonly used for the main floor, reached by steps from the courtyard to the piazza; the story above that—if it existed—was a hot, low-ceilinged, unventilated attic storeroom.

Thomas J. Farnham, who had met McLoughlin on the Columbia, spent a week at Fort Vancouver, where he was known as "a jovial, jolly fellow in Bachelors' Hall." He said that when the bell rang for dinner, "the company officers dined in state in a spacious room on the second floor, ceiled with pine above and at its sides. In the south west corner of it is a large close stove, sending out sufficient caloric to make it comfortable." In this room, at the end of a twenty-foot table, stood the Chief Factor, directing the gentlemen and guests to their places according to rank. After giving thanks to God, all were seated, to dine on "Roast beef and pork, boiled mutton, baked salmon, boiled ham, beets, carrots, turnips, cabbage, and potatoes, and wheaten bread," served on "a dinner set of elegant queen's ware," with decanters of wine. "Course after course goes round. The cloth and wine are removed together, cigars are lighted, and a strolling smoke around the premises, enlivened by a courteous discussion of some mooted point of natural history or politics, closes the ceremonies of the dinner hour at Fort Vancouver."

The Bachelors' Hall had also been built by then—a row of small, one-story cottages under one roof, for housing Chief Traders and clerks with their families, as well as visitors. It contained the smoking room, where "weapons, dresses, curiosities of civilized and savage life, and various implements of the fur trade" were on display. Voyageurs, trappers, and navigators met there, "smoking, joking, singing, and story telling; and in every way banishing *dull care*." In addition, it held a supply of books and magazines purchased by the officers, to supplement the company-owned library kept in the office.

Having settled into his rooms in the new Big House, McLoughlin plunged into work. On October 24, only a week after his arrival, he told the Governor and Committee that it "affords me the greatest pleasure to be able to inform your Honors that I find the business in a most prosperous state, which does the utmost credit to Mr. Douglas—and the other Gentlemen in charge of the different Departments." With characteristic generosity, he repeated his commendation six months later, after he had checked the accounts of the various posts and discovered that their profits had increased, "which is a proof of Chief Trader Douglas's good management and of the good conduct & zealous co-operation with him of the gentlemen in charge of these Districts."

Douglas well deserved the praise. He had supervised expeditions and supplied forts, had coped with a severe spring flood and an epidemic of measles, had sent lumber and salmon to the Sandwich Islands, and was preparing to put up a gristmill powered by water. He had also had the sawmill rebuilt "at the suggestion of Chief Factor McLoughlin," although it was still "an imperfect structure, subject to continued accidents, which, give rise to a thousand vexatious interruptions." Farther afield, Douglas had improved the farm on the Cowlitz by adding a spacious barn to its earlier buildings, had made plans to cultivate more than seven hundred acres, and had "as many ploughs agoing, and was sowing as much fall wheat as the means of the place afforded." In addition, before McLoughlin left the Columbia, five hundred head of cattle had been imported from California, and six hundred sheep had recently been sent on the *Nereide*. With these additions, Douglas said, the livestock were "too numerous for the limited pastures" around Fort Vancouver, and had been separated into herds.

The Columbia District was prospering, but McLoughlin was nevertheless facing a challenge, for the agreement with Russia required him to furnish
far more agricultural produce than his farms had ever before attempted. The
most difficult demand was the one for as much butter "as might be convenient for us to provide" in 1840, to be increased to 160 cwt. [16,000 pounds] per
year for the nine years after that—a huge amount for a fur-trading company
in a primitive area, with limited agricultural resources and a herd of an inferior breed. It weighed on McLoughlin. Only a few days after his return, he "set
about building three Dairies on Wapatoo [Sauvie] Island and sent one of the
English families to each of the following places, the Cowelitz Farm, Nisqually
and Fort Langley." They were to start dairies—one at Cowlitz, one at Nisqually,
and two at Fort Langley.

McLoughlin considered the expansion in farm products so important that
he decided to make a personal inspection. On November 18, barely a month
after his return, he folded his long legs into a canoe and set out—down the
Columbia to the mouth of the Cowlitz River and then up that stream to the
company farms. After examining their fields, herds, and new barn, he gave
specific directions for managing the dairy, and with obvious satisfaction said
that "as Mr. [John] Tod had all the ploughs which we could employ agoing, I
had only to allow him [to] proceed."

Next he went overland by horseback to Fort Nisqually, on a long southern
arm of Puget Sound, where he found the cattle and sheep in good condition
and the farming under William Kittson "going on well, and though the soil is light
it is well adapted to grazing and sheep pasture." From there he "embarked
one of the English servants with his family and 29 Cows on board the Steamer"
and took passage himself, to chug northward along the shore of the sound. At
Fort Langley, just above the mouth of the Fraser River, he again found the business prospering and gave instructions to the manager, James Murray Yale.

Pleased that all three posts had crops in the ground, animals thriving, and
their dairies well under way, McLoughlin made a brief excursion to examine
the north end of Vancouver Island as a possible site for the new depot the
Committee wanted him to found. After seeing an area that had a very fine
harbor but was otherwise "not a place suitable for our purpose," he set out for
home, and reached Fort Vancouver in time for Christmas. His trip had relieved
his worry about fulfilling company commitments, except for the persistent
shortage of butter. "I am afraid we will not be able to produce the quantity
we require; our cows are very bad milkers," he told Sir George. "Indeed some
of them do not give above a pint [of] milk a day."

Since McLoughlin's farms were well-staffed and thriving, he was free to turn his attention elsewhere, and agriculture was only part of his job. He was also to expand in the north by establishing two trading posts, one on the previously forbidden Stikine River, near today's Wrangel, and one at Taku, near today's Juneau. This time, thanks to the new agreement with Russia, he could freely cross the coastal strip to reach them.

His choice of officers for the Stikine River post shows how highly he valued it and how confident he felt, for he decided to send three members of his own family there—Eloisa's husband, William Glen Rae, to be its head; his son John to be Rae's assistant; and Eloisa herself to accompany her husband. In addition, he decided the time was right to establish a new fort at Taku, to be directed by Dr. John Kennedy, who had served in the north for several years. To build and equip two new posts would require a large expedition, and to lead this McLoughlin chose James Douglas, recently promoted to the rank of Chief Factor. On April 26, 1840, when everything was ready, Douglas, Dr. Kennedy, a crew of thirty-three men, and the members of McLoughlin's family took off from Fort Vancouver by canoe.

By all accounts, McLoughlin was pleased with this new venture, but young John approached it with reserve. Being assistant to the head of a fort was a giant step up, and yet his post would be distant, in a cold, unknown land. "I am going farther this year than ever," he told John Fraser, saying he would in the future "only write once in two years and then I will not be sure of even that time it will reach you." Later on, David gave it a different slant when he wrote, "I believe he is well satisfied with his situation being far away from the old Gentleman." If this carried a hint of resentment, perhaps because of his summary removal from England, McLoughlin seemed unaware of it.

He had ordered Douglas to lead the groups by canoe and overland to Fort Nisqually, board the *Beaver* there, and sail out of Puget Sound and north along the coast, taking a shipment of grain to the Russians. They made a detour, however, because while they were on the Cowlitz portage, they met a messenger who said Fort Langley had just burned to the ground. Since Douglas had ample manpower, he had the *Beaver* take them to the fort, where they stayed long enough to help replace the bastion, "and squared the wall pieces sills & beams of a new building 48 x 24 feet."

The party then boarded the *Beaver* and splashed on north to the Stikine River, in a land of mountains and fjords, where glittering chunks of blue ice crashed down from the glaciers and floated in the narrow straits. This time resistance came not from the Russians but from the natives, who were afraid the change would cut into their lucrative trade in furs. They laid siege and threatened to destroy the fort until the Russians assured them they would not suffer. Then, with peace restored, the British moved into the Redoubt St. Dionysius and renamed it Fort Stikine. McLoughlin later reported to the Committee that "we found them [the Russians] as Anxious to oblige and accomodate us as we could possible desire and you may depend that our utmost endeavour will be exerted to maintain this friendly disposition."

Douglas, however, was less sanguine. Having seen it firsthand, he considered Stikine a hazardous post, with a garrison "barely enough for its protection," defenses that were "not formidable," and Indians nearby who were "rude and turbulent." He reported that when he left, the natives "threatened violence broke the dam of a small water mill at the Fort, cut off its external supply of water, and did all the mischief in their power."

Right from the start, Eloisa detested Fort Stikine, and stayed there only to be with her husband. "It was a miserable place, a Russian establishment," she said. "There were only flat rocks and not trees around close. Within half a mile, just bare rocks. . . . The water was not close by the Fort there. We had a trough made with two boards for half a mile to bring in water." No attempt at agriculture was made at Stikine, but the area offered an ample supply of meat. Eloisa confirmed it. "There was very good living," she wrote, "plenty of game, deer, elk and fish brought by the Indians."

McLoughlin had told Douglas that after taking over Stikine, he was to go farther north and "establish a Post at the River Tacow on our territories, if the river is navigable . . . but, if this not practicable, he will build at the entrance of the River, or as nigh as circumstances will admit." The new post was named Fort Durham, although it was commonly called Fort Taku or merely Taku, often spelled "Takow" or in various other ways.

Dr. John Kennedy had charge of it, assisted by Roderick Finlayson, an able twenty-two-year-old clerk. Douglas delivered his cargo of grain and returned without mishap to Fort Vancouver, after which McLoughlin reported with great satisfaction, "Mr. Douglas left this with a party to go by the Cowelitz embark at Nisqually in the Steamer *Beaver* to proceed to the Coast and I have now the pleasure to inform your Honors that he returned here on the 2d Oct. after having fully accomplis[h]ed the object of his voyage."

This was almost certainly the happiest and most contented time of McLoughlin's life. His superiors had warmly endorsed him; the agricultural company that he had proposed so long ago was at last begun; his chain of coastal establishments had been extended by two; and one of them was staffed by his own son and son-in-law. One of his main goals—to penetrate the north—was within his grasp.

~ 3 ~
"The Germe of a Great State"
1838–1840

I n the spring of 1838, when McLoughlin left for his furlough, Jason Lee also went east, in order to secure recruits for his mission and urge the American government to take over Oregon. At that time Lee asked for passage with the company brigade, but the Chief Factor refused. "The Dr. could not grant my request," Lee said, "and expressed himself 'doubly mortified'; because he could not do me the favour, and should also be deprived of my company." The reason for McLoughlin's refusal is not known, but perhaps the brigade could not accommodate an additional passenger, or he may have hesitated to appear at York Factory with Lee—an American—in tow. At any rate, McLoughlin set out on the northern route, while Lee arranged to go as far as Fort Hall with "Messrs. Ewing & Edwards"—the settler F. Y. Ewing, and Philip L. Edwards of the mission.

Before leaving, Lee called a meeting at Mission Bottom and presented a petition he had prepared with the aid of Edwards and the Reverend David Leslie. McLoughlin knew of it through his French Canadian pipeline, and James Douglas probably expressed the prevailing opinion at the fort when he said it "will not, I presume, attract much attention . . . but it discovers the natural bias of our neighbours."

It was the earliest and mildest of several petitions by settlers, and while it did not attack McLoughlin or his company, it urged the United States to take "formal and speedy possession" of the area. It acknowledged the fact that conditions so far were peaceful due to "feelings of honor, to the feeling of dependence on the Hudson's Bay Company, and to their moral influence." Predicting that the company's ability to maintain order would inevitably decline as the population increased, it said,

> By whom, then, shall the country be populated? By the reckless and unprincipled adventurer . . . by the Botany Bay refugee; by the renegade of civilization from the Rocky Mountains; by the profligate

deserted seaman from Polynesia; and the unprincipled sharpers from Spanish America? We flatter ourselves that we are the germe of a great state . . . and are anxious to give an early tone to the moral and intellectual character of its citizens.

The fundamental cause of the petition was the system of joint occupation, under which settlers had no way to register their land claims and therefore feared the loss of their farms. The petition also reflected a small but rising tide of resentment against McLoughlin and his company, based on his early refusal to sell cattle, and the all too human envy of ill-equipped American farmers for the prosperous British fort. Still another—and potent—factor was religious bias, fed by the doctor's ties with the Catholic French Canadians, whom the staunchly Protestant residents scorned.

So far the schism was small, but it was destined to grow, because the settlers and the company were by their very natures at cross-purposes. As James Douglas put it, "The interests of the Colony, and Fur Trade will never harmonize, the former can flourish, only . . . by establishing a new order of things, while the fur Trade, must suffer by each innovation." In this climate Lee had prepared his petition, and it was signed by all nine male missionaries, by eighteen American settlers, and by nine French Canadians.

It is of interest that the two most important leaders in the Columbia— the British businessman, the American missionary—left in the same week, and that while they were gone, both would spur the area's growth. McLoughlin, who set out on March 22, 1838, would take part in a major expansion of the Columbia District's business. Lee, with the petition in a small trunk strapped to his horse's side, started on March 26, for a tour that would fan interest in the West and more than double the size of his mission's staff.

The early part of Lee's trip was uneventful, but tragedy was in store, for his wife was pregnant, and within three months of his departure she died in childbirth, along with her infant son. By then McLoughlin was in Europe, but James Douglas sent a messenger posthaste, who caught up with the minister at Pawnee Mission in the Middle West and handed him the letter edged with black. In spite of his grief, Lee knew he could accomplish nothing by turning back, so he pressed on toward the Atlantic.

In the East he lectured to huge crowds, as at Hartford, Connecticut, where "hundreds went away unable to gain admittance into the church." His message fell on fertile soil, for the United States was restless and growing fast. By 1838 it included twenty-six states; its neighbor Texas was an independent republic, flirting with the idea of annexation; the campaign for the abolition of slavery was catching fire; and a few railroads were being built. In Bangor, Maine, for example, a steam train ran twelve miles in two and one-half hours, with a fare of thirty-seven and a half cents. Interest in the West Coast had already been aroused by the writings of Hall Kelley, William Slacum, and others, and Lee's listeners were riveted by his vivid, on-the-spot reports.

During that winter, while McLoughlin was in Paris and London, Lee met with the Methodist Missionary Society in New York City. His plea for help was published in the *Christian Advocate*, resulting in an avalanche of cash and also of recruits—more than Lee wanted, hastily enrolled and poorly screened. Five years later, in 1844, he said, "both the Board, and myself as their agent, must have taken leave of our senses. . . . A great mistake was made in selecting some of those who were sent out. . . . I forewarned the Oregon Committee that if the persons who applied for situations were not examined by a proper committee the plan would fail. Such proved to be the case."

In addition to his efforts to strengthen his mission, he had the petition presented to Congress—a somewhat naive gesture, because under joint occupation the United States could not legally extend its laws to Oregon. Nevertheless, the document was printed and widely read, becoming one more impetus to American fascination with the Northwest.

George Simpson, who was also in New York, happened to meet Lee on October 1, 1839. As was his habit, the governor gleaned all the information he could, and he later informed the London Committee that Lee was "on the eve of sailing for the Columbia River with about 30 other Missionaries and their families, in a vessel called the *Lausanne*." He also said another party of two hundred "contemplated migrating from the State of Massachussets . . . next summer, with the view of becoming Settlers on the Wilhamet River." The tempo of American migration was speeding up.

That fall, while Lee's recruits were beginning their slow journey around the Horn, McLoughlin returned to Oregon, and the following May, he was informed that the *Lausanne* had safely crossed the bar of the Columbia. In a characteristic gesture, he immediately sent an employee to meet the ship near Fort George, to see that she made it safely to Fort Vancouver and to take its people "some excellent fresh bread and butter"—a special treat after the long sea voyage. The ship then sailed slowly upstream, piloted by a river-wise Chinook "who pointed out the channel in a very accurate manner."

On the afternoon of June 1, the missionaries reached Fort Vancouver, having been seven months at sea. As Daniel Lee described it,

After the ship was anchored, Dr. McLaughlin came on board, and was introduced to the mission family, and gave them a very kind invitation to partake of the hospitalities of the fort, which is situated on the north side of the river, about one quarter of a mile, or perhaps less than that, from the water. On the following day all were comfortably roomed in the fort, and nothing was lacking on the part of the ladies and gentlemen of the establishment to render our sojourn comfortable and pleasant.

The helpful "ladies of the establishment" undoubtedly included Marguerite McLoughlin and Amelia Douglas, who would have an important role in welcoming the guests, especially the women and children, and looking after their needs.

For a while McLoughlin's domain was lively with its visitors of all ages. Reports vary, but Daniel Lee said the newcomers, sometimes called "the great reinforcement," consisted of fifty-one souls, including "five missionaries and a number of laymen, such as mechanics, farmers, and physicians, and young ladies for teachers." Most of the men were accompanied by their wives, and some by their children. One member was Jason Lee's second wife, Lucy Thompson, whom he had married shortly before leaving the East.

Full of guests as the fort was, within two days it was housing still more—missionaries from the Willamette Valley and The Dalles. Accommodating so many would be difficult, but McLoughlin managed to put them up, probably in the new "Bachelors' Quarters." He also provided a hall for a meeting on June 3, at which they received their assignments: to strengthen Lee's headquarters on the Willamette; to enlarge the small station at The Dalles; and to found new missions on the Nisqually River, on the Umpqua River, and at the mouth of the Columbia. In a move that would prove disastrous for McLoughlin, Lee told the Reverend A. F. Waller to establish a branch at Willamette Falls, where the Chief Factor and George Simpson had claimed land in 1828 and where McLoughlin had hewn timber, planted potatoes, blasted a millrace, and put up a small bark-covered hut and a mill.

At this time Lee made another major change. Mission Bottom was marshy, close to the Willamette River and plagued with insects, as Thomas J. Farnham learned when he spent a night with Lee "more to the apparent satisfaction of 3 pecks of fleas than ourselves. These creature comforts abound in Oregon." Before going to the States, Lee had erected a mill about ten miles farther south, on a well-drained, fertile expanse beside a good stream. Called Chemeketa, the site was so promising that soon after his return he moved his school to it.

The *Lausanne* passengers marked the beginning of an accelerated influx of Americans, which strengthened Lee's mission and caused McLoughlin's influence to wane. According to James Douglas, in 1838 the Willamette Valley had contained 51 men of European descent—only adult males were counted—including 23 French Canadians, 10 missionaries, and 18 other American "stragglers from Calefornia &c." In the following year a few more Americans came in, mainly "from the Rocky Mountain Trapping Parties"; and in 1841 George Simpson estimated the number of men other than missionaries as 126— 65 Americans and 61 Canadians, who with their families brought the total to about 500. Counting the population was difficult, with farms scattered and communication slow, but these admittedly inaccurate figures give an idea of the area's rapid growth.

Farnham stayed in the area less than two months, but while he was there, the settlers enlisted his help in securing an American government. When they asked him why the United States did not offer the area protection, he replied that he could not give an answer "exculpatory of their national delinquency," but he advised the residents to send a petition to Washington, and agreed to deliver it.

They then prepared a memorial, which was signed by sixty-seven men, including nearly every male resident of the Willamette Valley, both Americans and French Canadians. Stronger than Lee's petition, it said the inhabitants were at the mercy of savages and "OTHERS THAT WOULD DO THEM HARM"—a covert attack on McLoughlin and his company. It indulged in a bit of creative journalism by reporting that "the crimes of *theft, murder, infanticide, etc.,* are increasing among them to an alarming extent." It praised the land, protested the strength of the Hudson's Bay Company, begged for "the high privileges of American citizenship; the peaceful enjoyment of life; the right of acquiring, possessing and using property; and the unrestrained pursuit of rational happiness." For this, it said, "your petitioners will ever pray."

In early December 1840, Farnham took passage in the company brig *Nereide* to the Sandwich Islands. He forwarded the document from there to Washington, and when it arrived, Senator Lewis F. Linn of Missouri presented it to Congress. Because of the treaty of joint occupation, Congress could not act on it, but Farnham's petition and the books he later wrote were a further spur to interest in Oregon.

In this growing conflict, McLoughlin, who had semiofficial but shrinking control of the area, was the quintessential man in the middle, caught between

the contradictory needs and rights of the settlers and his company. He foresaw further growth, and with ever an eye on business, tried to persuade the
Governor and Committee to use it as a new and lucrative resource. "If it is
Your Honors wish, to maintain our footing in the Country, we must supply the
wants of the trade," he warned the officers in London. "We will furnish their
little wants, so as to keep up a good feeling with them, but . . . there will be a
greater or less influx of people, from the United States every year, and the
trade will be taken up by other Merchants, if we do not anticipate them." It
would be a major shift—from fur trade to retail business—but he knew the
tide could not be stemmed, and that his company must adapt.

~4~

The Stirring of Government
1841

I n February 1841, eight months after the arrival of the *Lausanne*, Ewing
Young was taken sick with "a pressure on the brain and died a somewhat
violent death at his home." His death posed a problem, because he left "a
large and very unsettled estate, without having made the least provision for
its administration," and there were neither laws nor courts.

After the cattle drive of 1837, Young had become one of the most afflu-
ent farmers in the Willamette Valley, owner of a large land claim northwest of
French Prairie, a sawmill, and a sizeable herd of livestock. Previous deaths,
which had been among the French Canadian farmers, had been easily handled, because they were British citizens, and Parliament's Acts of 1820–21
had given the Hudson's Bay Company the right to administer law in the Northwest. In 1835, for example, after a former company trapper named Louis
Shangaratte "burst a blood vessel in the lungs and died almost immediately,"
the Chief Factor had asked Jason Lee to attend to the orphaned children and
"the little property that fell to the heirs," and no one had objected. In addition
to McLoughlin's legal power, his practice of carrying company retirees on company books "serves as an Encouragement to them to behave Well," as he put
it. But the only American organization was that of the missions, which had no
legal status, and the need to dispose of Young's wealth crystallized the wish
for laws.

Although surviving accounts vary in details, it appears that shortly before or after Young's death a group of settlers, mainly connected with the mission, had a caucus to discuss the situation—the Reverend Gustavus Hines placed it "on the very day" of the burial, while J. Quinn Thornton said it was a week before, on February 7. Little was accomplished except the selection of a "committee of arrangements" to set up a public meeting that would consider the problems of administering Young's estate and adopting a system of laws.

Hastily summoned by the committee, a larger number of Willamette Valley residents met on February 17, probably at Young's grave. With Jason Lee as chairman, they talked about a constitution, nominated officers, and adjourned until the following day, when "nearly every male inhabitant south of the Columbia, of full age" came by horseback or boat to the Methodist mission. McLoughlin, in his fort north of the Columbia, did not attend, nor was he expected to.

At this meeting, led by the Reverend David Leslie, the settlers chose a committee of nine with the ambitious goal of "framing a constitution and drafting a code of laws." They tried to broaden support by naming as committeemen three Methodist missionaries, three French Canadians, one American settler, and one Englishman, with Father Blanchet, McLoughlin's friend, as chairman.

Before adjourning, they elected officers—the Reverend Gustavus Hines as secretary, a clerk of courts, a "high sheriff," three constables, and a "supreme judge, with probate powers." But they had one major stumbling block: the choice of governor. William H. Gray, steward of the Methodist mission, gave an explanation in his *History of Oregon*, which is rabidly anti-Catholic and sometimes inaccurate, but still of value as the most complete eyewitness record, supplying details not found in other accounts. In Gray's opinion, "Bailey [the anti-mission candidate] could not be trusted, and Hines [the mission candidate, serving as secretary] could not be elected; hence the office of governor was discarded, and the committee instructed to prepare a constitution and laws, to be executed without an executive." Hines himself, in his terse official account, was more circumspect, saying only, "As it was not deemed necessary to elect a Governor that office was set aside."

Blanchet's committee was directed to report at another public meeting on "the first Thursday in June, at the new building near the Roman Catholic church"—today's town of St. Paul. But on that day, he informed the settlers that "in consequence of his not having called the committee together, no report had been prepared." The priest later said that while he was not opposed to a government, he thought there were too few inhabitants to warrant it, "and as far as his people were concerned there was certainly no necessity for one nor had he any knowledge of crime having been committed."

Many colonists thought McLoughlin had influenced Blanchet. Gray said that *"divide and conquer,* the policy adopted by the Hudson's Bay Company," was supported "heart and soul" by the priest, a view that was corroborated by a letter from George Simpson to the Governor and Committee. It said, "This last summer they [the Americans] made a strong effort to form a constitution for themselves, but the Company's influence over the Canadian settlers in a large measure defeated that object." Although McLoughlin's methods are not on record, he and Blanchet were friends, and he undoubtedly had a hand in the decision. He assisted the settlers in many ways, but as a loyal British subject and trusted employee of a British company, he could not promote a government that would strengthen the claim of the United States.

Disappointed but undeterred, the settlers elected Dr. William J. Bailey to replace Blanchet and try again. Since an American exploring expedition under Lieutenant Charles H. Wilkes had recently arrived, Bailey and his committee were told to confer with "John M'Loughlin" and with Wilkes "concerning the propriety of forming a provisional government in Oregon." But with the influential priest opposed and no report to act on, they were unable to do anything decisive, so they merely annulled the previous election of officers and set up another meeting for October 1841.

Although for the time being the pro-government forces were stalled, their efforts had not been entirely wasted. Dr. Ira L. Babcock, who had been elected "supreme judge," had appointed an administrator for Young's estate, and this official continued to function. During the next three years, Young's assets were auctioned for about five thousand dollars, to be held in trust in case heirs were found but used in the meantime for community benefit—specifically, to build a jail on land donated by McLoughlin. It would be Oregon's first government building.

The October meeting was not held, partly because the progovernment settlers were not numerous enough to organize without the help of the French Canadians, who were restrained by McLoughlin, and partly because the visiting American, Charles Wilkes, disapproved. Discouraged, the settlers temporarily gave up. In the words of Robert Newell, a trapper turned farmer, "As thare is no laws in this country, we do the best we can." The venture had failed, but it was important, because it was the first organized attempt to form a government in the Oregon Country. From then on the idea grew, taking deep root.

The failed attempt deepened the split between McLoughlin and the settlers, because they believed he had opposed them, and it reinforced the official company attitude. For several years Governor Simpson and the London officers had been aware of the growing number of Americans in the Willamette Valley, and they needed no great acumen to realize that the newcomers were a potential danger to the company's comfortable monopoly. The white-sailed Hudson's Bay ships, crisscrossing the Atlantic, carried many worried discourses on the American threat and how best to meet it. As early as 1839, the Governor and Committee had developed a highly skeptical outlook, and wrote to McLoughlin:

> With regard to Mr. Lee and his Missionary Brethren however much they may profess friendship and goodwill towards us, and notwithstanding their high eulogiums upon us for hnspitality and kind offices; it is quite evident they have promoted the present mania for emigration to the Columbia, which is likely to prove so troublesome and injurious to us. . . . they are employed as pioneers for the overflowing population of the New England States, who have it in view to repay us for our good offices, by possessing themselves of the fruits of our labors, as soon as they may be in a condition to wrest them from us by main strength.

The London Committee said that as long as the missionaries confined themselves to their "avowed objects," McLoughlin was to give them "such absolute necessities in clothing &c. as they may require, if they be in a condition to pay for the same." But they warned him to be cautious "unless they can assure us of more regular payment than we have hitherto received as there is a tardiness in honoring their Bills, which is neither regular nor convenient."

At that time McLoughlin and his company were in agreement, for he knew the missionaries received adequate stpport from their board, and therefore he could in conscience charge them for medical help and supplies. He replied, "Your view of the Revd. Mr. Lee and his Missionary Brethren . . . I believe to be correct and you may depend we will regulate our intercourse with them in any manner you direct."

In 1841, when the Americans were making their first attempt to form a government, the Governor and Committee were still of the same mind, considering the settlers as business rivals, to be dealt with severely but fairly, and discouraged from intruding on the company domain. The London officers instructed McLoughlin that "the supplies they obtain from us be charged for ready money or secure payment at as high a rate as may be considered expedient." They advised him that if foreign ships—meaning Americans—arrived with trade goods, he was to sell his merchandise "at such reduced prices for ready money as will prevent these adventurers deriving any profit from their speculation and deter others from entering into the trade."

Again McLoughlin consented, because the settlers were generally able to raise their own food with a sufficient surplus to exchange at the fort for their other needs, and he was as eager as the Committee to discourage competition. "The plan you direct in regard to our dealings with the Settlers in the Wallamette, is the one we have followed all along," he replied, "and I am extremely happy to find it Corresponds with your views."

He was comfortable in his role as a trader, approaching it from a businessman's point of view. But he had not yet faced bands of settlers who arrived without funds and in actual want. That dilemma was still to come.

~5~
An American Lieutenant
1841

The American who came to the West Coast in 1841 was Charles Wilkes— tall, dark-haired, with the erect carriage of a military officer. The U.S. Navy had sent him on a four-year expedition, 1838–42, with ambitious orders to explore the entire Pacific Ocean, including the Fiji Islands, South America, the Antarctic, Japan, and the Northwest Coast. He had a well-equipped entourage of six vessels, with a crew that included naturalists, botanists, a taxidermist, philologist, mineralogist, and several artists.

When Wilkes, with his flagship the *Vincennes* and the brig *Porpoise*, reached the Columbia, he found the bar so rough that he called it "one of the most fearful sights that possibly can meet the eye of a sailor." Instead of trying to cross it, he took his ships to Fort Nisqually, on Puget Sound, from which he sent exploring parties to various sections of the Northwest. He himself, with four men, rode Hudson's Bay horses to the Cowlitz Farm and then went by company canoe to Fort Vancouver.

Although McLoughlin was absent when they arrived, Wilkes said they were "politely invited in," and after a few minutes McLoughlin "came galloping up and gave us a most warm reception. . . . He is a fine looking person of robust frame, with a frank open countenance about 50 years of florid complexion his hair white . . . enthusiastic in disposition and I should think of great energy of character and well suited for the situation he occupies which requires no small talent and industry to fill."

McLoughlin, as always a generous host, invited Wilkes to tea, "a profusion of good fare served in an ample hall," where half a dozen "gentlemen" were seated according to rank, with the doctor at the head of the table. He also showed Wilkes to sleeping quarters in a log building, "scaled of one story with French windows & exceedingly comfortable except the bunks instead of bed—that is made of pine boards."

The fort had continued to grow. According to Wilkes, the palisade enclosed thirty-four buildings, including houses, a brick powder magazine, and shops for blacksmiths, carpenters, wheelwrights, coopers, and tinners. He listed forty-nine cabins for laborers in the outer village, as well as a hospital, distillery, gristmill, boathouse on the shore, large barn with seven outbuildings, and a threshing machine. He spoke of the beautiful river, "winding its way across the untouched forest backed by the distant blue hills and the striking snowy peak of Mt. Hood an object which one seldom tires in viewing." And he described the fort's busy early-morning life:

> At early dawn the bell is rung for the working parties, who soon after go to work: the sound of the hammers, click of the anvils, the rumbling of the carts, with tinkling of bells render it difficult to sleep after this hour. The bell rings again at 8, for breakfast; at 9 they resume their work, which continues till one; then an hour is allowed for dinner, after which they work till six, when the labours of the day close, at five o'clock on Saturday afternoon the work is stopped, when the servants receive their weekly rations.

McLoughlin offered Wilkes every possible assistance. "I feel that my expressions are few in comparison with the numerous kindnesses we all received," the lieutenant said. "Even Billy Bruce the gardener made us his debtor, by sending us repeatedly some of the fine fruit and vegetables grown under his care."

The lieutenant investigated French Prairie and the Willamette Valley, using a company boat and crew. At Willamette Falls the missionaries had built a log house, and he shrewdly forecast the future conflict by explaining that it was done "in order to secure the right of site or privileges." He also said the Hudson's Bay Company had "gone to considerable expense in blasting the rock for a mill race for the same purpose," and "have a trading-post here, and are packing fish, which the Indians catch in great quantities. This is said to be one of the best salmon-fisheries on the river."

He had a meal at the home of the Reverend Waller, and having seen Mrs. Waller's skill with her stove, the commander observed, "No engineer ever knew his engine better or could manage it with more adroitness." After meeting Father Blanchet and several neighboring farmers, he continued south to the Methodist mission at Chemeketa. It did not make a good impression.

> We dined a la Methodist on Salmon, Pork, potted cheese, and straw-berries, tea & hot cakes, they were all brothers and sisters some with coats, some without, red flannel shirts, and dirty white arms, hig-gledy piggledy. I shall not soon forget the narrow cramped up table more crowded round it than it would hold. . . . The meal was eaten by us all in brotherly love, but hunger assisted me or I never should have been able to swallow mine.

He found the buildings in poor condition, the hospital used as a residence, the school poorly attended, and a threshing machine standing neglected "in the public road over which all the travel passed."

While Wilkes was there, the settlers consulted him in hopes he would help them achieve an American government, but he said he found the country free of crime, with no need for laws, and he was sure the French Cana-dians did not want any. To the settlers' chagrin, he advised them "to wait until the government of the United States should throw its mantle over them"—a major disappointment, and an important factor in the temporary collapse of their effort. Father Blanchet agreed, saying his flock had no need for legal regulations, "nor had he any knowledge of crime having been committed."

During the next several months, McLoughlin provided boats and horses, with which Wilkes sent his men up and down the coast and inland to the Whit-man and Spalding missions. While the commander was at the fort, the Snake brigade arrived, singing as it came, and he was fascinated by the voyageurs, "who were to be seen lounging about in groups, decked in gay feathers, ribands, &c., full of conceit, and the flaunting air of those who consider themselves the beau-ideal of grace and beauty; full of frolic and fun." McLoughlin had him taken up the Cowlitz in a company boat to attend a July 4 barbecue held by sailors from the American ships that were anchored at Nisqually. The doctor meant to join him there, but arrived a day late.

While Wilkes was in the area, several young settlers were building a small vessel, the *Star of Oregon*, which they hoped to sail to California and exchange for cattle. They lacked rigging, however, and McLoughlin refused to sell it to them because they knew so little about ships that he thought they "were making a coffin for themselves." In their predicament they appealed to Wilkes, who checked their credentials and decided one of them, Joseph Gale, had sufficient seagoing experience to head the venture. He gave them several maritime instruments, along with American papers for clearing Mexican ports, and persuaded McLoughlin to sell them what they needed. In this way the doctor—able but reluctant—furnished cordage and sails for the first ocean-going vessel built in the Northwest as a commercial venture. And to his surprise the young crew made the trip safely, although with difficulty. They sold their vessel, hired extra hands, and brought back a total of 1,250 cattle, 600 horses, and nearly 3,000 sheep—a valuable addition to the area's stock.

On July 17, 1841, the sloop of war *Peacock*, of the Wilkes expedition, was wrecked on the bar, with the loss of all its equipment but no lives. The situation alarmed McLoughlin, because he heard that its captain had no replacement ship and therefore might discharge the crew and leave them in the area, with neither resources nor supervision. In dismay he wrote that "if these sailors had remained, they would have got into trouble . . . they would have remained idle, spoilt the Indians, and been ready to join the first that came to oppose us."

It happened that an American coaster, the *Thomas Perkins* under Captain Varney, was in the Columbia, and McLoughlin, to protect his own trade, had purchased the brig's entire cargo of molasses, sugar, and salt, to be paid in salmon at ten dollars per barrel. After the *Thomas Perkins* was partly loaded with his fish, McLoughlin learned that Wilkes wanted to buy the ship as a station for his idle crew—a possibility that delighted the Chief Factor. "I took back 360 barrels Salmon from Varney on his paying five hundred dollars," he told the Governor and Committee, "to enable him to sell his Vessel to Commodore Wilkes, to take away the crew of the *Peacock*."

As he hoped, when the ship was freed, Wilkes purchased her, renamed her the *Oregon*, and staffed her with the idled sailors. Hoping to forestall criticism, McLoughlin told the governor and Committee that it would have been disastrous to set unsupervised men free with no one to "prevent their getting into quarrels with the natives, and bringing the whole country into trouble . . . so important did I conceive it, for us to get these men away, that I would have considered myself justified to have given up the five hundred dollars." Nevertheless, when the Committee heard of it, they wrote the Chief Factor a sharply critical letter. "It would be offering speculators too much induce-ment to visit the Columbia River, were you to purchase any large cargo at so great an advance. You should have furnished us with an invoice or list of the goods." But Governor Simpson differed, and said McLoughlin had made the arrangement "with that excellent judgment which has generally characterized his management."

In late summer, while Wilkes was still in the area, the McLoughlins had an important family event—the marriage of seventeen-year-old Catherine Sinclair, Marguerite's granddaughter, to Francis Ermatinger, the Hudson's Bay officer who had criticized McLeod's expedition against the Clallams. The breach had not been permanent, for Ermatinger liked and admired the doc-tor. "I have never had more respect for any man in my life," he once wrote to his brother, and his letters show that he had for years hoped to marry Mc-Loughlin's daughter Maria Eloisa. In 1832 he had written, "My thoughts are much occupied upon the young Lady." In 1834 he had "not given up Maria." In 1836, "Two things have influenced me, Miss Maria and a Tradership. For these I have been working." But by 1838 he had abandoned hope. "My appli-cation for Miss Maria was answered with a no. . . . I am too gray for the young Lady." He was then forty-one, and his problem would have been more touch-ing if he had not in the meantime formed an alliance with a Pend d'Oreille woman.

Although he was much older than Catherine, and George T. Allan called him a "regular jolly jovial Cockney whom we sometimes styled Bardolf from the size and colour of his nose," Ermatinger was a capable officer, successful and well liked. McLoughlin apparently approved of the marriage, for he, James Douglas, "and several others" journeyed to Fort George, where the Reverend Joseph Frost, who had a mission nearby, performed the service on August 10. Existing records do not show whether Marguerite McLoughlin attended, but it is unlikely, for she was not named. Neither do any documents explain the reason for holding the ceremony at Fort George instead of Vancouver. It may have been for the sake of convenience, because Ermatinger was to assume management of the farm at the Cowlitz.

After the ceremony McLoughlin returned to Fort Vancouver, and George Simpson arrived there on August 25 on one of his periodic tours of inspec-tion. He had a new title—Sir George Simpson—bestowed by Queen Victoria for his outstanding service to his company and hence to the nation.

While he was there, he met Lieutenant Wilkes at a formal banquet, with "all the functionaries of the company" present—an occasion that Wilkes found gastronomically impressive, but dull. "Like all dinners, it was stiff and formal," he said. "Sir George Simpson occupied the head of the table, and there were none but men present." He echoed other visitors in noticing that the "wives seem to be little thought of, but for what reason I could not imagine, as many of them were highly worthy of notice." He particularly mentioned their devoted care for their husbands.

This was McLoughlin's final contact with Wilkes. Shortly afterward, the American sailed down the Columbia, to continue his explorations and return to the United States. But his departure did not mean the end of his influence, because he sent a report to the secretary of the navy and published several books. In these, his judgment of the missionaries remained harsh, particularly when he spoke of their drive to form a government. "Their principal reasons appear to me to be, that it would give them more importance in the eyes of others at a distance, and induce settlers to flock in, thereby raising the value of their farms and stock. I could not view the subject in such a light, and differed with them entirely as to the necessity or policy of adopting the change."

But he gave unstinted praise to the Chief Factor and the Hudson's Bay Company, whom he found abundantly generous. The Americans' anti-McLoughlin prejudice puzzled him. He said that "every facility has been at all times extended to newcomers and settlers; it is sufficient that they are of good character, and the use of cattle, horses, farming utensils, and supplies is invariably extended . . . until such time as they are able to provide for themselves." They could not, he said, "adduce any instance of the wrong application of his power. He is notwithstanding extremely unpopular among all classes of our countrymen, but for what reason it is difficult to conceive."

In several ways, Wilkes was important to McLoughlin. His report and other writings served as a counterweight to the criticisms of other visitors. He praised the Oregon Country—its beauty, its climate, its opportunities. He was influential in persuading the American government not to accept the Columbia as a boundary, but to insist on access to Puget Sound. And by discouraging the settlers' attempts to form a government, he helped the Hudson's Bay Company retain its dominance in the Northwest, at least for a time.

~6~

Golden California
1839–1841

E ven while McLoughlin was starting the agricultural company and northern posts, he turned his sights on California, which was then a territory
of the Republic of Mexico, with its northern boundary at the forty-second
parallel—today's border with Oregon. California had two ruling officials: the
civil governor, Juan Bautista Alvarado; and the military commander, General
Mariano Guadalupe Vallejo, Alvarado's uncle, who was said to have "unbounded influence." A relatively small number of Europeans, chiefly of Spanish
descent, lived in California. Many were aristocratic, some were wealthy, and
they occupied large inland cattle ranches or little towns along the coast. Mc-
Loughlin saw the area as potentially profitable, not only in furs, but also as an
outlet for general trade.

For more than a decade he had considered moving to the south, and as
early as 1827 he had sent Captain Æmelius Simpson to explore the area around
Monterey. On his return, Simpson had reported a ready market for both salmon and timber, which tempted McLoughlin. Being short of ships, however,
he made no further moves until 1830, when he sent Simpson south again,
instructing him,

> You will endeavour to ascertain if there are any settlers on the Bona-
> ventura [Sacramento], and if there would be any objections to our
> sending a party of Trappers to that part of the country or to the Bay
> of St. Francisco . . . you will also endeavour to learn if we could be
> allowed to take Cattle, Horses and Mules out of California. . . . If you
> become acquainted with any of the Missions you may tell them we
> will undertake to import any article they may wish from England.

This time the captain secured extensive information, and brought back
the disappointing report that "the only way in which business is done along
the South American coast is by barter as money is so very scarce." He said
California had only one big business—cattle—and that in consequence, "we
can only export our deals to be paid in hides and Tallow." This was so unprom-
ising that for several years McLoughlin dispatched only an occasional ship to
the southern ports.

He did, however, have his overland brigades go to the interior of California, led by A. R. McLeod in 1829 and afterward by Peter Skene Ogden, John Work, and Michel Laframboise. They trapped in the thinly populated Sacramento Valley, where no one pressed them for permits, and therefore they secured none. It was a frustrating job. Having no nearby fort as a source of supplies, they could not venture as far as the lower Colorado River, which "abounds with Beaver"; and having no licenses, they could hunt only "by stealth spending much of their time in unavoidable inaction, and travelling backwards and forwards to the Columbia for supplies." Even so, during the 1830s they took 10,860 beaver and 3,234 sea otters.

Like McLoughlin, the Governor and Committee had been interested for some time in a California post. The Chief Factor later said that "when it was first suggested to me in 1835" he had opposed it, thinking he would not be allowed the "necessary latitute" to build a profitable business, but that when it was proposed again while he was in London, "I agreed and made out a requisition by your direction, and in compliance with my instructions." He said that during their discussions, the company officials had told him to undertake a California venture, either by securing licenses for company ships or through a trading post. And in March 1839, about the time he started home, the London Committee informed George Simpson that "we think a store for the sale of British manufactured goods and other articles might be opened with advantage" at San Francisco or Monterey. As a further benefit, they believed a trading post could supply their brigades.

Still seeking advice, when McLoughlin passed through Red River in June 1839, he conferred with the Council of the Northern Department. They were interested, and since Alexander Simpson—Governor Simpson's young cousin—had just been transferred to Fort Vancouver, they passed a resolution sending him to California, "with a view of enabling us to form a Commercial Establishment there."

With all this backing, in the summer of 1840, only a few months after his return, McLoughlin decided it was the time for action, and he sent Alexander Simpson south. His instructions were broad—"to collect all the information you can about Calefornia, how business is carr[i]ed on; how and on what conditions foreigners are allowed to settle, &c."

In the fall, when Simpson made his report, McLoughlin was gratified and somewhat surprised at its optimism. It said California contained very large farms where wheat was raised only as feed for the herds of cattle, and that "nearly all the Hides collected in Calefornia" were exported by a mercantile

firm based in Boston. The laws of Mexico, Simpson said, allowed no foreign-
er to own land unless he became a Mexican citizen, but the local residents
had "a strong desire" for some foreign company to come in and reduce the high
prices of the present system. Simpson thought trading ships would be unprofitable at first, but he recommended a post at San Francisco, where there was
"only one small retail Shop . . . the Trade being carried on by vessels touching
and generally remaining some months in the Port." He thought a sales outlet
stocked with British goods could collect hides, tallow, beaver, and wheat and
set up a profitable trade with Lima (Peru), besides sending flour to Oahu and
helping fulfill the company's commitment of flour and wheat to the Russians.

   While in California, Simpson had met Captain John A. Sutter, owner of the
most substantial fort on the Sacramento River. He was a perplexing character—flamboyant—powerful—ambitious—but known for the generous aid he
gave to traders and trappers of any stripe. Sir George called him a former
"Grog shop keeper" who had "decamped in debt" from the United States and
had run up bills in California "to the amount of nearly 100,000$," including—
the unforgivable sin—a large sum owed to the Honourable Company. There
was some truth in Simpson's complaint, for Sutter had fled from his native
Switzerland to escape the threat of debtors' prison. In California, however, he
had prospered. His fort was lavish and slated for fame in 1849, with the discovery of gold in its millrace.

   Sutter said he had received "from the Civil Government a right to exclude
all Trapping Parties," but that the military authorities had not acknowledged the
right, and therefore he had "neither the will nor the power to interfere" with Hudson's Bay brigades. This meant that the trappers in the field could continue their
operations. And in regard to permissions, Alexander Simpson told McLoughlin
that Governor Alvarado "expressed himself very favorably on the subject" and
offered to help the company obtain a license "on the conditions which I offered
to him, i.e. our paying the legal municipal Duty (half a dollar p. Beaver) on
the hunts of the Trapping party, and of giving 20 p. Cent of the returns of the
Sea Otter hunt, the amount of which tribute to be paid in Goods." Whether
Alvarado would follow through, Simpson thought, "will be difficult to say; at
all events we have the credit and satisfaction of making a fair proposal."

   Paying duties skin by skin would be a considerable change from the brigades' former free-and-easy practice of ignoring licenses, and the charges
they faced were high. Americans had worked out their own system for dodg-
ing the exorbitant fees—with the full knowledge and consent of authorities,
they licensed their ships in the names of Mexican citizens, which "relieves

them entirely from the onerous charges levied exclusively on foreigners."
McLoughlin had not decided whether to use a similar system or find another,
but he was ready to move ahead, and in December 1840 he sent James Douglas
to California with instructions to make trade arrangements with the Mexican
government, if he could.

When Douglas returned, he said that in his meeting with General Vallejo,
"the first topic introduced was a delicate one," relating to the Laframboise
brigade, which had been trapping in the valleys. It must indeed have been
"delicate," for Vallejo was not happy with the brigades' practice of taking
without licenses "as much as we can, and as quick as possible, while it is in
our power"—an extension of the scorched-earth policy practiced on the
Snake. The general was disturbed because the British were exterminating the
once-plentiful beaver, as the Russians had exterminated the sea otter, but
Douglas was a skilled negotiator. After interviewing both Vallejo and Alvarado,
he was rewarded with promises that

> the whole trade of the country will be thrown open to us; a free grant
> of land for the erection of warehouses with other privileges will be
> conceded to the Company in their own name and right, within the
> harbour of San Francisco. Parties of Beaver hunters may be intro-
> duced through the regular Port of Entry, who will receive Passports,
> and be licensed to hunt in all parts of the uncultivated frontier, every
> such person being compelled by the authorities to execute fully the
> conditions of their agreement with the Company.

In order to receive these advantages, Douglas said, the company would
be required "to sail a vessel under the flag of Mexico," and the men must
become Mexican citizens. But the authorities had promised to furnish licenses for Hudson's Bay ships and passports for its hunters "until they obtain letters of naturalization, in due form, after 12 months residence in the country."

Having given McLoughlin the legal picture, Douglas, with unconcealed
enthusiasm, described the twelve trading vessels that were then operating along
the California coast. Owned by Mexicans, by the Boston firm of Bryant and
Sturgis, or by British subjects living in California, these ships were "all fitted
with commodious trading rooms, where goods can be displayed to advantage,"
and staffed by salesmen who, on their "arrival in harbour, post off to range through
the length & breadth of the country, calling at every house as they pass with their
books of tempting samples, to procure orders from the wealthy farmers."

Douglas considered the California trade so desirable that he had already made tentative arrangements with Jacob Primer Leese, Governor Alvarado's brother-in-law, to buy a choice piece of waterfront property on San Francisco Bay.

Although McLoughlin had been skeptical about prospects in California, he had great respect for Douglas's judgment, and this glowing report quieted his last doubts. He wrote to the Governor and Committee that "Mr. Douglas fully accomplished the object of his voyage and indeed more than I expected, as he succeeded in obtaining for the Company a permit to trap through all Calefornia." He asked the London officials to supply him with extra men and shipping, and estimated that they "could employ a hundred trappers there for the next three or four years."

He wanted to found the post immediately, but he was in a quandary, for he was, as usual, short of experienced officers. The solution he ultimately reached was to transfer his son-in-law, William Glen Rae, from Fort Stikine to the new establishment, leaving his son John in Rae's former position as head of the northern post. He hesitated, because Stikine was a high-risk assignment, remote from assistance and staffed by roughnecks, most of whom had been in trouble at other stations. "The worst characters among our men on the Coast," McLoughlin later called them, and said they had been "especially selected for that place because Mr. Rae and my son being stout men were considered better able to manage them."

But competent administrators were so scarce that McLoughlin had little choice. During John's four years as a company clerk, he had proven himself trustworthy and capable, with a reputation as a good disciplinarian. He had served a year as Rae's second in command, and McLoughlin gave him a strong assistant by transferring dependable young Roderick Finlayson from Taku to Stikine. With that done, confident that the two could handle their unruly men, the Chief Factor issued orders for Rae to go south.

Although Simpson later criticized John's promotion, the records show no grounds for attributing it to favoritism, and McLoughlin said he promoted his son "Merely from a sense of Duty," to "avail myself of his abilities to manage a Post for which he was Best qualified." He went further than that. Insisting that he did not want John to make a lifetime career of the fur trade, he said, "It is well known that I Intended on the Expiration of his contract that he should Leave the country and go some where Else to shift for himself."

His haste in setting up the California post has never been fully explained, for Sir George Simpson was to visit Fort Vancouver within a few months, and McLoughlin might have avoided trouble if he had waited for the governor's

Portrait thought to be Eloisa McLoughlin. This shows Eloisa as a young woman, probably in the early years of her marriage to William Glen Rae. OHS ORHI CN 56638

explicit consent. But the Chief Factor thought he had adequate backing, because the Committee had approved the project, and the Council of the Northern Department had directed Alexander Simpson to help found a California post. Furthermore, McLoughlin knew that with only a short season for securing hides—June to August—a few weeks of lost time would cost most of the trade for an entire year. "I acted on the full conviction that it was the intention of the Company to carry on a regular business at that place," he later wrote to Sir George Simpson, "and if I did not wait till you came, it is because the nature of the business would not admit of delay."

In the spring of 1841, when Rae and Eloisa left Stikine and started south on the *Beaver*, John Work's wife was with them, for Eloisa was pregnant, and McLoughlin had asked Mrs. Work to temporarily leave Fort Simpson and look after his daughter. While the little ship was making its slow and noisy trip through the Inland Passage, Eloisa gave birth to a baby girl, Margaret Glen. The child was only three days old when they landed at Fort Vancouver, where Eloisa could once more have the comfort of home and her mother's capable assistance. Somehow they all crowded into the Chief Factor's residence, with McLoughlin, Marguerite, David, Eloisa, and her family in one set of rooms while James and Amelia Douglas and their children occupied another.

But it was not for long. "Mr. Rae stayed only a few weeks when he went to California by way of the Sandwich Islands," Eloisa said later. "I stayed at Vancouver. He went to California to trade in hides and tallow and to open a

store." She and her children—two-year-old John and the infant Margaret—
were planning to follow him soon.

When Rae reached his new post, he found it would be expensive to buy
a raw site and erect a building, so he implemented the deal Douglas had set
up with Governor Alvarado's brother-in-law. For forty-six hundred dollars he
bought one of the few structures in Yerba Buena, the downtown area of
today's San Francisco. Eloisa later said that nothing in Yerba Buena was laid
out, that only the one block was fenced in, and that it "had on it a large house
. . . about half of it a store and the other half a dwelling house. . . . The building was about thirty by eighty feet, with the hall in the middle opening on the
side. The hall was very wide. In the back part there were four bed rooms and
the front was a dining room and sitting room. The kitchen was back of all."

Here, on the shores of San Francisco Bay, Rae established the company's
newest venture. In a short two years since the end of his furlough, McLoughlin had taken giant strides. He had implemented cooperation with Russia, expanded agriculture, and started the Puget's Sound Agricultural Company. He
had founded forts on the Stikine and Taku Rivers in the far north, and was reaching toward the south as well. But he had moved in haste, spreading his resources
thin, and he had assigned his son and son-in-law to positions of high risk.

McLoughlin's California post was at Yerba Buena on San Francisco Bay, in the heart of today's
business district of San Francisco. As shown in this 1846-47 drawing, Montgomery Street
fronted on the waters of the bay. The HBC property was the fenced property on Montgomery
Street. HUDSON BAY COMPANY ARCHIVES, PROVINCIAL ARCHIVES OF MANITOBA, HBCA 1987/363-C22/1 [N78-52]

CHAPTER 9

Stikine

Sir George Simpsons Visit . . . has cost me Dear.

DR. JOHN MCLOUGHLIN

~ 1 ~

Upheaval
1841–1842

On August 25, 1841, Governor Simpson, who was making a trip around the world, came to the Columbia and brought Chief Factor John Rowand as his guest. Sir George had been friendly in the past, and since McLoughlin was forging ahead on all fronts—the northern posts, Yerba Buena, and the agricultural venture—he had every reason to expect a pleasant visit.

Simpson remained at Fort Vancouver for less than a week. On September 1 he, with James Douglas and Chief Factor Rowand, left by canoe for Nisqually, where they boarded the *Beaver* and headed north to inspect the company posts. Sir George—always curious—was doubtless interested in trying out the steamer, but her captain, William McNeill, did not consider her seaworthy. He issued a warning that "*possibly* . . . the Boilers will take us to Sitika and back again to this place after performing the trading voyage," but that he would "not be answerable for what may happen. . . . I think we can risk to make both before mentioned trips, but no human knowledge can foretell the consequence." McLoughlin had meant to go along, but he changed his plan, for an unexplained reason.

Except for the *Beaver*'s condition, he had no reason to anticipate trouble, but his peace of mind was destroyed in late October when Simpson returned. After a stop at Sitka to discuss trading arrangements with the Russians, Sir George had continued up the coast, inspecting company forts. In the past he had approved of fixed establishments, but on this trip he found the business climate so changed that by the time he returned to Fort Vancouver, he had made a drastic decision—to completely reorganize the coastal trade.

The difference in the north had resulted from the agreement with the Russians. Under it, they were buying supplies from the British, and most Americans had withdrawn, because they could no longer reap a profit by selling goods to the tsar's forts. Simpson therefore thought the company no

George Simpson had a long career with the Hudson's Bay Company, 1820-1858, and during nearly all of that time he was director of field operations for the entire concern. By the time he retired, he was ill and nearly blind, and he died only two years later. *Sir George Simpson*, painted in 1857 by Stephen Pearce. HUDSON BAY COMPANY ARCHIVES, PROVINCIAL ARCHIVES OF MANITOBA, HBCA PICTURE COLLECTION, P-206 [N5394]

longer needed to attract the Indians to permanent posts, but could trade by ships and merely receive skins as the natives brought them in.

In addition, the company's affairs in London had taken an unfavorable turn, because silk had replaced beaver as the preferred material for gentlemen's hats, causing the international fur market to collapse. The Governor and Committee predicted "no very cheering prospect for the future, unless the tide of fashion change. . . . Economical management is our only resource under present circumstances." Aware of both factors—the world market and the change in coastal trade —Sir George had decided to close all of the posts except Fort Simpson, which he wotld retain as a northern supply depot. He reported to the Governor and Committee:

> The trade of the coast, cannot with any hope of making it a profitable business, afford the maintenance of so many establishments . . . nor does it appear to me that such is necessary, as I am of opinion that the establishments of Fort McLoughlin, Stikine & Takow, might be abandoned without any injury to the trade, and that the establishment of Fort Simpson alone, with the *Beaver* Steamer, will answer every necessary & useful purpose. . . . Under this arrangement, the Steamer would be constant-

ly employed, in visiting the principal trading stations. . . . indeed I am
of the opinion, that when once the Steam vessel comes into regular
operation . . . the returns of the Coast will materially increase.

He meant to have the *Beaver* call six times per year at regular times and locations, offering trade goods to the Indians and collecting furs.

Although to Simpson this was merely a sensible adaptation to change, to
McLoughlin it was a shattering blow. He had for years contended with inept
captains and vessels that failed to turn up on time or sank altogether, giving
him a bone-deep scorn for ships in general. And he considered the *Beaver* a
nuisance as well as a frightful expense, a vessel of skimpy size, forever breaking down, and "entirely at the mercy of the Engineer . . . who may act as whim
or caprice may induce him."

Moreover, after laboring for fifteen years, he had at last achieved a chain
of northern posts, and documents show that he had done it in accordance
with orders. In 1836 the Council at Norway House had said, "The Governor
and Committee being desirous that a Post should be established as early as
possible on Pelly's (supposed) Stikine River . . . an officer and 6 men [should]
be forwarded with Outfit 1837." In London in 1838–39, McLoughlin and the
company officers had discussed it and come to an agreement, as shown by a
letter in which the Governor and Committee said, "We were glad to learn that
Stikine & Takow were established agreeably to instructions."

The London officers, however, blew hot and cold. In 1843, long after the
posts had been closed, they wrote:

> We are decidedly of opinion that the trade with the Natives should be
> carried on from Posts established on the shore wherever that is practi-
> cable. . . . While we derive benefit from the natives, it must never be
> forgotten that it is our sacred duty to confer benefit on them: and this
> duty cannot be formed so well by the periodical visits of a ship as by
> the permanent residence of our officers and men in the country.

They specified that the "Officers & men, stationed at those posts, should be
persons of good character and exemplary conduct, to whom the natives can
look up with respect and confidence," and said that if the company could not
provide people of this type, "we should prefer having no posts at all."

McLoughlin in 1841 was of a similar mind, and he did not surrender easily. He protested Simpson's plan with vigor, saying that dependable posts gave

the company influence over the Indians and that "the Establishments being on the spot, will get more Furs & trade them cheaper, than the *Beaver*." If they relied on ships, he said, "when our Indians require an article, they will not wait for us, but trade it with the Russians." And he predicted that if they used only the steamer, when she "is laid up as she has been since Fall 1841 . . . all the Trade of the N.W. Coast, north of Vancouver's Island will be lost."

The disappointment of losing his posts was exacerbated because while in the north, George Simpson had held meetings with James Douglas, John Rowand, Captain McNeill of the *Beaver*, and John Work, who was Chief Factor at Fort Simpson. Even though McLoughlin would have been included if he had gone on the tour, even though it was Sir George's invariable practice to consult every knowledgeable person he met, the Chief Factor interpreted the meetings as actions taken behind his back. It is unlikely that his presence could have changed the outcome, but if he had been there, he might have accepted it more easily. As it was, he felt so insulted that he accused the governor of "wanting in the courtesy to which the situation he occupied in the Service entitled him"—a reaction that seemed to surprise Simpson. In consulting the others, he said, he "had not had the remotest intention" of being rude.

He also stood firm, apparently convinced that McLoughlin would eventually drop his objections and support company policy, as he had in the past. In November, while he was still at Fort Vancouver, Sir George wrote to Andrew Colvile, deputy governor of the company, "The Doctor is as much opposed to the abandonment of the posts on the N.W. Coast . . . as he has all along been to the Steamer, & for no other reason that I can discover, than that the measure did not originate with himself. To do him justice, however, although he never ceases talking about any measures which are forced upon him, he nevertheless pushes them when determined upon, with as much energy as if his own."

In the midst of this dispute, the governor dredged up the old question of where to locate permanent headquarters. As early as 1835, the Governor and Committee had told McLoughlin they considered the bar of the Columbia "too great a risk to be run by the Annual Ships from and to England." Even then they wished to send the supply ships somewhere else, although they realized that Fort Vancouver must be retained as a depot for the interior posts.

More recently, as Americans swept into the Willamette Valley, Simpson was afraid they might attack Fort Vancouver for its supplies, or that the boundary settlement might give both banks of the Columbia to the United States. Moving headquarters to Vancouver Island, he thought, would solve all problems, for it had no perilous bar, was certain to be on British soil when the boundary was set, was safely out of the settlers' reach, and would help ensure British title to the entire island, with access to Puget Sound.

Although McLoughlin acknowledged all of this, he believed that Fort Vancouver was "the most economical and efficient" location for the main depot, and he envisioned it as a future center for a profitable trade with the settlers. In the past he had made a desultory search for a new site, considering various places in Puget Sound or the Strait of Juan de Fuca but seeing problems with them all. He was more pleased with a spot that Captain McNeill, on a tour with James Douglas, had recently found at the south end of Vancouver Island—"a secure harbor accessible to shipping at every season, of good pasture, and, to a certain extent, of improvable tillage land." McLoughlin was willing to build an establishment there, but he considered it only a link in his northern chain, and he had not yet drafted a definite plan.

In addition to these major changes, Simpson made still another decision, one that at the time seemed small. On his visit to Fort Simpson he had found its head, John Work, "in ill health, laboring under the effects of a recent very dangerous rupture," and his chief aide "in a decline." The governor was concerned, and when he continued to Fort Stikine and found things there in apparently good condition, he ordered young John McLoughlin's assistant, Roderick Finlayson, to go at once to Fort Simpson, to help John Work.

The transfer disturbed McLoughlin, because it left his son with no dependable aide, and Stikine was known to be a dangerous post. In Eloisa's words, "When the Indians got drunk . . . they would destroy the trough so that we could not get water. . . . They were buying liquor and fighting all the time among themselves outside the Fort. . . . Of liquor a big hogshead four feet high was emptied in one day." John Rowand, who had gone north with Governor Simpson and stayed nearly two weeks at Stikine, was also worried. Later on, McLoughlin said Rowand had warned him that John was "exposed to very great danger, a circumstance that I mentioned to Sir George Simpson. . . . But the truth is I was at the time so affected at Sir George's plan to abandon Tacow, Fort McLoughlin (and at that time Stikine) . . . that it rendered me unable to think of any thing else."

Ominous though it was, the danger in John's situation was lost in the greater conflict. For several weeks, while Simpson remained at Fort Vancouver, the arguments raged back and forth, with the governor rigidly set in his decision and the Chief Factor as rigidly opposed. Finally, since Sir George was on a long trip and wanted to press ahead, they decided to go together as far as California and Oahu, continuing their discussions on the way.

~ 2 ~

Oahu
1842

In January 1842, when McLoughlin traveled to California with Sir George Simpson, he took Eloisa along. "I went with my father to go to my husband," she explained, and said the doctor "and a good many other gentlemen went to San Francisco with a vessell"—the *Cowlitz*. McLoughlin did not waste time aboard ship. He was armed with copies of company reports, and as the sails billowed overhead, he worked out a detailed set of facts and figures to show the value of posts.

Their first stop was Yerba Buena, where Simpson consulted Francis Ermatinger, leader of the California brigade, and received a bleak report on probable profits. It annoyed him. Next they went to Monterey, the only Mexican post open to foreign ships, from which all consignments for California ports were supposed to be carried in local vessels. There six customs collectors "flocked down to our vessel like vultures to their prey," demanding a fee, but were told it had already been paid. Disappointed, they left, to return the next morning with a fresh demand. Although Simpson at first refused, in the end, "after a good deal of chaffering and haggling," he had to remit two hundred dollars for taking goods back to Yerba Buena—the same goods, to the port they had just left. This offended Sir George's thrifty soul. When they set sail again, he was brooding, and soon after they reached Oahu, he dropped another bomb: he was going to close not only the northern forts, but also the new establishment at Yerba Buena.

McLoughlin was stunned, because "in California and all the way to Oahu Sir George Simpson held out that the Business was to be carried on an adequate scale." His protests, however, were of no avail. Simpson was in high dudgeon, and the customs duties plus Ermatinger's report had induced him to write off the southern market. "I believe you fully agree with me as to the inexpediency of persevering in our attempt to form a business in California," he told McLoughlin in a note. "By the accompanying letter to Mr. Rae, you will see that I have requested the business be wound up with the least possible delay." Never one to do things by halves, he also decided to discontinue the California brigade, because "it is quite evident that no good can arise from prosecuting the Fur trade or maintaining the trapping parties in those districts."

John McLoughlin started building business relations with the Sandwich Islands in 1830.
He was there with Sir George Simpson when he learned that his administrative responsibilities would be drastically reduced. *Port of Honolulu*, lithograph by G.H. Burgess, ca. 1857.

McLoughlin and Simpson stayed in the Sandwich Islands for about a
week, engaging in heated discussions that plowed back and forth over the
same ground. Since Simpson wanted their reasoning on record, he requested written memoranda, and these reveal how far apart the two men were,
with McLoughlin groping for a defense and Sir George icily confident.

Part of the argument was the still-festering issue of posts versus the
Beaver. McLoughlin presented his painfully prepared facts and figures showing that in 1836–40, the steamer had traded furs to a value of £13,401, but
was so expensive to operate that she had a net loss of £4,347. He further estimated that if the company had been using land establishments instead, "they
would have cleared £8027," and that even if the expense of erecting a new
post were deducted, "the company would have cleared £6527." His document, long and confusing, was little more than a rough estimate. The fur
trade depended on many variables, and if all of them could have been included, the *Beaver* would probably have shown a smaller loss.

McLoughlin, however, believed his figures were sound. All the gentlemen who understood the business of the coast agreed with him, he said,
"except one, who on my producing the accounts said without examining
them, 'Oh it is of no purpose, whatever you may say, the Directors are decid-

ed on carrying it, and it will be carried on.'"

Having spent so much time drawing up the document, he was incensed when Simpson rejected it, but the governor refused to budge. "After the best consideration I have been able to give the subject, my views or sentiments remain unaltered," he said. In addition, he instructed McLoughlin to "take the necessary steps" to have the southern coast of Vancouver Island examined as a site for the future headquarters. And he reiterated his decision to close Forts McLoughlin and Taku, "removing the officers and people of those establishments to the new depôt [on Vancouver Island] . . . which I have to beg may be placed under the charge of C.F. Douglas."

As for the expenses of the *Beaver*, Simpson said that no matter where she went, her costs were fixed, that they would change very little if she gathered more furs, and that she therefore would pay a profit if the posts were eliminated. Moreover, he believed she "had more effect in overawing the natives of the Coast and expelling opposition therefrom, than any other means that could have been adopted."

McLoughlin was clearly on the losing side of this argument, for company officers, both in London and in the field, were gradually developing admiration for the noisy little ship. Alexander C. Anderson, for example, a clerk who had served in the north, said, "It is, I know, become quite general to decry the merits of that valuable craft . . . but my own partial experience induced me to conclude that it is to the Steamer, chiefly, that we are indebted for the recent absence of competition in that direction." And the Governor and Committee said they had always expected the steamer to cost more than a sailing ship, but that she was valuable because the natives were "overawed by the exhibition of a power, which they cannot comprehend, but which they know to be irresistible."

As the Oahu meetings continued, Simpson became ever more caustic. He carped over details. He criticized the condition of salmon McLoughlin had shipped as "losing character, from some neglect or defect in the curing." He said the salmon casks were "weak and badly coopered." He called McLoughlin's permission for Rae to sell goods without cash payments "ill-judged," saying that no one in the trade had ever "in so short a time had so much credit on the books." He brusquely told the Chief Factor to send no more materials to Yerba Buena, where every transaction had brought "loss and inconvenience." And he said, "I do not see that any good can arise from you or Mr. Douglas revisiting California; on the contrary, I think that both your time and the time of that Gentleman would be much more usefully employed by remaining at your posts." Some of his complaints were sharply personal, as when he said business matters should be decided in advance instead of "either upon the impulse of the moment, or on loose & vague information," and that while Rae was winding up the affairs in California, he should be there "*alone*, unencumbered by family or followers of any description." Through it all, the Chief Factor was floundering, stubborn, out-argued but unconvinced.

At one point the two men discussed McLoughlin's possible retirement, and Simpson told the doctor that if he withdrew, the company "would feel disposed to put him on the footing of the most favored Chief Factor who had up to that period retired from the Service." McLoughlin later asked for more information about the "most favorable" terms, but nothing came of it.

One blatant mistake by Sir George was his objection to the purchase of the California site, for he said the company would never have consented to buying "some 100 or 150 yards frontage by as many in depth, at the wretched place of Yerba Buena, which of all others is the least adapted in point of situation & climate for an Establishment." He could scarcely have been more wrong. The "wretched place" is now in the heart of San Francisco's downtown district—the square bounded by Montgomery, Clay, Kearny, and Sacramento Streets. Today it is separated from the bay by several blocks of filled land, but in McLoughlin's time Montgomery Street skirted the water's edge.

As the days passed, the doctor tried to defend what he had done. Lacking Simpson's rapier tongue, he protested somewhat clumsily that he had founded the post at Yerba Buena because he thought the company intended "to carry on a regular business at that place (and which I believe it to be inferred from their correspondence) and not merely to make an adventure." He insisted that he had not "heard of a single dealer in hides & tallow in Calefornia who was not obliged to give credit, merely because cattle can be killed to advantage, only at one season in the year"; and that he had moved fast in order not to lose a year's trade. He admitted that the California venture did not "afford so good a prospect for business for the Hudsons Bay Company as I expected. . . . But now we are in it, I would advise to give the business a fair trial." To abandon the land brigade without a year's warning would be costly, he said, resulting in the loss of the men's valuable traps, which the company would have to replace. Simpson advocated sending a small party to retrieve them, but this, McLoughlin told him, would not work, because "every man hides his traps by himself, so as not to be robbed by others, & therefore none but himself can find them."

But all the Chief Factor's efforts failed, and at one point, totally exasperated, he chided Simpson for having made up his mind before the sessions began. "I am not aware that these subjects have been discussed, as it is perfectly out of the question, to talk of discussion, when there are only two persons . . . and one has the power to decide as he pleases and does." He was angry and hurt. "The only apology I can give for troubling you again with this subject, is the natural feeling of pain it must give me to see my labor time & money lost to no purpose whatever."

Although Sir George did not seem to realize how deeply McLoughlin was wounded, James Douglas did. Over the years, the Chief Factor had been loyal and generous to his aide, and in 1843 Douglas returned the favor by writing Sir George a personal letter:

> You seem to think that the Doctor is labouring under some extraordinary delusion, in regard to that subject, but to me his feelings appear perfectly natural . . . the slashing paragraphs in your report, denouncing abuses on shore and afloat gave him inexpressible pain, as they were so many indirect attacks on his management, and he lost thereby, in the exact ratio that you acquired merit. In some points of that sort, your remarks were rather severe.

Simpson's displeasure was indeed "severe." On March 4, 1842, after several days of heated arguments and notes, Simpson wrote, "I do not consider it necessary to occupy your time or my own on the other points noticed in your much valued communication, further than to say that no fresh light has been thrown upon them." Refusing to make any change "in the remarks and instructions I have deemed it my duty to give upon those subjects," he brought the meetings to an end by writing, "and these statements, I think, ought to be sufficient."

The two men then parted, never to meet again. McLoughlin later said he wrote to Sir George "informing him our private correspondence must cease," which he considered better than to "act the part of a Hypocrite and pretend a Regard for a man which I could not feel." Although the letter has not been found, Simpson mentioned it later, saying he greatly regretted it, "as it puts an end to the good understanding that has for many years subsisted between us, and terminates our private correspondence, which has so long been useful in our business relations."

While the governor continued his round-the-world journey, McLoughlin sailed back to Fort Vancouver, to face the distasteful job of closing his posts.

It was less than three years since he had returned in triumph from London, to set in motion a complicated set of new projects. But his status had plunged. He was embroiled in conflict with the strongest officer of the company, a man who had once been his firm advocate. He was to lose his posts in the north, lose Yerba Buena in the south, lose the California brigade. He must in the future depend on the detested ships. It was a stinging defeat.

~3~
"A Rack to Ones Feeling"
1842–1843

In March 1842, when Governor Simpson took the *Cowlitz* north from Oahu, he planned to sail to Siberia and travel overland from there to London. At Sitka, however, he had to wait for a ship, so he decided to pay one more visit to the northern posts, including Fort Stikine.

In the meantime McLoughlin, humiliated and indignant, returned to work at Fort Vancouver. There, in June, he received two crushing letters written by Simpson on April 27 at Fort Stikine. One was a personal note, which has disappeared. The other, an official dispatch several pages long, said in part:

On arrival . . . off the little Anchorage at this place, my mind was filled with apprehension that all was not right, by observing that both the English and

A portrait of the adult John McLoughlin, first child of Dr. John and Marguerite McLoughlin. John was the stormy petrel of the family. As a boy he was frequently in trouble, and the efforts to help him were related in numerous letters. Although he eventually became a dependable company employee, misfortune dogged him. The way McLoughlin dealt with his grief over his son's tragedy irreparably damaged his career. The miniature belongs to the McLoughlin Memorial Association and resides at the McLoughlin House National Historic Site. OHS ORHI 267

Russian Flags on the Fort were half mast high, and that Mr. John McLoughlin, the Gentleman left in charge, did not appear on the platform; the stillness that prevailed on shore,—one man only belonging to the Establishment having made his appearance at the gate, evidently showing that there was a mournful tale to relate, and on landing, I was more shocked than words can describe to learn that Mr. McLoughlin was no more, having fallen on the night of the 20/21 Instant in a drunken fray, by the hand of one of his own men.

The letter bluntly said that "the whole conduct & management of Mr. McLoughlin were exceedingly bad, and his violence when under the influence of liquor, which was very frequently the case," amounted to insanity. It referred to "the night in question, when this unfortunate young man was hurried into eternity by a gunshot wound from one of his own men,—this dreadful act being done, I firmly believe, under the influence of terror, as a measure of self preservation." And it expressed the belief that "any Tribunal by which the case could be tried, would find a verdict of 'Justifiable Homicide' . . . I consider it due to the people to say, that as a body, their conduct throughout has been fully better than could have been expected under such inhuman treatment as they were frequently exposed to."

Sir George included depositions from the fort's workmen, who accused young McLoughlin of mistreating his men. In midsummer Simpson wrote an even more caustic report to the Governor and Committee, saying that young McLoughlin "had become a slave to licentiousness and dissipation," that his treatment of his people was "very frequently cruel in the extreme," and that the business of the fort "was entirely neglected."

After John's success as a company clerk, the report was an overwhelming blow. In pride and sorrow, McLoughlin wrote to Edward Ermatinger, "My son John was Intelligent, active—had the faults of youth, was inconsiderate and thoughtless—at least had been so but this was wearing away. At the same time he had the Good qualities and Virtues of youth—though I say it. He was frank, open, firm—but Kind and Generous." The wound did not easily heal. Later, in one of the few times he referred to his wife in official correspondence, he said, "To die is the fate of all, but to lose ones Son in the way we lost him is more than painfull it is a Rack to ones feeling."

The "rack" must have been made heavier by the harshness of Sir George's report. Both men had been furious when they parted, and Simpson was no doubt influenced by his memory of John's early problems, along with a realization that he himself had removed young McLoughlin's only dependable aide. He accepted at face value the workmen's explanation that John had brought on his own death. He arrested only Urbain Heroux—the workman who pulled the trigger—and after hastily collecting the depositions, he continued his trip. He took Heroux as far as Sitka, because the murder had occurred in territory leased from Russia, which supposedly had jurisdiction, but he left the others at Stikine.

McLoughlin's initial grief was soon followed by anger and a grim determination "as a Father, & as an honest man" to justify his son's conduct and punish the guilty. He was especially bitter because after Finlayson's transfer, John's remaining assistants had been Thomas McPherson, "a poor soft half Breed Lad . . . so Dull and Stupid that I Doubt if he understood what Sir George asked him," and Philip Smith, who was "so soft and timid that the Men used to impose on him . . . and I had to interfere to protect him." McLoughlin was convinced that in leaving John with aides like these, Simpson had caused the young man's death.

Sometime during those difficult months, he received word that his mother had died on July 31, 1842, only a few months after John's murder. Little is known about Angélique McLoughlin, but a grandniece said a portrait made in her old age showed "traces of her beauty, which time had not been able to destroy," that she showed "remarkable affability toward her family and friends" and spent her last years in doing "good works." McLoughlin obviously loved her. He had gone to see her when he could and had faithfully helped her by sending money, and although his reaction is not recorded, her loss must have been a further blow.

His attention, however, was still focused on clearing his son's name. During the long summer days, he pored over the laborers' depositions and discovered gaping holes, after which he wrote "a thundering epistle to their honours at home." He called the depositions "the most Extraordinary Documents of the kind I ever saw, the Witnesses are not cross questioned." He said the murderer had kept his gun loaded, planning the murder; that John had taken up his own weapon only "in Justifiable self defense"; and that Pierre Kanaquassé—a ringleader—was "well known to be one of the Greatest villains in the country and whom necessity alone has obliged us to Employ." He described the previous conduct of Urbain Heroux as "so bad . . . that his Relations had been obliged to put him in Prison for Burglary and Robbery and Dropped the prosecution only on condition he would leave the country."

And he quoted a sentence from Simpson's private note, the only surviving part. "I have no Doubt on my mind that Urbain Heroux fired the fatal shot

But I think it is better not to bring it home to him." The governor doubtless gave this advice in hopes of inducing McLoughlin to drop the matter and thus avoid adverse publicity for the company, but it puzzled the doctor. He said he did not understand it, but that if Sir George meant the murderer was not to be punished, he must dissent, and would do everything he could "to Investigate this to me most painful affair so as to ascertain the truth."

However, distraught as he was, McLoughlin tried to carry on the work of the fort. "In the meantime I have a Duty and with the Blessing of God will perform it to the utmost of my abilities and means," he wrote, and reported a host of details, such as the lack of pemmican west of the Rockies and the ever-growing American menace. Even though he disagreed with Governor Simpson's recent orders, he was too experienced a company man to risk outright defiance, so he took measures to close the posts. By the following summer, he wrote that "Chief Factor Douglas is returned from the Coast, Forts Durham [Taku] and McLoughlin are abandoned, and Chief Trader Ross is erecting an Establishment on the place selected by Chief Factor Douglas on the south end of Vancouver's Island." The question of the northern forts would no longer figure in company correspondence, and Fort Victoria was begun.

It was an important venture, but nevertheless McLoughlin's overwhelming desire was to wipe the stain from John's reputation. During the summer of 1842, as word of the murder spread from post to post, it became evident that the doctor was not the only one to doubt Simpson's verdict. The Stikine workmen were sent to various posts and ships, and one of them, Pierre Kanaquassé, was held on the *Cadboro* and told James Douglas his version of the murder. Douglas, impressed, wrote it out for McLoughlin, after which the Chief Factor decided to meet the *Cadboro* at Nisqually and examine the prisoner for himself.

The interview was formal, with not only McLoughlin and Douglas present, but also Chief Trader Donald Manson, Captain McNeill, and the Reverend Jason Lee. It was apparent to them all that Kanaquassé might be a "villain," but that nevertheless his statements rang true and demolished the charges against John. Kanaquassé said the men of Stikine were incensed because young McLoughlin refused to let them receive Indian women inside the post, or leave it at night, and because he punished them for "scaling the Piquets" after dark and giving their Indian girls presents stolen from the fort's stores. The men, said Kanaquassé, had drawn up an agreement to murder their leader unless the company removed him from his post. All but one had signed it, and he himself had tried three times to make the fatal shot.

With considerable satisfaction, McLoughlin forwarded a transcript of Kanaquassé's testimony. If this is true, he said, "the depositions made before Sir George Simpson are false and must lead to a very erroneous decision." Pointing out various discrepancies, he said he would continue his investigation, because "without doubt if this melancholy affair is passed over, and not thoroughly examined, we will soon have more of them." He then sent Chief Trader Manson north with a fresh crew for Fort Stikine, directing him to interrogate the others and hand them over to the Russian authorities at Sitka.

It is not surprising that at this troubled time McLoughlin sought help through religion. At his Grandfather Fraser's insistence, he had been brought up in the Church of England, but he had been baptized a Catholic, his childhood family had belonged to that faith until Fraser interfered, and his beloved sister was a nun. As Chief Factor he had regularly read the Bible to his French Canadian employees in lieu of church services, and even though he was still a Protestant, he had attended Mass when the priests held it at the fort. With this background, heavy with grief, he made a business trip to Fort Nisqually in November 1842, and while there he chanced upon a book—*The End of Religious Controversy*, by John Milner—that offered him the consolation he badly needed. The event was recorded by Archbishop Francis Norbert Blanchet.

> He read it with avidity and was overcome and converted by it at once. On his return to Fort Vancouver he made his objuration and profession of Faith at the hands of the Vicar General, on November 18, 1842. He made his confession, had his marriage blessed on the same day, and prepared himself for his first communion by fasting during the four weeks of Advent. . . . Being thus prepared, he made his first communion at Fort Vancouver at midnight Mass on Christmas, with a large number of faithful women and servants of the Hudson's Bay Company. The little chapel was then full of white people and Indians; it was beautifully decorated and brilliantly illuminated; the *plain chant* was grave; the chant of the canticles of Noel in French and Chinook jargon, alternately by two choirs of men and women, was impressive, as well as was the holy performance around the altar.

Even though McLoughlin's new faith brought him consolation, he was still determined to clear John's name. He continued to examine every witness, every document, and eventually his blizzard of inquiries brought results. William Glen Rae and Roderick Finlayson, who had both spent time at Stikine, contradicted the depositions. Others who had been there attested that young John's personal allowance of liquor was scarcely touched—a fact that squared with his previous record, for during all his troubles in Paris and Canada, he had never been accused of intoxication.

They also said John was not cruel; that he punished his men only for sufficient cause, such as stealing company goods or sleeping while on watch; and that the punishments were not unduly severe. McLoughlin, in fact, related one instance in which Governor Simpson himself had "tickled Cadotte, the guide's shoulders, with a canoe pole," one in which he flogged a man, and another in which he knocked a man down. In all of these, the Chief Factor considered the punishments "richly deserved," but nevertheless he cited them as evidence that if necessary, even Sir George would use force.

A curious about-face was made by Chief Factor Rowand, who had fallen ill on the northern trip and had therefore spent two weeks at Stikine. He informed McLoughlin that he "did not see the deceased take a Single Glass while I was at Stikine and as for Beating his men I saw nothing of the kind . . . I never dreamed he was in danger of losing his life by his own men no far from that But hearing what kind of Indians he had to deal with I thought it was not safe for one Gentleman to be left alone."

However, after Sir George Simpson asked for "the precise words," Rowand dodged. "The fact is if the Deceased had misbehaved I was too sick to pay attention to any thing at all," he replied to Simpson. But he was uncomfortable, and plaintively added, "I wish I had acted as some of my Columbian friends, they took great care not to touch upon that affair at all."

Among the documents McLoughlin turned up were John's letters from Stikine to Roderick Finlayson and to Chief Trader John Work, who as head of Fort Simpson was John's immediate superior. In June 1841, concerned about his crew, he had written, "The more I see of the men the more I have to complain of them. I am obliged to mark every thing that is to be done—if not I am sure that it will be spoiled I have tried them in every way—and I am sorry to say that it is from my strict discipline that I get them to attend to their duty."

In the fall, when Simpson removed his aide, the young man wrote to Work, "I am sorry to say that Mr Finlayson is taken away from this post to your place, and the one that is left in his place will never answer the purpose . . . but I shall endeavour to do the Best of my abilities to give the best satisfaction until some young gentleman is sent."

By December he was considering a resignation. "I am daily on the look out for our Steamer to see what sort of a Trader I am going to get. If he is no

better than the two assistants I have now, the company must find another gentleman to take charge of this post," he told Work. "I have had scarcely any
rest, night and day I am up—it is to much for one. . . . I have not yet renewed
my contract till I see what assistant I shall get."

On the same day he wrote to Finlayson, "I am happy to tell you that the
Gallery is finished and when I get the Blue devils I can now stretch my legs
at nights . . . I am still amongst the living of this troublesome post though
reports says that I am going to be despatched to the *Sandy Hills*—all that does
not trouble me much—but it keeps me on my guard."

In February he told Finlayson, "I wish with all my heart to see you at Stikine
again . . . I have had all the troubles that a man could have since I have been alone."

The final letter—again to Finlayson—sounded a note of despair. "I cannot trust to no one . . . their never was an establishment on this coast so little
attention paid to as this place is . . . I am sure if it was some other gentleman
they would not be [left] so destitute as I have been." Later testimony by his
native wife said he knew of the men's plot to kill him and had predicted, "If
the Steamer does not come soon, I will not see her."

Besides assembling documents, McLoughlin marshaled other witnesses
who said they had never seen John drunk and that he had punished men only
for sufficient cause. The post journal had been kept up to April 19, one day
before the murder, with accounts showing a discrepancy of only ten pounds.
"I am now forty years in the Indian country," McLoughlin wrote to Governor
Simpson, "and . . . I never saw so small a defficiency on such an amount." He
dwelt on John's lack of a trustworthy staff. "I had sent the most turbulent of our
men to that Post, as Mr. Rae and the deceased being strict men could keep them
in order without having recourse to extreme measures, as many others would
require." And he repeatedly insisted that Sir George had caused John's death,
by removing Finlayson. Others thought so, too. John Work, who knew the situation, courageously wrote to Simpson himself, "I am convinced had he [Finlayson]
remained at Stikeen the catastrophy there would not have taken place."

McLoughlin's evidence was so formidable that in spite of Sir George's persistent accusations, the Governor and Committee began to see things in a different light. Although their public announcements were cautious, in June 1843
the company secretary, Archibald Barclay, wrote a personal letter to Simpson:

> The crime was clearly long premeditated and if ever men deserved
> hanging, Urbain Heroux, Pierre Kanaquassé, and the scoundrel Mc-
> Pherson, ought to be *strung up*. It is evident that the charges of

habitual intoxication and excessive severity were trumped up after
the deed was committed as a screen to the villany of the culprits.

Three months later he wrote again:

> I have read attentively every thing within my reach on the subject and
> I have come to the conclusion that McLoughlin was not a habitual drunk-
> ard, that the punishments he inflicted . . . were not of excessive severity,
> and that he was very vigilant and strict in keeping the men to their duty
> day and night. I think there was a plot formed to destroy him. . . .
>
> The evidence taken since you were at Stikine is no doubt loose,
> irrelevant often little to be depended upon, but it is not nearly so bad
> as that given before yourself at Stikine. That these worthless men should
> after what had happened unite in giving the deceased a bad charac-
> ter is natural enough but who can believe them when we see them
> contradicting themselves as they do on other points? . . . their pun-
> ishment whether it affect their lives or their liberty would be a most
> salutory, I may say necessary measure under all circumstances—and
> this is the determination which the Board have come to.

Unfortunately, however, McLoughlin displayed the same single-track obsti-
nacy he had shown years before when he badgered his uncle over the terms
of his contract. He used each new bit of evidence as an excuse for reviewing
the entire matter with wearisome details until even his friends lost patience,
and most of the officers at Fort Vancouver began to correspond in private with
Governor Simpson. James Douglas felt the strain. He tried in vain to dissuade
the doctor from his antagonistic—and hence dangerous—course by telling him
that the removal of Finlayson was "a necessary measure," because of Work's
poor health. "I have said every thing that could be said on the subject," Douglas
told Simpson in 1845, and a year later he spoke of "the fag and wear and tear
of the work, as has fallen to my share for the last five years. In fact I am harassed
beyond reason, and see no prospect of relief."

Interest in the quarrel spread to other posts. Archibald McDonald, at
Fort Colvile, told Simpson that "the pile upon pile of papers the unhappy
father has laboured to fill up upon this harrassing question to prove his son to
have been what in my opinion he was not, is truly astonishing. . . . I cannot
however disguise my dread of the attack that will be made upon me this
Summer if I go down, to bring me into his own way of thinking as I believe is

his habitual practice with every one with whom he comes in contact." In another letter McDonald said, "I fear we have got ourselves into a bobble." And McLoughlin's friend John Tod wrote to Edward Ermatinger in 1845:

> How the matter will end, is at present uncertain, but assuredly our interests can never be well looked after, when two of the first Characters in the Country are so much at variance—every allowance ought to be made for the feelings of a father, in such a case as this, but I fear the Dr. has not only compromised his dignity in this affair but has also failed to excite the Sympathy of the greater part of his friends, from his very excess.

In a contest between any employee and Simpson, the latter was certain to win, because he managed the company's affairs with such consummate skill that he was virtually indispensable. Furthermore, he had trumpeted his opinion so publicly that he found it impossible to retreat—and the company had to back its man. In September 1843, the Governor and Committee wrote to McLoughlin that his feelings were "too deeply interested to give them the calm consideration which they require, while their continued agitation gives rise to angry recrimination which is bad for the service."

They especially defended Simpson. "We cannot dismiss this painful subject without expressing our regret that throughout your letters, relating to it, you should have evinced so strong a disposition to throw the blame of your Son's death on Sir George Simpson, without, as it appears to us, the least shadow of reason." They conceded Sir George's error in removing Finlayson, but reminded McLoughlin that he had not protested at the time, which indicated that he was not worried about John's safety. This, they said, "refuted your own charge and acquitted Sir George Simpson of any blame that does not equally attach to yourself." The extent of McLoughlin's fall was shown in a private letter from Barclay to Simpson assuring him that the Committee had censured McLoughlin, and that "he has not been allowed to triumph."

For a year and more, the Governor and Committee hoped the Russian authorities would try Heroux and Kanaquassé, but in late 1843 Baron Wrangel sent word that they could not do so, because the crime had occurred "in that part of the Russian dominions which are given in Bail to the Hudsons Bay Comp."—an attitude that Secretary Barclay called "fudge alleged to get rid of the business." The Russians returned the two men to Hudson's Bay jurisdiction, which posed the question of what to do with them. Although they might be taken to Canada for trial, Barclay called it "an expense and inconvenience to get them and the witnesses transported thither." And yet everyone agreed that letting the matter drop would be a dangerous precedent.

While the question was being debated, Simpson ordered McLoughlin to release the prisoners who were still being held at various posts, but the doctor refused. Instead, he transmitted copies of all relevant documents to his agent, George Moffatt of Montreal, told Moffatt to prosecute the case if the company failed to do so, and sent Heroux, Kanaquassé, and eleven others to Norway House as witnesses. It was an unauthorized and expensive move. Adam Thom, Recorder of Rupert's Land, said it brought the company "the most serious perplexities," because Canada had no jurisdiction west of the Rockies and could deal with only its own citizens—but some of these men were from the Sandwich Islands, one was a Scot, and Kanaquassé was an Iroquois. After anguished consideration of all options, Thom recommended sending Heroux and Kanaquassé to McLoughlin's agent at Lachine and returning the islanders to the Columbia, the Scot to Scotland if he so desired, and the Canadians and Iroquois to their own country. In reporting to the Governor and Committee on Thom's opinion, Simpson lamented that there was no course by which the company could "avoid popular censure in this most untoward business," and said that if the prisoners were not suitably punished, McLoughlin would be responsible "for the odium which he will have heaped, and the injury which he will have inflicted, on the honorable company."

In a more practical vein, Simpson recommended that the doctor make up a list of expenses, "so that your honors may be able to decide whether the burden is to fall on the Fur trade or on Mr. McLoughlin himself." The Governor and Committee agreed, and even Secretary Barclay, McLoughlin's former defender, said that in sending the men east, the doctor had "acted like a fool." They warned him that they would hold him responsible for all costs, but for some reason they relented, and his account shows that no charges were actually levied against him.

The threat, however, gave McLoughlin pause. He wrote to Chief Trader Edward Ermatinger expressing his wish for a trial, but saying, "as it would cost to send the case to England where alone it can be tried at Least ten thousand pounds which is more than I can spare I must drop proceedings."

Simpson had undoubtedly shown good judgment in reorganizing the northern trade to meet new conditions, but his letters and reports lead to the inescapable conclusion that he was a business genius—and a flawed human being. W. Kaye Lamb in the introduction to McLoughlin's correspondence with his company, says, "If Simpson was right regarding trading matters he was just as certainly wrong in his policy following the murder of McLoughlin's son. His action was arbitrary and callous, and constitutes one of the most serious blots on his career."

That year—1842—was the turning point in McLoughlin's professional life, and from then on, his star began to fade. If he could have moderated his complaints, he might have avoided catastrophe, for at one time Barclay and the Committee were close to accepting his point of view. But he alienated even his friends by his persistence. His quarrel with Simpson interfered with his handling of the Columbia District's affairs; Barclay said the doctor's reports were so occupied with his son's death that they were "exceedingly meagre and unsatisfactory in other respects." Before the end of 1842, Sir John Pelly, governor of the Hudson's Bay Company, told him that he must resolve his feud with Simpson, or move to another department or retire. As McLoughlin said, "Sir George Simpsons Visit here in 1841 has cost me Dear."

CHAPTER 10

The American Dream

We deem it highly expedient for this comlunity
to take immediate measures to destroy all
Wolves, Bears & Panthers and such animals as are
known to be destructive to Cattle, Horses Sheap & Hogs.

REPORT TO MEETING, MARCH 6, 1843

~ 1 ~

Willamette Valley
1842

Even while McLoughlin was lost in grief and struggling to clear his son's name, he had to maintain relations with the American settlers, many of whom still wanted to establish an American government. They made no moves for two years after the death of Ewing Young, but they did not abandon their goal.

Three distinct groups were living in the Willamette Valley. The strongest was the Methodist mission under Jason Lee, which had its own organization, its teachers, ministers, and workmen. In addition to his headquarters at Chemeketa, Lee had branches at Willamette Falls, The Dalles, Nisqually near Puget Sound, and Clatsop on the coast. Although his people received provisions and funds from the Mission Board in New York, their records contain numberless references to McLoughlin's aid. When Daniel Lee was ill, "Dr. M'L. kindly offered him a passage, gratis," to the Sandwich Islands in a Hudson's Bay ship, and Lee returned in the company's *Nereide*. The missionaries used "rough fir boards which we obtained at Fort Vancouver" for a house on the coast. If they were seriously ill, McLoughlin had them cared for at the fort hospital, as when "Mrs. Kone's health was such that medical aid would soon be indispensable" and she was taken to Fort Vancouver to be safely delivered of her child. Jason Lee and McLoughlin were on good personal terms, and occasionally backed one another. Lee, for example, had attended the interview with Pierre Kanaquassé after the murder of the doctor's son.

The two Lees and their original party were apparently idealists, but those who came on the *Lausanne* or later were primarily interested in colonizing. McLoughlin said, "No men, in my opinion, could exert themselves more zealously than they did till 1840, when they received a large reinforcement of 40 or more persons; then the new-comers began to neglect their duties." Lee himself recognized the change, and laid it to the Mission Board's lack of care in select-

Jason Lee's mission built the school Chemeketa in 1840 as an Indian school but 'bandoned it in 1844 for lack of students. Although it had cost $10,000, it was sold to the Oregon Institute for $4,000. In 1853, the Oregon Institute received its charter from the Oregon legislature as Willamette University. OHS ORHI 564 & 565

ing recruits. In 1842 the missionaries had only a few Indian students, and they established a school for white children, housing it in a large frame building at Chemeketa—today's Salem. Named the Oregon Institute, it became important not only as a seat of learning, but as a hub of activity, often used for settlers' meetings.

The second group in the Willamette Valley were the independent farmers—retired mountain men plus a few others, such as Nathaniel Wyeth's followers. A French visitor, Eugene Duflot de Mofras, called them "backwoodsmen from the western United States," and said they were "courageous and patient, more skilful at hunting, wood cutting and carpentry than at agriculture." Living on small, scattered farms, they bought supplies and marketed grain at Fort Vancouver. Some padded their pocketbooks by taking an occasional break from the plow to join Hudson's Bay brigades—a casual plan that benefited both parties. One of the most prominent was Joe Meek, a black-haired, burly Virginian who said "bar" for "bear" and "thar" for "there," and was always ready for an adventure or a joke.

The third group, closely aligned with McLoughlin and about equal to the Americans in number, were the French Canadians, chiefly Hudson's Bay retirees. "They have very pretty orchards of apple trees, and some peach trees," said the settler Joel Palmer. "Their wives are native of the country. . . . But few of them speak English fluently; they mostly talk French and Chinook jargon." One of them was a newcomer, Francis Xavier Matthieu from Terre-bonne—home of McLoughlin's favorite uncle, Simon Fraser. Matthieu had been involved in the abortive Canadian rebellion of 1837–38, and when he needed a pass to get out of the country, Dr. Fraser secured it for him.

The French Canadians liked and trusted McLoughlin, who was fluent in their language and had adopted their religion. Because he carried them on the company books, which enabled them to stay in the Columbia District, his influence was great. Medorem Crawford, an immigrant of 1842, said, "The old doctor would go down to Champoeg, and whatever he told them to do, they would do. If they were shiftless, he would not give them half what they want-ed. If they were industrious, even if they were not successful, he would give them what they wanted. . . . If they went around horse-racing he would lec-ture them severely and make them afraid to do so. There were no laws or rules. If there were any disputes, he settled them arbitrarily. Just what he said was the law." Being Canadian subjects and liking McLoughlin's rule, they did not share the missionaries' zeal for government, and preferred the status quo.

Although at first the Chief Factor was on excellent terms with the set-tlers, by the early 1840s some of them were pulling away. In spite of Mc-Loughlin's generosity, they could not forget that he had refused to sell them cattle, that he was British, that he was a Catholic, and a friend of the French Canadians. Convinced that Oregon rightfully belonged to the United States, they regarded him as an interloper, unfairly blessed with well-stocked posts, in contrast to their own privations. "They look on us as intruders on their soil," McLoughlin said. "To hear them talk, they consider 54° North as the bound-ary, and that at least we ought not to pass 49° North."

They were especially resentful because his fort was their only market. Daniel Lee, at The Dalles mission, said that "to get our wheat ground we had to go to Fort Vancouver mill, a journey of seventy-five miles." Once they were there, it was salt in the wound that McLoughlin paid for their wheat in cred-it, not cash, at the rate of three shillings per imperial bushel—about 60 to 62½ cents, a price they considered atrociously low. However, he had no alter-native, because there was almost no currency in the area, and he tried to allow a favorable ratio between payments and prices. In 1841 Lieutenant Charles Wilkes said the purchase price "is supposed . . . to be equal to one dollar and twelve cents per bushel; but it is difficult for the settlers so to understand it, and they are by no means satisfied with the rate." When compared with wages, the payments were generous, for according to Wilkes, a good mechan-ic could earn only $2.50 to $3.00 per day, and a common laborer a dollar.

A further irritation was McLoughlin's method of measuring grain. As was common in Canada, he used the imperial bushel, which was larger than the American measure, and he insisted on having it filled with wheat and then kicked or tapped with a stick to settle the contents, after which it was refilled to the brim. As to kicking or striking the half-bushel, he said it was the custom in his native section of Canada.

To quiet the settlers' complaints, he had his container checked before witnesses and found it accurate, so he continued to use it. But when he had some of their wheat weighed and found it heavier than standard, he raised his price. "The truth is," he said, "when I was first asked the price of wheat I said 2/6 as I calculated the Bushel to weigh 60 lbs. but finding on measuring it that it weighed 72 lbs. I told them without their asking it I would give them 3/ [3 shillings] per Bushel. I thought my character as an honest man was beyond suspicion."

A tale that was told and retold with glee said that once, when McLoughlin himself was overseeing the measurement, he thought his agent was tapping the measure too lightly, so he uttered his usual "Tut, tut" and gave the container a resounding thump with his cane. But this blow, says the legend, "to his chagrin and the vast enjoyment of the bystanders, instead of settling the grain only shook it up. And with that the settlers were well pleased."

By the 1840s, the American population was growing so fast that the south bank of the Columbia seemed almost certain to fall to the United States when the boundary was settled. Not wanting to lose the north bank too, the Governor and Committee decided to strengthen the claims of Great Britain by bringing in settlers from Red River and placing them at Nisqually and on the Cowlitz.

The idea appalled McLoughlin. "I regret to see you intend to send 20 families to this place," he wrote to the Governor and Committee in November 1840. "We have no Prairie Land on the Cowelitz on which to place them and as to placing them on wood Land it would be worse than useless." He said timber on the Columbia was so heavy that inexperienced axemen could not cut it, that it "requires several years to rot the roots before the ground can be cleared," and that the "Plains of Nisqually" were adapted only to pasturing sheep.

Nevertheless the company persisted, saying that "houses will be erected for them,—Stock, such as Cattle, Sheep, Horses, &c. provided, likewise Agricultural Implements, without any advance being required." In the fall of 1841, when a party from Red River came to Fort Vancouver on the way to their farms, McLoughlin was skeptical, but followed instructions as best he could. Sending seventy-seven people to Nisqually and thirty-eight to the Cowlitz, he showed them "every indulgence . . . that could be possibly made

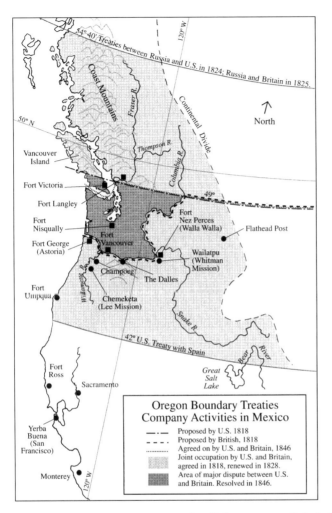

54° 40′ Treaties between Russia and U.S. in 1824; Russia and Britain in 1825.

120° W

Coast Mountains

Fraser R.

Continental Divide

50° N

↑
North

Vancouver
Island

Thompson R.

Columbia R.

Fort Victoria

49°

Fort Langley

Fort
Nisqually

Fort
Nez Perces
(Walla Walla)

Flathead Post

Fort George
(Astoria)

Fort
Vancouver

Wailatpu
(Whitman
Mission)

Champoeg

The Dalles

Fort
Umpqua

Willamette R.

Chemeketa
(Lee Mission)

Snake R.

42° U.S. Treaty with Spain

Bear River

Fort
Ross

Great
Salt
Lake

Sacramento

Yerba
Buena
(San
Francisco)

Monterey

120° W

Oregon Boundary Treaties
Company Activities in Mexico

—·— Proposed by U.S. 1818
—— Proposed by British, 1818
·········· Agreed on by U.S. and Britain, 1846
    Joint occupation by U.S. and Britain,
    agreed in 1818, renewed in 1828.
    Area of major dispute between U.S.
    and Britain. Resolved in 1846.

to induce them to remain." And still the attempt failed, for crops were poor and the Willamette inviting. A few families stayed on the Cowlitz, but those at Nisqually soon moved to the south side of the river, or left the country. "The fact is," McLoughlin said, "from the first moment I saw them, after their arrival from Red River, from their manner of speaking, I felt convinced they were desirous of going to the Wallamette."

The company had not succeeded in strengthening its hold on the Columbia's north bank, and the British had good cause to be concerned, for American interest in Oregon was growing. Travelers who had visited the Northwest wrote books and articles. Newspapers printed glowing stories about the climate, the opportunities, the rich, deep soil. Emigration societies were being formed.

Mixed with the praise were criticisms of McLoughlin and his company, often from those he had assisted. One of these was the report of William Slacum, the American captain who had inspected the Columbia in 1836, posing as a tourist. Slacum said the company encouraged slavery among the natives and incited them to attack Americans—baseless accusations, distressing to Mc-Loughlin. "I could not believe that people could have been found to Slander us in this manner," he said.

Even worse was the diatribe by Josiah Spaulding, captain of the *Lausanne*—the ship McLoughlin had greeted with fresh bread and a tub of butter. Spaulding's report to Congress was favorable to the doctor personally, whom he called "a gentleman of pleasing address, possessing great urbanity of manners and unbounded hospitality, opening his house to all strangers who can furnish any recommendations, or who have any claim, as men of character, upon his hospitality." But the captain issued a barrage of accusations against the company, saying that its trappers marked every step of their way "with violence blood & murder," and that Hudson's Bay brigades "commit every depredation, upon the poor, defenceless and peaceful Indians, living within the defined and acknowledged jurisdiction, of the United States, actually murdering hundreds of them, every year."

Insulted, incredulous, McLoughlin ironically told the Governor and Committee that "Capt. Spaulding has bestowed upon me a more flattering character than I desire," and that it seemed "somewhat inconsistent in him to suppose that a person deserving of such high commendation should have permitted the H.B.Co. Servants who are under his orders to commit the worst crimes that have disgraced the history of man." He pointed out the safety—even for strangers—of travel on the Columbia, which proved that the Indians had not been "butchered," as Captain Spaulding said. Moreover, he was aware that the captain's report, false as it was, would bolster similar charges by Hall Kelley and the somewhat milder but nevertheless critical statement of Slacum, fanning the anti-Hudson's Bay bias. It "has had the effect of exciting a great feeling of hostility towards us in the United States, & indeed in the opinion of every feeling man who reads it," McLoughlin told the London Committee.

Inevitably, as interest in Oregon grew, an increasing number of Americans decided to see it for themselves. In the fall of 1842, while the Red River settlers were struggling with the tough sod of the Cowlitz, the first large, organized group of American immigrants reached the Columbia. Numbering about

125 people, of which fifty-five were men over the age of eighteen, they had started from Missouri with a train of wagons, but left them at Fort Laramie or Fort Hall and finished the trip by packhorse. Until then the number of French Canadians and Americans had been roughly equal, and many of this immigration soon left, but enough remained to tilt the balance. For the first time, the Americans in the Willamette Valley were the dominant group.

An event of national importance occurred that summer. Fifteen years before, when the agreement of joint occupation was extended, it carried a proviso that either country could terminate it by giving a year's notice. American sentiment to take action was rising, and in 1841 Senator Lewis F. Linn of Missouri introduced a resolution in Congress directing the president to notify England that America intended to make that move. His resolution did not pass, but the following year, while the wagons were lurching over the plains, the governments of Britain and the United States tried again.

The United States was determined to retain Puget Sound, because the mouth of the Columbia was considered "a barred and indifferent harbor," and San Francisco Bay was held by Mexico. In addition, the Americans demanded an exclusive right to the Columbia River, while the British were equally determined to retain use of the main channel for access to their inland posts.

Sharp as these differences were, the Oregon boundary was only one facet of the problem, because parts of the U.S.-Canadian line east of the Rockies were also in dispute: the segments between Maine and New Brunswick, between New Hampshire and Quebec, and just west of the Great Lakes. The American Daniel Webster and Lord Ashburton of Britain, who met in Washington in April 1842, solved most of those questions. But they could not agree on the West Coast, and renewed the convention of joint occupation "indefinitely."

When the news finally reached Fort Vancouver, McLoughlin could feel somewhat relieved, because for at least a few years he would retain the right to conduct business on both banks of the river. But as the population of the Willamette Valley increased, so did the need for laws, courts, and ownership of land—meaning that if the United States and Great Britain could not make an agreement, the settlers must find a solution for themselves. McLoughlin well knew that whatever form that took, it would inevitably affect the north bank of the Columbia, involving him and his fort.

~ 2 ~

The Wolf Meetings
1842–1843

Because of disagreements on the trail, the immigration of 1842 arrived under two leaders, one of whom was Lansford W. Hastings, an attorney. By then McLoughlin had become uneasy about the land at Willamette Falls. He had claimed it for the company in 1829, but it was in the area that would probably become American, and the number of settlers was increasing. He therefore hired Hastings to safeguard the claim, and since another immigrant, J. M. Hudspeth, was a surveyor, the doctor hired him also, to establish boundaries and lay out streets and lots of the area's first town—Oregon City.

It was on two levels, a rocky strip along the river and a forested upper ledge. Until then the settlement had consisted of little more than the Methodist mission and the company mill, but the immigrants began at once to move in, clearing trees and riding horses along the muddy lanes. By December 1842, McLoughlin had sold at least one homesite and directed his lawyer to draw up the deed. The growth was astonishing. In the spring Hastings said, "In all there are about 14 buildings." And in August the Reverend Joseph Frost wrote that the mission contained a log dwelling for Mr. Waller, "a very good framed store-house," and a frame dwelling for George Abernethy, who was managing the mission's small store. In addition, he said, "there are at that place two saw-mills and a flouring-mill, and about twenty-six other buildings, principally frame." One of these was a retail outlet for the company, which the Governor and Committee had directed McLoughlin to build.

Besides Hastings, the other leader of the immigration was Dr. Elijah White, a slightly built man with ingratiating manners—fair of skin and blue-eyed, with abundant dark hair. This was his second visit to the Columbia, for he had come in 1837 as physician to the Willamette mission, but left three years later after a falling-out with Jason Lee. During his interim in the United States, he had secured a semiofficial appointment from the American government as subagent for the Indians west of the Rocky Mountains—a dubious title, because America had no legal jurisdiction there. In October McLoughlin told the Governor and Committee, "On Dr. White's arrival in the Wallamette he called a meeting of the Settlers to whom he shewed his Commission . . . and told them the United States intended to take them under their protection, which information was received with pleasure by the American Citizens, but with great coolness by the Canadians."

The tribes of the Willamette Valley had been all but wiped out by disease, but those farther inland—Cayuses and Nez Perces—were still strong. Even though they did not fear the British, they had heard about the greed of Americans in the East, and the influx of settlers worried them. Later that fall, a rumor said the Indians east of the Cascades intended to mount an attack, and White went up the Columbia to meet with them. Not wishing to support an alliance of immigrants against his Indian friends, McLoughlin warned Archibald McKinlay, head of Fort Nez Perces, that if Dr. White came to the fort, he was to be recognized only "as a private Individual, and as such, treated with all the courtesy his conduct deserves. But you cannot permit his holding Council with Indians in the Fort."

When White met with the Indians, he succeeded in calming their fears, even though they rightly saw his appointment as a threat to their lands. McLoughlin told the Committee, "A momentary excitement broke out among the Nez Percés and cayuse Tribes . . . caused by a report spread among them that White . . . had said he would take their lands from them." He said it was "certain" that White had never made such a claim, and that another report, of Indian threats to attack the settlers, was also false. Rather than stirring up the tribes, he said, White had met with them, "principally spoke to them of Religion, and advised them to become Farmers . . . the assembly eventually broke up quietly, and every thing by last accounts is quiet in the interior."

Spurious as White's title was, he was the first American official in the Northwest, and his presence revived the settlers' hopes of establishing a government. Their attempt of 1841 had failed, but many of them were still eager to act, even though they could not agree on a plan. Some wanted to declare a separate nation and fend for themselves; some, mainly the French Canadians, were satisfied with McLoughlin's loose rein; and still others favored a temporary arrangement, to last only until the boundary was determined and the United States took control.

The political ferment was expressed in a debating society, the Oregon Lyceum of Oregon City, in which the "question of a provisional government was . . . debated warmly for several evenings and finally voted down." Although McLoughlin was not present, he was said to be on "the side of an independent government," and the mission storekeeper George Abernethy, who had come on the *Lausanne* as a mission steward, claimed that "this independent government move was a prominent scheme of Dr. McLaughlin." There is, in fact, no evidence of a Hudson's Bay "scheme," but it is known that Lansford Hastings, McLoughlin's attorney, participated in the debates and offered an

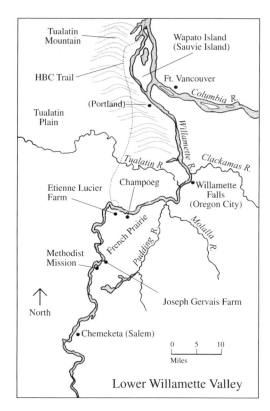

Lower Willamette Valley

unsuccessful resolution "that it is expedient for the settlers on this coast to establish an independent government."

The meetings were chiefly notable for expressing the settlers' concern and the wide divergence of their opinions. Hastings thought the flow of ideas "resulted in a determination to organize," and they may have influenced a few, or solidified beliefs. McLoughlin himself was less interested in the immigrants' politics than in fostering their good will as future customers. "An influx of Settlers will cause a great increase of business in the place," he informed the Governor and Committee, "which we can in the main Secure if we have the means of supplying the wants of the settlers and can procure a market for their produce."

In the spring of 1843, about half of the previous autumn's newcomers left for California or returned to the States. Although population estimates varied widely, one resident of that year thought the valley held about 200 French Canadians and 275 adult Americans, male and female, of whom about fifty were planning to leave. With this American majority and a growing interest,

the time seemed right for a fresh attempt to organize, and the settlers decided to act. McLoughlin, across the river in Fort Vancouver, played no part, but
his farmer son Joseph and the French Canadians doubtless kept him informed.

Remembering their earlier failure, the progovernment forces adopted a
roundabout approach based on a universal concern—wolves. "Our idea was,
to get an object before the people upon which all could unite, and as we advanced, secure the main object,—*self preservation, both for property and
persons*," explained William H. Gray.

According to him and others who were there, the activists called a meeting for February 2, 1843, in Gray's home at the Oregon Institute, and wisely
decided to focus on wolves. The meeting was "fully attended, and all took a
lively interest in it, for there was not a man in the settlement that had not
been a loser from wild animals." Little was attempted at that time except to
discuss the problem and appoint a committee of six to call a public meeting
for the first Monday in March at the home of Joseph Gervais, a French Canadian farmer. He was a member of the committee, as were his friend, Etienne
Lucier, and Gray.

On the appointed day, March 6, the settlers gathered at ten o'clock in the
morning, with no clergy invited and no representative of McLoughlin's company, who were thought to be in opposition. The Gervais house—on French
Prairie, halfway between Chemeketa and Champoeg—was substantial, about
eighteen by twenty-four feet, built of "square hewed logs," lighted by three
small windows "covered with fine thinly dressed deer skins," and warmed by
"a large fireplace, built of sticks tied together with buckskin thongs, and covered with a stiff plaster made of clay and grass." The backers of the movement
left no stone unturned. They took the chairman, James O'Neil, aside to see
that he was "informed of the main object, and requested to hurry through the
'wolf meeting' business as soon as possible."

The first part of the meeting went smoothly. Eloquent in the dim light,
they talked about wolves, and decided to establish a system of bounties—fifty
cents for a small wolf, $3.00 for a large one, $1.50 for a lynx, $2.00 for a bear,
and $5.00 for a panther. They were to be financed by voluntary contributions
and administered by two collectors, who could retain five percent of receipts.
These were promptly elected, and with that out of the way, the group got down
to their real object. The official notes are brief—scarcely more than an outline—but Gray's account contains an excerpt from an ardent address by one
speaker, probably Gray himself. It was a thinly disguised attack on McLoughlin
and his company.

How is it, fellow-citizens, with you and me, and our children and wives? . . . Is there any power or influence in the country sufficient to protect us and all we hold dear on earth from the worse than wild beasts that threaten and occasionally destroy our cattle? . . . We have mutually and unitedly agreed to defend and protect our *cattle and domestic animals;* now, fellow-citizens, I submit and move the adoption of the two following resolutions that we may have protection for our persons and lives as well as our cattle and herds.

The first resolution was "that a committee be appointed to take into cunsderation the propriety of taking measure for the civil & military protection of this colony." The second was "that this committee consist of 12." The settlers passed both and chose twelve committeemen, again including Gervais and Lucier.

These two assemblies, known as the Wolf Meetings—at the homes of Gray and Gervais—were important links in the chain that led to a local government. They were followed by a meeting of the committee of twelve on March 17 at the Falls of the Willamette—the name the Americans insisted on using for Oregon City, because they refused to recognize McLoughlin's right to found the town. When about fifty people showed up instead of the expected twelve, the committee decided to let everyone take part in the discussions.

McLoughlin, as before, was not present, but this time Jason Lee was, and for an unknown reason he and the storekeeper, George Abernethy, were "disposed to ridicule the proposed regulation as foolish and unnecessary." However, in spite of their opposition, the meeting proceeded with its agenda. The settlers discussed the thorny question of having a governor, and since each group insisted on its own candidate, they decided to have an executive committee of three. With that accomplished, they agreed unanimously to call a public meeting at Champoeg on May 2, 1843, "for the purpose of taking steps to organize themselves into a civil community."

When McLoughlin heard about the meeting, he was neither alarmed nor offended. Three days later, on March 20, he told Sir George Simpson that the settlers had met, that they planned to "erect a temporary Government," and that

though none of the Canadians were present at the meeting . . . yet they must admit the strength of the argument used by the Americans that they must now that people are coming here from different Countries adopt some plan to keep peace in the Country and that while the Canadians are bound, those who come from the states are amenable to no authority—and that they want to empower the authorities whom they elect to decide in cases between individuals—and in criminal cases to deliver the accused for trial to the Country to which he belongs.

McLoughlin was still a loyal British subject, but he realized that the rapidly growing American settlement needed more than the loose supervision that he, a Canadian, could provide. He was its storekeeper, its miller, its banker, its friend, and he was satisfied with that role.

~ 3 ~

Champoeg
1843

In early April 1843, McLoughlin received a letter from his lawyer, and when he read it, he was first incredulous, then furiously angry. Hastings had written:

> Dear Sir, I have now a remark to make in reference to a most novel and rediculous matter, about which you probably have heard nothing & of which I had not had even a hint until very recently; it is this; this Missionery Clan has recently got up and put in circulation a petition to the Congress of the U. States, the pretended object of which, is to have the U. States extend their jurisdiction over this Country, but Sir, to the astonishment of all honest men of Oregon, they have, in the most minute manner, set forth all manner of pretended grievances which they say they have received at the hands of yourself, and your Company; I must refer to a few of these complaints.

Hastings then quoted parts of the petition—that McLoughlin refused to supply cattle to the settlers, that he used an oversize wheat measure, that he kicked the half-bushel, that he priced his lumber unfairly, and a "general false assertion that you & your Company have always opposed all the interests of the Citizens & of the Country; how ungenerous, how exaggerated, how false." Hastings said he was even more surprised that the petition had been signed by many "otherwise respectable men," including some of his own emigration party, and that when asked, they told him the petition had been presented as a simple request for the United States to extend its jurisdiction to Oregon. "Even now," he said, "upon conversing with them I find they would not hesitate to sign a counter petition, the thing is most rediculous most scandalous."

This petition was far more hostile than those of Lee and Farnham. "I am astonished that there should be one person in the Country to say such a thing of me," McLoughlin spluttered after the initial jolt. He told Hastings that he lent cattle freely but would sell none in order to let the herd increase, that he had advanced money for the California cattle drive, and that "so anxious was I to replenish the Country with Cattle, that I killed none till 1838." He pointed out his care in measuring wheat and his increase in the price when he discovered the superior weight of the settlers' grain. As to opposing their interests, he said, "really, really, the Citizens are themselves the best judges if we did so or not." He asked Hastings to "take the measure you think most advisable which I presume would be by a meeting expressing their opinion on it or on the line of conduct I have pursued."

The petition had been sponsored by Robert Shortess, a settler of 1839 who had recently experienced a religious conversion. "My mind was full of enmity against God and man," Shortess had written to the Reverend Daniel Lee of The Dalles. "The world appeared to me a vast desert, in which was nothing desirable. Life seemed a curse, and I had no hope beyond it. . . . But through his [God's] mercy . . . I soon found a degree of peace of mind and love to him and all mankind."

Shortess may have loved mankind, but he had a fanatic hatred for McLoughlin and the Hudson's Bay Company, and after drawing up his petition, he had called a meeting at which he and its other backers persuaded sixty-five Americans to sign their names. Some residents objected. Elijah White informed the Bureau of Indian Affairs that a petition with "bitter accusations" was on its way, and said, "The gentlemen of the company have been fathers and fosterers of the Colony, ever encouraging peace, industry and good order and have sustained a character for hospitality and integrity too well established to be easily shaken."

The document had been produced in such haste that settlers in Tualatin Plains, north of French Prairie, did not sign it "for want of time to circulate it in that section," and Shortess had made no provision for sending it to Washington. William C. Sutton, however, had just left for the States, so Shortess started after him posthaste, caught up with him at the Cascades, and handed him the paper. Sutton eventually delivered it to Congress through Senator Linn, and it was entered in the national record.

Historians have speculated about its authorship—whether Shortess actually created it, or merely accepted responsibility for a statement by the Reverend Waller or George Abernethy. Shortess, in his letters to McLoughlin, implied that he himself was the originator, and much later, in 1867, he told the historian Elwood Evans that "without consulting any one," he decided on the petition, drew up a summary, "and showed it to one or two persons." He also said he had asked Abernethy "to write it in proper form, which he did, but refused to sign or allow it to be circulated in his handwriting, fearing it might injure the mission. I had it copied by A.E. Willson. It was circulated and, through his assistance, sent to Washington. . . . I will state that he wrote it at my request and from my notes."

This statement—if it is completely candid—points to Shortess as the originator, although it omits the identity and role of the "one or two persons" who saw the document. More important than the authorship was its backing, for many settlers and most of the missionaries signed it, Shortess was close to the mission party, and most people ascribed it to the party's influence. Even though Jason Lee and George Abernethy refused to sign, it was an unmistakable indication of the growing antipathy to McLoughlin, and a cruel blow.

On April 13, five days after receiving the letter from Hastings, the appalled Chief Factor wrote to Shortess asking "in common fairness" for a copy of the petition with names of the signers. Shortess immediately replied that he could not send it, "as the document and Signatures belong to the Signers & I have no right to make use of either without the consent of all concerned." McLoughlin then repeated his request, "so as I might be better able to vindicate my conduct," saying that if the signers did not wish to give their names, he would like at least a copy of the petition. Again Shortess refused, with a sarcastic suggestion that "perhaps the person who has given you the information mentioned in your notes can give that which you seem so anxious to obtain."

Two years earlier, McLoughlin had probably persuaded Father Blanchet not to support the settlers' first attempt to form a government, but at that time the Chief Factor had not seemed greatly concerned. Even in March 1843, when he learned they were planning a public meeting to make a stronger attempt, he spoke with considerable sympathy of their need "to adopt some plan to keep peace in the Country." The French Canadians had also been friendly with the Americans. The second Wolf Meeting had been held at the home of Gervais, and two of them, Gervais and Lucier, had been on the committee of twelve. But after the Shortess petition, the French Canadians withdrew their support, and popular opinion held that McLoughlin had persuaded them to do so.

William H. Gray said that in the time between the Wolf Meetings and the settlers' assemblage of May 2 at Champoeg, "the priests and the Hudson's Bay Company were not idle. They held two distinct meetings, one at the falls and one at Vancouver, and two in the French Prairie at the Catholic church." He also said that by May 2 the "Hudson's Bay Company had drilled and trained their voters for the occasion, under the Rev. F.N. Blanchet and his priests." George Le Breton wrote that the Canadians, "at the instigation doubtless of the Officers of the HB Company refused to join in these measures stating that they would be protected by the compy, and that it was the 'Bostons' only that the Indians intended to make war upon."

McLoughlin himself described a document that has disappeared. In a letter to Captain John Gordon of HMS *America*, he said an invitation to join the government was made "in the spring of 1843, and also declined by the Canadians, who drew out and delivered to the Americans a written declaration of their reasons and views for remaining separate." Their paper must have been drafted by a priest or member of the Hudson's Bay Company, because most of the French Canadians could neither read nor write. Although its details are lost, McLoughlin was obviously familiar with it.

As head of his company's Columbia District, he had great influence with these retirees, and since the population was nearly in balance, his opposition was significant. Whatever he or the priest told the retirees—suspicious Americans said they had been primed to vote no on every motion—many French Canadians joined the assemblage on May 2, when about a hundred booted and generally bearded men rode horses to the meeting place or swung their boats up to the shore.

Although Champoeg was not yet a town, it was a well-known, relatively level area at the north end of French Prairie, one of the few places where inhabitants could reach the Willamette River without hacking their way through a forest. The early Astorians and Nor'Westers had from time to time set up temporary trading posts in the vicinity, and McLoughlin's California brigades sometimes camped there while preparing and packing their gear.

Since it was a handy site for settlers to load their produce into canoes for shipment to Fort Vancouver, McLoughlin had recently had his workmen build a warehouse on the bank, overhanging the water, and he kept an agent there to receive, store, and ship wheat and maintain a small trading post to supply the settlers' needs. Even more imposing was the mill owned by Thomas McKay, who had a farm nearby, probably on the small Chehalem Creek. Besides these two large structures, a scattering of residences stood along the river,

F.X. Matthieu had lived in Terrebonne, and knew Mc-Loughlin's uncle, Dr. Simon Fraser. Matthieu came to Oregon in 1842 and remained there for the rest of his life. He had a prominent role in the formation of the Provisional Government, and much later, in 1900 he pointed out the location of the Champoeg meeting of May 2, 1843. He also helped reconstruct the list of pioneers who had been present. OHS ORHI 51292

ranging from log huts to substantial painted frame buildings amid small fields and orchards.

In 1843 there were approximately two hundred male Europeans living in the valley—one estimate said 83 French Canadians and 125 Americans—and about one hundred came to the May meeting, which indicates that in spite of the unrest, only half of the residents showed up. McLoughlin himself was not there, but Francis Xavier Matthieu, who was present, said it was held "in a Hudson's Bay building, just over the bluff, at the landing. . . . The meeting, however, was very informal, being called to order in the house, but the final vote being taken out of doors."

There, standing in the soft grass of spring, the settlers elected Ira L. Babcock as chairman and chose three men as secretaries—William H. Gray, George W. Le Breton, and William H. Willson. All three secretaries were sufficiently anti-McLoughlin and anti-Hudson's Bay to have signed the Shortess petition, but Judge Babcock had not. With him in charge, according to Le Breton's minutes, "The committee made their report, which was read, and A motion was made, that it be accepted, which was lost. Considerable confusion existing in consequence."

At this, mild-mannered Le Breton, struggling to enumerate the unruly crowd, moved that the meeting divide to be counted. And it was then that Joe Meek, big Joe Meek of the loud voice and powerful frame, made his mark in history. As William H. Gray told it in his *History of Oregon*:

Says Le Breton, 'We can risk it; let us divide and count.' 'I second that motion,' says Gray. 'Who's for a divide?' sang out old Joe Meek, as he stepped out; 'all for the report of the committee and an organization, follow me.' This was so sudden and unexpected that the priest and his voters did not know what to do, but every American was soon in line. Le Breton and Gray passed the line and counted fifty-two Americans, and but fifty French and Hudson's Bay Company

Joe Meek. OHS ORHI 10126

men. They announced the count—
'fifty-two for, and fifty against.' 'Three
cheers for our side,' sang out old Joe
Meek. Not one of those old veteran
mountain voices were lacking in that
shout for *liberty*. They were given
with a will, and in a few seconds the
chairman, Judge I.L. Babcock, called
the meeting to order, when the priest
and his band slunk away into the cor-
ners of the fences, and in a short time
mnunted their horses and left.

The story has sometimes been relegat-
ed to the rank of legend, but in addition to Gray's account, it was told by Meek
himself, by the French Canadian Matthieu, by the independent missionary
J. S. Griffin, and by the articulate settler John Minto, all of whom were present. J. Quinn Thornton, who made a careful study of the area's early history,
also recorded it, but he came to Oregon three years later, in 1846, so he had
to rely on settlers' reports.

All the eyewitnesses gave the same basic facts. Matthieu, for example,
said that he remembered well "how old Joe Meek strode forth, and by the
simple power of voice and example gained control." The minutes themselves
are a characteristically brief version of the same event, without naming Meek.
According to these, "It was moved by Mr. Le Breton, and seconded by Mr.
Gray, that the meeting divide, preparatory to being counted; those in favour
of the objects of this meeting taking the right, and those of a contrary mind
taking the left, which being carried by acclamation, and a great majority being
found in favour of organization, the greater part of the dissenters withdrew."

Matthieu added his own touch by saying that the vote at first was 50 for
and 52 against, but that he told the Canadians he was going to switch, and urged
Etienne Lucier to join him. Lucier, he said, was "quite suspicious" of heavy
American taxes, such as a levy on windows, but Matthieu told him that American laws were "entirely just and liberal, and under them all men were equal."
With this assurance, Lucier "followed him and now the vote stood 52 for and
50 against." The various counts of the ayes and nays disagreed. Le Breton's offi-

This imaginative view of the Champoeg meeting of May 5, 1843, was painted as part of a mural in the Oregon State Capitol. It looks south from the Hudson's Bay Company mill, away from the Willamette River, toward the hills. Seated in the foreground is Etienne Lucier, urging F.X. Matthieu to support the formation of a government. Near them is bearded Joe Meek, holding his rifle and calling for the settlers to divide. *Who's For Divide?* by Barry Faulkner. OREGON STATE ARCHIVES cial minutes said the measure passed by "a great majority," Gray and Matthieu called it a majority of two, and Robert Newell, also present, said five.

The specific number matters very little; the crucial point is that the settlers decided to form a government, without specifying its form. They elected several officers and appointed a legislative committee of nine to make a report to another public meeting, on July 5 at Champoeg. The sizeable attendance was evidence of the Americans' growing strength.

But it did not change the course of history. It was not a culmination, but a single step in a long progression. The future of the Oregon Country did not hang on this one vote, for Americans were sweeping in, and if they had lost in 1843, they would have doubtless tried again—and again. Neither did the Champoeg vote "save Oregon for the United States," as has been claimed, nor did it doom McLoughlin and his company. It was not a choice between Britain and America, but merely a sensible decision to set up some kind of government to defend the colony, to maintain law and order, and to safeguard land claims until a political decision at the national level established the border.

Nevertheless, the new system brought McLoughlin a profound change, because it meant he was no longer the area's strongest authority. His control was limited to British subjects, and when the Americans united, they greatly increased their clout. They would have their own laws, elect their own officials, and mete out their own penalties.

When the news was brought by horse and canoe to the fort, McLoughlin could not have been surprised, because he had long realized that it was only a matter of time until his loyal Canadians were outvoted. The fledgling government was small and limited in scope, and it lay outside the Hudson's Bay Company holdings. It might not survive. In one respect it would help McLoughlin, for the settlers now had an official organization that he could call on in case of trouble, instead of having to maneuver his way through a conglomerate of individuals with no one in charge.

But it also handed him a problem—what stance to take in the new relationship, how to be loyal to his company and fair to the Indians and friendly with this untried entity, all at once. Moreover, his town beside the falls was south of the Columbia, in the heart of the new government's domain. It was slipping beyond his control.

~4~

The Provisional Government
1843

E ven though the meeting at Champoeg had authorized a government, the harder job lay ahead—to transform a vague plan into specific laws. McLoughlin could not take part in the process, but he had an enormous stake in it as chief executive of the largest business in the area, with property both north and south of the Columbia. He was concerned, and he kept the London Committee informed.

As a first step, the settlers at Champoeg elected a legislative committee of nine. To McLoughlin, its roster had an ominous ring, because one of its members was Robert Shortess, three of the others had signed the Shortess petition, and it included no French Canadians. The committeemen were ordered to draft laws but were not told when or where to meet, merely that they should not spend more than six days, for which they would receive $1.25 per man per day, raised by voluntary subscription.

The problem of dredging up salaries was solved by the members themselves, who agreed to donate their per diem allowance, and the place was decided when the Methodist mission offered without charge its old storehouse at low-lying Mission Bottom. This was a barnlike structure "sixteen by thirty feet . . . with one square room in front, and the balance used for a granary . . . the upper part was for storing and sleeping use." It had served at various times as schoolhouse and church, and there, on May 16, 1843, the first Legislative Assembly in the Oregon Country met.

Its initial act was to elect as speaker sixty-two-year-old Robert Moore, gray-haired and portly, who presided over the meetings "sitting by a square-legged table or stand, in a chair with square posts, and strips of rawhide for bottom; dressed in fustian pants, large blue vest, and striped shirt, and a common brown coat." A resident since 1840, he was older than most immigrants, and his land claim, "Robin's Nest," was on the west side of the Willamette River, across from McLoughlin's claim at the falls. Some members of the committee suggested holding their sessions behind closed doors, "as they did not want to expose their ignorance of making laws," and "might be ashamed of what we had done." But after considerable discussion they decided to keep their sessions open, to show their willingness to take advice "from any source."

They were not as ill-prepared as they feared. Although the group included no lawyer, Chairman Moore had served in the Missouri legislature, Shortess had been educated as a schoolteacher, and James O'Neil had a copy of the statutes of the Territory of Iowa, which also contained the Iowa Organic Laws, the Declaration of Independence, and the Constitution of the United States. Armed with these, the committee met in two sessions, May 16–19 and June 27–28. They pared the job to size by assigning themselves to subcommittees—Judiciary, Land Claims, Military Affairs, Districts, Ways and Means—each of which worked out details for its own field. For McLoughlin, it was unfortunate that Shortess was a member of the subcommittee on land.

The clerk—young, bespectacled George Le Breton—included few details of the group's deliberations, because "from the deep interest he took in the discussions, he seemed to forget his work." Consequently, many of his minutes were bare statements such as "Moved and carried the Report be accepted," without a hint of what the report contained.

Nevertheless, he recorded the recommendations of the various subcommittees, and they were presented to a public meeting on July 5. Skimpy as they are, Le Breton's minutes make it clear that, drawing heavily on the Iowa law, this inexperienced but hard-working committee had crafted a legal system based on the traditional American branches of government—legislative, executive, and judicial—with one important difference: an executive committee of three instead of a governor. At this point in Le Breton's minutes, the words "and give the reason's for the same" were added but crossed out. There is a hint of official squabbles in two of the committee's rules, which say, "No member of the House shall be allowed to speak more than twice upon any subject except by permission of the House" and "Each Member shall respectfully address the chair."

By midsummer, at least some of the dissatisfied French Canadians had swallowed their anger, and on the Fourth of July "nearly all the Americans in the country, and many of the French and English," gathered at Champoeg for a celebration and potluck dinner. The Reverend Gustavus Hines, who was the featured speaker, disappointed his listeners because they wanted to hear about their own plans, and he "dwelt principally on the subject of temperance" and the "glorious deeds of our forefathers on the other side of the Rocky Mountains." But when he finally stepped down, the celebration was enlivened by races, food, and social mingling, and after enjoying the day "in the true spirit of liberty," most of the settlers camped for the night. Although McLoughlin was not there, a number of his French Canadian friends were, and his son Joseph.

The next morning the settlers gathered beside the Hudson's Bay warehouse as they had in May, and with considerable discussion, sometimes heated,
they considered the code known as the Organic Law of 1843—"organic" referring to the process of organization. They decided that the new government
would contain four districts, all south of the Columbia, which meant that Mc-
Loughlin's fort and farm on the north bank would not be included, although
his land at the falls would. W. H. Gray, in his *History of Oregon*, explained
why the Americans limited their reach: the committeemen feared that if they
included Fort Vancouver, they might become "an English or Hudson's Bay
Company settlement"; they thought they were well able to manage their own
affairs without the company's help; they expected another large immigration
in the fall and could extend their area then, if they chose. With a nod to Mc-
Loughlin's importance, Gray made the revealing comment that:

> Another prominent, and perhaps the most prominent reason of all
> was, we were afraid to attempt to enforce any laws we might . . . think
> necessary among ourselves, upon the servants of the company. We
> did not acknowledge their right to enforce any English laws over us,
> and we . . . wisely concluded if they would not openly interfere with
> us, we would not openly interfere with them, till we were strong
> enough to outnumber and control them.

At least for the time being, McLoughlin would have little part in and
receive little interference from the new organization.

With lively debate at every point, the settlers voted on, amended, and
passed the reports of the various subcommittees. They elected officers, including David Hill, Alanson Beers, and Joseph Gale as the Executive Committee.
McLoughlin's son Joseph was present and moved the adoption of Article I of
the report of the Judiciary Committee: "No person demeaning himself in a
peaceable and orderly manner shall ever be molested on account of his mode
of worship, or religious sentiments, in the said Territory."

Some of the old missionary idealism was reflected in the judiciary section,
which said that "the utmost good faith shall always be observed towards the
Indians; their lands and property shall never be taken from them without their
consent, and in their property, rights, and liberty, they shall never be invaded or
disturbed unless in just and lawful wars." Another paragraph declared that "there
shall be neither slavery nor involuntary servitude in said Territory, otherwise
than for the punishments of crimes." The settlers' charity, however, stopped short

of a universal franchise, for they restricted the vote to "every free, male inhabitant, descendant of a white man, of the age of twenty one years and upwards,
who shall have been an inhabitant of the territory at time of its organization."

The section that most affected McLoughlin was the one on land, and there
the hand of Shortess was all too evident, for it was an overt attack on the doctor's
rights at Willamette Falls. No one, it bluntly said, could "hold a claim of more than
one Square Mile," and "No person shall be entitled to hold such a claim upon City
or Town sites, extensive Water Privileges or other situations necessary for the transaction of Mercantile or Manufacturing Opperations and to the detriment of the
Community." When this was read for public discussion, the settlers accepted the
part about "Water Privileges," but the limitation of holdings to one square mile
set off a furor, because it would infringe on the claim of the mission. Pioneer ingenuity, however, was equal to the occasion. After heated discussion, they adopted the section, but sweetened it with a specific exemption: "provided that nothing in these laws shall be so construed, as to affect any claim of any Mission of
a Religious character made previous to this time of an extent not more than six
miles square." This protected the holdings of the Methodist mission while retaining the original, anti-McLoughlin provision. If implemented, it would deprive
him of his Oregon City property at the falls, including his entire town.

In November McLoughlin informed the Governor and Committee about
the new organization, but his letter, incomprehensibly, failed to mention the
unfavorable land law. Whether he believed he could have it modified later, or
expected the settlers to change it themselves, or simply thought it unworkable, is not known, but his report is oddly calm:

> The American population of the Wallamette had a political meeting
> last May, and invited the Canadians to unite with them in organizing
> themselves into a community, the Canadians who are fully as many
> as the others, told them they would positively take no part in their
> plans of organization, and government. The American party with a
> few Englishmen, who came by way of the States, and some
> Foreigners, formed themselves into a body, elected three men as an
> executive Board, three others as Magistrates, and three Constables,
> but so far, I am happy to say, every thing is quiet.

The new government, with its rules and officers, had begun operating on
the other side of the river. Conditions were changed, but McLoughlin did not
yet know what it would mean to him.

~5~

The First Great Immigration

1843

F ive years earlier, when Jason Lee took his 1838 petition to Washington, he gave it to Senator Lewis F. Linn of Missouri, who was particularly interested in Oregon. Linn presented it to the Senate in January 1839, and a month later he made a speech calling for the protection of American citizens on the West Coast. From then on, he never lost sight of the Northwest, but produced a spate of bills and memorials urging abrogation of the agreement of joint occupation, or the settlement of Oregon, or its establishment as a territory. None of his Oregon measures was enacted into law, but he was nevertheless a powerful figure.

His most significant attempt was a bill of January 1842 advocating extension of the laws of the United States to Oregon and a spectacular grant of 640 acres of free land to every male settler who would cultivate it for five years.

A view of Mt Hood from The Dalles. Then, as now, the beauty and majesty of Mt. Hood was impressive. This view shows the treeless, rolling land along the Columbia, backed by the 11,000-foot peak. This rendering is from Henry Warre's 1845 *Sketches in North America and the Oregon Territory.* OHS ORHI 790

The Columbia River at The Dalles, showing its danger. At this point the entire volume of the river is compressed into a narrow chute, creating one of the most dreaded sections of the entire Oregon Trail, a hazard that claimed a number of lives. This lithograph is from Maj. Osborne Cross's *Report in the Form of a Journal to the Quartermaster General, of the March of the Regiment of Mounted Rifleman to Oregon, May 18 to October 5, 1849.* OHS ORHI 81098

This lure was so strong that in early 1843, while the settlers were preparing to vote at Champoeg, hundreds of American families gathered in western Missouri, buying oxen, buying supplies, reinforcing wagons for a trek across the plains. They started in the spring, and in the fall they reached the Columbia.

They numbered approximately 875, so many that McLoughlin told the Governor and Committee, "the Country is filling up rapidly." Certain that they would eventually spread into land north of the Columbia, he begged the officers in London to seek protection from the British government, and asked for power to "take such measures as may appear to us, necessary for the Security of our property, until the question of jurisdiction be settled by treaty." He was astonished at the size and audacity of the group. One early settler said McLoughlin told him, in one of his occasional jests, "The Yankees are here, and the first thing you know they will yoke up their oxen and drive to the mouth of the Columbia and come out at Japan."

Many newcomers were prejudiced against McLoughlin because they had read adverse reports, including those of Hall Kelley and Captain Spaulding. Linn himself had fueled the hostility by an impassioned speech to the Senate.

Covered wagon on flatboat near Beacon Rock on Columbia River. Drawing by Alfred B. Burr.
OHS ORHI 5229

Calling Oregon "our soil," he had accused the Hudson's Bay Company of unfair trading practices, of committing "murder, oppression and every species of inhuman depradations," and of "training on their savage dependants to way lay our wanderers, to burn our settlements, exterminate the Settler."

The immigrants themselves may have brought the copy of the speech that fell into McLoughlin's hands. However it arrived, he was incensed, stormed that "This is a foul calumny," and said no American could call the area "our soil" when both countries had "the same right" to be there. He cited the fact that trappers and missionaries worked safely under his company's protection, and said, "we moreover call upon Dr. Linn for proofs of his sweeping charges, which we are confident he cannot give."

He entertained no illusions about the travelers' beliefs. "They expected when they left the States they would have to fight with us on arriving here," he said, "and to build Forts to protect themselves from the Indians whom we would, they supposed, excite against them." He told the Governor and Committee that one immigrant had stated, "It is true these are good folks and treat me kindly, but somehow or other I cannot like them, and moreover do not like those who like them." And he cited another who, before returning to the States, said his only regret "was that he did not burn Vancouver, as he had left the States with that intention."

The immigrants necessarily camped all along the Oregon Trail, and while most of them found it an ordeal, a few considered it one long picnic. The camps were alike in purpose, but different in detail, being places to rest, have meals, tend the stock, and perhaps do a bit of laundry. OHS ORHI 5231

Regardless of their bias, however, the immigrants were in desperate need, because the problems of the last hundred miles were nearly insurmountable. Some drove their cattle on an Indian trail from The Dalles to Oregon City, swimming them across the Columbia when the south bank became impassable and ferrying them back when they were near Fort Vancouver. Others left their stock at Fort Nez Perces and dared the chutes at The Dalles, where the Columbia was compressed into a "deep, frightful, cavernous channel," through which the water poured "with the velosity of lightning, and the roar of thunder." The majority came down the river, generally by leasing Indian boats or by felling trees to make rafts, on which they placed wagons with the wheels removed. At the Cascades, an impassable stretch for rafts, the early arrivals spent two weeks hacking out an incredibly rough wagon road around the rapids, a path so forbidding that Elizabeth Smith, a pioneer woman, wrote, "I carry my babe and lead, or rather carry another through snow mud and water almost to my knees. It is the worst road a team could possibly travel."

This immigration was the first of several to which McLoughlin gave massive aid, saving many who would otherwise have been lost. Some of the rafts were becalmed, and on one of these waterborne wagons a child was born.

The Columbia River flows through the Cascade mountains, and narrows at this point. Legend says these rapids were formed thousands of years ago by the collapse of a natural bridge over the Columbia. Because this segment of the river was impassable, the early immigrants built a rough wagon road on the north shore of the Columbia. PHOTO BY LEE MOORHOUSE. OHS CN 008374

One group was wind-bound so long on the river that its riders were reduced to eating boiled rawhide. A man who was stranded on his way upriver to aid another party passed the place where he had eaten breakfast a few days before, and there he "searched upon his knees, in the snow, for crumbs that might have fallen, weeping bitterly, and expecting to perish." A letter published in the *Oregon Spectator* said the immigrants experienced far more hardships between The Dalles and the Willamette Valley than in all the rest of the journey combined, and that "many were relieved from perishing by the benevolence of the Hudson's Bay Company."

The ones who managed to reach Fort Vancouver told about those who were stranded upriver, and whenever McLoughlin heard of a group in trouble, he immediately sent out company boats with blankets, food, and room for passengers. Jesse Applegate wrote, "the first full meal my party of 70 had for three weeks was out of the bounty of Dr. McLoughlin." Countless journals and letters contain vivid accounts of this impressive man with his shock of white hair and a tendency to stammer, who bustled back and forth, somewhat testy, but giving generous aid.

As one example, Marguerite's grandson, Dr. William McKay, told about the family of William Beagle, who arrived at the fort penniless, with Beagle himself ill of typhus. McLoughlin ordered McKay, who had recently completed his medical education, to treat the father. He also housed and fed the mother and several children for two months, and when Beagle recovered and asked for his bill, the Chief Factor replied, "Tut, tut, tut! bill, bill, bill! Take care of yourself, sir! That is the bill!" At this Beagle protested that he meant to pay, but McLoughlin again replied, "Tut, tut, tut! You do the best you can for some other man who is in trouble, and that will pay me!" He sent the family to the Willamette, free of charge, and sold them supplies on credit.

A similar story was told by John M. Shively:

> We are all in dirt and rags and have about us some ticking. Company Doctor McGloghlin sent for us to come to the fort. . . . We felt embarrassed in our rags, but this great and good man was so much of a gentleman that he made us feel easy in his presence. . . . After congratulating us on making the trip, he asked each of our names, went to his desk and gave each of us an order to his clerk at the store and told us to go to the store and get what we wanted. You bet we went. I bought a fine suit of clothes from the crown of my head to the sole of my feet, and went to the river, took a bath, put on my fine clothes, burned my buggy rags. Who now but me!

Even when these destitute immigrants were brought downriver, the problem was not solved, because they numbered nearly a thousand, doubling the European population in the Willamette Valley, and they needed food and shelter for the long winter months. Although the missionaries gave what assistance they could, neither they nor the other settlers had resources to care for so many, and it was the Canadian McLoughlin who stepped into the gap, feeding and clothing them, furnishing seed grain and supplies, and treating the sick in the company hospital. Marguerite's role is not on record, but she was the ranking woman at the fort. Letters and journals often refer to her unfailing kindness, and it is beyond belief that in this desperate situation she—along with Amelia Douglas and the other officers' wives —would be idle. It was a crisis, and everybody pitched in.

One newcomer was Peter Burnett, who told of stopping at Fort Nez Perces, where Chief Trader Archibald McKinlay agreed to keep his trail-worn cattle and replace them from Fort Vancouver stock. This spared Burnett the labor of taking them down the Columbia, but when he reached the fort and handed over McKinlay's order, McLoughlin was indignant. As Burnett told it:

Peter Burnett, formerly district attorney in Missouri, came to Oregon in the immigration of 1843. He was instrumental in shaping the Provisional Government, and a loyal friend to McLoughlin. He left Oregon in 1848, went to the California gold mines, and became the first governor of California. OHS ORHI 46162

"Are you aware?" said he to me, "that our Spanish cattle are much inferior to yours?" I told him I thought they were from the specimens I had seen at his place. "And you have learned," continued he, "that cattle may be safely driven from Walla Walla to this post?" I admitted that the success of our emigrants in bringing through their stock, had convinced me of the fact. "Mr. McKinley has done very wrong," said he, shaking his head, "very wrong indeed! Your cattle are superior to those I should be obliged to give you, and you would be much the losers by the arrangement. I will not consent to profit by your reliance on our good faith."

The Chief Factor then sent McKinlay orders to care for the cattle and restore the same animals later, after Burnett had established his residence.

While he was striving to care for the immigrants, McLoughlin had a visitor of a different sort—Lieutenant John Charles Frémont of the U.S. Army. Handsome, dark-eyed, lightly built but sinewy and active, Frémont was on his second exploring expedition, with orders to go as far as the Columbia River and then swing south to California. He said that when he reached Fort Vancouver, McLoughlin received him "with the courtesy and hospitality for which he has been eminently distinguished, and which makes a forcible and delightful impression."

Although he was inundated with immigrants, McLoughlin agreed to furnish the supplies Frémont needed, including cattle, horses, and mules; foodstuffs such as flour, peas, and tallow; and a large boat, two canoes, and enough men to transport the goods to the Americans' camp at The Dalles. Because the lieutenant was unable to pay in cash, McLoughlin accepted U.S. govern-

Methodist mission at The Dalles. Jason Lee's first and strongest branch mission was here, headed by his nephew the Reverend Daniel Lee. After the Mission Board in New York disbanded the mission, the establishment at The Dalles was transferred to the American Board of the Presbyterian Church, under Dr. Marcus Whitman of Waiilatpu. This lithograph is from Maj. Osborne Cross's 1850 *Report*. OHS ORHI 58874

ment vouchers for a bill that eventually came to more than two thousand dollars, including goods obtained from Forts Boise and Nez Perces. He invited the American to stay at Vancouver as a guest, but after two days Frémont left, with his boatloads of supplies. In one important way, he was different from many other visitors: his report was not critical of the British or McLoughlin, but spoke only of his kindness and generosity.

In that fall, while the settlers were arriving, Mt. St. Helens put forth a spectacular eruption—one of several during the 1840s and 1850s. The Reverend Daniel Lee, who observed it from the Dalles mission, said, "Ashes were falling with a mist-like appearance, coating the leaves, fences and stones with a gritty substance like hoar frost." Another missionary, the Reverend J. L. Parrish, described rolling clouds of black smoke, and reported that red-hot lava poured down the mountainside into the Cowlitz River, killing the fish.

Dramatic as the scene was, few settlers mentioned it in their journals and letters, probably because their main preoccupation was the elemental need to survive the winter. McLoughlin gave them massive aid. In previous years he had made loans of only two or three pounds sterling at a time, with no second advances until the first were paid off. But in the fall of 1843 the needs were so great that he issued quantities of goods with neither payment nor security. By the following spring, he had advanced a total of £6,606 to more than three hundred immigrants, which Sir George Simpson called "an enormous sum, a large portion of which, I fear, will turn out a bad debt." The Governor and Committee, being distant and unable to conceive the extent of the newcomers' misery, were displeased. Secretary Barclay crisply informed Mc-Loughlin that they disapproved of "so lax a system of credit," and that it "should be gradually discontinued, and one of prompt payment, either in cash or goods, substituted."

The Chief Factor, however, was convinced that lenience was not merely kind, but also the wisest course—the only sensible course—because many of the Americans were vigorous young frontiersmen who would not sit idly by while their families starved and lifesaving supplies were locked up in the fort. He told the Governor and Committee, "if I had acted Differently to what I had and refused assistance to the first Immigrants, Vancouver would have been taken and the Companys property in it and the Companys Business in the Department Destroyed and for which Robbery and Outrage the Company would never have recovered a farthing of Indemnification."

In addition, being a merchant with ever an eye to profits, he said the influx "will cause a great increase of business in the place & which we can in the main Secure if we have the means of supplying the wants of the settlers and can procure a market for their produce." The newcomers were active, resourceful, and bent on progress. James Douglas wryly said that "the restless Americans are brooding over a thousand projects, for improving the navigation, building steam Boats, erecting machinery and other schemes that would excite a smile, if entertained by a less enterprising people, with the same slender means."

Another of McLoughlin's responsibilities became more difficult that winter—acting as a buffer between settlers and Indians, who, in spite of Elijah White's efforts to reassure them, resented the growing number of whites. By 1842 the Nez Perces at the Lapwai mission had pulled down Spalding's mill and assaulted him with a gun, while the Cayuses at Waiilatpu had plucked Marcus Whitman's beard, threatened to destroy his house, and tried to strike him with an axe.

The missionaries, moreover, were at loggerheads among themselves, and therefore, in November 1842, Whitman left for the States to ask his board for advice and support. While he was away, a renegade tribesman forced himself into Narcissa's bedroom. He was driven away by "John," a Sandwich Islander staying in the house, but it frightened Narcissa so severely that she took refuge for the winter in the Methodist mission at The Dalles. Even when Whitman returned in the following year, the situation did not improve, because he was helping guide the immigrant train—a betrayal, in the eyes of the Cayuses.

The growing tension alarmed McLoughlin. In a document found among his private papers after his death, he said he had prevented an Indian attack in the fall of 1843, when the first canoes brought the immigrants to the fort. As they drew near, he noticed an unnatural excitement among the natives on the shore. His manuscript continues:

> One of them bawled out to his companions, "It is good for us to kill these Bostons." Struck with the excitement I had seen in the countenances of the Indians since they had heard the report of the immigration coming, I felt certain they were inclined to mischief, and that he spoke thus loud as a feeler to sound me . . . I immediately rushed on them with my cane, calling out at the same time, "Who is the dog that says it is a good thing to kill the Bostons." The fellow, trembling, excused himself, "I spoke without meaning harm, but the Dalles Indians say so." "Well," said I, "The Dalles Indians are dogs for saying so, and you also," and left him. . . . I had done enough to convince them I would not allow them to do wrong to the immigrants with impunity.

The incident was corroborated by Francis Xavier Matthieu, who said the doctor heard them plotting, "raised his cane and threatened condign punishment," causing the Indians to scatter and give up their "evil plan."

The year this occurred, 1843, was a landmark. In spring the settlers decided to have their own government. In summer they gave it form, a primitive form but nevertheless a definite system, accepted by popular vote, with officers, laws—and a somewhat wobbly prognosis. Finally, in autumn, the settlement reeled from its first great surge of population.

It was of enormous significance to McLoughlin, for it gave the American settlers a decisive majority and further weakened the power of the French

Canadians. He still had strong influence with the Indians, and he was still un-challenged on the north bank of the Columbia. But within the settlement, even within his town beside the falls, he must accept a smaller role.

~6~

The Oregon City Land Claim
1829–1844

B eginning in 1841, McLoughlin was caught up in a struggle over the land claim at Oregon City. It was a complex problem that must be discussed in some detail, because that property became his home and place of business during the last decade of his life and was the basis for his final, crushing defeat.

His first visit to the falls of the Willamette is not on record, but he had been interested in them from his earliest years on the Columbia. They were spectacular, a roaring, foaming cataract over immense gray rocks. One valuable feature was a rocky island of four to five acres in low water and two or three acres in ordinary high water, conveniently close to the east bank, where it would be of immense help in developing the water power.

In 1829, when McLoughlin took George Simpson to see it, they decided to claim the waterfall and island by building a sawmill. However, after the wreck of the *William and Ann* and the subsequent trouble with natives of the coast, the Chief Factor built his mill near Fort Vancouver, on a creek flowing into the Columbia. He did not abandon Willamette Falls, but "had a party residing there the whole winter, they built three Log Houses & prepared the wood for a Saw Mill . . . and in the Spring of 1830 had potatoes planted there." At that time there was no doubt as to who was claiming the land. George Simpson said later that they had decided "to take possession of part of this waterfall for the Company."

They could not file a claim, however, because under joint occupation all land was held merely by the settlers' unwritten agreement to honor the rights of the first person on the premises. Even after formation of the provisional government, its laws were a stopgap, to function until one nation or the other took possession. No land titles in the Pacific Northwest would be legal until enactment of the Donation Land Law in 1850.

McLoughlin was not blind to the value of the falls. Saying they were "destined by nature to be the most important place in this country," he con-

To fishermen Willamette Falls was a lucrative spot, blessed with runs of salmon who had
come up the Columbia and Willamette Rivers, to spawn in their home streams. Here, as
at Celilo Falls near The Dalles, the Indians stood on wooden platforms over the falls, and
fished with dip nets on long poles. This was a major source of food. Above, the lithograph
"Willamette Falls" from *Narrative of the United States Exploring Expedition* by Charles
Wilkes (OHS ORHI 86385) and opposite, a ca. 1841 sketch by Joseph Drayton for the Wilkes
expedition. OHS ORHI 968

tinued his activity there, having his men fish, cut timber, and plant small
plots. Nathaniel Wyeth noted in 1832 that "the H. B. Co. are erecting a saw
mill to which they contemplate adding a grist mill." In the same year, Eugene
Duflot de Mofras noticed that the company had "a little wooden house, kept
by one man," at the falls. And McLoughlin said, "In 1832 I had the Mill race
blasted and in the Spring of 1838 I got all the squared timber hauled to the
spot, and a small building erected to serve as a house & store."

Two years later Jason Lee acknowledged the claim. Shortly after the *Lausanne* brought the load of recruits, he decided to start a branch at the falls,
and asked McLoughlin for permission to use company land. Since some
squared timber was lying on the ground, he also asked to borrow part of that
for the house, and McLoughlin not only agreed, he sent Dr. William F.
Tolmie to point out the exact site where Lee might build. The Chief Factor
was willing to help the mission, but he was canny enough to protect his own
claim, so he wrote:

Vancouver, 21st July, 1840

To the Rev'd Jason Lee.

Dear Sir:

Yesterday I was informed that You intend to establish a Mission
at the Falls of the Wallamette. I beg to inform You that in 1830, as is
well known to most of the old Settlers in the Wallamette, I took possession of the side of the Falls on which I got a Mill race blasted,
from the upper end of the Falls across to the Clackamas River and
down to where the Clackamas falls into the Wallamette including the
whole point of land and the small Island in the Falls on which the
portage is made and which I intend to claim when the Boundary line
is drawn. . . .

Private P.S. Of course this is not to prevent Your building the Store,
as my object is merely to establish my claim.

Having been warned, and presumably agreeing to the terms, Lee erected
the building with company wood on company land. Later that summer, in "an
evil moment for McLoughlin," he sent Reverend Alvan F. Waller, who had

The Reverend A.F. Waller came to Oregon in 1840 with the Great Reinforcement. At that time, Lee assigned him to lead a mission at the falls of the Willamette River, and it was Waller who set off the furor over McLoughlin's land claim there. In other respects, Waller was successful. After the missions were disbanded, the Methodist church maintained congregations in the area and operated the Oregon Institute. Waller was a member of its Board of Trustees. OHS ORHI 391

come on the *Lausanne*, to establish a mission branch at the falls and set up a small trading post, stocked with goods brought on the ship.

For the next year, the missionaries and men of the Hudson's Bay Company lived side by side and at peace. In 1841 Lieutenant Wilkes noted that the company had a trading post, salmon fishery, packing plant, and millrace, which they had blasted at "considerable expense." The fuzzy legal situation, however, was about to become a major problem, because the land was being claimed by the Hudson's Bay Company. This was acceptable in Britain, and under the convention of joint occupation the rights of both nations were to be retained. But according to laws of the United States, a corporation could not hold land by preemption—that is, by occupation in order to establish a title.

The first trouble arose in 1841, when a mission employee named Felix Hathaway built a house on the island without permission. As soon as McLoughlin heard of it, he "gave him formal notice" of the company's prior claim, and himself put up a small building there. Hathaway "desisted," but a group of mission employees immediately organized the Island Milling Company with multiple owners, three-quarters of whom were from the mission. Disregarding the doctor's claim, this company built a sawmill on the island, in the belief that when the boundary was settled and American law prevailed, the Hudson's Bay Company could not establish title.

The British objected, because they thought all claims would be honored, according to the laws of both countries. In that year, when Sir George Simpson came to Fort Vancouver and learned what was happening, he wrote a sarcastic report about missionaries who attend "more to temporal than spiritual affairs,

& exercise good judgment in reference to commerce." He told the Governor and Committee that a company ship was bringing machinery from England to be used at the falls, "and to that end, C. F. [Chief Factor] Douglas has been instructed to recover entire possession of the scite originally occupied by the Company."

At that time, McLoughlin and the company officers agreed that they must hold the land at the falls. Simpson told McLoughlin to vigorously oppose the Methodists and to erect the sawmill, install the machinery, and operate it—a directive the Chief Factor was happy to follow. He did not, however, oust Waller and the milling company, because, he later said, "I could not believe that persons calling themselves Ministers of the Gospel would do what their countrymen of the most humble station in life having the least regard for right would condemn."

Although Waller was quiet during the summer of 1842, he wrote a letter to his brother deriding McLoughlin's position.

> The Hudson's Bay Company seem determined to monopolize everything as long as possible. . . . They made a claim at the falls, on the side where I now am, about twelve years since by digging a short mill-race, hewing a quantity of timber, and so forth,—a few years since they put up a small house, and covered it with bark. Last fall an American took possession of a small island in the Falls; but no sooner was it known at Fort Vancouver than a company of men was sent off with boards to put up a hut, and soon the governor of the Fort came up, greatly incensed, called the man a pilferer, and any thing but good; he however went on.

McLoughlin received a further indication of trouble in the fall of 1842, when Stephen H. L. Meek, Joe Meek's brother, wanted to build a house in Oregon City. "I told him to select a lot," McLoughlin said. "He accordingly went to the Falls but returned in a few days to tell me that Mr. Waller had opposed his making a selection & had told him that he was much obliged to me for giving away Lots in his Claim." Alarmed at last, McLoughlin asked the Reverend Jason Lee to intercede.

Lee's loyalty, however, was split. He knew the Hudson's Bay Company had been there first, that British subjects and American citizens had equal rights, and that to the land-hungry colonists, jumping a claim was a serious offense. But he sympathized with his friends at the mission. He replied that he had talked the problem over with Waller, who would not make a claim unless the area became American and the government refused ownership to a British citizen. In that case, Lee said, Waller "considered that he had a better right than *any other* man, and should secure a title if he could." And then Lee masterfully straddled the issue. "From what I have since heard, I am inclined to think I did not understand Mr. Waller correctly, but I am not certain it is so . . . I had not the most distant idea when I stationed Mr. Waller there that he would set up a private claim to the Land." He suggested that McLoughlin confer directly with Waller, and ended with the pious hope that "a mutual understanding will produce mutual satisfaction."

Since the Chief Factor was at the falls when he received Lee's letter, he met with Waller, who assured him he was not making a counterclaim, but merely wished to retain the land he had cleared. He said that since he had given away some lots, he wanted to allow the recipients to keep them, and McLoughlin consented with one proviso: that he should receive an equal amount of land from Waller's adjoining claim. Waller first agreed—then backtracked, saying "I will keep mine, keep you yours"—and then changed his mind again, agreeing to make the exchange after all.

During that fall of 1842, as has been shown, McLoughlin hired Lansford W. Hastings to defend the land claim and had J. M. Hudspeth lay out Oregon City. In the following spring, amid the hammering and sawing of rapid construction, Hastings supposedly settled the dispute by paying Waller twenty-five dollars for having cleared a piece of land "on the west side of middle or main street." A deal with Waller, however, was build on sand. Before long, he demanded one hundred dollars for clearing the east side of the road, and again McLoughlin agreed, although Jason Lee, acting as agent, considered the amount so exorbitant that he would accept only half of it. McLoughlin then posted a notice "in the most public place in this town" offering written deeds to all who had bought land from him, or received it as a gift.

By this time McLoughlin was decidedly uneasy, and found himself in a dilemma. His duty was to his company, but it might be legally unable to hold title to the land, and he did not want to lose it altogether. In March 1843 he wrote a puzzled note to Simpson:

> In acting as I have done, I have only been actuated by a desire to
> secure it more effectually to the concern and to have less disputes
> about it, as I think it can be more effectually secured in the name of
> an individual than in that of the Company, and I wish to know
> Can the Company secure this place in their own name?

If they cannot, can I secure it for them in my name? If either of these can be done, I will do it at once. If the Company cannot keep it in their name, nor I cannot keep it for them in mine, I will then keep it in my own name on my own account. In the meantime till I hear from you, I will go on as if it was mine.

The intricate question stumped Sir George. He referred it to Adam Thom, Recorder of Rupert's Land, who produced a meticulously correct exposition saying, "the legal capacity of that body to hold in any way the real property aforesaid must depend on the code of the new territory, which whether it may proceed from the National Congress, or from a local legislature or from both, has not as yet any existence." In other words, the question could be answered only after the boundary settlement had been made and the new government took the helm. Although the answer was legally impeccable, it did not tell McLoughlin what the company wanted him to do, and he querulously complained, "As to the Falls of the Wallamette, I really do not understand Mr. Thoms opinion." He was not the only baffled one. Douglas called the opinion "as vague and mysterious as the oracles of Delphi," while the Governor and Committee ignored it, leaving McLoughlin on his own.

During that spring, the settlers created the provisional government and adopted the land law that—if upheld—would prevent both McLoughlin and his company from claiming townsites or "extensive Water Privileges." In May 1843, Hastings set out for California, and in the fall another lawyer, John Ricord, came with the immigration. After becoming Lee's attorney, Ricord offered McLoughlin a proposal for what he called "an amicable arrangement" to settle the land claim. Its terms, however, would transfer so much of it to Waller, Lee, and the Island Milling Company that McLoughlin declined, with a wry comment that it "appeared to propose an amicable arrangement in which all the sacrifices were to be made by me."

By then Lee and his mission were in serious trouble. The ministers at the branch missions as well as his own staff—in uncomfortable posts, frustrated, jealous—had sent numerous complaints to the Mission Board about his reports, expenses, and relationships with colleagues. Knowing of these complaints, in December 1843 Lee sailed in a company ship to the Sandwich Islands, and from there he went to the East Coast of the United States in order to confer with his superiors in New York and defend his own stewardship.

While he was in Oregon, he had posed as McLoughlin's friend, but in the East he visited Washington, D.C., and recorded Waller's land claim. "Please tell

Bro. Waller that his claim is filed in the Office of the Commissioner General of the land office," he wrote to Gustavus Hines. "This will probably secure it to him." From Washington he went to New York for extensive meetings with the Mission Board, then visited his family home in Canada, and while there, on March 12, 1845, he died unexpectedly from a respiratory ailment.

Ricord had left Oregon, on the same ship as Lee, but before sailing, he had written a lengthy anti-McLoughlin proclamation, which was publicly posted in Oregon City after his departure. Completely disregarding McLoughlin's early claim—his buildings, mill, crops, fishery, and production of timber—it said Waller had taken possession in 1840; that his was the prior claim; that he had raised crops until December 1842, when McLoughlin had Waller's land surveyed "for the purpose of setting it in subdivisions to American Citizens"; and that Waller was not at that moment cultivating his farm because "it was wrested from him." Ricord cited—correctly—the fact that the doctor did not live on the land, but he ignored the provisional government's law that permitted the use of agents in residence, a condition McLoughlin had met. Ricord said without basis that American law forbade a Canadian subject to claim land by preemption. And he warned settlers against buying lots from McLoughlin, saying the doctor had no legal right to issue a deed. The document, which was long and pretentious, stimulated interest in the controversy, but it was so obviously false that it had little permanent effect.

It did, however, further emphasize the dubious status of the claim, because one section said, "The Hudsons Bay Company a Foreign Corporation, is in fact the claimant while Dr. McLoughlin only lends his name well knowing, that a corporation . . . cannot acquire a preemption."

Faced with this direct challenge, and receiving little help from his superiors, McLoughlin decided that the best way to keep the land was to place it in his own name, and in March 1844 he wrote a long statement in which he reviewed the entire controversy and quoted many documents. Referring to ownership, he said, "I am not claiming the Land for the Hudsons Bay Company but for myself. . . . There are many people here who can swear that since 1829/30 I have repeatedly spoken to them of the Falls of the Wallamette as being my claim." The accuracy of this was obviously open to doubt.

Nevertheless, his fellow officers accepted it, and James Douglas explained to Simpson that "the site at Wallamette Falls . . . is held in Mr. McLoughlins own name, as the Company's right would not be respected one moment. The people here are well aware that the claim of an English Corporate Body to lands in the Wallamatte, would not be established in the American Courts, and it is clearly imprudent in the Company to engage in any land speculation south of the Columbia."

Sir George Simpson went a bit further. He told McLoughlin he was not "prepared to sanction any expenditure" at the falls, and he washed his hands of the affair by placing all costs—for erecting mills and securing legal advice—in a "John McLoughlin Suspense account." It was his opinion that the only way the company could secure title was to persuade the British government to have a special clause inserted in the boundary settlement, when that day came.

In the spring of 1844, four months after Ricord left, Dr. Elijah White, the American agent for Indian affairs, heard about the situation. White, who genuinely liked McLoughlin, suggested that since he was going to the falls, he would speak to Waller and try to arrange an arbitration. When McLoughlin agreed, White set up a meeting of the Chief Factor, Waller, the Reverend David Leslie (acting head of the mission), and three others—Douglas, White himself, and Major W. Gilpin, a former officer in the U.S. Army. In this meeting, McLoughlin bought out Waller's claim. As the Chief Factor explained it:

> After they had a good deal of discussion . . . I consented to give five acres & five hundred dollars to Mr. Waller, and 14 Lots to the Methodist Mission . . . I found them [the terms] so exorbitant I said, "Gentlemen you have bound me". "No, No," says Mr. Gilpin, "Well" said I "Mr. James (alluding to Mr. Douglas) this is your doings: "Yes", says he, "I think for your sake, it is better to give you one good fever and have done with it". I acceded to the terms & signed the papers.

This transaction was definite and clear. If by any chance a future government honored Waller's claim, McLoughlin had bought it and paid Waller for it, in a signed and witnessed deed.

Nevertheless, White was still troubled, and he wrote to T. Hartley Crawford, commissioner of Indian affairs, that "had any gentleman disconnected with the Hudson's Bay Company been at half the pains and expense to establish a claim at the Willamette falls, very few would have raised an opposition." Similarly, he told Secretary of War J. M. Porter, "I hope . . . his claim will be honored in such a manner as to make him conscious that we, as a nation, are not insensitive to his numerous acts of benevolence and hospitality to our countrymen."

Shortly after that, Waller left the Willamette to take charge of the Methodist branch at The Dalles. The mission itself had never contested the claim, and with Waller gone, the controversy ceased, although the Island Milling Company continued to operate its gristmill.

Even before Lee went to New York, the Mission Board—alerted by his assistants' complaints—had sent the Reverend George Gary to Oregon to liquidate the organization there. Gary arrived in early 1844, and within a few days he confronted McLoughlin with a fresh demand. As the doctor glumly reported to the Governor and Committee, the missionary "offered to sell me the Lots in Oregon City now occupied by the Methodist Mission & . . . wished to know what I would give for them. I replied that I let the Methodist Mission have them in the first instance . . . the fairest way would be for the mission to return me my Lots & I would pay them for their improvements." But Gary refused, saying he considered the lots as mission property.

In the end, McLoughlin paid $5,400—apparently a reduction from $6,000—for all the mission lots and buildings within Oregon City, even though he had given them the land. It grieved him that "the first violation of the rights of another in this Country is committed by a Minister of the Gospel," and he thought that as a result of the long struggle, the Methodist mission had "lost all influence in the Country."

Whether or not that was true, there was no doubt that McLoughlin had legally bought Waller's claim and all the mission property in Oregon City, paying for them with company money and acquiring undisputed ownership. However, a knotty problem was left: American strength was growing, and when the boundary was decided, the south bank of the Columbia would almost certainly fall to the United States. Would the McLoughlin-Hudson's Bay Company claim be honored under American law?

CHAPTER 11

The Fall

*I trust when the truth is known, it will be found
that I have acted with as much zeal as if my life
had been at stake, and justice will be done me.*

DR. JOHN MCLOUGHLIN

~ 1 ~

On His Own
1844–1845

In 1844, while McLoughlin and the mission were locking horns over the Oregon City land claim, the French Canadians decided to issue another political statement. Sometime during that winter and spring, probably with McLoughlin's blessing and possibly with his active help, they conferred with their priest, Father Louis Langlois, and worked it out.

Their declaration of the year before—which has disappeared—had opposed the provisional government, but after the immigration of 1843, they realized they were outnumbered and must cooperate. Their second statement therefore expressed a wish for laws, an assurance that they did not "intend to rebel," and a shrewd list of engagingly candid conditions on which they would support the new regime: They would not sign a petition to Congress until the boundary was settled. They did not approve of the present land laws. They considered the existing government "too self-interested . . . overloading the colony instead of improving it." They wanted laws limited, because the more there were, "the more opportunity for knavery on the part of lawyers." They wanted the government small, because "the more men employed and paid by the public, the less remains of industry." And they concurred with people everywhere that all laws "burthensome and oppressive . . . must be avoided. Such are imposts, useless taxes, all kinds of registration."

Father Langlois, who had "drawn out" the paper, presented it to a general but poorly attended meeting at Champoeg on March 4, 1844. Although little information has survived, it is known that the settlers agreed to accept the paper and that the Canadians voted in the next election.

In his report to the Governor and Committee, McLoughlin explained that in 1843 the Canadians had refused to join the government, but this year, "seeing the increasing number of Americans, and that it would be impossible to maintain peace and order in the Country without organizing themselves," they consented. He acknowledged his part in their decision, saying the Americans and British "had hitherto lived in the Country in a peaceable manner," each according to its own customs, but now the growing population made it "absolutely necessary to organize." As an example of potential trouble, he told of an immigrant who publicly confessed that he had "belonged to a band of Robbers in the State of Arks-ans-as" and that several of his former band were also in the area. It was because of this man and others like him, McLoughlin said, that "I no longer opposed the organization,—and the Canadians joined it."

At this time a wave of nationalism was sweeping the United States, where expansionists were casting hungry eyes not only on Oregon, but also on Texas and northern Mexico—today's California. In 1844 the Democratic party, insisting that America's title to the entire Northwest was "clear and unquestionable," trumpeted the slogan "54-40 or fight"—a demand for a boundary at 54 degrees, 40 minutes of latitude. It was popular, but so extreme that it was never a likely prospect. The real question was whether the line could be held at the forty-ninth parallel, and James K. Polk became president on the promise to annex Texas and establish American ownership of Oregon.

"Manifest Destiny"—the inevitable spread of the United States from the Atlantic to the Pacific—had become a popular cry, with its vision of one nation stretching across mountains and deserts. Although Britain and America both claimed discovery of the Columbia, thoughtful citizens of each country knew that population would probably outweigh historical precedent in setting the boundary. Secretary of State John C. Calhoun said, "Let us encourage emigration . . . and let the West send off its swarms; fill Oregon with our citizens, and it will become ours as certainly as a ripe peach drops to the ground in autumn." James Douglas voiced the same opinion when he wrote to the Governor and Committee, "I am sorry to hear that the Settlement of the Boundary question is likely to drag on, from year to year . . . as the Americans will soon leave nothing to settle."

Politicians then were cut from the same cloth as politicians today—and Manifest Destiny was a bountiful subject for speeches, letters and papers, of which quantities poured forth. The correspondence and journals of the immigrants themselves, however, show that while some of those who made the cross-country trek were moved by patriotism, most were mainly concerned with their own affairs.

These were as varied as the people themselves. The lure of adventure was one factor often cited by immigrants, as when Jesse Applegate wrote, "But for myself and those of my class I claim no higher motive for coming here than the inherent restlessness of our nature." Some had already emigrated several times. Robert Moore, who became prominent in the formation of the pioneer government, had previously moved from Pennsylvania to Missouri and from there to Illinois.

Many had a double motive. The pioneer Lucy Ann Henderson Deady said, "Most of the immigrants were going to Oregon to secure free land, yet there was a strong political feeling, and some of the men had painted different mottoes on their canvas wagon sheets, such as '54-40—All or None.'" R. W. Morrison, who came in 1844, said in one document that he came to Oregon chiefly to save it from the British, but in another he admitted that in Missouri "I am compelled to sell all I can make every year, in order to make ends meet," and he was therefore going west.

And Peter Burnett wrote that while living in Missouri, "I saw that a great American community would grow up, in the space of a few years, upon the shores of the distant Pacific, and I felt an ardent drive to aid in this most important enterprise." But he also remembered that he was greatly in debt with no chance of reducing it, that his wife was ill, and that in the fall of 1842, when he read the Linn bill with its offer of land, he felt a surge of hope. "If Dr. Linn's bill should pass, the land would ultimately enable me to pay up," he said. "In staying where I was, I saw no reasonable probability of ever being able to pay my debts. . . . Putting all these considerations together, I determined . . . to move to Oregon."

These and other records show that the settlers' overriding motive was the desire for space—a chance to start over. To leave a checkered past. Elude their creditors. Build a new life. Seize the brass ring. They came for land, deep and rich, waiting for their plows. It was significant that after Senator Linn's promise of free land, the immigration of 1843 made a sevenfold increase from the one of the year before, and that streams of immigrants continued to pour in long after the boundary had been set, so that Oregon's nationality was no longer in doubt.

McLoughlin, well aware that a yeasty mix was gathering, treated the settlers with caution. "In this Country I have always found it best to be watchful without appearing to be so," he wrote to the Governor and Committee. Realizing that the boundary was a sensitive issue, he avoided discussing it, "merely telling those who spoke to us on the subject that I did not understand the merits of the case But as it was an affair that would be settled without asking my opinion and still less my consent I did not trouble my head about it."

In November 1844, aware that his men were outnumbered and might be in actual danger, he warned Sir J. H. Pelly, governor of the company, that on the Columbia there was "no prospect of forming a British party sufficiently strong to take the lead in the country." The immigrants, he said, included "many upright respectable men, yet there are many of a different character." And he believed that unless the boundary could be decided soon, the Americans "will declare themselves an independent state, and if a few more of their countrymen get into California and make their footing good north of the Bay of San Francisco, they will unite with those."

In the previous November, McLoughlin had asked his company to obtain official protection from the British government, and on July 15, 1844, he thought his plea had been answered when the eighteen-gun sloop HMS *Modeste* sailed up the river under Captain Thomas Baillie. Pleased by "the appearance at this place of a British Man of War," McLoughlin had James Douglas take Baillie and his officers on a tour of the Willamette Valley, to brief them on the situation there. But it was a disappointment, because the visitors were courteous and agreeable but "had more taste for a lark than for a 'musty' lecture on politics or the great national interests in question." Like McLoughlin, Douglas was profoundly disturbed by British lethargy. He told Simpson that while the Americans were "pouring petition after petition into the hands of their government . . . we are doing nothing; British feeling is dying away so much, that Englishmen, in the Wallamette, are either afraid or ashamed to own their country."

Welcome as the *Modeste* was, she did not stay in Oregon for long. McLoughlin supplied her crew with beef, vegetables, and "several articles of sea store not to be procured at Oahu," and agreed to furnish future supplies if given advance notice. Captain Baillie then sailed away, leaving the Chief Factor as vulnerable as before.

Soon after that, in early fall, a searing wind blew for days from the parched lands of eastern Oregon, making the air so dry that 6,061 pounds of beaver skins stored at Fort Vancouver, shrank to 5,548—a costly loss, although McLoughlin hoped they "would regain their weight on the voyage home." In late September, with the air still dry, the nearby forests caught fire, and a hot blaze swept westward, threatening Fort Vancouver itself. The barn was "almost instantly wrapped in flames, the clover field caught fire, the fence [of wooden rails] burnt fiercely, the orchard was in a blaze, and for upwards of an hour the Establishment was menaced with apparently inevitable destruction." Everyone toiled until, after "immense exertion," the workers arrested the fire within a scant three hundred feet of the stockade.

Although the resulting loss was heavy, McLoughlin reported that it would not interfere with company business, and "when we consider the great danger to which our property was exposed, we have every reason to be grateful to Providence for being merciful to us." Human nature has not changed. Two men "took advantage of the moment when we were all busily engaged with the fire, to rifle several of the Gentlemen's rooms; and afterwards broke into the Depense and got brutally drunk." McLoughlin had them imprisoned, and punished "as their conduct deserved."

After the fire he ordered a fire engine, an advanced piece of machinery for its time, "capable of discharging from 80 to 100 gallons per minute by 18 or 20 men, with mahogany cistern and Cast Iron wheels . . . copper rivetted leather hose 40 feet each with brass screws a moveable Copper Strainer 2 wrenches & Straps," at a cost of £138. Before delivery, a copper cistern was substituted for the wooden one.

Late in the fall of 1844 a still larger immigration arrived, numbering twelve hundred persons. They were somewhat less prejudiced than those of the previous year, because earlier arrivals had sent back word that the malicious anti-Hudson's Bay accusations were not true. Even so, many of the newcomers were edgy. The following spring, in March 1845, McLoughlin wrote, "In the Month of January last some Americans seeing us repair our pickets erect a bastion, our Blacksmiths making small Axes for the Indian Trade, spread a report among their Countrymen that we were fortifying the Fort and making axes to set the Indians against the Americans, which excited alarm among the Immigrants of 1844, but the old residents told them, they were mistaken, and dispelled their aprehensions."

Again the wayfarers were in distress. John Minto, one of three who came ahead on horses to seek help, took a boatload of provisions to the Cascades, where he said he found "men in the prime of life lying among the rocks seeming ready to die. . . . There was scarcely a dry day, and the snow-line was nearly down to the river."

And McLoughlin, as before, shouldered the major burden of rescue. One man, Joseph Watt, said his people were brought to Fort Vancouver by "Mr. Hess" in a company boat. "We had eaten the last of our provisions at our last camp, and were told by Hess that we could get plenty at the fort, with or without money;—that the old Doctor never turned people away hungry." He said that when they reached the fort, McLoughlin sat at a small table and offered to supply the immigrants' needs, while they stood in a line extending nearly around the room. He asked each man what his family required, wrote out orders for supplies, and said they could settle their accounts by delivering wheat to the fort after they were established.

John Minto's "Reminiscences" showed, as did other accounts, the Chief Factor's odd mannerism of repeating words or phrases. As Minto described it, "Doctor McLoughlin was on the porch or stoop, of the residence building, and beckoned us to him. He asked if we were the young men who had applied for a boat to assist our friends down the river. We replied we were. He said, 'Young men, young men—I advise you, if you can, take your boat above the cascades and bring all the people down to the cascades—not your own friends only, and I'll see—I'll see they are brought from there.'"

Anticipating this influx, McLoughlin had made a special effort to raise extra food and seed, and had urged the farmers of the valley to do the same. But still the arrival of so many strained the area's resources. Although nobody was starving, supplies such as clothing were impossible to obtain at any price, and Peter Burnett wrote, "At any public gathering it was easy to distinguish the new from the old settlers. . . . They were dressed in broadcloth, and wore linen bosomed shirts and black cravats, while we wore very coarse, patched clothes; for the art of patching was understood to perfection in Oregon. But, while they dressed better than we did, we fed better than they."

In December 1844, McLoughlin extended help to the provisional government by donating land for a jail—"all that point [in Oregon City] laying between fourth and fifth Cross street between Water street and the River for the purpose you Request—and to Revert to me when not used as a Gaol." The building was financed with money from the Ewing Young estate, three payments totaling $875 being made to P. W. Dawson, Contractor, "for services rendered in constructing a publick jail," plus one payment of $150 from the Treasury of Oregon. The structure, however, saw little if any use, for it apparently burned within a few months.

In February 1845, McLoughlin saw a graphic example of his company's vulnerability when two young Americans, Henry Williamson and Isaac Alderman, put up a log hut within half a mile of Fort Vancouver and nailed a placard "upon an adjoining tree." It quoted an old rhyme:

Feby 15th 1845

Meddle not with this house or claim
For under is the Master's name.

Henry Williamson

This was a significant incursion onto Hudson's Bay land. "We must keep in mind," McLoughlin said, "that these men are animated with strong nation-

Gustavus Sohon made this drawing of Fort Vancouver in 1854 while on a surveying expedition to look for a railroad route from the Mississippi to the Pacific. This sketch shows the orchards and the lush gardens that McLoughlin helped to create around the fort. OHS ORHI 4287

al feelings and strongly opposed to British interests, and that the conduct of a few like Williamson might lead to very serious and important consequences." He sent a party to tear down the cabin and remove the sign, at which the two stormed over to Fort Vancouver to argue their case with the doctor himself.

Fortunately, said McLoughlin, "Dr. White . . . the Revd. Mr. Hines, Mr. Pettygrove, and several other American Gentleman, chanced to be here on business, and were present during Williamson's interview with me, as they heard every thing that passed." This included a threat "to burn the finest building in Oregon"—meaning the fort—and the young man's boast that "he was perfectly fearless about the consequences."

When the interview ended with no solution, McLoughlin sent a report to the three-man executive committee of the provisional government—William Bailey, Osborne Russel, and P. G. Stuart—asking them to remove Williamson from the company premises "in order that the unanimity now happily subsisting between the American Citizens and British subjects . . . may not be disturbed or interrupted." He and Douglas also sent a circular to the citizens of Oregon reminding them that the Hudson's Bay Company was there under a lawful treaty, that its presence protected both British and Americans, and that its men wanted to maintain harmony but would not allow their rights to be infringed upon. As McLoughlin had hoped, the trespassers withdrew, after which the committee expressed regrets and thanked him for his amicable cooperation.

By then it was nearly a year and a half since McLoughlin had asked his company for help, and when the reply finally came, it was a disappointment. Instead of offering governmental aid, Secretary Barclay merely said, "No such protection can be obtained in the existing state of the Boundary Question, of which there is little prospect of an early settlement. You must therefore make use of the best means within your power for the preservation of the Company's rights."

This was alarming, for McLoughlin had at most two hundred men at the fort, while there were several times as many settlers. He therefore recounted the Williamson incident to William Miller, the British consul general at Honolulu, and said, "I would also take the liberty of recommending, in the strongest terms, the propriety of a Government Vessel being sent to this River, for the protection of British Interests" until the boundary was settled.

But again no help appeared. Miller merely wrote that he had "given due consideration" to McLoughlin's letter, and "had a conversation with Sir Thomas Thompson the Senior Naval Officer amongst these Islands" about sending a ship of war. He gave no indication of Thompson's reply or what action, if any, might be taken. McLoughlin was on his own.

~ 2 ~

Yerba Buena
1841–1845

During the early 1840s, while immigrants were spreading into the Willamette Valley, McLoughlin's son-in-law William Glen Rae was in charge of the Hudson's Bay post in California. Eloisa was there too, living with her husband in the company house on San Francisco Bay. She liked it.

> I found everything nice in San Francisco in the Winter. The flowers covering the hills. . . . We had a great many parties there. You know the Spanish ladies were there a great many of them. They were very sociable there. They gave parties; and of course we went to see them;

and when friends of ours came we gave little parties too and of course we invited them to come. I went across the bay once to a wedding when Captain Hinckly was married. . . . It was quite a large wedding. They danced three nights and then they had bull fights. The first time I ever saw bull fights—everyday. . . . The place was very small at that time. They never called it San Francisco in those days; it was "Yerba Buena" all the time.

Matters in California, however, were less idyllic than Eloisa thought, partly because Yerba Buena had unusual problems, and partly because Governor Simpson disapproved of the entire venture.

During the disastrous Oahu conferences of 1842, he had told McLoughlin that Rae should "remain at his post until after the killing season of 1843," and then sell out. A vessel, Sir George said, should be sent to take the equipment and personnel back to Vancouver, and on no consideration should the Chief Factor "prolong the winding up of this losing business beyond the autumn of 1843." Although these were definite instructions, McLoughlin discounted them, because he knew they had been issued in the heat of a quarrel. Moreover, he was occupied with the distasteful job of closing the northern posts and creating a supply system large enough to satisfy the Russians' demands. He was angry at Simpson, absorbed in clearing his son's name, and convinced that the California post had originally been authorized by the Governor and Committee as well as by Sir George himself. It would succeed, he thought, if given a fair chance, so he temporized.

Ignoring the governor's orders was risky at best, and it was made infinitely worse by Yerba Buena's peculiar situation. Its major problem was a shortage of shipping—a surprising shortage, for the Governor and Committee knew McLoughlin's responsibility was being expanded both north and south, and that he would need extra vessels. In 1842 they sent the 350-ton supply ship *Valleyfield*, intending that she remain for the California trade, but she was late leaving London, late reaching the Columbia, and further delayed because she brought new boilers for the *Beaver*. Since McLoughlin's only available ship, the *Vancouver*, could not carry these large items without cutting "two of her beams," the *Valleyfield* had to take them to the steamer at Nisqually. And while she was there, workmen discovered not only that her own boilers were rusty, but that a seven-foot seam had been left uncaulked, so she was "put on shore in Puget Sound" for repairs.

She could not leave Puget Sound until October. "If she had been here in the spring as she ought," McLoughlin later told the Governor and Committee, "she would have been in time for the Calefornia trade, as any vessell to be of use for collecting Hides on the coast of Calefornia ought to be there by May." She was so late that when she finally reached Yerba Buena, Rae said he had to send her to Oahu without a cargo, because he lacked sufficient furs to "authorize me to pay the demurrage and tonnage duties. Had a vessel arrived at the time specified by Sir George Simpson and C. Factor McLoughlin, I could have obtained sufficient freight, but being uncertain as to the time of the Vessel's arrival, I could not make fixed arrangements."

In the following year, 1843, McLoughlin could not spare a vessel, because he "had to send the *Columbia* with the Russian Goods to Sitka," but the supply bark *Vancouver* made a side trip from the Columbia to Oahu, and stopped at Yerba Buena on her way back. With her was William Sinclair, Catherine Sinclair's sixteen-year-old brother, and he remained at Yerba Buena as a clerk. By this time Rae had amassed a quantity of goods and had sent hides to Oahu, but the ship had left them there "in consequence of not being able to take them on board."

She did, however, deliver Rae's accounts, which showed a loss of £900 in 1841—approximately equal to the $4,600 he had paid for the property—and a respectable profit of £2,363 for the following year. McLoughlin felt vastly encouraged to learn that Yerba Buena "showed a fairer prospect than any branch of business, that I had seen the fur trade enter." He "thought it probable their Honors would consider it advantageous to continue the trade," and that it would be wise to "keep the business agoing till their Honors decision was known." Again he put off closing the post.

In the following summer, 1844, he seemingly found a messenger, because Captain Thomas Baillie of the British warship *Modeste* was going from Fort Vancouver to California. The Chief Factor seized the chance to dispatch letters to the south, and Baillie actually saw Rae, but—in an incredible lapse of memory—he "forgot to deliver [the letters] and took them to Woahoo."

Contacts for the rest of the year were no better. In July McLoughlin wrote, "I have not heard from Mr. Rae since May 1843, at which I am not surprised, as we have no communication with that place." During the summer and fall he could not send a ship south, "as the Russians required so much wheat, that we had to send the *Cowelitz* and *Columbia* to the North West Coast, so that Mr. Rae found himself all the time without a Vessel to go along the Coast to collect hides."

By that year, 1844, the London officers were distinctly annoyed because of the skimpy news from Yerba Buena and McLoughlin's delay in having it closed. In April Secretary Barclay sent definite orders to have Rae abandon the post "with as little delay as possible," and by the time the Chief Factor received the word, he had decided that with communication so difficult and returns so poor, he would close the port as soon as he had an available ship. In January 1845, when the *Cowlitz* was at last going to Oahu, he wrote that "on the way she will call at S. Francisco to Deliver a Letter to Chief trader Rae instructing him to Wind up the Hudson Bay Companys affairs in Calefornia as soon as possible."

But the time lag, as always, interfered. Even though McLoughlin had taken this step, the London officers did not know it, and in the fall Barclay wrote again with obvious annoyance that the subject had been so "fully discussed" and "unequivocally declared" that it was not "necessary to revert to it, further than to express the hope that the instructions you have repeatedly received to wind up the concern have been carried into effect." At the same time, he privately told Simpson that the Chief Factor seemed to be "carrying on an underhand correspondence with Rae and quietly keeping up the Estabt. at its full amount." An "underhand correspondence" was unlikely, for there were few contacts between Fort Vancouver and Yerba Buena, but W. Kaye Lamb, in the introduction to McLoughlin's published letters, says the doctor "did not send copies of all his letters to or from Rae to London." This indicates that private notes may have been included in the occasional mail pouch.

McLoughlin was aware of the difficulties with shipping, but he had no way of knowing how serious the administrative problem at Yerba Buena had become. Although Rae had done well as head of rough-and-ready Fort Stikine, California was a foreign country, with unfamiliar laws and an entrenched system of trading alliances. He had to contend with the prejudice of powerful General Vallejo, who disliked the Hudson's Bay Company for its former practice of overtrapping beaver "to the point of extinguishing the species." Moreover, the Southwest was embroiled in a political upheaval that would eventually lead to the Mexican War, because Texas, having seceded from Mexico, was clamoring for annexation to the United States, while American settlers in California were determined to follow suit. And Rae, with his lack of experience, had to maneuver through the morass without supervision or advice.

In early spring 1845, the *Cowlitz* at last set sail for Yerba Buena, carrying McLoughlin's orders to close the post, but they arrived too late. In June, when the bark returned to Fort Vancouver, she brought staggering news. James Alexander Forbes—the British vice consul at San Francisco—had been called in to handle an emergency at the company post, and on January 21 he had written:

This silhouette is the only known picture of William Glen Rae, Mc-Loughlin's son-in-law. It is on a bracelet that belonged to Eloisa, and is owned by the McLoughlin Memorial Association. It is on display at the McLoughlin House National Historic site in Oregon City.
PHOTOGRAPH BY AUTHOR

It becomes my painful duty to inform you of the death of the Honble. Hudson's Bay Company's Agent at this place, W. G. Rae Esquire, who on the morning of Sunday 19th Instant [January] put a period to his existence with a pistol, the ball of which passed through his brain, and instant death ensued. This dreadful intelligence reached me the same night, and instantly I took my horse, and arrived at Yerba Buena at daylight. . . . You will perceive by the document marked A that the unfortunate Gentleman declares having become involved in difficulties from which he could not extricate himself, and the causes thereof.

Eloisa sent her father more details: that Rae had been unable to sleep for several nights; that he feared "they were going to attack him that same day, to tie and beat him to death"; that "all he wished was that they would not injure her and her children"; and that he would "sooner take his own life than suffer himself to be abused." While she watched, he put a pistol to his forehead and drew the trigger. When it failed to go off he threw it down, "and seizing another pistol with six barrels, he snapped it three times before she could get to him, when she caught him with both her hands by the collar of his waistcoat, and fell to the ground in a swoon."

Her nephew, young William Sinclair, was still a clerk at the post. When he heard the noise he rushed in and helped Rae carry his wife to bed, after which she revived and "clung to him until he promised not to repeat the attempt."

Eloisa McLoughlin Rae Harvey, date unknown. Eloisa returned to Oregon City after her husband William Rae committed suicide. She later married Daniel Harvey, one of McLoughlin's valued aides.
OHS ORHI 38305

But soon afterward, when she saw a pistol in her husband's pocket and asked what he was going to do with it, he "made no answer, but rushed into the next room, put the pistol to his forehead, fired, and fell instantly dead."

During the next few months, through various reports and letters, McLoughlin learned how unstable Rae had been. He had threatened the lives of Eloisa and the children. His clerk, Montrose McGillivray, who had himself been fired for drinking, said that "from the very first day of my landing in Calefornia till the day of my Departure, [he] has not been to my knowledge, sober two days of a week." And a young employee referred to only as "Mr. Ridley," who had "insinuated himself" into Rae's confidence, was of such a doubtful character that Forbes reported, "I am certain he has told Mr. Rae many untruths, and contributed greatly to involve that gentleman in many difficulties."

Much of Rae's predicament had been rooted in the seething unrest of local politics, coupled with his own lack of judgment. Having met the former civil governor, Juan Alvarado, who was rebelling because he had been replaced, Rae had allowed himself to be drawn into the insurrection. He had furnished lances to the rebels, sold them ammunition, and become so involved in their schemes that when the weak uprising collapsed, he feared he might be captured, punished, and perhaps executed. Most of the Fort Vancouver officers— blessed with hindsight—decided that the young man had been a disturbed individual, placed in a situation he could not handle. Peter Skene Ogden, for example, said, "The great mystery attached to Rae's death so far as I can learn was the dissapated life he led and to such an excess was it carried as to deprive him of reason . . . but not the slightest restraint was imposed on him he had his full sway and thus unfortunately terminated his existence."

McLoughlin himself attributed the problem to the lack of communication. He said his letters to Rae were not delivered, that coastal traders had been accused of destroying them, and that in consequence Rae felt neglected, which "preyed on his mind and drove him to the desperate act."

Both factors—Rae's instability and his isolation—undoubtedly contributed to his collapse. He left a note saying,

> I hereby declare that I have got myself into difficulty through the intrigue and malice of others, but that I have never intentionally wronged the Hudson's Bay Coy. a single farthing, that their property will be squandered, books destroyed, and no outstanding debts appear remg. after I am no more I am satisfied of, but this the Company ought to blame themselves for as they have entirely neglected the Calefa. trade in not sending Vessels here to receive the Returns. . . . This is the truth, so help me God.

McLoughlin had Eloisa brought home, but not for several months, probably because of the lack of ships. Rae had shot himself in January 1845, the news had come in June, and finally, on December 15, David McLoughlin left Fort Vancouver to help close the post at Yerba Buena and escort his sister to the Columbia. Her three children came with her: John, Margaret Glen, and Maria Louisa, ages six, four, and three. The boy William Glen Rae, born a few days after Rae's death, had lived only a short time and was buried in the Mission Dolores churchyard, Yerba Buena.

In her brief biography of her father, Eloisa said she sailed away from California "just as the Mexican War commenced. There was great excitement in San Francisco—or Yerba Buena as it was still called." Having had little to do with business affairs, she had only a sketchy idea of what had gone wrong. "I know a great many debts were left there," she said, "and there were a great many creditors that would not pay when we left. The place was not very profitable there. It was always credit—everything we sold was always on credit. The hides and tallow were not regarded as very good pay. We wanted furs. And wheat was still worse than hides. It was poor wheat and mixed with dirt."

Since McLoughlin and his wife had moved to Oregon City in January 1846, David brought Eloisa and the children there, not to Fort Vancouver, and they all settled down in the family's big house. Eloisa's homecoming was one bit of joy in an otherwise disastrous year, because she was dear to her parents, and for the rest of their lives they would have her and her brood nearby.

~3~
Joining Hands
1845

During the 1840s, McLoughlin occasionally visited his village at the falls, sitting "aloft in the stern of a bateau, erect and dignified, dressed in a long blue coat with brass buttons, buff waistcoat, dark trousers, and gray beaver hat, made in London. When he reached Oregon City he clambered up the rocky path and paced the single street carrying a gold-headed cane." He found his town lively and growing, with homes and shops being built along its muddy streets.

Its first rapid spurt of growth came with the immigration of 1843. Some of these newcomers were renegades, but many were men like Peter Burnett and Jesse Applegate—honest, experienced, and forceful. Burnett had been a district attorney in Missouri, and after five years in Oregon, where he was elected its supreme judge, he would move to California and become that state's first governor. Applegate, a surveyor, was within a year a member of Oregon's legislative committee—a respected member with great influence. Both of them were McLoughlin's friends.

The immigrants, who began at once to claim land, build cabins, and clear fields, were so numerous that they had considerable power. Within a few months they were chafing at the defects in the existing laws, especially the ill-fashioned section on land, which required recent claimants to record their tracts "within Twenty days from the time of Marking said claim" but allowed those already in possession "one year from the passage of this Act." Other problems were the government's uncertain—or nonexistent—finances and its constricted jurisdiction, which stopped at the Columbia and therefore did not include Fort Vancouver, with its potential tax revenue.

In the general election of May 1844, several of the recent immigrants were elected to the legislative committee—so many that they constituted about half of the membership—and they promptly began a major revision of the Organic Law. Two of their goals were to make the registration of claims more fair, and to include the Hudson's Bay Company in the provisional government. This would be awkward, because it was strongly pro-American, while most Hudson's Bay men were British subjects, and loyal to the queen.

During the summer, the new legislative committee worked out an extensive revision of the laws, and they met again in December to make further changes. Considering the system wholly inadequate, they decided that at the next general election, they would ask the voters to approve a convention for the purpose of drawing up a constitution. "There is a call for a convention of the people, to meet in June to form a constitution," McLoughlin told the Governor and Committee in March 1845. When June came, however, this proposal was defeated, because many Americans feared it would lead to an independent government, and they wanted to be part of the United States. The legislators then called a special election for July 25.

There the revised code was accepted *viva voce*, creating the Organic Law of 1845, which used parts of the earlier system, with additions and revisions. Peter Burnett said the registration of claims was dispensed with because it was "an onerous burden on new immigrants." Instead of an executive committee, there was to be a governor, and George Abernethy, formerly a lay worker at the Methodist mission, was elected to that position. The legislature was to meet at "Willamette Falls"—the missionaries' name for Oregon City. The favorable treatment for the mission, however, was eliminated, by cutting its land grant from six square miles to one—a change of little importance, because Lee's establishment had been dissolved.

Of special interest for McLoughlin, the new code omitted the clause depriving him of his property, and it specifically said, "all laws heretofore passed in regard to land claims be, and the same are hereby repealed." Another act authorized him to construct a canal at the falls, "sufficiently safe and wide for the passage of boats of the width of 13 feet or less." This, said Burnett, "enabled him to bring the water to propel his extensive flour mill, and was of much public benefit." One surprise was the choice of Francis Ermatinger—Catherine Sinclair's husband—as treasurer. Since by then Ermatinger was in charge of the Hudson's Bay post in Oregon City, his election indicated improvement in company-settler relations.

Among other innovations of the new Organic Law were a "pole Tax" of fifty cents, and property taxes of one-eighth of one percent on "Improvements on Town Lots, Mills, Pleasure Carriages, Clocks, Watches, Horses, Mules, Cattle and Hogs." It was given teeth by the provision that anyone who refused to pay taxes "should have no benifits of the Law of Oregon" and could not vote. The first tax collector was Sheriff Joseph L. Meek, who had a roll of 400 names for the poll tax and 345 for the property tax. McLoughlin was listed as the largest owner, with his mill valued at $7,000, his town lots at $4,200, cattle at $1,000, and merchandise at $2,500, for a total valuation of $12,212—on which his total tax was $15.77. Meek's report said his job was difficult "owing to the unsettled state of the publick mind," that Robert Shortess was among those who refused to comply, and that one indignant settler bluntly vowed, "Darn my sole if I pay."

The former Organic Law had required government officers to swear loyalty to the United States, a pro-American pledge that British subjects such as McLoughlin and Douglas could not make. Realizing this, and needing more revenue, the newly elected legislators changed the oath to a simple promise to support the organic laws of the provisional government of Oregon, so far as they were "consistent with my duties as a citizen of the United States, or a subject of Great Britain."

In August 1845, after the new code had been adopted, Jesse Applegate made an overture to McLoughlin. As the doctor explained it to the Governor and Committee, "the idea of a union for the purpose of mutual protection was suggested to me while on a visit to the Wallamette Falls, by the following letter from Mr. Applegate, an American, much respected by his countrymen, and a Member of the Provisional Legislature." He enclosed the letter, which asked whether, if the company joined, it would cooperate "by the payment of taxes, and in other respects complying with the laws of this provisional government."

After the trespass by Williamson and Alderman, McLoughlin knew how vulnerable his company was. "A crisis was evidently fast approaching," he said, "which would drive us to the painful necessity of yielding to the storm, or of taking the field openly, arms in hand, with means so unequal, compared to those arrayed against us, as to leave no hopes of success." Even so, he moved with caution, telling Applegate he could not decide so important a point without consulting his officers.

He then returned to Fort Vancouver, where Douglas agreed with him that since the association no longer required an oath of loyalty to the United States, joining it would not violate their duty as British subjects or the honor of the company. On the contrary, they thought membership would promote "the security of the Company's property, and the peaceful maintenance of its rights," and on August 15 McLoughlin sent a letter of acceptance, which he and Douglas both signed.

It said that since neither the British nor American government seemed ready to extend jurisdiction over the region, and since the oath no longer interfered with loyalty to their own country, "we the Officers of the Hudson's Bay Company, consent to become parties to the articles of compact." They exacted two conditions: the company would pay taxes only on sales to settlers, not on its entire holdings; and the district north of the Columbia would be called Vancouver instead of Lewis and Clark, the name the settlers had chosen. This name, McLoughlin said, "gave rise to many angry discussions," but the company's choice was adopted.

The new arrangement benefited both parties, for it provided the provisional government with a much-needed source of revenue and gave protection to McLoughlin's company in case of trouble with squatters. Nevertheless, the decision had not been easy, and in a long letter to the Governor and Committee, the Chief Factor set forth his reasons: the refusal of the British government to send aid; the provisional government's protection of members only; the difficulty in collecting from American debtors; the probability that the provisional government would expand north of the Columbia; and the need for a shield from "desperate and reckless characters . . . outcasts of society, who have sought a refuge in the wilds of Oregon. With their natural turpitude of disposition embittered by national hostility." But even with the government's aid, McLoughlin thought trouble might erupt. For safety's sake, he had the 1845 harvest of skins stored at Fort Victoria instead of Fort Vancouver, saying that "the Furs from the Interior will be sent there as soon as the *Cadboro* . . . can be spared for the purpose." And Sir George Simpson, equally cautious, urged him to keep all goods "as much as possible out of reach of the troublesome people by whom you are surrounded at present."

This growing antagonism was not confined to the Columbia, for relations between Britain and the United States had become so tense that war was being discussed on both sides of the Atlantic. Sir Robert Peel, the British prime minister, recommended "an additional frigate at the mouth of the Columbia, and a small artillery force on shore." President Polk wrote in his diary, "A grave discussion took place in view of the contingency of war with Great Britain, growing out of the present critical state of the Oregon question. Mr. Buchanan [Secretary of State] said it was his conviction that the next two weeks would decide the issue of peace or war." Polk also told his brother, "The only way to treat John Bull is to treat him firmly and look him straight in the eye." And an editorial in the *New York Morning News* quoted Andrew Jackson as having said, "There must be no arbitration but at the cannon's mouth!" Aware of the situation, McLoughlin said he had joined the provisional government because he thought it "the only means of preventing scenes of violence and contention," which might drag the two countries into war.

It was ironic that just after he made his decision, two arrivals indicated that Her Majesty's Government was after all interested in Oregon. First, two officers of the British armed forces came to the Columbia in late August and remained until spring. Second, while they were there, a British fleet entered the Strait of Juan de Fuca, and two of the officers spent a week at Fort Vancouver.

The first, who came on August 25, 1845, were Lieutenants Henry J. Warre and Mervin Vavasour, escorted from Red River to Oregon by Peter Skene Ogden. In briefing Ogden for his role as guide, Sir George Simpson told him that Warre and Vavasour were on a secret mission to reconnoitre the Pacific Coast and explore "the practicability of forming military stations therein and conveying troops thither," in case a military occupation became necessary. The mission was so secret that even to McLoughlin they were presented as private travelers, bent on "the pleasure of field sports and scientific pursuits," but he guessed their true purpose. They were difficult guests. Ogden said they were "most disagreeable companions," given to "constant grumbling and complaining . . . I would rather for ever forego the pleasure of seeing my Friends than submit to travel over the same road with the same companions."

While they were in the area, they visited—with McLoughlin's assistance—the Willamette, Fort George, Vancouver Island, "Nesqually," and Walla Walla. They shopped at the Fort Vancouver stores for such luxuries as "superfine beaver hats, figured vests, pipes, toiletries, and extract of roses." In the spring they left with a Hudson's Bay brigade, accompanied by Francis Ermatinger, to cross the mountains and go to England. On June 16, 1846, while they were at Red River, they wrote a long report that was harshly critical of the Hudson's Bay Company and of McLoughlin. He would hear from them again.

The other arrival was a fleet of sixteen British vessels that sailed into the Strait of Juan de Fuca, with HMS *America* as flagship. Her captain, John Gordon, had orders to show the people of the United States that the British were "prepared in case of necessity to oppose them," a promise that vastly relieved McLoughlin. He told Gordon he would "with great pleasure" inform the settlers of the *America's* mission.

The ship's officers who came to Fort Vancouver—Lieutenant Parke and Lieutenant William Peel, son of Prime Minister Sir Robert Peel—had orders to assure British subjects that Her Majesty's Government would give them protection. McLoughlin offered them the facilities of the fort, provided a guide to the Willamette and back, and had long talks with them, although the young men's belligerence worried him. George Roberts, a participant, said that during a discussion about the possible war, one of the officers threatened that if it came to blows, "we will hit them a good deal harder than we would other people." He was in uniform—vigorous—and he said it with such fire that the peace-loving McLoughlin replied with a distressed, "Oh, Captain Park! Captain Park!"

They had arrived on September 8, and on the sixteenth they returned to their ship. Peel then made a report favorable to the company, saying that many settlers arrived with a hostile feeling, "but in the course of a twelve-month, from feeling their dependence on the Company as a market, and how much they are indebted to them for the peaceful conduct of the Indians their opinions greatly change."

Captain Gordon, however, was a man of a different stripe. McLoughlin had James Douglas accompany the lieutenants when they returned to the *America*, and he remained on board for three days, conferring with the captain. "The old Gentleman was exceedingly kind," Douglas later said, "but no wise enthusiastic about Oregon or British interests. He does not think the country worth five straws and is surprised that Government should take any trouble about it. He assured me that he could not interfere, with trespassers squatting on our claims and in such cases advised a settlement by arbitration, a very wise plan truly,—to lose every thing we hold. . . . He did not appear at all friendly to the Hudsons Bay Company, and told me plainly that we could not expect to hold the entire country."

The report Gordon sent to England spoke fervently of the need to keep the Strait of Juan de Fuca; and it criticized McLoughlin, saying that he and his company had treated the settlers "in the most liberal manner," which encouraged American immigration. He also censured the doctor's decision to join the provisional government, because in his opinion "the Company's people were sufficiently strong to protect themselves."

Warre and Vavasour and the British fleet had been welcome indications of the British government's interest in the Columbia, but they gave McLoughlin no tangible help, and Captain Gordon bluntly refused to interfere. After they had gone, the Chief Factor was in the same position as before—a loyal subject of the Crown, trying to serve his country and his company in difficult times. England's indifference—its failure to leave a permanent force on the Columbia—made his position untenable. The provisional government, having outgrown its roots in the Willamette Valley, was reaching toward Hudson's

Bay soil. It had a workable code of laws, a system of taxation, a governor. And he, the most powerful man on the Northwest Coast, had therefore become its active, although somewhat reluctant, ally.

~4~

The Trap
1845

After 1844, when McLoughlin bought out Waller and the Methodist mission, he no longer faced a local challenge to his land claim, but it still presented a problem—whether to hold it in the company's name or his own. He was not the only one perplexed. James Douglas said that in the present political regime, the land was merely "a sink of capital," and he asked Simpson whether there was any objection to having the doctor take it on his own account, merely reserving the stores and granary for the company.

McLoughlin himself, having asked for advice and received Adam Thom's inscrutable reply, mulled it over for several months and finally decided that the wisest course was to keep the title himself—or at least appear to do so. On March 20, 1845, he sent Sir George Simpson two drafts on his account—£685.12.2, the company's outlay at the falls in 1843, and £3487.19.4, the outlay in 1844, for a total of £4173.11.6. With them he sent a long, puzzling letter.

One part of it seemed to express a simple decision to purchase the property, saying that since his query about the claim had not been answered, "I inferred that they left me to my own Discretion to keep it for the Company or myself as, I might consider most advisable," and that since the firm probably could not hold it under American law, he felt justified in placing it in his own name. But in another part, he indicated that his offer was a ruse, saying he would hold the land "in trust for the Company . . . and when I left the Company I could transfer it to another and he would hold it in the same way." He gave assurance that he would "transfer it to whoever the Company wishes as to keep it in their own name is quite out of the question." He explained that he did not expect to profit from the land because "at my time of life I cannot be desirous of beginning a new Business," and that he only wished "to further the Interests of the Company and Extend British influence." He evidently realized he was taking a risk, for he said, "If I have done Wrong it proceeds from their Honors Silence. . . . I hope I will not be allowed to suffer."

McLoughlin's reasons for making this move are not clear, and even the men who knew him were uncertain on this point. Dugald Mactavish, who had personally discussed the matter with him, thought he genuinely wanted to buy out the claim, while Peter Skene Ogden made the somewhat muddled comment that he first thought the offer to hold it for himself was sincere, but that "from what he now states it appears quite the contrary altho I must confess I am rather sceptical in my belief."

Countless letters and journals depict McLoughlin as a man of rigid fairness and integrity in both personal and business dealings, as when he insisted that Peter Burnett's valuable cattle must be returned to him and when he took pains to credit even drunken sea captains with whatever virtues they possessed. He was, however, resourceful, self-confident—and aggressive. He had a strong respect not only for the letter of the law, but also for fairness and fundamental rights, and in the past he had been devious when he thought a small subterfuge would prevent a greater injustice. As previous examples, in 1808 he had adopted Roderick McKenzie's suggestion of resorting to a "stratagem" in order to get the salary he thought the company was unjustly withholding, and which he needed in order to help his brother. In 1829, faced with a dangerous shortage of guns, he had told Donald Manson, "Of course this must be Kept a secret . . . Evade the Demand by saying you omitted to write for them or that I did not send them or that I object to sell our Guns for four Skins—as may best suit your purposes." In the 1830s he had dodged regulations by carrying French Canadian retirees on the company books, with no salaries and no work requirements, in order to spare them an arduous and senseless trek across the Rockies.

His handling of the land claim, therefore, was entirely consistent with several questionable—but fair—solutions he had found in the past. Having to act alone, with no advice from his superiors, he tried in 1845 to foresee and forestall a grab for land that he thought he and his company rightfully owned, having found it, claimed it, and developed it according to the laws of the time. He was determined to keep it out of the hands of those who were trying to jump the claim. Afterward, he frankly said he had offered to cover the costs so that "if called into Court I would be able to swear the place was mine—and that I had paid for it so as to avoid every difficulty." The consequences of sending the bank drafts would be immensely important to McLoughlin's future, but he could not have known it at the time, nor did he seem to realize how far his prestige had fallen.

The plunge had begun in 1841, when he had a quarrel with Sir George Simpson—a quarrel that was still simmering. In 1844 Simpson told him that the Columbia had developed such a bad reputation for severe punishments that he could not find high-caliber men willing to serve there—a charge McLoughlin indignantly denied. The difficulty, he insisted, was the reduction in wages under the policy of strict economy, and the location of the employment center at Lachine. "Is it to be expected," he asked, "that a man who has the opportunity of engaging at Montreal will take the trouble to go to La Chine? most certainly he will not, and the Hudson's Bay Company's Office . . . ought to be in Montreal, as the North West Company's was."

Simpson also dredged up an apparent discrepancy in the doctor's annual reports, which listed the net gains for the outfits of 1841–43 as £22,974, £16,982, and £21,726, while Simpson calculated them as £1,474, £4,003, and £3,156. The differences were not due to error by McLoughlin, for he had kept accounts as directed, using prescribed tables. But Sir George had allowed for estimated errors in valuation.

The quarrel, however, was not the only cause of the company's dissatisfaction. The doctor's official reports were so loaded with complaints about the Stikine investigation that they had become "exceedingly meagre and unsatisfactory in other respects." He had delayed in following instructions to close Yerba Buena and the northern posts, had incurred heavy costs on property at the falls, and had advanced £6,600 in credit to American immigrants. In addition, fur-trade revenues had sagged, and the Puget's Sound Agricultural Company had not met expectations. In 1845 Simpson said "the profits of the Columbia business are by no means so great as the accounts represent, while the exertions that are made to meet its demands are exceedingly embarrassing & injurious to every other branch of the business." In most of these areas, McLoughlin had contended with special problems, some of them insoluble, but his results nevertheless displeased the Committee. In March 1844, Secretary Barclay told Sir George Simpson that "nothing will now do but McLoughlin's removal."

The Chief Factor received his first indication of serious dissatisfaction in June 1845, when the *Cowlitz* returned from California with the report of Rae's suicide in her mail packet. That, however, was not the only bad news. She also brought a letter from Secretary Barclay—businesslike and coldly blunt—saying the Governor and Committee had decided that the expected advantages from placing the entire Columbia under one person had not been realized. It continued:

It is not advisable that the cargo of so extensive a District should be confided to one individual however experienced; they have therefore resolved that the Country shall be divided into two or more Districts, each to be represented by a commissioned officer. . . . the Allowance of £500 per annum which was granted to you beyond your emoluments as a Chief Factor, in consideration of the great extent and consequent responsibility of the charge committed to you, shall cease on the 31st May 1845.

McLoughlin would suffer not only a humiliating reduction of power and prestige, but a financial loss as well.

He immediately sprang to his own defense. He denounced the plan to split the district, saying it could bring only "the same results as occurred in it during the time of the late North West Company, division and discord, which ruined the business." He furiously objected to the cut in pay, maintaining that "it is a part of the conditions on which I renewed my Agreement." As for aiding the settlers, he said that if he had refused supplies and they attacked the fort in order to seize what they needed, the world would have said the company "deserved to suffer"; and if some of the immigrants had perished, "we would have incurred such a load of odium as would have been ruinous to us."

It was June when he learned of Rae's suicide and the reduction in his own district. In the fall he received another blow—this time a dispatch from Governor Simpson acknowledging receipt of his drafts. It said, "Your letter on this subject is not, to my apprehension, quite distinct, but I draw from it . . . that, your object is to purchase the Mills in question from the Company at their cost, handing the bills in payment." The matter, Simpson said, had been laid before the Council at Red River, who had decided to accept it; the company was therefore relinquishing all title to the mills, and McLoughlin's drafts were to be "charged to that gentleman's account." Whether or not McLoughlin had intended to actually purchase the land, it was his, and his money was gone.

He reacted with shock and dismay, insisting that he did not want title to the land, explaining that he had only tried to hold it for the company, and pleading for Simpson to have the decision reversed. But the unwanted purchase was not the final catastrophe of that disastrous year. In November still another numbing letter reached him. This one said the Council of the Northern Department at Red River had decided that McLoughlin was no longer to be in full charge of the Columbia District, but would be replaced by a three-man Board of Management—Douglas, Ogden, and the doctor himself. The board's duties, Simpson said, would begin immediately, and he suggested:

Should C. F. McLoughlin's altered position, arising from his purchase of the Willamette Mills, render it desirable for him to devote the whole of his time & attention to his own affairs during the current year, we have no objection to his having leave of absence during the remainder of the year, say from the receipt of this communication until the close of the Outfit, when he may enter upon the Rotation of Furlough . . . but, should he be disinclined to accept that Rotation of Furlough & feel disposed to continue his duties in the service, we have, in that case, to beg that, he may come across the mountains next Spring, in order to attend the Council for the Northern Dept. to be held at Red River Settlement in the early part of June, to the end that he may be appointed to a charge on the East side of the mountains, as it is considered probable that his presence at Fort Vancouver, where he has so long had the sole charge, might be productive of embarrassment in many points of view.

This was a ruthlessly matter-of-fact presentation of his transfer to another post and possible retirement, and Simpson's intent was crystal clear. It was inconceivable—as he well knew—for McLoughlin to stay at Fort Vancouver in a subordinate role, after his proud years in absolute charge. Sir George also knew that the doctor had just spent a very large sum for the land at the falls, and that American law required him to reside in the Columbia area in order to hold his claim. Nevertheless, the company had decided that if the Chief Factor remained active, he must transfer to a post east of the Rockies—which he could not do without losing his land. It left him no choice except to resign. Crushed, McLoughlin wrote to George Pelly, company agent at Oahu,

If at the time I had known my Salary of five hundred pounds was stopped and that I was recalled to the East side of the Mountains I would not ever have thought of becoming possessed of this property, and Sir George Simpson seeing the change in my circumstances and situation ought to have sent my Draft Back to me so as I might Decide reject or take as I pleased and which if he had Done most assuredly I would not be at present here. . . . I could not meet your Views in Regard to settling in the Willamette as that would oblige me to Retire which I did not wish to do.

He regretted the whole unhappy transaction, did not want the land, and pleaded, "I hope your Honors . . . will Allow me to Return it to you if I cannot sell it." His request was denied. Simpson had already notified London of the purchase, and on August 22, 1845, McLoughlin's personal account was debited by two payments totaling £4173.11.6, "for his Bill dated Fort Vancouver 19th Mar." The sum was so large that it depleted his lifetime savings to less than two thousand pounds.

The blows of that year had fallen on McLoughlin with crushing weight. In March—worried, uncertain—he had sent the drafts. In June he heard of Rae's suicide and that he himself was to be replaced as head of the Columbia District, losing his bonus. In early fall his offer to buy the land was accepted and absorbed. And in November he was told that he would be transferred to a post east of the Rockies, which meant he must abandon either his partnership or his investment. It had been only six years since he had returned from his furlough in a seemingly impregnable position, loaded with honors. But in that short time his son was murdered, his son-in-law committed suicide, his salary was cut, his position was diminished, and he was forced to resign.

The life of the fort, however, swept on, and even while McLoughlin was preparing to leave, he had to confront another influx of settlers—this time nearly three thousand souls. Like those of the past two years, they were exhausted and in need, and in spite of his own troubles, the Chief Factor sent them boats and food and supplies.

It was the last immigration that had to come down the Columbia, for one small group, led by Samuel K. Barlow and William H. Rector, managed to overcome inconceivable hardship and bring wagons around the south shoulder of Mt. Hood from The Dalles to Oregon City. By the next fall, 1846, Barlow had obtained a charter from the provisional government and laid out his famous toll road, enabling settlers to choose between the perilous route down the Columbia and the almost equally horrendous passage by land. It was rough, deep in mud, or snow and ice, and in places so steep that the drivers had to tie ropes to their wagons and snub them around trees, to ease the vehicles down the grade. But the families came through—by river, by the trail—entrusting themselves to fragile boats or slogging beside the wagons and sometimes putting their shoulders to the wheels. Whichever route they chose, the Hudson's Bay Company was no longer their only source of safety and support, because the population of the Willamette Valley had grown so much that its residents were able to provide the necessary care.

While the immigration was arriving, McLoughlin wrote a long letter, his last official report to the Governor and Committee. Much of it was a dogged effort to convey essential business news—the movements of ships, condition of pelts, supply of flour and wheat for Russia, problems of personnel. He also reiterated the time-worn accusations about young John's murder and Simpson's role, for these still rankled. He ardently justified his assistance to the settlers, saying that if he had refused help and some had perished, "such an outcry would justly have been raised against us here, that even you in London would have suffered by it . . . I have not only fulfilled the dictates of humanity, but most effectually promoted the best interests of the Company." And he remind-ed the Committee that as for the settlers, "they had the same right to come as I had to be here."

Other, deeply moving passages related his efforts to perform his duty. "I beg to repeat my request that you oblige me by informing me what act of mine has caused you to decide as Mr. Secretary Barclay writes. . . . I trust when the truth is known, it will be found that I have acted with as much zeal as if my life had been at stake, and justice will be done me."

A misconception widely believed at one time was that McLoughlin resigned because he had been ordered to turn his back on the immigrants, regardless of their need. This belief was voiced by Horace S. Lyman in an address of 1886 to the Oregon Pioneer Association, in which he quoted the doctor as saying, "Gentlemen, if such be your orders, I will serve you no more." However, Lyman made the statement four decades after the fact, and he acknowledged it as rumor by beginning, "It is said that . . ." These were Lyman's words, not McLoughlin's, and they did not fit the facts.

Documents show that the London officers, as businessmen, objected to extending credit to the immigrants, and that the Chief Factor ardently defend-ed his practices, but there is no evidence that the company advocated allow-ing anyone to suffer. McLoughlin, in fact, agreed at first with the official pol-icy. In 1845 he wrote to the Governor and Committee, "I am by no means surprised that you find our amount of outstanding debts great, as they are greater than I wish, but this is entirely owing to the circumstances in which we were placed." Although he was profoundly sympathetic toward the immi-grants, he handled accounts on a business basis as long as he could, and he eased his demands only when it became necessary in order to avoid hardship. It was not aid to immigrants that caused his dismissal. He was finessed out of his position because the affairs of the Columbia District were not going well, partly because of circumstances beyond his control, but also because of his own temperament.

Another misconception is the belief that the company charged Mc-Loughlin for the settlers' debts. Although many of his contemporaries believed it and said as much in their letters and journals, they were mistaken. His daughter Eloisa had heard the rumor, but she was doubtful, and said, "I never knew whether they made him pay. Once after my father died I asked if they made him pay. The gentleman I spoke to did not answer me." McLoughlin himself did not make the claim, and his company accounts show no such deductions, nor any costs arising from young John's murder. The records of his estate listed settlers' debts, but these were for loans made later, while he was in business in Oregon City.

The company actually gave him generous economic treatment, for his special salary of five hundred pounds was continued for an additional year, until mid-1846—after which he would have a year's furlough followed by a two-year leave of absence, so that his formal retirement would not start until June 1, 1849. For one year more, according to the regular company practice, he would receive a full Chief Factor's share of profits, and a half-share for the next five years.

Nevertheless, McLoughlin had been maneuvered into a humiliating resignation, and at the age of sixty-two, after a lifetime of service, he had reached a tragic milestone. He must give up his position of authority, turn his back on his career, live among people of another nation, and forge a new life.

CHAPTER 12

The City Beside the Falls

I have Drunk and am Drinking
the cup of Bitterness to the very Dregs.

DR. JOHN MCLOUGHLIN

~ 1 ~

Starting Over
1846–1847

During the last weeks of 1845, while McLoughlin and Marguerite were preparing for their move to Oregon City, the doctor engaged carpenters to erect a house on his land claim—a large house, to accommodate their suddenly expanded family. Eloisa and her three children would be living permanently in the new house as soon as they returned from California. Young William McKay, who had recently completed his medical studies in the East, would be with the McLoughlins at least for a time. And Marguerite's granddaughter Catherine Ermatinger would also be with them, because her husband, Francis, had been called to York Factory for reassignment. Since Catherine had a little girl, Fanny, the household would have four children under the age of six, which may have been the reason the doctor wrote somewhat disconsolately about finding himself "at the age of Sixty three . . . in danger of becoming a pauper with two orphan families on my hands."

By early 1846 the house was habitable, so on January 4, McLoughlin and his wife went down to the Fort Vancouver landing. There they boarded company bateaux, to go four miles down the broad Columbia to the mouth of the Willamette, and then twenty miles upstream between its forested banks to Oregon City. The logistics of the move were formidable, for they had a great deal of furniture and household goods, all of which had to be transported by water. On the way they passed a single log cabin, covered with shingles, recently built by Francis W. Pettygrove and Asa Lovejoy. It functioned as a store, with a small stock of items for sale, and its owners, by the flip of a coin, had named it Portland. The site was blessed with deep water for ships, and its founders were planning a plank road to the west, through a canyon and over a range of steep hills, into the wheat-growing area of Tualatin Valley. Portland was destined to grow.

McLoughlin's Oregon City house was a substantial one of two stories, luxurious for its time—a frame structure with high ceilings, a large living room and dining room downstairs, four bedrooms upstairs, and four fireplaces for heat. It contained no running water, and the kitchens were separate buildings. McLoughlin later stated in an affidavit that he had spent $4,368 for a dwelling house, $950 for an office, $70 on one kitchen, and $50 on another, and that "a large portion of the work was executed by himself." Most of the lumber came from his own mills, and undocumented but credible tradition says the ceiling, doors, window frames, and trim came around the Horn from New England.

The house was not on the waterfront, but in the second block —number 29—one of the parcels McLoughlin had recovered from the Methodist mission when he settled his land claim with the Reverend George Gary. The house faced west toward the river, with the kitchens, woodshed, quarters for servants, "necessary," and other buildings on the adjoining lot to the south, and another house to the north. In addition, McLoughlin owned a sizeable cluster of businesses nearby. Three stores and one "old building" were on the block across the street, and adjacent to these was the "mill reserve," itself as large as several blocks. It contained the gristmill with its race, basin, and "appurtenances," the sawmill with its race, the store known as the French store, the granary, and the foundry building. McLoughlin operated one store as his own business, and he had a half interest in the "French store," started by Captain Menes of *L'Etoile du Matin* to dispose of goods salvaged after the vessel foundered on the Columbia bar.

Here, on the low bench of land overlooking the falls, the McLoughlins took up a new life, surrounded by their young family. Caring for so many was a great deal of work, and Marguerite was aided by several Indian servants. She was, as always, quiet and reserved, keeping in the background, but greatly admired in the community and loved by her husband. One of their pleasures was attendance at the Catholic church. It had been recently built on land donated by McLoughlin, and it was dedicated on February 8, soon after their move. Small as the church was, it offered one taste of luxury, for McLoughlin sent to England for its pipe organ.

The doctor's correspondence from Oregon City often contained references to his family, especially to his wife and Eloisa, sometimes to Catherine Ermatinger. In a note to James Douglas, for example, he said, "I was sorry to learn Mrs Douglass was unwell. I hope she is better please Remember Mrs McL Mrs Rae Mrs E [Catherine Ermatinger] to her not forgetting   Yours Respectfully

Marguerite Wadin McKay McLoughlin. The only known picture of McLoughlin's wife, taken at an unknown date, but certainly late in her life. She had become heavy, but she also suffered from a kidney ailment, which caused considerable swelling. OHS ORHI 260

Eloisa and Daniel Harvey had three children, Daniel, Mary Angelica, and James William McLoughlin. With her three children by Rae, six children lived in the Oregon City house. This picture is of Eloisa and her youngest child, Mary Angelica Harvey. (Courtesy of McLoughlin House National Historic Site) OHS ORHI 260

Jn McLoughlin." Similarly, to W. A. Leidesdorff, his business agent in California, he wrote, "Mrs Rae Begs to be remembered to you and the Children still Remember you and Both prefer San Francisco to Oregon." And to Captain David Dring of the *Janet*, he made an intriguing but unexplained personal request. "Pray do not forget to send Back the Key for the piano."

For all his gracious phrases, however, the move to Oregon City was a wrenching comedown, from the management of the entire Columbia District to handling real estate, supervising three mills, and operating a small retail store—the former Hudson's Bay Company store—in a primitive frontier town. Even though McLoughlin was financially secure, most of his friends thought he had taken a deplorable fall. "I regret to hear that he lowers himself by keeping a shop and retailing out trifling articles to the Yankees," wrote John Work, while McLoughlin himself was inconsolable. Brooding incessantly, he wrote to the Governor and Committee, "I have Drunk and am Drinking the cup of Bitterness to the very Dregs."

New as it was, Oregon City in 1846 had attained the substantial population of five or six hundred—estimates vary. Joel Palmer, who had come with the immigration of 1845, said there were "about one hundred houses, most of them not only comodious, but neat," as well as "quite a number of carpenters, masons, &c., in constant employment," reflecting the area's explosive growth. He listed "one hatter, one tannery, three tailor shops, two cabinet- makers, two silversmiths, one cooper, two blacksmiths, one physician, three lawyers, one printing office . . . one lath machine, and a good brickyard in active operation," along with two churches—neatly counterbalanced by two taverns. Three American merchants were active—John H. Couch, Francis W. Pettygrove, and George Abernethy, who had bought "the brick store" from the mission.

Because the first "gaol" had burned, the provisional legislature, on December 24, 1846, decided to build a substantial log jail and voted "to receive a lot donated by John McLoughlin for the purpose of erecting said jail." The project dragged, however, and a year later one of the legislators, James Nesmith, "reported they deemed it inexpedient in the present embarrassed condition of finances to incur the expense of a jail." Somehow it was eventually built, as shown on Oregon City's town plat.

For McLoughlin, as for other businessmen, the most serious problem was a shortage of money, so severe that in 1845 the provisional legislature had passed an act saying that "approved orders on solvent merchants and good merchantable wheat . . . shall be lawful tender." As a consequence, business transactions became so awkward that storekeepers and shoppers used various substitutes, some ingenious, some a nuisance. George Abernethy in his brick store made change in the form of rocks on which he pasted papers stating his name and the value of that particular piece. Several kinds of paper currency were circulated—scrip of the provisional government, which was not quite trusted, and orders on merchants. A debtor might pay in Abernethy, Couch, or Hudson's Bay currency—or other merchants—all having different values. A premium favoring cash was common. In 1846 Lieutenant Neil M. Howison said it was "worth 12% more than bills," and a year later the Hudson's Bay Company was selling flour at $2.50 per hundredweight for cash, or $3.00 for currency. The first significant amount of money in the area was a barrel of silver dollars, brought on the British ship *Modeste* for paying her crew.

Oregon City was the major settlement on the Willamette, but several rivals were springing up, the largest being Salem, about twenty miles south, the successor to Jason Lee's "Chemeketa." Salem was thriving even though its progress was slowed because Willamette Falls blocked ships, and all their cargo had to be loaded into the wagons that lumbered up and down the narrow portage road connecting with the upriver boats.

In addition to these sizeable towns, two small villages were rising on the other side of the river: Linn City, named in honor of Senator Linn, and Multnomah City, after the Indian tribe. Two ferries crossed the river, operated by Hugh Burns and Robert Moore, who charged 6¼ cents for "a single footman," 12½ cents for a man and horse, 3 cents per head for sheep or hogs, and 3 cents per 100 pounds of "Goods or other freight." But a wagon and team came high at $1.50, a pleasure carriage was 75 cents, and sawed lumber was 25 cents per thousand feet. Although McLoughlin did not own the ferries, he had an interest in them, because his holdings included the "ferry landing and privilege."

During the doctor's last weeks at Fort Vancouver, he was planning to go east to the Council at Red River or even to London, "to demand as a right a full examination into my conduct." After he had spent a few months at Oregon City, he decided such a trip would not be wise, because under American law a long absence might invalidate his land claim, but he thought he might sell out entirely. "I may not be able to leave the Country before selling," he said, "as if I do . . . I may lose the property." It was in midsummer 1846, after six months in Oregon City, that he gave the company formal notice of his decision not to resume active duty.

Still uneasy about his tenure of the land for which he had paid so dearly, he asked Peter Burnett, who had been elected Chief Justice, to give him the oath of allegiance to the United States. Burnett, however, replied that since the provisional government had no legal standing in America, he lacked the necessary authority. And when McLoughlin asked what measures he might take "to get rightful possession of Abernethy Island"—the island portion of his claim, taken over by the Island Milling Company—Burnett warned him that "agitating the question then might lead to trouble in this Country." He recommended deferment until the American government established jurisdiction.

McLoughlin decided to wait rather than cause friction, but he was bitter—uncertain—depressed. In April 1846, he told his agent in San Francisco that he did not yet have his affairs in order, because of "a Kind of Indecision from a Desire of selling out and a Desire to join you in California." Three months later he informed the company officers that he felt "disgraced and Degraded," and that "though the people are very kind to me yet if I had my money I would not Remain here if a present was made of it to me." He plugged away at his businesses, operating them as best he could, but without any real interest. In March 1847, Ogden told Sir George Simpson that the doctor was "so melancholy that serious apprehensions were entertained [he] would lose his reason."

McLoughlin, however, was a doer by nature, and he found plenty to do. In February, just a month after his move, a fire at his mills destroyed a thousand feet of sawn lumber, but was "extinguished by the efforts of the Americans, English, Irish, Kanakas (alias Sandwich Islanders) and Indians." He then leased both sawmills to Walter Pomeroy and Absalom Hedges at a thousand dollars per year for two years, but continued to operate the sales shop and gristmill for himself. This mill was a source of pride—a huge new structure, started in 1843 and at last nearing completion. It was the largest and finest in Oregon— sixty-three by forty-three feet, square-timbered, with three pairs of French burrstones, each pair able to grind a hundred barrels of flour per day. He also dealt in real estate, because he owned much of Oregon City, with lots and buildings for sale or rent.

With assets like these—mills, stores, a growing town—McLoughlin's interest in life gradually returned, and he cast a wide net, for his years at Fort Vancouver had given him contacts in London, the Sandwich Islands, California, and Montreal. His chief exports were lumber and wheat, which he tried to sell to markets as distant as Manila and Tahiti. George Pelly, in Honolulu, acted as agent for him as well as for the Hudson's Bay Company, supplying sugar, syrup, rice, salt, molasses, coffee, and special items such as cups and saucers, paint, linseed oil, and cut-glass lamps. The settler George Luther Boone said the McLoughlin store was "stocked with goods from England, molasses, corduroy pants, striped hickory shirts, Honolulu sugar black as tar and Brazilian rope tobacco so strong it would make your head swim or stop a clock. Frenchmen from Champoeg were trading there, Canadian voyageurs in blue knit tasseled caps." As a chief factor, McLoughlin had successfully juggled myriad aspects of the fur trade, and now—an acute businessman—he handled his own enterprise well.

Even though Fort Vancouver was being displaced by Fort Victoria as district headquarters, it continued to serve as the center for company stores and posts farther up the river. Peter Skene Ogden and James Douglas were the fort's joint managers, and McLoughlin obtained part of his stock from them, including sheet tin, iron, canvas, spikes, and nails. At first it was a friendly arrangement, but not long after his move, when he asked Douglas and Ogden to give David employment "merely for his Victuals till I could get him regularly admitted to the Service so as that in the mean time he should not be Idle," he received a rude surprise. As he told Sir John Henry Pelly, governor of the Hudson's Bay Company, his request was refused, "and this by Gentlemen particularly Mr. Douglass who knows every thing I did to promote the Interest of the Company."

Eloisa possibly referred to this when she wrote, "My father always liked him [Douglas]. Towards the last something happened I do not know what; I could not learn what it was. He was against my father in something, and my father was very angry about it. It was just about the time my father left." A letter Douglas wrote to Sir George Simpson in 1845 contains a possible clue, for it discusses the decision to remove Roderick Finlayson from Fort Stikine and have him assist Work, who was ill, leaving young John McLoughlin essentially alone. "Poor John was a strong active man, in sound health, Work a suffering invalid," the letter said. "The arrangement met with my full approbation." McLoughlin continued to blame Simpson for his son's death, and if he heard of Douglas's remark, it may have led to the falling-out.

Hurt as he was by the Douglas-Ogden refusal to employ his son, McLoughlin soon turned the situation to his own advantage. He needed employment for David, and since it was difficult to secure shipping space for bulky goods—flour, wheat, and lumber—he paid the American firm of F. W. Pettygrove & Company twenty thousand dollars for a partnership for David, which enabled him to ship goods on that company's bark, the *Toulon*. David often went with the vessel to handle the business, and his father entrusted him with considerable responsibility. "You will sell what [produce] you have unless you have good Reasons for leaving it to be sold by Mr Leidsdorff," one of his letters said, and after giving rather loose instructions for handling the money, it continued, "You may perhaps find some opportunity of transferring the Bargain at a profit."

Because the fiscal year didn't end until May, McLoughlin's retail store—the former Hudson's Bay store—was in both names, his and the company's, with the profits of £3,854 divided according to the amount each had invested. This was £1,053

A 1901 photo of David McLoughlin, Dr. John McLoughlin's youngest son. After several years as his father's assistant, David went to the gold fields in 1849, and eventually moved to Porthill, Idaho. There he married Annie Grizzly, daughter of a Kootenai chief, and was father of a large family. In 1901 he visited Portland, made a major speech, granted several interviews and wrote memoirs that furnish otherwise unknown information. He died two years later, still a resident of Porthill. OHS ORHI 1268 to McLoughlin, based on the purchase price of the property, and £2,801 to the company, based on the inventory value of goods furnished during that year. In May McLoughlin took over the entire business, but since a sizeable stock of goods remained, and moving it to Fort Vancouver would be expensive, the company rented a granary from him at £121 per year, to be used as a Hudson's Bay retail store.

In February 1846, shortly after McLoughlin moved, a group of local businessmen organized the Oregon Printing Association and founded the *Oregon Spectator*, first issued on February 5, 1846. One prominent member of the group was Francis W. Pettygrove, co-founder of Portland; George Abernethy was treasurer; and W. G. T ' Vault was the editor. The new paper was a four-page journal, fifteen by eleven inches, issued semi-monthly and blessed at its beginning with 155 subscribers. This was a fortuitous time for setting up a press, because the area was undergoing great change, the boundary was still undecided, and the future was bound to be lively. With the avowed aim of promoting "good morals, temperance, and education," the newspaper piously claimed to be nonpolitical, although it was generally hostile to McLoughlin and the British. Nevertheless, the doctor was interested in the *Spectator*, and for several years he occasionally contributed a letter or news item to its columns. The first American newspaper on the Pacific Coast—eagerly read and often controversial—it symbolized the growing importance of his town.

~ 2 ~

The Boundary Treaty
1846–1847

HMS *Modeste*, which had visited the Columbia in 1844, came again in November 1845, just before McLoughlin's move. For eighteen months she lay at anchor at Fort Vancouver, as a reminder that England had an interest in the Columbia and in protecting British subjects. Her most notable activity was the role of goodwill embassy, for she hosted a series of entertainments to which all the settlers were invited.

These were elaborate productions, with scenery painted by the crew, and several roles taken by young ladies of the area. The plays included popular dramas of the day, such as *Three Weeks after Marriage, The Deuce Is in Him,*

McLoughlin, date unknown, but in his later years. All his portraits show his outstanding feature—the mane of white hair, falling almost to his shoulders. It was this, plus his hot temper, that caused the Indians to call him "the White-Headed Eagle." OHS ORHI 69600

Love in a Village, and *The Meek Doctor*, with at least one orchestra of violin, flute, and bagpipe.

In addition to plays, the ship's young officers arranged horse races, balls, and games. McLoughlin furthered the rapport by allowing his new gristmill—finished at last—to be used for a community ball sponsored by young Americans, many of whom had helped erect the building. Even at a dance, however, with the men of the *Modeste* in glamorous uniform and the ship's band playing, people did not forget their prickly politics. While the dancers were bowing and twirling, one young ship's officer met the settler Robert Newell and wagered a bottle of wine that in case of war, most of the men present would fight on the British side—a strange bet in that predominantly American town. It must have surprised no one that the officer lost.

Disagreement over politics, however, did not interfere with the prevailing good will. McLoughlin expressed the general warmth by writing to Captain Baillie:

> I am informed the Modeste Sails on Monday next. Allow me to Wish
> you a pleasant Voyage home and a happy meeting with your friends
> and to assure you that I consider that the presence of HMS Modeste
> at Vancouver Your Conduct and that of your officers the Good Behaviour
> and Discipline of your Crew have been the Means of preventing trou-
> ble in the Country. . . . Permit me to state a fact that since I am in the
> Country I have known no ships Crew Conduct themselves in so order-
> ly a Manner as that of HM Ship Modeste under your Command.

A less pleasant reminder of the volatile international scene came in late 1846 or early 1847, when McLoughlin's old comrades Douglas and Ogden sent him part of the report of Lieutenants Warre and Vavasour. It was so critical of the Hudson's Bay Company that the British government had forwarded it to the London Committee, and Governor Simpson had referred it to Fort

Vancouver. Sir George said the company wanted "to relieve the concern from the grave imputations thus brought against them," and that McLoughlin was to be consulted for "such observations thereon as he may think proper."

The doctor read the report with interest at first, then with disbelief and growing anger. It accused him and the company of poor judgment, of possible disloyalty, and of showing special favors that promoted the immigration of American settlers. "We are convinced that without their assistance not thirty American families would ever have been in the settlement," the report said. It asserted that McLoughlin had cooperated with the settlers' government, had sold goods to citizens of the United States "at even a more advantageous rate than to the British Subjects," and that as a result, "the Gentlemen of the Hudson's Bay Company . . . now require the protection of the British Government against the very people to the introduction of whom they have been more than accessory."

Stung by the criticism and offended by the report's inaccuracies, Mc-Loughlin wrote a long rebuttal, in which he pointed out that many Americans had come without the company's assistance, and that his aid was a humane policy, necessary in the isolated Northwest and wise from a business stand-point. "As people will not allow their families [to] starve, when provisions are in their reach," he said, "if we had not assisted them Vancouver would have been destroyed, the world would have said we were treated in the manner our inhuman conduct deserved, the Character of the Hudsons Bay Company and its Officers . . . would be censured with obloquy, and the Company's business in this department would be ruined." He reminded the officials that he had joined the provisional government because when he asked for British support, he was told to protect company property "in the best way I could." And as for aiding the settlers, he insisted that it was necessary, because "we had no right or power to drive them away."

He was especially infuriated because he had been required to accommo-date Warre and Vavasour without being warned that they were government agents. If the spies had consulted him, they would have received more reli-able information, he tartly said, and suggested that they should have at least handed him their report "for perusal, that I might have an opportunity to explain, and not have as it were, my character assasinated in the dark."

When Douglas and Ogden received McLoughlin's statement, they were delighted, because it demolished the accusations against the company and justified their own conduct. In March 1847 they sent it to Simpson, telling him that it was a pleasure to do so because it "furnishes so full and complete a

A view of Oregon City, looking downriver, along the east shore of the Willamette River. The falls, McLoughlin house, and mills are out of the picture, to the right. The Catholic church with square bell tower, is near the center, and the Methodist church is farther left on the point of land. The snowcap in the background is Mt. Hood. *Oregon City, 1845*, by Henry Warre. OHS ORHI 791

refutation of the absurd and unfounded statements made by Messrs. Warre and Vavasour, that we deem it superfluous to make any further remarks on the subject."

Neither the British government nor the company followed up on the report. The episode was irritating but insignificant, because by the time slow-moving ships carried McLoughlin's statement to London, the boundary negotiations were in their final stages, and the Warre-Vavasour report had no discernible impact on the location of the line or the company's reputation.

It did, however, reflect the increasingly tense international situation. The British doggedly insisted that the boundary follow the forty-ninth parallel to the Columbia and that river to the sea. In 1842 the British negotiator, Lord Ashburton, had written, "I shall make no settlement in this case on any other terms." And in April 1845 Lord Aberdeen, Secretary for Foreign Affairs, had offered to make the ports south of the forty-ninth parallel free to both countries, but said, "Beyond this degree of compromise Her Majesty's Gov't could not consent to go." Meanwhile, the United States gave up its extreme demand for 54°40', but refused to yield an inch below the forty-ninth parallel, all the way to the Pacific.

One great sticking point was still the wish for deep-water ports, because the Northwest Coast has so few. San Francisco Bay then belonged to Mexico. The Columbia was blighted by its bar. And the next port north, the coveted jewel, was Puget Sound, surrounded by forests and mountains—deep—spacious—blessed with many arms. Both nations were determined to have it, and on this issue statesmen dug in their heels. The U.S. government considered placing artillery at the mouth of the Columbia, and Her Majesty's navy sent a fleet of warships to the Pacific.

In the impasse, the British suggested arbitration, which the Americans at first angrily refused for fear of losing Puget Sound. "The United States might almost as well abandon the whole territory as consent to deprive themselves of these harbors," said Secretary of State James Buchanan, while the *New York Evening Post* predicted that if arbitration were tried and went amiss, America would be left "high and dry on the rock-bound shore of the Pacific, without a shelter for a skiff."

Even for those days of colorful hyperbole, some of the prose was amazing. The *Ohio Statesman*, for example, wrote:

> Withered be the hand that dismembers Oregon, and palsied the tongue that consents to an act so treasonable, foul and unnatural. Let Freedom's holy banner be planted upon the farthest ice-bound cliff, to which our title is clear and unquestionable, and our answer to our arrogant foe be given in the words of Vasa—'Here will we take our stand.'

With less elegance but just as much ardor, the *Oregon Spectator* printed a bold headline, "A WAR WITH ENGLAND!" and asked, "Who wants a parcel of low flung, 'outside barbarians' to go in cahoots with us, and share alike a piece of land that always was and always will be ours?"

By 1846, however, both countries had problems severe enough to soften their belligerence. In Britain, the potato crop of Ireland failed, the harvest of grain was expected to be below average, and the country was bitterly divided over the repeal of its "corn laws"—import duties on grain. In America, the independent republic of Texas was agitating for admission to the union, and as a result the United States was facing a probable war with Mexico—a contingency that was more pressing than the Oregon boundary.

As a result, responsible diplomats on both sides of the Atlantic softened their tone. Lord Aberdeen in England disparaged "a cause so preposterous and absurd as the possession of a few miles of pine swamp" and told Edward Everett, the former ambassador to Britain, "I cannot believe it possible that the Government of the United States could venture to drive matters to extremity, and incur the heavy responsibility of a war." An editorial in the London *Times* said traditions of kinship, language, laws, and morals "bind the two nations together by ties which it would be atrocious to sever by the sword. We are two people, but we are one family." And Daniel Webster, senator from Massachusetts, said war would be "an act at once of stupendous folly and enormous crime."

In a retreat from its previous insistence on the Columbia River boundary, the British government then suggested a line on the forty-ninth parallel from the Rocky Mountains to Puget Sound, and from there to the Pacific via the Strait of Juan de Fuca. Both nations accepted these terms, which preserved their access to the Strait of Georgia and Puget Sound. Britain would relinquish the north bank of the Columbia but receive all of Vancouver Island, and the Hudson's Bay Company would be allowed navigation rights in the river. The United States would give up its insistence on 54°40'—a small concession, because the forty-ninth parallel was the line American diplomats had offered periodically ever since 1818. On this basis they divided approximately half a million square miles—the size of today's Great Britain, Ireland, France, Germany, Holland, and Belgium combined.

Neither country obtained all it wanted, but neither lost everything, for each received about one-half of the area and preserved Pacific outlets through the Columbia and Puget Sound. The United States kept the section where its people were in a majority, while Britain retained the rich fur lands and canoe routes in New Caledonia, the "possessory rights" of its citizens south of the Columbia, and rights of navigation in that river.

Although the treaty was ratified by the Senate on June 15, 1846, the news did not reach the Columbia until late October, when David McLoughlin returned from Hawaii on the *Toulon*. As soon as the ship crossed the bar of the Columbia, he disembarked, to hurry to Oregon City by canoe and give his father a newspaper clipping from the *Polynesian* dated August 29, 1846. McLoughlin considered it so important that he took it at once to the editor of the *Spectator*, who published it in the next issue with the statement, "We are indebted to the politeness of Dr. McLaughlin for the following."

The clipping was brief and not entirely accurate, but it contained the main facts: the boundary treaty had been signed. And "the 49th degree is to

This view of Oregon City, ca 1850-52, looks upriver toward the falls. At the south (left) end of Main Street, just beyond the church, is McLoughlin's house with several related structures, probably including a separate kitchen. The large tract beyond the house is the Mill Reserve, which contains a scattering of buildings and extends to the river bank. The small settlement across the river is West Linn, which was then known as Linn City. *Oregon City on the Willamette River*, by John Mix Stanley. AMON CARTER MUSEUM, FORT WORTH, TEXAS

run on to the Straits of Fuca the whole Island of Vancouver being left in the possession of England, and the said Straits of Fuca, Pugeth Sound, &c., remaining free to both parties." The Columbia River would also be free.

The settlers had fretted over the boundary for years, and when they heard this long-awaited news, they broke into a frenzy of jubilation. As the *Spectator* described it, "The only piece of ordnance owned in any way by the territory— a twelve pounder, presented to the city by B. Stark Jr., Esq., was quickly mounted upon the rocks, on the river's bank, and a salute of twenty-one guns fired under the direction of our mayor A.L. Lovejoy Esq. The reports were the loudest, and the rejoicing echoes of the old hills of the Willamette the longest, that the most patriotic could wish to hear."

McLoughlin himself was well pleased. "As to the treaty It seems to me the British subjects in the Country have every Reason to be satisfied with it," he wrote to James Douglas, "and I do Believe that the Conduct we pursued has tended to our obtaining such favourable terms and prevented Britain and the United States being Involved in Horrors of War." His belief that by keeping peace on the Columbia he had saved both nations from a major conflict was an enormous satisfaction to him, one he retained for life and often mentioned.

He had, in fact, understandable reasons for pride. History can never be rewritten, and although it seems unlikely that the two nations would have actually gone to war, they were longtime adversaries—jealous—suspicious— each with a faction that was spoiling for a fight. It is possible that if a tactless or ruthless Chief Factor had been in charge of the Columbia during those critical years, an angry incident, especially one costing immigrants' lives, might have been the spark that set off a blaze.

The first report of the treaty had included its main terms only, but in the spring a more complete account came, and was printed in the *Spectator* for April 1 and 15, 1847. Two articles of the treaty undoubtedly gave McLoughlin a profound sense of relief, for they confirmed land titles for him and his fellow Britons:

> Art. III. . . . the possessory rights of the HBC and all British subjects who may be already in the occupation of land or other property lawfully acquired within said territory, shall be respected.

> Art. IV. The farms, lands, and other property . . . belonging to Puget's Sound Agricultural Company, on the north side of the Columbia River, shall be confirmed to the said Company.

At long last, McLoughlin's title to his land claim seemed to be secure. But envious men in the Willamette Valley were still casting their eyes on that valuable property. He was certain to hear from them again.

~3~

An American Citizen
1847–1849

After his discouraging first year as a private citizen, McLoughlin entered a busy and reasonably contented period, walking up and down the boardwalks in his long dark coat, serving customers, weighing merchandise, buying and selling and shipping. He became interested in the life around him—his family, friends, and especially the children. One day, for example, while

John McLoughlin commissioned F. G. Bowman to paint this portrait of his sister, Marie Louise, Sister Saint Henry of the Ursulines. It still hangs in the Ursuline Monastery in Quebec. COLLECTION URSULINES DE QUÉBEC

he and Sam Barlow were on their way to have a plane blade sharpened, they met young Benjamin Bonney with another small boy. Stopping to talk and pat their heads, McLoughlin said, "if you will go with Mr. Barlow and turn the grindstone while he sharpens that plane bit, I will give you each a handful of candy." They eagerly agreed, and when the job was done, he led them into his store for their reward—a handful of candy hearts printed with mottoes, a never-to-be-forgotten treat.

A darker note was sounded by several deaths within McLoughlin's family. The first was that of his uncle, Dr. Simon Fraser—the good angel—which happened just before the move to Oregon City. As David said, it "grieved us much."

The next was that of McLoughlin's sister Marie Louise, who died in Quebec on July 3, 1846—a genuine loss, for he loved her. Throughout the years they had kept in touch. As Sister St. Henry, Mother Superior of the Ursuline convent, she had taken care of his daughter Eliza, and he and his brother David had sent her globes, maps, and games as aids for her classes. A tangible reminder of his interest is her portrait, commissioned for the convent "at the special request of her brother, Dr. [John] McLoughlin."

And in April 1847, a letter from P. C. Michaud said Michaud's mother—the doctor's sister Julienne—had died in debt. Although McLoughlin had maintained little contact with this sister, she had been living on one of his farms at Rivière-du-Loup, and he wrote to Michaud, "I allowed my Mother (and I Believe your Mother lived with her) for a Number of years before her Death £150 per Annum and the Revenue of my farms at River du Loup. . . . Since my Mothers' Death I allowed your Mother [to] Enjoy the Revenue of my farms on the same Conditions as I did to my Mother." In a characteristic response to a family need, he told his nephew that he could remain on the farm on the same terms.

At about that same time, the doctor was delighted when his old friend Nathaniel Wyeth sent him "Cuttings seeds Newspapers and Thiers life of

Napoleon"—a thoughtful gift, because McLoughlin was especially interested in the French dictator. Years before, while Wyeth was at Fort Vancouver, the two men had enjoyed arguing about him, and the doctor had named the principal street at Champoeg "Napoleon Boulevard." Wyeth asked for help in establishing his title at Fort William, on today's Sauvie Island, and McLoughlin told him, "I will do myself the pleasure to attend to your Claim there are several Squatters on it." He wrote again in a few months to explain that the provisional government allowed claims only for actual settlers, but that he had recorded Wyeth's piece and had taken care to "state that you Claim it and that I lease it from you."

In June 1847, McLoughlin granted Ogden and Douglas an extension of their lease for the company outlet, because their Oregon City store had so much merchandise that moving it to Fort Vancouver would be expensive. But a year later, when the lease of his sawmills to Pomeroy and Hedges expired, he did not renew it, explaining that "though Mr Pomeroy is a good honest man and has done me justice, still . . . I may take them [the mills] into my own hands as I think I can do better by them." He estimated that his two plants could produce one million board feet per annum, and that he had sufficient water power at the falls to erect three or four more, if they were needed.

After taking over the operation, he hired John Minto as assistant, one of the main jobs being to catch logs from upstream as they went into the millrace. It was hard, dangerous work, at which McLoughlin sometimes lent a hand, assisted by young Dr. William McKay, who was still with the McLoughlin family. Minto described the white-haired doctor moving from point to point beside the stream, and said that one day, when logs jammed in the gateway to the flumes, he and McKay both tackled the jumbled mass with long levers and "worked with a will" until they broke it up. At this McLoughlin was so delighted that he dropped his pole, clasped William in his arms, and kissed him on the cheek.

McLoughlin had a special pleasure that summer when he received a medal from the Pope, brought by Father Blanchet, who had been in Rome and returned as Archbishop of Oregon City. With the medal was a brief that said the doctor had been accepted into the order of the Knights of St. Gregory, because "you are esteemed by all for your upright life, correct morals and zeal for religion." For the rest of his life, these were McLoughlin's most treasured possessions.

As always, he had family responsibilities. In March 1848, when Catherine Ermatinger and her children left to join her husband at Fort Chipewyan on

Lake Athabasca, McLoughlin arranged for her journey. "They will proceed with the Express if the Route is safe," he told Francis Ermatinger, "but if . . . danger is apprehended they will Return here and proceed with the Summer Brigade."

She left as planned, but the big house remained lively, with Eloisa's family there, as well as David and McKay. The doctor and Marguerite acquired a reputation for hospitality. George Luther Boone, grandson of Daniel Boone, came to Oregon City in 1848, and said that he "soon knew all the boys in town especially Billy McKay, clerk in the Hudson's Bay Store. . . . McKay boarded at McLoughlin's and often asked me to stay all night with him. Plenty of beds upstairs at the McLoughlin house."

Eloisa gave a brief picture of her father as a sociable and outgoing citizen. "He was fond of children; very fond of ladies company; fond of talking and visiting. Especially when he went to church in the morning he would go and visit at one place and then at another. He said he had no time to do it on week days. He was very busy all the time till he died."

Even though McLoughlin had bought out the mission's claim to his land, the problem was revived in midsummer 1847 by George Abernethy, the provisional governor, who had bought the equipment of the Island Milling Company. Without asking for permission, Abernethy started to haul logs to his island mill over the top of McLoughlin's dam—an intrusion that alarmed the doctor. He wrote to his friend Chief Justice Peter Burnett, saying, "I state to you how affairs are and hope you will do the Needful." Burnett's response is not on record, but the irritation subsided in September with the opening of a public bridge from the end of Main Street to the Abernethy mill. The incident was trivial, but significant in showing that the controversy over the doctor's claim was still alive.

The old conflict was revived again by a farmer named A. J. Vickers, who registered a rival claim on part of McLoughlin's Oregon City land. When the doctor protested, Vickers first cited the obsolete law that no individual could hold townsites or water privileges, then said that even though McLoughlin had recorded his title in 1843, he should have done so again in 1845, when the Oregon law was changed. "This man had got three or four Men to join him," the doctor told Wyeth, "and though the Community Disapprove their Conduct still it is Extremely harrassing to be Annoyed in this Way." He explained that no one who had recorded land under the old law had reregistered it; and he placed a notice of ownership in the *Spectator*, which was countered by a notice from Vickers. The spat became a *cause célèbre*. Businessmen held a meeting to discuss ways to handle claim jumpers, and supporters of both men vented their opinions in letters to the editor. Lively as the dispute was, however, it faded out, leaving no record of the outcome.

During the past several years, the Indians of eastern Oregon had grown increasingly resentful of the ever larger, ever more destructive wagon trains. The tribes at Waiilatpu—the Whitman mission near Walla Walla—were increasingly restive, and McLoughlin, with his network of friends and business acquaintances, heard about it. In October 1847 he wrote to U.S. Secretary of War William L. Marcy strongly recommending that every company from Missouri should have a conductor "well Acquainted with the percautions Necessary to be taken by persons travelling from there to Fort Hall." The government, he said, should establish a post there with an Indian agent, who "ought to have ten or twelve steady Judicious Men well Acquainted with the Indians." These must be men whom the Indians knew and respected, and he suggested "Mr Robert Newel an Old Rocky Mountain trader as a person well qualified for the office of Agent at Fort Hall and he should select the Conductors." He urged the use of the southern route explored in 1846 by Levi Scott and Jesse Applegate. It was somewhat longer but less rugged than the northern trail, and "out of the Range of the Nez perces Cayouses and Walla Walla tribes the Best Armed Most Numerous and the Most Warlike tribes on this side of the Rocky Mountains."

Five days later McLoughlin wrote again, because several immigrants had been "pillaged of their property" between Walla Walla and The Dalles. As before, he recommended that each group have a competent leader, saying that when he was at Fort Vancouver he never sent out a party without an officer who knew the natives well. "In Justice to the Indians," he continued, "I must say I have known Many and Many a White Man as Ready to impose on the Indians when in their power as Indians in Similar situation to impose on Whites. . . . Among Indians the Majority will support Right—and Reprobate and punish Wrong." In addition, he was troubled by "a Report that the Half Breeds will not be allowed to have claims of land"—a restriction that would "Blast the Prospects of these people" and force them to retire among their Indian relatives. This, he said, would retard the settlement of the country, and was both unjust and unnecessary, because they were "as peaceable orderly and Industrious as any settlers in the Country."

McLoughlin had great respect for the natives and profound knowledge about their problems and beliefs. If his advice had been taken, it might have

John McLoughlin's letter book copy of his Oct. 16, 1847 letter to the Secretary of War, William L. Marcy. The letter begins, "Sir, My residence in this Country and the situation I held as officer in Charge of the Hudson Bay Co Business in it from 1824 to1846 has afforded me opportunity to acquire some Knowledge of the Character and Disposition of the Indians in this Territory...." His advice, even if it had been heeded, was much too late to avoid an attack on the Whitman Mission in Waiilatpu on November 29, 1847. FORT VANCOUVER NATIONAL HISTORIC SITE

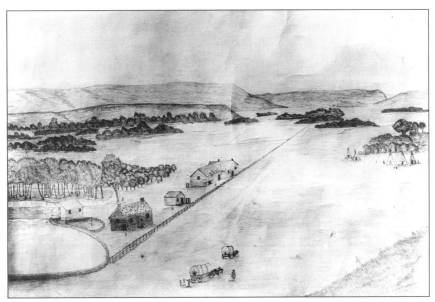

A drawing of the Whitman mission, made from memory by Nancy A. (Osborn) Jacobs, who was a child there and survived the attack. She said, "According to the best of my recollection, the above is a correct representation of the mission building at the time of the massacre, Nov. 29, 1847." OHS ORHI 637

avoided at least some of the tragedies of the next few decades. But it was ignored, and in any case it came too late. On November 29, 1847, infuriated by a measles epidemic, a group of Cayuses killed Dr. Marcus Whitman and his wife, Narcissa, along with eleven other men and two children, and took forty-seven captives.

William McBean, in charge of Fort Nez Perces, sent the news by a messenger, who reached Fort Vancouver on December 6. On the following day three boats started upriver under the leadership of Peter Skene Ogden, with Thomas McKay as his aide. Ogden—white-haired by then but still vigorous and courageous—had sixteen boatmen, a load of blankets, ammunition, and other goods with which to ransom the prisoners, but no soldiers. When the Cayuse chiefs had gathered, he made a speech that has become famous, in which he bluntly told them he could not make promises. "The Company have nothing to do with your quarrel," he said. "If you wish it, on my return I will see what can be done for you; but I do not promise to prevent war. Deliver me the prisoners to return to their friends, and I will pay you a ransom, that is all." After a lengthy conference, he secured the release of the captives, whom he rushed down the Columbia to safety, along with the members of the Spalding mission at Lapwai.

In Oregon City, the legislative committee passed a bill authorizing Abernethy to set up an army, finance it by contributions, and send it upriver to capture the Indians who were responsible. At first McLoughlin thought the venture would fail, and he refused to contribute, explaining that "if the winter of 1847–48 were as severe as those of 1826–27, and the Columbia froze, it would be impossible to take provisions to the troops in the Cayuse Country, and they must inevitably perish from hunger and cold." He advocated waiting for warmer weather, but when he heard that the volunteers had set out and were in want of provisions, he sent them "106 head of beef cattle and all the flour the commissary required." The volunteer army then went upriver, to wage a brief campaign and return in the spring.

While they were still in the field, an event of national importance occurred in California. On January 24, 1848, gold was found in Sutter's millrace, about forty-five miles from his mill near today's Sacramento.

McLoughlin and his fellow merchants felt the effects almost at once, for within a few weeks men began to leave in droves for the mines, and those who stayed behind struggled to satisfy the greedy new market. In 1849 more than fifty vessels came up the Columbia River to carry back grain, flour, lumber, and other products. The price of wheat rose to $2 a bushel from its former 62 cents, lumber to $100 per thousand board feet. Goods became so scarce that in February 1849 the Reverend William Roberts of Oregon City wrote, "Not a Blanket, or Kettle, or tin pan or pair of boots or strong coat or pants or hat fit to wear or pound of Sal Eratica [baking soda] or tea can be bought anywhere in the territory that I know of at any price." In January 1849, the *Spectator* reported the influx of $400,000 in gold dust, and the following March David McLoughlin wrote to his cousin:

> I believe both California & Oregon is covered with Gold. . . . I am now on the eve of starting for the gold region with large numbers of Indians hired to me for a year I hope then to be satisfied for the remainder of my life every one has to do his own work in these days, silver or Gold being no object to any one. . . . This time last year men that would be very glad to get employment are now walking about the Street too proud to touch any thing. believe me Money is flying about here in large quantities especially Gold dust I have made for my share these last five months about twenty thousand dollars.

Miners at work in California. The gold rush had an immense effect, both good and bad, on Oregon. It brought in business and capital, because shoring up the mines consumed quantities of lumber, and the miners needed Oregon-grown food. The demand for goods also created shortages of commodities of every kind, and monopolized shipping. From John C. Van Tramp's *Prairie and Rocky Mountain Adventures*. OHS ORHI 87176

Even though gold dust was valuable, it was a nuisance as a medium of exchange. People carried it in leather pouches, and stores set up jewelers' scales for weighing it. F. X. Matthieu said it was "like dirt" and that "I have seen the Hudson's Bay store at Oregon City take in a four-quart pan of dust in one day."

Before long, annoyed at the inconvenience, a group of citizens, including George Abernethy, established an unauthorized mint on a street near the river. There workers melted dust on a common blacksmith's forge, poured it into molds, rolled it into thin bars, and stamped out five- and ten-dollar gold pieces, called Beaver Money for their crude sketch of that animal. The makeshift mint produced about $30,000 in ten-dollar coins and $25,000 in five-dollar coins, enough to ease the shortage if they had been circulated. But they contained more gold than their face value, and consequently people melted them, or sent them to the U.S. Mint.

In the summer of 1849, in the midst of the gold fever, the Cayuses surrendered five men, who were brought to Oregon City for trial. McLoughlin was called to the stand, where he testified that as early as 1840 or 1841 he had warned Whitman of his danger and advised him to move to the Willamette Valley. According to Father Blanchet, one of the accused Indians had not been present at the killings, and the others declared they were innocent but had surrendered to save their people from further war. They were, however,

A tongue-in-cheek rendition of Joseph Meek in Washington. After the attack on the Whitman mission, Meek made a mid-winter trip to the national capital to appeal for help from the U.S. Government. With his frontier accent and dress he captivated those whom he met, and being a distant relative of President Polk's wife, he had entree to state functions. From *River of the West* by Francis F. Victor. OHS ORHI 98826

found guilty and executed by hanging, with Joseph Meek in the unenviable role of executioner. McLoughlin had made every effort to prevent violence, but it had nevertheless occurred, and he left no comment on the outcome.

Although it was not apparent at the time, the Whitman massacre was an important step in the sequence that would eventually lead to McLoughlin's final tragedy. In late 1847, as soon as the provisional legislature heard about the uprising, they sent Joseph Meek to Washington, D.C., on a daring midwinter ride, to report the event to the federal government. Meek's leather clothes, his backwoods accent—and his relationship to his distant cousin, President Polk's wife—created a sensation, prompting Congress to pass an act that established Oregon Territory. Besides providing for a governor, attorney, marshal, three judges, and other officers, all appointed by the president, it called for an elected delegate, who was to offer advice on legislation affecting the territory. This—the introduction of American law—was the event McLoughlin had been awaiting for years, with a mixture of hope and dread.

After signing the bill on August 14, 1848, President Polk appointed General Joseph Lane, a veteran of the Mexican War, as governor, and gave Meek

Joseph Lane was appointed governor when Congress, stirred to action by the attack on the Whitman mission, made Oregon a Territory. This shows him and Joseph Meek riding mules across the desert of the southwest, on their way to Oregon. from *River of the West* by Francis F. Victor. OHS ORHI 98827

the job of escorting the general to his new realm. They went by boat from Lane's Indiana home to Missouri, then to Santa Fe with ten mule-drawn wagons and fifty-five mounted men, and continued west by pack mule. The trip was a near disaster. They were plagued by winter cold and desert drought; mules died, soldiers deserted, and the remaining few had to walk the last miles to Los Angeles, where they boarded a ship for San Francisco. Finding it so over-run with gold miners that transport was in short supply, the last seven men took the small vessel *Jeanette* to Astoria and went upriver to Oregon City, reaching it on March 2, 1849.

On the following day Lane issued a proclamation saying that the Oregon Country—until then formless and unnamed—was now Oregon Territory. Tra-dition holds that he made his announcement from the balcony of the Rose farm near Oregon City, after which a huge barbecue was held, with music by two violins and a clarinet, and a hearty meal based on whole steers roasted in pits.

Peter Burnett, Chief Justice for the provisional government, had lacked legal authority to administer an oath, but Lane was fully accredited. On May 13 he ap-pointed territorial judges, and McLoughlin moved at once to secure his land. On May 30 he went to the court and "filed my intention to become an American citizen," his declaration being "drawn up by the Clerk of Judge Bryants Court." In it he promised to support the Constitution of the United States, and renounced

John McLoughlin's declaration of intent to become a citizen of the United States. He signed the following: "I, do solemnly swear, that I renounce all allegiance and fidelity to all and any foreign prince, potentate, state and sovereignty, whatever and particularly to Victoria, Queen of the United Kingdom of Great Britain and Ireland, and that I will support the Constitution of the United States, and the provision of 'An act to establish the Territorial Government of Oregon", so help me God." OHS ORHI 98792 "all allegiance and fidelity to all and any foreign prince, protector, State and Sovereignty whatever, and particularly to Victoria Queen of the United Kingdom of Great Britain and Ireland." Although he would have a two-year waiting period before completion of citizenship, he had taken the first, highly significant step.

With that achieved at last, he could rest more easily than he had for years. The terms of the boundary settlement had clearly stated that "the possessory rights of . . . all British subjects" would be respected, which should safeguard his claim, but the property of an American citizen was even more secure.

~4~
"The Companionship of Adders"
1849–1851

I n 1849 McLoughlin's application for citizenship had not yet become final. "Foreigners," however, could legally vote in Oregon Territory provided they had taken the oath to become citizens, and therefore he was able to cast a ballot in the general election of June 1849. But he made a mistake.

The problem had begun with George Abernethy, the provisional governor. After coming with Jason Lee on the *Lausanne* in 1840, he opened the mission store in Oregon City, bought it when the mission was disbanded, and became manager of the mission-based Island Milling Company, which had built the mills on the rocky island that was part of McLoughlin's claim. The company at first had multiple owners, but in 1846 Abernethy bought the other investors' shares, ignoring the doctor's rights. The island was subsequently known as Abernethy Island or Governor's Island.

Three years later Abernethy sold the company's mills and logs to W. P. Bryant, Oregon's new federal judge, for thirty thousand dollars. The situation dismayed McLoughlin, because if he took his land claim to court, the man on the bench would be Judge Bryant, purchaser of the mills, and Bryant's ownership depended on the validity of Abernethy's claim. McLoughlin therefore decided not to "bring the case forward till the bench was full," and merely wrote to Bryant saying that the island was part of his claim, that it was recorded in the book of land claims, and that he expected to recover it "as soon as it shall meet the pleasure of my adopted government to act in the matter."

Abernethy's right to the island and sale to Bryant were supported by a group commonly called the mission party, because many of its members had belonged

This view of Oregon City was painted by Paul Kane, who visited the area in 1847. It shows McLoughlin's Mill Reserve, a very large tract just south of his house, which contained the gristmill, saw mill, granary, French store, foundry, "and appurtenances." The mill race is the glimpse of water near the lower center, behind the cluster of buildings, and just beyond it is the disputed island, with a pair of mills and stacks of lumber. The McLoughlin house is out of the picture, to the right. *The Mills of Oregon City* by Paul Kane. STARK MUSEUM OF ART, ORANGE, TEXAS

to Lee's mission until 1844, when the Reverend Gary dissolved it. Although Gary had dismissed its laymen, he had given each a passage home or its equivalent—about eight hundred to one thousand dollars—and most of them had stayed in Oregon as businessmen or farmers. They were intensely interested in politics.

Dissolution of the mission did not stop the growth of the Methodist church. It remained active, supporting several congregations and administering the Oregon Institute, which became Willamette University. With its interests focused on religion and education, the church did not belong to the mission party, and it had no part in politics.

As a territory, Oregon could send a delegate to advise Congress in drawing up laws for the area, and Abernethy wanted a spokesman who would uphold his claim to the island and the sale of mills and logs to Bryant. With this in mind, he and the mission party chose as their candidate Samuel R. Thurston— personable, well educated, handsome—a bearded young newcomer to Oregon who was known as a master of fire-eating oratory. It was said that at one public confrontation, when his opponent "moved forward, Thurston pointed his finger straight at him . . . and said, 'Don't you take another step, or a button-hole will be seen through you.'" And the other man stopped.

Thurston's eloquence and the mission party's prestige were a powerful combination. In addition, with scores of settlers in the California mines, many of the voters were recent arrivals, who did not know McLoughlin or under-stand the politics of the land claim but were aware that Thurston had strong supporters. As a result, he received 470 votes and his nearest rival, Columbus Lancaster, 321. It sounded an ominous note for the doctor, because Thurston, being indebted to Abernethy and the mission party, hoped for their backing in future elections.

The doctor, being well aware of Thurston's tie to Abernethy and the mis-sion party, had not only voted for Lancaster, he had urged his French Cana-dian friends to do the same. His mistake had been to openly admit it. "I voted, and voted against him, as he well knew, and as he seems well to remember," the doctor later said. The consequence was that Thurston's pro-Abernethy slant was intensified by a personal grudge.

Soon after the election, the Legislative Assembly adopted a memorial to Congress pleading for a land law, for money to pay its debts and the costs of the Cayuse War, and for roads and public buildings. With this memorial in his luggage, Thurston set out for Washington by way of Panama. At about the same time, Judge Bryant also left for Washington, supposedly to lobby for a land bill, although he would actually help Thurston, in order to protect his own purchase of the island mills.

In late 1849 Thurston crossed the Isthmus of Panama by mule, but because he was ill and unable to watch his baggage while on the rugged trail, his goods, including the memorial, were either lost or stolen. Undaunted, when he reached Washington, he replaced the memorial with a set of resolutions as he remembered them, and began a complex process of studying congres-sional procedures, making contacts, and meeting with committees, aided by Judge Bryant. Finding the legislators so preoccupied with the issue of slavery that they had little interest in Oregon, he worked tirelessly to remind them of the territory's needs. He was an able man—eloquent, smart, and effective.

However, his talents were marred by a streak of sleaze, which showed in small things. He wrote to his wife that her brother Frank was emigrating to Oregon, and that "I promised Frank I would not tell you, but it is too good to keep." He sent her a "gold bosome pin," saying, "you may tell them [it] cost twenty dollars, tho I paid but ten for it." And he told her about his trick on

Robert Moore, for whom he was carrying five hundred dollars in gold dust. "Old father Moore will suppose his gold is lost, as I wrote him and you it was. I wanted to see what the old Coon would have to say whether he would blame me or not. . . . I now inform you that it is not [lost]."

The same streak was evident in his efforts to ensure his own reelection by cementing his ties to the Abernethy group. The best way to do this, he thought, was to help the governor eradicate McLoughlin's entire land claim, because if the doctor retained his legal rights on the mainland, his right to the island would also be established.

American settlers could not acquire official title to the land while it was owned by the natives, and therefore one of Thurston's early moves, in January 1850—aided by Judge Bryant—was to promote a bill to "extinguish" Indian titles "to all the land between 42 and 49 north latitude, west of the Cascade Mountains, and to remove the indians East of the Cascades." This, he said, "is the first step towards our land law." As a territorial delegate, he could not present the bill or vote, but he could—and did—help shape it.

He followed this in May or early June with a long letter to the House of Representatives pointing out the wishes of the settlers in many areas—courts, roads, postal system, public buildings, and education. Much of it was sound, adhering to acknowledged needs, but part of it urged the passage of a land bill that would seize McLoughlin's entire claim. Long and polished, this section was remarkable for its convincing eloquence and breezy disregard for truth. It said the Methodist mission had made the claim first but had been "forced to leave it under the fear of having the savages of Oregon let loose upon them," that McLoughlin "held it by violence and dint of threats," that he had sold lots worth $200,000, and that he "still refuses to file his intentions to become an American citizen." It described the island as "of no value" and as only "two acres of barren rock," which had been sold to George Abernethy and should be confirmed to him because of the gristmill that stood there. Otherwise, the letter said, "Dr. McLoughlin will hold, as he has heretofore held, the bread of the people of the Territory in his own fist."

Its most cunning feature was a plan for Congress to transfer McLoughlin's land claim to the territory, to be sold for educational funds and thus "save their capital, their county seat, and the balance of that noble water power from the grasp of this British propagandist." Warming to the subject, it continued:

> The children of my Country are looking up to you with countenances
> flashing eloquence, clamoring to be educated, and asking you, in sim-

ple but feeling language, where your charity begins. They call you 'fathers,' and ask you whether you will put the moral weapons of defence in your children's hands in the shape of education.

It was a clever plan, to wrap McLoughlin's loss in a cloak of respectability—even virtue—as a benefit for youth.

On May 28, 1850, when the House debated its Oregon bill, Thurston delivered a speech—equally creative—concerning McLoughlin's land. As printed in the *Congressional Globe*, it said,

> This company has been warring against our government for these forty years. Dr. McLoughlin has been their chief fugleman, first to cheat our government out of the whole country, and next to prevent its settlement. . . . He has driven men from claims and from the country. . . . How, sir, would you reward Benedict Arnold, were he living? . . . this bill proposes to reward those who are now, have been, and ever will be, more hostile to our country—more dangerous, because more hidden, more jesuitical.

He told the lawmakers they could consult the Supreme Judge of the Territory for proof of his allegations, and Bryant wrote a letter to Congress stating that they were true.

Having obtained copies of the letter and the debate, Thurston sent them to his contacts in Oregon, along with his proposed land bill. On the back of the parcel he wrote, "Keep this still till next mail, when I shall send them generally. . . . keep dark."

Throughout that summer of 1850, McLoughlin was unaware of his opponents' strategy. He attended the Fourth of July celebration, featuring a procession and an oration by the Honorable K. Pritchett, who was acting as governor because Lane had resigned and left for California. After the program and a community dinner in the "dining salon," many of the guests offered toasts. One of these was McLoughlin, who proposed, "Oregon, from the fertility of its soil, the salubrity and mildness of its climate; the finest place in North America for the residence of civilized man." These are the words of a confident man, participating in community life, pleasant, successful, at ease.

But the clouds were gathering. His opponents had said he did not vote in the previous election, prompting him to write to its judges for confirmation. He had not anticipated trouble, but—although witnesses had seen him cast a ballot—the election judges replied that his vote "was rejected because the Law of the Territorial absolutely prohibited you . . . the right of voting." McLoughlin then appealed the decision to Orville C. Pratt, Associate Judge of the Supreme Court of Oregon, who had been appointed for the southern part of the territory, but served the entire area after Bryant went to Washington. As the doctor expressed it, Pratt "decided that my declaration of intention was legal and that I had the right to vote—I voted and have done so ever since." Favorable as Pratt's reply was, the episode indicated that McLoughlin still had problems, and he soon learned how serious they were. It was May 1850 when the election judges rejected him, and in late August or early September Thurston's packet of papers arrived: the letter, debate, and proposed bill.

When the delegate sent it to Oregon and asked his contacts to "keep dark," he either made no allowance for human nature, or he wanted his plan exposed. The documents were promptly passed from one reader to another, and rumors about them began to circulate. Thurston's supporters insisted they could not be true, as did the editor of the *Oregon Spectator*, who wrote, "We venture the assertion that the story was started by some malicious or mischief-making persons." When a copy fell into McLoughlin's hands, he was furious at Thurston's accusations and horrified to discover that the proposed bill would deprive him of his entire claim.

Stunned, he wrote a long and ardent letter of rebuttal to the newspaper, which printed it on September 12, 1850, with Thurston's papers in the same issue. The doctor staunchly defended himself and the Hudson's Bay Company, saying that under the treaty of joint occupation they had held the legal right to conduct business, had maintained friendship with the Indians, and had made it safe to travel in the area. Stung by being called "chief fugleman," he said, in one of his occasional descents into sarcasm, "This is a term which he probably gathered from the vocabulary in which he found the word 'gumption,' with which he recently garnished another dish, and which he seems to have prepared for appetites similar to his own . . . I am an old man, and my head is very white with the frost of many winters, but I have never before been accused as a cheat."

He recounted his provision of boats, cattle, clothing, food, farming utensils, and seed to the immigrants. He referred to many who had praised his efforts—Wilkes, Frémont, and others—and said he had been criticized in England for helping Americans too much.

"If I had acted differently," he said, "the Government would have had difficulties, and this community would perhaps not have enjoyed the peace it has, nor be in so prosperous a condition as it is . . . the country could never have been colonized as easily as it was, but for the timely, ample, and continuous assistance rendered by me, to them, with the means of the Hudson's Bay Company under my charge."

He reminded readers that he had claimed the land in 1829 and had taken numerous measures to hold it, while the Methodists had not come until 1840. He told of his many donations. "I have given away lots to the Methodists, Catholics, Presbyterians, Congregationalists, and Baptists. I have given 8 lots to a Roman Catholic Nunnery, 8 lots to the Clackamas Female Protestant Seminary, incorporated by the Oregon Legislature."

As for being a British propagandist, he said, "If I was an Englishman, I know no reason why I should not acknowledge it; but I am a Canadian by birth, and an Irishman by descent. I am neither ashamed of my birth-place or lineage—but it has always appeared to me that a man who can only boast of his country has little to be proud of."

He recited his efforts to attain citizenship and his prompt exercise of the right to vote. He asked whether the people of Oregon City could "believe Mr. Thurston did not know . . . that Mr. Abernethy had sold his rights, whatever they were to Judge Bryant," and that if Congress were to donate the island, "they would be donating it to Judge Bryant, his heirs and assigns."

And he lamented the attempt "to take from me my property, and to leave me in the decline of life, and in the decrepitude of old age, to the companionship of adders, who—when they were benumbed with frost, I gathered from the hedges and warmed into life, to feel, when alas! too late, the stings of their ingratitude."

His letter and Thurston's were widely read and set off a furor. Many landowners were relieved that their claims would be confirmed, and some were pleased at the seizure of British land, but others were shocked. As one example, William J. Berry wrote in the *Spectator* that he had formerly admired Thurston, but that in relation to the land claim, "I think he had placed himself in the position of the old cow, who, after giving a fine pail of milk, kicked it all over." Berry then dissected Thurston's argument, saying that the mission, and hence Abernethy, never had a right to the claim, "unless jumping constitutes right." And Asahel Bush, editor of the *Oregon Statesman*, wrote to the delegate, "there is not a press in the country now in favor of you. . . . The *Spectator* would not publish those little scraps you sent me."

According to the land bill, Oregon City lots were safe if they had been bought from McLoughlin before March 4, 1849—when President Polk's term of office expired and the administration of President Taylor began—but settlers who had made later purchases feared for their claims. On September 19, 1850, they held a public meeting in Oregon City at which they passed resolutions declaring that the eleventh section of the bill, relating to McLoughlin, was unjust and uncalled for; that the doctor "merits the gratitude of multitudes of persons in Oregon for the timely and long-continued assistance tendered by him in the settlement of this Territory"; and that the bill would cause a "severe, inequitable, unnecessary, and irremediable injustice." A total of fifty- six persons signed the memorial.

Another public meeting, however, was held in Salem, fortress of the mission party, and this group "highly approved" of Thurston's actions. The children of Oregon, they said, had "a better right to the balance of that claim than Dr. McLoughlin."

Although the favorable memorial was sent to Congress, neither trains nor telegraph wires yet crossed the Rockies, and in September 1850—long before the memorial arrived—Congress passed, and President Fillmore signed, the Donation Land Law. It stated that every male American citizen over the age of eighteen, including "half-breed Indians," could claim 320 acres, provided he met certain conditions; and that if he had a wife, she could receive the same.

As McLoughlin feared, the law also said Abernethy Island was "confirmed to the legal assigns of the Willamette Milling and Trading Companies," while the rest of his land claim, except for lots given away or sold before March 4, 1849, was to be "at the disposal of the Legislative Assembly, the proceeds thereof to be applied . . . to the establishment and endowment of a university, to be located at such place in the territory as the Legislative Assembly may designate." Thurston had prepared the legislators so cleverly that when this section came to a vote, they knew only that it had the unqualified backing of the territory's elected delegate and Chief Justice. They were unfamiliar with Oregon, no knowledgeable person was on hand to tell them the truth, and with not a glimmer of opposition, they passed the bill.

It was a heady achievement for Thurston, who gloated to his wife that "their present defeat is my triumphant success . . . which arms me with a force against which they cant stand. Truly, dear, never did a Delegate come out of his first session so lucky and so successfully as I have. . . . I see the scattered bones of D M Laughlin, the HB Company and their actors."

Even though his bill had passed, Thurston continued to seek support, in hopes of being reelected as delegate. He wrote to McLoughlin's friend Nathaniel Wyeth asking for information about the doctor, calling him "odious" and accusing him of an attempt "to cripple" Oregon's growth. Wyeth—both loyal and astute—sent Thurston a warm endorsement of McLoughlin's generosity and asked Congressman Robert C. Winthrop to investigate. But Winthrop learned little. He replied a month later that he had asked Thurston "what there was pending before Congress or the Executive," and that Thurston "would tell me nothing."

The transactions involving Abernethy Island are not clear. Bryant had bought its mill, and later on Abernethy said that before the Donation Land Law was passed, he and his son had transferred title to the island itself to Joseph Lane, governor of the territory. However, Abernethy owned it again by 1850, having apparently repossessed it, for an unknown reason. Whether he had actively assisted Thurston, or collaborated in devising the plan, or merely profited from it, he must have known what was being done, and he accepted it.

For McLoughlin, the mechanics of the sale were of little consequence. The significant point was that Abernethy and Bryant would benefit financially by taking the island, while Thurston—ambitious for power—was indebted to Abernethy for his political backing. Therefore they cleverly and successfully attacked the entire claim, by presenting a barrage of falsehoods to the United States Congress. Francis Fuller Victor, author of Bancroft's *History of Oregon*, bluntly asserted that Bryant was bribed, and it is known that he was "in reduced circumstances" when he came to Oregon but was "well off financially" when he left six months later.

Abernethy continued to expand his business, buying ships and inaugurating a wholesale venture for the import of merchandise from New York. Although he prospered, neither Bryant nor Thurston returned to Oregon, or lived long to enjoy the fruits of their scheme. Bryant, whose health was poor, went from Washington to his home in Indiana, resigned his judgeship, and died within a few months. Thurston set out for the Northwest, but in April 1851 he died on the steamer *California*, near Acapulco. His grave was in Mexico until two years later, when his remains were brought to Salem and reburied there.

McLoughlin might have sought justice through the boundary treaty of 1846, which had provided that the possessory rights of British subjects were to be respected, but Thurston had inoculated his bill against that possibility by including a section that forbade anyone from making a land claim under both treaty and land law. However harmless this appeared, it tied McLoughlin's hands, because he had declared his intention to become an American citizen, which prevented him from asking for "possessory rights" as a British citizen.

He was entirely without recourse.

His anguish was intensified by the realization that after all he had done to help American settlers, many had turned against him. He still had supporters, however—strong supporters—who clung to the idea that perhaps the deed could be undone. With this faint hope, but in a bitter mood, he continued to operate his store and his mills, not knowing when they might be seized.

~ 5 ~

"A Dieu"
1850–1857

McLoughlin was in despair. When his claim was threatened in 1844, he saved it by buying out Waller and the mission. When he was maneuvered out of his job as Chief Factor, he built a successful business on his own. But he could not stand against the American government. In his torment, he wrote:

> My own claim and home, and the only one I have on earth, was reserved; and as if to propitiate the intended outrage upon me individually and to approve the good and the just, an appeal was made to their sense of the value of education by donating this home of mine and last resting place to the endowment and uses of a University! . . . unseen and unheard, thousands of miles away from Washington, it was precipitated upon me and mine just as I was stepping into the grave and least prepared to meet and avert the consequences of such a stunning calamity.

He was stunned because so many settlers—the people he helped—had deserted him. "If the American immigrants had been my brothers and sisters, I could not have done more for them," he said, "yet after acting as I have, spending my means and doing my utmost to settle the country, my claim is reserved, while every other settler in the country gets his."

His desolation was increased by the loss of two sons. On December 14, 1848, while Governor Lane was making his way to Oregon, Joseph McLoughlin died. As told by David:

> He went with Thomas McKay on a hunting expedition through Southern Oregon into California as far south as Sacramento Valley. Before

returning the party was camped on a tributary of Cow Creek where there was a high bank. Seeing a fire across the stream he started to walk to it, when he accidentally fell down the bank and was seriously injured inwardly, which eventually caused his death. This accident gave the name of Jump off Joe to the place.

Joseph, age forty-one, was his firstborn son, a solid, dependable man and a valued worker, accompanying brigades, acting as storekeeper at Fort Vancouver, and farming near Champoeg. He had kept in contact with his father, and McLoughlin would miss him.

The second death was that of Thomas McKay, who perished—probably from tuberculosis—sometime between November 18, 1849, when he signed a dated bill, and April 19, 1850, when the settler G. Groom was appointed administrator of his estate. McKay had been entrusted with many important assignments for the company and had lived nearby, managing his horse farm near the mouth of the Willamette, farming on French Prairie, building and operating a large mill near Champoeg. His loss undoubtedly left a hole in the lives of McLoughlin and his wife.

The other son, David—age twenty-eight—was away, having gone to the California gold mines as he had planned. David would never return to Oregon for long. From California he went to mines in British Columbia and from there to Porthill, Idaho, where he made his permanent home.

The brightest spot in the McLoughlin family picture was the marriage of Eloisa in 1850 to Daniel Harvey, whom McLoughlin knew well and liked. Harvey, the former superintendent of the Fort Vancouver farm, had been in charge of the sawmill at the time of the forest fire of 1844, which he had helped fight. More recently, he had managed McLoughlin's mills in Oregon City, and after the marriage he became the doctor's trusted aide.

During the next few years, Eloisa and her new husband had one daughter and two sons, making a total of six children under the McLoughlin roof:

John Rae	b. 1839
Margaret Glen Rae	1841
Maria Louisa Rae	1842
Daniel Harvey Jr.	1851
Mary Angelica Harvey	1854
James William McLoughlin Harvey	1856

Of these, Maria Louisa Rae was McLoughlin's favorite, a clever, laughing girl with a strong sense of humor. He gave her an exquisite melodeon, and toward the end of his life, when rheumatism made it difficult for him to write, she transcribed his letters and helped with his accounts.

Since no officials in the territory were willing to actually dispossess Mc-Loughlin, he retained his house, his mills and store, but business profits had been only part of his income, and when he could no longer sell lots, his revenues shrank. For several months he was badgered for refunds by those who had bought land after March 1849, too late for their titles to be confirmed under the land law. In the fall of 1850, however, he received relief from their demands, because the legislature responded to numerous requests by ratifying his later sales.

Many residents were in debt to McLoughlin for credit he had extended as a private merchant, and while most of them were honest, a few were not. Records of the Clackamas County Circuit Court show that he brought several suits to recover sizeable amounts. Three of these, against Matthieu Richardson, Egbert Wolcott, and William Singer, were "discontinued" with a signed promise to pay, the one against Singer being dated June 10, 1857, only a few months before McLoughlin's death.

Three others were against men who had left the area—William Riley, Thomas Purves, and William M. Card. They resulted in "writs of attachment," entitling McLoughlin to revenue from their remaining lands and goods. One was against J. G. Gray and Bissell, Maxwell, and Stevens, "owner of Steamer Multnomah, wherever they may be found." In his plea McLoughlin said they were not local residents, "as he verily believed" when he extended credit, and that Gray was about to move his property "outside the jurisdiction of this Court, with intent to Defraud his creditors." The case was "discontinued," presumably because the men and steamboat had indeed taken off, for there was no record of payment. And another, against Alfred and Francis W. Pettygrove—co-founder of Portland—who "have not answered the Summons of the court," ended with the return of a town lot to the doctor.

After he died, his account books showed debts of more than two hundred settlers and the small number of suits in a decade of business, indicates that McLoughlin resorted to litigation, but only against those who had left the area or owed him large sums with no apparent attempt to pay. His grievances were so well founded that no recorded case was decided against him.

During the 1850s, while the doctor was busy with his store and mills, Oregon grew with dizzying speed, because settlers continued to pour in, tak-

McLoughlin with his grand-daughters Margaret Glen Rae and Maria Louisa Rae. The gentlemen behind are George Warren Hyde and Dan O'Neill. OHS ORHI 45701

ing up farms in the Willamette Valley and gradually pushing south. To accom-modate them and handle their crops, small towns sprang up along the rivers, laced together after 1851 by steamboats. Their base was Canemah, just above Willamette Falls, where they accepted freight from the large vessels of the lower river. It was a slow, back-breaking process—to unload the cargo, pack it into wagons, haul it up the narrow portage road, and transfer it to river-boats. Shipping lay at anchor, piers hummed with activity, and so many wag-ons were needed that a parade of them plodded up and down the road, lit at night by huge flares. In 1844 the provisional legislature had given McLoughlin the right to construct a canal around the falls, "sufficiently safe and wide for a passage"—presumably equipped with locks. Although he did not finish it, he built a "wing" above the falls, and this gave ships on the upper river a safe place to anchor.

Nevertheless, the growth of Oregon City lagged, largely because McLough-lin's land was in question. By 1850, with a population of 697, it was outdis-tanced by the newer settlement downstream—Portland, which had two hun-dred more, thanks to two great advantages: a corduroy road that was bone-shaking, but nevertheless gave access to farms of the Tualatin Valley; and a deep-sea port. Oregon City could not be reached by oceangoing ships, because of the rocky shallows where the Clackamas River flowed into the Willamette, but its lusty rival had unobstructed access to the Columbia.

During the past few years, as the growing population made Oregon a profitable outlet for trade, its contact with the East Coast had improved.

Barks and brigs and an occasional steamer left the Portland docks and connected to larger vessels at San Francisco. For freight, clipper ships sailed around the Horn. For passengers and mail, steamers chugged from San Francisco to Panama, packhorses and packmules crossed the isthmus, and steamers traveled up the East Coast. Time for the Oregon-New York trip shrank to about a month, and a more or less regular mail service began.

The growth and change inevitably affected McLoughlin's town. In 1851–52 the territorial capital was moved from Oregon City to Salem, but before long it was transferred to the newer town of Corvallis, where it remained less than a year and then moved back to Salem to stay.

Amid all this ferment, McLoughlin was undecided what to do. Still operating his store and mills, he was a familiar figure on the streets of Oregon City, trudging along in his ample black coat, thumping his cane, doffing his hat to the ladies. He had sufficient support to be elected mayor in April 1851, receiving forty-four votes while the incumbent, William K. Kilborne, had twenty-two. But after holding office only six months, the doctor resigned for an unknown reason, and placed an advertisement in the *Oregon Spectator* saying that since he intended to leave "for the United States," his debtors and creditors should settle their accounts. And then—still with no recorded explanation—he changed his mind, staying in Oregon City after all. On September 5, 1851, he became a full citizen, and the following year the Oregon legislature, by an official act, accepted the "donation" of his land.

Although this had the ring of finality, McLoughlin did not quite give up hope of recovering his property, and with the help of friends he tried various plans. In July 1851 he wrote to Alexander H. H. Stuart, "Secretary of State for the Home Department," outlining the story of his claim, his pending citizenship, and his voting record. Recounting the actions of Thurston and Judge Bryant, he said his conduct had been "misrepresented by malicious and designing persons," and he asked to have his title restored. "Every upright honest Citizen of this Territory acquainted with its History," he said, would verify his aid to the immigrants. "But for my exertions, there sufferings would have been much greater—having acted in good faith I trust the Government will do me justice and not allow me to be the victim of Malice." Oregon, however, was merely a distant territory with no votes in Congress and no political clout. Secretary Stuart apparently took no action, and nothing was done.

In 1853, in a pathetic attempt to strengthen his position, McLoughlin sent a set of seven questions to a number of early settlers, asking them to verify his help. "Do you think the first settlers could have begun the settlement without my assistance?" "Have you not heard it stated that I did all I could to assist the first settlers and immigrants?" Nothing more is on record—how many replies he received or what he did with them—and the attempt was fruitless. It was about that same time—1853–54—that the resident Orlando Humason offered a resolution to the Oregon legislature asking it to thank the doctor for his many acts of assistance. The lawmakers, however—torn by their conflicting desires—talked and dallied, and postponed even this mild measure.

Two years later, McLoughlin's supporters achieved a measure of success when they again presented a memorial to the Legislative Assembly, outlining his efforts in the settlers' behalf and pleading for relief. This time the legislators passed an act—number 30 in a long list of measures—"praying Congress to restore to Dr. McLoughlin certain school lands in Oregon City and to grant to the University fund two townships of land instead." It was doubtless a satisfaction to the doctor, for it indicated friendship, or at least tolerance, in his own town. A territorial legislature, however, had no means to pressure the federal government, which as before did not respond.

As the years passed, the population of Oregon continued to grow, with a fresh influx of settlers every fall—so many that in 1853 the northern section was split off to form Washington Territory. Farms spread across most of the arable land in the Willamette Valley; steamboats operated on the Willamette and Columbia rivers, with portages at the Cascades and The Dalles; stage coaches rumbled from Oregon City to Corvallis and by 1856 to Eugene.

Change also came to Fort Vancouver, which was still functioning, although on an ever more restricted scale. Most of McLoughlin's friends were gone. John Work remained, but James Douglas had become Chief Factor of the new Hudson's Bay Company headquarters at Fort Victoria, while Peter Skene Ogden made an extensive trip east, returned briefly to Fort Vancouver, and then built a house on his donation land claim south of Oregon City. Naming it The Cliffs because of its location on a bluff over the river, he moved there in 1853—a bittersweet pleasure for McLoughlin, who visited him regularly until 1854, when his old friend died.

On a happier note, Dr. Forbes Barclay, who had been McLoughlin's colleague at Fort Vancouver, retired and moved to Oregon City. There he built a house that was splendid for its day, with multi-paned windows and brass hardware brought from England. The Barclays had been married at Fort Vancouver, with McLoughlin himself signing their certificate, and now the two families were able to resume their friendship, for their homes were only a few blocks apart. Andrina Catherine Barclay—Katie—remembered that when she was a child, a wedding was held at her home, and she sat on a sofa beside McLoughlin. The doctor, she said, "was fond of children and was most indulgent with them," and "gave me a little sip from his glass." Another wedding, that of Mr. Le Forest, keeper of the Hudson's Bay store, was held in the McLoughlin home, and it was a grand affair, "fruits and wines being specially ordered from San Francisco." The host himself—impressive in his best dark coat—presided at the head of the table, and the bride, Mrs. Mary Le Forest, said later that on this occasion McLoughlin "for the first time in his life tasted champagne."

Although the doctor seldom touched "spirits," a story was told by the steamboat captain George Cole, who frequently brought grain downriver to the mill. After delivering his cargo, the captain would accompany Mr. McKinlay, manager of the McLoughlin store, to the owner's home, where the doctor would prepare three goblets of rum. The first was one-third full, the second contained half as much, the third contained half of that, and "two parts of water were added to each part of rum." McLoughlin would hand Cole the glass with the smallest amount, give McKinlay the medium glass, and keep the largest for himself as the men settled down to discuss business affairs. But Cole was curious. Why, he finally asked McKinlay, did the doctor give himself the best serving? To which the manager replied, "Well, Captain, he dealt that out medicinally and not for sociability. Being a man of ripe years, he took the most himself, me being next in age, the second sized dose, and you being the youngest, the smallest dose. That's his way."

A vexatious problem arose in 1854, relating to the Red River settlers who had come to the Nisqually and Cowlitz more than a decade earlier on the basis of lavish promises by the Hudson's Bay Company of housing, land, and supplies. Within a few months they had moved to the Willamette Valley, but "unfortunately, none were called upon to cancel the contract," and over the years they had often expressed their dissatisfaction. In 1854, one of them—John Otchin—brought suit against Dr. William Tolmie as agent of the Puget's Sound Agricultural Company "for non-fulfillment of the agreement." A jury awarded Otchin four thousand dollars in damages, but on appeal the Supreme Court of Oregon Territory rescinded it. In the following year, Otchin and others brought suit again, this time against McLoughlin, Tolmie, Dr. Barclay, and Richard Lane, "as partners in the Company."

Justice in those days moved with exemplary speed: the trial "came off in Portland in May." Before the end of the month, the "judge decided on not allowing the case to go to a Jury." Otchin appealed to the Supreme Court, and by July of that same year the court "sustained the decision." For McLoughlin, no harm was done, but it was an added worry in those troubled times.

In 1854–57 his contentious family in Quebec involved him in a long dispute. Having heard that on his three farms at Rivière-du-Loup "everything was going to ruin," he asked John Malcolm Fraser, one of Grandfather Fraser's second brood, to sell them, and sent Fraser a power of attorney. Later, since McLoughlin had not received a receipt, he sent a second power of attorney to his daughter Eliza, telling her that if John Malcolm would handle the affair, "you must not act." Eliza, however, disregarded his instructions and sold one of the farms to another relative, John Fraser of St. Mark, for £1,350, causing John Malcolm to set up a vigorous protest. Eventually, after trying in vain to straighten it out, McLoughlin explained that the feckless buyer "has not paid her of this money a cent," and sent John Malcolm money to redeem the land. It was a three-year entanglement, complicated by the long distance, in which it appears that John Fraser of St. Mark was a family maverick, deeply in debt. Eliza's reason for the ill-advised sale was not explained.

By 1857, worn out and brooding over his problems, suffering from diabetes, the doctor had become a semi-invalid—seventy-two years old, noticeably gaunt, frail, and bent. In late summer, having become bedfast, he was told that La Fayette Grover, delegate to the U.S. Congress, was passing his house, and the sick man sent a request for a visit. Grover later said that as soon as he arrived, McLoughlin explained.

> "I shall live but a little while longer and this is the reason I sent for you. I am an old man and just dying, and you are a young man and will live many years in this country. . . . As for me, I might better have been shot"—and he brought it out harshly—"I might better have been shot forty years ago!" After a silence, for I did not say anything, he concluded: "than to have lived here, and tried to build up a family and an estate in this government. I became a citizen of the United States in good faith. I planted all I had here, and the government has confiscated my property. Now what I want to ask of you is that you will give your influence after I am dead to have this property go to my children. I have earned it as other settlers have earned theirs, and it ought to be mine and my heirs." I told him I would favor his request, and did.

At that time McLoughlin was being cared for by Marguerite and Eloisa, with his old friend Dr. Forbes Barclay and his nephew, Dr. William DeChesne, as his medical attendants. French was the language of the family, and on September 5, 1857, when DeChesne entered the sickroom, he asked as always, "Comment allez vous?" The phrase is commonly interpreted as "How are you?," but McLoughlin replied to its literal meaning of "How are you going?" He replied, "A Dieu" [To God].

They were his last words.

~ 6 ~

Last Things

McLoughlin's funeral was held at the Catholic Church of St. John the Apostle in Oregon City on Saturday, September 7, 1857—a rainy day when roads were so thick with mud that the spring wagon used as a hearse was mired down. His coffin, therefore, "was carried on men's shoulders" from his house to the church, and from there "to the grave" by eight stalwart men, friends of his last hard years. After the funeral Mass, he was buried in the churchyard, and a stone was later placed at his head saying, "The Pioneer and Friend of Oregon. Also The Founder of This City."

McLoughlin's will was simple.

He gave all his property in the parish of Rivière-du-Loup to his daughter Eliza Eppes, "to be used and enjoyed by her during the term of her natural life" and then to be divided equally among her children. This bequest—three farms totaling about 676 acres—included the land she had sold to John Fraser of St. Mark. Since neither the property nor income from its sale appears in the inventory of the estate, the transaction was evidently allowed to stand, and Eliza may have collected the money directly from Fraser, by-passing the will's provision for her children. Her father had been generous to her, with payments from his Hudson's Bay account of one hundred to four hundred pounds made at irregular intervals over the years. She was widowed, with several children living on the half-pay of her army-officer husband, and McLoughlin may have thought she was in need.

In personal possessions, the doctor gave his household goods, including furniture, linen, china, and glassware, to his wife, "to hold to her as her own absolute property." His silver—a valuable collection—went to Eloisa, but Marguerite was granted its use.

He assigned the rest of his estate to three legatees—Eloisa Harvey, Daniel Harvey, and David McLoughlin—"to be divided equally between, share and share alike, and to their respective heirs forever." There was one proviso: they were to pay their mother one thousand dollars per year and allow her to live in the house "with the garden and privileges thereunto belonging to be used and enjoyed by her during her life."

Finally, McLoughlin specified that Daniel Harvey was to be executor, and that in case of "any difference dispute, question or controversy," Harvey's decision was to be as binding "as if I myself had made and expressed the same in this my will."

The appraisers—A. L. Davis, John H. Couch, and Amory Holbook—disregarded the as-yet-unenforced seizure of McLoughlin's land and listed all of it as assets. According to their records, McLoughlin's real estate in the business district of Oregon City was located in blocks 1 and 2 of the city plat and in the large waterfront tract labeled "reserved." It contained:

Gristmill, millrace, appurtenances, basin, granary	$30,000
Sawmill, race, and appurtenances	5,000
Store known as French store and lot	1,000
Foundry buildings and lots	2,500
Two stores and "old building"	10,000
One old store	3,000
Ferry landing and privilege	4,000

His home, adjacent to the reserve, was on lot 6, block 29, with other buildings on lot 5. These would be the kitchen, one or more "necessaries," the woodshed, and other household structures. In this block he also owned the house identified as "formerly Sur. Gen. office" and all the remaining lots except one, for a total valuation of $11,000. In addition to the downtown property, his real estate in Oregon City included approximately 100 scattered lots valued at $50 each, 24 complete blocks valued at $80-200 each, small properties above the falls at Canemah, and others at Linn City, across the river.

In addition to real estate, McLoughlin's business assets included flour and grain bags, 1 scale, 1 grindstone, shovels, bushel measures, a quantity of wheat, 18,000 feet of lumber, 16 hogs, 1 cow, 1 steer, 1 calf, an "Inn Safe," and 1 "proof staff"—probably a tool for measuring the depth of wheat in a bin.

In personal goods, for which the appraisers did not specify a value, he had furniture, silver plate, and a gold watch and chain. The silver, bought while on furlough in London in 1838–39, included a pair of "Candlearbra," 12 pearl-handled knives and forks, 6 large spoons, 29 large tablespoons, 4 "Decanter Holders," 3 pairs sugar tongs, 12 ladles, 2 sugar-creamer sets, 2 each coffee and tea pots, 4 "Knife Resters," 3 "Fish slicers," and many other pieces. The furniture was not listed, but some had been brought from Fort Vancouver, the most impressive being a magnificent mahogany table that seated twelve.

The above were tangible assets. Besides these, McLoughlin's books showed unexpired interest in the Hudson's Bay Company, ten shares in the "Puget Sound Agri. Co.," and scrip of Clackamas County. That was rated at full face value, but for some reason the scrip of Washington and Oregon Territories was discounted by about two-thirds. There were several promissory notes of considerable size and approximately two hundred accounts receivable, one group of which the appraisers cautiously designated as "of doubtful or no value" and another as "of no value." The appraisers made the following summary of assets, both personal and business:

Summary

Real Estate	$86,170.00
Personal Estate	2,525.10
Furniture & Silver	1,544.00
Cash and shares	13,613.12
Script	3,720.46
Promissory notes	9,053.63
Accounts Receivable	25,958.71
Total (Considered Good)	142,585.02
Doubtful promissory notes	5,517.35
Doubtful account receivable	23,896.91
Grand total	$171,999.28

This was a sizeable sum, the more surprising because McLoughlin had given so much away. Approximately half of the property, however, might be seized at any time.

While the estate was being settled, the Harvey family remained in the Oregon City house with McLoughlin's widow. Their position was difficult, because they were unable to sell any land, even though the legislature had not formally taken it over. During that time, Daniel Harvey, as executor, paid claims of slightly more than twenty-five thousand dollars, and he reported the gristmill and granary as "still in use," which implies that they were producing revenue. In 1859 David sold his share of the estate to Eloisa and her husband for twenty-five thousand dollars, and the next year Marguerite McLoughlin died, to be buried in the churchyard beside her husband. Eloisa and Daniel Harvey were then the sole heirs, with the final accounting incomplete. Burt Brown Barker, who made a detailed study of the estate, concluded:

> Thus Daniel Harvey and his wife Eloisa became possessed of the entire estate of Dr. McLoughlin. It may be that being so in possession of the entire estate he paid the claims and was excused from filing a report of distribution. No record of any orders was found so that this part remains in the realm of presumption. David McLoughlin being out of the picture there was no one to object and probably all orders were waived.

In the year of Marguerite's death—1860—the Hudson's Bay Company abandoned McLoughlin's old headquarters. For the first decade after his departure, Fort Vancouver had been a profitable company post, buying goods from both London and New York and selling chiefly to the settlers. The gold rush had been a bonanza, so lucrative that George Simpson estimated the post's 1849 profits as more than seventeen thousand pounds.

But by the late 1840s settlers had begun to encroach on the company farms, and the U.S. Army moved in. In 1850 the Regiment of Mounted Rifles erected substantial buildings on the bluff behind the fort, calling it Camp Vancouver. The military—being in full charge—considered the British firm a bothersome interloper on American soil and stepped up pressure until the company decided to withdraw, and on May 7, 1860, the steamer *Otter* left with a final load of "full freight." The name "Camp Vancouver" was discontinued, the original "Fort Vancouver" was restored, the site became a post of the U.S. Army, and the old Hudson's Bay buildings gradually decayed until in 1866 the crumbling remnants burned.

Meanwhile, Eloisa and Daniel Harvey had precarious tenure in the Oregon City house, because their property might be taken at any time. Oregonians, however, were uncomfortable with the seizure of McLoughlin's land. In 1859 the territory became a state, and three years after that, since Congress still offered no remedy, the Oregon legislature took matters into its own hands. It had already sold a number of lots for a total of nearly ten thousand dollars,

Fort Vancouver in 1860. By then it was under control of the U.S. army, and its buildings were in a state of disrepair. Most of them burned soon after this picture was made, and were not rebuilt until much later, when the National Park Service made an extensive restoration, on the original site. OHS ORHI 55089

assigned to the University Fund, and it lacked authority to abrogate a federal law. It was, however, free to market the property, and therefore in 1862 it partly remedied the injustice by passing an act, with no negative votes in the House and only two in the Senate, which were later reversed. This act enabled McLoughlin's heirs to buy all his remaining land claim except Abernethy Island, and required them to pay only the token sum of one thousand dollars to the University Fund. The Harveys could have reduced their cost by paying in greenbacks, which were discounted, but they scorned to do so, and handed over the full sum in coins of gold. McLoughlin's land again belonged to his family.

They did not stay on it long. Two years later, Eloisa and her husband sold the lot across the street to the Oregon City Woolen Manufacturing Company, in which Daniel Harvey was a shareholder. The company at once built an enormous, two-story mill, cutting off the view, and the Harveys moved a few miles down the Willamette to the thriving young village called Portland.

The doctor was dead. His family had moved. His house was in decay. His fort was crumbling. For a lesser man, it might have meant oblivion, but the McLoughlin legacy was strong.

This bronze statue of Dr. John McLoughlin stands in the national capitol, Washington, D.C. Sculpted by Gifford MacG. Proctor, it was given by Oregon to the nation in 1953. OHS ORHI 11121

In 1867 a group of former immigrants founded the Oregon Pioneer Society, which was reorganized in 1873 as the Oregon Pioneer Association. They held annual meetings, made speeches, and published articles, in which scores of tributes to McLoughlin were paid.

"If he had not helped us we could not have lived in Oregon," wrote Daniel S. Holman.

"His benevolent work was confined to no church, sect nor race of men, but was as broad as suffering humanity, never refusing to feed the hungry, clothe the naked, and provide for the sick and toilworn," said Willard H. Rees.

One of the most perceptive comments was that of Peter Burnett, who recounted the doctor's dilemma in trying to please company directors while serving the needs of humanity. He said, "No possible line of conduct could have escaped censure."

Some were couched in the florid language of the time. J. Quinn Thornton said, "Old white-haired John McLoughlin . . . is in sublimity of character, a Mount Hood towering above the foot hills into the regions of eternal snow and sunshine."

And his friend Dr. William Tolmie mourned him as "the late great and good Dr. John McLoughlin, the head and front, the life and soul, the guide and chief director."

As the years passed, the pioneers' descendants became increasingly interested in the man who had saved so many lives. Whether he had prevented war—as he thought—was debatable, but no one doubted that without him, the early settlement of the Oregon Country would have been immeasurably more difficult. Instead of being brought safely downriver in company boats, settlers might have lost their lives in the roaring Columbia River rapids. Without company food and medicine and hospital care, they might have perished from disease.

Before long, people began to write about him. In 1887 money was raised by popular subscription for a portrait, painted by William Cogswell and presented by the Oregon Pioneer Association to the State of Oregon. It hung in the state capitol until 1935, when the building burned. In 1905 "McLoughlin Day" was an event of the Lewis and Clark Exposition. In 1909 the McLoughlin Memorial Association was formed, and his house was moved to the city park and opened to the public. Officials named things for him: a street—a school—a building. In 1933 a span over the Clackamas River was built and marked with a brass plaque saying, "The Dr. John McLoughlin Memorial Bridge." A decade later, the PTA and schoolchildren of the state paid for a bronze bust and set it up at Willamette Falls. In 1957 the state legislature officially entitled him the "Father of Oregon."

By then the federal government had become involved. In 1925, honoring the Fort Vancouver centennial, the U.S. Mint issued a silver half-dollar with McLoughlin's bust on one side—the only doctor of medicine shown on a U.S. coin. In 1941 his house was designated a National Historic Site maintained by the McLoughlin Memorial Association. Seven years later his old fort was made a National Monument, and in 1961 it became a National Historic Site. Its visitors' center offers exhibits of the fur trade and early settlement. The palisade and several buildings have been reconstructed on the original site. Early flowers and vegetables grow in the garden, and during the summer, workers in period dress demonstrate fur-trade occupations. Since every state is entitled to have statues of two citizens in the nation's capitol, the voters of Oregon selected McLoughlin and Jason Lee for that honor. The state legislature commissioned the works and in 1953 the two were put in place, the missionary in Statuary Hall, and the doctor in a nearby room.

In the Northwest today, his name is often seen. Residents drive on McLoughlin Boulevard, McLoughlin Avenue, McLoughlin Way. Students attend several McLoughlin Schools. Picnickers drive up the Columbia to McLoughlin Park, while hikers and campers head for Mount McLoughlin. Actors portray the Chief Factor in pageants and plays. Two elaborate Oregon Trail centers have opened, in Oregon City and Baker City, featuring the time when the hot-tempered, kindly doctor, white-haired and tall, welcomed the settlers at trail's end.

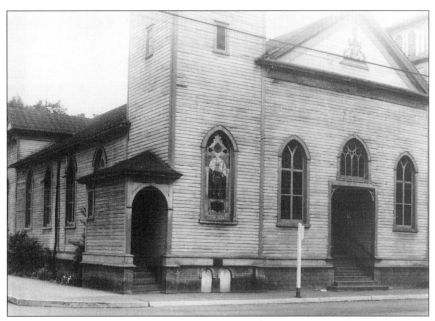

The west front of St. John's Catholic Church in Oregon City, with the McLoughlin headstones embedded in the new section of foundation. The graves themselves were inside the
addition, under the floor. OHS ORHI 98790

For nearly half a century, the only disturbance of his burial site occurred
in 1900, when the Church of St. John the Apostle was enlarged, the graves of
McLoughlin and his wife were covered by the new floor, and the headstones
became part of the new foundation. The second disturbance—more extensive—occurred in 1948, when the church membership decided to raze the
building and replace it with a new one at Fifth and Washington Streets. In July
of that year, the bodies of McLoughlin and his wife were exhumed "in well
preserved condition, from beneath the historic church soon to be disman-
tled," and placed in new gray wooden caskets. With "three hundred fifty towns
people and others present"—including the Most Reverend Edward D. Howard,
Archbishop of Portland, six other priests, the priests' choir, and fifteen servers,
acolytes, crossbearers, and assistants—an elaborate ceremony opened with a
"solemn pontifical requiem mass," while rain dripped through the old church's
roof. The assemblage—priests, archbishop, townspeople, acolytes, choir—then
formed a long procession and walked to the site of the future church.

There, beneath a white canvas shelter, the president of the McLoughlin
Memorial Association read a letter written in 1900 by Hugh Burns, who had

attended the services of 1857. Dr. Burt Brown Barker, president of the Oregon Historical Society and vice-president emeritus of the University of Oregon, gave an address. The archbishop blessed the new site, and the bodies were "again lowered into hallowed ground."

But even this was not trail's end. Although an impressive memorial was erected, incorporating the headstones, the other plans did not materialize. The church was built elsewhere, and in 1970 its land at Fifth and Washington was sold to the city, meaning that the bodies had to be moved again.

This time they were placed in new bronze caskets, and on Sunday, August 31, 1970, the Most Reverend Robert J. Dwyer, Archbishop of Portland, celebrated a Requiem Mass at the church, attended by a large congregation. As before, the assemblage formed a long procession, and, led by the archbishop and by Thomas Vaughan, director of the Oregon Historical Society, they walked several blocks to the grounds of the McLoughlin House.

The first reburial of John and Marguerite McLoughlin, in July 1948. OHS ORHI 98789

The headstones were moved to their final location in 1970, on the grounds of the Mc-Loughlin House National Historic Site, high above the falls in Oregon City. OHS ORHI 21056

It was a resplendent day of blue skies and sunshine. When all were gathered, the archbishop blessed the new graves "in the garden park next to the famous couple's home," and the Chief Factor was again laid to rest, with his beloved Marguerite at his side.

Graced by fir trees, edged with native shrubs, the site was high above the falls on land he himself had reserved for a park. It was close to the house he had planned, the house in which he had spent his final, most private years. Dr. John McLoughlin had come home.

Abbreviations

CPT	John A. Hussey, *Champoeg: Place of Transition*
FTE	Frederick Merk, *Fur Trade and Empire: George Simpson's Journal*
G&C	Governor and Committee, Hudson's Bay Company, London
GS	Sir George Simpson
HBC	Hudson's Bay Company
HBCA	Hudson's Bay Company Archives, Provincial Archives of Manitoba, Winnipeg
HBRS	Publications of the Hudson's Bay Record Society
HBRS 4	*Letters of John McLoughlin, First Series*
HBRS 6	*Letters of John McLoughlin, Second Series*
HBRS 7	*Letters of John McLoughlin, Third Series*
JD	James Douglas
McL	Dr. John McLoughlin
ME	Burt Brown Barker, *The McLoughlin Empire and Its Rulers*
NWC	North West Company
OHQ	*Oregon Historical Quarterly*
OHS	Oregon Historical Society
OHSL	Oregon Historical Society Library, Portland, Ore.
OPAT	*Oregon Pioneer Association, Transactions*
OQ	Frederick Merk, *The Oregon Question*
PAC	Public Archives of Canada, Ottawa
SF	Dr. Simon Fraser
WHQ	*Washington Historical Quarterly*

Notes

Some references for the Hudson's Bay Company Archives, Provincial Archives of Manitoba (HBCA, PAM) differ from those in previously published works, to conform with the archives' current system.

Unless otherwise indicated, all archival numbers in the references are for HBCA.

Prologue: The House

xv   *Decline of McLoughlin House* *Morning Oregonian*, 12 May 1899, 2; Smelser, "History of the McLoughlin House," 36–38.

          Oregon City vote Prosch, "Efforts to Save the Historic McLoughlin House," 41. The vote was 100 for and 360 against.

xv–xvi   *The mill* The fire was set because—it was said but not proved—many of the mill workers were Chinese.

xvi   *"McLoughlin's former home..."* "To the Voters and Taxpayers of Oregon City," political pamphlet, quoted in Smelser, "History of the McLoughlin House," 37.

          "a haunt of wandering..." "Restoration of the McLoughlin House," political pamphlet, quoted in Smelser, "History of the McLoughlin House," 37–38.

          Injunctions *Oregon City Enterprise*, 2 April 1909; Zumwalt, "Old Home," 8; see also p. 7.

          Moving McLoughlin House Hastings, "The Moving of the McLaughlin Home."

xvii   *Customs of Columbia Indians* Ross, *Adventures of the First Settlers*, 87–120; Clarke, *Pioneer Days*, 1:89–99, 123–25.

xviii   *"White-Headed Eagle"* David McLoughlin to Eva Emery Dye, 10 April 1892, Eva Emery Dye Papers, MSS 1089, OHSL; Allan, "Reminiscences," 76.

          "He put men in irons..." Harvey, "Biography of Her Father," 6.

          Joint occupation *OQ*, 51–53.

          Kanakas These were hired by the HBC on trading voyages to the Sandwich (now Hawaiian) Islands.

xviii–xix   *"I am of opinion..."* McL to Sir J. H. Pelly, 12 July 1846, A.10/22, HBRS 7:171.

xix   *"spanned a continent..."* Lamb, Introduction to HBRS 7:lxii–lxiii.

"sound and well built...loaded the inside..." Hastings, "The Moving of the McLaughlin Home."

Time needed for moving house Zumwalt, "Old Home," 8.

xx *Dedication of house* Holman, "Dedication of the McLoughlin House," 385.

Chapter 1–1: The Litigious Frasers

3 *Fraser family* ME, 55–57; Deloge, "Fraser (ffraser), Malcolm," and Prince, "Mc-Loughlin, Marie-Louise," both in Wallace, *Dictionary of Canadian Biography,* 7:330–31, 573.

Scottish rebellion and Battle of Culloden ME, 56–57; Gray, *Lord Selkirk of Red River,* 12; Prebble, *The Highland Clearances,* 13.

Malcolm Fraser ME, 57, 60–61, 67–71.

4 *Battle of Quebec* Wrong, *Canadian Manor,* 30.

Fraser receives seigneury ME, 57–58; Wrong, *Canadian Manor,* 37–38.

5 *Property in Quebec* Deloge, "Fraser (ffraser), Malcolm," in Wallace, *Dictionary of Canadian Biography,* 7:331. In addition to rural properties, Fraser owned five houses on rue des Grisons in Quebec and one on rue de la Fabrique. He set up the Madawaska Company, as partner, and engaged in lending money. Some of his properties were mortgaged, most were for rent.

Malcolm Fraser's marriage and children Yvon Deloge says Marie Allaire was Fraser's "common law wife" (ibid.); Burt Brown Barker says Fraser "married Marie Allaire," but that the certificate has not been found (*ME,* 60); W. Kaye Lamb calls Marie Allaire Malcolm Fraser's "young French Canadian wife" (HBRS 4:xxx).

Estate lifestyle Wrong, *Canadian Manor,* 207–11.

"Monsieur, il était..." Ibid., 210.

5–6 *Fraser at Battle of Quebec* ME, 68; Fraser's account in Wrong, *Canadian Manor,* 29–30, 251–62 (Fraser's journal is printed on pp. 249–71).

6 *John McLoughlin, grandfather* ME, 23–24; Pelletier, "Extracts from Rivière-du-Loup Records," 1. The parish records say, "John McLoughlin, agriculteur...ne vers 1714" and, in a different hand, "in Ecosse ou in Irlande?" McLoughlin called himself "an Irishman," and a letter from his nephew, Dr. Henri DeChesne (in the David McLoughlin Papers at OHSL), says the grandfather was "from the nord of Ireland—he was Scotch Irish."

Spellings McLauchland: Wyeth, *Correspondence and Journals,* 176; McGlaucland: ibid., 53, 181; McGloghlin: Shiveley, "Memoir," *OHQ* 81 (Spring 1980): 25; McLauchlan: Morrison, *North West Company in Rebellion,* 30 n. 22; Mac-Lochlan: Scouler, "Journal," *OHQ* 6 (June 1905): 168.

Lease of land Henry Caldwell, "Seignior of the Seigniories of Côte Lauzon and other places," to François Tannau, inhabitant of Rivière-du-Loup, 25 March 1775. Printed in *ME,* 277–78. The other witness was one "John McLoughlin," identity unknown, but he was not Angélique Fraser's future father-in-law. He signed the lease in the well-formed hand of an educated man, and the father-in-law later used only his mark in signing a deed.

7   *Grandfather could not write* ME, 26; deed of land, with "John McLoughlin his mark," *ME*, plate 14 and pp. 283–86.

        Fraser's war journal ME, 57.

        Religious differences Ibid., 95; John McLoughlin (father) letter, 27 July 1796, ibid., 143; Prince, "McLoughlin, Marie-Louise," in Wallace, *Dictionary of Canadian Biography*, 7:573.

        Angélique Fraser's marriage Pelletier, *Album Historique*, 67, quoted in *ME*, 24, 30.

        "Malcolm Fraser was..." Pelletier, *Album Historique*, 67.

Chapter 1–2: Across the St. Lawrence

8   *Birth and baptism of McL* Société Historique de Kamouraska, "Qui Etait John McLoughlin?" 1, 3; *ME*, 23. An extract from the parish records of Kamouraska says that John was born in Rivière-du-Loup "du dix-neuf du mois d'octobre" and baptized "le cinq du mois de décembre" in Kamouraska. Pelletier, "Extracts from Rivière-du-Loup Records."

        McLoughlin farm ME, 310–13; reproduction of town plat showing three McLoughlin farms, 310.

9   *The seigneur rears Marie Louise* Prince, "McLoughlin, Marie-Louise," in Wallace, *Dictionary of Canadian Biography*, 7:573; *Glimpses of the Monastery*, 357, quoted in *ME*, 32.

        "almost by force...attending the Sunday services..." Glimpses of the Monastery, 357, quoted in *ME*, 32.

        McLoughlin children Church records of Rivière-du-Loup and certificate by Vicar of Quebec, cited in *ME*, 26.

10   *Donation of land* ME, 24.

11   *Malcolm Fraser's second family* Ibid., 60–62; Société Historique de Kamouraska, "Qui Etait John McLoughlin?" 3; Deloge, "Fraser (ffraser), Malcolm," in Wallace, *Dictionary of Canadian Biography*, 7:331. Deloge says Fraser had five children by Marie Allaire and three by "Marie Ducros." The will of Malcolm Fraser (*ME*, 292) numbers four by Marie Allaire and four by "Mary Dugros" (the spelling in the will). Each gives a total of eight children, plus several others by unknown Indian women. Deloge cites W. Stewart Wallace, "Notes on the Family of Malcolm Fraser," *Bulletin des Recherches Historiques*, May 1933, 267–71.

        "My Grandmother and Mother..." McL to SF, 28 July 1814, *ME*, 165.

        "because she has lived..." ME, 292 (Fraser's will is printed on pp. 286–94).

        "Honoured Sir..." Dr. John McLoughlin's father to Malcolm Fraser, 27 July 1796, *ME*, 143.

12   *Marie Louise to Quebec* Prince, "McLoughlin, Marie-Louise," in Wallace, *Dictionary of Canadian Biography,* 7:573; *ME,* 95.

Granddaughter's belief Maria Louisa Rae Myrick, interview, in Lockley, "Impressions."

Scottish atmosphere Wrong, *Canadian Manor,* 211; *ME,* 60.

"The Doctor..." Allan, "Reminiscences," 76.

"of John McLoughlin's..." Tolmie, *Journals,* 87; Tolmie, "Letter" 30.

13   *Alexander and Simon Fraser ME,* 72–73.

Marie Louise's religion Prince says that when she first went to the Ursulines, her grandfather threatened to disinherit her and her family if she became a Catholic. "McLoughlin, Marie-Louise," in Wallace, *Dictionary of Canadian Biography,* 7:573.

"storm raised...while the irascible..." Glimpses of the Monastery, 357–59, quoted in *ME,* 32.

"radiant with smiles" Glimpses of the Monastery, 403, quoted in *ME,* 99.

"try to prevent..." Glimpses of the Monastery, 361, quoted in *ME,* 96.

Chapter 1–3: A Very Young Doctor

14   *Dr. James Fisher ME,* 33; "The Hospital #21," Old Fort William Training Manual, 4.

"The grand preventive..." Journal and Correspondence of Dr. Abel Edwards, William Auld to Edwards, 7 February 1814, B.C. Provincial Archives, quoted in Cole, *Exile,* 23.

David a student Photostat of David's Return of the Services, in *ME,* opposite 277; 82.

15   *Dr. Simon Fraser ME,* 72–73.

McL petition Ibid., plate 10.

"This will certify..." Ibid., plate 11.

"do certify..." Ibid., plate 12.

Dates of documents Ibid., plates 10–12; McL contract with McTavish, Frobisher.

16   *"I will tell..."* DeChesne to Dye, 6 October 1893, Dye Papers, MSS 1089, box 1, OHSL. DeChesne's account was paraphrased in Dye, *McLoughlin and Old Oregon,* 67.

"I cannot accuse..." McL to SF, 1 July 1808, *ME,* 147.

"People talk of..." McL to SF, 28 July 1814, *ME,* 165.

"What and how...should retribute..." Alexander Fraser to SF, 20 July 1808, *ME,* 151.

18   *"reported and confirmed..."* Beaver, "Experiences," 32.

"I would much..." McL to SF, 1 July 1808, *ME,* 147.

Montreal Campbell, *North West Company,* 15–18; Jenkins, *Montreal,* 204, 253–57.

McTavish, Frobisher Rich, *Fur Trade,* 189.

Simon McTavish Campbell, *The North West Company,* 19, 20; MacKay, *Honourable Company,* 109–10; Newman, *Caesars,* 110–12.

18–19   *"good wine..."* David MacMillan, "'The Marquis'—King of the Fur Trade," *Canadian Banker,* July-August 1978, 29, quoted in Newman, *Caesars,* 10.

19   *McL's decision to enter NWC* Morrison and Morrison, "John McLoughlin," 377–89.

20   *"whenever whereunto...with the Consent..."* McL contract with McTavish, Frobisher, 1.

Chapter 1–4: To the Fur Country

20   *Montreal* Campbell, *North West Company,* 15–18; Jenkins, *Montreal,* 217.

Departure of canoes Jenkins, *Montreal,* 217.

Flotillas Nute, *Voyageur,* 23–28; Innis, *Fur Trade,* 230, 242–43; Harmon, *Journal of Voyages,* 2–3.

22   *Voyageurs' songs* Nute, *Voyageur,* 103–55.

"Unto the crystal fountain..." Printed in Bryce, *Remarkable History,* 306.

23   *"Dedacated to St. Ann..."* Peter Pond, diary, *Wisconsin Historical Collections* 18 (1908): 326, quoted in Nute, *Voyageur,* 39.

"the poor fellow..." *Journal of Duncan McGillivray,* ed. Arthur S. Morton, 11, 12, quoted in Nute, *Voyageur,* 66.

24   *Voyageurs' appearance* Nute, *Voyageur,* 13–20, 46–48; Robinson, *Great Fur Land,* 106–34.

"seemed to have..." Bigsby, *Shoe and Canoe,* 1:133.

Voyageurs' pay Innis, *Fur Trade,* 242–43. Nute cites 400 livres per paddler but 1,200 for a foreman or steersman (*Voyageur,* 36).

"reloaded, cooked breakfast..." Thomas L. McKenney, *Sketches of a Tour,* 417–18, quoted in Nute, *Voyageur,* 14.

"I have now..." Quoted in Ross, *Fur Hunters,* 234–47. Ross did not name the voyageur.

25   *Travel with voyageurs* Nute, *Voyageur,* 50–59.

"During our first day..." "Robert Kennicott," *Transactions of the Chicago Academy of Sciences* 1 (1869), part 2:155–59, quoted in Nute, *Voyageur,* 68.

26   *Activities of voyageurs* Nute, *Voyageur,* 31, 48; Harmon, *Journal of Voyages,* 30 April, 10 May 1800, 2, 4.

"cursing, singing..." Campbell, *North West Company,* 40.

Chief Solomon Nanuwan of Chiboogama, HBC, "Solomon Voyageur," 162.

Food, living habits of voyageurs Robinson, *Great Fur Land*, 106–34; Nute, *Voyageur*, 35–74.

Route from Montreal Nute, *Voyageur*, 63, 64; Harmon, *Journal of Voyages*, 29 April–13 June 1800, 1–14.

27   *Crosses* Harmon, *Journal of Voyages*, 15, 23 May 1800, 6, 10.

Sault Ste. Marie Franchère, *Voyage*, 275; Harmon, *Journal of Voyages*, 30 May 1800, 12.

Canoe lock Rich, *Fur Trade*, 195; Harmon, *Journal of Voyages*, 30 May 1800, 12; observations of Isaac Todd and Simon McTavish, in Payette, *The Northwest*, 136. The Nor'Westers' original route through Sault Ste. Marie was along the south shore, over flat land. But in 1796 that bank reverted to the United States, and the NWC built a canal around the difficult portage on the north shore.

XY Company at Sault Ste. Marie Rich, *History of the Hudson's Bay Company*, vol. 2, HBRS 22:224.

Shore of Lake Superior Harmon, *Journal of Voyages*, 1–12 June 1800, 13–4; Nute, *Voyageur*, 64.

Fort Kaministiquia Rich, *Fur Trade*, 195. The modern spelling is *Kaministikwia*, but McLoughlin himself used the older spelling.

Chapter 2–1: The Fur Companies

29   *"The Expectations..."* McL to SF, 28 July 1806, *ME*, 145.

32   *Canadian Shield* Rich, *Fur Trade*, 3–6.

"The waterways..." Martin, introduction to GS, *Journal of Occurrences*, HBRS 1:xvii–xviii.

33   *Early beaver robes* Campbell, *North West Company*, 2, 3; Innis, *Fur Trade*, 10–11.

Processing beaver Campbell, *North West Company*, 3; Rich, *Fur Trade*, 45–46.

34   *"the appearance of..."* Vancouver, journal, extract in Greenhow, *Oregon and California*, 232.

David Thompson Nute, *Highway*, 26–32; Rich, *Fur Trade*, 183–84. Thompson returned from the West to Fort William (as Fort Kaministiquia was later renamed) in 1812 and retired in 1813. He had charted the source of the Mississippi, the Columbia River system, and the upper Missouri. For nearly two years he worked on a ten-foot map showing the North West Company's domain and canoe routes; this map hung for years in the partners' dining room. Thompson surveyed again from 1816 to 1826, on the U.S.-Canadian border.

Alexander Mackenzie Rich, *Fur Trade*, 184–85; Ormsby, *British Columbia*, 31–33; MacKay, *Honourable Company*, 112–15; Henry, *New Light*, 2:776–77 n. 43.

35   *History of NWC* Campbell, *North West Company*, 67–68; Rich, *Fur Trade*, 173–74.

36   *NWC names* Bryce, *Remarkable History*, 158.

"The names..." Wallace, introduction to *Documents*, 35.

Growth of NWC General Return of Departments and posts, in Payette, *The Northwest*, 226–27; Rich, *Fur Trade*, 188–89.

The Beaver Club MacKay, *Honourable Company*, 118; Wilson, "Beaver Club," 21, 24.

37   *"By four o'clock..."* Landmann, journal, quoted in Wilson, "Beaver Club," 20–21.

Comparison between NWC and HBC Rich, *Fur Trade*, 188.

Comparison between NWC and XYC Ibid., 195.

"all were merry..." Henry, *New Light*, 15 September 1809, 2:542.

38   *"The music consisted..."*"Robert Kennicott," *Transactions of the Chicago Academy of Sciences* 1 (1869), part 2:160, quoted in Nute, *Voyageur*, 84.

"I had the honour..." John McKay to HBC Committee, 25 December 1799, quoted in MacKay, *Honourable Company*, 131.

Trickery Bancroft, *Northwest Coast*, 1:572.

Murders on frontier Morton, *History of the Canadian West*, 513; Rich, *Fur Trade*, 173, 175; Rich, *History of the Hudson's Bay Company*, vol. 1, HBRS 22:118, 122, 229; Wallace, *Documents*, 8–9, 11–12, 68–75; MacKay, *Honourable Company*, 110; Campbell, *North West Company*, 136. *Wadin* is also spelled *Waden, Wadden,* and *Waddens*.

Chapter 2–2: Fort Kaministiquia

38   *Fort Kaministiquia* Campbell, *North West Company*, 127, 138; Franchère, *Voyage*; Rich, *Fur Trade*, 195–96; MacKay, *Honourable Company*, 111.

39   *"elegantly constructed..."* Franchère, *Voyage*, 266.

40   *U.S.-Canada boundary* Nute, *Highway*, 14–18; Rich, *Fur Trade*, 189–90; Innis, *Fur Trade*, 232. The Webster-Ashburton Treaty of 1842 decided the boundary, but the survey was not finished until 1926.

"and from thence..." Treaty of Paris, quoted in Nute, *Highway*, 14.

Officers' gathering Bryce, *Remarkable History*, 157; Franchère, *Voyage*, 268–69; Rich, *Fur Trade*, 188, 197; MacKay, *Honourable Company*, 111.

41   *Physical plant at fort* Cox, *Columbia*, 332; Bryce, *Remarkable History*, 155–57; Franchère, *Voyage*, 266–67; Selkirk's Plan of Fort William, in "The Hospital #21," Old Fort William Training Manual.

Voyageurs' regale Bryce, *Remarkable History*, 156; Franchère, *Voyage*, 267.

"women, soldiers..." Cox, *Columbia*, 333.

42   *"carried up..."* Irving, *Astoria*, 10.

"the great emporium..." Cox, *Columbia*, 330.

Athabasca..."The Athabasca" was the valley of the Athabasca River, which drained to Great Slave Lake, the Mackenzie River, and the Arctic Ocean. Chipewyan was an important fort there. Rich, *Fur Trade*, 179.

Ball at headquarters Bryce, *Remarkable History,* 157; Morrison, *North West Company in Rebellion,* 30.

43 *McL only physician* McL to SF, 1 July 1808, *ME,* 147; McL to SF, 2 August 1810, ibid., 155. "Dr. McLoughlin's House and the Apothecary's Shop #2" says Dr. Henry Munro was also at the fort part of the time, but "devoted almost all of his time to the company's affairs" (5).

Chapter 2–3: An Apprentice Again

43 *Medical equipment at the fort* "Dr. McLoughlin's House and the Apothecary's Shop #2," 8–13.

"*among my patients…*" McL to SF, 11 August 1806, *ME,* 145. "Dr. Darwin" was not the Charles Darwin of evolution fame, but his grandfather, Erasmus Darwin.

44 "*petrifid fir…I must again…*" McL to SF, 16 July 1805, *ME,* 144.

"*I read much…*" McL to SF, 11 August 1806, *ME,* 146.

"*I would not trouble…*" Ibid.

Family letters The file kept by Simon Fraser contains 118 letters written between 1796 and 1857, many by McLoughlin. His Uncle Simon's son John married his Uncle Alexander's daughter Elisabeth. When Simon died, John Fraser inherited the letters, and when he died, Elisabeth gave them to her brother William. Eventually William's daughter, Mrs. Alice Prevost, discovered them and gave them to the McLoughlin Memorial Association of Oregon City, Oregon. *ME,* 20.

"*that you wish'd…*" McL to SF, 28 July 1806, *ME,* 145.

45 *Quarrel between Mackenzie and McTavish* Rich, *Fur Trade,* 190–92; Campbell, *North West Company,* 117–23, 129.

Rivalry and merger of NWC and XYC Rich, *Fur Trade,* 193–95; Campbell, *North West Company,* 151. Documents on the merger are printed in Payette, *The Northwest,* 229–37.

Harmon's estimate of McL's age HBRS 4:xxxii; Harmon, *Sixteen Years,* 9 November 1807, 108.

Winters at outposts "Dr. McLoughlin's House and the Apothecary's Shop #2," 5; McL letters, in *ME,* 144, 154, 156, 158; Harmon, *Sixteen Years,* 108–9.

"*came to see…*" Chaboillez, journal, 13 January 1798, printed in Payette, *The Northwest,* 179.

46 *Gallons of liquor brought in* Rich, *Fur Trade,* 194. Further comparisons are in MacKay, *Honourable Company,* 221–30; and Innis, *Fur Trade,* 233.

"*we do not mix…*" Henry, *New Light,* 2:542.

47 "*To behold…*" Harmon, *Journal of Voyages,* 19 November 1800, 35.

48 "*drunken Indians…*" MacKay, *Honourable Company,* 222.

"*that baneful source…*" Henry, *New Light,* 2:711.

"*Good Sir, it grieves…*" Petition of William Tomison and fellow officers, quoted in Rich, *History of the Hudson's Bay Company,* vol. 2, HBRS 22:227.

"could hardly stand..." McKenzie, journal, quoted in Bryce, *Remarkable History,* 164.

"Of all people..." Harmon, *Journal of Voyages,* 25 December 1802, 73.

"hid themselves..." Ibid., 1 January 1811, 162–63.

"I believe I will..." McL to SF, 16 July 1805, *ME,* 144.

49   *"past a much better..."* McL to SF, 28 July 1806, *ME,* 145.

"I would if You..." Ibid. William McKay was a brother of Alexander McKay, who had crossed North America with Alexander Mackenzie.

Crossing height of land Campbell, *North West Company,* 41–42; Nute, *Voyageur,* 66–67.

50   *"our people are..."* Harmon, *Sixteen Years,* 1 September 1807, 107.

"We are in..." Ibid., 9 November 1807, 108.

"great numbers..." Ibid., 4 December 1807, 108.

"nearly nine-tenths..." Ibid., 29 April 1804, 80.

McL visits Red Lake Ibid., 28 December 1807 and 14 January 1808, 108–9.

51   *"The Dr. &c. are returned..."* Ibid., 19 February 1807, 109.

GS's trip Rich, *Fur Trade,* 244; Rich, *History of the Hudson's Bay Company,* vol. 2, HBRS 22:416.

Chapter 2–4: Brother David

51   *Birth of son Joseph ME,* 15, 329. The David McLoughlin Papers at OHSL say Joseph was born "about 1808"; the register at St. Paul's Catholic Church in French Prairie, Oregon, says he died on December 14, 1848, at the age of "about 38 years."

McL's first marriage David McLoughlin Papers, OHSL.

Value of native wives Van Kirk, *"Many Tender Ties,"* 51. Van Kirk calls the abandonment of fur-trade families "a severe trial to the feelings."

52   *Nancy McKay certificate* List of papers seized by Selkirk at Fort William, from Archives Nationales du Quebec a Montreal, NWC Papers, H. Doucet, Notary, 4032½, 29 January 1817, printed in "Dr. McLoughlin's House and the Apothecary's Shop #2."

"I understand he..." John Work to Edward Ermatinger, 15 February 1837, in Dye, "Old Letters," *WHQ* 2 (April 1908): 259.

"How could I spend..." Harmon, *Journal of Voyages,* 28 February 1819, 231.

Alexander Fraser's children ME, 61.

53   *"I think they may..."* McL to SF, 1 July 1808, *ME,* 147.

"this sad Experiment..." Ibid., 147–48.

"My Dear Davie" McL to Dr. David McLoughlin, 20 March 1827, *ME,* 182.

"There is one thought..." McL to SF, 13 July 1808, *ME*, 149.

"Stratagem," "something handsome" McL to SF, 1 July 1808, *ME*, 148.

54　　*"no promise..."* McL to SF, 13 July 1808, *ME*, 150.

"I told him..." Ibid., 149.

"It was and is still..." Ibid., 149–50.

McL's poor pay HBRS 4:xxxiv.

McL accepts offer McL to SF, 16 July 1808, *ME*, 150.

"Nothing but my brother's..." McL to SF, 11 August 1808, *ME*, 151.

55　　*"by the first..."* McL to SF, 2 August 1809, *ME*, 153.

"I am sorry to find..." Ibid.

"I am sorry you did not..." McL to SF, 27 June 1810, *ME*, 154.

"Mr. McTavish told me..." SF to McL, 20 May 1810, quoted in McL to SF, 2 August 1810, *ME*, 155.

56　　*Family efforts to finance David's education* Various letters in *ME*, 150–60.

"disappointments by those..." Malcolm Fraser to SF, 26 September 1808, *ME*, 152.

"sent him a Shilling..." James Ker to Malcolm Fraser, 3 April 1811, *ME*, 339.

"£120—, to keep him..." James Ker to Malcolm Fraser, 22 April 1811, *ME*, 341.

57　　*"It is very strange..."* McL to SF, 12 August 1811, *ME*, 155–56.

"Your letter surpris'd me..." McL to SF, 12 August 1812, *ME*, 159–60.

"I am sorry to find..." McL to SF, 6 August 1813, *ME*, 163–64.

"I am happy to find..." McL to SF, 28 July 1814, *ME*, 164.

"Be assured had it not..." McL to SF, 12 August 1811, *ME*, 156.

Chapter 2–5: Physician-Clerk

58　　*Marguerite McKay* Elliott, "Marguerite Wadin McKay McLoughlin," 338–47.

McL's marriage David McLoughlin Papers, OHSL; Elliott, "Marguerite Wadin McKay McLoughlin," 341–47.

"was remarkable...when the exuberance..." Dr. William McKay, interview, in Clarke, *Pioneer Days*, 1:192.

"come in for a Share... offers to go..." McL to SF, 22 March 1812, *ME*, 159.

McKay daughters David McLoughlin Papers, OHSL.

59　　*"In a few days..."* McL to SF, 12 August 1811, *ME*, 156. This Vermilion Lake is in today's St. Louis County, Minnesota. It is about twenty miles long; the Vermilion River flows from it into Rainy Lake. Fort Vermillion was near the Peace River, west of Lake Athabasca.

"traitorous meetings..." Wrong, *Canadian Manor*, 160.

Malcolm Fraser in War of 1812 Malcolm Fraser, journal, printed in Wrong,

Canadian Manor, 147, 160; *ME,* 69; Deloge, "Fraser (ffraser), Malcolm," in Wallace, *Dictionary of Canadian Biography,* 7:331.

"our Southern bad Neighbours..." Malcolm Fraser to James Ker, 10 November 1812, *ME,* 345.

"to send as many..." Minutes of 1812 rendezvous, quoted in Campbell, *North West Company,* 188–89.

60   *"fleet of 44 loaded..."* Franchère, *Voyage,* 278.

Route of flotilla through Great Lakes Ibid., 278–79; Campbell, *North West Company,* 188–89.

"I am Greatly...I receiv'd no letter..." McL to SF, 12 August 1812, *ME,* 160.

David McLoughlin David received his diploma from the College of Surgeons, Edinburgh, on March 20, 1809, and his medical degree from the University of Edinburgh on June 24, 1810. After joining the British armed forces, he was in six battles in three years, in the war with Spain. He retired to half pay in 1819, achieved a remarkably successful private practice in France, and fully retired from the British army in 1824. *ME,* 83–85.

Birth of son John ME, 38; Parish Records, St. James Church, Vancouver, Washington, photostat copy at OHSL.

NWC property destroyed Franchère, *Voyage,* 274.

Deaths of father and grandfather ME, 39, 312.

"This year is a Year..." McL to SF, 6 August 1813, *ME,* 163–64.

61   *Alexander Fraser bought seigneury ME,* 61.

"give my Mother 50£..." McL to SF, 6 August 1813, *ME,* 164.

"Nothing can do...It certainly grieves...Sea Otter..." McL to SF, 28 July 1814, *ME,* 165, 166.

Chapter 3–1: The Honourable Company

63   *"I cannot think..."* McL to SF, 10 October 1817, *ME,* 169.

65   *Radisson and Groseilliers* Rich, *Fur Trade,* 19–20, 22–23; Rich, *Hudson's Bay Company,* 1:21–34; MacKay, *Honourable Company,* 15–32.

66   *"You are to saile..."* Instructions to captains, quoted in MacKay, *Honourable Company,* 23–24.

Eaglet *and* Nonsuch Rich, *Hudson's Bay Company,* 1:36–42; MacKay, *Honourable Company,* 22–26.

Formation of HBC and granting of charter Rich, *Fur Trade,* 28–30; MacKay, *Honourable Company,* 37–38; Williams, "Highlights," 4–8; Rich, *History of the Hudson's Bay Company,* vol. 1, HBRS 21:52–53.

"Governor and Company..." Rich, *Hudson's Bay Company,* 1:53.

"true and absolute...all those Seas...with any Prince..." HBC charter, quoted in MacKay, *Honourable Company,* 39; and Rich, *Hudson's Bay Company,* 1:52–54.

| 67 | *Token payments* MacKay, *Honourable Company*, 40; photograph of Queen Elizabeth II receiving payment in Assiniboine Park, Winnipeg, July 24, 1959, in *The Beaver*, Autumn 1959, 31. |

67–68   *"like great wasps..."* James Knight, journal, quoted in MacKay, *Honourable Company*, 73.

68   *Decline in HBC profits* Rich, *Fur Trade*, 186; Tables of Dividends, 1670–1863, in MacKay, *Honourable Company*, 339–44.

"On one side..." Davies, "From Competition to Union," 166.

"and even overturn..." Andrew Graham's Observations on Hudson's Bay, 1767–1791, HBRS, quoted in Williams, "Highlights," 28.

69   *"Sleep by the Frozen Sea"* Joseph Robson, *Account of Six Years Residence in Hudson's Bay*, quoted in Rich, *Hudson's Bay Company*, 1:589.

Value of furs Rich, *Fur Trade*, 188.

Profits to HBC field men Ibid., 204.

Number of employees, 1811 Ibid., 188–89; "General Return of Departments and Posts occupied by the North West Company," printed in Payette, *The Northwest*, 226–27.

Time lag for NWC shipping Isaac Todd and Simon McTavish, "Memoir," printed in Payette, *The Northwest*, 135; Bancroft, *Northwest Coast*, 1:551–59; Bryce, *Remarkable History*, 120–21. Innis suggested an elapsed time up to forty–two months (*Fur Trade*, 233).

Ships on Lake Superior Rich, *Fur Trade*, 188.

Nor'Westers call HBC charter illegal FTE, xxxvi; Rich, *Fur Trade*, 192–93, 202, 205.

70   *"it would be very difficult..."* Rich, *Fur Trade*, 193.

Efforts to use Hudson Bay Rich, *Fur Trade*, 192; Campbell, *North West Company*, 139–41, 158; Bancroft, *Northwest Coast*, 2:301.

Mackenzie efforts Rich, *Fur Trade*, 205.

71   *"Two of the Hudson's..."* Harmon, *Journal of Voyages*, 30 January 1807, 123.

Chapter 3–2: Lord Selkirk's Colony

71   *Earl of Selkirk* Martin, *Lord Selkirk's Work*, 15–20; Douglas, *Lord Selkirk's Diary*, HBRS 35:ix–xiv.

Highlanders displaced Martin, *Lord Selkirk's Work*, 57; Douglas, *Lord Selkirk's Diary*, HBRS 35:x–xi; Gray, *Lord Selkirk of Red River*, 8, 12; Prebble, *The Highland Clearances*, 16, 98, 111, 145.

Jean Wedderburn Gray, *Lord Selkirk of Red River*, 51.

72   *Selkirk's early colonies* Martin, *Lord Selkirk's Work*, 21–24; MacKay, *Honourable Company*, 134; Rich, *Fur Trade*, 207.

Pemmican Robinson, *Great Fur Land*, 117–18.

"Take the scrapings..." Ibid., 117.

Need for pemmican Gray, *Lord Selkirk of Red River,* 94.

"are on the eve..." Henry, *Journal,* 12 July 1806, 1:201. See also Henry, *New Light,* 1:302–3.

Fort Gibraltar Innis, *Fur Trade,* 189; Bryce, *Remarkable History,* 189.

Métis Williams, "Highlights," 39; Gray, *Lord Selkirk of Red River,* 94; Rich, *Fur Trade,* 219.

72–73 *Mackenzie and Selkirk cooperation* Rich, *Fur Trade,* 205; Gray, *Lord Selkirk of Red River,* 53–54, 58.

73 *Selkirk and NWC maneuvers* Rich, *Fur Trade,* 205–8; Martin, *Lord Selkirk's Work,* 32–34; Campbell, *North West Company,* 140, 176.

"Even if..." Simon McGillivray, quoted in Rich, *Fur Trade,* 210.

NWC petitions Petition for NWC charter, 22 June 1811, 30 June 1812, printed in Payette, *The Northwest,* 312–14, 327, 335–42; Jean Morrison, *North West Company in Rebellion,* 8–9.

Selkirk receives grant, terms Rich, *Fur Trade,* 209; Martin, *Lord Selkirk's Work,* 34; Halkett, *Statement,* 2.

74 *Size of grant* Rich, *Fur Trade,* 209; Rich, *History of the Hudson's Bay Company,* vol. 2, HBRS 22:300; Martin, *Lord Selkirk's Work,* 34.

HBC's previous plans for colony Rich, *Fur Trade,* 205–6.

"It will require..." Simon McGillivray to NWC partners, 7 April 1812, quoted in Martin, *Lord Selkirk's Work,* 55.

75 *First settlers* Martin, *Lord Selkirk's Work,* 42, 43; Rich, *History of the Hudson's Bay Company,* vol. 2, HBRS 22:302–3; Rich, *Fur Trade,* 210–12; Gray, *Lord Selkirk of Red River,* 67–73.

"standing alone..." William Auld, from Selkirk Papers, quoted in Martin, *Lord Selkirk's Work,* 56 n. 1.

Condition of settlers, NWC assistance Campbell, *North West Company,* 205–7; Bryce, *Remarkable History,* 211; Rich, *Fur Trade,* 213.

"were grubbing with hoes..." Campbell, *North West Company,* 206.

76 *Three forts* Martin, *Lord Selkirk's Work,* 53; Rich, *Fur Trade,* 212–13.

"McTavish McGillivrays..." Extract from minutes of NWC rendezvous, 1814, copied in Simon McGillivray's notebook for 1815, in Morrison, *North West Company in Rebellion,* 44–45; "Minutes of Transactions of the North West Company at Fort William, 1807–14," in Wallace, *Documents,* 290.

"no person trading..." Pemmican proclamation, excerpts and discussions in Rich, *Fur Trade,* 218–19; Halkett, *Statement,* ii; Martin, *Lord Selkirk's Work,* 67–70; Gray, *Lord Selkirk of Red River,* 91–93.

"crush all the Nor'Westers..." Miles Macdonell, quoted in Campbell, *North West Company,* 210.

"an act of madness" Bryce, *Romantic Settlement*, 91. The governor recognized his own folly and wrote of his "imprudence," saying, "I beg therefore that your Lordship be not prevented from any delicacy to send a suitable person to take my situation." Macdonell to Selkirk, 24 July 1814, quoted in Martin, *Lord Selkirk's Work*, 75 n. 6.

77   *Attempt at compromise* Rich, *Fur Trade*, 219; Halkett, *Statement*, iii; Martin, *Lord Selkirk's Work*, 73; Gray, *Lord Selkirk of Red River*, 96.

"We will do…" Alexander Macdonell to Montreal partners, 5 August 1814, Martin, *Lord Selkirk's Work*, 79; Halkett, *Statement*, 11.

"Captain, Voyageur Corps…" Duncan Cameron to Archibald McDonald, 3 April 1815, printed in Halkett, *Statement*, 19. This letter is one example of Cameron's use of the title.

Campaign to lure colonists away Halkett, *Statement*, 12–16; Bryce, *Remarkable History*, 219–21; Martin, *Lord Selkirk's Work*, 78; Rich, *Fur Trade*, 219–20; Morrison, *North West Company in Rebellion*, 12–13.

"I wish that some…" Alexander Macdonell to James Grant, March 1816, quoted in Martin, *Lord Selkirk's Work*, 107.

"though distant from…" McL to SF, 28 July 1814, *ME*, 164–65.

78   *"with his Knowledge…"* Ibid., 165.

"I neither advised…" McL to SF, 16 August 1815, *ME*, 166–67.

"bring to it their…" Franchère, *Voyage*, 262.

Rainy Lake post Miles Macdonell, in Selkirk Papers, MG 19 E1, p. 17054, PAC, quoted in Morrison, *North West Company in Rebellion*, 30 n. 22.

"It has always…" McL to SF, 28 July 1814, *ME*, 165.

Macdonell order to vacate posts Campbell, *North West Company*, 211; Gray, *Lord Selkirk of Red River*, 107.

Arrest of Macdonell and Spencer Halkett, *Statement*, iii, 22, 26; Rich, *Fur Trade*, 220.

"on a criminal charge…" "Transaction Relative to a Seizure of Provisions by Mr. Miles Macdonnell," printed in Halkett, *Statement*, iii.

McL and Bethune deplore violence Rich, *Fur Trade*, 233; Gray, *Lord Selkirk of Red River*, 104.

"I could not help…" James Hughes to McL, 24 January 1816, Selkirk Papers, p. 8739, PAC, quoted in Martin, *Lord Selkirk's Work*, 88 n. 1; see also Gray, *Lord Selkirk of Red River*, 133.

79   *"had their belly full"* McL to Dugald Cameron, 16 August 1814, Selkirk Papers (C8), p. 8621–2, PAC, quoted in Gray, *Lord Selkirk of Red River*, 104.

McL at rendezvous Simon McGillivray's notebook, 16 July 1815, printed in Morrison, *North West Company in Rebellion*, 24. This is one of many examples of contemporary spellings of McLoughlin's name.

"All is fun..." Ibid., 20 July 1815, 30.

"Last night..." Miles Macdonell, in Selkirk Papers, MG 19 E1, p. 17061, PAC, quoted in Morrison, *North West Company in Rebellion*, 31 n. 25.

Winterers' dissatisfaction Simon McGillivray's notebook, 17 July 1815, printed in Morrison, *North West Company in Rebellion*, 26–28.

"would be most injurious..." Ibid., 27.

"It is therefore..." Ibid.

80   *"was considered extraordinary..."* Ibid., 18 July 1815, 28.

"Dr. McLaughlin refuses...threatens a prosecution..." Ibid., 29.

McL agrees to Athabasca Ibid., 19 July 1815, 29–30.

"The Dr. exhibits..." Ibid., 30.

"Dr. McL since his appointment..." Ibid., 22 July 1815, 31–32.

Chapter 3–3: The Battle of Seven Oaks

81   *"Removed so far..."* McL to SF, 16 August 1815, *ME*, 166–67.

Doctor's quarters Franchère, *Voyage*, 267; "Dr. McLoughlin's House and the Apothecary's Shop #2," 3.

82   *"When you are..."* Quoted in Gray, *Lord Selkirk of Red River*, 134.

"a frothy trifling..." GS, Character Book, HBRS 30:169.

Robertson leads flotilla Jean Morrison, *North West Company in Rebellion*, 10–11; Martin, *Lord Selkirk's Work*, 97; Williams, "Highlights," 41–42.

Robertson's actions at Red River Martin, *Lord Selkirk's Work*, 97–99, 106–8; Rich, *Fur Trade*, 220–21; Williams, "Highlights," 41–42; Gray, *Lord Selkirk of Red River*, 112, 114, 131–35.

"A storm is..." Alexander Macdonell to Duncan Cameron, 13 March 1816, quoted in Halkett, *Statement*, 71.

"God only knows..." Alexander Macdonell to Dugald Cameron, 13 March 1816, quoted in Gray, *Lord Selkirk of Red River*, 135; also in Halkett, *Statement*, 72.

Robertson opens mail Gray, *Lord Selkirk of Red River*, 134–35.

"The plan I am..." Robertson, diary, quoted in Williams, "Highlights," 42.

83   *Gibraltar demolished* Martin, *Lord Selkirk's Work*, 108; Gray, *Lord Selkirk of Red River*, 142–43.

"The sight of..." Campbell, *North West Company*, 215.

Archibald McLeod Morrison, *North West Company in Rebellion*, 49.

"You will, as soon..." McLeod, Henry, and McL to Grant, Morrison, and Roussin, 3 June 1816, printed in Halkett, *Statement*, 100–102; Gray, *Lord Selkirk of Red River*, 137.

84   *NWC partners meet colonists* "Deposition of Michael Heden," in Halkett, *Statement*, lviii; Rich, *Fur Trade*, 222.

"son of Colonel..." Pritchard, narrative, extracts in Halkett, *Statement*, 83. Two witnesses listed "Thomas McKay" among the Métis without further identification, but Pritchard specifically said, "A half-breed (son of Colonel William M'Kay)." Halkett, *Statement*, 83, 154, xxx.

"The orders were..." "Declaration of Boucher," extracts in Payette, *The Northwest*, 449.

Semple meets Métis Pritchard, narrative, extracts in Halkett, *Statement*, 82; Martin, *Lord Selkirk's Work*, 110–12.

85   *Battle of Seven Oaks* Pritchard, narrative; "Deposition of Michael Heden"; "Declaration of F. F. Boucher," French original with translation, all in Halkett, *Statement*, 82–85, lv–lx, xcix–c; Gray, *Lord Selkirk of Red River*, 144–48. Pritchard was saved by a Canadian named Lavigne, who pleaded with other Métis to spare him; Boucher's horse dragged him away from the firing.

"the fire was begun..." "Declaration of F. F. Boucher," in Halkett, *Statement*, c.

Heden's escape "Deposition of Michael Heden," in Halkett, *Statement*, lvi.

"a shot was..." Ibid.

86   *"almost immediately..."* Pritchard, narrative, in Halkett, *Statement*, 83.

Gifts to Métis William McGillivray, testimony at trial, extract in Payette, *The Northwest*, 456–58; Rich, *Fur Trade*, 222.

"I thank Providence..." Robert Henry to Alexander Henry, 22 July 1816, quoted in Martin, *Lord Selkirk's Work*, 110; Gray, *Lord Selkirk of Red River*, 148.

"every neutral person..." J. D. Cameron, 14 July 1816, Selkirk Papers, p. 2377, quoted in Martin, *Lord Selkirk's Work*, 116.

McL's encounter with Fraser "Deposition of Alexander Fraser," dictated to J. M. Mondelet, J.P., 6 March 1817, printed in Halkett, *Statement*, xcv–xcvii.

Chapter 3–4: The Storming of Fort William

87   *Selkirk in Montreal* Martin, *Lord Selkirk's Work*, 115; Rich, *Fur Trade*, 222–24; Campbell, *North West Company*, 219–20. While Selkirk was in Montreal, he served as mouthpiece of the HBC by approaching William McGillivray to offer "for a pepper corn rent" the right to trade in the Athabasca and in land south of the colony, provided the Nor'Westers recognized the charter. Since this territory was not within Rupert's Land and therefore not the company's to dispose of, McGillivray was not impressed. He made a counteroffer that the two firms unite, with the NWC assuming two-thirds of costs and profits while the HBC retained one-third. The HBC, as McGillivray expected, declined. Campbell, *North West Company*, 219.

Selkirk cannot obtain a guard Exchange of letters between Selkirk and Sir John Sherbrooke, Governor of the Canadas, March and April 1816, printed in Halkett, *Statement*, 44–51.

Selkirk's mercenaries Rich, *Fur Trade*, 224; G. A. Fauche, "Account of the Transaction at Fort William on Lake Superior, in August 1816," printed in

Halkett, *Statement*, lxxxiv–lxxxv, 60.

"give the officers..." Fauche, "Account," in Halkett, *Statement*, lxxxiv.

Selkirk's route Halkett, *Statement*, 61–63; Martin, *Lord Selkirk's Work*, 117.

Macdonell released Martin, *Lord Selkirk's Work*, 116–17; Rich, *Fur Trade*, 222.

Selkirk meets Macdonell Gray, *Lord Selkirk of Red River*, 151.

"brought the dismal..." Fauche, "Account," in Halkett, *Statement*, lxxxv.

88   *"obtain more complete..."* Selkirk to Sir John Sherbrooke, 29 July [1816], printed in Halkett, *Statement*, 63.

"It is a business..." Selkirk to his wife, n.d., Correspondence at St. Mary's Isle, vol. 3, p. 405, quoted in Martin, *Lord Selkirk's Work*, 231; also in Gray, *Lord Selkirk of Red River*, 208.

"in a batteau..." "Narrative of Mr. John McNabb," 17 August 1816, printed in Halkett, *Statement*, xcii.

Selkirk arrests partners Ibid; Fauche, "Account," in Halkett, *Statement*, lxxxvi–lxxxvii; Gray, *Lord Selkirk of Red River*, 156.

"with much alacrity..." "Narrative of Mr. John McNabb," printed in Halkett, *Statement*, xciii.

"on their word..." Ibid.

"We received the intelligence..." Fauche, "Account," in Halkett, *Statement*, lxxxvii. This destruction of NWC papers left a serious gap in the historical record.

89   *"criminality...such as to justify..."* Ibid., lxxxvii.

Daniel McKenzie remains at Fort William Campbell, *North West Company*, 230; "Deposition of D. M'Kenzie," summarized, with extracts, in Halkett, *Statement*, 143–48; Gray, *Lord Selkirk of Red River*, 162–63.

"I was in a state..." "Deposition of D. M'Kenzie," in Halkett, *Statement*, 145.

Marriage certificate List of papers seized by Selkirk at Fort William, from Archives Nationales du Quebec a Montreal, NWC Papers, H. Doucet, Notary, 4032½, 29 January 1817, printed in "Dr. McLoughlin's House and the Apothecary's Shop #2," 2.

"One canoe in which three..." Wilcocke, *Narrative of Occurrences*, 102, extract in Halkett, *Statement*, 179.

90   *"on asking whether..."* Fauche, "Account," in Halkett, *Statement*, lxxxvii.

"was taken lifeless..." Nicholas Garry, diary, in *Transactions of the Royal Society of Canada*, 1900, sec. 2, p. 113, quoted in HBRS 4:xxxix.

"a Mr. Grover..." McL to Edward Ermatinger, 1 February 1835, 3 March 1837, in "Letters of Dr. John McLoughlin to Edward Ermatinger," 366, 370.

"had gone on his circuit..." Fauche, "Account," in Halkett, *Statement*, lxxxviii–lxxxix.

"accused of the highest..." *Montreal Herald*, 21 September 1816, quoted in

Payette, *The Northwest,* 414.

"I Know my Grandmother..." McL to SF, 27 February 1817, *ME,* 167.

"the Ritz Carlton..." Landmann, journal, quoted in Wilson, "Beaver Club," 20–21.

91   *McL in Beaver Club* Wilson, "Beaver Club," 64.

Selkirk's mistakes Rich, *Fur Trade,* 225–26; Martin, *Lord Selkirk's Work,* 122–25; Campbell, *North West Company,* 232–35.

"Old Sleepy Head" Martin, *Lord Selkirk's Work,* 122.

Selkirk resists arrest Selkirk to Gore, Lieutenant-Governor of Upper Canada, 12 November 1816, printed in Halkett, *Statement,* 150–51; Martin, *Lord Selkirk's Work,* 128–30; Rich, *Fur Trade,* 226.

"an affidavit..." Selkirk to Governor-General of Upper Canada, 12 November 1816, printed in Halkett, *Statement,* 150.

"The consequences..." Selkirk to his wife, quoted in Martin, *Lord Selkirk's Work,* 125; also in Gray, *Lord Selkirk of Red River,* 207.

"If we are to be poor..." Lady Selkirk to John Halkett, quoted in Martin, *Lord Selkirk's Work,* 158.

"For Heaven's sake..." Lady to Lord Selkirk, 1816, extract in Gray, *Lord Selkirk of Red River,* 192–94. Quotation is on p. 194.

Selkirk at Red River Bryce, *Remarkable History,* 246–47; Rich, *Fur Trade,* 227; Martin, *Lord Selkirk's Work,* 132–33; Gray, *Lord Selkirk of Red River,* 237.

"Dr McClougholin..." Journal of J. Lemoine, 10 November 1817, PAC MG 19(G) B–231–a1, Pointe de Meuron Journals (PMJ), HBCA, translated at Old Fort William.

"disbanded, intoxicated..." Campbell, *Fur Trade Tactics,* 35.

"Dr. McLoughlin struck him..." Journal of J. Lemoine, 9 March 1818, PAC MG 19(G) B–231–a2, Pointe de Meuron Journals (PMJ), HBCA, translated at Old Fort William.

92   *"9 quarts of bleached corn...to the interior..."* Ibid., 23–24 April 1818. A later entry recounts violent treatment by "the Doctor & Taite" (22 November 1818, B–231–a4), but this was Dr. Scott, who was then at Fort William. McLoughlin had left in early summer 1818 to attend his trial of October 30, 1818.

"disorganisation...has issued...very unwell..." McL to SF, 10 October 1817, *ME,* 169.

93   *"Our family at..."* McL to SF, 5 October 1818, *ME,* 170.

"Between you and me...When I come..." Ibid., 171.

"my Uncle Alexander..." Ibid., 170.

"All becomes..." Samuel Gale to Lady Selkirk, 30 October 1818, quoted in Martin, *Lord Selkirk's Work,* 154.

Three divisions of suits Ibid., 142; Campbell, *North West Company,* 238.

List of accusations *Montreal Courant*, no date given, quoted in Campbell, *North West Company*, 238; Martin, *Lord Selkirk's Work*, 147.

The trial Rich, *Fur Trade*, 228, 238; Campbell, *North West Company*, 237–39; HBRS 4:xl; partial transcript printed in Payette, *The Northwest*, 437–65. The five who stood trial with McLoughlin were Alexander Mackenzie, Hugh McGillis, John McDonald, Simon Fraser (a Nor'Wester, not McLoughlin's uncle), and John Siveright. The last was also charged as an accessory before the fact.

94   *"the unscrupulous land-grabber"* *Montreal Gazette*, no date given, quoted in Campbell, *North West Company*, 232.

"unconscionable and potentially..." Campbell, *North West Company*, 238.

"not alleged..." Partial transcript of trial, 30 October 1818, printed in Payette, *The Northwest*, 437.

"had reduced our stocks...All the canoes..." McGillivray, testimony, ibid., 453, 457.

Verdicts Campbell, *North West Company*, 238–39; Rich, *Fur Trade*, 238.

Selkirk's costs Martin, *Lord Selkirk's Work*, 133 n. 2.

95   *Belief in courts' prejudice* Rich, *Fur Trade*, 228.

Selkirk estate At Selkirk's death the estate had a debt of £160,000 and owned £26,000 in HBC stock. His heirs later returned the Assiniboine grant to the HBC for £1,500 of stock. Martin, *Lord Selkirk's Work*, 175.

"let the wicked..." Lady to Lord Selkirk, 15 November 1818, quoted in Gray, *Lord Selkirk of Red River*, 304.

Chapter 3–5: The End of an Era

95   *McL income and NWC accounts* Barker, *Financial Papers*, 37–40; HBRS 4:xxxvi.

96   *Winterers' dissatisfaction* HBRS 4:xli.

NWC former agreements Campbell, *North West Company*, 128; Rich, *Fur Trade*, 195; list of shares with dates due, in Morrison, *North West Company in Rebellion*, 39.

97   *"left Fort William..."* Samuel Gale to Lady Selkirk, September 1819, Selkirk Correspondence, 6500, from photostats in PAC, quoted in HBRS 4:xlii.

"firmness of character...a good dinner..." Robertson to Moffat, about 15 February 1819, Robertson, *Correspondence Book*, HBRS 2:82.

McL contacts Moffat and Gale HBRS 4:xlii–xlv.

"possesses influence..." Gale to Lady Selkirk, September 1819, Selkirk Correspondence, 6500–6501, from photostats in PAC, quoted in HBRS 4:xlii.

Ellice offer Martin, *Lord Selkirk's Work*, 167.

98   *"seemed to alter..."* Selkirk to Colvile, 8 January 1820, quoted in Rich, *History of the Hudson's Bay Company*, vol. 2, HBRS 22:civ.

HBC rejects Ellice offer Lamb, Introduction to HBRS 4:xliii.

Conflict on frontier MacKay, *Honourable Company*, 150; Rich, *Fur Trade*,

229–33; Campbell, *North West Company*, 243–64.

HBC indebtedness Campbell, *North West Company*, 266.

"Rival posts fought..." FTE, xxxvii.

McL demoted Lamb, Introduction to HBRS 4:xliv.

"The Doctor..." McGillivray to J. G. McTavish, 15 July 1820, HBCA, Folder of North West Company Letters, quoted in HBRS 4:xliv.

99 *McL and Bethune represent winterers* Lamb, Introduction to HBRS 4:xliv; Rich, *Fur Trade*, 243. Bethune was the grandson of Jean Etienne Wadin, through Wadin's daughter Veronica. McLoughlin's wife Marguerite was Wadin's daughter through an Indian woman. *ME*, 221 n. 98.

McL takes children to Montreal McL to SF, November 1821 [1820], *ME*, 171–72; McL to SF, 5 May 1822, *ME*, 172; *ME*, 43.

Selkirk's death The earl had gone to Pau, France, hoping to regain his health, but he died there on April 8, 1820. Martin, *Lord Selkirk's Work*, 175.

"the Montreal Houses..." Gale to Colvile, 28 October 1820, Selkirk Correspondence, 6994, from photostats in PAC, quoted in HBRS 4:xlv.

"if Mr. McLoughlin..." Ibid., 6994–95.

Purpose of trip Ibid.

"notwithstanding their appearance..." Gale to Colvile, Robertson, 28 October 1820, Selkirk Correspondence, quoted in HBRS 4:xlvii n. 1.

100 *"bears a strong..."* Robertson to Moffat, n.d. but before 20 June 1821, Robertson, *Correspondence Book*, HBRS 2:148.

"Mr. Glens...I hope when you come..." McL to SF, November 1821 [1820], *ME*, 171.

Robertson's capture and escape Robertson to Moffat, about 12 February 1819, Robertson, *Correspondence Book*, HBRS 2:78–79.

"In the evening..." Robertson to Moffat, December 1820, ibid., 139.

101 *"The cloth being..."* Ibid.

"I am afraid..." Robertson to Moffat, probably the last week of December 1820, ibid., 142.

McL visits David, receives power of attorney Abstract of title, Barker Papers, cited in *ME*, 86.

102 *McL loses status* Rich, *Fur Trade*, 241.

Coalition HBRS 4:xlvi–xlviii; Rich, *History of the Hudson's Bay Company*, vol. 2, HBRS 22:397; MacKay, *Honourable Company*, 158–62; Rich, *Fur Trade*, 239–42; Campbell, *North West Company*, 265–67.

Attempt to penalize McL and Bethune Rich, *Fur Trade*, 241.

103 *"The feudal state..."* Irving, *Astoria*, 11.

Chapter 3–6: Coalition

103   *Nicholas Garry* HBRS 4:xlviii; MacKay, *Honourable Company*, 165–68; Campbell, *North West Company*, 267–69, 273–74.

McL revisits brother ME, 43; HBRS 4:xlix–l; William McGillivray to John George McTavish, 5 March 1822, B.239/c/1, fos. 65–67, printed in Fleming, *Minutes of Council*, HBRS 3:406.

Meeting at Fort William MacKay, *Honourable Company*, 168–70; Campbell, *North West Company*, 270; Rich, *Fur Trade*, 242.

104   *New HBC organization* Campbell, *North West Company*, 270–71; Rich, *Fur Trade*, 242; MacKay, *Honourable Company*, 158–63. Twenty shares were allotted to HBC directors, twenty to Montreal partners, five to the estate of Lord Selkirk, and 2½ each to Simon McGillivray and Edward Ellice, as compensation for their former profits as NWC agents.

Departments of HBC Rich, *History of the Hudson's Bay Company*, vol. 2, HBRS 22:406–7.

Protest against coalition Campbell, *North West Company*, 272–73.

"Amalgamation!" Willson, *Great Company*, 433.

MacKay, *Honourable Company*, 203; Rich, *Hudson's Bay Company*, 3:411.

105   *"With reduced means..."* Speech of Simon McGillivray in 1825, extract in MacKay, *Honourable Company*, 156–57.

"the yearly disbursements..." McGillivray to Reverend John Strachan, July 1821, extract in MacKay, *Honourable Company*, 164.

"To Let, for three..." Montreal Herald, 25 September 1824, printed in Payette, *The Northwest*, 507.

106   *Fort William's subsequent history* Fort William was used by the HBC as a subsidiary post until the late nineteenth century, when it was abandoned, its remains were torn down, and the land became a freightyard for the Canadian Pacific Railway. Today the Ontario government operates Old Fort William, an authentic replica located seven miles upstream from the original site. There workers in period costumes demonstrate canoe making, fur beating, baking, carpentry, etc. The voyageur trail from Montreal to Lake Superior was unused until the Canadian Pacific Railway laid tracks along part of the original route. Newman, *Caesars*, 210; documents from Old Fort William.

Meeting at York Factory Rich, *Hudson's Bay Company*, 3:415.

"One of them..." John Tod, "Reminiscences of 1821," manuscript in Bancroft Library, quoted in Newman, *Caesars*, 219.

"Dear Sir I shall..." GS to McL, 1 December 1821, D.4/1, fo. 14–14d, HBRS 4:xlix.

107   *Acts of 1821* Printed in Martin, *Lord Selkirk's Work*, 218–22; see also Rich, *Fur Trade*, 240–41; Rich, *Hudson's Bay Company*, 3:401–3; FTE, xii, xiii.

"Home via Canada..." Officers' Ledger, A.16/59, fo. 18, quoted in HBRS 4:l.

McGillivray letter William McGillivray to John George McTavish, 5 March 1822, B.239/c/1, fos. 65–67, printed in Fleming, *Minutes of Council*, HBRS 3:405.

McL's request for funds William Smith to McL, 8 January 1822, A.5/6, fo. 179d, HBRS 4:xlix–l.

McL returns to London Fleming, *Minutes of Council*, HBRS 3:406.

108   *"I hope that you..."* McL to SF, 5 May 1822, *ME*, 172.

McL's children SF to Thomas Thain, 27 December 1822, *ME*, 173; *ME*, 44, 45.

"gambled sang and fought..." MacKay, *Honourable Company*, 185.

McL *delivers documents* GS to G&C, 15 August 1822, printed in Fleming, *Minutes of Council*, HBRS 3:365.

"on an Exploring..." McL to SF, 14 September 1823, *ME*, 174–75.

109   *John Tanner* McL, Journal of Lac la Pluie, vol. 2, entries for 1, 3, 4, 9 September 1823, B.105/a/9, quoted in HBRS 4:li.

McL increases returns Lamb, Introduction to HBRS 4:li.

"the best early accounts" Nute, *Highway*, 62.

Rainy Lake area and people McL, "Indians from Fort William," 9–10, 12, 14.

Family goes to York Factory Harvey, "Biography of Her Father," 1.

York Factory gathering MacKay, *Honourable Company*, 105.

110   *"at St. Mary's..."* David McLoughlin Papers, OHSL.

McL assigned to Columbia HBRS 4:li–lii; "Minutes of Council held at York Factory," 10 July 1824, *FTE*, 217, 229. The minutes are printed on pp. 215–40.

Chapter 4–1: John Jacob Astor's Company

113   *"As you ascend..."* McL to SF, 15 March 1825, *ME*, 176.

115   *"not sanguine..."* G&C to GS, February 1822, *FTE*, xlix–l. Company documents often mention abandoning the Columbia, as in J. H. Pelly to Lords of the Committee of the Privy Council for Trade, 7 February 1838: "Several of the leading and most intelligent persons in the country strongly recommended that the company should abandon it altogether." *FTE*, 343.

Early ships along Northwest Coast Samuel N. Dicken, "Oregon Geography before White Settlement, 1770–1840," and Donald C. Cutter, "Spain and the Oregon Coast," in Vaughan, *Western Shore*, 1, 30–44. The Cabrillo-Ferrelo expedition of Spain in 1542–43 and Sir Francis Drake of England in 1579 probably sighted Oregon, but did not record details.

116   *Heceta sights Columbia* Cutter, "Spain and the Oregon Coast," in Vaughan, *Western Shore*, 41; Heceta's report, translated extract in Greenhow, *Oregon and California*, 430–33; *OQ*, 2.

"bore away and run in..." Log of Gray's *Columbia*, 11 May 1792, in Greenhow, *Oregon and California*, 434. The log itself has disappeared, but extracts from it were copied in 1816 by Mr. Bullfinch of Boston, one of the ship's owners,

and were published in newspapers and reports to Congress, with an affidavit by Bullfinch to their exactness.

"stood clear of the bars..." "John Boit's Log of the Columbia," 311. Boit was one of three crewmen who kept journals.

Gray and Vancouver OQ, 3–5.

"in no respect remarkable" Elliott, "Oregon Coast," 388.

American trade with Asia FTE, xlvii–xlviii; OQ, 142–46; James R. Gibson, "Bostonians and Muscovites on the Northwest Coast, 1788–1841" in Vaughan, *Western Shore*, 86–88.

U.S. and British claims OQ, 1–6.

117   *Pacific Fur Company* Ross, *Adventures of the First Settlers*, 2–10; Franchère, *Voyage*, li–liii, 2–8.

Men on Tonquin Ross, *Adventures of the First Settlers*, 7–8, 13; Franchère, *Voyage*, 8. Ross says he and Robert Stuart were clerks who had been promised partnership "at the end of the third year," but Franchère lists young Stuart as a partner.

Age of Thomas McKay Baptismal record at Glengarry, cited in Elliott, "Marguerite Wadin McKay McLoughlin," 339. Thomas was born in 1797.

Captain Thorn Ross, *Adventures of the First Settlers*, 14, 68, 166; Clarke, *Pioneer Days*, 1:42–43. Both Ross and Franchère cite Thorn's irrational behavior, such as marooning a boatload of men.

Crossing bar Ross, *Adventures of the First Settlers*, 54–62.

Building Fort Astoria Ibid., 71–73; Franchère, *Voyage*, 65, 79–80, 86, 90.

"boiled fish..." Ibid., 73–75.

Franchère's account Franchère, *Voyage*, 68.

118   Tonquin *leaves* Ibid., 68; Ross, *Adventures of the First Settlers*, 81.

Story of interpreter Ross, *Adventures of the First Settlers*, 159–65; Franchère, *Voyage*, 133–38. The accounts of Ross and Franchère generally agree, except Franchère says the captain insulted the chief by slapping his face with a bundle of furs and that the explosion happened a day later instead of almost at once. The accounts were based on interviews with the interpreter, the only firsthand witness. Ross said Weeks, the ship's armorer, blew up the ship, while Franchère did not name the individual.

Astor's other posts These included Okanogan, She Whaps (near Kamloops), Spokane (about ten miles northwest of today's Spokane), Kootenai (in today's Montana), Flathead (Montana), Nez Perce (on the Snake River), and Wallace House (near Salem, Oregon). Ross, *Adventures of the First Settlers*, 142–45, 200, 202, 206, 208; Carey, *General History*, 207–8.

McL offered post McL to SF, 22 March 1812, ME, 159.

"Mr. Pillet fought..." Cox, *Columbia*, 116.

Beaver *and* Lark *lost* Ross, *Adventures of the First Settlers*, 239–41, 260–61.

Decision to abandon Fort Astoria Ibid., 220, 239–41, 244–46.

Sale of Astoria Ibid., 252–54; Franchère, *Voyage*, 143; Carey, *General History*, 210–18. Astor estimated the value as $200,000, which is generally regarded as too high.

119   *"What! Is this..."* Franchère, *Voyage*, 151. The original is in French. This version is as translated by Milo Milton Quaife. Franchère's own translation, quoted in Henry, *New Light*, 2:771, says, "What! is this the Fort I have heard so much of! Good God...!" But Ross says Black was "never once heard to utter an oath or indecorous expression all the time he was in the river." *Adventures of the First Settlers*, 259. When Elliott Coues, editor of the Henry journals, encountered the conflicting forms, he exclaimed, "And it is thus that history is written!" *New Light*, 2:771.

"a bottle of Madeira..." Henry, *New Light*, 2:770. See also Franchère, *Voyage*, 150.

"taken by either..." Treaty of Ghent, quoted in *OQ*, 8.

Biddle and Prevost *OQ*, 17–18, 22–24; Elliott, "An Event," 181–87.

120   *"We nailed up..."* Journal of Lieut. J. H. Aulick, in Elliott, "An Event," 183.

"that of the United States..." Cox, *Columbia*, 77.

120–21   *Russian ukase* *OQ*, 129–32; *FTE*, 72 n. 128; HBRS 4:xvii; Gibson, "Bostonians and Muscovites," in Vaughan, *Western Shore*, 110.

121   *Spain cedes coast* *OQ*, 37, 124. On February 22, 1819, Spain signed the Adams-Otis Treaty ceding to the United States its claims to the Pacific Northwest north of the forty-second parallel. Mexico won independence from Spain in 1821, and on October 24, 1824, the Mexican parliament signed the constitution that made the country a republic.

Treaties with Russia *OQ*, 124, 132; *FTE*, 72 n. 128; HBRS 4:xxii; Gibson, "Bostonians and Muscovites," in Vaughan, *Western Shore*, 111.

Chapter 4–2: Over the Stony Mountains

121   *McKay daughters* The David McLoughlin Papers at OHSL list the husbands of the three daughters but omit the girls' names. The Red River Register of Baptisms gives the date of the marriage of Mary McKay and William Sinclair as June 21, 1823. Elliott, "Marguerite Wadin McKay McLoughlin," 339. Nancy's marriage certificate was listed among the papers seized by Selkirk from McLoughlin's desk at Fort William in 1816 (Archives Nationales du Quebec a Montreal, NWC Papers, H. Doucet, Notary, 4032½, 29 January 1817, printed in "Dr. McLoughlin's House and the Apothecary's Shop #2"). Since McKay had left the Fort William area in 1808, his youngest daughter was born not later than the following year, and was at least fifteen in 1824—marriageable age by the standards of that time.

Joseph at Sault Ste. Marie David McLoughlin Papers, OHSL.

"advanced," "for a life of work..." Sister St. Henry to SF, 18 May 1826, *ME*, 180.

122   *"My object is not..."* McL to SF, 15 March 1825, *ME*, 176.

        "I do not know..." Ibid.

        Northern Department HBRS 4:xii; Fleming, *Minutes of Council*, HBRS 3:xi.

        New Caledonia attached to Columbia HBRS 4:liv; *FTE*, xxxviii, 72, 83. For examples of Simpson's and McLoughlin's use of "Columbia Department," see *FTE*, 66, 83, 187; and HBRS 4:88, 183, 199.

        GS's background FTE, xliii–xlvi.

123   *"shrewd, purposeful..."* Rich, *Fur Trade*, 233–34.

        Physical description of GS Bancroft, *Northwest Coast*, 2:489; Galbraith, *Little Emperor*, 22.

        GS's measures of economy FTE, xlvi.

        GS as traveler Teisendorf, "George Simpson, Canoe Executive," 39.

        Canoeman holds GS in water FTE, xlv.

        "two Light Canoes..." GS, journal, 15 August 1824, *FTE*, 3–4. Simpson did not write the journal in daily entries, but several days at a time. Some of the dates are approximate.

        "We went from..." Harvey, "Biography of Her Father," 1.

124   *McL's route, GS's route* GS, journal, 15 August 1824, *FTE*, n. 5.

        "This channel was..." Ibid., about 25 August 1824, 8.

        "In Lake Primeau..." Ibid., 2 September 1824, 16.

        "The Dr is still..." Ibid., about 5 September 1824, 18.

        "It was unsafe..." Ibid., 20 September 1824, 20.

        "Mr. McMillan and I..." Ibid., 22 September 1824, 22.

125   *"On the 26th..."* Ibid., 26 September 1824, 23.

        "which is productive..." Ibid., 3 April 1825, 131.

        "Continued our route..." Ibid., 27 September 1824, 23.

        "George Simpson came..." Harvey, "Biography of Her Father," 1.

128   *"extremely unwell...the remainder of the day"* GS, journal, 2 October 1824, *FTE*, 27–28.

        "strong and steady..." Ibid., 10 October 1824, 29.

        "beautifully Wild..." Ibid., 11 October 1824, 30.

        Meeting McKay Ibid., 10–11 October 1824, 29–31.

        "a tall very dark..." Roberts, "Round Hand," 208.

        "a cavalcade..." GS, journal, 14 October 1824, *FTE*, 32.

        Athabasca Pass Ibid., 12–17 October 1824, 32–36.

129   *"this basin should..."* Ibid., 17 October 1824, 34.

        The Grande Côte Ibid., 35.

"for making canoes" Henry, *New Light,* 2:903; also see 796, 834, 836, 840. Traders' journals and letters often refer to cedar brought by ship from Canada, and to cedar-plank boats propelled by paddles, not oars.

"called Boats but are..." GS, journal, 21 October 1824, *FTE,* 38.

130   *"and our provisions..."* Ibid.

"in two Boats...bold and strong..." Ibid., 22 October 1824, 38–39.

"The Weather cold...Raining in torrents..." Ibid., 22, 23 October 1824, 40.

"Heavy Rain..." Ibid., 25 October 1824, 41.

"I do not know..." Ibid.

Spokane House Ibid., 28 October 1824, 43–49.

"left to a self sufficient...in the hands of..." Ibid., 46.

Ogden leads brigade Ibid., 46–47.

"perfectly independent..." Ibid., 27 October 1824, 42.

131   *"Hundreds of... thought nothing..."* Ibid., 6 November 1824, 61.

"great numbers...nearly opposite...No sooner had we..." Ibid., 6 November 1824, 62.

"placed a great..." Ibid., 7 November 1824, 63.

"after Supper all...about 10 P.M...." Ibid., 8 November 1824, 64.

Chapter 4–3: Winter at Fort George

132   *Layout of Fort George* Sketch, 1818, by Lieutenant Mervin Vavasour, in Elliott, "Surrender at Astoria,"; following p. 270; Biddle, "Log of the U.S.S. *Ontario,*" 310–11; sketch of fort, in Schafer, "Warre and Vavasour's Military Reconnaissance," 99.

"During the rainy..." Henry, *New Light,* 2:776.

Inventory J. D. Cameron to GS, 5 April 1822, D.4/116, fo. 92, HBRS 4:xvi.

"altogether an air..." GS, journal, n.d., *FTE,* 65. The middle part of the journal, pp. 65–124, is a long, undated report.

"There was hardly..." Harvey, "Biography of Her Father," 2.

"I cannot say..." McL to SF, 15 March 1825, *ME,* 176.

133   *Concomely* Harvey, "Chief Concomly's Skull," 161; Santee, "Comcomly and the Chinooks."

Concomely's sons-in-law Santee, "Comcomly and the Chinooks," quoting Ranald MacDonald, 275. They were Duncan McDougal, former partner at Fort Astoria; Archibald MacDonald, father of Ranald MacDonald; Louis Rondeau, HBC trapper; and Thomas McKay, son of Marguerite McLoughlin. Merk lists only two, Duncan McDougal and "A. McKenzie," HBC clerk. *FTE,* 87 n. 43.

Chinook Indians Ross, Adventures of the First Settlers, 87–101; Paul Kane, "Address to Canadian Institute," 4 March 1845, printed in *Toronto Daily Colonist,*

6–9 August 1845, reprinted in Vaughan, *Paul Kane,* 20–50.

Chinook Jargon Father Francis Norbert Blanchet, *Dictionary of Chinook Jargon* (Portland, 1853), reprinted in Vaughan, *Paul Kane,* 55–65. Blanchet's *Dictionary* is a miniature book, about three by five inches and forty pages long, but it was widely used, and printed in several editions.

134   *"as none but..."* GS, journal, n.d., *FTE,* 96. For further details of Simpson's dalliances, see Galbraith, *Little Emperor,* 68–71, 95, 108–12.

"are generally considered..." Paul Kane, "Address to Canadian Institute," 4 March 1845, printed in *Toronto Daily Colonist,* 6–9 August 1845, reprinted in Vaughan, *Paul Kane,* 20–50. Quotation is on p. 25.

Joint occupation, negotiations OQ, 39–45, 164–78; Nute, *Highway,* 12–18.

British vs. American demands OQ, 48–53, 130–32.

135   *"I view it..."* Jefferson to Astor, 9 November 1813, from *The Writings of Thomas Jefferson,* ed. Andrew A. Lipscomb and Albert E. Bergh, quoted in *OQ,* 14.

"fit only for..." *New York Gazette,* 16 March 1822, quoted in *OQ,* 119.

"a convenient...Along the back..." Speech of Senator Thomas Hart Benton, 1 March 1825, *Congressional Debates,* 18th Cong., 2d sess (1824–25), 712, quoted in *OQ,* 117.

"As the Americans are..." G&C to Chief Factors in Charge of Columbia Dep't, 22 July 1824, *FTE,* 240.

136   *"shewn an extraordinary..."* GS, journal, 28–30 October 1824, *FTE,* 47.

Decision to move Hussey, *Fort Vancouver,* 43; GS, journal, n.d., *FTE,* 87.

"it became necessary..." GS, journal, n.d., *FTE,* 92–93.

"either high perpendicular..." Ibid., 87.

"After Mr. Kennedy and I..." McL to G&C, 6 October 1825, D.4/6, fos. 45–56, HBRS 4:4.

137   *Site of first Fort Vancouver* Hussey, *Fort Vancouver,* 39–40. It was not at today's Belle Vue Point, but sloped from the present-day State School for the Deaf (2901 East 7th Street, Vancouver, Washington) to the river. The buildings were where the school now stands; the lower land was fields and orchards.

"the noble river..." Wilkes, *Narrative,* 4:335.

"A Farm to any extent..." GS, journal, n.d., *FTE,* 87.

Construction Hussey, *Fort Vancouver,* 43–44, 48; Clarke, *Pioneer Days,* 1:184.

"very large and ungainly..." Dr. William McKay, interview, in Clarke, *Pioneer Days,* 1:182.

"actually shed Tears..." GS, journal, 16 March 1825, *FTE,* 122. On starting east, Simpson again dated his journal.

Journey to Vancouver Ibid., 16–19 March 1825, 122–24.

Spellings of "Willamette" Old spellings include *Wallamet, Wallamitte,* and

Wilarmet. Lewis A. McArthur says Charles Wilkes in the 1840s "appears to have crystallized government use in favor of Willamette." *Oregon Geographic Names*, 909. McArthur lists numerous early spellings.

138   *"too young & delicate..."* Ibid., 17 March 1825, 123.

"built on the same plan..." Scouler, "Journal," *OHQ* 6 (June 1905): 174. For further comparison to Fort George, see Hussey, *Fort Vancouver*, 43–44.

"The Establishment is..." GS, journal, 18 March 1825, *FTE*, 123–24.

"in a half-finished state" David Douglas, *Journal*, 16 November–26 December 1824, 152.

"Saturday, March 19th..." GS, journal, *FTE*, 124.

Chapter 5–1: Up the River

141   *"I have shipped..."* McL to G&C, 6 October 1825, D.4/6, fos. 45–56, HBRS 4:16.

143   *"old scow," "new scow"* Work, "Journal," ed. Pipes, 22 March 1825, 140.

The Otter Ibid., 140 n. 2; Ross, *Adventures of the First Settlers*, 153.

Transfer of equipment Work, "Journal," ed. Pipes, 140–46.

144   *"a queer looking..."* GS, Character Book, A.34/2, fos. 18d–19, quoted in biography of Work, appendix B, HBRS 4:358.

"Friday 8. Stormy..." Work, "Journal," ed. Pipes, 8–10 April 1825, 144.

"The wind blew..." Ibid., 22–23 March, 1 April 1825, 141–42.

"forewith... old and crazy... so rotten" Ibid., 4–5 April 1825, 143.

"thick and hazy" Ibid., 7 April 1825, 144.

145   *McL's explanation of tribal war* McL to G&C, 6 October 1825, D.4/6, fos. 45–56, HBRS 4:5.

"an Indian of..." Work, "Journal," ed. Pipes, 23–24 March 1825, 141.

"To revenge this..." Scouler, "Journal," *OHQ* 6 (June 1905): 165.

"collecting about the place..." McL to G&C, 6 October 1825, D.4/6, fos. 45–56, HBRS 4:5.

Delay caused by ship Ibid., HBRS 4:2–3; HBRS 4:lxix; Hussey, *Fort Vancouver*, 48.

146   *"trifling"* G&C to GS, 2 June 1824, A.6/20, fos. 160d–164, extract in *FTE*, 210.

"a very inferior quality" McL to G&C, 6 October 1825, D.4/6, fos. 45–56, HBRS 4:l.

Bricks used for chimneys Hussey, *Fort Vancouver*, 49.

"constantly employed" McL to G&C, 6 October 1825, D.4/6, fos. 45–56, HBRS 4:6.

"a state of ruin..." Scouler, "Journal," *OHQ* 6 (September 1905): 277.

Chapter 5–2: The First Fort Vancouver

146   *"a fair, florid..."* George Roberts to Frances Fuller Victor, 28 November 1878, in Roberts, "Round Hand," 188.

Douglas's arrival Douglas, *Journal*, 8 April 1825, 103. Most entries in Douglas's journal summarize several days or weeks.

"The chief factor..." Ibid., 19 April 1825, 106.

"at 8 o'clock morning..." Ibid.

"a tent was kindly..." Ibid., 107.

"out of our power..." McL to G&C, 6 October 1825, D.4/6, fos. 45–56, HBRS 4:15.

"thirty quires of paper..." Douglas, *Journal*, February 1826, 157.

"to prevent me..." Ibid., September 1825 (written October 3), 142.

Killed and ate eagle Ibid., 143.

"rain fell in such..." Ibid., December 1825, 152.

148   *"Big House"* Hussey, *Historic Structures*, 1:89–91.

"took an airing..." Douglas, *Journal*, December 1825, 152.

"we saw little..." Ball, "Across the Continent," 16 November 1832, 100.

"I cannot forbear..." Douglas, *Journal*, 20 March 1827, 242.

McL accompanies brigade Ibid., 242–47.

"and returned at dusk..." Ibid., 17 April 1827, 247.

Medal Property of the McLoughlin Memorial Association, at the McLoughlin House in Oregon City.

149   *Governor John Henry Pelly* Pelly was seven years older than McLoughlin, having been born in 1777. He served in the East India Company, became a ship's mate and then captain for the HBC, and was elected a Committee member in 1816, deputy governor in 1812, and governor in 1822. His tenure outlasted that of McLoughlin, for he served until his death in 1852. In 1840 he became a baronet, and was known to his friends as "Sir Pelly" rather than "Sir John." A brief biography is in HBRS 6:399–401.

Posts of Columbia District Hussey, *Fort Vancouver*, 32; GS, journal, *FTE*, 66; GS to H. U. Addington, 5 January 1826, Corres. with Government No. 721, extract in *FTE*, 264. The list in Simpson's letter to Addington includes both Columbia and New Caledonia posts.

150   *"about Eight Days..."* GS, journal, 1 November 1824, *FTE*, 51.

Posts in New Caledonia GS to Addington, 5 January 1826, *FTE*, 264; Merk's explanation is on p. 24 n. 54.

"serious loss...a store keeper...for the information..." GS to McL, 10 March 1825, D.4/7, fo. 98d, HBRS 4:liii–liv.

"invested with discretionary..." G&C to GS, 23 February 1826, A.6/21, fos. 73d–80d, extract in *FTE*, 267.

"*only such Buildings…*" McL to G&C, 1 September 1826, B.223/b/2, fos. 20–28d, HBRS 4:32.

151 *Standard of trade* GS, journal, *FTE*, 171–74.

152 *McLoughlin's varied jobs* Barker, *Letters*, iii; McL to G&C, 6 October 1825, D.4/6, fos. 45–56, HBRS 4:1–22; other letters in the same volume.

Lima, Valparaiso McL to G&C, 11 October, 24 November 1830, 28 October 1832, 28 May 1834, HBRS 4:88, 95, 105, 120.

"*The additional Shot…*" McL to G&C, 1 September 1826, B.223/b/2, fos. 20–28d, HBRS 4:27.

"*I also sent ninety…*" McL to G&C, 6 October 1825, D.4/6, fos. 45–56, HBRS 4:7.

First harvest McL to Governor, Chief Factors, and Chief Traders, 20 March 1826, D.4/115, fos. 40d–46, extract in *FTE*, 270.

Shipment of seeds Hussey, *Fort Vancouver*, 51; McL to G&C, 1 September 1826, B.223/b/2, fos. 20–28d, HBRS 4:31.

"*Our farming goes…*" Ibid.

"*Our Stock of pigs…* McL to G&C, 6 July 1827, B.223/b/3, fos. 4d–10d, HBRS 4:44.

153 "*the Wolves…*" McL to GS, 20 March 1827, D.4/120, fos. 48–58d, *FTE*, 291.

Orders to set up coastal trade HBRS 4:lxix.

Staff at Fort Vancouver McL to G&C, 6 October 1825, D.4/6, fos. 45–56, HBRS 4:11.

"*I hope…*" McL to SF, 15 March 1825, *ME*, 175–76.

"*I have in mind…*" McL to SF, 19 March 1826, *ME*, 179.

"*consisting of 9 boats…*" Work, "Journal," ed. Elliott, 5 July 1826, *WHQ* 6 (January 1915): 27.

"*on hearing that the Doctor…*" John Warren Dease to the Governor, Chief Factors, and Chief Traders, Athabaska Portage, 15 October 1826, D.4/120, fo. 16, HBRS 4:xcviii.

154 "*mechanics of various…*" Smith, Jackson, and Sublette, Letter to Eaton, 29 October 1830, 397.

154–55 "*great stump…looked on…*" Dr. William McKay, interview, in Clarke, *Pioneer Days*, 1:185.

155 *Wheat-growing* Hussey, *Fort Vancouver*, 51, 203. For a detailed discussion of McL's early mills, see 203–6.

"*On visiting the mill…*" Narcissa Whitman to her mother, September 1836, in Elliott, "White Women," *OHQ* 37 (June 1936): 182.

"*There was a gentleman…*" Harvey, "Biography of Her Father," 7–9.

"*A gentleman…*" Narcissa Whitman to her mother, September 1836, in Elliott, "White Women," *OHQ* 37 (June 1936): 180.

"says he has..." Hiram Bingham to Jeremiah Evarts, treasurer of the American Board of Commissioners for Foreign Missions, 16 February 1829, in Blue, "Green's Missionary Report," 264.

"a fine garden..." Smith, Jackson, and Sublette, Letter to Eaton, 29 October 1830, 397.

156   *"Here we find fruit..."* Narcissa Whitman to her mother, September 1836, in Elliott, "White Women," *OHQ* 37 (June 1936): 179–80.

Chapter 5–3: The Snake Brigade

156   *Fur desert* Rich, *History of the Hudson's Bay Company*, vol. 2, HBRS 22:584; Hussey, *Fort Vancouver*, 34–35; Merk, "Snake Country Expedition," 107.

"extremely desirable..." G&C to GS, 12 March 1827, A.6/21, fos. 116–123d, extract in *FTE*, 286.

"It is in our interest..." Fleming, *Minutes of Council*, HBRS 3:154 n. 1.

"It is scarcely...well may it be said..." Ogden, *Snake Country Journals*, 24 [25] April 1829, HBRS 28:144.

Snake Country OQ, 74–75, frontispiece (map).

157   *"neither falsetto, tenor..."* Elliott, "Peter Skene Ogden," 272.

"the humorous, honest..." Cox, *Columbia*, 29. Cox obviously used "gay" in its classical meaning, as "merry."

Ogden's background Elliott, "Peter Skene Ogden."

HBC accepts Ogden, Grant, and Black GS to Colvile, 8 September 1823, Dominion Archives, Selkirk Transcripts, XXV, 8011, extract in *FTE*, 203; see also Lamb, Introduction to HBRS 4:xx.

GS and McL met Ogden GS, journal, 28 October 1824, *FTE*, 43–49.

158   *"the very scum..."* Ibid., 45.

159   *Freemen's indebtedness* Merk, "Snake Country Expedition," 106; McL to G&C, 1 September 1826, B.223/b/2, fos. 20–28d, HBRS 4:34.

Fur trappers' life Ogden, "Journals," ed. Elliott; Elliott, "Peter Skene Ogden"; Ogden, *Snake Country Journals*, HBRS 13, 23, 28; Robinson, *Great Fur Land*, 243–52; Ross, *Adventures of the First Settlers*, 203–7.

160   *"suddenly seized with a violent..."* Ogden, *Snake Country Journals*, 25 March 1826, HBRS 13:146–47.

Ogden's brigade HBRS 4:lx.

Americans accompany Ogden Merk, "Snake Country Expedition," 99.

"that damn'd all–cursed..." Ogden to Governor, Chief Factors, and Chief Traders, 27 June 1824 [1825], D.4/119, fos. 10d–12, HBRS 4:297.

Americans guided troublemakers Ogden to Governor, Chief Factors, and Chief Traders, 10 July 1825, D.4/119, fos. 12–15, printed in Merk, "Snake Country Expedition," 112.

161   *"Tues. Jan. 10th..."* Ogden, "Journals," *OHQ* 10 (December 1909): 348, 353;
        11 (June 1910): 209.

        "All have been killed..." Ogden, "Snake Country Journals," 1 January 1829,
        HBRS 28:20.

        McL receives Ogden's letter McL to Chief Factors and Chief Traders, 10 August
        1825, excerpt in *FTE*, 254; Merk, "Snake Country Expedition," 103.

        Ogden's route Merk, "Snake Country Expedition," 99–100.

        Great Salt Lake Ibid., 100. Tradition says Jim Bridger discovered Great Salt
        Lake in 1824–25, and Étienne Provost, under William H. Ashley, may have
        reached the lake about then. Merk says Ogden's discovery is the earliest with
        documentary proof.

        Ogden meets Americans Ogden to Governor, Chief Factors, and Chief Traders,
        10 July 1825, D.4/119, fos. 12–15, printed in Merk, "Snake Country Expedition,"
        109–12; Ogden to Governor, Chief Factors, and Chief Traders, 27 June 1824
        [1825], D.4/119, fos. 10d–12, HBRS 4:296–99.

162   *American payments* Ogden to Governor, Chief Factors, and Chief Traders, 10
        July 1825, D.4/119, fos. 12–15, printed in Merk, "Snake Country Expedition,"
        112.

        "for not a freeman...waggons overland..." Ogden to Governor, Chief Factors,
        and Chief Traders, 27 June 1824 [1825], D.4/119, fos. 10d–12, HBRS 4:299;
        extract in Merk, "Snake Country Expedition," 115–16.

        "Mortifying intelligence..." McL to other posts, 10 August 1825, B.223/b/1,
        fos. 19–21, HBRS 4:302–3.

163   *"The freemen it seems..."* McL to G&C, 6 October 1825, D.4/6, fos. 45–56,
        HBRS 4:10.

        "killed on the East side..." McL to G&C, 7 October 1825, D.4/6, fos. 57–57d,
        HBRS 4:24.

        Habitual trespass Merk, "Snake Country Expedition," 103–5.

        "Letters from Mr. Ogden..." GS, journal, 7 April 1824, *FTE*, 134.

        "hunt all the head branches..." McL to GS, 20 March 1827, D.4/120, fos.
        48–58d, excerpt in *FTE*, 289.

        "all collisions..." G&C to GS, 20 September 1826, A.6/21, fos. 98–100,
        excerpt in Merk, "Snake Country Expedition," 118.

        "this should on no account..." G&C to McL, 20 September 1826, A.6/21, fos.
        101–102d, excerpt in Merk, "Snake Country Expedition," 119.

        G&C's reluctance to seek redress Ibid., 118–19.

        McL meets Ogden HBRS 4:lxiv; McL to G&C, 1 September 1826, B.223/b/2,
        fos. 20–28d, HBRS 4:27–28.

        "very handsome" Lamb, Introduction to HBRS 4:lxiv. This figure is from McL
        to GS, 20 March 1826, D.4/19, fo. 45, HBRS 4:lxiv. This differs from McLough-
        lin's report to the Governor and Committee, in which he reported that the

hunt of the whole party brought 3,577 beaver skins, of which the "servants" brought 2,188 made beaver and 79 made beaver in otters. McL to G&C, 1 September 1826, B.223/b/2, fos. 20–28d, HBRS 4:27.

164   *McL checks accounts* HBRS 4:lxv.

"incurred by desertion..." McL to GS, 20 March 1827, D.4/120, fo. 52d, HBRS 4:lxv.

Trappers' pay Ibid.; McL to G&C, 6 July 1827, B.223/b/3, fos. 4d–10d, HBRS 4:40–41.

"Several have Killed..." McL to G&C, 1 September 1826, B.223/b/2, fos. 20–28d, HBRS 4:34.

McL changes rates Ibid; HBRS 4:lxv–lxvi.

"I can only say..." McL to GS, 20 March 1827, D.4/120, fo. 52, HBRS 4:lxvi.

165   *McKay with Ogden* Ogden to Governor, Chief Factors, and Chief Traders, 10 October 1826, D.4/120, fos. 14–15d, excerpt in *FTE*, 283.

"All obliged to sleep..." Ogden, *Snake Country Journals,* 14 March 1827, HBRS 23:94. Ogden's journal was a day off.

"It is to be regretted..." Ogden to Governor, Chief Factors, and Chief Traders, 10 October 1826, D.4/120, fos. 14–15d, excerpt in *FTE*, 283.

"The American is now..." Ogden, "Journals," 23 January 1828, *OHQ* 11 (December 1910): 370.

"They are making..." Ibid., 25 January 1828, 371. The Americans survived.

"sorry they had left..." McL to G&C, 6 July 1827, B.223/b/3, fos. 4d–10d, HBRS 4:41.

166   *"we can afford..."* G&C to GS, 12 March 1827, A.6/21, fos. 116–123d, excerpt in Merk, "Snake Country Expedition," 119–20.

Chapter 5–4: Ships & Their Captains

166   *William and Ann* HBRS 4:1 n. 3; Barker, *Letters,* 331.

"I am sorry to say..." McL to G&C, 6 October 1825, D.4/6, fos. 45–56, HBRS 4:1.

167   *"sent a share of every..."* Ibid., 3.

Voyage of William and Ann HBRS 4:lxix–lxx.

"Captn Kelly was..." McL to Governor, Chief Factors, and Chief Traders, 20 March 1826, D.4/119, fos. 40d–46, extract in *FTE*, 270.

Brought back few furs Hussey, *Fort Vancouver,* 60; Lamb, Introduction to HBRS 4:lxx.

"venture to enter..." McL to GS, 20 March 1826, D.4/119, fo. 41d, HBRS 4:lxx. Portland Canal and Observatory Inlet are large arms of the Pacific, near the mouth of the Nass River in present-day central British Columbia.

168   *"amounted to pusillanimity"* GS, 1826 report, D.4/89, fo. 6, HBRS 4:lxx.

"direct[ed] him to come..." McL to G&C, 6 October 1825, D.4/6, fos. 45–56, HBRS 4:21.

"It is unfortunate..." McL to Hanwell, [September 1825], B.223/b/1, fo. 30, HBRS 4:lxx.

"very much disappointed..." McL to G&C, 6 October 1825, D.4/6, fos. 45–56, HBRS 4:16, 17.

Information from Kelly HBRS 4:lxx, lxxi.

"There must be..." McL to GS, 20 March 1826, D.4/119, fo. 44, HBRS 4:lxxi.

168–69   *"The late arrival..."* McL to G&C, 1 September 1826, B.223/b/2, fos. 20–28d, HBRS 4:25.

169   *"Of Several Articles..."* McL to G&C, 6 July 1827, B.223/b/3, fos. 4d–10d, HBRS 4:42.

"We can never..." McL to G&C, 10 July 1828, B.223/b/4, fos. 8d–13, HBRS 4:61–62.

"if an opposition..." McL to G&C, 11 October 1830, B.223/b/6/, fos. 13–18d, HBRS 4:87.

"had the benefit of freight..." J. H. Pelly to William Huskisson, 25 July 1826, A.8/2, fos. 9–11d, extract in *FTE*, 279.

East India monopoly and NWC agreement with Perkins & Company FTE, xlix; HBRS 4:xxvii.

HBC agreement with East India Company G&C to Chief Factors, 22 July 1824; G&C to GS, 11 March 1825; G&C to GS, 23 February 1826; G&C to A. L. Johnstone & Co., 31 March 1826, all in *FTE*, 240, 251, 268, 271–72; HBRS 4:xxvii.

"after some negociation" G&C to GS, 12 March 1824, A.6/20, fos. 133d–142, 148d–149, extract in *FTE*, 207.

"losing concern..." G&C to GS, 23 February 1826, A.6/21, fos. 73d–80d, extract in *FTE*, 268.

"operated against us..." McL to G&C, 6 October 1825, D.4/6, fos. 45–56, HBRS 4:13.

Broughton *and* Vancouver McL to G&C, 1 September 1826, B.223/b/2, fos. 20–28d, HBRS 4:lxxi, 29.

"to be decked..." Ibid., 29.

170   *"the want of Iron..."* GS, 1829 report, D.4/93, fo. 61d, HBRS 4:29 n. 2.

Dryad's arrival McL to G&C, 1 September 1826, B.223/b/2, fos. 20–28d, HBRS 4:24–25.

"I am sorry to have to..." Ibid., 25.

"Captn Davidsons talent..." GS, journal, n.d., *FTE*, 119.

"is as much addicted..." McL to G&C, 1 September 1826, B.223/b/2, fos. 20–28d, HBRS 4:35–36.

Relationship of Lieut. Simpson and GS MacKay, *Honourable Company,* 236; Harvey, "Biography of Her Father," 7. After Æmelius Simpson's mother died, his father married Mary Simpson, George's aunt, and the children were brought up as members of the family. HBRS 30:199 n. 1.

171   *The Cadboro* HBRS 4:42 n. 2.

"fifty-six feet long..." Bancroft, *Northwest Coast,* 2:476.

"The 'Cadboro' is quite..." GS to William Smith, 17 November 1828, D.4/16, fos. 4d–8d, extract in *FTE,* 301.

Cargo in 1827 McL to G&C, 6 July 1827, B.223/b/3, fos. 4d–10d, HBRS 4:42.

"The following year..." McL to G&C, 10 July 1828, B.223/b/4, fos. 8d–13, HBRS 4:55.

GS prefers Fraser River GS, journal, n.d., *FTE,* 73–77; GS to Colvile, 9 August 1824, extract in *FTE,* 244; GS to McLeod, 1 November 1824, extract in *FTE,* 247; HBRS 4:lviii–lix.

"become our principal..." GS to McL, 9 July 1827, D.4/90, fo. 98d, HBRS 4:lviii.

Hanwell's refusal HBRS 4:lxxii.

"proceeded by the Cowlttz..." McL to G&C, 6 July 1827, B.223/b/3, fos. 4d–10d, HBRS 4:44.

Simpson meets land party Hussey, *Fort Vancouver,* 63; McL to G&C, 6 July 1827, B.223/b/3, fos. 4d–10d, HBRS 4:44.

Fort Langley founded Rich, *History of the Hudson's Bay Company,* vol. 2, HBRS 22:613–14.

"untill the Stockades..." McL to G&C, 14 November 1827, B.223/b/3, fos. 21–22, HBRS 4:53.

172   *"saw few furs..."* Ibid.

Attack on crew of Cadboro Ibid.

"shocking proof...a Vessel must be..." McL to GS, 20 March 1828, D.4/121, fo. 33d, HBRS 4:lxxii.

"to Exchange into..." Lieut. Simpson to McL, 23 June 1827, B.223/b/3, fo. 12, HBRS 4:lxxii.

173   *"about three hundred Bushels..."* McL to G&C, 14 November 1827, B.223/b/3, fos. 21–22, HBRS 4:54.

"we must avail..." McL to G&C, 5 August 1829, B.223/b/5, HBRS 4:xcii.

Lieut. Simpson's report HBRS 4:lxxiii.

Shipment of salmon and lumber Hussey, *Fort Vancouver,* 64; HBRS 4:lxxiii; Lomax, "Hawaii-Columbia River Trade," 332–34; Throckmorton, *Argonauts,* 11. The HBC had recently opened an establishment in Hawaii.

"The expense of keeping..." McL to G&C, 15 November 1838, B.223/b/12, fos. 2–11, HBRS 4:155.

GS predicts profits GS to Lieut. Simpson [c. October 1828], D. 4/16, fos. 3–4, extract in *FTE*, 298.

"might prove as profitable..." GS, paraphrased in Hussey, *Fort Vancouver,* 64.

"the Russian Establishment..." McL to G&C, 5 August 1829, Barker, *Letters*, 37.

"to Lima..." McL to G&C, 11 October 1830, B.223/b/6, fos. 13–18d, HBRS 4:88.

174 *"to find a passage..."* McL to G&C, 18 November 1834, B.223/b/10, fos. 35–37, HBRS 4:128–29.

Chapter 5–5: Establishing Peace

174 *"and fully understood..."* McL to G&C, 15 November 1843, B.223/b/30, fos. 46–50, HBRS 6:117.

"We are traders..." Ibid., 118.

175 *"The whites themselves..."* Harvey, "Biography of Her Father," 6.

"Tie him to that cannon..." Matthieu, "Reminiscences," 96.

"The Indians we found..." Ball, "Across the Continent," 99.

"God forbid..." McL to Simon McGillivray, 27 February 1832, Barker, *Letters*, 255. This Simon McGillivray was the mixed-blood son of William McGillivray, former Montreal agent of the NWC.

"all the Chiefs..." McL to G&C, 1 September 1826, B.223/b/2, fos. 20–28d, HBRS 4:26.

Belief in retaliation G&C to McL, 28 October 1829, A.8/22, fos. 45–49d, paraphrased in *FTE*, 318; Johansen, "McLoughlin and the Indians." Reid, "Restraints of Vengeance," has an excellent discussion of Indian beliefs about retaliation and their applications.

176 *Hood Canal* This is a narrow waterway parallel to Puget Sound and extending south from Admiralty Inlet, near Whidbey Island.

Attack by Clallams McL to G&C, 10 July 1828, B.223/b/4, fos. 8d–13, HBRS 4:57; McL to G&C, 7 August 1828, B.223/b/4, fos. 19d–22d, HBRS 4:63; HBRS 4:lxxix.

"without having had..." McL to G&C, 10 July 1828, B.223/b/4, fos. 8d–13, HBRS 4:57.

"To pass over such..." Ibid.

177 *Tribes offer help* Ibid.

Arrival of the Eagle Ibid., 55 n. 2.

"strong burthensome Vessel" Ibid.

"to come to the Columbia..." Ibid., 58.

"vitiate the Insurance" Ibid.

"cautious and prudent," "get the Woman..." Repeated in McL to Simpson [March 1830], Barker, *Letters*, 81–82.

"the influence her father...her liberty was..." Ermatinger, journal, 26 June 1828, Ermatinger, *Fur Trade Letters*, 105. The journal is printed on pp. 97–114.

"accomplished the object..." McL to G&C, 7 August 1828, B.223/b/4, fos. 19d–22d, HBRS 4:63.

"a few Cannon Shot...burnt the Village..." Ibid., 64.

Attack on second village Ibid., 65; Ermatinger journal, 8 July 1828, Ermatinger, *Fur Trade Letters*, 113. Reports of the number killed do not agree. Ermatinger said the Indians reported twenty-five, including two that they themselves killed in retaliation for the attack on McKenzie, but he doubts the number (*Fur Trade Letters*, 113). McLoughlin cited a total of twenty. McL to G&C, 7 August 1828, B.223/b/4, fos. 19d–22d, HBRS 4:65.

177–78   *"it is certainly...It is a duty..."* McL to G&C, 7 August 1828, B.223/b/4, fos. 19d–22d, HBRS 4:65.

178   *"a failure"* William Todd to Edward Ermatinger, 15 July 1829, in Dye, "Old Letters," *WHQ* 1 (July 1907): 258.

"For my part..." Ermatinger, quoted in McL to GS, [March 1830], Barker, *Letters*, 83.

McLeod orders journal Francis Ermatinger to Edward Ermatinger, 5 March 1829, Ermatinger, *Fur Trade Letters*, 95.

Ermatinger's complaints Ermatinger, journal, *Fur Trade Letters*, 99, 105–8, 111–12, 113, 114.

"at the price..." Ibid., 105.

"I wish we..." Ibid., 113.

Disagreement between McL and Ermatinger McL to GS, [March 1830], Barker, *Letters*, 85; McL to Ermatinger, 20 March 1830, Barker, *Letters*, 99, 102, 103.

"There seems...conceive that..." McL to GS, [March 1830], Barker, *Letters*, 85, 83.

179   *"there must be..."* G&C to McL, 28 October 1829, paraphrased in *FTE*, 318. Ermatinger remained in the HBC's employ, on good terms with McLoughlin; and on August 12, 1841, he married Marguerite McLoughlin's granddaughter, Catherine Sinclair. Elliott, "Marguerite Wadin McKay McLoughlin," 388; Barker, *Letters*, 306–7; Francis Ermatinger to Edward Ermatinger, 4 March 1843, Ermatinger, *Fur Trade Letters*, 250.

Report of Arthur Black McL to G&C, 10 August 1828, B.223/b/4, fos. 23–24d, HBRS 4:68–69; Sullivan, *Jedediah Smith, Trader*, 178.

Jedediah Smith's escape McL to G&C, 10 August 1828, B.223/b/4, fos. 23–24d, HBRS 4:68–69; Sullivan, *Jedediah Smith, Trader*, 175–77. The "Bridge River" was a tributary of the Umpqua.

"a few wild berries..." McL, "Autobiography," in Clarke, *Pioneer Days*, 1:216, originally published as "Document Found among the Private Papers of the Late Dr. John McLoughlin," *OPAT*, 1880, 46–55.

"secured an Indian...two skirmishes..." McL to G&C, 10 August 1828,

B.223/b/4, fos. 23–24d, HBRS 4:70.

Killings by Smith party Ibid.; Sullivan, *Jedediah Smith, Trader,* 158, 167–70, 174; Smith, journal, in Sullivan, *Travels,* 31, 51, 65, 81, 82, 83.

Jedediah Smith Sullivan, *Jedediah Smith, Trader,* 2, 3, 208–10.

180 "*melancholy intelligence...*" McL to G&C, 10 August 1828, B.223/b/4, fos. 23–24d, HBRS 4:70.

"*I know many people...*" McL to McLeod, 12 September 1828, printed in Sullivan, *Travels,* 110–11.

Goods lost by Smith McL to G&C, 10 August 1828, B.223/b/4, fos. 23–24d, HBRS 4:70.

Expeditions of Ogden and McLeod Douthit, "The Hudson's Bay Company and the Indians of Southern Oregon," 33–36; Ogden, *Snake Country Journals,* HBRS 23:3–134; McLeod, journal, September 1826–15 February 1827, HBRS 23:175–219.

"*no intention but...*" Ogden, *Snake Country Journals,* 18 March 1827, HBRS 23:96.

"*grumble at our presumption...*" McLeod, journal, 27 November 1826, HBRS 23:193.

Indian killed Douthit, "The Hudson's Bay Company and the Indians of Southern Oregon," 35.

McLoughlin's instructions McL to McLeod, 12 September 1828, Sullivan, *Travels,* 110–11; HBRS 4:lxxviii.

"*McLeod knows these Indians...*" McL to Smith, 12 September 1828, Sullivan, *Travels,* 110.

181 "*You know those Indians...*" McL to McLeod, 12 September 1828, Sullivan, *Travels,* 111.

"*This was not...*" William Todd to Edward Ermatinger, 15 July 1829, in Dye, "Old Letters," *WHQ* 1 (July 1907): 257.

"*were Enemies destroying...*" GS, report to G&C, 1 March 1829, Sullivan, *Travels,* 148.

181–82 *Kelawatsets' grievances* Sullivan, *Travels,* 123; GS to Smith, 26 December 1828, extract in *FTE,* 303; Douthit, "The Hudson's Bay Company and the Indians of Southern Oregon," 31, 44–45.

182 "*wishing to ride...*" McLeod, journal, 11 October 1828, Sullivan, *Travels,* 123.

"*where we were intruders...*" GS, report to G&C, 1 March 1829, Sullivan, *Travels,* 148.

"*aiding and assisting...*" McLeod, journal, 11 October 1828, Sullivan, *Travels,* 123–25.

"*to gratify their passion...*" McL, "Autobiography," in Clarke, *Pioneer Days,* 1:216.

GS report GS to G&C, 1 March 1829, Sullivan, *Travels,* 143–50.

183   *"from 7 to 800 Beaver..."* Ibid., 149; HBRS 4:lxxviii.

McLeod brings Smith's property to Fort Vancouver McL, letter, recipient not
stated, 24 March 1829, Barker, *Letters,* 78. Barker states that the recipient is
George Simpson, but McLoughlin signed it, "I am Dear Sir Yours truly," as in
other letters of his to Ogden, not "Your obe^dt humble Servant," as in other
letters to Simpson. It refers to "my letter of the 6th Sept," which is the date
of a letter to Ogden; no known letter to Simpson is of that date.

"the Gentlemen..." GS to Smith, 26 December 1828, *FTE,* 302–6.

Smith rejoins his company Sullivan, *Jedediah Smith, Trader,* 191; Sullivan,
Travels, 152.

Smith's agreement with HBC Sullivan, *Jedediah Smith, Trader,* 195. In 1830
Smith's company took the first wagons over the eastern portion of what was
later known as the Oregon Trail, but did not cross South Pass or the Rockies.
Ibid., 198, 203–4, 216, 226 n. 63.

Death of Smith Ibid., 216; Sullivan, *Travels,* 153.

"loitered his time..." McL, probably to Ogden, 24 March 1829, Barker, *Letters,*
78.

"I neaver meant..." McL to McLeod, 3 March 1830, Barker, *Letters,* 79.

McLeod expedition HBRS 4:xciv; Douthit, "The Hudson's Bay Company and
the Indians of Southern Oregon," 45–46; McL to GS, 24 March 1829, enclosed
in McL to McLeod, 23 February 1830, Barker, *Letters,* 76.

184   *McLeod transferred to Mackenzie* HBRS 4:xciv.

McLeod's promotion denied Barker, *Letters,* appendix A, 316.

Wreck of William and Ann Log of *Owhyhee,* in Howay, "The Brig Owhyhee,
1829–30," 11; Rich, *History of the Hudson's Bay Company,* vol. 2, HBRS 22:623.

"split from stern...a few triffles..." McL to Archibald McDonald, Chief Trader
at Fort Langley, 22 March 1829, Barker, *Letters,* 6.

"I send you...evade the demand..." McL to Donald Manson, 28 March 1829,
Barker, *Letters,* 10–11.

McL lends his rifle McL to Donald Manson, 18 August 1829, Barker, *Letters,* 46.

"reluctant to Supply..." McL to Donald Manson, 16 October 1829, Barker,
Letters, 63.

"defferred taking...all the crew..." McL to G&C, 5 August 1829, B.223/b/5,
fos. 8–13, HBRS 4:71–72.

Chief's report Ibid., 71.

Expedition against Clatsops Ibid., 72.

"his Messenger returned...fired at...Rum in Canoes..." Ibid.; Barker, *Letters,* 30.

185   *Discovery of bodies and McL's conclusion* McL to G&C, 5 August 1829,
B.223/b/5, fos. 8–13, HBRS 4:73; McL to G&C, 5 August 1829, Barker, *Letters,*
31. The latter source, on pp. 21, 31, and 38, contains two almost identical ver-

sions, the first saying "I am of opinion the crew were murdered" and the second reading "I am of opinion the crew were not murdered." McLoughlin may have omitted "not" in the first version through error, or he may have found new evidence and changed his mind. The second draft, containing "not," was the one sent to London.

"there was no mark..." McL to G&C, 5 August 1829, Barker, *Letters,* 31.

"still several of..." McL to G&C, 13 August 1829, B.223/b/5, fos. 13d–14d, HBRS 4:82.

GS believes it was murder HBRS 4:lxxviii n. 1.

Wreck of Isabella Ibid., lxxxi; McL to G&C, 11 October 1830, B.223/b/6, fos. 13–18d, HBRS 4:83.

Indian camp Tolmie, *Journals,* 5, 12 May 1832, 171, 178. George Allan also described Indians dancing in rings near the fort. "Reminiscences," 79.

"giving as a reason..." McL to G&C, 24 November 1830, Barker, *Letters,* 163.

"bad medicine..." McL to GS, 20 March 1841, B.223/b/28, fos. 22–26d, HBRS 6:247.

Losses to Blackfoot tribe McL to G&C, 7 August 1828, B.223/b/4, fos. 19d–22d; 28 October 1832, B.223/b/8, fos. 26d–30; 31 October 1837, B.223/b/17, fos. 39–46, cont. in B.223/b/18, fo. 2, HBRS 4:66, 103, 215.

Expedition against Tillamooks McL to Laframboise, [April 1832]; McL to Samuel Black, 8 May 1832, both in Barker, *Letters,* 268, 270.

Confrontations with southern tribes Douthit, "The Hudson's Bay Company and the Indians of Southern Oregon," 46–47; McL to G&C, 15 November 1843, B.223/b/30, fos. 46–50, HBRS 6:116; JD to G&C, 18 October 1838, B.223/b/20, fos. 2–28d, HBRS 4:241–42.

Fort Umpqua Douthit, "The Hudson's Bay Company and the Indians of Southern Oregon," 47.

186   *"prevented the numberless..."* JD to G&C, 18 October 1838, B.223/b/20, fos. 2–28d, HBRS 4:252.

"it was not considered..." McL to G&C, 15 November 1843, B.223/b/30, fos. 46–50, HBRS 6:118.

"Indeed your whole..." G&C to McL, 28 October 1829, A.8/22, fos. 45–49d, excerpt in *FTE,* 318–19.

"Your whole administration..." GS to McL, 15 March 1829, D.4/16, fos. 25d–35d, extract in *FTE,* 308.

Chapter 6–1: The Grand Emporium

187   *"In a word..."* Dunn, quoted in Clarke, *Pioneer Days,* 1:186.

189   *"a high and rugged road"* Hussey, *Vancouver,* 69–70.

"The wheels of his wagon..." Dr. William McKay, interview, in Clarke, *Pioneer*

Days, 1:183.

British-American boundary negotiations OQ, 164–78.

China trade Ibid., 142–46. The East India Company's monopoly was due to expire in approximately a decade

"a rebellious and ungrateful..." Ibid., 150.

Military station Ibid., 120–21, 172.

190   *"establish a Post..."* McL to G&C, October 6, 1825, D.4/6, fos. 45–56, HBRS 4:12, 19.

"the whole of the Snake..." McL to GS, 20 March 1827, D.4/120, fos. 48–58d, extract in *FTE,* 287–88.

Joint occupation renewed HBRS 4:lx; *OQ,* 178.

"a fine large..." GS, journal, n.d., *FTE,* 117, 119.

"difficult and dangerous" McL to G&C, 1 September 1826, B.223/b/2, fos. 20–28d, HBRS 4:32.

" it is not my opinion..." GS to H. U. Addington, British secretary for foreign affairs, 5 January 1826, extract in *FTE,* 265.

"if the navigation..." GS to McL, 9 July 1827, D.4/90, fo. 94, HBRS 4:lviii.

Simpson's entourage McDonald, *Peace River,* 1, 2, 4; MacKay, *Honourable Company,* 273–74.

GS in Fraser gorge McDonald, *Peace River,* 37; Rich, *History of the Hudson's Bay Company,* vol. 2, HBRS 22:168. Amazed Indians clung to high viewpoints as they watched this breakneck journey, for the natives here seldom used canoes, even to fish for salmon. Instead, as the terrified Archibald McDonald explained, the tribes reached the river by ladders, which they climbed again after their "hazardous communication with the fish."

"shot like the flight..." GS, *Part of Dispatch,* HBRS 10:37.

191   *"I should consider..."* GS, 1829 report, D.4/93, fo. 34, HBRS 4:lix.

Moving Fort Vancouver Hussey, *Fort Vancouver,* 70–71.

Reuse of structures Hussey, *Fort Vancouver,* 71 n. 76; Hussey, *Historic Structures,* 1:89.

"three hundred feet..." Smith, Jackson, and Sublette, Letter to Eaton, 29 October 1830, 397.

Housing in tents John Warren Dease, "Memorandum Book, 1829," quoted in Hussey, *Historic Structures,* 89.

"began to put up...ready to enter" Ibid.

William Fraser Tolmie Bancroft, *Northwest Coast,* 2:616.

191–92   *"admiring the rich groves..."* Tolmie, *Journals*, 8 May 1832, 174–75.

192   *Size, structure of Fort Vancouver* Hussey, *Fort Vancouver*, 117–72; Hussey, *Historic Structures;* Townsend, *Narrative*, 187.

193   *Agriculture at other forts* Gibson, *Farming the Frontier*, has extensive post-by-post details of productivity.

          "cut down a breadth..." London, *Encyclopoedia of Agriculture*, 425. The Fort Vancouver Library has an original copy of the *Encyclopoedia of Agriculture*, edition of 1835—not a large book but enormously thick, 1,378 pages. This is undoubtedly the book McLoughlin used, although it may not be the same edition. A description of the reaping machine is on p. 439.

          "Even if they cost..." McL to G&C, 4 April 1836, B.223/b/15, fo. 75, HBRS 4:143–44.

          Slacum's observation Slacum, "Report on Oregon," 186.

          "a mammoth..." Farnham, *Travels*, 265–66.

194   *"on three poles..."* Harvey, "Biography of Her Father," 9.

          Activity at Fort Vancouver Roberts, "Round Hand," 195, 197, 199–200; Dunn, *Oregon Territory*, 145–47.

          "There was great..." Harvey, "Biography of Her Father," 4.

          "not stuck up...When the voyageurs..." David McLoughlin to Eva Emery Dye, 10 April 1872, Dye Papers, OHSL, MSS 1089.

195   *"his family has taken care..."* Francis Ermatinger to Edward Ermatinger, 24 February 1834, Ermatinger, *Fur Trade Letters*, 173.

          "Sent calico & tartan..." Tolmie, *Journals*, 8 May [1832], 174.

          GS and McL visit falls Hussey, *Fort Vancouver*, 64; HBRS 4:xcii.

          "There are here..." Townsend, *Narrative*, 191–92.

          "Saws enough could..." GS, 1829 report, D.4/93, fo. 57d, HBRS 4:xcii.

          GS and McL choose location McL to GS, 16 March 1831, D.4/125, fos. 77–79, HBRS 4:228.

          "sawed sufficient Lumber..." McL to G&C, 1 July 1846, A.10/22, fos. 1–8, HBRS 7:157.

          "eatables and drinkables" Lamb, Introduction to HBRS 4:lxxv, from GS, 1829 report.

          "In short, never did..." GS, 1829 report, D.4/93, fos. 48d, 49d, HBRS 4:lxxv.

196   *Fall burning* Clarke, *Pioneer Days*, 1:89–92; Douglas, "Sketch of a Journey," *OHQ* 6 (March 1905): 78–79.

          "The whole country..." Townsend, *Narrative*, 246.

197   *Willamette Valley* CPT, 43–47.

           "as the country..." McL to G&C, 16 November 1836, B.223/b/23, fos. 70–83d,
           HBRS 4:173.

           Company license CPT, 45.

           Lucier starts with express Ibid., 48–49.

           "so as to remove..." McL to G&C, 16 November 1836, B.223/b/12, fos.
           70–83d, HBRS 4:173.

           McL aids Lucier Ibid., 172–73; *CPT*, 48–51.

198   *"I considered..."* McL to G&C, 16 November 1836, B.223/b/12, fos. 70–83d,
           HBRS 4:173.

           "Discouraged our people..." Ibid.

           "whatever way we view..." Ibid., 172.

           "It remains for..." Ibid., 174.

           McL's restrictions Ibid., 173–74; *CPT*, 51; Rich, *History of the Hudson's Bay
           Company*, vol. 2, HBRS 22:660–61.

           "answerable for them..." McL to G&C, 4 December 1843, A.11/70, fos.
           41–46, HBRS 6:189.

199   *French Prairie* CPT, 7.

Chapter 6–2: "An Immensity of Trouble"

199   *Previous visit of* Owhyhee HBRS 4:lxx, lxxix.

           "Captain Dominie gives..." McL to G&C, 6 July 1827, B.223/b/3, fos. 4d–10d,
           HBRS 4:45.

           Owhyhee *and* Convoy Barker, *Letters*, 330, 331. The *Owhyhee* was a brig, two-
           masted, square-rigged on both masts. The *Convoy*, a hermaphrodite brig, was
           two-masted, square-rigged on the foremast, and fore-and-aft-rigged on the
           mainmast. The other types of ship commonly named in fur-trade documents
           are the sloop (single-masted, fore-and-aft-rigged), the schooner (two or more
           masts, fore-and-aft-rigged on all lower masts), and the bark (three or more
           masts, square-rigged on all but the aftermost mast, which is fore-and-aft-
           rigged). Ships were so important to traders that they habitually specified their
           rigging by saying "the brig *Owhyhee*," for example.

           Josiah Marshall Morison, "Salmon Trade," 112–13.

           "it would require 40 or 50..." Dominis to Marshall, 4 March 1829, ibid., 121.

           Captain Dominis A. S. Twombly, *Hawaii and Its People*, 328, quoted in Morison,
           "Salmon Trade," 112–13.

200   *"the English Company..."* Thompson to Marshall, 26 March 1829, ibid., 122.

"the company have very few…" Dominis to Marshall, 14 June 1829, ibid., 123.

"Our prospects this Season…" Thompson to Marshall, 26 March 1829, ibid., 122.

"We then considered…" McL to G&C, 5 August 1829, Barker, *Letters*, 35.

"repassed on her way…" McL to GS, 20 March 1830, D.4/123, fo. 94–101, *FTE*, 322

"to oppose them" Ibid.

"On our arrival…" Thompson to Marshall, 26 March 1829, Morison, "Salmon Trade," 123.

"reduced the price…" McL to G&C, 5 August 1829, B.223/b/5, fos. 8–13, HBRS 4:76; also in Barker, *Letters*, 33, 35–36.

201 *"I am sorry…extremely obliging…"* McL to G&C, 5 August 1829, B.223/b/5, fos. 8–13, HBRS 4:79; also in Barker, *Letters*, 36–37.

"his conduct was…" G&C to McL, 10 November 1830, A.6/22, fo. 78, quoted in HBRS 4:lxxxvi.

"mistook Chinook Point…" HBRS 4:lxxxi; McL to G&C, 11 October 1830, B.223/b/6, fos. 13–18d, HBRS 4:83.

"all the remaining…It is unnecessary…" Ibid., 83–84.

202 *"caused a great commotion…"* J. F. Harriott to John McLeod, 25 February 1831, in Dye, "Old Letters," *WHQ* 1 (July 1907): 260.

Eagle *and* Dryad *are late* HBRS 4:lxxiv, lxxxvi; McL to G&C, 11 October 1830, B.223/b/6, fos. 13–18d, HBRS 4:85, 87.

Activity of Owhyhee *and* Convoy HBRS 4:lxxix–lxxx; Morison, "Salmon Trade," 123

"brought his vessel…" McL to GS, 20 March 1830, *FTE*, 323.

"20 Men, one Clerk…" Ibid.

"to give Indns… ." McL to G&C, 5 August 1829, B.223/b/5, fos. 8–13, HBRS 4:78; also in Barker, *Letters*, 35–36.

McL gives assistance Log of *Convoy,* extracts in Howay, "The Brig Owhyhee, 1829–30," 15.

"on what terms…could not carry…" McL to GS, 20 March 1830, Barker, *Letters*, 92.

"to buy up…" Ibid., 93.

"In the Columbia…" Ibid.

203 *"as you well…"* McL to Samuel Black, 23 September 1829, Barker, *Letters*, 57.

"of course I am…" McL to Samuel Black, 20 March 1830, Barker, *Letters*, 100.

"in spite of…" McL to Samuel Black, 29 June 1830, B.223/b/6, fo. 3d, HBRS 4:lxxx.

"an idle indolent..." GS to J. G. McTavish (private), 30 July 1830, B.135/c/2, fo. 48, quoted in HBRS 4:xcix.

"the worst man..." Francis Ermatinger to Edward Ermatinger, 15 March, 24 February 1834, Ermatinger, *Fur Trade Letters,* 180, 172.

"his intemperate habits..." "Minutes of Council, 1836," paragraph 80, printed in Oliver, *Canadian North-West,* 2:737.

204   *"could not acceede...It may be said..."* McL to GS, 20 March 1830, Barker, *Letters,* 97, 98.

Death of Dease Ermatinger, *Fur Trade Letters,* 103 n. 11.

"went as far..." GS to McTavish, 30 July 1830, B.135/c/2, fo. 48, HBRS 4:c.

"is quite a changed..." GS to McTavish, 15 August 1831, B.135/c/2, fo. 69d, HBRS 4:c.

GS's tragedy Simpson had recently married Frances Simpson, a Scottish girl whom he adored. Following the birth of their son, her health was poor, and the infant lived only a few months. Galbraith, *Little Emperor,* 116–17.

"a very bustling..." GS, Character Book, in Williams, *Hudson's Bay Miscellany,* HBRS 30:176. The subjects of these evaluations were not identified until Simpson's list was discovered among his private papers after his death.

205   *"great exertions indefatigable..."* GS, 1832 report, D.4/99, fo. 22d, HBRS 4:ci.

American ships leave McL to G&C, 11 October 1830, B.223/b/6, fos. 13–18d, HBRS 4:92; McL to John Rowand, 3 August 1830, Morison, "Salmon Trade," 115.

"an immensity of trouble" McL to John Rowand, 3 August 1830, Morison, "Salmon Trade," 115. Rowand was Chief Factor in charge of the Saskatchewan District.

Skins taken by American captains Morison, "Salmon Trade," 125.

Sale of salmon in Boston Ibid., 115–16. The salmon were of poor quality, perhaps because they were stale when salted or were shipped near sperm oil and beaver skins, which affected the flavor. In addition, the ship's owner had to pay duty on "foreign-caught fish," because the Columbia was "not claimed as a part of...the United States."

"been obliged to Keep..." McL to G&C, 11 October 1830, Barker, *Letters,* 145.

"as to restoring..." McL to Donald Manson, clerk at Fort George, 9 November 1829, Barker, *Letters,* 65.

Restoration of tariff HBRS 4:lxxxi.

Chapter 6–3: The Intermittent Fever

206   *Changes in company policy* G&C to McL, 28 October 1829, A.6/22, fo. 46,

HBRS 4:lxxxiv.

"This is the first..." McL to Rowand, 3 August 1830, D.4/125, fos. 76d–77, HBRS 4:lxxxiv–lxxxv. The *Eagle* reached Fort Vancouver on June 10, 1830, and the *Dryad* on August 16.

207   *"subject to your orders..."* G&C to McL, 28 October 1829, A.6/22, fo. 46, HBRS 4:lxxxiv.

James Douglas Sage, *Douglas,* 18–19; Ormsby, *British Columbia,* 511–12; biographical sketch in HBRS 7:309–14.

Douglas family in McL's house Hussey, *Historic Structures,* 1:99; McL to G&C, 15 November 1836, B.223/b/12, fos. 2–11, HBRS 4:161.

208   *"a stream chain..."* McL to G&C, 24 November 1830, B.223/b/6, fos. 23d–25d, HBRS 4:97.

"In the course..." McL to G&C, 11 October 1830, Barker, *Letters,* 143–44.

"seeing all my endeavours..." Ibid., 143.

"We highly approve..." GS to McL, 2 July 1831, D.4/18, fo. 68, HBRS 4:91 n. 1.

"miserably lame..." GS, 1832 report, D.4/99, fo. 14d, HBRS 7:lxxxvii.

Declining returns McL to G&C, 11 October 1830, B.223/b/6, fos. 13–18d, HBRS 4:86. In this letter, McLoughlin describes the decline, including observations by Ogden and McLeod.

Simpson to Nass Harbor Captain Simpson's Report, 30 September 1830, B.223/c/1, fos. 19–24d, HBRS 4:305–13; McL to Rowand, 3 August 1830, D.4/125, fos. 76d–77, HBRS 4:lxxxiv–lxxxv.

209   *"began to shake..."* Lee and Frost, *Ten Years,* 132.

Fever spreads McL to Donald Manson, 15 November 1830; McL to Archibald McDonald, 9 December 1830, both in Barker, *Letters,* 153, 175.

"a disease of..." Townsend, *Narrative,* 197.

"exclusive of women..." McL to Archibald McDonald, 9 December 1830, Barker, *Letters,* 153.

"I had to attend..." McL to G&C, 24 November 1830, Barker, *Letters,* 163–64.

"But praise be..." McL to Manson, 15 November 1830, Barker, *Letters,* 153.

210   *Allan hands out medicine* Allan, "Reminiscences," 79.

"But the fellow mistaking..." Ibid.

"Plomondo says that..." Douglas, journal, 1840–41, 3, 4, quoted in Bancroft, *Northwest Coast,* 2:503–4. "Plomondo" was Simon Plomondon, an *engagé* since 1821. In 1837 he became one of the first farmers in today's Washington, taking up land in the Cowlitz valley on McLoughlin's advice. Douglas said Plomondon's account was "perhaps overcharged, but in the main I firmly believe cor-

rect, as the ague has been a fruitful source of death to every Indian tribe exposed to its attacks."

McL's estimate McL to G&C, 11 October 1830, Barker, *Letters,* 140.

"Taking the sickly state..." McL to Archibald McDonald, 9 December 1830, Barker, *Letters,* 175.

211   *"Every man in this..."* McL to G&C, 20 October 1831, Barker, *Letters,* 216–17.

"the mortality..." McL to Heron, 9 September 1831, Barker, *Letters,* 213.

"I request will you..." McL to Charlton, 27 October 1831, Barker, *Letters,* 225.

"Taking one..." Townsend, *Narrative,* 233–34.

"I am sorry to inform..." McL to Pierre Chrysologue Pambrun, clerk at Walla Walla, 1 September 1832, Barker, *Letters,* 296.

212   *"The Indians..."* Townsend, *Narrative,* 223.

Chapter 6–4: Moving North

212   *American and Russian traders* HBRS 4:lxxxiii.

Treaties on selling arms, liquor, and ammunition OQ, 132; HBRS 4:xxii, lxxxiii, civ

"notwithstanding the terms..." GS to G&C, 25 November 1841, D.4/110, fos. 18–18d, HBRS 6:56 n. 4.

Routes to New Caledonia FTE, 349–50.

213   *Russians purchase American goods* HBRS 4:lxxxiii.

"enable us..." GS to His Excellency the Gov of the Russian Fur Compys Establishment, 20 March 1829, Barker, *Letters,* 16, 17.

Report of Lieutenant Simpson 1 October 1829, D.4/123, fos. 8d–20, FTE, 314–17.

"could supply..." Ibid.

"be a fruitless contest" Lieutenant Simpson to G&C, 16 September 1829, extract in FTE, 313.

"either did not appear..." Report of Lieutenant Simpson, 1 October 1829, D.4/123, fos. 8d–20, FTE, 314–17.

214   *"annually at cost..."* William Smith to Chief Manager and Directors, Russian American Company, 16 December 1829, *Appendix to the Case of the United States,* 260, quoted in HBRS 4:lxxxiv.

"as high Up as you..." McL to Captain Æmelius Simpson, 7 July 1830, Barker, *Letters,* 109–10.

"a good Southern...in great abundance..." Captain Simpson, report, 23 September 1830, B.223/c/1, fos. 19–24d, HBRS 4:309.

"too rapid for...Arms & ammunition..." Ibid., 311–13.

McL sends out Dryad *and* Vancouver McL to G&C, 24 November 1830, Barker, *Letters,* 165.

Instructions to Simpson McL to Captain Simpson, 10 April 1831, Barker, *Letters,* 194–95.

Fort Simpson Binns, *Ogden,* 242–43.

Simpson's death Ibid., 245; HBRS 4:xxxv.

215 *"By his death..."* McL to G&C, 20 October 1831, Barker, *Letters,* 214.

Marine superintendent HBRS 4:lxxxv–lxxxvi.

"never hold out..." Wrangell to Directors, Russian American Company, 6 May 1832, *Alaskan Tribunal Boundary, App. to Counter Case of U.S.,* 1–2, quoted in HBRS 4:lxxxvii.

"tell them that..." McL to Ogden, 15 December 1831, B.223/b/7, fo. 10d, HBRS 4:lxxxvii.

216 *"a Land Establishment..."* McL to Ogden, 5 October 1832, B.223/b/8, fos. 18–20, HBRS 4:315.

"the wear & tear...With posts we become..." McL to G&C, 28 May 1834, B.223/b/10, fos. 13–15d, HBRS 4:119.

"a cargo to...Of course I am..." McL to G&C, 16 June 1832, B.223/b/8, fos. 4–4d, HBRS 4:99.

"provide salt..." Memoranda for Finlayson, n.d., Barker, *Letters,* 277–78.

Open letter McL to Finlayson (Letter No. 269), 17 July 1832, Barker, *Letters,* 287–88.

Sealed letter McL to Finlayson (Letter No. 270), 17 July 1832, Barker, *Letters,* 288–90.

"the man's superior..." Ibid., 288.

217 *"I tremble for..."* Finlayson to James Hargrave, 21 February 1833, Glaze-brook, *Hargrave Correspondence,* 106.

"must on no account..." G&C to GS, 1 March 1833, A.6/23, fo. 11, HBRS 4:116 n. 5.

"get quit of those..." G&C to McL, 1 May 1833, A.6/23, fo. 22d, HBRS 4:lxxxix.

"If there is any..." McL to G&C, 28 May 1834, B.223/b/10, fos. 13–15d, HBRS 4:117.

McL receives approval HBRS 4:lxxxix.

Sandwich Island agency Ibid., xcii–xciii.

George Pelly Biography in HBRS 4:353. Pelly was agent in the Sandwich Islands until his retirement in 1851.

Forts McLoughlin and Nisqually HBRS 4:xc.

Ogden explores Stikine Ibid.

218   *"for which purpose..."* McL to Ogden, 6 May 1834, B.223/b/10, fos. 7–7d, HBRS 4:316.

Redoubt St. Dionysius HBRS 4:civ.

"merely a few cedarbark..." Tolmie, *Journals,* 20 June 1833, 284.

"He did not deny..." P. S. Ogden's Report of Transactions at Stikine, 1834, A.11/69, fos. 3–6, HBRS 4:318–19.

"He was a thin...by guessing and conjecturing" Tolmie, *Journals,* 20 June 1833, 283.

Ogden's protest P. S. Ogden's Report of Transactions at Stikine, 1834, A.11/69, fos. 3–6, HBRS 4:317–22.

"This morning the Chiefs..." Ibid., 319.

219   *"to cut off..."* GS, 1834 report, D.4/100, fos. 10d–11d, HBRS 4:civ.

"However galling..." P. S. Ogden's Report of Transactions at Stikine, 1834, A.11/69, fos. 3–6, HBRS 4:322.

"derangement...while the Russians..." McL to G&C, 14 March 1835, A.11/69, fos. 1–2, HBRS 4:135.

G&C's reception of McL's reports HBRS 4:cvi.

G&C's instructions to McL G&C to McL, 28 August 1835, B.223/c/1, fos. 39–43, HBRS 4:cvi.

"prosperous and highly promising..." Minutes of Temporary Council held at York Factory, July 1834, B.239/k/2, fo. 38, quoted in HBRS 4:cii.

220   *Bonus* Minutes of G&C, 2 March 1836, A.1/59, fo. 105; G&C to GS, 9 March 1836, A.6/24, fo. 24, both in HBRS 4:cii–ciii. For the outfits of 1824 to 1833, McLoughlin's first decade on the Columbia, his yearly income had ranged from somewhat less than £600 to slightly more than £1,000, for an average of approximately £835. HBRS 4:cii–ciii.

"Before bringing this..." McL to G&C, 15 November 1836, B.223/b/12, fos. 2–11, HBRS 4:164.

Chapter 6–5: My Son John

221   *McL's finances* Barker, *Financial Papers,* 47–60. This volume contains McLoughlin's NWC account, on pp. 43–46, and his HBC account, on pp. 54–87.

222   *"Bill to Simon Fraser...Cash paid..."* Ibid., 56, 58.

Uncertainty over Elisabeth McL to SF, 15 March 1825, *ME,* 176.

"happy to find..." GS to SF, 17 November 1826, *ME,* 181–82.

"astonished..." SF to McL, 20 April 1827, *ME*, 184.

"soiling [his] breeches" SF to John McLoughlin, 12 January 1836, *ME*, 219.

"Mr Essoms school..." McL to SF, 19 March 1826, *ME*, 178

"Messrs Glen Walker...corrupted the morals..." SF to John McLoughlin, 12 January 1836, *ME*, 219.

"I do not know..." McL to SF, 19 March 1826, *ME*, 178.

"a sufficient Knowledge...as I before..." Ibid., 183.

223 *"I thought and do..."* Ibid.

"I do not think...the Girl cannot be..." Ibid., 183–84.

Thain's illness *ME*, 180 n. 67.

"succombed to an attack..." Wallace, *Documents*, 33.

McL's account and power of attorney Barker, *Financial Papers*, 57 n. 11, 58 n. 12.

"George Simpson's Bill..." McL's HBC account, 21 January 1828, in Barker, *Financial Papers*, 58.

"a dividend along..." SF to McL, 20 April 1827, *ME*, 183.

"take the young man..." SF to GS, 16 October 1827, *ME*, 184–85. A biography, "John McLoughlin—the Son," is in *ME*, 107–25.

224 *"unmercifully..."* GS to SF, 14 March 1828, *ME*, 186–87.

"even and mild..." Ibid., 187.

"I am Dear John..." SF to John McLoughlin, [July 1828], *ME*, 188 n. 78.

"surpris'd after the refusal..." McL to John McLoughlin, 1 February 1830, *ME*, 190–91.

225 *John goes to Paris* *ME*, 111–12

"If I fail..." John McLoughlin to John Fraser, 8 August 1833, *ME*, 199.

"I have passed..." John McLoughlin to SF, 24 February 1833, *ME*, 197.

Dr. David McLoughlin's income *ME*, 115

"You cannot imagine..." John McLoughlin to John Fraser, 18 May 1832, *ME*, 193.

Disturbances in Paris *ME*, 113.

"three memorable..." John McLoughlin to John Fraser, 8 August 1833, *ME*, 199–200.

226 *"The reason why I did..."* John McLoughlin to SF, 26 October 1831, *ME*, 191.

"Since my arrival..." John McLoughlin to John Fraser, 18 May 1832, *ME*, 192.

"Ah what can be..." John McLoughlin to SF, 24 February 1833, *ME*, 196–97.

"You cannot think..." John McLoughlin to SF, 26 October 1831, *ME*, 192.

"Great satisfaction..." McL to SF, 4 February 1837, quoting letter of 1833 by Dr. David McLoughlin, *ME*, 233.

"This is too painful..." McL to SF, 14 February 1836, *ME*, 223–24.

"He writes me..." McL to John Fraser, 14 February 1836, *ME*, 221–22.

227 *"my Brother found him..."* McL to John McLeod, 1 February 1836, from McLoughlin Letters in the McLeod Correspondence, PAC, extract in *ME*, 220.

Financial arrangements for John ME, 114–15.

"was the cause of..." McL to SF, 4 February 1837, citing Finlayson's opinion, *ME*, 235.

McL's explanation of dismissal McL to SF, 14 February 1836, *ME*, 222.

"My Brother does not write..." Ibid.

John leaves Paris ME, 115.

Chapter 7–1: The Boston Ice Man

229 *"It was a Rule..."* McL to G&C, 16 November 1836, B.223/b/12, fos. 70–83d, HBRS 4:170.

231–32 *"This morning a party..."* McL to G&C, 29 October 1832, B.223/b/8, fo. 31, HBRS 4:108–9.

Wyeth and ice business Cummings, *American Ice Harvests*, 18–25.

"I will lose my scalp..." Wyeth to Frederic Tudor, 6 September 1835, Wyeth, *Correspondence and Journals*, 150.

232 *Wyeth enrolls with Kelley* Wyeth to Hall Kelley, 30 August 1831, Wyeth, *Correspondence and Journals*, 1, 36.

Wyeth's preparation Wyeth, *Correspondence and Journals*, 1–47. Details are on pp. 25, 27, 29, 34, 50.

"about $800...how salmon are pickled..." Ibid., 50, 29.

"The bugle of which..." Wyeth to S. K. Livermore, 23 January 1832, ibid., 25.

233 *"half boat...an amphibium..."* John B. Wyeth, *Short History*, 10, 11.

"a coarse woolen..." Ibid., 12.

Wyeth's journey Wyeth, *Correspondence and Journals*, 6 June–29 October 1832, 155–76.

234 *"gray and my face..."* Ibid., 6 June 1832, 155.

Site of rendezvous Graustein, *Thomas Nuttall*, 279; Wyeth, *Correspondence and Journals*, 159.

"All my men..." Wyeth, *Correspondence and Journals*, 6 July 1832, 159. This is a summary entry covering July 6–26.

Contact with Sublette Ibid., 6 July, 29 August 1832, 159, 165.

"in the most hospitable..." Ibid, 13–20 October 1832, 173.

"to his own table..." Ball, "Across the Continent," 99–100.

235   *"Here I was received..."* Wyeth, *Correspondence and Journals,* 29 October 1832, 176.

"I could not refuse..." Ibid., 6–18 November 1832, 178.

"eating and drinking..." Ibid., 19 November 1832, 178.

"3 or 4 Canadians..." Ibid., 29 November 1832–4 January 1833, 179.

235–36   *"Doct J. McGlaucland"* Ibid., 23 January 1833, 181.

Tibbetts and Smith settle in Oregon CPT, 63–68.

"Of course I gladly..." Ball, "Across the Continent," 100. Ball's daughter, Kate Ball Powers, listed six boys taught by Ball, including David McLoughlin and "Billy" McKay. Letter to the *Oregonian,* 1932.

236   *"I parted with feelings..."* Wyeth, *Correspondence and Journals,* 31 January–3 February 1833, 181.

"50 pr ct..." Wyeth to GS, 12 March 1833, ibid., 56–58.

Green River Townsend called it "Green River, Siskadee, or Colorado of the West." *Narrative,* 79. Wyeth wrote letters while there and dated them "Ham's Fork of the Colorado of the West." *Correspondence and Journals,* 133–40.

Wyeth's trip home Wyeth, *Correspondence and Journals,* 3 February–30 September 1833, 181–219.

"To day the thing is..." Supplement of letter to Leonard I. Wyeth, 20 November 1833, ibid., 85.

Contract with Milton Sublette Wyeth to Henry Hall and Mess. Tucker and Williams, 8 November 1833; Wyeth to Milton Sublette, 9 October 1833, both in Wyeth, *Correspondence and Journals,* 77, 71. The contract has disappeared.

236–37   *"Every man in the company..."* Townsend, *Narrative,* 31.

237   *William Sublette refuses contract* Wyeth to Milton Sublette, 1 July 1834, Wyeth, *Correspondence and Journals,* 140.

"and named it Fort Hall..." Wyeth, *Correspondence and Journals,* 6 August 1834, 227.

"We manufactured..." Wyeth to Leonard Jarvis, 6 October 1834, ibid., 146.

Men remain at Fort Hall Wyeth, *Correspondence and Journals,* 6 August 1834, 227.

Fort Hall to Fort Vancouver Ibid., 6 August–14 September 1834, 227–33; Townsend, *Narrative,* 120–86; Lee and Frost, *Ten Years,* 121–24. Wyeth went from Fort Nez Perces to The Dalles in the missionaries' barge and engaged canoes there.

"received us..." Wyeth, *Correspondence and Journals,* 14 September 1834, 233.

237–38   *"On the beach..."* Townsend, *Narrative,* 185–86.

Loan of a boat Ibid., 190–95.

Townsend as surgeon McL to G&C, 31 October 1837, B.223/b/17, fos. 38–46; B.223/b/18, fo. 2, HBRS 4:203.

"Mr. Wyeth..." McL to GS, 3 March 1835, D.4/127, fo. 70, quoted in HBRS 4:cvii.

"meet them fairly..." GS to McL, 15 March 1829, HBC Journal no. 950A, extract in *FTE,* 308.

McL accepts Wyeth's proposal HBRS 4:cviii–cix.

238–39   *Fort Boise built* HBRS 4:cix. McLoughlin said McKay passed the winter of 1834–35 near Wyeth's Fort Hall and would also pass the winter of 1835–36 there, at the site of Fort Boise. McL to G&C, 30 September 1835, B.223/b/11, fos. 35d–39, HBRS 4:141–42.

"put him down" G&C to McL, 1 February 1834, A.61/23, fo. 63, HBRS 4:cvii–cviii

Soundness of McL's policy Rich, *History of the Hudson's Bay Company,* vol. 2, HBRS 22:651, 673.

239   *Wyeth's misfortunes* Wyeth, letters to "Friend Weld," Frederic Tudor, "Friend Brown," "Bro. Charles," "Parents," and "Dear Wife," *Correspondence and Journals,* 148–54

"by drowning and disease..." Wyeth to his wife, 22 September 1835, *Correspondence and Journals,* 154.

Wappattoo Island Wyeth to Weld, 3 April 1835, *Correspondence and Journals,* 148.

"I have no good news..." Wyeth to brother Leonard, 6 October 1834, Wyeth, *Correspondence and Journals,* 145.

"I assure you the Fort..." Wyeth to Tudor, 6 October 1834, Wyeth, *Correspondence and Journals,* 143.

"We have failed..." Wyeth to Jas. W. Fenno, 6 October 1834, Wyeth, *Correspondence and Journals,* 143–44.

Wyeth's new proposal HBRS 4:cix–cx; Wyeth to McL, 5 May 1836, B.223/b/12, fos. 33–34, HBRS 4:340–41.

240   *McL consults officers* McL to G&C, 5 May 1836, B.223/b/15, fos. 16d–17, HBRS 4:149.

Wyeth to specify goods HBRS 4:cxi.

"vigorously..." GS to McL, 25 June 1836, quoted in McL to G&C, 16 November 1836, B.223/b/12, fos. 70–83d, HBRS 4:170.

"Is it possible..." McL to G&C, 16 November 1836, B.223/b/12, fos. 70–83d, HBRS 4:170, 177.

240–41   *McL polls officers* HBRS 4:cxii. Replies are enclosed in McL to G&C, 18 November 1836, B.223/b/12, fos. 54–55, HBRS 4:178–82.

"Wyeth is obliged..." McL to G&C, 16 November 1836, B.223/b/12, fos. 70–83d, HBRS 4:171.

Wyeth returns to ice business Cummings, *American Ice Harvests*, 25.

241 "*had given over...very properly...brough[t] down his Furs*" McL to G&C, 31 October 1837, B.223/b/17, fos. 38–46, continued in B.223/b/18, fo. 2, HBRS 4:208.

"*I have this day...*" McL to G&C, 11 January 1838, B.223/b/18, fo. 17, HBRS 4:216.

Wyeth's men as farmers CPT, 71.

Chapter 7–2: The Macedonian Cry

242 *Jason Lee* Bancroft, *Oregon*, 1:56–57.

"*a thin bony...*" Ibid., 58.

Visit of Flatheads Lee and Frost, *Ten Years*, 109–10; Brosnan, *Jason Lee*, 2–10; Josephy, *Nez Perce Indians*, 85–95.

"*sincere searchers after truth...*" G. P. Disosway, 19 January 1833, *Christian Advocate*, 1 March 1833, quoted in Josephy, *Nez Perce Indians*, 93.

"*immediately we endeavoured...*" Acts 16:9, 10.

"*a high-wrought account...*" Lee and Frost, *Ten Years*, 110–11.

243 *Jason Lee party* Ibid., 109, 113–14; Brosnan, *Jason Lee*, 32–34, 46–47.

First Protestant services Brosnan, *Jason Lee*, 64.

"*sat upon the ground...*" Townsend, *Narrative*, 118

Arrival at Fort Vancouver Lee and Frost, *Ten Years*, 124; Brosnan, *Jason Lee*, 69.

243–44 "*We received every...*" "The Diary of Reverend Jason Lee," OHQ 17 (September 1916): 262.

244 "*it was too dangerous...*" McL, "Autobiography," in Clarke, *Pioneer Days*, 1:220.

McL assists Lee Lee and Frost, *Ten Years*, 124.

"*a mixed congregation...*" "The Diary of Reverend Jason Lee," 28 September 1834, OHQ 17 (December 1916): 399.

"*Could I but know...*" Ibid., 24 September 1834, 398.

245 *Lee's equipment on* May Dacre Lee and Frost, *Ten Years*, 113, 124–25; Brosnan, *Jason Lee*, 35.

"*seven oxen, one bull...*" Brosnan, *Jason Lee*, 75.

HBC contribution McL to Lee, 1 March 1836, printed in Holman, *Dr. John McLoughlin*, 57; Hines, *Missionary History*, 16.

"*about a dozen...*" Lee and Frost, *Ten Years*, 125.

"*a gown...*" Shepard, letter, 10 January 1835, *Zion's Herald* 6 (28 October 1835): 170, quoted in Brosnan, *Jason Lee*, 76.

McL provides medical help Lee and Frost, *Ten Years,* 196–98, 303; Gay, *Mrs. Jason Lee,* 26; "Mission Record Book," 238, 246, 254.

246   *Samuel Parker* MSS by Parker's son, Dr. Samuel J. Parker, original at Cornell University, in Drury, *Marcus and Narcissa,* 1:27–28.

"a man of good..." Gray, *History of Oregon,* 107. This book by William H. Gray, a lay missionary who came with the Whitmans, is biased, vitriolic, sometimes inaccurate, and marred by implacable hatred for the Hudson's Bay Company and Catholics. However, it contains historical details which would otherwise be lost and which, when checked against other accounts, seem fairly reliable despite his bias.

Whitman's training Drury, *Marcus and Narcissa,* 1:71–82, 160; Robertson, "Reminiscences of Alanson Hinman," 268–70.

"with high cheek bones..." Robertson, "Reminiscences of Alanson Hinman," 268

"took up his Residence..." McL to G&C, 16 November 1836, B.223/b/12, fos. 70–83d, HBRS 4:175.

"a very good old..." Roberts to Frances Fuller Victor, 28 November 1878, in Roberts, "Round Hand," 195.

"a man of piety..." McL in Private Papers, MS, 2d ser. 6, quoted in Bancroft, *Northwest Coast,* 2:536 n. 19.

McL aids Parker McL to G&C, 16 November 1836, B.223/b/12, fos. 70–83d, HBRS 4:175.

Parker leaves Drury, *Marcus and Narcissa,* 1:192, 348–49.

"a good teacher..." Jonathan S. Green, Secretary to the American Board of Commissioners for Foreign Missions, to Whitman, 9 March 1836, quoted in Hulbert, *Overland,* 6:197.

247   *"As the boats..."* Gray, *History of Oregon,* 149.

"We are now in..." Narcissa Whitman, "Journey," 62.

"put his Daughter..." Narcissa Whitman, journal, printed in Elliott, "White Women," *OHQ* 37 (September 1936): 184.

"lived separate..." Harvey, "Biography of Her Father," 12–13.

248   *"Mrs. McLoughlin has..."* Narcissa Whitman, journal, printed in Elliott, "White Women," *OHQ* 37 (September 1936): 188.

"gentleman fashion..." Ibid., 185.

"Doct. McLaughlin..." Ibid., 183–84.

"as cheap as..." Narcissa Whitman to her family, 1 November 1836, printed in Elliott, "White Women," *OHQ* 37 (September 1936): 189–90.

"buoyant in spirits..." David McLoughlin to Eva Emery Dye, 20 March 1892,

in Dye Papers, MS 1089, OHSL.

McL's decision to cooperate Rich, *History of the Hudson's Bay Company*, vol. 2, HBRS 22:661.

249   *"If you refuse..."* McL to G&C, 16 November 1836, B.223/b/12, fos. 70–83d, HBRS 4:174–75.

Whitman-Spalding antagonism Drury, *Marcus and Narcissa*, 1:218–19.

Whitman and Spalding missions Ibid., 1:218.

"fether bed" Narcissa Whitman to her mother, 5 December 1836, printed in Elliott, "White Women," *OHQ* 38 (March 1937): 47.

250   *Methodist reinforcement* Brosnan, *Jason Lee*, 87–88; Lee and Frost, *Ten Years*, 146.

"The next morning..." Pittman to sisters and brothers, 11, 15, 18 May 1837, printed in Gay, *Mrs. Jason Lee*, 152–53.

"a light blush..." Allen, *Ten Years*, 66–67; Gay, *Mrs. Jason Lee*, 53.

Canoe trip Allen, *Ten Years*, 68.

Indian children Gay, *Mrs. Jason Lee*, 55.

"we found things..." Pittman to parents, 5 June 1837, ibid., 156–57.

"I was told..." "The Diary of Reverend Jason Lee," 28 July 1838 (written on his way east), *OHQ* 17 (December 1916): 409.

251   *"she was eminently..."* Ibid.

"holy institution...And now, my friends..." Ibid., 411–12.

Lee's marriage "Mission Record Book," 264; Lee and Frost, *Ten Years*, 149.

McL leads services in French HBRS 4:cxviii.

Petitions of French Canadians O'Hara, *Catholic History*, 17.

"sad spiritual conditions" Ibid.

HBC wants Catholic mission north of Columbia GS to Bishop of Quebec, 17 February 1838, MS in General Land Office Records, Old Townsites Series, Docket 1 (165), Box No. 31, printed in O'Hara, *Catholic History*, 18–19.

"give his assurance..." Ibid.

252   *"such facilities..."* GS to Bishop of Quebec, summer 1837, quoted in Hussey, *Fort Vancouver*, 177.

Appointment of Blanchet and Demers Hussey, *Fort Vancouver*, 177–78; O'Hara, *Catholic History*, 19–20, 23–24.

"black-haired, brown-eyed..." Gray, *History of Oregon*, 180.

Mass and mission at Fort Vancouver O'Hara, *Catholic History*, 21–22; Hussey, *Fort Vancouver*, 177.

Church of St. Paul's O'Hara, *Catholic History*, 25, 29.

253 *"and you are therefore..."* Blanchet, *Historical Sketches*, 91.

Catholic headquarters Hussey, *Fort Vancouver*, 178.

Chapter 7–3: The Reverend Beaver

253 *Rev. Beaver* Gray, *History of Oregon*, 162; Brosnan, *Jason Lee*, 64.

Beaver chosen by GS Beaver, "Mr. Beaver Objects," 10; Clark, "Editorial Comment," 66; HBRS 4:cxvii.

"a church bell, a pulpit..." Hussey, *Fort Vancouver*, 174; *The Beaver*, December 1940, 11–12; Clark, "Editorial Comment," 68.

Rev. Beaver's arrival Lee and Frost, *Ten Years*, 137–38; Hussey, *Fort Vancouver*, 174.

254 *Accommodations for Beaver* Hussey, *Fort Vancouver*, 180–81; Beaver to G&C, 10 November 1836, printed in Beaver, "Mr. Beaver Objects," 10.

"above a dozen..." Beaver to Benjamin Harrison, 19 March 1838, Beaver, *Reports and Letters*, 68, 73.

"appear perhaps extraordinary..." McL to G&C, 15 November 1836, B.223/b/12, fos. 2–11, HBRS 4:161. This was the "old house," which had been moved board by board from the first Fort Vancouver.

"the deals composing..." Tolmie, *Journals*, 172.

Beaver's decision to leave; petition Beaver to G&C, 10 November 1836, Beaver, "Mr. Beaver Objects," 10–11; Beaver, "Experiences," 26–27.

Beaver's dissatisfactions Hussey, *Fort Vancouver*, 175; HBRS 4:cxvii–cxviii; Beaver, "Mr. Beaver Objects," 12.

"I understand the Revd... ." McL to G&C, 16 November 1836, B.223/b/12, fos. 70–83d, HBRS 4:175–76.

255 *Beavers' second house* Hussey, *Fort Vancouver*, 181; Gray, *History of Oregon*, 150, 163.

Beavers share house JD to G&C, 5 October 1838, B.223/b/21, fos. 4–12, printed in Douglas, "Report on 'The Beaver Affair,'" 20, 21.

"too filthy..." Gray, *History of Oregon*, 163.

Priests occupy house Hussey, *Fort Vancouver*, 181.

Preparation of salmon Beaver, probably to McL, 10 August 1837, Beaver, "Mr. Beaver Objects," 13; JD to GS, 5 October 1837, printed in Douglas, "Report on 'The Beaver Affair,'" 16.

"His Expenditure of Wine..." McL to G&C, 16 November 1836, B.223/b/12, fos. 70–83d, HBRS 4:176.

"exceedingly inconvenient..." Beaver to G&C, 10 November 1836, Beaver, "Mr. Beaver Objects," 10.

256   *"a French Bible..."* McL to Beaver, 17 December 1836, B.223/b/15, fo. 65, HBRS 4:cxviii.

"the very strong-hold..." Beaver, "Experiences," 23.

"change in our mode..." McL to Beaver, 16 December 1836, B.223/b/15, fo. 64, quoted in HBRS 4:cxviii.

"few of the Canadians..." McL to Beaver, 30 December 1836, Beaver, "Mr. Beaver Objects," 13.

"In the first place..." McL to Beaver, 16 December 1836, B.223/b/15, fo. 64, quoted in HBRS 4:cxviii; also in Beaver, "Mr. Beaver Objects," 13.

"without reference..." McL to G&C, 15 November 1836, B.223/b/12, fos. 2–11, HBRS 4:162.

Beaver teaches school HBRS 4:cxvii–cxviii; McL to G&C, 15 November 1836, B.223/b/12, fos. 2–11, HBRS 4:162.

"an almost general desertion..." McL to G&C, 15 November 1836, B.223/b/12, fos. 2–11, HBRS 4:162. Beaver was also determined to teach the Church of England catechism to children whose French Canadian fathers were absent or had died. Beaver, "Experiences," 23–24.

"unless I am permitted..." Beaver to McL, 30 September 1836, quoted in HBRS 4:cxviii.

"neither common sense..." Lamb, Introduction to HBRS 4:cxviii.

257   *"I sing about an hour..."* Narcissa Whitman, "Diary," quoted in Drury, *Marcus and Narcissa*, 1:217.

Beaver's objection to teaching by others Ibid.; Beaver, "Mr. Beaver Objects," 12; Beaver, *Reports and Letters*, 10, 11.

"is under my sole..." Beaver to McL, 30 September 1836, Beaver, *Reports and Letters*, 7.

"unusual in England..." Beaver to Mesdames Whitman and Spalding, 1 October 1836, "Mr. Beaver Objects," 12; also in Beaver, *Reports and Letters*, 11.

McL and Beaver exchange letters Beaver, "Mr. Beaver Objects," 12, 13; HBRS 4:cxviii.

Beaver dismissed from school McL to G&C, 15 November 1836, B.223/b/12, fos. 2–11, HBRS 4:162; Beaver, "Experiences," 24.

"I enjoy the privaledge..." Narcissa Whitman to Rev. L. Hall, 25 October 1836, Northwest and Whitman College Archives, Penrose Memorial Library, Whitman College.

"shocked not at..." Beaver to Benjamin Harrison, 15 November 1836, quoted in Drury, *Marcus and Narcissa,* 1:230; also in Beaver, *Reports and Letters,* 22.

"rather fierce..." "George T. Allen," *Pacific Express* (Portland), 12 April 1888, quoted in Hussey, "Women of Fort Vancouver," 293.

"did not come here..." Thomas M. Anderson, "Army Episodes and Anecdotes; or Life at Vancouver Barracks...," 467–68, MS at Beinecke Rare Book and Manuscript Library, quoted in Hussey, "Women of Fort Vancouver," 293; Beaver, *Reports and Letters,* xiv–xv.

"very kind" Roberts to Frances Fuller Vibtor, 11 November 1878, Roberts, "Round Hand," 196.

258   *"a first rate..."* Francis Ermatinger to Edward Ermatinger, 16 March 1837, Ermatinger, *Fur Trade Letters,* 195.

Mrs. Beaver makes dresses Clark, "Editorial Comment," 70; Hussey, "Women of Fort Vancouver," 294.

"a proper wedding ceremony" Clark, "Editorial Comment," 70.

Beaver and McKay After McKay left the fort, they each wrote one letter to the other, and Beaver sent McKay a copy of the title page of a book he hoped to write. Beaver, *Reports and Letters,* xiv.

Beaver's sealed reports McL to G&C, 19 November 1836, B.223/b/12, fo. 64, HBRS 4:184; GS to Beaver, 30 June 1837, D.4/23, fo. 55, HBRS 4:184 n. 2.

JD and McL remarry HBRS 4:cxix; Clark, "Editorial Comment," 70.

"a female of..." Beaver to G&C, B.223/b/19, fos. 9d, 10d, quoted in HBRS 4:cxx.

"If, Dr. McLoughlin,..." George Roberts to Frances Fuller Victor, 28 November 1878, in Roberts, "Round Hand," 196.

"I was walking..." Beaver, "Experiences," 31; see also HBRS 4:cxx.

259   *"Mr. Beaver, I make...Dr. McLoughlin, I won't accept..."* Roberts to Frances Fuller Victor, 28 November 1878, in Roberts, "Round Hand," 196; see also Beaver, Fourth Report to G&C, 20 March 1838, in Beaver, *Reports and Letters,* 93.

"certain passages" JD to GS, 5 October 1837, printed in Douglas, "Report on 'The Beaver Affair,'" 23.

"I declined holding..." JD to G&C, 18 October 1838, B.223/b/20, fos. 2–28d, HBRS 4:266–67.

Use of wine JD to GS, 5 October 1837, printed in Douglas, "Report on 'The Beaver Affair,'" 20.

"Mrs. McL., who is...decent, married..." Ibid., 21, 20.

Parish duties Ibid., 27.

260   *Departure of Beaver* JD to G&C, 18 October 1838, B.223/b/20, fos. 2–28d,

HBRS 4:267.

"entirely upon his own..." Ibid.

HBC releases Beaver Beaver, "Experiences," 35.

"it has been reported..." Ibid., 32.

Chapel Ibid., 28.

Chapter 7–4: Bonneville, Kelley, & Young

260
Bonneville expedition Bancroft, *Northwest Coast,* 2:568–70; Carey, *General History,* 292–97; Johansen and Gates, *Empire,* 141.

261
Wyeth's offer Wyeth to Bonneville, 22 June 1833, 1 September 1834, Wyeth, *Correspondence and Journals,* 58–60, 141–42.

Pambrun's refusal McL to G&C, 30 September 1835, B.223/b/11, fos. 35d–39, HBRS 4:141; McL to G&C, 31 October 1837, B.223/b/17, fos. 38–46, HBRS 4:195–96.

"As to Bonnaville..." McL to G&C, 31 October 1837, B.223/b/17, fos. 38–46, HBRS 4:195–96.

"with a small party..." McL to G&C, 30 September 1835, B.223/b/11, fos. 35d–39, HBRS 4:141.

Washington Irving and Bonneville Bancroft, *Northwest Coast,* 2:568.

262
Bonneville's accomplishments Johansen and Gates, *Empire,* 141.

Bonneville's return to Fort Vancouver Hussey, *Fort Vancouver,* 211.

"In the latter part..." Figueroa to McL, 9 September 1834, quoted in HBRS 4:127 n. 1. McLoughlin acknowledged receipt of the letter in McL to G&C, 18 November 1834, B.223/b/10, fos. 33–37, HBRS 4:127.

"I would have nothing..." McL, report, quoted in Bancroft, *Northwest Coast,* 2:550 n. 1.

Kelley obsessed with Oregon Johansen and Gates, *Empire,* 141–44. On Kelley's prolific writings, see Bancroft, *Northwest Coast,* 2:554.

262–63
Kelley's journey to Oregon Johansen and Gates, *Empire,* 148; Kelley, *Oregon,* xiv–xv, 100; Bancroft, *Northwest Coast,* 2:548–49.

"a band of marauders..." Kelley, *Oregon,* 100. Every writer gives a slightly different number of men and horses, and Kelley's own accounts disagree. Young (quoted in Bancroft, *Northwest Coast,* 2:548 n. 4) says he had 77 horses and mules, Kelley and the others had 21, and those who joined them had 56.

"so unwell that...out of humanity...a few old clothes..." McL's remarks on Caleb Cushing's report, in McL to William Miller, British Consul at Oahu, 24 March 1845, B.223/b/33, fos. 40–46, HBRS 7:278–79. The report of Cushing, chairman

of the House of Representatives' Committee on Foreign Affairs, included Jason Lee's memorial to Congress, Lee's letter to Cushing, Wyeth's memoir on Oregon, William Slacum's report to John Forsyth of 26 March 1837, Kelley's memoir of his Oregon expedition, and other documents. HBRS 7:269 n. 2.

"a white slouched hat..." George Roberts to Frances Fuller Victor, 28 November 1878, in Roberts, "Round Hand," 185.

Kelley's housing Kelley, *Oregon*, 181; McL's remarks on Cushing's report, B.223/b/33, fos. 40–46, HBRS 7:279.

"a cabin, opening..." Kelley, *Oregon*, 181.

"The persecuting monster..." Ibid., 180.

264   *"overhaul my baggage..."* Ibid., 145.

"his only object..." Ibid., 186.

McL gives Kelley passage to Hawaii Kelley, *Oregon*, 186–87; McL's remarks on Cushing's report, B.223/b/33, fos. 40–46, HBRS 7:282.

"the colonization..." Kelley, *Oregon*, 135.

"neither a great..." Bancroft, *Northwest Coast*, 2:544–45.

"He alone was stirring..." Clarke, *Pioneer Days*, 1:274.

Young carries Shakespeare Powers, *Oregon Literature*, 91. At the "sail" of Young's estate, C. M. Walker bought the two books for $3.50. Young, "Ewing Young," 280.

"a very candid..." Walker, "Sketch of Ewing Young," 58.

265   *Wyeth requests supplies* Ibid.

"while these accusations...It is not so easy..." McL's remarks on Cushing's report, B.223/b/33, fos. 40–46, HBRS 7:277, 278.

"Mr. Young had been..." Ibid., 277.

"had no hand in..." Ibid.

Young and Kelley exonerated Geer, *Fifty Years*, 47; McL's remarks on Cushing's report, B.223/b/33, fos. 40–46, HBRS 7:277. Courtney Walker said Figueroa wrote to McLoughlin the following fall "withdrawing the charges." "Sketch of Ewing Young," 57.

"that bane that changes..." Lee and Frost, *Ten Years*, 140.

Oregon Temperance Society Lee and Frost, *Ten Years*, 140–42; Bancroft, *Oregon*, 1:98–99; "Mission Record Book," 248–51; *CPT*, 133, 349 n. 6.

Petition by settlers Lee and Frost, *Ten Years*, 141.

"with feelings of..." "Mission Record Book," 248–49.

"tyrannizing oppression..." Ibid., 250–51.

266   *"felt that if...It is due..."* Lee and Frost, *Ten Years*, 140–41.

Chapter 7–5: The Willamette Cattle Company

266   *President Jackson sends Slacum* Bancroft, *Oregon*, 1:100; *CPT*, 123; Slacum, "Report on Oregon," 177; HBRS 4:cxxii, 185 n. 2.

Slacum's request Slacum, "Report on Oregon," 183.

"He never gave me..." McL's remarks on Cushing's report, B.223/b/33, fos. 40–46, HBRS 7:270–71.

267   *"including officers' dwelling–houses..."* Slacum, "Report on Oregon," 185–86.

"almost every house..." Lee and Frost, *Ten Years*, 144; *CPT*, 82.

"although they were located..." Slacum, "Report on Oregon," 185.

"a cloud hung...on the same terms..." McL's remarks on Cushing's report, B.223/b/33, fos. 40–46, HBRS 7:276, 278.

268   *Slacum transmits HBC offer to Young* Ibid., 276; Slacum, "Report on Oregon," 195; *CPT*, 349 n. 6. Finlayson had been on the Columbia since 1831 and was one of McLoughlin's most important aides.

"I found that nothing..." Slacum, "Report on Oregon," 196.

"we had not the number..." McL's remarks on Cushing's report, B.223/b/33, fos. 40–46, HBRS 7:278.

"As to Beef..." McL to G&C, 31 October 1837, B.223/b/17, fos. 38–46, HBRS 4:206–7.

McL refuses beef to Belcher Belcher, *Voyage*, 1:296; Bancroft, *Oregon*, 1:140 n. 2; Clarke, *Pioneer Days*, 1:305.

"If I sold, they..." McL, "Autobiography," in Clarke, *Pioneer Days*, 1:220.

"was in contemplation" Lee and Frost, *Ten Years*, 144.

Willamette Cattle Company Slacum, "Report on Oregon," 196; Bancroft, *Oregon*, 1:141; *CPT*, 83; Lee and Frost, *Ten Years*, 145.

269   *"so that by purchasing..."* McL, "Autobiography," in Clarke, *Pioneer Days*, 1:221. Bancroft says that with McLoughlin's donation, the figures for the amount raised and amount spent tally, but without it $880.00 is unexplained. *Oregon*, 1:141. Lee and Frost say the cost was $2,480 for 800 cattle at $3 per head and 40 horses at $12 each. The drivers were paid $1 per day. *Ten Years*, 146.

269–70   *"The last month..."* P. L. Edwards, diary, MS 24, quoted in Bancroft, *Oregon*, 1:146.

Cattle drive McL, "Autobiography," in Clarke, *Pioneer Days*, 221; Edwards, diary, quoted in Bancroft, *Oregon*, 1:142–50; Lee and Frost, *Ten Years*, 146; *CPT*, 83.

Young prospers Bancroft, *Oregon*, 1:151; *CPT*, 136.

"kept the tame..." McL, "Autobiography," in Clarke, *Pioneer Days*, 1:221.

Slacum report Slacum, "Report on Oregon," 175–224. McLoughlin discussed this report at length in McL to William Miller, 24 March 1845, B.223/b/33, fos. 40–46, HBRS 7:270–78.

"unauthorized introduction..." Slacum, "Report on Oregon," 185.

"subject to the protection..." Ibid., 197.

270 *"is calculated..."* Ibid., 188.

"It is incorrect..." McL's remarks on Cushing's report, B.223/b/33, fos. 51d–62d, HBRS 7:271.

"the wives made a present..." Ibid., 275.

"they also attack ours..." Ibid., 273.

"we made it a point..." Ibid., 273–74.

"the finest grazing..." Slacum, "Report on Oregon," 202.

Military post Ibid., 205.

271 *"our whalers from the coast..."* Ibid.

"I hope our claim..." Ibid., 204; HBRS 4:cxxiii.

Petition not taken by Slacum CPT, 349 n. 9; Pike, "Petitions," 216–18.

Chapter 7–6: Sails & Steam

Arrival of Nereide McL to G&C, 28 May 1834, B.223/b/10, fos. 13–15d, HBRS 4:116

Langtry appointed G&C to McL, 1 May 1833, A.6/23, fo. 22d, HBRS 4:cxiii.

"unnecessary with the number..." McL to G&C, 28 May 1834, B.223/b/10, fos. 13–15d, HBRS 4:117.

Repairs to Nereide Ibid., 116.

"did not immediately..." Ibid., 121.

"from the Lords..." Langtry to McL, 18 May 1834, B.223/b/10, fo. 16, HBRS 4:121 n. 2.

McL sends Langtry to England HBRS 4:cxiii.

Finlayson in charge Ibid., cxvi.

272 *Early interest in steamer* McL to GS, 20 March 1826, D.4/119, fo. 45d, HBRS 4:lxxiv.

"a small steam boat..." McL to GS, 20 March 1827, D.4/119, fo. 53d, HBRS 4:lxxiv. 4:111.

McL thinks company agrees McL to Ogden, 28 October 1833, B.223/b/9, fo. 19, HBRS 4:111 n. 1.

"would not pay..." McL to G&C, 18 November 1834, B.223/b/10, fos. 33–37,

HBRS 4:124.

"As to the Steam Boat..." McL to G&C, 30 September 1835, B.223/b/11, fos. 35d–39, HBRS 4:139.

McL's query to GS McL to GS, 3 March 1835, D.4/127, fo. 69, HBRS 4:cxiv.

"most substantially..." Bancroft, *Northwest Coast,* 2:600.

Equipment of Beaver Ibid., 601. She was 101.4 feet in length and 11 feet deep, with a 20-foot beam. OHS neg. OrHi 109.

Beaver's tryout Clarke, *Pioneer Days,* 1:205–6; Bancroft, *Oregon,* 1:123; Parker, *Journal,* 310–11.

273   *"Our progress was..."* Finlayson to McL, 29 September 1836, B.223/b/12, fos. 16–24d, HBRS 4:327.

"when not supplied..." Ibid., 328.

274   *"she will give..."* Ibid.

Decline of returns HBRS 4:xciv–xcv.

Seven ships HBRS 4:cxv.

"built as strong..." G&C to McL, 28 August 1835, B.223/c/1, fos. 39–43, HBRS 4:cxiii. A carronade is a short, large-bore cannon, chiefly used on ships.

McL uses Nereide McL to G&C, 15 November 1836, B.223/b/12, fos. 2–11, HBRS 4:163; JD to GS, 18 March 1838, B.223/b/20, fos. 68–83d, HBRS 4:274.

"she draws so much..." McL to G&C, 15 November 1836, B.223/b/12, fos. 2–11, HBRS 4:154.

"little more than..." McL to G&C, 24 October 1839, A.11/69, fos. 1–2, HBRS 6:5.

Mutiny on Nereide McL to G&C, 26 October 1837, B.223/b/18, fos. 3d–5, HBRS 4:189–93; JD to GS, 18 March 1838, B.223/b/20, fos. 68–83d, HBRS 4:274–75.

"that no Court..." JD to GS, 18 March 1838, B.223/b/20, fos. 68–83d, HBRS 4:274.

275   *"mann the windless"* McL to G&C, 26 October 1837, B.223/b/18, fos. 3d–5, HBRS 4:191–92.

"to be fed..." Ibid.

"It is true..." Ibid., 193.

"we were forced..." JD to GS, 18 March 1838, B.223/b/20, fos. 68–83d, HBRS 4:274–75.

"your orders for..." JD to G&C, 18 October 1838, B.223/b/20, fos. 2–28d, HBRS 4:247.

Nereide *accident* JD to GS, 18 March 1838, B.223/b/20, fos. 68–83d, HBRS

4:275–76.

"from the wrinkled...in rough weather..." Ibid.

Nereide *called home*   G&C to JD, 31 October 1838, A.6/25, fo. 12d, HBRS 6:5 n. 2.

"vexatious annoyance...It is not only..."   Finlayson to McL, 29 September 1836, B.223/b/12, fos. 16–24d, HBRS 4:323, 330.

276   *"Your individual opinion..."*   G&C to McL, 28 August 1835, A.6/23, fos. 138d–139, quoted in McL to G&C, 9 April 1836, B.223/b/15, fos. 10–12, HBRS 4:144–45.

"I know of no difference..."   McL to G&C, 9 April 1836, B.223/b/15, fos. 10–12, HBRS 4:145.

McL called to London   HBRS 4:cxxvi.

Strain in McL's relations with G&C   Rich, *History of the Hudson's Bay Company,* vol. 2, HBRS 22:668, 670.

276–77   *"I see that you..."*   "Letters of Dr. McLoughlin to Edward Ermatinger," 1 February 1835, 366.

277   *"to pay a visit..."*   McL to GS, 20 March 1837, B.223/b/15, fo. 78, HBRS 4:cxxv.

"I would be extremely..."   McL to G&C, 2 November 1837, B.223/b/18, fo. 5d, HBRS 4:215.

Building project   Hussey, *Fort Vancouver,* 118–27, 142 n. 67, 150, 162; Gray, *History of Oregon,* 149, 150.

"a good and commodious..."   Francis Ermatinger to Edward Ermatinger, 19 March 1838, Ermatinger, *Fur Trade Letters,* 202.

New "Big House"   Hussey, *Fort Vancouver,* 150, 162; Hussey, *Historic Structures,* 1:93–95; Gray, *History of Oregon,* 149–50.

Move into new house   Hussey, *Historic Structures,* 1:89; Beaver, *Reports and Letters,* 82, 120.

"more commodious..."   Beaver to G&C, 2 October 1838, printed in Beaver, *Reports and Letters,* 120.

Chapter 7-7: Daughters & Sons

277   *McKay daughters*   David McLoughlin Papers, OHSL.

"I received a letter..."   John McLoughlin to SF, 24 February 1833, *ME,* 197.

William Randolph Eppes   *ME,* 129; David McLoughlin Papers, OHSL.

"a very fine..."   GS, Character Book, quoted in biographical notes, HBRS 4:353–55.

Rae at Vancouver   Harvey, "Biography of Her Father," 14.

"I have a clear..." David McLoughlin to John Fraser, 7 April 1843 [1842], *ME*, 246.

David sent to Paris David McLoughlin Papers, OHSL; McL to John Fraser, 14 February 1836, *ME*, 221; *ME*, 132.

"in consequence of..." McL to SF, 4 February 1837, *ME*, 235.

"for any sum..." McL to SF, 14 February 1836, *ME*, 223.

"My youngest son..." McL to John McLeod, 1 February 1836, extract in *ME*, 220.

"My Brother writes..." McL to John Fraser, 14 February 1836, *ME*, 221.

Thomas McKay *CPT*, 93–99; Bird, "Thomas McKay" and "Will of Thomas McKay."

279 *"It rained..."* Allan, "Reminiscences," 77.

Joseph McLoughlin *ME*, 329 n. 9; biography in HBRS 4:350.

"there was no..." McL to G&C, 31 October 1837, B.223/b/17, fos. 38–46, continued in B.223/b/18, fo. 2, HBRS 4:194.

John with Simon Fraser *ME*, 115–21; family letters in *ME*, 201–28.

John enrolls at McGill Photocopy of class roster, 1834, provided to author by McGill University. He was listed only one term.

"If no letter..." John McLoughlin to SF, 14 March 1835, *ME*, 204–5.

"On the receipt..." John McLoughlin to John Fraser, 25 March 1835, *ME*, 205.

279–80 *"You will on receipt..."* SF to John McLoughlin, 12 April 1835, *ME*, 208.

280 *"I am extremely..."* Sister St. Henry to SF, 11 May 1835, *ME*, 210.

"anxious to know..." I. H. Trudeau to SF, 7 April 1835, *ME*, 207.

"having been deceived..." Confectioner Connet to SF, 1 June 1835, *ME*, 211.

"that you would be..." J. F. Pelletier to SF, 1 July 1835, *ME*, 215.

"a complete set..." John McLoughlin to John Fraser, 28 August 1835, *ME*, 217.

281 *"I am convinced..."* SF to John McLoughlin, 12 January 1836, *ME*, 218–19.

"as he was actually..." McL to SF, 4 February 1837, *ME*, 232.

"It is impossible..." Ibid., 232–33.

"He has applied..." Ibid., 233–34.

"if a hundred and fifty..." McL to SF, 8 February 1837, *ME*, 235.

282 *Dickson expedition* *ME*, 119–22; HBRS 6:xxvii–xxix.

"Major of the Cavalry...interesting..." *ME*, 120.

"worked with silver..." John McLoughlin to John Fraser, 11 October 1836, *ME*, 231.

"they would occasion...set them at variance...you will have less..." GS to Christie,

4 September 1836, D.4/22, fos. 74d–75, HBRS 6:xxviii.

"your Father requested..." GS to John McLoughlin, 7 September 1836, D.4/22, fo. 70, HBRS 6:xxviii.

"desist from his foolish..." Sister St. Henry, quoted in John Fraser to McL, 13 April 1837, *ME*, 237.

282–83   *"is considered by all..."* John Fraser to John McLoughlin, 16 April 1837, *ME*, 238, 39.

283   *"We hired dogs..."* John McLoughlin to John Fraser, 8 August 1837, *ME*, 240–41.

John goes to Fort Vancouver *ME*, 122; HBRS 6:xxix.

"I perfectly agree..." John McLoughlin to John Fraser, 29 July 1838, *ME*, 241. Written at Norway House, during John's trip with McL.

Chapter 8–1: McLoughlin in England

287   *"The interests of the Colony..."* JD to G&C, 18 October 1838, B.223/b/20, fos. 2–28d, HBRS 4:242.

289   *Ogden, Black, Douglas as substitutes* HBRS 4:cxxvii; Rich, *History of the Hudson's Bay Company*, vol. 2, HBRS 22:645–46.

"Fort Vancouver and the lower..." Minutes of Council, June 1837, A.6/24, fos. 113d–114, printed in Oliver, *Canadian North-West*, 2:767.

"a stout powerful..." GS, Character Book, in Williams, *Hudson's Bay Miscellany*, HBRS 30:204–5.

G&C displeased Rich, *History of the Hudson's Bay Company*, vol. 2, HBRS 22:645.

"less system..." G&C to JD or the Officer superintending the Columbia Department, 15 November 1837, A.6/24, fos. 113d–114, quoted in HBRS 4:cxxvi–cxxvii.

290   *McL stops at Walla Walla* Drury, *Marcus and Narcissa*, 1:272–74; Brosnan, *Jason Lee*, 97.

"numerous favors...We cannot speak..." Whitman to Secretary Green, 12 March 1838, in Houghton Library, Harvard University, quoted in Drury, *Marcus and Narcissa*, 1:274, 2:368.

Thomas McKay and sons Drury, *Marcus and Narcissa*, 1:272–73.

"I would succeed better..." McKay, "Additional Light," 92.

"I do myself the pleasure..." McL to G&C, 20 November 1840, B.223/b/28, fos. 58–65, HBRS 6:13. The Governor and Committee, who forwarded the request to McLoughlin, did not further identify the Geographical Society.

"came out this spring..." John McLoughlin to John Fraser, 29 July 1838, *ME*, 241.

Canadian rebellions ME, 242 n. 122. Insurrections occurred in 1837–38 in Lower and Upper Canada—some at St. Eustache, near Terrebonne, where McLoughlin's relatives lived.

291   *"The Doctor, who has..."* John Tod to Edward Ermatinger, 12 July 1838, Ermatinger Papers, Archives of B.C., quoted in HBRS 4:cxxvii.

         "to day at 1 P.M....I intend to start..." McL to G&C, 1 August 1838, A.10/7, fos. 57–58, HBRS 4:218.

         Great Western HBRS 4:cxxviii, 218 n. 1.

         "in time to come...you may depend..." McL to Elisabeth Fraser, 12 August 1838, ME, 242.

         Death of Alexander Fraser ME, 78.

         Elisabeth and John Fraser marry McL to John Fraser, 17 February 1844, ME, 251. See also ME, 20, 78, 242 n. 124.

292   *"Paris 13th Sept... ."* McL to G&C, 13 September 1838, A.10/7, fos. 121–22, HBRS 4:219.

         Payments to Catherine O'Gorman Barker, *Financial Papers*, 68–82.

         O'Gorman letters A.10/16, fos. 180–81, quoted in HBRS 4:219 n. 2; Barker, "The Dr. John McLoughlin House."

         Marguerite's daughters David McLoughlin Papers, OHSL; Elliott, "Marguerite Wadin McKay McLoughlin," 339; Barker, "The Dr. John McLoughlin House," 2. In 1812, near Sault Ste. Marie, Gabriel Franchère met "Captain McCargo, whose Great Lakes schooner had been burned in the War." Franchère, *Voyage*, 273.

293   *"as if it obtains..."* G&C to JD, 31 October 1838, A.6/24, fos. 172–75, HBRS 6:209–10 n. 1.

         Negotiations in London Rich, *History of the Hudson's Bay Company*, vol. 2, HBRS 22:651–55.

         Pressure by Foreign Office HBRS 7:xii.

         Agreement between companies HBRS 6:27 nn. 1, 2; HBRS 7:xi–xii; Oliver, *Canadian North-West*, 2:791–96.

         "as annual rent..." Oliver, *Canadian North-West*, 2:793.

294   *Advantages in agreement* HBRS 6:xi–xii; HBRS 7:xii; Oliver, *Canadian North-West*, 2:791.

         Puget's Sound Agricultural Company Carey, *General History*, 249–50; HBRS 7:xiii–xv.

         First agents of PSAC HBRS 7:xiii.

         "The Government is favorable..." G&C to GS, 20 March 1839, A.6/25, fo. 28, HBRS 6:15–16 n. 2.

         "unfolded his views..." Tolmie, *Journals*, 178.

McL's 1832 proposal D.4/100, fos. 30–31d, HBRS 7:xiv; Rich, *History of the Hudson's Bay Company*, vol. 2, HBRS 22:661–62.

"that cattle rearing..." GS to G&C, 27 August 1834, D.4/100, fos. 22d–23d, HBRS 4:137 n. 3.

"would be detrimental..." G&C to McL, 10 December 1834, A.6/23, fos. 100–100d, HBRS 4:137–38 n. 3.

"I see nothing..." McL to G&C, 30 September 1835, B.223/b/11, fos. 35d–39, HBRS 4:137.

295   *"Mr. McLoughlin presents..."* McL to G&C, 28 February 1839, A.10/8, fo. 75, HBRS 6:1.

"the Chief Factor..." Minutes of G&C, 27 February 1839, A.1/61, fos. 51–51d, HBRS 6:xii.

"could not hesitate..." McL to SF, 4 February 1837, *ME*, 233.

David's education David McLoughlin Papers, OHSL; see also *ME*, 46, 132–33.

296   *"resigned the service..."* Commonwealth Relations Office to Barker, 31 July 1954, quoted in *ME*, 133 n. 18.

"Agent of Gt. Western..." Barker, *Financial Papers*, 70–71. It was not a personal cost, because McLoughlin had been given three hundred pounds for "Travelling Expenses, Outfit 1838."

Book to SF McL to SF, 24 February 1840, *ME*, 244.

"I much regret..." Ibid.

Council at Red River HBRS 6:1 n. 2. The Council of the Northern Department met at various posts, including York Factory, Norway House, and Red River.

McL to Norway House and York Factory Ibid.

297   *"I arrived here..."* David McLoughlin to SF, 11 July 1839, *ME*, 243. David's reason for staying in Montreal has not been explained, but he may have wanted to spend some time with his cousin, John Fraser. His means of transportation is also unknown. The HBC, with headquarters at York Factory, did not send brigades to Montreal, but there was business communication, because George Simpson lived at Lachine, and the company's employment office was also there.

Catherine Sinclair Elliott, "Marguerite Wadin McKay McLoughlin," 338; Sampson, *Business Correspondence*, 131; Ermatinger, *Fur Trade Letters*, 248. It is known that she was at Fort Vancouver shortly after this time, and this would have been the most logical time for her to make the trip.

"the big Doctor has..." John Tod to Edward Ermatinger, February 1840, Ermatinger Papers, vol. 2, p. 73, National Archives of Canada.

"at the foot of..." McL to GS, 20 March 1841, B.223/b/28, fos. 22–26d, HBRS 6:250.

"a hearty old gentleman..." Farnham, *Travels*, 91.

Blankets for sails These would be the famous HBC blankets.

298   *McL's arrival at Fort Vancouver* McL to SF, 24 February 1840, *ME*, 244.

"resumed sole charge..." Tolmie, "Letter," 27.

Chapter 8–2: Reaching Out

298   *"a young man..."* JD to G&C, 14 October 1839, A.11/69, fos. 72–89, HBRS 6:219–20.

298–99 *"travelling on horseback..."* John McLoughlin to John Fraser, 15 March 1840, *ME*, 245.

299   *"I still feel..."* David McLoughlin to John Fraser, 7 April 1843 [1842], *ME*, 247.

"I brought back David..." McL to John Fraser, 24 October 1840, *ME*, 246.

Eloisa's son John Rae was born February 3, 1839, at Fort Vancouver. Maria Louisa Rae Myrick, interview in Lockley, "Impressions," *Oregon Journal*, 20 September 1929; Anne Billeter, "Genealogy," printed in Wilson, *Dr. John McLoughlin*, 183–84.

McL's and JD's families in Big House Lieut. George Foster Emmons, journal, 25 July 1841, cited in Hussey, *Historic Structures*, 1:99. Douglas and his wife would eventually have five daughters, but in 1839 there were only two.

"singing, dancing...ball in the evening..." Thomas Lowe, journal, 25 December 1844, 1 January 1845, 31 December 1845, quoted in Hussey, *Historic Structures*, 1:97–100.

Use of term "upstairs" Information from officers at Fort Vancouver National Historic Site.

"a jovial, jolly..." Roberts, "Round Hand," 195.

"the company officers..." Farnham, *Travels*, 103–4.

300   *Bachelors' Hall* Hussey, *Historic Structures*, 2:131.

"weapons, dresses...smoking, joking, singing..." Dunn, *Oregon Territory*, 145.

"affords me the greatest..." McL to G&C, 24 October 1839, A.11/69, fos. 90–91, HBRS 6:3. The same letter establishes McLoughlin's return date as October 17, 1839.

"which is a proof..." McL to GS, 20 March 1840, B.223/b/26, fos. 1–5d, HBRS 6:234.

"at the suggestion..." JD to G&C, 18 October 1838, B.223/b/20, fos. 2–28d, HBRS 4:259–60.

JD's improvements on Cowlitz JD to G&C, 14 October 1839, A.11/69, fos. 72–89, HBRS 6:220–21.

"as many ploughs..." McL to GS, 20 March 1840, B.223/b/26, fos. 1–5d,

HBRS 6:230.

Cattle and sheep McL to G&C, 2 November 1837, B.223/b/18, fo. 5d, HBRS 4:216; JD to G&C, 18 October 1838, B.223/b/20, fos. 2–28d, HBRS 4:250; JD to GS, 18 November 1838, B.223/b/20, fos. 60–83d, HBRS 4:284.

"too numerous..." JD to GS, 18 March 1838, B.223/b/20, fos. 68–83d, HBRS 4:284.

301 *Contract for butter* Article 4 of 1839 agreement with Russians, summary in HBRS 6:27 n. 2. Butter was so difficult to supply that the Governor and Committee shortly persuaded Wrangel to accept a smaller amount. G&C to McL, 31 December 1839, A.6/25, fo. 53, quoted in HBRS 6:27 n. 2.

"as might be convenient..." G&C to McL, 31 December 1839, A.6/25, fo. 53, quoted in HBRS 6:27 n. 2. See also McL to G&C, 31 October 1842, B.223/b/29, fos. 75–91, HBRS 6:72–73; and McL to GS, 20 March 1840, B.223/b/26, fos. 1–5d, HBRS 6:236.

"set about building..." McL to GS, 20 March 1840, B.223/b/26, fos. 1–5d, HBRS 6:230.

Tour of inspection Ibid., 230–31.

"as Mr. Tod..." Ibid., 231.

"going on well..." Ibid.

"not a place..." Ibid.

"I am afraid..." Ibid., 236.

302 *Appointments to Stikine* McL to GS, 20 March 1841, B.223/b/28, fos. 22–26d, HBRS 6:246.

Douglas party departs McL to G&C, 23 May 1840, B.223/b/27, fos. 16d–17, HBRS 6:8.

"I am going farther..." John McLoughlin to John Fraser, 15 March 1840, *ME*, 245.

"I believe he is..." David McLoughlin to John Fraser, 7 April 1843 [1842], *ME*, 247.

"and squared the wall..." McL to G&C, 23 May 1840, B.223/b/27, fos. 16d–17, HBRS 6:8.

303 *"we found them as Anxious..."* McL to G&C, 20 November 1840, B.223/b/28, fos. 58–65, HBRS 6:24.

"barely enough for..." JD, report to McL, 1 October 1840, in Leader, "Douglas Expeditions," *OHQ* 32 (December 1931): 368.

"It was a miserable..." Harvey, "Biography of Her Father," 9.

"establish a Post..." McL to GS, 20 March 1840, B.223/b/26, fos. 1–5d, HBRS 6:232.

Roderick Finlayson JD to GS, 6 April 1846, HBRS 6:389, biographical note.

"Mr. Douglas left..." McL to G&C, 20 November 1840, B.223/b/28, fos. 58–65, HBRS 6:23.

Chapter 8–3: "The Germe of a Great State"

304 *"The Dr. could not..."* "The Diary of Reverend Jason Lee," 28 July 1838, *OHQ* 17 (December 1916): 404.

"Messrs. Ewing & Edwards" Ibid., 405.

Lee's petition Pike, "Petitions," 218–20; Drury, *Marcus and Narcissa,* 1:286.

"will not, I presume,..." JD to G&C, 18 October 1838, B.223/b/20, fos. 2–28d, HBRS 4:241.

"formal and speedy..." Brosnan, "Oregon Memorial," 75–76; Pike, "Petitions."

305 *"The interests of..."* JD to G&C, 18 October 1838, B.223/b/20, fos. 2–28d, HBRS 4:242.

Message to Lee Canse, "Jason Lee," 260–61. William H. Gray says he received notice at Fort Hall and paid "Richardson" $150 to take the news to Lee. *History of Oregon,* 182.

"hundreds went away..." Brosnan, *Jason Lee,* 116.

306 *Railroad in Maine* White, *Essays,* 208–9.

Lee reports to Methodist Missionary Society, presents petition Pike, "Petitions," 220; Brosnan, *Jason Lee,* 219.

"both the Board..." Lee, statement to Mission Board, in Brosnan, *Jason Lee,* 248.

"on the eve of...contemplated migrating..." G&C to McL, 31 December 1839, A.6/25, fo. 51, HBRS 6:14 n. 2.

Methodist recruits; the Lausanne Lee and Frost, *Ten Years,* 216–17; Brosnan, *Jason Lee,* 142–46. Rev. J. L. Parrish, a passenger on the *Lausanne,* and Rev. H. K. Hines, the brother of a passenger, said the U.S. government subsidized the ship, but no record of this has been found. Drury, *Marcus and Narcissa,* 1:295–96.

Arrival of Lausanne McL to G&C, 20 November 1840, B.223/b/28, fos. 58–65, HBRS 6:14.

"some excellent fresh..." Lee and Frost, *Ten Years,* 224. In 1851 Washington settled in today's state of Washington, became a well-to-do farmer, and founded the city of Centralia on his land claim. Taylor, "Slaves and Free Men," 160.

"who pointed out..." Lee and Frost, *Ten Years,* 225.

307 *"After the ship..."* Ibid., 225–26.

"five missionaries..." Ibid., 216–17; see also Brosnan, *Jason Lee,* 145–47; Carey,

General History, 294. Their numbers differ slightly.

Lee remarried Drury, *Marcus and Narcissa,* 1:296–97.

Housing at fort Hussey, *Historic Structures,* 2:131.

Meeting and assignments Lee and Frost, *Ten Years,* 226; Brosnan, *Jason Lee,* 176.

McL's activity at falls GS to G&C, 25 November 1841, long extract in "Letters of Sir George Simpson," 82; Waller to his brother, 6 April 1842, printed in Brosnan, *Jason Lee,* 178–79; HBRS 7:xl, xlii; Wilkes, "Diary," *WHQ* 17 (January 1926): 44.

"more to the apparent..." Farnham, *Travels,* 95.

307–8 *Chemeketa* Bancroft, *Oregon,* 1:192.

308 *Population estimates* JD to G&C, 18 October 1838, B.223/b/20, fos. 2–28d, HBRS 4:240; JD to G&C, 14 October 1839, A.11/69, fos. 72–89, HBRS 6:226; GS to G&C, 25 November 1841, D.4/110, fo. 28, HBRS 7:xxxiv.

"exculpatory of..." Farnham, *Travels,* 175.

"OTHERS THAT WOULD..." Petition of 1840, printed in Gray, *History of Oregon,* 194–96; *CPT,* 135–36.

Farnham petition Pike, "Petitions," 221–24; *CPT,* 135–36; Farnham, *Travels,* 94; Gray, *History of Oregon,* 194–96; Bancroft, *Oregon,* 1:231–34.

309 *"If it is Your Honors..."* McL to G&C, 18 November 1843, B.223/b/30, fos. 74–95, HBRS 6:171, 174.

Trade with Americans Rich, *History of the Hudson's Bay Company,* vol. 2, HBRS 22:672.

Chapter 8–4: The Stirring of Government

309 *"a pressure..."* Geer, *Fifty Years,* 168.

"a large and very unsettled..." Hines, *Life on the Plains,* 418, excerpt in Duniway and Riggs, "Oregon Archives," 219.

Young's death and estate Hines, *Life on the Plains,* 417–20; Duniway and Riggs, "Oregon Archives," 219; Geer, *Fifty Years,* 168–69, 172; *CPT,* 136; Young, "Ewing Young," 171–305.

"burst a blood vessel...the little property..." Lee and Frost, *Ten Years,* 132–33.

"serves as an Encouragement..." McL to G&C, 16 November 1836, B.223/b/12, fos. 70–83d, HBRS 4:174.

310 *"on the very day"* Minutes of Meeting, February 18, Hines, *Life on the Plains,* 417–20, printed in Duniway and Riggs, "Oregon Archives," 218.

Date of February 17 meeting Thornton says a preliminary meeting was held on February 7, Young died on February 15, the funeral was on February 17, and the first meeting was held that day. "Provisional Government," 50. Hines, who was present, says the meeting was on the day of the funeral. *Life on the Plains*, 418. Hussey discusses conflicting accounts in *CPT*, 349 n. 10. Grover, in *Oregon Archives*, details the meeting but without reference to Young.

"nearly every male..." Hines, *Life on the Plains*, 418; Duniway and Riggs, "Oregon Archives," 220.

Minutes of February 17 meeting Grover, *Oregon Archives*, and Hines, *Life on the Plains*, both in Duniway and Riggs, "Oregon Archives," 216–21. Grover and Hines are the best primary sources for the formation of government, and their relevant sections are reprinted by Duniway and Riggs in "Oregon Archives," 211–80. Hines, who was secretary at the early meetings, probably referred to his notes in writing his book. Grover was authorized by the Legislative Assembly in 1853 to gather and publish the documents. Other eyewitness accounts are Gray, *History of Oregon*; Matthieu, "Reminiscences"; and Labonte, "Reminiscences." Another valuable source is J. Quinn Thornton, who was not present during the first years of the government, but wrote *Oregon and California* and "Provisional Government" with the aid of participants. *CPT*, 370–74, discusses sources in detail.

"framing a constitution..." Grover, *Oregon Archives*, 5–7, excerpt in Duniway and Riggs, "Oregon Archives," 217.

"Bailey could not..." Gray, *History of Oregon*, 201.

"As it was not deemed..." Hines, *Life on the Plains*, 418; Duniway and Riggs, "Oregon Archives," 220.

"the first Thursday..." Minutes of Meeting, February 18, Hines, *Life on the Plains*, 417–20, printed in Duniway and Riggs, "Oregon Archives," 220. The Grover version of the same meeting says "to meet on the first Tuesday of June." Duniway and Riggs, "Oregon Archives," 218.

"in consequence..." Hines, *Life on the Plains*, 419; Duniway and Riggs, "Oregon Archives," 220.

311   *"and as far as..."* Wilkes, *Narrative*, 4:350.

"divide and conquer..." Gray, *History of Oregon*, 202.

"This last summer..." GS to G&C, 25 November 1841, long extract in "Letters of Sir George Simpson," 81.

"John M'Loughlin...concerning the propriety..." Gray, *History of Oregon*, 202.

Disposal of Young's estate CPT, 138.

"As thare is no..." Newell, *Memoranda*, 40.

312   *"With regard to..."* G&C to McL, 31 December 1839, A.6/25, fo. 52d, HBRS 6:18–19 n. 2.

"*avowed objects...*" Ibid.

"*Your view of...*" McL to G&C, 20 November 1840, B.223/b/28, fos. 58–65, HBRS 6:18–19.

313   "*the supplies they obtain...*" G&C to McL, 1 December 1841, A.6/25, fo. 157, HBRS 6:74 n. 4.

"*The plan you direct...*" McL to G&C, 31 October 1842, B.223/b/29, fos. 75–91, HBRS 6:73–74.

Chapter 8–5: An American Lieutenant

313   *Wilkes expedition* Clarke, *Pioneer Days,* 2:398. Wilkes's *Narrative,* vols. 4 and 5, contain extensive material on the Northwest.

"*one of the most...*" Wilkes, *Narrative,* 4:293.

"*politely invited in....*" Wilkes, "Diary," 28 [May] 1841, *WHQ* 16 (July 1925): 217.

314   "*a profusion...*" Ibid., 220.

Fort Vancouver buildings Wilkes, *Narrative,* 4:326–27.

"*winding its way...*" Wilkes, "Diary," 28 [May] 1841, *WHQ* 16 (July 1925): 220.

"*At early dawn...*" Wilkes, *Narrative,* 4:329.

"*I feel that...*" Wilkes, *Columbia River,* 25.

315   "*in order to secure...*" Wilkes, *Narrative,* 4:344.

"*No engineer ever...*" Wilkes, "Diary," *WHQ* 17 (January 1926): 44.

"*We dined a la...*" Ibid., 50–51.

"*in the public...*" Ibid., 48.

"*to wait until...*" Wilkes, *Narrative,* 4:353.

"*nor had he any knowledge...*" Ibid., 4:350.

"*who were to be...*" Ibid., 4:364.

316   *Star of Oregon* Account written by Joseph Gale, printed in Clarke, *Pioneer Days,* 2:617–27.

"*were making a coffin...*" Ibid., 619.

Wreck of Peacock McL to G&C, 17 September 1841, A.11/70, fos. 17–18, HBRS 6:41; Howerton, "Peacock"; Wilkes, "Diary," *WHQ* 17 (July 1926): 227.

"*if these sailors...*" McL to G&C, 4 November 1842, B.223/b/29, fos. 93–98d, HBRS 6:97.

McL buys cargo McL to G&C, 24 May 1841, A.11/70, fos. 13–16d, HBRS 6:37, 96–97. Wilkes said that McLoughlin had made a charter agreement with Captain Varney and had loaded goods, but surrendered the charter for "a small consideration, if the goods...were delivered at Vancouver." Wilkes, *Narrative,*

4:495.

"I took back..." McL to G&C, 4 November 1842, B.223/b/29, fos. 93–98d, HBRS 6:96.

Wilkes buys ship Wilkes, *Columbia River*, 5; McL to G&C, 17 September 1841, A.11/70, fos. 17–18, HBRS 6:41; McL to G&C, 4 November 1842, B.223/b/29, fos. 93–98d, HBRS 6:98.

316–17   *"prevent their getting..."* McL to G&C, 4 November 1842, B.223/b/29, fos. 93–98d, HBRS 6:96–97.

317   *"It would be offering..."* G&C to McL, 30 March 1842, A.6/26, fo. 8d, HBRS 6:96 n. 1.

"with that excellent..." GS to G&C, 25 November 1841, D.4/110, fo. 30, HBRS 6:96 n. 1.

Catherine Sinclair's marriage Frost, "Journal," *OHQ* 35 (December 1934): 369; Francis Ermatinger to Edward Ermatinger, 4 March 1842, Ermatinger, *Fur Trade Letters*, 250; Elliott, "Marguerite Wadin McKay McLoughlin," 338–40.

"I have never had..." Francis Ermatinger to Edward Ermatinger, 24 February 1834, Ermatinger, *Fur Trade Letters*, 173.

"My thoughts are much..." Francis Ermatinger to Edward Ermatinger, 24 March 1832, Ermatinger, *Fur Trade Letters*, 158.

"not given up Maria" Francis Ermatinger to Edward Ermatinger, 24 February 1834, Ermatinger, *Fur Trade Letters*, 172–73.

"Two things have influenced..." Francis Ermatinger to Edward Ermatinger, 11 March 1836, Ermatinger, *Fur Trade Letters*, 186.

"My application..." Francis Ermatinger to Edward Ermatinger, 19 March 1838, Ermatinger, *Fur Trade Letters*, 202.

"regular jolly jovial..." Allan, "Reminiscences," 80.

"and several others" Francis Ermatinger to Edward Ermatinger, 4 March 1842, Ermatinger, *Fur Trade Letters*, 250.

GS knighted HBRS 6:xiv.

318   *"all the functionaries..."* Wilkes, *Columbia River*, 12.

"Like all dinners...wives seem to be..." Wilkes, *Narrative*, 5:122.

"Their principal..." Ibid., 4:352.

"every facility..." Wilkes, *Columbia River*, 26.

Wilkes report Wilkes, "Report"; HBRS 6:143 n. 1.

Chapter 8–6: Golden California

319   *"unbounded influence"* JD to G&C, 18 October 1838, B.223/b/20, fos. 2–28d,

HBRS 4:249.

"You will endeavour..." McL to Captain Æmelius Simpson, 24 November 1830, B.223/b/6, fos. 22d–23, excerpt in *FTE*, 332.

"the only way..." McL to GS, 16 March 1831, D.4/125, fos. 77–79, HBRS 4:226. This letter reports Captain Simpson's recent arrival from Monterey.

320   *Early California brigades* HBRS 7:xix.

"abounds with Beaver...by stealth spending..." JD to G&C, 14 October 1839, A.11/69, fos. 72–89, HBRS 6:225, 207.

Harvest of furs McL to GS, 7 April 1841, B.223/b/28, fos. 2–5d, HBRS 6:257.

"when it was..." McL to GS, 20 March 1844, printed in Judson, "Documentary," 223.

"we think a store..." G&C to GS, 20 March 1839, A.6/25, fo. 28, HBRS 7:xxi.

"with a view..." Minutes of Council, 1839, in Oliver, *Canadian North-West*, 2:786. Alexander Simpson was Æmelius Simpson's half-brother, the stepson of Sir George's aunt, Mary Simpson.

"to collect all the..." Alexander Simpson to McL, 1 October 1840, quoting McL's instructions, B.223/b/28, fos. 34–39, HBRS 6:241.

"nearly all the Hides..." Ibid., 242–44.

321   *San Francisco trade* JD to McL, 23 March 1841, B.223/b/28, fos. 8–11d, HBRS 6:255.

"Grog shop keeper..." GS to G&C, 1 March 1842, D.4/110, fos. 55d–56, extract in HBRS 6:240–41 n. 1.

"from the Civil Government..." Alexander Simpson to McL, 1 October 1840, B.223/b/28, fos. 34–39, HBRS 6:240–41.

"expressed himself very..." Alexander Simpson to McL, 1 October 1840, B.223/b/28, fos. 34–39, HBRS 6:240.

321–22   *"relieves them entirely..."* JD to G&C, 14 October 1839, A.11/69, fos. 72–89, HBRS 6:206.

322   *"the first topic..."* JD, diary, 3 January 1841, MS quoted in HBRS 7:xxviii n. 1.

"as much as we..." McL to GS, 7 April 1841, B.223/b/28, fos. 2–5d, HBRS 6:258.

Vallejo's concern Tays, "Mariano Guadalupe Vallejo," 57.

"the whole trade..." JD to McL, 23 March 1841, B.223/b/28, fos. 8–11d, HBRS 6:252.

"to sail a vessel..." Ibid., 253–54.

"all fitted with commodious..." Ibid., 254.

323   *JD's tentative purchase* HBRS 7:xxiv.

       "*Mr. Douglas fully...*" McL to GS, 7 April 1841, B.223/b/28, fos. 2–5d, HBRS 6:257–58.

       Rae to California HBRS 7:xxiii.

       "*The worst characters...*" McL to G&C, 31 October 1842, B.223/b/29, fos. 75–91, HBRS 6:88.

       John McLoughlin's qualifications HBRS 6:xxx.

       GS criticizes promotion McL to GS, 1 February 1844, D.5/10, fos. 125–61, HBRS 6:377. This letter contains a number of quotations from letters written by GS to McL.

       "*Merely from a...*" Ibid., 378.

324   "*I acted on the full...*" McL to GS, 7 March 1842, B.223/b/29, fos. 71–73, HBRS 6:282–83.

       Eloisa delivers child David McLoughlin Papers, OHSL.

       "*Mr. Rae stayed only...*" Harvey, "Biography of Her Father," 27.

325   *Purchase of building* McL to G&C, 4 November 1842, B.223/b/29, fos. 93–98d, HBRS 6:104.

       "*had on it a large...*" Harvey, "Biography of Her Father," 21.

Chapter 9–1: Upheaval

327   "*Sir George Simpsons Visit...*" McL to J. H. Pelly, 12 July 1846, A.10/22, fos. 33–41d, HBRS 7:171.

329   *Arrival of GS* McLoughlin said the date was August 24 (McL to G&C, 17 September 1841, A.11/70, fos. 17–18, HBRS 6:40); Simpson said it was August 25 (GS to G&C, 25 November 1841, D.4/110, fo. 7, HBRS 6:40 n. 5).

       "*possibly...the Boilers...*" Captain McNeill, 2 May 1841, quoted in McL to G&C, 24 May 1841, A.11/70, fos. 13–16d, HBRS 6:36.

       Simpson's decision HBRS 6:xv.

330   *Silk hats replace beaver* HBRS 6:387.

       "*no very cheering...*" G&C to McL, 27 September 1843, A.6/26, fos. 78d–85, HBRS 6:306.

       "*The trade of the...*" GS to G&C, 25 November 1841, D.4/110, fos. 15–15d, HBRS 6:xvi.

331   "*entirely at the mercy...*" McL to G&C, 31 October 1842, B.223/b/29, fos. 75–91, HBRS 6:71.

       "*The Governor and Committee...*" Resolution passed by the Council at Norway House, June 1836, in Oliver, *Canadian North-West*, 2:727.

"*We were glad...*" G&C to McL, 8 September 1841, A.6/25, fo. 145, quoted in McL to G&C, 31 October 1842, B.223/b/29, fos. 75–91, HBRS 6:70.

"*We are decidedly...Officers & men...*" G&C to McL, 27 September 1843, A.6/26, fos. 78d–85, HBRS 6:309.

332   "*the Establishments...*" McL to G&C, 4 November 1842, B.223/b/29, fos. 93–98d, HBRS 6:100.

Conferences with GS HBRS 6:xv–xvi.

"*wanting in the courtesy...had not had...*" GS to Pelly, 23 November 1842, D.4/61, fo. 9d, HBRS 6:xvi.

"*The Doctor is as much...*" GS to Colvile, 15 November 1841, D.4/113, fos. 378–380d, HBRS 6:xvii.

"*too great a risk...*" G&C to McL, 8 December 1835, A.6/23, fos. 154–154d, HBRS 4:154 n. 1.

Reasons for moving headquarters HBRS 6:xviii.

333   "*the most economical...*" McL to G&C, 15 November 1836, B.223/b/12, fos. 32–32d, HBRS 4:155.

Sites for headquarters G&C to McL or officer in charge, 21 December 1842, A.6/26, fos. 34–39d, HBRS 6:297; HBRS 6:xviii.

"*a secure harbor...*" JD to GS, 18 March 1838, B.223/b/20, fos. 68–83d, HBRS 4:287.

"*in ill health...*" GS to G&C, 5 January 1843, B.223/b/29, fos. 23–28d, HBRS 6:350.

"*When the Indians...*" Harvey, "Biography of Her Father," 19–20.

"*exposed to very...*" McL to G&C, 31 October 1842, B.223/b/29, fos. 75–91, HBRS 6:88, 89; see also McL to GS, 1 February 1844, D.5/10, fos. 125–61, HBRS 6:374.

Chapter 9–2: Oahu

334   "*I went with my...*" Harvey, "Biography of Her Father," 22.

Monterey an open post HBRS 7:xxiii.

"*flocked down...after a good deal...*" GS, *Narrative*, 1:343, 357.

GS closes Yerba Buena GS to McL, 1 March 1842, D.4/27, fos. 3–9d, HBRS 6:266–68.

"*in California and all...*" McL to J. H. Pelly, 12 July 1846, A.10/22, fos. 33–41d, HBRS 7:168.

"*I believe you fully...*" GS to McL, 1 March 1842, D.4/27, fos. 3–9d, HBRS 6:266, 267.

335   *GS requests memoranda* HBRS 6:xviii.

             McL's estimate of Beaver's cost McL to GS, 10 February 1842, D.4/111, fos. 84–91d, HBRS 6:xix.

             "they would have cleared..." Ibid.

335–36   *"except one, who..."* McL to GS, 1 March 1842, B.223/b/29, fos. 67–70, HBRS 6:276.

336   *"After the best..."* GS to McL, 1 March 1842, D.4/27, fos. 3–9d, HBRS 6:262–63.

             "had more effect..." GS to G&C, 25 November 1841, D.4/110, fos. 16d–17, HBRS 6:xix.

             "It is, I know,..." A. C. Anderson to GS, 16 June 1841, D.5/6, fos. 154–57, HBRS 6:xix–xx.

             "overawed by the exhibition..." G&C to McL, 27 September 1843, A.6/26, fo. 81, HBRS 6:xxi.

             "losing character...weak and..." GS to McL, 1 March 1842, D.4/27, fos. 3–9d, HBRS 6:265.

             "ill-judged...in so short...loss and inconvenience" GS to McL, 3 March 1842, D.4/27, fos. 12–16, HBRS 6:278.

336–37   *"I do not see...either upon...alone, unencumbered..."* Ibid., 278–79.

337   *"would feel disposed..."* GS to Pelly, 23 November 1842, relating discussion with McL, D.4/61, fo. 15, HBRS 7:lix.

             "some 100 or 150..." GS to McL, 3 March 1842, D.4/27, fos. 12–16, HBRS 6:277.

             Streets bounding HBC property HBRS 7:xxix; Harvey, "Biography of Her Father," 21.

             "to carry on a regular...heard of a single..." McL to GS, 7 March 1842, B.223/b/29, fos. 71–73, HBRS 6:282–83.

             "afford so good..." McL to GS, 1 March 1842, B.223/b/29, fos. 67–70, HBRS 6:273.

             "every man hides..." McL to GS, 7 March 1842, B.223/b/29, fos. 71–73, HBRS 6:284.

338   *"I am not aware..."* Ibid., 285.

             "The only apology..." McL to GS, 1 March 1842, B.223/b/29, fos. 67–70, HBRS 6:276.

             "You seem to think..." JD to GS, 16 November 1843, D.5/9, fos. 229–36, HBRS 6:xvii.

             "I do not consider it...in the remarks..." GS to McL, 3 March 1842, D.4/27, fos. 12–16, HBRS 6:282.

"and these statements..." GS to McL, 7 March 1842, D.4/27, fos. 17d–19, HBRS 6:288.

"informing him..." McL to Pelly, 12 July 1846, A.10/22, fos. 33–41d, HBRS 7:167.

"as it puts an end..." GS to Pelly, 23 November 1842, D.4/61, fos. 9–9d, HBRS 7:167 n. 1.

Chapter 9–3: "A Rack to Ones Feeling"

339   *GS goes north* HBRS 6:xxii.

"On arrival..." GS to McL, 27 April 1842, D.4/27, fos. 41–42d, HBRS 6:343. Simpson relates his approach to the fort in *Narrative*, 2:181.

340   *"the whole conduct..."* GS to McL, 27 April 1842, D.4/27, fos. 41–42d, HBRS 6:344–45.

"had become a slave..." GS to G&C, 6 July 1842, D.4/110, fos. 98d–99, HBRS 6:xxxi.

"My son John..." McL to Edward Ermatinger, 1 February 1843, University of British Columbia, Special Collections, printed in Ermatinger, "Tragedy," 131.

"To die is the fate..." McL to Edward Ermatinger, 16 February 1846, National Archives of Canada, Ermatinger Estate fonds, MG 19, A 2, ser. 2, vol. 1, p. 220.

341   *GS at Stikine* HBRS 6:xxxi.

"as a Father..." McL to G&C, 4 December 1843, B.223/b/30, fos. 157–60, HBRS 6:181.

"a poor soft half Breed..." McL to G&C, 24 June 1842, B.223/b/29, fos. 2–18, HBRS 6:44, 52.

Death of McL's mother ME, 49, 60.

"traces of her beauty..." Sister Marie de St. Thomas d'Aquin, "Conquered by Faith," printed in Pelletier, *Album Historique*, 71.

"a thundering epistle..." John Tod to Edward Ermatinger, 1 September 1842, MS in Provincial Library, Victoria, B.C., extract in Ermatinger, "Tragedy," 132.

"the most Extraordinary..." McL to G&C, 24 June 1842, B.223/b/29, fos. 2–18, HBRS 6:43–46.

"I have no Doubt..." Ibid., 43.

342   *GS suggests dropping case* HBRS 6:xxxii.

"to Investigate..." McL to G&C, 24 June 1842, B.223/b/29, fos. 2–18, HBRS 6:43.

"In the meantime..." Ibid., 53.

"Chief Factor Douglas..." McL to G&C, 2 August 1843, A.11/70, fo. 31, HBRS 6:109.

Kanaquassé report "Pierre Kanaquassé's Narrative...On Board Schooner Cadboro

21 June 1842," B.223/b/29, fos. 48–53, HBRS 6:xxxiii–xxxiv; McL to G&C, 7 July 1842, B.223/b/29, fos. 29–30, HBRS 6:60–61.

343   *"the depositions made..."* McL to G&C, 19 August 1842, B.223/b/29, fos. 39–41d, HBRS 6:67, 68.

Fresh crew at Stikine Ibid., 67.

McL attends Mass George B. Roberts to Frances Fuller Victor, 23 May 1879, Roberts, "Round Hand," 209.

"He read it with avidity..." Blanchet, *Historical Sketches*, 75.

Evidence discovered HBRS 6:xxxvii.

344   *"tickled Cadotte..."* McL to G&C, 18 November 1843, B.223/b/30, fos. 74–95, HBRS 6:175–76.

"did not see..." Rowand to McL, 11 March 1843, D.5/10, fos. 126–27, quoted in McL to GS, 1 February 1844, D.5/10, 125–61, HBRS 6:355–56.

"the precise words" GS to Rowand, 15 June 1844, D.4/31, fo. 81d, quoted in HBRS 6:xxxix.

"The fact is if..." Rowand to GS, 16 August 1844 (private), D.5/12, fos. 184–85, HBRS 6:xxxix.

"The more I see..." John McLoughlin to Work, 3 June 1841, Howay collection, University of British Columbia.

"I am sorry..." John McLoughlin to Work, 2 October 1841, HBCA, John McLoughlin, jnr., Folder.

344–45   *"I am daily..."* John McLoughlin to Work, 2 December 1841, HBCA, John McLoughlin, jnr., Folder.

345   *"I am happy..."* John McLoughlin to Finlayson, 2 December 1841, B.201/c/1, fos. 1–2, HBRS 6:xxxvi.

"I wish with all..." John McLoughlin to Finlayson, 14 February 1842, B.201/c/1, fos. 3–4, HBRS 6:xxxvii.

"I cannot trust..." John McLoughlin to Finlayson, 26 February 1842, B.201/c/1, fos. 5–6, HBRS 6:xxxvii.

"If the Steamer..." McL to G&C, 31 October 1842, quoting his son's wife, B.223/b/29, fos. 75–91, HBRS 6:85.

"I am now forty..." McL to GS, 1 February 1844, D.5/10, fos. 125–61, HBRS 6:360.

"I had sent..." McL to GS, 20 March 1843, D.5/8, fos. 151–62, HBRS 6:xxxvii.

"I am convinced..." Work to GS, 5 July 1842 (private), D.5/7, fos. 94–95, HBRS 6:xxxviii.

345–46   *"The crime was clearly..."* Barclay to GS, 1 June 1843, D.5/8, fos. 274–75,

HBRS 6:xli.

346   *"I have read attentively..."* Barclay to GS, 4 September 1843, D.5/8, fos. 502–3, HBRS 6:xli–xlii.

"a necessary measure...I have said..." JD to GS, 5 March 1845, D.5/13, fos. 17–24, HBRS 7:177–78.

"the fag and wear..." JD to GS, 20 March 1846, D.5/16, fos. 460–65, HBRS 7:lviii n. 2.

"the pile upon pile..." McDonald to GS, 27 April 1843, D.5/8, fos. 246–47, HBRS 6:xliv.

347   *"I fear we have..."* McDonald to Edward Ermatinger, 15 June 1848, Ermatinger, "Tragedy," 132.

"How the matter..." John Tod to Edward Ermatinger, 10 March 1845, Ermatinger Papers, transcript in Library of the University of British Columbia, quoted in HBRS 6:xliv.

"too deeply interested..." G&C to McL, 27 September 1843, A.6/26, fos. 78d–85, HBRS 6:308.

"We cannot dismiss..." Ibid., 312.

"he has not been..." Barclay to GS, 4 September 1843, D.5/8, fos. 502–3, HBRS 6:xlii.

"in that part..." Pelly to GS, 3 November 1843, D.5/9, fos. 170–71, HBRS 6:xlv.

347–48 *"fudge alleged...an expense..."* Barclay to GS, 18 November 1843 (private), D.5/9, fo. 246, HBRS 6:xlv.

348   *McL sends documents and men east* HBRS 6:xlvi.

Opinion of Thom GS to G&C, 21 June 1844, A.12/2, fos. 398–428, quoted in HBRS 6:xlvi.

"the most serious..." Ibid.

"avoid popular..." Ibid., xlvii.

"so that your honors..." Ibid.

"acted like a fool" Barclay to GS, 19 August 1844, D.5/12, fos. 193–94, HBRS 6:xlviii.

Threat to charge costs to McL Barclay to McL, 30 November 1844, A.6/26, fo. 140, HBRS 6:xlviii.

"as it would cost..." McL to Edward Ermatinger, 16 February 1846, National Archives of Canada, Ermatinger Estate fonds, MG 19, A 2, ser. 2, vol. 1, p. 222.

349   *"If Simpson was right..."* Lamb, Introduction to HBRS 6:xlix.

McL alienates friends Rich, *History of the Hudson's Bay Society,* vol. 2, HBRS

22:716.

"exceedingly meagre..." Barclay to GS, 1 June 1843, D.5/8, fos. 274–75, HBRS 6:xlix.

Pelly's warning to McL McL to Sir John Pelly, 12 July 1846, A.10/22, fos. 33–41d, HBRS 7:164.

"Sir George Simpsons Visit..." Ibid., 171.

Chapter 10–1: Willamette Valley

349   *"We deem it highly..."* Report to Meeting, 6 March 1843, printed in Duniway and Riggs, "Oregon Archives," 226.

351   *Methodist missions* Lee and Frost, *Ten Years*, 152, 226, 269, 275; Carey, *General History*, 295.

"Dr. M'L. kindly..." Lee and Frost, *Ten Years*, 134.

Lee returns in Nereide Ibid., 137.

"rough fir boards..." Ibid., 295.

"Mrs. Kone's health..." Ibid., 296.

"No men, in my opinion,..." McLoughlin, "Document," 50; Clarke, *Pioneer Days*, 1:220.

352   *School for whites* Lee and Frost, *Ten Years*, 303–4. The Oregon Institute later became Willamette University.

"backwoodsmen from the..." Pipes, "Extracts," 189. The French government sent de Mofras to Oregon to investigate its commercial possibilities.

"They have very pretty..." Palmer, *Journal*, 85.

353   *Matthieu and Dr. Fraser* Matthieu, "Reminiscences," 75, 102.

"The old doctor..." Crawford, "Missionaries," 10–11.

"They look on us..." McL to G&C, 18 November 1843, B.223/b/30, fos. 74–95, HBRS 6:160.

"to get our wheat..." Lee and Frost, *Ten Years*, 249.

Price for wheat McL to G&C, 15 November 1843, B.223/b/30, fos. 52–67, HBRS 6:124–25. A clipping from the *Times* (London), 15 December 1843, said that wheat "is worth 80 c. per bushel at Fort Vancouver" and that it was paid "in goods, at a low rate." A.11/70, fo. 122A, HBRS 7:256.

"is supposed..." Wilkes, *Narrative*, 4:365.

356   *Measuring wheat* Matthieu, "Reminiscences," 90; Lansford W. Hastings to McL, 8 April 1843, in Correspondence regarding the Shortess Petition, B.223/b/31, fos. 16–19d, HBRS 7:252; Shortess petition, printed in Duniway and Riggs, "Oregon Archives," 230.

Kicking bushel McL to Hastings, 10 April 1843, in Correspondence regarding the Shortess Petition, B.223/b/31, fos. 16–19d, HBRS 7:253. Elijah White confirmed McLoughlin's measurement. Allen, *Ten Years,* 201.

"The truth is..." McL to Hastings, 10 April 1843, in Correspondence regarding the Shortess Petition, B.223/b/31, fos. 16–19d, HBRS 7:253–54.

"to his chagrin..." Matthieu, "Reminiscences," 90; see also *CPT,* 113–14.

G&C's plan to strengthen claims G&C to Duncan Finlayson and the Councils of the Northern and Southern Departments, 1 June 1842, A.6/26, fos. 14–14d, HBRS 6:77 n. 2.

"I regret to..." McL to G&C, 20 November 1840, B.223/b/28, fos. 58–65, HBRS 6:17.

"houses will be..." HBCA, PSAC Deeds and Agreements, 1841, quoting instructions of GS, 10 September 1840, HBRS 6:78 n. 3.

Red River settlers GS to G&C, 25 November 1841, D.4/10, fos. 24–24d, HBRS 7:xxxv n. 1.

356–57 *"every indulgence..."* McL to G&C, 15 November 1843, B.223/b/30, fos. 46–50, HBRS 6:120.

357 *Settlers move to Willamette* JD to GS, 10 March 1843, D.5/8, fos. 143–44, HBRS 7:xxxv; Galbraith, "Puget's Sound Agricultural Company," 255–56.

"The fact is..." McL to G&C, 15 November 1843, B.223/b/30, fos. 46–50, HBRS 6:120.

358 *"I could not believe..."* McL to G&C, 21 November 1840, B.223/b/28, fos. 66–67, HBRS 6:32–33.

"a gentleman..." Spaulding Report, House of Representatives, Report No. 830, 27th Cong., 2d sess., pp. 56–57, quoted in HBRS 6:119 n. 1.

"with violence blood..." Spaulding Report, quoted in McL to G&C, 15 November 1843, B.223/b/30, fos. 68–72, HBRS 6:143, 145.

"Capt. Spaulding has..." McL to G&C, 15 November 1843, B.223/b/30, fos. 46–50, HBRS 6:118–19. McLoughlin wrote four letters to the Governor and Committee the same day, doubtless because he was upset.

"has had the effect..." McL to G&C, 12 August 1844, B.223/b/31, fos. 103d–106, HBRS 7:4.

358–59 *Immigration of 1842* McL to G&C, 31 October 1842, B.223/b/29, fos. 75–91, HBRS 6:75–77; Crawford, "Occasional Address," 14; Bancroft, *Oregon,* 1:255–62.

359 *American majority* GS to G&C, 25 November 1841, D.4/110, fo. 28, HBRS 7:xxxiv.

Linn resolution Senate Journal, 27th Cong., 2d sess., 1841–42, p. 81, cited in *OQ*, 192.

"a barred and indifferent..." Ashburton to Lord Aberdeen, 25 April 1842, quoted in *OQ*, 205.

Boundary disputes OQ, 191.

Webster-Ashburton negotiations OQ, 189–215.

Joint occupation renewed OQ, 215.

Chapter 10–2: The Wolf Meetings

360 *McL hires Hastings and Hudspeth* McL, Statement on Land Claim, B.223/b/31, fos. 2–14, HBRS 7:202; Correspondence regarding the Shortess Petition, B.223/b/31, fos. 16–19d, HBRS 7:251; Hastings, *Emigrants' Guide*, 56.

Town on two levels Corning, *Willamette Landings*, 32.

McL sells lots McL, "Notice," 27 March 1843; McL, Deed to Pomeroy, 2 March 1843; McL, Deed to Wilson, 26 December 1842, all in Duniway and Riggs, "Oregon Archives," 233–36.

"In all there are..." Hastings, *Emigrants' Guide*, 54.

"a very good..." Lee and Frost, *Ten Years*, 330.

HBC store McL to G&C, 1 July 1846, citing instructions of 1842, A.10/22, fos. 1–8, HBRS 7:155.

Elijah White Bancroft, *Oregon*, 1:155.

White as subagent McL to G&C, 31 October 1842, B.223/b/29, fos. 75–91, HBRS 6:76; Johansen and Gates, *Empire*, 186, 189; Bancroft, *Oregon*, 1:155.

"On Dr. White's..." McL to G&C, 31 October 1842, B.223/b/29, fos. 75–91, HBRS 6:76; see also *CPT*, 350 n. 20.

361 *Rumor of attack CPT*, 143–44.

"as a private..." McL to Archibald McKinlay, 14 April 1843, enclosed in McL to G&C, 15 November 1843, B.223/b/30, fos. 52–67, HBRS 6:129.

"A momentary excitement..." McL to G&C, 15 November 1843, B.223/b/30, fos. 52–67, HBRS 6:128–29.

Oregon Lyceum Gray, *History of Oregon*, 261; Bancroft, *Oregon*, 1:296–97; Johansen and Gates, *Empire*, 188; Hastings, letter in *Saint Louis New Era*.

"question of...the side of an..." Gray, *History of Oregon*, 261.

361–62 *"this independent government...that it is expedient..."* Abernethy to Gray, 11 March 1866, printed in Gray, *History of Oregon*, 269.

362 *"resulted in a determination..."* Hastings, letter in *Saint Louis New Era*.

"An influx of..." McL to G&C, 4 July 1844, B.223/b/31, fos. 95–101, HBRS

6:200.

Willamette population "Documents," *OHQ* 1 (September 1900): 327–28, including "Extract of Letter Dated Wilhamet, February 19, 1842," from New York
Tribune, 18 January 1842. It lists 125–30 adult white males, including 50 Americans and 75–80 French Canadians. Thornton estimates that in 1840 there were
63 French Canadians, including 3 priests, and "an aggregate of 137 Americans."
"Provisional Government," 45. George Simpson's estimate was 500 souls—60 Canadians and others with Indian wives, and 65 American families. *Narrative*, 1:249.

363   *"Our idea was,..."* Gray, *History of Oregon*, 261.

Meeting of February 2 W. H. Willson, Minutes, in Duniway and Riggs, "Oregon
Archives," 221–22; Grover, *Oregon Archives*, 8. The minutes contain only
measures that were adopted, with no record of discussions or discarded ideas.

"fully attended, and all..." Gray, *History of Oregon*, 261.

Meeting of March 6 Duniway and Riggs, "Oregon Archives," 222–27; Gray,
History of Oregon, 262–67; Grover, *Oregon Archives*, 9–11.

"square hewed logs..." Labonte, "Reminiscences," 174. Gervais, who had come
to the Columbia in 1811 with Astor's overland expedition, was sometimes employed as *engagé* in a company brigade. *CPT*, 53–54.

"informed of the main..." Gray, *History of Oregon*, 263.

Bounties Duniway and Riggs, "Oregon Archives," 222, 226–27; Grover, *Oregon
Archives*, 9–11.

364   *"How is it, fellow-citizens,..."* Gray, *History of Oregon*, 266–67.

"that a committee..." Duniway and Riggs, "Oregon Archives," 223, 226; Grover,
Oregon Archives, 11.

Meeting of March 17 McL to G&C, 20 March 1843, enclosed in GS to G&C,
21 June 1843, FO 5/401, quoted in Clark, *Willamette Valley*, 1:793–94; Gray,
History of Oregon, 268; *CPT*, 147, 351 n. 26.

"disposed to ridicule..." Gray, *History of Oregon*, 268, 270.

Decision not to have governor Ibid., 269–70.

"for the purpose..." Duniway and Riggs, "Oregon Archives," 238, from notes
taken by Grover.

"erect a temporary...though none..." McL to GS, 20 March 1843, enclosed in GS
to G&C, 21 June 1843, FO 5/401, extracts in Clark, *Willamette Valley*, 1:793–94.

Chapter 10–3: Champoeg

365   *"Dear Sir, I have..."* Hastings to McL, 8 April 1843, in Correspondence regarding the Shortess Petition, B.223/b/31, fos. 16–19d, HBRS 7:251–52.

366   *"I am astonished..."* McL to Hastings, 10 April 1843, in Correspondence

regarding the Shortess Petition, B.223/b/31, fos. 16–19d, HBRS 7:253–54.

"My mind was full..." Quoted in Lee and Frost, *Ten Years*, 263. Shortess died in 1877 near Astoria, "where he had lived as a recluse." *Ashland (Oregon) Tidings*, 14 September 1877, quoted in Bancroft, *Oregon*, 1:207 n. 31.

"bitter accusations..." White to T. Hartley Crawford, Commissioner of Indian Affairs, 1 April 1843, printed in White, *Concise View*, 172; Allen, *Ten Years*, 200–201.

"for want of time..." Gray, *History of Oregon*, 297.

Sutton gives petition to Senator Linn Clipping from the *Times* (London), 19 July 1845, quoting *Springfield (Illinois) Journal*, A.11/70, fo. 122A, HBRS 7:256.

367		*"without consulting any one..."* Shortess to Elwood Evans, 1 September 1867, Evans, *Pacific Northwest*, 1:243.

Authorship of petition Carey says it was "probably" drafted by Abernethy. *General History*, 332. Duniway and Riggs put a star beside Waller's name as "signature of author." "Oregon Archives," 232.

"in common fairness...as the document...so as I might...perhaps the person..." McL to Shortess, 13, 23 April 1843; Shortess to McL, 14 April, 24 July 1843, Correspondence regarding the Shortess Petition, B.223/b/31, fos. 16–19d, HBRS 7:254–56.

"to adopt some..." McL to G&C, 20 March 1843, enclosed in GS to G&C, 21 June 1843, FO 5/401, extract in Clark, *Willamette Valley*, 1:793–94.

McL's pressure on Canadians Thornton said the Canadians "held one meeting at Vancouver, one at the Willamette Falls, and two at the Catholic Church in the French Prairie," and that "a system of hostile measures [was] agreed upon." "Provisional Government," 61. Thornton was not in Oregon at that time, but arrived shortly after.

368		*"the priests and..."* Gray, *History of Oregon*, 273, 279.

"at the instigation..." Le Breton to Caleb Cushing, 1 December 1843, Cushing Papers, Library of Congress, quoted in Johansen and Gates, *Empire*, 189.

"in the spring of..." McL to Captain John Gordon, 15 September 1845, printed in Scott, "Report of Lieutenant Peel," 57.

Champoeg CPT, 43–61.

HBC warehouse CPT, 109–10; Geer, *Fifty Years*, 175; Matthieu, "Reminiscences," 102. The warehouse was apparently built after the fall of 1841, when Charles Wilkes and Eugene Duflot de Mofras both referred to the HBC post at the falls but not to one at Champoeg, and before the spring of 1843, when, according to Matthieu, he helped build an addition to it.

HBC store at Champoeg CPT, 112; HBRS 7:138 n. 2.

Settlement at Champoeg CPT, 116–17.

369   *Population* Clark, *Willamette Valley,* 1:283.

"*in a Hudson's Bay...*" Matthieu,"Reminiscences," 92.

"*The committee made...*" Duniway and Riggs, "Oregon Archives," 236; Grover, *Oregon Archives,* 14.

"*Says Le Breton,...*" Gray, *History of Oregon,* 279.

370   *Meek's role* Meek's part in the meeting is affirmed in Gray, *History of Oregon,* 279; Geer, *Fifty Years,* 175; Bancroft, *Oregon,* 1:303–4; Matthieu, "Reminiscences," 94; and Victor, *River of the West,* 321. Thornton said Joe Meek "thundered out with an earnestness not less than he would manifest in an attack upon a grizzly bear, 'who's for a divide?'" "Provisional Government," 61–62. Others, including John Minto and the Reverend J. S. Griffin, are cited in CPT, 353 n. 14. See Thomas, "Truth and Fiction," 222–24.

"*how old Joe Meek...*" Matthieu, "Reminiscences," 94.

"*It was moved by...*" Minutes of the May 2 meeting, Duniway and Riggs, "Oregon Archives," 236–37; Grover, *Oregon Archives,* 14.

"*quite suspicious...*" Matthieu,"Reminiscences," 89. A monument at Champoeg names those who voted pro "as far as obtainable." The fifty-two names were compiled in 1901 by George H. Himes of the OHS through correspondence with old settlers, with Matthieu's help. For many years, the annual programs for services at the monument contained revised lists, as errors were discovered. The fifty-third name on the monument, Adam Hewitt, was inscribed later. CPT, 243–53.

372   *Election of officers, decision to meet on July 5* Duniway and Riggs, "Oregon Archives," 236–38.

Significance of Champoeg vote CPT, 157–60.

Chapter 10–4: The Provisional Government

373   *Legislative committee* This committee consisted of Robert Moore (chairman), David Hill, Robert Shortess, Alanson Beers, Thomas J. Hubbard, William H. Gray, James A. O'Neil, Robert Newell, and William Dougherty. Gray, Hubbard, O'Neil, and Shortess had signed the Shortess petition. Duniway and Riggs, "Oregon Archives," 237, 232–33.

Payments to committee Every member subscribed his own per diem pay, and in addition "Alanson Beers, Rev. J. L. Parish, and Dr. Ira Babcock subscribed the full amount for board of the whole nine." Gray, *History of Oregon,* 336.

"*sixteen by thirty...*" Ibid.

"*sitting by a square-legged...*" Ibid.

Robert Moore Dobbs, *Men of Champoeg,* 115–19; Bancroft, *Oregon,* 1:237–38 n. 29. Born in Pennsylvania in 1781, Moore emigrated to Missouri in 1822, served in that state's legislature, moved to Illinois in 1835, and went to Oregon in 1840.

"as they did not want..." Gray, *History of Oregon,* 338.

374   *Qualifications of committee* CPT, 160; Bancroft, *Oregon,* 1:237–38 n. 29.

"from the deep interest..." Gray, *History of Oregon,* 339.

"Moved and carried..." Duniway and Riggs, "Oregon Archives," 245.

Decisions of committee Ibid., 240–51.

"and give the reason's..." Ibid., 246.

"No member of the House..." Ibid., 248.

"nearly all the Americans..." Hines, *Life on the Plains,* 425; CPT, 161–62.

"dwelt principally...glorious deeds..." Gray, *History of Oregon,* 346.

"in the true spirit..." Hines, *Life on the Plains,* 425.

375   *Four districts* Duniway and Riggs, "Oregon Archives," 266.

"an English or...Another prominent,..." Gray, *History of Oregon,* 340–41.

Executive Committee Duniway and Riggs, "Oregon Archives," 254, 258.

"No person demeaning himself..." Ibid., 253, 257.

"the utmost good faith..." Report, Committee on the Judiciary, Article III, adopted 5 July 1843, ibid., 257.

"there shall be neither..." Ibid., Article IV, paragraph 1, 258.

376   *"every free, male ..."* Ibid., paragraph 4.

"hold a claim..." Report, Committee on Private Land Claims, adopted 5 July 1843, in Duniway and Riggs, "Oregon Archives," 267. The minutes say the report was adopted "with a proviso" (255); an editor's note on the report says "Proviso not found" (267).

"provided that nothing..." Organic Laws, Fair Copy, Rearranged after May 1844, Article 2nd, Section 17th.—Land Claims, in Duniway and Riggs, "Oregon Archives," 279.

"The American population..." McL to G&C, 15 November 1843, B.223/b/30, fos. 52–67, HBRS 6:129–30.

Chapter 10–5: The First Great Immigration

377   *Senator Linn* Johansen and Gates, *Empire,* 180–81, 184, 186, 191; Bancroft, *Oregon,* 1:176, 217–18, 370–81.

Free land Johansen and Gates, *Empire,* 184, 186; Bancroft, *Oregon,* 1:379; Carey,

General History, 447.

378   *Immigration of 1843* Holman, *Dr. John McLoughlin,* 70–78; Bancroft, *Oregon,* 1:406–19.

         "the Country is...take such measures..." McL to G&C, 15 November 1843, B.223/b/30, fos. 52–67, HBRS 6:140–41.

         "The Yankees are here..." Rev. J. L. Parrish, quoted by Rev. I. D. Driver, "Annual Address," 26–27; see also Clarke, *Pioneer Days,* 1:213.

         Anti-HBC prejudice Rich, *History of the Hudson's Bay Company,* vol. 2, HBRS 22:703.

379   *"our soil..."* Linn, speech to Senate, January 1843, quoted in McL to G&C, 4 December 1843, A.11/70, fos. 41–46, HBRS 6:184, 186. This letter, printed on pp. 184–92, discusses Linn's speech at length.

         "This is a foul..." McL to G&C, 4 December 1843, A.11/70, fos. 41–46, HBRS 6:186.

         "They expected when..." McL to G&C, 19 July 1845, A.11/70, fos. 112–21, HBRS 7:86–87.

380   *Hardships of immigrants* "Ford's Road-Makers," MS in Bancroft Library, quoted in Bancroft, *Oregon,* 1:408–11; *Oregon Spectator,* 21 January 1847, 2.

         "deep, frightful..." Hastings, *Emigrants' Guide,* 29.

         "I carry my babe..." Geer, "Diary," 171; also in Geer, *Fifty Years,* 146. Elizabeth Smith, whose husband died on the trail, later married Theodore T. Geer.

381   *"searched upon his knees,..."* "Ford's Road-Makers," MS in Bancroft Library, quoted in Bancroft, *Oregon,* 1:411.

         "many were relieved..." *Oregon Spectator,* 21 January 1847.

         "the first full meal..." Jesse Applegate, "Views of Oregon History," MS, quoted in Bancroft, *Oregon,* 1:410 n. 37.

382   *"Tut! tut! tut!..."* Dr. William McKay, interview in Clarke, *Pioneer Days,* 1:226–27.

         "We are all..." "John M. Shively's Memoir," part 1, *OHQ* 81 (Spring 1980): 23–24. Shively's "ticking" referred to ticks or fleas.

         Population doubled No accurate census exists. *CPT,* 151, says a "reasonable estimate" for spring 1843 is about 215 adult males. Adult males in the fall immigration numbered about 290. *CPT,* 164. Bancroft, *Oregon,* 1:395 n. 4, cites various other estimates.

         Burnett's cattle Burnett, journal, printed in Wilkes, *The History of Oregon,* 90. Burnett's journal offended McKinlay, but McLoughlin assured him that he knew settlers often asked for such exchanges, and that those he had talked with expressed "the Warmest terms of Gratitude for the Very Kind Manner you had treated them." McL to Archibald McKinlay, 30 November 1847, Sampson, *Business Correspondence*, 74–76; see also 76 n. 127.

383   *"Are you aware?..."* Burnett, journal, in Wilkes, *The History of Oregon*, 98.

"with the courtesy..." Frémont, *Report*, 183, quoted in Egan, *Frémont*, 175.

Frémont at fort Egan, *Frémont*, 174–77.

384   *Mt. St. Helens eruptions* Scott, *History of the Oregon Country*, 4:120; Holmes, *Mount St. Helens*.

"Ashes were falling..." Lee and Frost, *Ten Years*, 257.

385   *Credit to settlers* HBRS 7:lii.

"an enormous sum..." GS to McL, 16 June 1844, D.4/31, fo. 95, HBRS 7:lii.

"so lax a system..." Barclay to McL, 30 November 1844, A.6/26, fo. 140d, HBRS 7:lii.

"if I had acted..." McL to Sir J. H. Pelly, 12 July 1846, A.10/22, fos. 33–41d, HBRS 7:162–63.

"will cause a great..." McL to G&C, 4 July 1844, B.223/b/31, fos. 95–101, HBRS 6:200–201.

"the restless Americans..." JD to G&C, 18 October 1838, B.223/b/20, fos. 2–28d, HBRS 4:241–42.

Trouble at missions Spalding, *Diaries*, 300, 307–8; Josephy, *Nez Perce Indians*, 205–6; Bancroft, *Oregon*, 1:333–35; Drury, *Marcus and Narcissa*, 1:95–97, 435.

386   *Narcissa Whitman frightened* Drury, *Marcus and Narcissa*, 2:14–18.

Whitman assists immigration Ibid., 76–83; Johansen and Gates, *Empire*, 172.

"One of them bawled..." McL, "Autobiography," in Clarke, *Pioneer Days*, 1:222.

"raised his cane..." Matthieu, "Reminiscences," 75.

Chapter 10–6: The Oregon City Land Claim

387   *Willamette Falls* Townsend, *Narrative*, 191–92; Palmer, *Journal*, 79.

Size of island Holman, *Dr. John McLoughlin*, 102.

GS and McL visit falls GS to G&C, 25 November 1841, D.4/110, fos. 37–37d, printed in "Letters of Sir George Simpson," 82.

First HBC mill Lamb, Introduction to HBRS 4:lxxiii.

"had a party..." McL, Statement on Land Claim, 1 March 1844, B.223/b/31, fos. 2–14, HBRS 7:199. The complete statement is printed on pp. 195–219.

"to take possession..." GS to G&C, 25 November 1841, D.4/110, fos. 37–37d, printed in "Letters of Sir George Simpson," 82.

"destined by nature..." McL to G&C, 20 November 1845, B.223/b/33, fos.

2–38, HBRS 7:119.

388   *"the H. B. Co. are erecting..."* Wyeth, *Correspondence and Journals,* 179.

"a little wooden..." Pipes, "Extracts," 160.

"In 1832 I had..." McL, Statement on Land Claim, 1 March 1844, B.223/b/31, fos. 2–14, HBRS 7:199.

Lee asks for land Ibid.

389   *"Vancouver, 21st July,..."* McL to Lee, 21 July 1840, in McL, Statement on Land Claim, 1 March 1844, B.223/b/31, fos. 2–14, HBRS 7:199–200.

"an evil moment..." Rich, Introduction to HBRS 7:xli.

390   *"considerable expense"* Wilkes, "Diary," *WHQ* 17 (January 1926): 44.

"gave him formal notice...desisted" McL, Statement on Land Claim, 1 March 1844, B.223/b/31, fos. 2–14, HBRS 7:200.

Island Milling Company Ibid., 218.

"more to temporal...and to that end,..." GS to G&C, 25 November 1841, D.4/110, fos. 37d–38, HBRS 7:xli–xlii.

391   *HBC decision to hold land* Rich, *History of the Hudson's Bay Company,* vol. 2, HBRS 22:706.

"I could not believe..." McL to G&C, 20 November 1845, B.223/b/33, fos. 2–38, HBRS 7:119.

"The Hudson's Bay Company..." Waller to his brother, 6 April 1842, Brosnan, *Jason Lee,* 178–79, reprinted from *Ohio Statesman,* 10 March 1843, first printed in *Christian Advocate and Journal,* 21 December 1842, 74.

"I told him..." McL to Jason Lee, 18 November 1842, printed in McL, Statement on Land Claim, 1 March 1844, B.223/b/31, fos. 2–14, HBRS 7:200–201.

392   *"considered that he..."* Lee to McL, 28 November 1842, ibid., 201–2.

McL meets Waller McL, Statement on Land Claim, 1 March 1844, B.223/b/31, fos. 2–14, HBRS 7:203.

"I will keep mine,..." Ibid.

McL pays Waller Ibid., 202–3.

"on the west side..." Ibid., 203.

"in the most public..." Appendix A to Shortess petition, Duniway and Riggs, "Oregon Archives," 234.

"In acting as I have..." McL to GS, 20 March 1843, quoted in McL to G&C, 20 November 1845, B.223/b/33, fos. 2–38, HBRS 7:121.

393   *"the legal capacity..."* Thom's opinion, B.223/b/30, fo. 96, HBRS 6:165 n. 1.

"As to the Falls..." McL to G&C, 18 November 1843, B.223/b/30, fos. 74–95,

HBRS 6:165.

"as vague and mysterious..." JD to GS, 4 April 1845, D.5/13, fos. 391–92, HBRS 7:190.

Land law of 1843 Duniway and Riggs, "Oregon Archives," 267.

Ricord in Oregon Bancroft, *Oregon,* 1:211–16; Holman, *Dr. John McLoughlin,* 212, 222.

Ricord's proposal Ricord to McL, 2 November 1843, in McL, Statement on Land Claim, 1 March 1844, B.223/b/31, fos. 2–14, HBRS 7:204–5.

"appeared to propose..." McL, Statement on Land Claim, 1 March 1844, B.223/b/31, fos. 2–14, HBRS 7:205.

Complaints against Lee Brosnan, *Jason Lee,* 244, 246, 248–51; Hines, *Missionary History,* 282–91.

393–94   *"Please tell Bro. Waller..."* Lee to Gustavus Hines, 1 July 1844, Brosnan, *Jason Lee,* 245.

394   *Lee's appearance before Mission Board* Brosnan, *Jason Lee,* 246–51; Hines, *Missionary History,* 306–13.

Lee's death T. T. Geer, *Fifty Years,* 59, 60; Brosnan, *Jason Lee,* 272. Sixty years later, in June 1905, Lee's body was reburied in the Lee Mission Cemetery in Salem, Oregon, near his wives and infant son.

"for the purpose..." Ricord proclamation, B.223/b/31, fos. 32–34d, HBRS 7:195–98; see also Holman, *Dr. John McLoughlin,* 212, 222.

"The Hudsons Bay..." Ricord proclamation, B.223/b/31, fos. 32–34d, HBRS 7:197.

"I am not claiming..." Notes on Mr. Records Letter, 8 December 1843, in McL, Statement on Land Claim, 1 March 1844, B.223/b/31, fos. 2–14, HBRS 7:211.

"the site at Wallamette..." JD to GS, private, 16 November 1843, D.5/9, fos. 229–36, HBRS 7:xlv.

395   *"prepared to sanction..."* GS to McL, 15 June 1844, D.4/31, fo. 82d, HBRS 7:xlvii.

"John McLoughlin Suspense..." GS to G&C, 21 June 1844, A.12/2, fos. 398–428, HBRS 7:xlvii.

"After they had..." McL, Statement on Land Claim, 1 March 1844, B.223/b/31, fos. 2–14, HBRS 7:214–15; Holman, *Dr. John McLoughlin,* 224–25. A manuscript copy is in the McLoughlin-Fraser Family Papers, OHSL, MS 927.

"had any gentleman..." White to T. Hartley Crawford, Commissioner of Indian Affairs, 1 April 1843, printed in Allen, *Ten Years,* 200.

"I hope..." White to J. M. Porter, Secretary of War, 15 November 1843, printed in Allen, *Ten Years,* 220.

Waller goes to The Dalles After the Dalles mission was closed, Waller returned to the Willamette Valley. Bancroft, *Oregon,* 1:190, 224.

396   *"offered to sell..."*   McL, Statement on Land Claim, B.223/b/31, fos. 2–14, HBRS 7:215.

McL's payment to mission   Gary valued the mission holdings at $6,000. Gary to McL, 15 July 1844, quoted in McL, Statement on Land Claim, B.223/b/31, fos. 20–23d, HBRS 7:216. McLoughlin told Captain John Gordon of HMS *America* that he paid $2,200 for lots and $3,800 for buildings. 15 September 1845, extract in Clark, *Willamette Valley,* 1:825. The Chief Factor told the Governor and Committee that he paid $5,400. McL to G&C, 20 November 1845, B.223/b/33, fos. 2–38, HBRS 7:122.

"the first violation..."   McL, Statement on Land Claim, 1 March 1844, B.223/b/31, fos. 2–14, HBRS 7:214.

"lost all influence..."   McL to G&C, 20 November 1844, B.223/b/31, fos. 198–234, HBRS 7:35.

Chapter 11–1: On His Own

397   *"I trust when the..."*   McL to G&C, 20 November 1845, B.223/b/33, fos. 2–38, HBRS 7:151.

399   *Canadians' document*   Frein, "Canadian Settlers." The document was incorrectly dated as March 4, 1843, in Grover, *Oregon Archives,* and in Gray, *History of Oregon,* 273–75; the 1844 date is now accepted. See McL to G&C, 4 July 1844, B.223/b/31, fos. 95–101, HBRS 6:199; HBRS 7:3 n. 3; Clark, "British and American Subjects," 151–57; and *CPT,* 354 n. 32.

Meeting of March 4   *CPT,* 166; McL to GS, 20 March 1845, extract in Clark, *Willamette Valley,* 1:807.

"seeing the increasing..."   McL to G&C, 20 November 1844, B.223/b/31, fos. 198–234, HBRS 7:32–33. Parts of this letter are identical to McL to G&C, 4 July 1844, B.223/b/31, fos. 95–101, HBRS 6:199.

400   *"clear and unquestionable"*   Polk, address to Democratic convention in Baltimore, 1844, excerpt in *OQ,* 282. The term was popular at that time, often repeated.

Presidential campaign of 1844   *OQ,* 338–47, 364–67.

Manifest Destiny   Ibid., 404; Throckmorton, *Argonauts,* 32–33; Baker, "Experience, Personality, and Memory," 229–30.

"Let us encourage..."   John C. Calhoun, speech to Congress, May 1843, quoted in JD to GS, private, 23 October 1843, D.5/9, fos. 114–21, HBRS 7:xxxi.

"I am sorry to hear..."   JD to GS, 5 March 1845, D.5/13, fos. 217–24, HBRS 7:178.

400–401   *"But for myself..."*   Applegate, "Letter to W. H. Rees."

401   *Robert Moore*   Bancroft, *Oregon,* 1:237–38 n. 29.

"Most of the immigrants..." Lucy A. H. Deady, interview in Lockley, "Impressions," *Oregon Journal,* 24 January 1929, p. 6.

R. W. Morrison Minto, "Occasional Address," 43; Minto, "Robert Wilson Morrison," 55.

"I am compelled..." Minto, "Reminiscences," *OHQ* 2 (June 1901): 130.

"I saw that a great..." Burnett, "Recollections," *OHQ* 5 (March 1904): 64.

"In this Country..." McL to G&C, 19 July 1845, A.11/70, fos. 112–21, HBRS 7:89.

"merely telling those..." McL to Sir J. H. Pelly, 12 July 1846, A.10/22, fos. 33–41d, HBRS 7:169.

402   *"no prospect of forming..."* McL to Pelly, 15 November 1844, extract in Clark, *Willamette Valley,* 1:803–4. McLoughlin expressed the same view in McL to GS, 20 March 1845, FO 5/443; and McL to Pelly, 2 April 1845, FO 5/435, 443, extracts in Clark, *Willamette Valley,* 1:807, 814.

"many upright respectable..." McL to G&C, 19 July 1845, A.11/70, fos. 112–21, HBRS 7:88, 89.

"will declare themselves..." McL to Pelly, 15 November 1844, FO 5/443, extract in Clark, *Willamette Valley,* 1:804.

Arrival of Modeste McL to G&C, 12 August 1844, B.223/b/31, fos. 103d–106, HBRS 7:1.

"the appearance at this..." McL to G&C, 20 November 1844, B.223/b/31, fos. 198–234, HBRS 7:35.

"had more taste...pouring petition after petition..." JD to GS, 5 March 1845, D.5/13, fos. 217–24, HBRS 7:180.

McL to supply Modeste McL to Baillie, 2 August 1844, extract in Clark, *Willamette Valley,* 1:802.

"several articles..." Thomas Baillie, Commander of HMS *Modeste,* to Sir George Seymour, Rear Admiral in command Pacific Station, 14 August 1844, Admiralty letters, 5/500, extract in Clark, *Willamette Valley,* 1:801.

"would regain their weight..." McL to G&C, 20 November 1844, B.223/b/31, fos. 198–234, HBRS 7:45.

"almost instantly wrapped..." JD to McL, 30 September 1844, included in McL to G&C, 20 November 1844, B.223/b/31, fos. 198–234, HBRS 7:40. Douglas wrote a long letter reporting details of the fire; it is pp. 37–44 of McLoughlin's letter.

"when we consider..." McL to G&C, 20 November 1844, B.223/b/31, fos. 198–234, HBRS 7:44.

403   *"took advantage of..."* JD to McL, 30 September 1844, quoted in McL to

G&C, 20 November 1844, B.223/b/31, fos. 198–234, HBRS 7:43.

"capable of discharging..." Moses Merryweather, estimate, 3 September 1845, A.10/20, fos. 186–87, HBRS 7:52 n. 1.

Copper cistern Archibald Barclay, Secretary of HBC, to Merryweather, 4 September 1845, A.5/15, p. 61, quoted in HBRS 7:52–53 n. 1.

Decrease in prejudice McL to G&C, 20 November 1844, B.223/b/31, fos. 198–234, HBRS 7:47.

"In the Month..." McL to GS, 20 March 1845, FO 5/443, extract in Clark, *Willamette Valley*, 1:809.

Minto comes ahead Bancroft, *Oregon*, 1:451–52.

"men in the prime..." Minto, "Camp Fire Orations," p. 15, MS quoted in Bancroft, *Oregon*, 1:454.

Narrative by Watt Watt, "Recollections of Dr. John McLoughlin," 24–25.

404   *"Doctor McLoughlin was..."* Minto, "Reminiscences," *OHQ* 2 (September 1901): 234–35.

McL's preparation for immigrants Holman, *Dr. John McLoughlin*, 78; Bancroft, *Oregon*, 1:456.

"At any public..." Burnett, "Recollections," *OHQ* 5 (June 1904): 172.

"all that point..." McL to A. L. Lovejoy, M. Gilmore, and R. Newell, 20 December 1844, printed in Young, "Ewing Young," 312–13.

"for services rendered..." Ibid.

"upon an adjoining tree" McL to William Miller, Consul General at Honolulu, 24 March 1845, B.223/b/33, fos. 40–46, HBRS 7:260.

"Feby 15th 1845..." Ibid.

"We must keep..." McL to G&C, 28 March 1845, B.223/b/33, fos. 170–72, HBRS 7:73.

405   *"Dr. White...to burn the finest..."* McL to Miller, 24 March 1845, B.223/b/33, fos. 40–46, HBRS 7:260–62; Allen, *Ten Years*, 251.

"in order that the unanimity..." McL to Executive Committee, 11 March 1845, included in McL to Miller, 24 March 1845, B.223/b/33, fos. 40–46, HBRS 7:262–63.

"No such protection..." Barclay to McL, 30 November 1844, excerpt in McL to G&C, 20 November 1845, B.223/b/33, fos. 2–38, HBRS 7:103.

"I would also take..." McL to Miller, 24 March 1845, B.223/b/33, fos. 40–46, HBRS 7:268.

"given due consideration..." Miller to Pelly and Allan, HBC Agents, 3 June 1845, included in McL to G&C, 20 November 1845, B.223/b/33, fos. 2–38, HBRS 7:102.

Chapter 11–2: Yerba Buena

406–7   *"I found everything…"* Harvey, "Biography of Her Father," 11.

407   *"remain at his post…"* GS to McL, 1 March 1842, D.4/27, fos. 3–9d, HBRS 6:268.

Previous approval of California post G&C to GS, 20 March 1839, A.6/25, fo. 28, quoted in HBRS 7:xxi; Resolution of Council of Northern Department, in Oliver, *Canadian North-West,* 2:786; McL to GS, 20 March 1844, printed in Judson, "Documentary," 223–24.

The Valleyfield G&C to McL, 1 December 1841, A.6/25, fo. 155d, HBRS 6:62 n. 2; Statement of Voyages Performed by Shipping Attached to Columbia Department, 1842–45, JD to GS, 4 April 1845, D.5/13, fos. 391–92, HBRS 7:192.

"two of her beams" McL to G&C, 19 August 1842, B.223/b/29, fos. 37–38, HBRS 6:62.

"put on shore…" McL to G&C, 31 October 1842, B.223/b/29, fos. 75–91, HBRS 6:75.

"If she had been here…" McL to G&C, 4 July 1844, B.223/b/31, fos. 95–101, HBRS 6:195.

408   *"authorize me…"* Rae to G&C, 1 November 1842, quoted in G&C to McL or Officer in Charge, 27 September 1843, A.6/26, fos. 78d–85, HBRS 6:314.

"had to send the Columbia…*"* McL to Barclay, 25 November 1844, A.11/70, fos. 91–93, HBRS 7:65.

William Sinclair Biographical supplement in HBRS 7:320. After Rae's suicide, Sinclair became apprentice postmaster at Fort Vancouver, and later served at various other posts. He retired in 1860, except for a brief return in 1864–65.

"in consequence of…" McL to Barclay, 25 November 1844, A.11/70, fos. 91–93, HBRS 7:65.

Yerba Buena finances McL to G&C, 15 November 1843, B.223/b/30, fos. 52–67, HBRS 6:122.

"showed a fairer prospect…thought it probable…" McL to Barclay, 25 November 1844, A.11/70, fos. 91–93, HBRS 7:66.

"forgot to deliver…" McL to G&C, 19 July 1845, A.11/70, fos. 112–21, HBRS 7:81.

"I have not heard…" McL to G&C, 4 July 1844, B.223/b/31, fos. 95–101, HBRS 6:194.

"as the Russians required…" McL to Barclay, 25 November 1844, A.11/70, fos. 91–93, HBRS 7:65.

409   *"with as little delay…"* Barclay to McL, 1 April 1844, A.6/26, fo. 112d, HBRS 7:xxvi n. 5.

"on the way she will…" McL to Pelly, 6 January 1845, A.11/70, fos. 98–100,

HBRS 7:68.

"fully discussed..." Barclay to McL, 30 November 1844, A.6/26, fo. 138, HBRS 7:xxvi n. 5.

"carrying on an underhand..." Barclay to GS, 3 April 1844, D.5/11, fos. 30–31, HBRS 7:xxvi n. 5.

"did not send copies..." Lamb, Introduction to HBRS 7:xxvi.

Prejudice of Vallejo HBRS 7:xxvii.

"to the point of..." Tays, "Mariano Guadalupe Vallejo," 57.

James A. Forbes Beginning about 1834, Forbes had several times performed services for the Hudson's Bay Company. In 1842, for an unknown reason, the company had become dissatisfied with him, and on May 28, 1843, McLoughlin had instructed Rae not to employ him in the future. B.223/b/30, fo. 13d, quoted in HBRS 7:76 n. 1.

410   *"It becomes my painful..."* Forbes to McL, 21 January 1845, B.221/b/33, fos. 187–91, quoted in McL to G&C, 19 July 1845, A.11/70, fos. 112–21, HBRS 7:75–76.

"they were going..." Eloisa to McL, paraphrased in McL to G&C, 19 July 1845, A.11/70, fos. 112–21, HBRS 7:80–81.

"clung to him..." Ibid.

411   *"from the very first..."* Montrose McGillivray to GS, 18 March 1844, D.5/10, fos. 453–54, HBRS 7:xxviii.

"insinuated himself...I am certain..." Forbes to McL, 21 January 1845, B.223/b/33, fo. 189d, HBRS 7:78 n. 3.

Rae in insurrection McL to G&C, 19 July 1845, A.11/70, fos. 112–21, HBRS 7:81–82; HBRS 7:xxviii.

"The great mystery..." Ogden to GS, private, 15 March 1847, D.5/19, fos. 366–72, HBRS 7:xxviii.

412   *"preyed on his mind..."* McL to G&C, 19 July 1845, A.11/70, fos. 112–21, HBRS 7:81.

"I hereby declare..." Note left by Rae, 18 January 1845, A.11/70, fo. 122, HBRS 7:78 n. 1.

David escorts Eloisa David McLoughlin Papers at OHSL; Maria Louisa Rae Myrick, interview in Lockley, "Impressions," *Oregon Journal*, 20 September 1929.

Eloisa's children Myrick, interview in Lockley, "Impressions," *Oregon Journal*, 20 September 1929; McLoughlin genealogy, in Wilson, *Dr. John McLoughlin*, 183, 184.

"just as the Mexican..." Harvey, "Biography of Her Father," 27.

"I know a great many..." Ibid., 24.

Chapter 11–3: Joining Hands

413 *"aloft in the stern..."* Molson, "Glimpses of Life," 160. McLoughlin's grand-daughter Maria Louisa Rae Myrick later said he wore "knee breeches with silver buckles." Interview in Lockley, "Impressions," *Oregon Journal,* 21 September 1929. If so, they were old-fashioned, for trousers in the 1840s were narrow and tapered. She possibly was remembering McLoughlin's accounts of his younger days, when breeches were fashionable; or perhaps he wore breeches and boots when working in his mill.

Burnett, Applegate Sampson, *Business Correspondence,* 36 n. 77; 50 n. 99; 66 nn. 123, 124.

"within Twenty days..." Duniway and Riggs, "Oregon Archives," 267.

414 *"There is a call..."* McL to G&C, 28 March 1845, B.223/b/33, fos. 170–72, HBRS 7:73.

Special election changes code McL to G&C, 4 July 1844, B.223/b/31, fos. 95–101, HBRS 6:200; *CPT,* 169–71.

Code of 1845 "Copy of the Oregon Laws," B.223/b/31, fos. 36–66, HBRS 7:219–50; Johansen and Gates, *Empire,* 191; *CPT,* 167–72. The "fair copy" of the first code, arranged after May 1844, is in Duniway and Riggs, "Oregon Archives," 273–80. It includes the anti-McLoughlin land law.

"an onerous burden..." Burnett, "Recollections," *OHQ* 5 (June 1904): 191.

Abernethy elected governor Carey, *General History,* 346; Johansen and Gates, *Empire,* 192; Sampson, *Business Correspondence,* 123.

"all laws heretofore..." "Copy of the Oregon Laws," B.223/b/31, fos. 36–66, HBRS 7:238.

"sufficiently safe..." Ibid., 239.

"enabled him to bring..." Burnett, "Recollections," *OHQ* 5 (June 1904): 195.

Ermatinger elected treasurer Sampson, *Business Correspondence,* 130; Barker, *Letters,* 306.

"pole Tax..." "Copy of the Oregon Laws," B.223/b/31, fos. 36–66, HBRS 7:221–22.

415 *Meek's tax report* Scott, "First Taxes"; Scott, "Oregon Tax Roll, 1844."

"owing to the unsettled..." "Report of J. L. Meek," in Young, "Financial History," 391; see also Tobie, "Joseph L. Meek," *OHQ* 40 (March 1939): 32.

"Darn my sole..." Scott, "First Taxes," 8. Meek made the report in December 1844.

"consistent with my duties..." Oath of office, 1845, quoted in Carey, *General History,* 349; see also *CPT,* 180; and McL to G&C, 30 August 1845, A.11/70,

fos. 153–54, HBRS 7:95.

"the idea of a union..." McL to G&C, 20 November 1845, B.223/b/33, fos. 2–38, HBRS 7:98–99.

"by the payment of..." Applegate to McL, 14 August 1845, quoted in McL to G&C, 20 November 1845, B.223/b/33, fos. 2–38, HBRS 7:99. McLoughlin gives the date of Applegate's letter as August 14, but context indicates that Applegate wrote it earlier.

"A crisis was..." McL to G&C, 20 November 1845, B.223/b/33, fos. 2–38, HBRS 7:98–100.

"the security of..." Ibid.

416   *"we the Officers..."* McL and JD to Legislative Committee, 15 August 1945, quoted in McL to G&C, 20 November 1845, B.223/b/33, fos. 2–38, HBRS 7:106.

"gave rise to..." McL to G&C, 20 November 1845, B.223/b/33, fos. 2–38, HBRS 7:106.

"desperate and reckless..." Ibid., 101.

"the Furs from the Interior..." McL to G&C, 19 July 1845, A.11/70, fos. 112–21, HBRS 7:89.

"as much as possible..." GS to McL, 1 January 1845, quoted in Merk, *OQ*, 246–47.

"an additional frigate..." Sir Robert Peel to Lord Aberdeen, 23 February 1845, Aberdeen Correspondence, privately printed, 1885, extract in Clark, *Willamette Valley*, 1:841.

"A grave discussion..." Polk, diary, 23 December 1845, quoted in Carey, *General History*, 458.

"The only way..." James Polk to William H. Polk, 27 March 1846, quoted in *OQ*, 346.

"There must be no..." Andrew Jackson, as quoted in *New York Morning News*, 4 July 1845, quoted in *OQ*, 232.

417   *"the only means..."* McL to G&C, 30 August 1845, A.11/70, fos. 153–54, HBRS 7:95.

"the practicability of..." GS to Warre and Vavasour, 30 May 1845, D.4/66, fos. 210–14, HBRS 7:96 n. 2. Documents on the Warre-Vavasour expedition are in Schafer, "Warre and Vavasour's Military Reconnaissance."

"the pleasure of..." GS to Ogden, 30 May 1845, D.4/32, fo. 11d, quoted in HBRS 7:96 n. 2.

"most disagreeable..." Ogden to GS, 20 March 1846, D.5/16, fos. 457–59, HBRS 7:146–47 n. 3. The commander of the British forces in Canada, in consultation with Simpson, had arranged for the Warre-Vavasour expedition.

"superfine beaver hats..." Schafer, "Warre and Vavasour's Military Reconnaissance," 3.

"prepared in case of..." Gordon to Secretary of the Admiralty, 19 October 1845, FO 5/459, extract in Clark, *Willamette Valley,* 1:835.

"with great pleasure" McL to Gordon, 15 September 1845, FO 5/459, extract in Clark, *Willamette Valley,* 1:823.

418   *"we will hit them..."* Roberts, "Round Hand," 201.

"but in the course..." Peel to Gordon, 27 September 1845, FO 5/459, printed in Clark, *Willamette Valley,* 1:829.

McL sends JD to the America McL to G&C, 20 November 1845, B.223/b/33, fos. 2–38, HBRS 7:147.

"The old Gentleman..." JD to GS, private, 20 March 1846, D.5/16, fos. 460–65, HBRS 7:liv.

"in the most..." Gordon to Secretary of the Admiralty, 19 October 1845, FO 5/459, extract in Clark, *Willamette Valley,* 1:834.

Chapter 11–4: The Trap

419   *"a sink of capital"* JD to GS, private, 5 March 1845, D.5/13, fos. 217–24, HBRS 7:185.

McL drafts McL to GS, 20 March 1845, D.5/13, fos. 320–23, HBRS 7:xlviii; GS to McL, 15 June 1845, D.4/67, fos. 51–51d, HBRS 7:xlix.

"I inferred that..." McL to GS, private and confidential, 20 March 1845, D.5/13, fos. 320–23, HBRS 7:xlviii. W. Kaye Lamb believes the offer was sincere and that McLoughlin later changed his mind. Lamb cites a statement by Ogden, who was at the Red River Council when it decided to accept McLoughlin's drafts. Introduction to HBRS 7:l–li. Simpson was also there, and may have influenced the decision. Whatever McLoughlin intended, his letters support both sides of the question.

420   *Mactavish's belief* GS to McL, 15 June 1845, D.4/67, fos. 51–51d, printed in Lamb, Introduction to HBRS 7:xlix.

"from what he now..." Ogden to GS, private and confidential, 20 March 1846, D.5/16, fos. 457–59, HBRS 7:l–li.

McL's previous deviousness See chapters 2–4, 5–5, and 6–1.

"if called into Court..." McL to George Pelly, 12 July 1846, A.10/22, fos. 33–41d, HBRS 7:164.

421   *Complaints about Columbia's reputation* G&C to McL, 27 September 1843, quoted in McL to G&C, 20 November 1844, B.223/b/31, fos. 198–234, HBRS 7:14.

"Is it to be expected..." McL to G&C, 20 November 1844, B.223/b/31, fos. 198–234, HBRS 7:15–16.

GS finds discrepancies GS to McL, Ogden, and Douglas, 16 June 1845, D.4/67, fo. 61, quoted in McL to G&C, 20 November 1845, B.223/b/33, fos. 2–38, HBRS 7:136.

"exceedingly meagre..." Barclay to GS, 1 June 1843, D.5/8, fos. 274–75, HBRS 6:xlix.

"the profits of..." GS to McL, Ogden, and Douglas, 16 June 1845, D.4/67, fos. 63d–64, HBRS 7:lvii.

London Committee displeased HBRS 7:lviii.

"nothing will now..." Barclay to GS, 4 March 1844, D.5/10, fos. 338–39, HBRS 7:lviii.

"It is not advisable..." Barclay to McL, 30 November 1844, A.6/26, fo. 139d, quoted in McL to G&C, 20 November 1845, B.223/b/33, fos. 2–38, HBRS 7:114.

422   *"the same results..."* McL to G&C, 19 July 1845, A.11/70, fos. 112–21, HBRS 7.89, 90.

"Your letter..." GS to McL, 15 June 1845, D.4/67, fos. 51–51d, HBRS 7:xlix.

423   *"Should C. F. McLoughlin's..."* GS to McL, Ogden, and Douglas, 16 June 1845, D.4/67, fos. 67–67d, HBRS 7:142 n. 2.

"If at the time..." McL to George Pelly, 12 July 1846, A.10/22, fos. 33–41d, HBRS 7:164.

"I hope your Honors..." McL to G&C, 1 July 1846, A.10/22, fos. 1–8, HBRS 7:159.

424   *"for his Bill dated..."* McL, Proprietary Account with HBC, 22 August 1845, printed in Barker, *Financial Papers,* 76.

Immigration of 1845 Johansen and Gates, *Empire,* 194; Holman, *Dr. John McLoughlin,* 81–83.

Barlow Road Carey, *History of Oregon,* 354, 397; Bancroft, *Oregon,* 1:521–22, 532; Edwards, "Oregon Trail," 146.

Residents provide aid Oregon Spectator, 21 January 1847.

425   *"such an outcry..."* McL to G&C, 20 November 1845, B.223/b/33, fos. 2–38, HBRS 7:128, 141.

"I beg to repeat...I trust when..." Ibid., 141, 151.

"Gentlemen, if such..." Lyman, "Dr. John McLoughlin," 53.

"I am by no means..." McL to G&C, 19 July 1845, A.11/70, fos. 112–21, HBRS 7:88.

Belief McL was charged Barker, *Financial Papers,* 50.

426   *"I never knew..."* Harvey, "Biography of Her Father," 33.

           McL's HBC account Barker, *Financial Papers*, 54–87.

           McL's pay in retirement HBRS 7:lx; Barker, *Financial Papers*, 50.

Chapter 12–1: Starting Over

427   *"I have Drunk..."* McL to Sir J. H. Pelly, 12 July 1846, A.10/22, fos. 33–41d,
           HBRS 7:166. This letter was written after McLoughlin moved to Oregon City,
           and he directed it to the governor himself, not the Committee.

429   *McKay living with McLoughlins* Dye, "Boone Family Reminiscences," 223.

           Ermatinger family McL to Francis Ermatinger, 15 March 1848, Sampson,
           Business Correspondence, 87–88, 131. The Ermatinger house, in which Catherine
           lived, is now a museum.

           "at the age of..." McL to G&C, 1 July 1846, A.10/22, fos. 1–8, HBRS 7:154.

           Move to Oregon City HBRS 7:lxi.

           Early Portland Bancroft, *Oregon*, 2:9.

430   *McLoughlin house* Smelser, "History of the McLoughlin House," 31–34; infor-
           mation from visits to McLoughlin House, Oregon City.

           Costs of house McL, "Costs of Improvements," 68–70.

           "a large portion..." Ibid., 69.

           Location on land recovered from the mission McLoughlin, Statement on Land
           Claim, 1 March 1844, B.223/b/31, fos. 2–14, HBRS 7:207, 216.

           Other buildings Barker, *Financial Papers*, 7, 15, 16; plat of Oregon City in
           Smelser, "History of the McLoughlin House," 30.

           French store The *L'Etoile du Matin*, owned by V. Marzion & Company of
           Havre de Grace, was so badly damaged on the bar in 1849 or 1850 that she was
           towed to Portland and unloaded, and her hull was burned. In 1850, McLoughlin
           became a partner in the store Menes opened. Barker, *Financial Papers*, 30;
           Bancroft, *Oregon*, 1:326–27 n. 18.

           Indians as household help Mrs. Mary Le Forest, interview in *Morning Oregonian*,
           12 May 1899.

           Catholic church on McL's land Maria Louisa Rae Myrick, interview in Lockley
           "Impressions," *Oregon Journal*, 20 September 1929.

           "I was sorry to learn..." McL to JD, 15 April 1847, Sampson, *Business Correspon-
           dence*, 17.

431   *"Mrs. Rae Begs..."* McL to Leidesdorff, 13 August 1847, Sampson, *Business
           Correspondence*, 42.

           "Pray do not forget..." McL to Captain David Dring, 12 August 1847, Sampson,

Business Correspondence, 39.

"I regret to hear..." John Work to Edward Ermatinger, 10 December 1849, printed in Phillips, "Family Letters," 40.

"I have Drunk..." McL to Pelly, 12 July 1846, A.10/22, fos. 33–41d, HBRS 7:166.

432 *"about one hundred..."* Palmer, *Journal,* 76.

Buildings in Oregon City David McLoughlin to John Fraser, 15 March 1845, *ME,* 252; *Oregon Spectator,* 19 February 1846; Sampson, *Business Correspondence,* xliii–xliv. By 1847 the *Spectator* was running an ad for "wagon cart tires for sale at the brick store."

"to receive a lot..." Geer, "Incidents," 371.

"approved orders..." "An Act Relative to the Currency, and Subjecting Property to Execution," passed by legislature of provisional government on 12 December 1845. See *Oregon Spectator,* 19 February 1846; Gilbert, *Trade and Currency,* 46–47; Sampson, *Business Correspondence,* xliii n. 62.

Abernethy's rocks Throckmorton, *Argonauts,* 60.

Forms of currency Bancroft, *Oregon,* 2:14–15.

Lower prices for cash Throckmorton, *Argonauts,* 60; Howison, "Report," 10; Gilbert, *Trade and Currency,* 56.

Barrel of dollars Roberts, "Recollections," MS, p. 8, cited in Bancroft, *Oregon,* 2:14–15.

433 *Linn City, Multnomah City* Palmer, *Journal,* 77, 78.

Ferries "Copy of the Oregon Laws," in HBRS 7:239–41; Palmer, *Journal,* 78; Barker, *Financial Papers,* 16.

Ferry landing Barker, *Financial Papers,* 7, 16.

"to demand as a right..." McL to G&C, 20 November 1845, B.223/b/33, fos. 2–38, HBRS 7:142.

"I may not be able..." McL to G&C, 1 July 1846, A.10/22, fos. 1–8, HBRS 7:158.

McL consults Burnett McL to Alexander H. H. Stuart, Secretary of the Interior, 15 July 1851, *ME,* 331; Jesse Applegate, MS, quoted in Bancroft, *Oregon,* 1:506.

McL's effort to take oath of citizenship McL to Stuart, 15 July 1851, *ME,* 330.

"to get rightful...agitating the question..." Ibid., 331.

"a Kind of Indecision..." McL to Leidesdorff, 10 April 1847, Sampson, *Business Correspondence,* 11.

"disgraced and Degraded..." McL to Pelly, 12 July 1846, A.10/22, fos. 33–41d, HBRS 7:171.

"so melancholy that..." Ogden to GS, private, 15 March 1847, D.5/19, fos.

366–72, HBRS 7:159 n. 1.

434   *"extinguished by the..."* *Oregon Spectator,* 19 February 1846.

Sawmill leased McL to Starkey, Janion and Company, 12 March 1848, Sampson, *Business Correspondence,* 85–86; Douglas to GS, D.5/18, 3 August 1846, HBRS 7:lxi.

Gristmill Sampson, *Business Correspondence,* xliv.

McL's extensive business Numerous letters in Sampson, *Business Correspondence:* pp. 16, 19, 20, 32, 42, and others.

"stocked with goods..." George Luther Boone, in Dye, "Boone Family Reminiscences," 223. George Luther Boone was a grandson of the famed Daniel Boone.

Fort Vancouver as secondary depot Hussey, *Fort Vancouver,* 92. The history of the fort from 1846 to 1869 is on pp. 91–114.

"merely for his Victuals...and this by Gentlemen..." McL to Sir J. H. Pelly, 12 July 1846, A.10/22, fos. 33–41d, HBRS 7:168.

435   *"My father always..."* Harvey, "Biography of Her Father," 37.

"Poor John was..." JD to GS, 5 March 1845, D.5/13, fos. 217–24, HBRS 7:178.

Partnership for David Francis W. Pettygrove, "Oregon in 1843," 21–23, Oregon manuscripts, Bancroft Library, cited in Sampson, *Business Correspondence,* xlv; Throckmorton, *Argonauts,* 58; Howison, "Report," 22–23.

"You will sell what..." McL to David McLoughlin, 10 April 1847, Sampson, *Business Correspondence,* 8–10.

McL and HBC share business JD and Ogden to GS, 19 March 1846, B.223/b/34, fo. 19, HBRS 7:lxi.

436   *McL rents granary to HBC* JD and Ogden to GS, 19 March 1846, D.5/16, fos. 434–49, HBRS 7:138 n. 1.

Oregon Spectator founded "To the Public," editorial in *Oregon Spectator,* 5 February 1846. The first story, covering most of page 1, was a reprint of the Organic Laws of Oregon. The second paper west of the Missouri was the *Californian* of Monterey, its first issue being 15 August 1846.

Chapter 12–2: The Boundary Treaty

436   *Visit of the* Modeste Knuth, "HMS *Modeste*"; *Oregon Spectator,* 19 February, 20 August 1846; 4 February, 3 May 1847; and many others.

437   *Orchestra for play* *Oregon Spectator,* 14 May 1846, quoted in Alice Henson Ernst, "Stage Annals of Early Oregon from 1846 to 1875," *OHQ* 42 (June 1941): 151–61.

Ball at McL's mill Minto, "Antecedents," 50–51; Chadwick, "Address," 26. Minto says the boastful officer was Lieutenant Peel, from the *America,* but that is an error. Peel left in September 1845 and was sent to London posthaste to deliver his report. The ball was in 1846.

"I am informed..." McL to Captain Thomas Baillie, 1 May 1847, Sampson, *Business Correspondence,* 25.

438   *"to relieve the concern..."* GS to Ogden, JD, and Work, 30 June 1846, D.4/68, fos. 114d–115, HBRS 7:285 n. 2.

"We are convinced..." Warre and Vavasour, report, enclosed in Ogden and JD to GS, 16 March 1847, D.5/19, fos. 373–74, HBRS 7:286–87.

"As people will not..." McL's reply, enclosed in Ogden and JD to GS, 16 March 1847, D.5/19, fos. 373–74, HBRS 7:296, 292, 288.

"for perusal..." Ibid., 298.

"furnishes so full..." Ogden and JD to GS, 16 March 1847, D.5/19, fos. 373–74, HBRS 7:286.

439   *"I shall make..."* Ashburton to Aberdeen, 25 April 1842, quoted in *OQ,* 208.

"Beyond this degree..." Aberdeen to Richard Pakenham, 18 April 1845, quoted in *OQ,* 250 n. 53.

440   *Desire for Puget Sound* *OQ,* 199, 234–35.

Negotiations over boundary Ibid., 395–417.

"The United States might..." Buchanan to Louis McLane, 26 February 1846, in Senate Doc. 489, 29th Cong., 1st sess., serial 478, pp. 40–41, excerpt in *OQ,* 225.

"high and dry..." Editorial in *New York Evening Post,* 25 March 1846, extract in *OQ,* 225.

"Withered be the hand..." *Ohio Statesman,* 15 June 1846, quoted in *OQ,* 330.

"A WAR WITH ENGLAND!..." *Oregon Spectator,* 28 May 1846.

Problems in England *OQ,* 309–36.

Threat of war with Mexico Ibid., 230, 389.

441   *"a cause so..."* Aberdeen to Hudson Gurney, 20 January 1846, from Aberdeen Correspondence, extract in Clark, *Willamette Valley,* 1:851.

"I cannot believe..." Aberdeen to Edward Everett, 3 January 1846, from Aberdeen Correspondence, extract in Clark, *Willamette Valley,* 1:850.

"bind the two nations..." Editorial in London *Times,* 3 January 1846, extract in *OQ,* 302.

"an act at once..." Daniel Webster to Evelyn Denison, 26 February 1846, quoted in Denison to Aberdeen, 24 March 1846, from Aberdeen Correspondence, extract in Clark, *Willamette Valley,* 1:857.

Division of Oregon Country *OQ,* 417.

David brings news Sampson, *Business Correspondence*, 141; *Oregon Spectator*, 12 November 1846. Its placement shows its importance—page 1, column 1.

"We are indebted..." *Oregon Spectator*, 12 November 1846.

"the 49th degree..." Ibid.

442   *"The only piece..."* Ibid.

"As to the treaty..." McL to JD, 15 April 1847, Sampson, *Business Correspondence*, 17.

443   *"Art. III..."* Johansen and Gates, *Empire*, 207–8.

Chapter 12–3: An American Citizen

444   *"if you will go..."* Lockley, "Recollections of Benjamin Franklin Bonney," 53.

"grieved us much" David McLoughlin to John Fraser, 15 March 1845, *ME*, 252.

Marie Louise's death *ME*, 96–99.

Globes and maps *Glimpses of the Monastery*, 357, cited in *ME*, 95.

"at the special request..." *Glimpses of the Monastery*, 363, quoted in *ME*, 105.

Death of Julienne McL to P. C. Michaud, 1 February 1848, Sampson, *Business Correspondence*, 80.

"I allowed my..." Ibid.

Offer to nephew Ibid., 80–81.

"Cuttings seeds Newspapers..." McL to Wyeth, 20 April 1847, Sampson, *Business Correspondence*, 21.

444–45   *Arguments about Napoleon* George T. Allan said that once, while the doctor was dressing his injured hand, "in the height of debate...he treated my poor hand so roughly that I heartily wished Napoleon and the Peace of Amiens far enough." "Reminiscences," 77–78.

Street at Champoeg Corning, *Willamette Landings*, 81. An Oregon State Highway Department map of June 1967 shows Champoeg in 1852, with Napoleon Street continuing as the road to Salem. Reproduced in *CPT*, following p. 222.

"I will do myself..." McL to Wyeth, 20 April 1847, Sampson, *Business Correspondence*, 22–23.

"state that you Claim it..." McL to Wyeth, 10 October 1847, Sampson, *Business Correspondence*, 57.

HBC lease renewed McL to Ogden and JD, 8 June 1847, Sampson, *Business*

"though Mr Pomeroy..." McL to Starkey, Janion and Co., 12 March 1848, Sampson, *Business Correspondence*, 86.

Mill capacity Ibid.

Minto at mill Minto, "What I Know of Dr. McLoughlin," 190–91.

Blanchet as archbishop O'Hara, *Catholic History,* 99–101.

Knight of St. Gregory Sampson, *Business Correspondence,* 30 n. 65; O'Hara, *Catholic History,* 36; Holman, *Dr. John McLoughlin,* 161–62. The breviary and medal are at McLoughlin House in Oregon City. A stained-glass window depicting St. Gregory and inscribed "In Memorium" to McLoughlin was in St. John's Catholic Church in Oregon City until the building was torn down and the window moved to the headquarters of the Clackamas County Historical Society.

"you are esteemed…" Translation of the patent of membership in Order of St. Gregory, original at OHSL.

446   *"They will proceed…"* McL to Francis Ermatinger, 15 March 1848, Sampson, *Business Correspondence,* 87–88. Catherine stopped at Fort Colvile, presumably because she and Fanny were ill with the measles, and joined her husband the following summer. It is said that she was pregnant when she arrived. For details of the stormy marriage, see Ermatinger, *Fur Trade Letters,* 266–93.

"soon knew all…" Dye, "Boone Family Reminiscences," 223.

"He was fond…" Harvey, "Biography of Her Father," 35.

"I state to you…" McL to Burnett, 28 July 1847, Sampson, *Business Correspondence,* 36–37.

Vickers jumps claim Sampson, *Business Correspondence,* 59–60 n. 115; *Oregon Spectator,* 29 April 1847.

"This man had got…" McL to Wyeth, 10 October 1847, Sampson, *Business Correspondence,* 60.

447   *Dispute* Sampson, *Business Correspondence,* 59–60 n. 115; *Oregon Spectator,* 15, 29 April, 27 May, 25 November 1847, 6 January 1848.

Indian unrest McL, "Autobiography," in Clarke, *Pioneer Days,* 1:223–24. Whitman told McLoughlin that the leader of the unrest was Thomas Hill, a Shawnee educated in the United States who had warned the Cayuses about seizures of tribal lands there. McLoughlin urged Whitman to leave Waiilatpu, but the missionary refused.

"well Acquainted…" McL to William L. Marcy, Secretary of War, 16 October 1847, Sampson, *Business Correspondence,* 65–68.

"pillaged of their property…" McL to Marcy, 21 October 1847, Sampson, *Business Correspondence,* 69–70.

449   *Whitman massacre* Drury, *Marcus and Narcissa,* 2:205–65; Drury, *First White Women,* 1:161–70; *Oregon Spectator,* 10 December 1847, 6, 20 January 1848; Sampson, *Business Correspondence,* 91 n. 141.

Ogden rescues hostages Drury, *Marcus and Narcissa,* 2:287–94; *Oregon Spec-*

tator, 20 January 1848.

"The Company have nothing..." Ogden, speech to Cayuses, printed in Bancroft, *Oregon,* 1:693–94; in *Oregon Spectator,* 20 January 1848; and in many other sources.

450   *Bill to raise army* *Oregon Spectator,* 6 January 1848.

"if the winter...106 head of beef cattle..." McL to editor of *Oregonian* (Portland), 22 July 1854.

Gold rush Johansen and Gates, *Empire,* 235.

Shortages Throckmorton, *Argonauts,* 94.

"Not a Blanket..." Rev. William Roberts to Cor. Sec'y of Mission Society of the M.E. Church, 14 February 1849, in Roberts, "Letters," *OHQ* 22 (September 1921): 248.

"I believe both California..." David McLoughlin to John Fraser, 18 March 1849, *ME,* 253.

451   *"like dirt..."* Matthieu, "Reminiscences," 103.

Unauthorized mint Lockley, *Oregon's Yesterdays,* 131; Lockley, "Recollections of Benjamin Franklin Bonney," 53–54; Johansen and Gates, *Empire,* 235; Dye, "Boone Family Reminiscences," 223.

Trial of Cayuses Blanchet, *Historical Sketches,* 141; Bancroft, *Oregon,* 2:96–99; *Oregon Spectator,* 18 May 1850; Brown, *Political History,* 323–24.

452   *Meek in Washington* Bancroft, *Oregon,* 1:676–79; Johansen and Gates, *Empire,* 226–27; Victor, *River of the West,* 434–68.

Oregon becomes territory Johansen and Gates, *Empire,* 227; *CPT,* 171.

452–53   *Trip of Meek and Lane* Bancroft, *Oregon,* 1:777–80; Victor, *River of the West,* 469–82.

453   *Function at Rose farm* *Enterprise* (Oregon City), 12 September 1935, article by granddaughter of Joseph A. Roman, who bought the house in 1919, clipping at OHSL.

"filed my intention..." McL to Alexander H. H. Stuart, Secretary of the Interior, 15 July 1851, *ME,* 330–31; see also Holman, *Dr. John McLoughlin,* 121. McLoughlin himself addressed Stuart as "Secretary of State for the Home Department."

455   *"all allegiance and fidelity..."* McL, Declaration of Intention to File for Citizenship, in Clackamas County records, microfilm.

Chapter 12–4: "The Companionship of Adders"

455   *"Foreigners"* McL, Declaration of Intention to File for Citizenship, in Clackamas County records, microfilm.

McL votes Holman, *Dr. John McLoughlin,* 121–22; McL, letter to *Oregon Spectator,* 12 September 1850, ibid., 239. The entire letter is on pp. 229–43.

Abernethy's background Lee and Frost, *Ten Years,* 217; Sampson, *Business Correspondence,* 122–24; Cogswell, *Capitol Names,* 81–82, 102; Throckmorton, *Argonauts,* 23–24, 50, 65–66. Abernethy was building a considerable business enterprise. In 1850 he bought a mill on the Columbia, about sixty miles from its mouth. He operated a store—the first brick store in Oregon, mortared with mud.

Abernethy buys and sells mills McL, letter to *Oregon Spectator,* 12 September 1850; McL to Alexander H. H. Stuart, 15 July 1851, *ME,* 332; Holman, *Dr. John McLoughlin,* 122, 240, 243; Throckmorton, *Argonauts,* 96–97; Sampson, *Business Correspondence,* xlvii. In 1842 Felix Hathaway had deeded his title to the island to the Island Milling Co., promising to defend it against all persons, "the Lord excepted." The deed is dated November 23, 1852, obviously a copyist's error for 1842. Book 2, Record of Deeds of Clackamas County, cited in Holman, *Dr. John McLoughlin,* 114–15.

"bring the case..." McL to Alexander H. H. Stuart, 15 July 1851, *ME,* 332.

"as soon as it..." McL to Bryant, 21 August 1849, included in McL, letter to *Oregon Spectator,* 12 September 1850, printed in Holman, *Dr. John McLoughlin,* 240.

456   *Mission workers remain* Hines, *Missionary History,* 349. The Methodist church remained active in the area. In 1849 the Oregon and California Mission Conference of the Methodist Church was organized. It supported several churches and maintained the Oregon Institute at Salem, which later became Willamette University. The church, however, did not have a role on the political scene. Ibid., 383.

Samuel Thurston Bancroft, *Oregon,* 2:114 n. 23; O'Dell, "Biography of Samuel R. Thurston"; Holman, *Dr. John McLoughlin,* 122–23.

457   *"moved forward..."* La Fayette Grover, "Public Life," MS, 96–97, quoted in Bancroft, *Oregon,* 2:115 n. 24.

Results of vote Bancroft, *Oregon,* 2:114 n. 22; Holman, *Dr. John McLoughlin,* 123.

McL supports Lancaster William Berry, letter to *Oregon Spectator,* 26 December 1850, printed in Holman, *Dr. John McLoughlin,* 245.

"I voted, and..." McL, letter to *Oregon Spectator,* 12 September 1850, Holman, *Dr. John McLoughlin,* 239.

Memorial Bancroft, *Oregon,* 2:73–75.

Bryant to Washington, D.C. Teiser, "First Chief Justice," 51; *Oregon Spectator,* 25 July 1850.

Thurston loses baggage Thurston to his wife, 15 December 1849, Thurston,

"Spousal Letters," 24.

"I promised Frank..." Thurston to his wife, 2 January 1850, Thurston, "Spousal Letters," 27.

"gold bosome pin" Thurston to his wife, 30 November 1850, Thurston, "Spousal Letters," 53.

458   *"Old father Moore..."* Thurston to his wife, 7 January 1850, Thurston, "Spousal Letters," 28.

"to all the land..." Thurston to his wife, 2 January 1850, Thurston, "Spousal Letters," 24.

"forced to leave..." Thurston to House of Representatives, May or early June 1850, printed in *Oregon Spectator,* 12 September 1850, Holman, *Dr. John McLoughlin,* 124–27.

"save their capital..." Ibid.

459   *"This company has..."* Thurston, debate, printed in *Congressional Globe,* 30 May 1850, 31st Congress, 1st session, vol. 21, pt. 2:1079, printed in *Oregon Spectator,* 12 September 1850, quoted in Holman, *Dr. John McLoughlin,* 129–30.

Letter from Bryant Shippee, "Federal Relations," *OHQ* 20 (December 1919): 362 n. 28.

"Keep this still..." Thurston, quoted in McL, letter to *Oregon Spectator,* 12 September 1850, Holman, *Dr. John McLoughlin,* 233–34.

Pritchett is acting governor Bancroft, *Oregon,* 2:98.

"dining salon...Oregon, from..." *Oregon Spectator,* 11 July 1850.

460   *"was rejected because..."* McL to A. Lovejoy, Horace Baker, and W. W. Buck, 4 May 1850; Horace Baker and Wm. Buck to McL, n.d., MS at Oregon State Archives.

"decided that my declaration..." McL to Alexander H. H. Stuart, 15 July 1851, *ME,* 331. Bryant had been appointed as Chief Justice to serve in the northern part of the territory, including Oregon City, and Pratt as Associate Justice, for the southern part. After Bryant went to Washington, D.C., Pratt served both areas unaided for nearly two years. See Bancroft, *Oregon,* 2:101–2.

"We venture the assertion..." Wilson Blain, editor of *Oregon Spectator,* 22 August 1850, quoted in Bancroft, *Oregon,* 2:125 n. 45.

"This is a term..." McL, letter to *Oregon Spectator,* 12 September 1850, Holman, *Dr. John McLoughlin,* 231.

"If I had acted..." Ibid., 232.

461   *"I have given away..."* Ibid., 238.

"If I was an Englishman..." Ibid.

"believe Mr. Thurston..." Ibid., 242–43.

"to take from me..." Ibid., 232–33.

"I think he had..." William Berry, letter to *Oregon Spectator,* 26 December 1850, printed in Holman, *Dr. John McLoughlin,* 243.

"there is not a press..." Asahel Bush to Thurston, 5 December 1850, excerpt in Turnbull, *Oregon Newspapers,* 79.

462   *Meeting in Oregon City* Bancroft, *Oregon,* 2:127; Holman, *Dr. John McLoughlin,* 137.

"merits the gratitude..." *Oregon Spectator,* 26 September 1850, printed in Holman, *Dr. John McLoughlin,* 137–38.

Meeting in Salem Bancroft, *Oregon,* 2:128; Holman, *Dr. John McLoughlin,* 138–39.

"highly approved..." Resolution adopted in Salem, quoted in Holman, *Dr. John McLoughlin,* 139.

Donation Land Law Bancroft, *Oregon,* 2:122; Johansen and Gates, *Empire,* 231–34. The law granted 320 acres to a male settler over age eighteen who had lived on and cultivated his land for four years before December 1, 1850; a like amount to his wife, if they married by December 1, 1851; and 160 acres to those at least twenty-one years of age who settled between December 1, 1850, and December 1, 1853. In 1853 it was extended to those who arrived by December 1, 1855.

"confirmed to the..." Section 11, Donation Land Law, quoted in Holman, *Dr. John McLoughlin,* 141–42.

"their present defeat..." Thurston to his wife, 29 September 1850, Thurston, "Spousal Letters," 51.

Thurston wants reelection Turnbull, *Oregon Newspapers,* 75, 80.

463   *"odious..."* Thurston to Wyeth, 16 November 1850, correspondence of Thurston, Wyeth, Winthrop, and McLoughlin, published in *Oregon Spectator,* 3 April 1851, reprinted in Holman, *Dr. John McLoughlin,* 256–57.

"what there was pending..." R. C. Winthrop to Wyeth, 28 December 1850, ibid., 260.

Records of sale Bancroft cites a deed of April 25, 1849, transferring the island to Lane. *Northwest Coast,* 1:254. Holman discusses Abernethy's sale of the company to Bryant, on May 29, 1849, for $30,000. Many letters by McLoughlin and others refer to the sale. Historians generally agree that Abernethy's role was unsavory. Throckmorton refers to the sale's "questionable purpose—to deprive Dr. McLoughlin of his claim." *Argonauts,* 96. Sampson says "a conspiracy was formed" by Abernethy and Thurston. *Business Correspondence,* xlvi.

Abernethy repossesses mills Sampson, *Business Correspondence*, 123; Throck-morton, *Argonauts*, 96.

Bryant's ethics Bancroft, *Oregon*, 2:122; Johansen and Gates, *Empire*, 243; Teiser, "First Chief Justice," 52–54; Throckmorton, *Astronauts*, 96–97.

"in reduced circumstances..." Johansen and Gates, *Empire*, 243.

Abernethy's later business Throckmorton, *Argonauts*, 90–93, 104–5, 217–19.

Death of Bryant Teiser, "First Chief Justice," 48.

Death of Thurston Bancroft, *Oregon*, 2:136–37; Thurston, "Spousal Letters," 28.

463–64   *McL cannot claim title* Holman, *Dr. John McLoughlin*, 128; Bancroft, *Oregon*, 2:123. The land law did not guarantee British claims, which the boundary treaty supposedly protected.

Chapter 12–5: "A Dieu"

464   *"My own claim..."* "Letter of Dr. John McLoughlin to *Oregon Statesman*, 8 June 1852," 297–98.

"If the American..." McL, "Autobiography," in Clarke, *Pioneer Days*, 1:225–26.

Death of Joseph Records of St. Paul's Church, St. Paul, Oregon, in HBRS 4:350; David McLoughlin Papers, OHSL.

"He went with Thomas..." David McLoughlin Papers, OHSL.

465   *Death of McKay* HBRS 4:349; *CPT*, 99; Bird, "Thomas McKay," 13–15. The pioneer George T. Himes later said Dr. William McKay had informed him that Thomas McKay died in 1849. Bird, "Will of Thomas McKay," 15.

Activities of McKay Bird, "Thomas McKay," 1–14; *CPT*, 92–99; biographical note in HBRS 4:347–49; "Copy of the Oregon Laws," HBRS 7:248–49;

David McLoughlin David McLoughlin Papers, OHSL; *ME*, 132–40; Sampson, *Business Correspondence*, 140–42.

Daniel Harvey ME, 127; McL to G&C, 20 November 1844, B.223/b/31, fos. 198–234, HBRS 7:38–43; Biography in HBRS 6:390–91.

Eloisa's children Wilson, *Dr. John McLoughlin*, 183–84; HBRS 6:391. The geneal-ogy on pp. 181–89 was compiled by Anne Billeter.

466   *Maria Louisa Rae* Maria Louisa Rae Myrick, interview in Lockley, "Impressions," *Oregon Journal*, 19–21 September 1929; information at McLoughlin House. The estate of Winifred Myrick, Maria Louisa's daughter, donated the melodeon to the McLoughlin House.

Legislature ratifies sale of lots Bancroft, *Oregon*, 2:131; *Oregon Spectator*, 13 February 1851.

McL's lawsuits Records of Clackamas County Circuit Court, John McLoughlin

Case File, Oregon State Archives.

467   *Canemah* Corning, *Willamette Landings*, 61–65.

"sufficiently safe..." "Copy of the Oregon Laws," HBRS 7:239. See also Bancroft, *Oregon*, 1:440.

468   *West Coast shipping* Throckmorton, *Argonauts*, 107–13.

Capital moves Corning, *Willamette Landings*, 108.

McL as mayor Oregon *Spectator*, 2 January, 10 April 1851; Sampson, *Business Correspondence*, xlviii n. 71.

McL's plans to go to U.S. Advertisement in *Oregon Spectator*, 14 October 1851 to 16 March 1852; Sampson, *Business Correspondence*, xlviii n. 72.

McL becomes citizen Sampson, *Business Correspondence*, xlvi; Holman, *Dr. John McLoughlin*, 121–22; *Oregon Spectator*, 12 September 1850.

Legislature accepts donation Bancroft, *Oregon*, 2:131.

"misrepresented by malicious..." McL to Alexander H. H. Stuart, 15 July 1851, *ME*, 330–33. McLoughlin was incorrect in addressing Stuart as "Secretary of State." He was Secretary of the Interior.

Questionnaire Belknap, "McMurtrie's Oregon Imprints," 248–49.

469   *Humason's resolution* Bancroft, *Oregon*, 2:131 n. 56; *Oregon Statesman*, 29 January, 5 February 1856.

"praying Congress to..." Number 30 in List of Acts "passed by the 7th Annual Legislative Assembly of Oregon," in *Oregon Statesman*, 5 February 1856; also discussed in *Oregon Statesman*, 29 January 1856.

Farms spread across... Throckmorton, *Oregon Argonauts*, 204–6.

Fort Vancouver changes Hussey, *Fort Vancouver*, 93–95.

Ogden's move and death Ibid., 95–96; Elliott, "Peter Skene Ogden," 266, 273; plaque on Highway 99 near Oregon City.

Dr. Barclay Nichols, "Fine Old Mansion," 38; information at Barclay House, Oregon City.

470   *"was fond of children..."* Andrina Catherine Barclay, in Nichols, "Fine Old Mansion," 41; Nichols, "Dr. Forbes Barclay."

Le Forest wedding Mary Le Forest, pioneer of 1852, in "Oldest House in Oregon City," *Morning Oregonian*, 12 May 1899, p. 2; Maria Louisa Rae Myrick, interview in Lockley, "Impressions," *Oregon Journal*, 21 September 1929.

"two parts of water..." Cole, *Early Oregon*, 72–73.

Red River trial HBRS 6:77–78 nn. 1, 2; Jackson, "Red River Settlers," 279–89.

"unfortunately, none...for non-fulfillment...as partners..." Dugald Mactavish

471

472

to W. G. Smith, HBC Secretary, 5 May 1855; Mactavish to GS, 21 July 1855, both from HBRS 6:77 n. 1, B.223/b/41, fos. 78–78d, 83d.

"came off in Portland..." Ibid.

"everything was going..." McL to John Fraser of St. Mark, 28 October 1856, *ME*, 254.

"you must not act" McL to Eliza Eppes, 23 July 1856, quoted in McL to John Fraser of St. Mark, 28 October 1856, *ME*, 254.

Sale of farm McL to John Fraser of St. Mark, 29 March 1854, 28 October 1856, 5 January 1857; McL to John Malcolm Fraser, 1 January 1857, 5 January 1857, all in *ME*, 78, 253–57.

"has not paid her..." McL to John Malcolm Fraser, 5 January 1857, *ME*, 256.

"I shall live..." La Fayette Grover to Frederick V. Holman, 14 September 1905, extract in Holman, *Dr. John McLoughlin,* 159. The same extract, almost verbatim, is in Bancroft, *Oregon,* 2:130–31 n. 53.

"Comment allez vous?" DeChesne to Eva Emery Dye, 6 October 1893, Dye Papers, MS 1089, OHSL.

Death of McL *Oregon Argus,* 5 September 1857.

Chapter 12–6: Last Things

472

McL's funeral Obituary, *Oregon Argus,* 5 September 1857.

"was carried on..." Hugh Burns to John March Smith, 6 September 1857, printed in *Oregon City Enterprise,* 7 July 1948, p. 1; Maria Louisa Rae Myrick, interview in Lockley, "Impressions," *Oregon Journal,* 21 September 1929.

McL's will Printed in *ME*, 302–4, from Book A, pp. 217–19, Records of Clackamas County, Oregon City.

Payments to Eliza McLoughlin's HBC account, in Barker, *Financial Papers,* 70, 72, 80, 82. The payments began August 23, 1839.

473

McL's estate Barker, *Financial Papers,* 5–35, contains a list of the entire estate, as appraised.

Real estate Ibid., 7–8.

Business assets Ibid., 8.

474

Personal goods Ibid., 9, 17.

McL's accounts Ibid., 9–15.

Appraisers' summary Ibid., 15.

475

"still in use" Daniel Harvey, report, ibid., 54.

David sells his share Barker, *Financial Papers,* 35. David was in the eastern part of Oregon Territory—today's Idaho.

Death of Marguerite ME, 17, 51–52.

"Thus Daniel Harvey..." Barker, *Financial Papers*, 35.

Last years of HBC at Fort Vancouver Hussey, *Fort Vancouver*, 98–114.

HBC leaves fort Hussey, *Fort Vancouver*, 110–14. The HBC and the Puget's Sound Agricultural Company presented claims of $5,449,936.67, including more than $1.2 million for their property at Vancouver. However, in 1869 the HBC was awarded $450,000 for all its "possessory rights and claims under the Oregon Treaty of 1846." The Puget's Sound Agricultural Company was allowed an additional $200,000, paid in 1870 and 1871. The negotiations involved 2,400 pages of printed evidence.

Previous sales of McL's land Bancroft, *Oregon*, 2:662. The University of Oregon, at Eugene, opened in 1876, $75,000 of its funds being derived from the sale of lands. Of this amount, nearly $10,000 was from sales from the McLoughlin claim.

476 *Land returned to Harveys* Holman, *Dr. John McLoughlin*, 159–61; Bancroft, *Oregon*, 2:131 n. 56.

Harveys sell property and move to Portland Smelser, "History of the McLoughlin House," 36; Zumwalt, "Old Home," 4.

477 *Oregon Pioneer Association* Bancroft, *Oregon*, 2:693. The association published the *Transactions of the Pioneer Association*, containing valuable source material, between 1874 and 1928. The pioneers held annual reunions; for the first one, on November 11, 1873, the "ladies had prepared bountifully for a feast." *OPAT* 1874, 7–8.

"If he had not helped..." Daniel S. Holman, in Holman, *Dr. John McLoughlin*, 280.

"His benevolent work..." Willard H. Rees, address to OPA, in *OPAT*, 1879:31.

"No possible line..." Burnett, "Recollections," *OHQ* 5 (March 1904): 93.

"Old white-haired John..." Thornton, "Provisional Government," 51.

"the late great and good..." Tolmie, *Journals*, 399.

478 *Portrait* Wilson, *Dr. John McLoughlin*, 163.

McLoughlin Day Ibid.

McLoughlin Memorial Association Smelser, "History of the McLoughlin House," 39.

Clackamas River bridge Wilson, *Dr. John McLoughlin*, 165.

McL's bust at the falls Ibid., 166.

"Father of Oregon" Oregon Blue Book, 1989–90:3

Half-dollar McClure, "The Good Dr. McLoughlin."

National Historic Site Wilson, *Dr. John McLoughlin*, 163.

Fort Vancouver Hussey, *Fort Vancouver,* vii–x; interview with David Hansen, archivist/historian.

479 *Church enlarged* "News Notes," *OHQ* 49 (September 1948): 257; *Oregon City Enterprise,* 7 July 1948; Wilson, *Dr. John McLoughlin,* 165.

First reburial The *Oregon City Enterprise* of 7 July 1948 has a news article and the address by Burt Brown Barker, both on p. 1. Other articles are in *Oregonian,* 7 July 1948, section 2:5; *Sunday Oregonian,* 4 July 1948, section 1:8; and *Journal* (Portland), 26 June 1948.

"in well preserved condition..." Oregon City Enterprise, 7 July 1948, 1.

480 *"again lowered..."* Ibid., 5.

Memorial erected Oregonian, 24 June 1970.

Second reburial Oregonian, 31 August 1970; Wilson, *Dr. John McLoughlin,* 166; author's interview with Thomas Vaughan.

481 *"in the garden park..."* Oregonian, 31 August 1970.

Sources

PUBLISHED WORKS

Aberdeen, George Hamilton-Gordon, Fourth Earl of. *Selections from the Correspondence of George Earl of Aberdeen, K.G., K.T., 1845.* Privately printed, 1885.

Allan, George T. "A Gallop through the Willamette." *OPAT* 1881:56-59.

———. "Journal of a Voyage from Fort Vancouver, Columbia River, to York Factory, Hudson's Bay, 1841." *OPAT* 1881:38-55.

———. "Reminiscences of Fort Vancouver on Columbia River, Oregon, as it Stood in 1832 ..." *OPAT* 1881:75-80.

Allen, Miss A. J., ed. *Ten Years in Oregon: Travels and Adventures of Doctor E. White and Lady...* Ithaca, N.Y., 1850.

Applegate, Jesse. "Letter to W. H. Rees, Secretary of OPA, 25 December 1874." *OHQ* 20 (December 1919): 397-99.

Arneson, James. "Property Concepts of Nineteenth Century Oregon Indians." *OHQ* 81 (Winter 1980): 391-422.

Bagley, Clarence B., ed. *Early Catholic Missions in Old Oregon.* 2 vols. Brussels, Belgium, 1847. Reprint, Seattle: Lowman & Hanford, 1932.

Baker, Abner S., III. "Experience, Personality and Memory: Jesse Applegate and John Minto Recall Pioneer Days." *OHQ* 81 (Fall 1980): 229-59.

Ball, John. "Across the Continent Seventy Years Ago: Extracts from the Journal of John Ball." Ed. Kate N. B. Powers. *OHQ* 3 (March 1902): 82-106.

———. *Autobiography of John Ball, Compiled by His Daughters, Kate Ball Powers, Flora Ball Hopkins, Lucy Ball.* Grand Rapids, Mich.: Dean-Hicks Company, 1925.

Bancroft, Hubert Howe. *History of the Northwest Coast.* 2 vols. San Francisco: The History Company, 1884, 1886.

———. *History of Oregon.* 2 vols. San Francisco: The History Company, 1886–88.

Barkan, Frances B. *The Wilkes Expedition: Puget Sound and the Oregon Country.* Olympia: Washington State Capital Museum, 1987.

Barker, Burt Brown. "The Dr. John McLoughlin House." Article written for the McLoughlin

Memorial Association, published in pamphlet form. At OHSL and McLoughlin House.

———. *The McLoughlin Empire and Its Rulers: Doctor John McLoughlin, Dr. David Mc-Loughlin, Marie Louise (Sister St. Henry)*. Northwest Historical Series, 5. Glendale, Calif.: Arthur H. Clark Company, 1959.

———. "Visit to the McLoughlin Country. The Annual Society Address." *OHQ* 51 (December 1950): 310-19.

———, ed. *The Financial Papers of Dr. John McLoughlin*. Portland: OHS, 1949. Reprinted from *OHQ*, March and September 1944, September 1949.

———. *Letters of Dr. John McLoughlin, Written at Fort Vancouver, 1829–1832*. Portland: Binfords & Mort, 1948.

Barry, J. Neilson. "Agriculture in the Oregon Country in 1795–1844." *OHQ* 30 (June 1929): 161-68.

———. "The Champoeg Meeting of March 4, 1844." *OHQ* 38 (December 1937): 425-32.

———. "First Local Government, 1841: Index to Primary Sources." *OHQ* 41 (June 1940): 195-202.

———. *The French Canadian Pioneers of the Willamette Valley*. Portland: Sentinel Press, ca. 1933.

Beaver, Herbert. "Experiences of a Chaplain at Fort Vancouver, 1836–1838." Beaver to Editor of *Church of England Protestant Magazine*, 1 February 1841, in issue of March 1841. Ed. R. C. Clark, reprinted in *OHQ* 39 (March 1938): 22-38.

———. "Mr. Beaver Objects . . . " Ed. Thomas E. Jessett. *The Beaver*, September 1941, 10-13.

———. *Reports and Letters of Herbert Beaver, 1836–1838*. Ed. Thomas E. Jessett. Portland: Champoeg Press, 1959.

Beck, Warren A., and Ynez D. Haase. *Historical Atlas of the American West*. Norman: University of Oklahoma Press, 1989.

Beckham, Stephen Dow. *Land of the Umpqua: A History of Douglas County, Oregon*. Roseburg, Ore.: Douglas County Commissioners, 1986.

Beidleman, Richard G. "Nathaniel Wyeth's Fort Hall." *OHQ* 58 (September 1957): 197-250.

Belcher, Edward. *Narrative of a Voyage around the World Performed in Her Majesty's Ship Sulphur, during the Years 1836–42...2 vols.* London: Henry Colburn, 1843.

Belknap, George N. "McMurtrie's Oregon Imprints: A Supplement." *OHQ* 51 (December 1950): 239-72.

Bibler, Stephen H. "Specimen of Abernethy Rock: A Medium of Exchange." *OHQ* 44 (September 1943): 249-52.

Biddle, Captain James. "Extract from Log of the U.S.S. *Ontario*, Captain James Biddle." Ed. T. C. Elliott. In "Documents," *OHQ* 3 (September 1902): 310-11.

Bigsby, John Jeremiah. *The Shoe and Canoe, or Pictures of Travel in the Canadas*. 2 vols. London: Chapman & Hall, 1850; New York: Paladin Press, 1850.

Binns, Archie. *Peter Skene Ogden: Fur Trader*. Portland: Binfords & Mort, 1967.

Bird, Annie Laurie. "Thomas McKay." *OHQ* 40 (March 1939): 1-14.

———. "The Will of Thomas McKay." *OHQ* 40 (March 1939): 15-18.

Blanchet, Archbishop Francis Norbert. *Historical Sketches of the Catholic Church in Oregon, during the Past Forty Years*. Portland: Sentinel Press, 1878.

Blue, George Verne. "Green's Missionary Report on Oregon, 1829." *OHQ* 30 (September 1929): 259-71.

———. "A Hudson's Bay Company Contract for Hawaiian Labor." *OHQ* 25 (March 1924): 72-75.

Boit, John. "John Boit's Log of the Columbia." Introduction by F. G. Young, notes by F. W. Howay and T. C. Elliott. *OHQ* 22 (December 1921): 257-351.

Bordwell, Constance. "Delay and Wreck of the *Peacock:* An Episode in the Wilkes Expedition." *OHQ* 92 (Summer 1991): 119-98.

Boyd, Robert. "The Pacific Northwest Measles Epidemic of 1847–1848." *OHQ* 95 (Spring 1994): 6-47.

Brewer, Henry Bridgeman. "The Diary of Henry Bridgeman Brewer. Being a Log of the Lausanne..." *OHQ* 29 (June, September, December 1928): 189-208, 288-309, 347-62; *OHQ* 30 (March, June 1929): 53-62, 111-19.

Bright, Verne. "The Folklore and History of the Oregon Fever." *OHQ* 52 (December 1951): 241-53.

Brosnan, Cornelius J. *Jason Lee: Prophet of the New Oregon*. New York: Macmillan, 1932.

———. "The Oregon Memorial of 1838." *OHQ* 34 (March 1933): 68-77.

Brown, J. Henry. *Brown's Political History of Oregon: Provisional Government*. Portland: Lewis & Dryden, 1892.

Brown, Jennifer S. *Strangers in Blood: Fur Trade Families in Indian Country*. Vancouver and London: University of British Columbia Press, 1980.

Bryce, George. *History of Manitoba*. Toronto and Montreal: The Canada History Company, 1906.

———. *The Remarkable History of the Hudson's Bay Company*. London: Sampson, Low, Marston, 1910.

———. *The Romantic Settlement of Lord Selkirk's Colonists (The Pioneers of Manitoba)*. New York: Musson Book Company, 1909.

Burnett, Peter. "Journal." *New York Herald*, December 1844–January 1845. Reprinted in George Wilkes, *History of Oregon, Geographical, Geological and Political;* and in George Wilkes, *An Account and History of the Oregon Territory*. Reprinted in *WHQ*, 1906-8.

———. "Letters," 10 November 1843 and 25 July 1844. *OHQ* 4 (June 1903): 180-83.

———. "Recollections and Opinions of an Old Pioneer." Chapters 3-6 of Burnett, "Journal," reprinted in *OHQ* 5 (March, June, September, December 1904): 64-99, 151- 98, 272-

305, 370-401.

Campbell, Marjorie Wilkins. *The North West Company*. Toronto: Macmillan of Canada, 1957.

Campbell, Susan J. *Competitive Fur Trade Tactics: Pointe de Meuron, 1817–1821*. In Thunder Bay Historical Museum Society Papers and Records, Thunder Bay, Ontario, vol. 1 (1973): 33-40.

Canse, John Martin. "Jason Lee: New Evidence on the Missionary and Colonizer." *WHQ* 6 (October 1915): 251-63.

Carey, Charles Henry. *General History of Oregon through Early Statehood*. Portland: Binfords & Mort, 1971. Originally published as *A General History of Oregon Prior to 1861*. 3 vols., Portland: Pioneer Historical Publishing Company, 1922. Reprint, 2 vols., Portland: Metropolitan Press, 1935–36.

———, ed. "Lee, Walker, and McLoughlin." *OHQ* 33 (September 1932): 187-213.

Caulfield, Vera. "Two Houses. How McLoughlin House Was Saved." *OHQ* 76 (September 1975): 299-301.

Caywood, Louis R. "The Archaeological Excavation of Fort Vancouver." *OHQ* 49 (March 1948): 99-116.

Chaboillez, Charles. "Journal of Charles Chaboillez, 1797–1798." In Payette, *The Northwest*, 142-217.

Chadwick, S. F. "Address to Oregon Pioneer Association." *OPAT* 1874:15-32.

Clark, Dan Elbert. "Manifest Destiny and the Pacific." *Pacific Historical Review*, 1932:1-17.

Clark, Robert Carlton. "Editorial Comment: Reverend Herbert Beaver." *OHQ* 39 (March 1938): 66-73.

———. *History of the Willamette Valley, Oregon*. 3 vols. Chicago: S. J. Clarke Publishing Company, 1927.

———. "How British and American Subjects Unite in a Common Government for Oregon in 1844." *OHQ* 13 (June 1912): 140-59.

Clarke, Samuel A. *Pioneer Days of Oregon History*. 2 vols. Portland: J. K. Gill Company, 1905.

Cogswell, Philip, Jr. *Capitol Names: Individuals Woven into Oregon's History*. Portland: OHS Press, 1977.

Cole, George. *Early Oregon*. Spokane, Wash.: private print, 1905.

Cole, Jean Murray. *Exile in the Wilderness: The Life of Chief Factor Archibald McDonald, 1790–1853*. Seattle: University of Washington Press, 1979.

Corning, Howard M. *Willamette Landings—Ghost Towns of the River*. Portland: Binfords & Mort, 1947.

———, ed. *Dictionary of Oregon History*. Portland: Binfords & Mort, 1956.

Cox, Ross. *Adventures on the Columbia River*. London, 1831. Reprint, ed. Edgar I. Stewart and Jan R. Stewart., Norman: University of Oklahoma Press, 1957.

Crawford, Medorem. *Journal of Medorem Crawford. An Account of His Trip across the Plains with the Oregon Pioneers of 1842.* Eugene, Ore.: Star Job Office, 1897.

———. "Occasional Address." *OPAT* 1881:9-19.

Cummings, R. O. *American Ice Harvests.* Berkeley: University of California Press, 1949.

Daniels, Roy. *Alexander Mackenzie and the North West.* London: Faber & Faber, 1969.

Davidson, Gordon Charles. *The North West Company.* New York: Russell & Russell, 1967.

Davies, K. G. "From Competition to Union." *Minnesota History* 40, no. 4 (Winter 1966): 166.

Davis, William Heath. *Seventy-Five Years in California.* Ed. Douglas S. Watson. San Francisco: John Howell, 1929.

Deloge, Yvon. "Fraser (ffraser), Malcolm." In Wallace, *Dictionary of Canadian Biography,* 7:330-31.

Dillon, Richard. *Siskiyou Trail: The Hudson's Bay Fur Company Route to California.* New York: McGraw-Hill, 1975.

Dobbs, Caroline C. *Men of Champoeg: A Record of the Lives of the Pioneers Who Founded the Oregon Government.* Portland: Metropolitan Press, 1932. Reprint, Cottage Grove, Ore.: Emerald Valley Craftsmen, 1975.

Douglas, David. *Douglas of the Forests: The North American Journals of David Douglas.* Ed. John Davies. Seattle: University of Washington Press, 1980.

———. *Journal Kept by David Douglas during his Travels in North America, 1823–1827.* London: Royal Horticultural Society, 1914. Reprint, New York: Antiquarian Press, 1959.

———. "Sketch of a Journey to the Northwestern Parts of the Continent of North America during the Years 1824–'25–'26–'27." *OHQ* 5 (September, December 1904): 230-71, 324-69; *OHQ* 6 (March, June 1905): 76-97, 206-27.

Douglas, James. "Douglas Expeditions, 1840–41." Ed. Herman A. Leader. *OHQ* 32 (March, June, September, December 1931): 1-22, 145-64, 262-78, 350-72.

———. "The James Douglas Report on 'The Beaver Affair.'" Ed. W. Kaye Lamb. *OHQ* 47 (March 1946): 16-28.

Douglas, Thomas, Fifth Earl of Selkirk. *Lord Selkirk's Diary, August 5, 1803 to December 15, 1804.* Ed. Patrick C. T. White. HBRS 35. Toronto: Champlain Society, 1958.

Douthit, Nathan. "The Hudson's Bay Company and the Indians of Southern Oregon." *OHQ* 93 (Spring 1992): 25-64.

Driver, Rev. I. D. "Annual Address." *OPAT* 1887:21-31.

Drury, Clifford M. *Marcus and Narcissa Whitman and the Opening of Old Oregon.* 2 vols. Pacific Northwest Parks and Forest Association, 1986.

———, ed. *First White Women over the Rockies: Diaries, Letters, and Biographical Sketches of the Six Women of the Oregon Mission Who Made the Overland Journey in 1836 and 1838.* 2 vols. Glendale, Calif.: Arthur H. Clark Company, 1963.

Duniway, David C., and Neil R. Riggs, eds. "The Oregon Archives, 1841–1843." *OHQ* 60 (June 1959): 211-80.

Dunn, John. *History of the Oregon Territory and British North-American Fur Trade, with an Account of the Habits and Customs of the Principal Native Tribes on the Northern Continent*. London: Edwards & Hughes, 1844.

Dye, Eva Emery. "Boone Family Reminiscences As Told to Mrs. Dye." *OHQ* 42 (September 1941): 220-29.

————. *Hudson's Bay Company Regime in the Oregon Country*. Bulletin of the University of Oregon Historical Series, vol. 1, no. 2, 1898.

————. *McLoughlin and Old Oregon*. Chicago: A. C. McClurg & Company, 1901.

————, ed. "Old Letters from HBC Officials and Employees from 1829 to 1840." In "Documents," *WHQ* 1 (July, October 1907; January, April 1908): 256-66, 40-43, 161-68, 254-64.

Edwards, G. Thomas. "The Oregon Trail in the Columbia Gorge, 1843–1855: The Final Ordeal." *OHQ* 97 (Summer 1996): 134 75.

Edwards, Phillip Leget. *California in 1837. Diary of Col. P. L. Edwards, Containing an Account of His Trip on the Pacific Coast in 1837*. Sacramento, Calif.: A. J. Johnson & Company, 1890.

————. *Sketch of the Oregon Country: Emigrants' Guide*. Liberty, Mo., 1842. Reprint, Fairfield, Wash.: Ye Galleon Press, 1971.

Egan, Ferrol. *Frémont: Explorer for a Restless Nation*. New York: Doubleday & Company, 1977.

Eide, Ingvard Henry. *The Oregon Trail*. Chicago, New York, San Francisco: Rand McNally & Company, 1972.

Elliott, Thompson Coit. "The Coming of the White Women, 1836." *OHQ* 37 (June, September, December 1936): 87-101, 171-91, 275-90; *OHQ* 38 (March, June 1937): 44-62, 206-23.

————. "Dr. John McLoughlin and His Guests." *WHQ* 3 (October 1908): 63-77.

————. "An Event of One Hundred Years Ago." Contains journal of J. H. Aulick. *OHQ* 19 (September 1918): 181-87.

————. "The Fur Trade in the Columbia River Basin Prior to 1811." *WHQ* 6 (1915).

————. "A Hudson's Bay Company Marriage Certificate." *OHQ* 10 (September 1909): 325-30.

————. "Marguerite Wadin McKay McLoughlin." *OHQ* 36 (December 1935): 338-47.

————. "The Oregon Coast As Seen by Vancouver in 1792." *OHQ* 30 (March, December 1929): 33-42, 384-94.

————. "Peter Skene Ogden, Fur Trader." *OHQ* 11 (September 1910): 229-78.

————. "The Surrender at Astoria in 1818." *OHQ* 19 (December 1918): 271-82.

Ermatinger, C. O., ed. "A Tragedy on the Stikene in '42." *OHQ* 15 (March 1914): 126-32.

Ermatinger, Francis. "Earliest Expedition against Puget Sound Indians." Ed. Eva Emery Dye. *WHQ* 1 (January 1907): 16-29.

————. *Fur Trade Letters of Francis Ermatinger Written to His Brother Edward during His Service with the Hudson's Bay Company, 1819–1853*. Ed. Lois Halliday McDonald. Glendale, Calif.: Arthur H. Clark Company, 1980.

Evans, Elwood. *History of the Pacific Northwest, Oregon and Washington, Embracing an Account of the Original Documents on the Pacific Coast of North America...in the Original Territory of Oregon.* 2 vols. Portland: North Pacific History Company, 1889.

Farnham, Thomas J. *Travels in the Great Western Prairies, the Anahuac and Rocky Mountains, and in the Oregon Territory.* Poughkeepsie, N.Y.: Killey & Lossing, 1841. Reprinted in *Early Western Travels, 1748–1846,* ed. Reuben Gold Thwaites, vols. 28, 29. Cleveland: Arthur H. Clark Company, 1906.

Fleming, R. Harvey, ed. *Minutes of Council, Northern Department of Rupert Land, 1821–31.* Introduction by H. A. Innis. HBRS 3. Toronto: Champlain Society, 1940; London, Hudson's Bay Record Society, 1940.

Franchère, Gabriel. *Narrative of a Voyage to the Northwest Coast of America, in the Years 1811, 1812, 1813, and 1814...*New York: Redfield, 1854. Reprint, New York: Citadel Press, 1968.

Francis, Daniel. *Battle for the West.* Edmonton: Hurtig, 1982.

Frein, P. J., trans. "Address by the Canadian Settlers of the Willamette Valley." Facsimile of original text and translation into English. *OHQ* 13 (September 1912): 338-43.

Frémont, John Charles. *Report of the Exploring Expedition to the Rocky Mountains in the Year 1842 and to Oregon and North California in the Years 1843–44.* Washington, D.C.: Gales & Seaton, 1845.

Frost, Rev. John H. "Journal of John [Joseph] H. Frost." Ed. Nellie Pipes. *OHQ* 35 (March, June, September, December 1934): 50-73, 139-67, 235-62, 348-75.

Galbraith, John S. "The Early History of the Puget's Sound Agricultural Company, 1838–43." *OHQ* 55 (September 1954): 234-59.

———. *The Hudson's Bay Company as an Imperial Factor, 1821–1869.* Berkeley and Los Angeles: University of California Press, 1957.

———. *The Little Emperor: Governor Simpson of the Hudson's Bay Company.* Toronto: Macmillan of Canada, 1976.

Gary, Rev. George. "Diary of Rev. George Gary." Ed. Charles Henry Carey. *OHQ* 24 (March, June, September, December 1923): 68-105, 153-85, 269-333, 386-433.

Gay, Theressa. *Life and Letters of Mrs. Jason Lee, First Wife of Rev. Jason Lee of the Oregon Mission.* Portland: Metropolitan Press, ca. 1936.

Geer, Mrs. Elizabeth Dixon Smith. "Diary Written on the Oregon Trail." *OPAT* 1907: 153-79.

Geer, Theodore T. *Fifty Years in Oregon: Experiences, Observations, and Commentaries upon Men, Measures, and Customs in Pioneer Days and Later Times.* New York: Neale Publishing Company, 1912.

———. "Incidents in the Organization of the Provisional Government." *OHQ* 2 (December 1901): 366-80.

Gibson, James R. *Farming the Frontier: The Agricultural Opening of the Oregon Country, 1786–1846.* Seattle and London: University of Washington Press, 1985.

Gilbert, James Henry. *Trade and Currency in Early Oregon: A Study in the Commercial and Monetary History of the Pacific Northwest*. Columbia University Studies in History, Economics and Public Law, vol. 26, no 1. New York: Columbia University Press, 1907.

Glazebrook, G. P. de T., ed. *The Hargrave Correspondence, 1821–1843*. Toronto: Champlain Society, 1938.

Glimpses of the Monastery. Scenes from a Brief Sketch of the History of the Ursulines of Quebec during Two Hundred Years, 1639–1839. By a Member of the Community. Quebec: D. Darveau, 1875. 2d ed., Quebec: L. J. Demers & Frère, 1897.

Glover, Richard, ed. *David Thompson's Narrative, 1784–1812*. Toronto: Champlain Society, 1962.

Graustein, Jeanette E. *Thomas Nuttall, Naturalist. Explorations in America, 1808–1841*. Cambridge: Harvard University Press, 1967.

Gray, John Morgan. *Lord Selkirk of Red River*. Toronto: Macmillan of Canada, 1963.

Gray, William H. *History of Oregon, 1792–1849, Drawn from Personal Observation and Authentic Information*. Portland: Harris & Holman; San Francisco: H. H. Bancroft & Company; New York: American News Company, 1870.

Greenhow, Robert. *The History of Oregon and California and Other Territories of the North-West Coast of North America Accompanied by a Geographical View...*Boston, 1844; Los Angeles: Sherwin & Freutal, 1970.

Grover, La Fayette, comp. *The Oregon Archives, Including the Journals, Governor's Messages and Public Papers of Oregon, from the Earliest Attempt...to Form a Government Down to and Inclusive of...Jan 26, 1853*. Salem, Ore.: A. Bush, 1853.

Hakola, John W., ed. *Frontier Omnibus*. Missoula: Montana State University Press, and Helena: Historical Society of Montana, 1962.

Halkett, John. *Statement Respecting the Earl of Selkirk's Settlement upon the Red River...* London: John Murray, 1817; New York: James Eastburn & Company, 1818; facsimile edition, Toronto: Coles Publishing Company, 1970.

Harmon, Daniel Williams. *A Journal of Voyages and Travels in the Interior of North America, between the 47th and 58th Degrees of North Latitude*. New York: A. S. Barnes & Company, 1903; ed. Daniel Haskell, Andover, Vt., 1820; American Explorers Series, New York: Allerton Book Co., 1922.

———. *Sixteen Years in the Indian Country: The Journal of Daniel Williams Harmon, 1800–1816*. Ed. W. Kaye Lamb. Toronto: Macmillan of Canada, 1957.

Harvey, A. G. "Chief Concomly's Skull." *OHQ* 40 (June 1939): 161-67.

Hastings, Lansford W. *The Emigrants' Guide to Oregon and California*. Ed. Charles Henry Carey. Princeton, N.J.: Princeton University Press, 1932.

———. Letter in *Saint Louis New Era*, 25 March 1844. Excerpted in *OHQ* 2 (June 1901): 202.

———. *A New History of Oregon and California; Containing Complete Descriptions of Those Countries, Together with...a Vast Amount of Information...* Cincinnati, Ohio: George

Conklin, 1847.

Henry, Alexander [the Younger]. *The Journal of Alexander Henry the Younger, 1799– 1814.* Ed. Barry M. Gough. Toronto: Champlain Society, 1988.

———. *New Light on the Early History of the Greater North West. The Manuscript Journals of Alexander Henry, Fur Trader of the Northwest Company, and of David Thompson* ... Ed. Elliott Coues. 3 vols. New York: Francis P. Harper, 1897; facsimile reprint, 2 vols., Minneapolis: Ross & Haines, 1965.

Hill, Douglas. *The Opening of the Canadian West*. New York: John Day Company, 1967.

Hill, William E. *The Oregon Trail: Yesterday and Today. A Brief History and Pictorial Journey along the Wagon Tracks of Pioneers*. Caldwell, Idaho: Caxton Printers, 1987.

Hines, Gustavus. *Life on the Plains of the Pacific: Oregon: Its History, Condition, and Prospects...* Buffalo, N.Y.: George H. Derby and Company, 1851.

Hines, H. K. *Missionary History of the Pacific North West, Containing the Wonderful Story of Jason Lee with Sketches of Many of His Co-laborers*. Privately published, 1899.

Holman, Frederick V. "Dedication of the McLoughlin House." *OHQ* 10 (December 1909): 384-85.

———. *Dr. John McLoughlin, the Father of Oregon*. Cleveland: Arthur H. Clark Company, 1907.

———. "Some Important Results from the Expeditions of John Jacob Astor to, and from, the Oregon Country." *OHQ* 12 (September 1911): 206-19.

Holmes, Kenneth. *Ewing Young, Master Trapper*. Portland: Binfords & Mort, 1967.

———. "Mount St. Helens, Recent Eruptions." *OHQ* 56 (June 1955): 197-210.

Howay, F. W. "The Brig Owhyhee in the Columbia, 1827." *OHQ* 34 (December 1933): 324-29.

———. "The Brig Owhyhee in the Columbia, 1829–30." *OHQ* 35 (March 1934): 10-21.

Howerton, N. A. "Untold Story of the Peacock Wrecked in 1841." *OHQ* 43 (June 1942): 129-34.

Howison, Lieut. Neil M. "Report of Lieutenant Neil M. Howison on Oregon, 1846." House Miscellaneous Documents, no. 29, 30th Congress, 1st sess. *OHQ* 14 (March 1913): 1-60.

Hulbert, A. B., and Dorothy F. Hulbert. *Overland to the Pacific*. 8 vols. Denver: The Stewart Commission of Colorado College, Denver Public Library, 1932–41.

Hussey, John A. *Champoeg: Place of Transition*. Portland: OHS, Oregon State Highway Department, and National Park Service, 1967.

———. *Fort Vancouver: The History of Fort Vancouver and Its Physical Structure*. Portland: Washington State Historical Society and National Park Service, 1957.

———. *Historic Structures Report, Fort Vancouver.* 2 vols. Denver Service Center, National Park Service, U.S. Department of the Interior, June 1972, April 1976.

———. "The Women of Fort Vancouver." *OHQ* 92 (Fall 1991): 265-308.

Innis, Harold A. *The Fur Trade in Canada: An Introduction to Canadian Economic History.*

New Haven: Yale University Press, 1930.

———. *Peter Pond, Fur Trader and Adventurer*. Toronto: Irwin & Gordon, 1930.

Irving, Washington. *Astoria*. Philadelphia, 1836. Reprint, Portland: Binfords & Mort, 1967.

Jackson, John C. "Red River Settlers vs. Puget Sound Agriculture Company, 1854–55." *OHQ* 85 (Fall 1984): 278-89.

Jenkins, Kathleen. *Montreal, Island City of the St. Lawrence*. New York: Doubleday, 1966.

Johansen, Dorothy. "McLoughlin and the Indians." *The Beaver*, June 1946, 18-21.

Johansen, Dorothy, and Charles M. Gates. *Empire of the Columbia: A History of the Pacific Northwest*. New York, Evanston, and London: Harper & Row, 1957.

Jones, Robert F. "The Identity of the *Tonquin's* Interpreter." *OHQ* 98 (Fall 1997): 296-314.

Josephy, Alvin M. *The Nez Perce Indians and the Opening of the Northwest*. New Haven: Yale University Press, 1965. Abridged edition, Lincoln and London: University of Nebraska Press, 1971.

Judson, Katharine B., ed. "Documentary, MCL to GS, March 20, 1844." *OHQ* 17 (September 1916): 215-39.

Kelley, Hall. *Hall J. Kelley on Oregon*. Ed. Fred Wilbur Powell. Princeton, N.J.: Princeton University Press, 1932. Reprint, New York: Da Capo Press, 1972.

Knight, James. *The Founding of Churchill: Being the Journal of Captain James Knight, Governor-in-Chief of Hudson Bay from 14th of July to 13th of September, 1717*. Ed. James F. Kenney, PAC. Toronto: J. M. Dent & Sons, 1932.

Knuth, Priscilla, ed. "HMS *Modeste* on the Pacific Coast, 1843–47: Log and Letters." *OHQ* 61 (December 1960): 408-36.

Labonte, Louis. "Reminiscences." Ed. H. S. Lyman. *OHQ* 1 (June 1900): 169-88.

Lalande, Jeff. *First over the Siskiyous: Peter Skene Ogden's 1826–1829 Journey through the Oregon-California Borderlands*. Portland: OHS Press, 1987.

Lamb, W. Kaye. Introduction to *Letters of John McLoughlin from Fort Vancouver to the Governor and Committee*. First, second, and third series, HBRS 4, 6, and 7. Toronto: Champlain Society, 1941, 1943, 1944.

Landerholm, Carl. *Vancouver Area Chronology, 1784–1958*. Vancouver, Wash., 1960.

Lang, H. O. *History of the Willamette Valley, Being a Description of the Valley and Its Resources... Together with Personal Reminiscences of Its Early Pioneers*. Portland: G. H. Himes, 1885.

Larpenteur, Charles. *Forty Years a Fur Trader on the Upper Missouri. The Personal Narrative of Charles Larpenteur, 1833–1872*. 2 vols. Ed. Elliott Coues. New York: Francis P. Harper, 1898. Reprint, Minneapolis: Ross & Hines, 1962.

Leader, Herman A. "Douglas Expeditions, 1840–41." *OHQ* 32 (March, June, September, December 1931): 1-23, 145-64, 262-78, 350-72.

———, ed. "McLoughlin's Answer to Warre Report." *OHQ* 33 (September 1932): 214-29.

Leary, David T. "Slacum in the Pacific, 1832–37: Backgrounds of the Oregon Report." *OHQ* 76 (June 1975): 118-34.

Lee, Daniel, and Joseph Frost. *Ten Years in Oregon*. New York: J. Collard, 1844. Reprint, Fairfield, Wash.: Ye Galleon Press, 1968.

Lee, Jason. "The Diary of Reverend Jason Lee." *OHQ* 17 (June, September, December 1916): 116-46, 240-66, 397-430.

Lockley, Fred. *Conversations with Pioneer Women*. Eugene, Ore.: Rainy Day Press, 1981.

———. "Impressions and Observations of the Journal Man." Column in *Oregon Journal*, 1929.

———. *Oregon's Yesterdays*. New York: Knickerbocker Press, 1928.

———. *Recollections of Benjamin Franklin Bonney*. Fairfield, Wash.: Ye Galleon Press, 1969. Reprinted from *OHQ* 24 (March 1923): 36-55.

Loewenberg, Robert J. *Equality on the Oregon Frontier*. Seattle: University of Washington Press, 1976.

Lomax, Alfred L. "Hawaii-Columbia River Trade in Early Days." *OHQ* 43 (September 1942): 328-38.

London, J. C. *An Encyclopoedia of Agriculture: Comprising the Theory and Practice of the Valuation, Transfer, Laying Out, Improvement, and Management of Landed Property*. 5th ed. London: Thompson, Rees, Orne, Brown, Green & Longman, 1835.

Lyman, Horace S. "Address to OPA." *OPAT* 1886:66-77.

———. "Dr. John McLoughlin." *OPAT* 1886:41-58.

McArthur, Lewis A. *Oregon Geographic Names*. 6th ed. Portland: OHS Press, 1992.

McClure, Dudley L. "The Good Dr. McLoughlin." *Numismatic News*, 23 June 1984, 692-94. Clipping at OHSL.

McDonald, Archibald. *Peace River: A Canoe Voyage from the Hudson's Bay to the Pacific by the Late Sir George Simpson*. Ed. Malcolm McLeod. Ottawa: J. Durie & Son, 1872. Reprint, Edmonton: M. C. Hurtig, 1971.

McGillivray, Duncan. *The Journal of Duncan McGillivray of the North West Company at Fort George on the Saskatchewan... 1794–5*. Ed. A. S. Morton. Toronto: University of Toronto Press, 1929.

MacKay, Douglas. *The Honourable Company: A History of the Hudson's Bay Company*. Indianapolis and New York: Bobbs-Merrill, 1936.

McKay, William. "Additional Light on the Whitman Matter." *OPAT* 1889:91-93.

McLeod, Alexander Roderick. "Journal of a Hunting Expedition to the Southland of the Umpquas under the Command of A. R. McLeod C. T. September 1826." In *Peter Skene Ogden's Snake Country Journals*, HBRS 23:175-219.

"McLoughlin House." Pamphlet at OHSL.

McLoughlin, John. "Autobiography." In Clarke, *Pioneer Days*, 1:215-26.

———. "Cost of Improvements Made by Dr. John McLoughlin at Willamette Falls to January

1, 1841." *OHQ* 14 (March 1913): 68-70.

———. "Document Found among the Private Papers of the Late Dr. John McLoughlin." *OPAT* 1880:46-55. Reprinted as "Autobiography" in Clarke, *Pioneer Days*, 1:215-26.

———. "Documentary: Doctor John McLoughlin to Sir George Simpson, March 20, 1844. Ed. Katharine B. Judson. *OHQ* 17 (September 1916): 215-39.

———. "Dr. John McLoughlin's Last Letter to the Hudson's Bay Company, as Chief Factor in Charge at Fort Vancouver, 1845." Ed. Katharine B. Judson. *American Historical Review* 21, no. 1 (October 1915): 104-34.

———. "The Indians from Fort William to Lake of the Woods." McGill University MS 2364, printed in *Amphora* (Alcuin Society, Vancouver, Canada) 8 (Spring-Summer 1971): 9-16.

———. *John McLoughlin's Business Correspondence, 1847–48*. Ed. William R. Sampson. Seattle and London: University of Washington Press, 1973.

———. "Letter of Dr. John McLoughlin, Published in the *Oregon Spectator,* Thursday September 12, 1850." In Holman, *Dr. John McLoughlin*, 229-43.

———. "Letter of Dr. John McLoughlin to *Oregon Statesman*, June 8, 1852." In McLoughlin Papers, MS 575, OHSL, reprinted in *OHQ* 8 (September 1907): 294-99.

———. *Letters of Dr. John McLoughlin, Written at Fort Vancouver, 1829–1832*. Ed. Burt Brown Barker. Portland: Binfords & Mort, 1948.

———. "Letters of Dr. McLoughlin to Edward Ermatinger." Ed. T. C. Elliott. *OHQ* 23 (December 1922): 365-71.

———. *The Letters of John McLoughlin from Fort Vancouver to the Governor and Committee, First Series, 1825–38*. Ed. E. E. Rich. *HBRS* 4. Toronto: Champlain Society, 1941.

———. *The Letters of John McLoughlin from Fort Vancouver to the Governor and Committee, Second Series, 1839–44*. Ed. E. E. Rich. *HBRS* 6. Toronto: Champlain Society, 1943.

———. *The Letters of John McLoughlin from Fort Vancouver to the Governor and Committee, Third Series, 1844–46*. Ed. E. E. Rich. *HBRS* 7. Toronto: Champlain Society, 1944.

———. "A Narrative of Events in Early Oregon Ascribed to Dr. John McLoughlin." *OHQ* 1 (June 1900): 193-206.

Maloney, A. B. "Hudson's Bay Company in California." *OHQ* 37 (March 1936): 9-23.

Martin, Chester. *Lord Selkirk's Work in Canada*. Oxford: Oxford University Press, 1916.

Matthieu, Francis Xavier. "Reminiscences." Ed. H. S. Lyman. *OHQ* 1 (March 1900): 66-104.

Memorial of the Legislative Assembly of Oregon Territory, Relative to Their Present Situation and Wants. Documents sent to 30th Congress, 1st sess., 10 August 1848. Fairfield, Wash.: Ye Galleon Press, 1972.

Merk, Frederick. *The Oregon Question: Essays in Anglo-American Diplomacy and Politics*. Cambridge: Belknap Press of Harvard University Press, 1967.

———. "Snake Country Expedition, 1824–25, an Episode of Fur Trade and Empire." *OHQ* 35 (June 1934): 93-122.

————, ed. *Fur Trade and Empire: George Simpson's Journal; Remarks Connected with the Fur Trade in the Course of a Voyage from York Factory to Fort George and Back to York Factory, 1824–1825.* Harvard Historical Studies, vol. 31. Cambridge: Harvard University Press, 1931.

Milln, Nadiene. "The First Bastile." *Clackamas County Historical,* 1968–69, 12-18.

Milner, John. *The End of Religious Controversy in a Friendly Correspondence between a Religious Society of Protestants and a Roman Catholic Divine.* London: Art and Book, 1842.

Minto, John. "Antecedents of the Oregon Pioneers and the Light These Throw on Their Motives." *OHQ* 5 (March 1904): 38-63.

————. "Champoeg, Marion County, the First Grain Market in Oregon." *OHQ* 15 (September 1914): 283-84.

————. "Early Days of Oregon." *OPAT* 1874:26-27.

————. "Occasional Address." *OPAT* 1876:35-50.

————. "Reminiscences of Hon. John Minto, Pioneer of 1844." *OHQ* 2 (June, September 1901): 119-67, 209-54.

————. "Robert Wilson Morrison." *OPAT* 1894:53-66.

————. "What I Know of Dr. McLoughlin and How I Know It." *OHQ* 11 (June 1910): 177-200.

"Mission Record Book of the Methodist Episcopal Church, Willamette Station, Oregon Territory, Commenced 1834." Introduction by Charles Henry Carey. *OHQ* 23 (September 1922): 230-66.

Molson, Mrs. William Markland. "Glimpses of Life in Early Oregon." *OHQ* 1 (June 1900): 158-64.

Morgan, Dale. *Jedediah Smith and the Opening of the West.* Indianapolis: Bobbs- Merrill, 1953.

Morison, Samuel Eliot. "New England and the Opening of the Columbia River Salmon Trade, 1830." *OHQ* 28 (June 1927): 111-32.

Morrison, Dorothy N., and Jean Morrison. "John McLoughlin, Reluctant Fur Trader." *OHQ* 81 (Winter 1980): 377-90.

Morrison, Jean, ed. *The North West Company in Rebellion: Simon McGillivray's Fort William Notebook, 1815.* PAC, Simon McGillivray Papers, MG 19 A35, vol. 7, notebook 4. Thunder Bay, Ontario: Thunder Bay Historical Museum Society, 1988.

Morton, Arthur S. *A History of the Canadian West to 1870–71 Being a History of Rupert's Land...and of the North-West Territory (Including the Pacific Slope).* London, 1939. Ed. Lewis G. Thomas, Toronto: University of Toronto Press, 1973.

Nanuwan of Chiboogama, Hudson's Bay Company. "Solomon Voyageur." *The Beaver,* March 1929, 162-63.

Nesmith, J. W. "Diary of the Emigration of 1843." *OHQ* 7 (December 1906): 329-59.

Newell, Robert. *Robert Newell's Memoranda: Travles in the Territory of Missourie; Travle to the Kayuse War; Together with a Report on the Indians South of the Columbia River.*

Ed. Dorothy O. Johansen. Portland: Champoeg Press, 1959.

Newman, Peter C. *Caesars of the Wilderness*. Vol. 2 of *Company of Adventurers*. Markham, Ont.: Penguin Books, 1987.

Nichols, M. Leona. "Fine Old Mansion." *Clackamas County Historical*, 1966–67, 36–43.

Nicolay, Charles Grenfell. *The Oregon Territory: A Geographical and Physical Account of That Country and Its Inhabitants; with Outlines of Its History and Discovery*. London, 1846. Reprint, Fairfield, Wash.: Ye Galleon Press, 1967.

Nute, Grace Lee. *The Voyageur*. New York and London: D. Appleton & Company, 1931; Reprint, St. Paul: Minnesota Historical Society, 1955.

———. *The Voyageur's Highway: Minnesota's Border Lake Land*. St. Paul: Minnesota Historical Society, 1941.

O'Donnell, Terence. *An Arrow in the Earth: General Joel Palmer and the Indians of Oregon*. Portland: OHS Press, 1991.

Ogden, Peter Skene. "The Peter Skene Ogden Journals." Ed. T. C. Elliott, copied by Agnes C. Laut from HBCA. 1825–26, *OHQ* 10 (December 1909): 331-65; 1826-27, *OHQ* 11 (June 1910): 201-22; 1827-28 and 1828-29, *OHQ* 11 (December 1910): 355-97.

———. *Peter Skene Ogden's Snake Country Journals*. Vol. 1, 1824 and 1825–26, ed. E. E. Rich, HBRS 13; vol. 2, 1826–27, ed. K. G. Davies, HBRS 23:3-134; vol. 3, 1827–28 and 1828–29, ed. Glyndwr Williams, HBRS 28. London: Hudson's Bay Record Society, 1950, 1961, 1971. Vol. 2 also contains A. R. McLeod's journal (HBRS 23:175-219).

———. *Traits of American Indian Life and Character, by a Fur Trader*. London, 1853. Reprint, San Francisco: Grabhorn Press, 1933.

O'Hara, Edwin V. *Catholic History of Oregon*. 3d ed. Portland: Catholic Book Company, 1925. First published as *Pioneer Catholic History of Oregon*.

Oliver, Edmund H., ed. *The Canadian North-West: Its Early Development and Legislative Records: Minutes of the Councils of the Red River Colony and the Northern Department of Rupert's Land*. 2 vols. Publications of the Canadian Archives. Ottawa: Government Printing Bureau, 1914–15.

O'Meara, Walter. *The Last Portage*. Boston: Houghton Mifflin Company, 1962.

Ormsby, Margaret A. *British Columbia: A History*. Vancouver, B.C.: Macmillan of Canada, 1958.

Palmer, Joel. *Journal of Travels over the Rocky Mountains, to the Mouth of the Columbia River; Made during the Years 1845 and 1846...* Early Western Travels, ed. Reuben Gold Thwaites, vol. 30. Cleveland, Ohio: Arthur H. Clark Company, 1906. Reprint, Fairfield, Wash.: Ye Galleon Press, 1983.

Parker, Samuel. *Journal of an Exploring Tour beyond the Rocky Mountain*. Ithaca, N.Y.: Mack, Andrus, & Woodruff, 1842.

Payette, B. C., ed. *The Northwest*. Montreal: Printed privately for Payette Radio, 1964.

———. *The Oregon Country under the Union Jack*. Montreal: Printed privately for Payette

Radio, 1962.

Pelletier, Abbé Edouard. *Album Historique et Paroissial de Notre-Dame du Portage, 1723 à 1940*. Quebec: Abbé Edouard Pelletier, 1942.

Phillips, Paul C. *The Fur Trade*. Norman: University of Oklahoma Press, 1961.

———, ed. "Family Letters of Two Oregon Fur Traders, 1828–1856." In *Frontier Omnibus*, ed. John W. Hakola. Missoula: Montana State University Press, and Helena: Historical Society of Montana, 1962.

Pike, C. J. "Petitions of Oregon Settlers, 1838–1848." *OHQ* 34 (September 1933): 216-35.

Pipes, Nellie. "Indian Conditions in 1836–38." *OHQ* 32 (December 1931): 332-42.

———, ed. and trans. "Extracts from the Exploration of Oregon Territory of Eugene Duflot de Mofras." *OHQ* 26 (June 1925): 115-90. Contains chaps. 7, 8 of Duflot, *Exploration du Territorie de l'Oregon, des Californies et de la Mer Vermeille*.

Pollard, Lancaster. "Site of the Smith Massacre of July 14, 1828." *OHQ* 45 (June 1944): 133-37.

Powers, Alfred. *History of Oregon Literature*. Portland: Metropolitan Press, 1935.

Prebble, John. *The Highland Clearances*. Martin Secker & Warburg, 1963; Hammondsworth, England: Penguin Books, 1963.

Prince, Suzanne. "McLoughlin, Marie-Louise." In Wallace, *Dictionary of Canadian Biography*, 573.

Prosch, Thomas. "Efforts to Save the Historic McLoughlin House." *WHQ* 1 (January 1907): 36-42.

Rasky, Frank. *The Taming of the Canadian West*. Toronto: McClelland & Stewart, 1960.

Rees, Willard H. "In Memorium of Willard H. Rees." *OHQ* 4 (December 1903): 386-91.

Reid, John Phillips. "Restraints of Vengeance: Retaliation-in-Kind and the Use of Indian Law in the Old Oregon Country." *OHQ* 95 (Spring 1994): 48-92.

Rich, E. E. *The Fur Trade and the Northwest to 1857*. The Canadian Centenary Series. Toronto: McClelland & Stewart, 1967.

———. *The History of the Hudson's Bay Company, 1670–1870*. Vol. 1, 1670–1763; vol. 2, 1763–1870. HBRS 21, 22. London: Hudson's Bay Record Society, 1958, 1959.

———. *The Hudson's Bay Company, 1670–1870*. Vol. 1: 1670–1763; vol. 2: 1763–1820; vol. 3: 1820–1870. Toronto: McClelland & Stewart, 1960.

Roberts, George B. "The Round Hand of George B. Roberts: The Cowlitz Farm Journal, 1845–51, and Letters to Mrs F.F. Victor, 1878–83." Ed. Thomas Vaughan and Priscilla Knuth. *OHQ* 63 (June-September [combined issue] 1962): 101-236.

Roberts, Rev. William M. "The Letters of the Rev. William Roberts, Third Superintendent of the Oregon Mission." Ed. Robert Moulton Gatke. *OHQ* 21 (March 1920): 33-48; *OHQ* 22 (September 1921): 225-51.

Robertson, Colin. *Colin Robertson's Correspondence Book, September 1817 to September 1822*. Ed. E. E. Rich, assisted by H. R. Fleming. HBRS 2. Toronto: Champlain Society, 1939.

Robertson, James R. "Reminiscences of Alanson Hinman." *OHQ* 2 (September 1901): 266-86.

Robinson, Henry Martin. *The Great Fur Land*. New York: G. P. Putnam's Sons, 1879. Reprint, Toronto: Coles Publishing Company, 1972.

Ross, Alexander. *Adventures of the First Settlers on the Oregon or Columbia River: Being a Narrative of the Expedition Fitted Out by John Jacob Astor...* London: Smith, Elder & Company, 1849. Reprint: Readex Microprint Corporation, 1966.

———. *The Fur Hunters of the Far West: A Narrative of Adventures in the Oregon and Rocky Mountains*. London, 1855. Ed. Kenneth A. Spaulding, Norman: University of Oklahoma Press, 1956.

———. *The Red River Settlement, Its Rise, Progress, and Present State, with Some Account of the Native Races and Its General History to the Present Day*. London, 1856. Reprint, Edmonton: Hurtig Publishers, 1972.

Sage, Walter N. *Sir James Douglas and British Columbia*. University of Toronto Studies, History and Economics, vol. 6, no. 1. Toronto: University of Toronto Press, 1930.

Sampson, William R. "Nathaniel Jarvis Wyeth." In *The Mountain Men and the Fur Trade*, ed. LeRoy R. Hafen, 5:381-401. Glendale, Calif.: Arthur H. Clark Company, 1968.

———, ed. *John McLoughlin's Business Correspondence, 1847–48*. Seattle and London: University of Washington Press, 1973.

Santee, J. F. "Comcomly and the Chinooks." *OHQ* 33 (September 1932): 271-78.

Schafer, Joseph, ed. "Documents Relative to Warre and Vavasour's Military Reconnaissance in Oregon, 1845–6." *OHQ* 10 (March 1909): 1-99.

Schwantes, Carlos A. *The Pacific Northwest: An Interpretive History*. Lincoln: University of Nebraska Press, 1990.

Schwantes, Carlos A., and G. Thomas Edwards, eds. *Experiences in a Promised Land: Essays in Pacific Northwest History*. Foreword by Robert E. Burke. Seattle: University of Washington Press, 1986.

Scott, Harvey. *History of the Oregon Country*. 6 vols. Cambridge: Harvard University Press, 1924.

Scott, Leslie M. "First Taxes in Oregon, 1844." *OHQ* 31 (March 1930): 1-10.

———. "Influence of American Settlement upon the Oregon Boundary Treaty of 1846." *OHQ* 29 (March 1928): 1-19.

———. "Oregon Tax Roll, 1844." *OHQ* 31 (March 1930): 11-24.

———, ed. "Report of Lieutenant Peel on Oregon, 1845–46." *OHQ* 29 (March 1928): 51-76.

Scouler, John. "Dr. John Scouler's Journal of a Voyage to N.W. America—Columbia—Vancouvre & Nootka Sound." Ed. Nellie Pipes. *OHQ* 6 (March, June, September 1905): 54-75, 159-205, 276-87.

"Secret Mission of Warre and Vavasour." In "Documents," *WHQ* 3 (April 1912): 131-53.

Shippee, Lester Burrell. "The Federal Relations of Oregon." *OHQ* 19 (June, September, December 1918): 89-133, 189-230, 283-333; *OHQ* 20 (March, June, September,

December 1919): 35-93, 173-218, 261-95, 345-95.

Shively, John M. "John M. Shively's Memoir." Parts 1, 2. Ed. Howard M. and Edith M. List. *OHQ* 81 (Spring, Summer 1980): 5-29, 181-95.

Simpson, George. Character Book. Ed. Glyndwr Williams. In *Hudson's Bay Miscellany,* HBRS 30:167-236.

———. *Fur Trade and Empire: George Simpson's Journal; Remarks Connected with the Fur Trade in the Course of a Voyage from York Factory to Fort George and Back to York Factory, 1824–1825* Ed. Frederick Merk. Harvard Historical Studies 31. Cambridge: Belknap Press of Harvard University Press, 1968.

———. *Journal of Occurrences in the Athabasca Department by George Simpson, 1820 and 1821, and Report.* Ed. E. E. Rich. Introduction by Chester Martin. HBRS 1. London: Champlain Society, 1938.

———. "Letters of Sir George Simpson, 1841–1843." Ed. Joseph Schafer. *American Historical Review* 14 (October 1908): 70-94.

———. *London Correspondence Inward from Sir George Simpson, 1841–42.* Ed. Glyndwr Williams. Introduction by John S. Galbraith. HBRS 29. London: Hudson's Bay Record Society, 1973.

———. *Narrative of a Journey around the World...1841 and 1842.* 2 vols. London: Henry Colburn, 1847. Republished as *An Overland Journey round the World...* Ed. Adam Thom and Archibald Barclay. Philadelphia, 1847.

———. *Part of Dispatch from George Simpson, Esq., Governor of Ruperts Land, to the Governor & Committee of the Hudson's Bay Company, London, March 1, 1829. Continued and Completed March 24 and June 5, 1829.* Ed. E. E. Rich. Introduction by W. Stewart Wallace. HBRS 10. Toronto: Champlain Society, 1947.

Slacum, William A. "Slacum's Report on Oregon, 1836–7." *OHQ* 13 (June 1912): 175-224.

Smelser, June. "A History of the McLoughlin House." *Clackamas County Historical,* 1960, 27-55.

Smith, Jedediah S., David E. Jackson, and William L. Sublette. Letter to Hon. John H. Eaton, Secretary of War, 29 October 1830. In "Documents," *OHQ* 4 (December 1903): 395-98. From Senate Executive Document 39, 21st Congress, 2d sess., pp. 21-23.

Spalding, Henry H. *The Diaries and Letters of Henry H. Spalding and Asa Bowen Smith, Relating to the Nez Perce Mission, 1838–1842.* Glendale, Calif.: Arthur H. Clark Company, 1958.

Sullivan, Maurice S. *Jedediah Smith, Trader and Trail-Breaker.* New York: Press of the Pioneers, 1936.

———. *The Travels of Jedediah Smith, a Documentary Outline Including the Journal of the Great American Pathfinder.* Santa Ana, Calif.: Fine Arts Press, 1934.

Sylvester, Avery. "Voyages of the Pallas and Chenamus." *OHQ* 34 (September, December 1933): 259-72, 359-71.

Taylor, Quintard. "Slaves and Free Men: Blacks in the Oregon Country, 1840–1860." *OHQ* 83 (Summer 1982): 153-70.

Tays, George. "Mariano Guadalupe Vallejo. A Biography and a History." *California Historical Society Quarterly,* September, December 1937, 216-55, 348-72; March, June, September 1938, 50-73, 151-67, 219-42.

Teisendorf, K. C. "George Simpson, Canoe Executive." *The Beaver,* Summer 1970, 39-41.

Teiser, Sidney. "The First Chief Justice of Oregon Territory, William P. Bryant." *OHQ* 48 (June 1947): 45-54.

Thomas, Russell B. "Truth and Fiction of the Champoeg Meeting." *OHQ* 30 (September 1929): 218-37.

Thornton, J. Quinn. "History of the Provisional Government of Oregon." *OPAT* 1874: 43-96.

———. *Oregon and California in 1848.* 2 vols. New York: Harper & Brothers, 1864.

Throckmorton, Arthur L. *Oregon Argonauts: Merchant Adventurers on the Western Frontier.* Portland: OHS Press, 1961.

Thurston, Samuel R. "Diary of Samuel Royal Thurston." Introduction by George H. Himes. *OHQ* 15 (September 1914): 153-205.

———"The Spousal Letters of Samuel R. Thurston, Oregon's First Territorial Delegate to Congress: 1847–1851." Ed. James R. Perry, Richard H. Chused, and Mary Delano. *OHQ* 96 (Spring 1995): 4-79.

Tobie, H. E. "Joseph L. Meek, A Conspicuous Personality." *OHQ* 39 (June, September, December 1938): 123-46, 286-306, 410-24; *OHQ* 40 (March, September 1939): 19-39, 243-64.

Tolmie, William Fraser. *The Journals of William Fraser Tolmie, Physician and Fur Trader.* Vancouver, B.C.: Mitchell Press, 1963.

———. "Letter from Dr. Tolmie." *OPAT* 1884:25-37.

Townsend, John Kirk. *Narrative of a Journey across the Rocky Mountains to the Columbia River.* Originally published 1839. Abridged in Reuben Gold Thwaites, *Early Western Travels,* 1905. Reprint of abridged version, Fairfield, Wash.: Ye Galleon Press, 1970. Reprint of Ye Galleon version, Lincoln: University of Nebraska Press, 1978.

Turnbull, George S. *History of Oregon Newspapers.* Portland: Binfords & Mort, 1939.

Van Kirk, Sylvia. *"Many Tender Ties": Women in Fur-Trade Society in Western Canada, 1670–1870.* Winnipeg: Watson & Dwyer Publishing, 1981.

———"Women and the Fur Trade." *The Beaver,* Winter 1972, 4-21.

Vaughan, Thomas, ed. *Paul Kane: The Columbia Wanderer.* Portland: OHS Press, 1971.

———. *The Western Shore: Oregon Country Essays Honoring the American Revolution.* Portland: OHS Press, n.d.

Victor, Frances Fuller. *Early Indian Wars of Oregon, Compiled from the Oregon Archives...* Salem, Ore.: F. C. Baker, 1894.

———. *River of the West.* Hartford, Conn., and Toledo, Ohio: R. W. Bliss & Company, 1870.

Walker, Alexander. *An Account of a Voyage to the Northwest Coast of North America in 1785 and 1786 by Alexander Walker*. Ed. Rovin Fisher and J. M. Bumsted. Seattle: University of Washington Press, 1982.

Walker, Courtney. "Sketch of Ewing Young." *OPAT* 1880:56-58.

Wallace, W. Stewart. "Notes on the Family of Malcolm Fraser." *Bulletin des Recherches Historiques* 39 (May 1933): 267-71.

———. *The Pedlars from Quebec and Other Papers on the Nor'Westers*. Toronto: Ryerson Press, 1954. Facsimile edition, New York: Greenwood Press, 1960.

———, ed. *Dictionary of Canadian Biography*. 11 vols. Toronto: University of Toronto Press, 1969–82.

———*Documents Relating to the North-West Company*. Toronto: Champlain Society, 1934. Facsimile edition, New York: Greenwood Press, 1968.

Waller, Alvin. "Letter to His Brother, 6 April 1842." *OHQ* 4 (June 1903): 178-79. From *Ohio Statesman*, 10 March 1843; first published in *Christian Advocate and Journal*.

Warren, Eliza Spalding. *Memoirs of the West: The Spaldings*. Portland: Marsh Printing Company, [1916?].

Watt, Joseph. "Recollections of Dr. John McLoughlin." *OPAT* 1886:24-27.

White, Elijah. *A Concise View of Oregon Territory, Its Colonial and Indian Relations...* Washington, D.C.: T. Barnard, 1846.

White, Elwyn Brooks. *Essays*. New York: Harper & Row, 1977.

Whitman, Narcissa. "A Journey across the Plains in 1836: The Journal of Mrs. Marcus Whitman." *OPAT* 1891:40-68.

———. *Letters and Journal*. Comp. T. C. Elliott. Portland: OHS Press, 1937.

Wilcocke, Samuel Hull. *A Narrative of Occurrences in the Indian Countries of North America...* London, 1817.

Wilkes, Charles. *Columbia River to the Sacramento*. Philadelphia, 1845. Reprint, Oakland, Calif.: Biobooks, 1958.

———. "The Diary of Wilkes in the Northwest." Ed. Edward S. Meany. *WHQ* 16 (1925): 49-61, 137-45, 206-23, 290-301; *WHQ* 17 (1926): 43-65, 129-44, 223-29.

———. *Narrative of the United States Exploring Expedition during the Years 1838, 1839, 1840, 1841, 1842*. 5 vols. New York: G. P. Putnam & Company, 1856.

———. "Report on the Territory of Oregon by Charles Wilkes, Commander of the United States Exploring Expedition, 1838–1842." *OHQ* 12 (September 1911): 269-99.

Wilkes, George. *An Account and History of the Oregon Territory; Together with a Journal of an Emigrating Party across the Western Prairies of America, and to the Mouth of the Columbia River*. London: William Lott, 1846. Chapters 3-6 are reprinted as Burnett, "Recollections and Opinions of an Old Pioneer."

———. *The History of Oregon, Geographical, Geological and Political, and Also an Account of the Characteristics and Present Condition of the Oregon Territory, by a Member of the Recently Organized Oregon Legislature.* New York: William H. Colyer, 1845. Reprinted in *WHQ*, October 1906; January, April, July, October 1907; January, April, July 1908. Chapters 3-6 consist of Burnett, "Recollections and Opinions of an Old Pioneer."

Williams, Glyndwr. "Highlights of the First Two Hundred Years of the Hudson's Bay Company." *The Beaver*, Autumn 1970, 4-63.

———, ed. *Hudson's Bay Miscellany, 1679–1870.* HBRS 30. London and Winnipeg: Hudson's Bay Record Society, 1975.

Willson, Beckles. *The Great Company, Being a History of the Honourable Company of Merchants-Adventurers Trading into Hudson's Bay.* Toronto: Copp, Clark Company, 1899.

Wilson, Clifford P. "The Beaver Club." *The Beaver*, March 1936, 19-24, 64.

Wilson, Nancy. *Dr. John McLoughlin: Master of Fort Vancouver, Father of Oregon.* Medford, Ore.: Webb Research Group, 1994.

Work, John. *Fur Brigade to the Bonaventura, John Work's California Expedition, 1832–1833 for the Hudson's Bay Company.* Ed. Alice Bay Maloney from original MS. Foreword by Herbert Eugene Bolton. San Francisco: California Historical Society, 1945.

———. "John Work's Journey from Fort Vancouver to Umpqua River, and Return, in 1834." Ed. Leslie M. Scott. *OHQ* 24 (September 1923): 238-68.

———. "Journal of John Work, April 30th to May 31st, 1830." Ed. T. C. Elliott. *OHQ* 10 (September 1909): 296-313.

———. "The Journal of John Work, March 21–May 14, 1825." Ed. Nellie Pipes. *OHQ* 45 (June 1944): 138-46.

———. "The Journal of John Work, November 1824–September 15, 1826." Ed. T. C. Elliott. *WHQ* 3 (July 1912): 198-228; *WHQ* 5 (April, July, October 1914): 83-115, 163-91, 258-87; *WHQ* 6 (January 1915): 26-49.

Wrong, George M. *A Canadian Manor and Its Seigneurs: The Story of a Hundred Years, 1761–1861.* Toronto: Macmillan of Canada, 1926. Part of Malcolm Fraser's journal is printed on pp. 149-71.

Wunder, John R., ed. *Historians of the American Frontier: A Bio-Bibliographical Sourcebook.* New York: Greenwood Press, 1988.

Wyeth, John B. *Oregon: Or a Short History of a Long Journey from the Atlantic Ocean to the Region of the Pacific, by Land.* Cambridge: Printed for John B. Wyeth, 1833. Reprint, Ann Arbor: University Microfilms, 1966.

Wyeth, Nathaniel J. *The Correspondence and Journals of Captain Nathaniel J. Wyeth, 1831–6.* Ed. F. G. Young. Eugene, Ore.: University Press, 1899.

Young, F. G. "Ewing Young and His Estate." *OHQ* 21 (September 1920): 171-315.

———"Financial History of Oregon." *OHQ* 7 (December 1906): 360-432.

Zumwalt, Mrs. W. Bruce. "The Old Home of Dr. John McLoughlin." Pamphlet at Clackamas County Historical Society, Museum of History, Oregon City, Ore.

MANUSCRIPTS

Abernethy, George. Papers. MS 929, OHSL.

Allan, George Traill. "Reminiscences of Fort Vancouver on Columbia River, Oregon, as it stood in 1832, and some account of the Hudson Bay Company's farm there at that period..." Typescript copy at Fort Vancouver National Historic Site, Vancouver, Wash., from originals in possession of the Corporation of the Township of Langley, Murrayville, British Columbia.

Applegate, Jesse. "Views of Oregon History." Yoncalla, Ore., 1878. Oregon Manuscripts, microfilm #4470, Bancroft Library, University of California, Berkeley.

Clackamas County Land Claim Records. Microfilm, Clackamas County Archives, Oregon City, Ore.

Crawford, Medorem. "The Missionaries and Their Work." Salem, Ore., 1878. MS, microfilm 176, Bancroft Library, University of California, Berkeley. At OHSL.

DeChesne, Dr. Henri. Letter to Eva Emery Dye, 6 October 1893. Dye Papers, MS 1089, OHSL.

"Dr. McLoughlin's House and the Apothecary's Shop #2." National Heritage Limited, 1075 Report, with Selkirk's sketch of Fort William. Report is at Old Fort William, Thunder Bay, Ontario.

Dye, Eva Emery. Papers. OHSL.

Ermatinger Correspondence. British Columbia Archives, Victoria.

Ermatinger Estate Records. National Archives of Canada, MG 19 A 2, series 2. Bound typescript copy at University of British Columbia Archives, HR F5820.1 E7 A1.

Harvey, Eloisa McLoughlin. "Biography of Her Father." MS, original at Bancroft Library, University of California, Berkeley. Typed copy at OHSL.

Hastings, Charles S. "The Moving of the McLaughlin Home in Oregon City, Oregon. June 28, 1839." MS, at McLoughlin House.

"The Hospital #21." Old Fort William Training Manual. National Heritage Limited, 1975. At Old Fort William, Thunder Bay, Ontario.

Lemoine, J. "Journal." In Pointe de Meuron Journals, HBCA Reel 1M152 B23a1, B23a2. Transcript by Fort William Archaeological Project, Thunder Bay, Ontario.

Lowe, Thomas. "Private Journal Kept at Fort Vancouver, June 15, 1843–January 3, 1846." Typescript. British Columbia Provincial Archives, Victoria.

McLoughlin, David. Papers. MS 1089, OHSL.

McLoughlin, John. Case file. Clackamas County Circuit Court Records, Oregon State Archives, Salem.

———. Contract with McTavish Frobisher & Co., 26 April 1803. Original at Old Fort William, Thunder Bay, Ontario.

———. Declaration of Intention to File for Citizenship. In Clackamas County Land Claim Records, Oregon City, Ore.

————. "Statement on Land Claim," 1 March 1844. Handscript copy in McLoughlin- Fraser Family Papers, MS 927, OHSL. Printed in HBRS 7:199-219, 223/b/31, fos. 2-14.

McLoughlin, John, Jr. Letters. Howay Collection, University of British Columbia Archives, Vancouver.

Nichols, M. Leona. "Dr. Forbes Barclay: Beloved Physician." MS, at McLoughlin House.

O'Dell, Mrs. W. H. (Thurston). "Biography of Samuel R. Thurston." Samuel Thurston Papers, MS 379, OHSL.

Pelletier, Louis J. "Extracts from Rivière-du-Loup Records." Bureau du Prolonotaire, Rivière-du-Loup (en bas), 16 déc. 1928, Archives Nationales du Québec. Photocopy at Old Fort William, Thunder Bay, Ontario.

Pettygrove, Francis W. "Oregon in 1843." Port Townsend, Wash., 1878. Oregon Manuscripts, microfilm #4774, Bancroft Library, University of California, Berkeley.

Roberts, George B. "Recollections of Hudson's Bay Co." MS, Bancroft Library, University of California, Berkeley.

Société Historique de Kamouraska. "Qui Etait John McLoughlin?" Article paru dans le "Pharo" numéro de mai 1958. Typescript at Old Fort William, Thunder Bay, Ontario.

Whitman, Narcissa Prentiss. Letter to the Rev. L. Hall, 25 October 1836. Northwest and Whitman College Archives, Penrose Memorial Library, Whitman College, Walla Walla, Wash.

Index

photo, 370

Meek, Stephen H.L., 391

Menes, _____, capt. of *L'Etoile du Matin*, 430

Merk, Frederick, 98

Methodist Missionary Society, 243, 244, 306, 353, 394

Métis, 72, 76, 77, 82, 83, 86, 88, 94

Mexican War, 409, 440

Michaud, Julienne McLoughlin (sister of Dr. John), 10, 444

Michaud, P.C., 444

Milbanke Sound, 217

Miller, William, 270, 406

Milner, John, 343

Minors, _____, capt. of *Dryad*, 208, 215

Minto, John, 370, 404, 445

Mission Bottom, 244, 250, 304, 373

Modeste (HMS), 402, 408, 432, 436-37

Moffatt, George, 97, 223, 278, 281, 348

Montcalm, Marquis de, 4

Monterey, 173, 214, 319, 320

Montgomery, Richard, 6

Montreal, 3, 18, 20-21, 60, 69, 82, 83, 90, 93

Moore, Robert, 373-74, 401, 433, 457-58

Mordelet, J.M., 86

Morrison, R.W., 401

Mount Hood:
Warre sketch, 377

Mount McKay, 38, 103

Mount Murray, 4-5, 12, 13

Mount Royal, 18

Mount St. Helens:
eruption, 384

Multnomah City, 433

Munro, Henry, 43, 53

Murray Bay, 5, 59

Nairne, John, 5

Nancy (HBCo. vessel), 60

Nass Harbor, 208, 214

Nass River, 210, 214, 215

Nelson River, 124

Nereide (brig), 271, 274, 275, 291, 300, 308

Nesmith, James, 432

New Archangel, 173

New Caledonia, 122, 150, 171, 184, 212, 217, 218, 270, 289, 294, 441

New North West Company, 45

Newell, Robert, 311, 372, 447

Neysmith, John L., 280

Nez Perces Indians, 242, 244, 249, 360, 385, 447

Nisqually River, 307, 353, 356

Nonsuch (ship), 66

North Bentinck Arm, 34

North West Company, 13, 15, 16, 18, 21, 27, 32-33:
founded, 35-36;
marriage certificates, 51-52;
merger with HBCo. 101-103, 104-107;

Colophon

The typeface used throughout OUTPOST is New Caledonia. Originally a Linotype face designed by William Dwiggins in 1939, Caledonia (the Latin name for Scotland) is one of the most widely used book types of all time. Dwiggins described the face as having "that simple, hard-working, feet-on the ground quality." In the late 1980s, Linotype released New Caledonia, removing some of the constraints placed on the original design when it was first produced in metal and augmenting the range of weights for the typeface.

The OHS Press would like to honor the "simple, hard-working, feet-on-the-ground quality" of those people who have helped to transform this book from an intellectual to a physical product.

Editing: Nancy Trotic

Design: Lori McEldowney Root

Maps: Christine Rains

Indexing: Jean Brownell

Scanning (Interior): Revere Graphics • Portland, Oregon

Scanning (Dust Jacket): Precision Digital Imaging • Tigard, Oregon

Printing: Bang Printing • Brainerd, Minnesota

Production Assistance: Bob Smith • BookPrinters Network

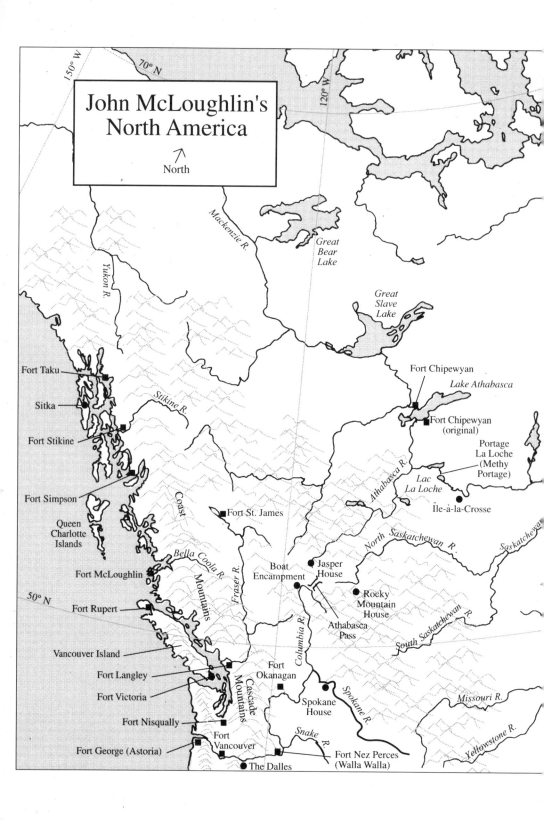

John McLoughlin's North America

↑ North

150° W
70° N
120° W

Mackenzie R.

Great Bear Lake

Great Slave Lake

Yukon R.

Fort Taku

Sitka

Stikine R.

Fort Stikine

Fort Simpson

Queen Charlotte Islands

Fort Chipewyan

Lake Athabasca

Fort Chipewyan (original)

Portage La Loche (Methy Portage)

Lac La Loche

Île-à-la-Crosse

Athabasca R.

Fort St. James

North Saskatchewan R.

Saskatchew

Coast

Bella Coola R.

Fort McLoughlin

Mountains

Fraser R.

Boat Encampment

Jasper House

Rocky Mountain House

Columbia R.

Athabasca Pass

South Saskatchewan R.

50° N

Fort Rupert

Vancouver Island

Fort Langley

Fort Victoria

Fort Nisqually

Fort George (Astoria)

Fort Okanagan

Cascade Mountains

Spokane House

Spokane R.

Missouri R.

Fort Vancouver

Snake R.

The Dalles

Fort Nez Perces (Walla Walla)

Yellowstone R.